"A sharply drawn, engaging book about air wars largely led by some colorful brigands."

—*Kirkus*

"Petzinger focuses on the people in the epic contest. And that's what makes the book so fun, and elevates *Hard Landing* above the typical aviation or business book."

—*Dallas Morning News*

"A wonderful book that explains why the airline business is such a crazy industry."

—*St. Petersburg Times*

"This riveting book is replete with little-known facts. . . . An important book [that] reads like a novel and leaves the reader eager for his next."

—*Pittsburgh Tribune-Review*

"Fascinating insights from a journalist who obviously well researched the topic."

—*Airliners*

"What makes this frank, matter-of-fact volume engaging is its detailed analysis of the politics and big-business duplicity behind those flashy ads."

—*Air & Space*

"Colorfully chronicles the changing alliances and enmities of these men as they battle to win at any cost and change the way the world travels."

—*Booklist*

"In this comprehensive exploration of the industry, Petzinger focuses on the brilliant but sometimes seriously flawed leaders who have revolutionized the business of moving people in flying cylinders. . . . Intriguing."

—*Orange County Register*

ALSO BY THOMAS PETZINGER, JR.

Oil and Honor: The Texaco-Pennzoil Wars

HARD LANDING

HARD LANDING

*The Epic Contest
for Power and Profits
That Plunged the Airlines
into Chaos*

Thomas Petzinger, Jr.

TIMES BUSINESS

RANDOM HOUSE

LIBRARY OF CONGRESS CATALOGING-IN-PUBLICATION DATA

PETZINGER, THOMAS, JR.
    HARD LANDING: THE EPIC CONTEST FOR POWER AND PROFITS THAT PLUNGED THE AIRLINES INTO CHAOS / THOMAS PETZINGER, JR.
    P. CM.
    INCLUDES BIBLIOGRAPHICAL REFERENCES AND INDEX.
    ISBN 0-8129-2835-0
    1. AIRLINES—UNITED STATES—HISTORY. 2. AERONAUTICS, COMMERCIAL—UNITED STATES HISTORY. 3. AERONAUTICS, COMMERCIAL—DEREGULATION—UNITED STATES HISTORY. I. TITLE.
HE9803.A4P48   1995
387.7'0973—DC20   95-13684

To Paulette

And to Beatrice, Eva, and Janis

It was a love of the air and sky and flying, the lure of adventure, the appreciation of beauty. It lay beyond the descriptive words of men—where immortality is touched through danger,` where life meets death on an equal plane; where man is more than man.
—CHARLES LINDBERGH,
The Spirit of St. Louis, 1953

This is a nasty, rotten business.
—ROBERT CRANDALL,
American Airlines, 1994

ACKNOWLEDGMENTS

I grew up around the airlines. As a teenager I handled baggage and freight for United Airlines. My late grandmother, Beatrice V. March, founded a travel agency in Ohio 40 years ago. My father, Thomas V. Petzinger, Sr., built it into a business well known for integrity and innovation. My brother, Charles C. Petzinger, is now building the business into a world-class operation. Over the years my mother, Jean March Petzinger, and my sister, Elizabeth Ann Holter, involved themselves in the agency whenever it required class.

My first thanks thus go to my relatives for exposing me to the delights of the travel profession. Only now, after researching this book, do I appreciate how hard they have had to work to extract a living from it.

I owe a tremendous debt to my sources, who are listed elsewhere. In addition to thanking them for their time, trust, and candor, I wish to extend my regrets to each and every one of them that this is not precisely the book any of them might have wished me to write.

At *The Wall Street Journal,* I thank Paul Steiger, the managing editor, who kept a job open for me while I disappeared to work on this project. News editor Cynthia Crossen helped assure a soft landing on my return. For their encouragement, moral support, and reporting assistance along the way, I thank my *Journal* colleagues Jill

Abramson, Laurie Cohen, Brian Coleman, Al Hunt, Bruce Ingersoll, Hal Lancaster, Laurie McGinley, Walt Mossberg, Alan Murray, Asra Nomani, Rick Wartzman, and David Wessel, as well as my former colleagues Eugene Carlson, Jim Stewart, and Peter Truell. I especially wish to thank the *Journal*'s Bridget O'Brian, who not only shared her insights but provided years of outstanding coverage on which this manuscript heavily relies.

Apropos of that, I am grateful to many other current and former *Journal* reporters whose trailblazing reporting precedes my efforts here. They include Teri Agins, Jeff Bailey, Buck Brown, Bryan Burrough, Harlan Byrne, Susan Carey, Gary Cohn, John Curley, Jon Dahl, Bob Davis, Steve Frazier, George Getschow, Dick Gibson, Roy Harris, Jim Hirsch, Al Karr, Scott Kilman, John Koten, Joann Lublin, Mike McCarthy, Priscilla Meyer, Daniel Pearl, Brett Pulley, Carl Quintanilla, Bob Rose, Dean Rotbart, Brent Schlender, Ron Shafer, Randy Smith, Roger Thurow, and Judy Valente. I would like to single out the *Journal*'s Bill Carley, who covered more big stories than anyone else during much of the period encompassed by this book.

There is a regrettable trend in business journalism to resist acknowledging the work of people at other publications. I am proud to cite the work of outstanding journalists from elsewhere, including, at *Fortune,* Kenneth Labich, Rush Loving, Jr., Louis Kraar, and Peter Nulty; at *Business Week,* Aaron Bernstein; John Byrne, Reggi Ann Dubin, James Ellis, Pete Engardio, Chuck Hawkins, and Jim Norman; at *Aviation Week,* James T. McKenna, James Ott, and Carole A. Shifrin; at *Crain's Chicago Business,* Mark Hornung; at the *Chicago Tribune,* Carol Jouzaitis and Jim Warren; at *The New York Times,* Adam Bryant and Agis Salpukis; at *Air Transport World,* Joan Feldman; at *The Washington Post,* Richard Weintraub; and writing in *Texas Monthly,* William P. Barrett, James Fallows, and Jan Jarobe.

Anyone who writes a book about commercial aviation owes an incalculable debt to Robert Daley, R.E.G. Davies, Robert Serling, and Carl Solberg, who have written outstanding histories. Two other authors—Dan Reed, who has written a biography of Robert Crandall, and Capt. John J. Nance, who wrote an account of Braniff's failure—generously shared insights with me.

I cannot mention everyone in the airline industry who provided help, but I would like to single out a few: at American Airlines, Al Becker, Iain Burns, Lizanne Peppard, and the infinitely patient and helpful John Hotard; at British Airways, Sandy Gardner, Peter Jones, John Lampl, Derek Ross, and David Snelling; at Southwest Airlines, Helen Bordelon, Ginger Hardage, Kristie Kerr, and Ed Stewart; at the Air Line Pilots Association, John Mazor and Kathy White; at United Airlines, Millie Borkowski and Jan Johnson. Thanks also to one of the greatest knowledge resources in the airline industry, Marion Mistrik, chief librarian at the Air Transport Association in Washington, D.C.

A number of my friends and associates read all or part of the manuscript and provided valuable comments; my thanks to Bob Cross, Katherine Field, Stephen Holter, Joe Meier, Bridget O'Brian, Carolyn Phillips, and Babak Varzandeh. Dick Tofel found bloopers that no one else would have caught. The toughest copy editor I know—my mother, Jean Petzinger—read every word a couple of times and improved more of them than I can count.

I have been blessed with intelligent and dedicated researchers. Cortney Murdoch rounded up records across the country. Babak Varzandeh endured the frustrations of the SEC. John Whittier joined me for countless hours over photocopiers. Jennifer Reingold, Colin Cowles, and Cass DuRant helped me accumulate a massive library of clippings.

Friends, family, and associates provided assistance in many other ways. Ed Upton, a model of virtue, helped me understand how the airline industry works and how an airplane flies. Lisa Petzinger helped me understand how reservation networks operate. I received valuable insights and information from Steve Frazier, Harry Litwin, Dina Long, and Bob Schettino; introductions from Karen Ceremsak, Henry Griggs, and Joe Jamail; and vital favors from Patrick Forte, Al Gibson, Chris Long, Robert Meeks, Jan Norris, Susan Purseley, Beth Shannon, Dominic Suprenant, Shelly Winebold, and the crew at Pan Atlas Travel Service.

At Random House and Times Books, Peter Osnos was a true believer in this book and never seemed to doubt the outcome, even when he probably should have. Miranda Brooks, Henry Ferris, Carie Freimuth, Diane Henry, Lesley Oelsner, Beth Pearson, Mary Beth

Roche, and Laura Taylor also were great allies. Copy editor Peg Haller made more spectacular catches than I wish to admit. But my deepest thanks go to Steve Wasserman, the editorial director of Times Books, who took on this project midway through the process and gave it the attention an adopted child requires. It will horrify the reader to know that at one point the manuscript of this book was nearly double its present length; the guidance, spirit, and talent of Steve Wasserman helped turn it into a real book.

I wish also to acknowledge my literary agent, Alice Fried Martell, the epitome of integrity and good humor, and a wonderful friend.

For their toleration and inspiration I thank my children, Beatrice, Eva, and Janis. And mostly I thank my wife, Paulette Thomas, who covered the story, nurtured the manuscript, defended my sanity, and kept our family whole. Though I deserved less, she never for a minute let me down.

CONTENTS

PROLOGUE: THE TIGHTROPE

Flying is an act of conquest, of defeating the most basic and powerful forces of nature. It unites the violent rage and brute power of jet engines with the infinitesimal tolerances of the cockpit. Airlines take their measurements from the ton to the milligram, from the mile to the millimeter, endowing any careless move—an engine setting, a flap position, a training failure—with the power to wipe out hundreds of lives. "A wink, a single gesture, is enough to topple you from the tightrope," wrote Antoine de Saint-Exupéry, the great French author and aviator.

This book is about the men who try to earn a profit from the tightrope act.

Like jet flight itself, the business of transporting people from city to city by air unites the massive with the microscopic. At the beginning of each day 4,500 giant aluminum vessels start their engines and fling themselves into the air over the United States. With paying passengers aboard, they fly at nearly the speed of sound to their destinations, disgorge themselves, fill up again, and fly on. They repeat this process through the day a total of 20,000 times, lacing the skies over America with a canopy of exhaust trails. Airline technicians monitor every cubic foot of atmosphere via satellite, to the point of logging each individual lightning bolt over the continental United

States. At the end of the day the airplanes cool down for an evening of gentle inspection and intricate care, like thoroughbreds after a hard day of training, having carried well over one million riders.

Repetitiveness on this scale means that success and doom occur in the margins of the airline business: bad business decisions have a way of becoming catastrophic; good calls look in retrospect like acts of genius. It costs anywhere from seven to fourteen cents to fly one passenger a mile, and with nearly a half-billion passengers a year flying nearly a half-trillion miles, the pennies have a way of disappearing quickly.

This frenetic daily exercise is repeated with such consistency and efficiency that the failures of the system call attention to its reliability. Many flights arrive late, of course, but in the majority of cases they do so in order to assure that an even greater number of passengers will arrive on time. Tragically, airliners do crash, although this happens so infrequently that a person is statistically less likely to die on a jet flight than by choking on a meal.

The airline industry reached this level of ubiquity within the space of human memory, making it younger than telecommunications, moviemaking, or automobile manufacturing. Yet already flying has become part of the furniture of modern-day American life, taken as much for granted as running water or interstate highways. Previously accessible only to the comfortably fixed or to those traveling on expense accounts, flying, in barely a decade's time, has become more affordable than driving. Although cars are often called the foundation of American culture, by the mid-1990s more adult Americans had flown in airplanes than owned automobiles.

Yet behind the commonplace routine of an airplane flight today are 25 years of pandemonium and confrontation—bankruptcies, labor strikes, lawsuits, liquidations, fare wars, firings, fines, mergers, divestitures, and congressional showdowns—any of which may reappear at any moment. The airlines have experienced more than their share of traumas, to be sure, but every crisis is rooted in a larger pressure bearing down on global culture or economics. The airlines of America (and a few overseas) provide an uncommonly clear window through which to view the social and economic upheavals sweeping the globe.

They cannot help revealing these changes, often in exaggerated ways. Airlines are service, information, and capital goods businesses all in one. They sell one of the few products consumed while it is being produced, right before the eyes of the customer. They exploit technology on a scale exceeded by no industry except perhaps medicine. They form the vital core of the world's biggest industry—travel and tourism, which accounts for one out of every 15 jobs. Airlines are managed as information systems and operated as networks. They embody, and can help us understand, some of the vexing paradoxes of modern economic life—why the value pricing revolution has given consumers unparalleled economic power, for instance, while at the same time causing the living standards of so many to decline.

The airlines also provide vivid case studies in corporate strategy. The terrific sums of capital at stake and the numbing repetitiveness of their operations make airlines uniquely sensitive to the commands of management. Even a question of substituting chicken Parmesan for chicken divan becomes a vital corporate matter—to say nothing of deciding to which continents an airline should fly, what fares it should charge, how many jets it should buy, or whether it should assent to the demands of a union or instead allow employees to go on strike. The thinness of the industry's margin of error is evident in how many names have vanished from the roster: Eastern, Pan Am, People Express, Frontier, Braniff, and Air Florida, to name some whose unhappy fates we will follow in this book. But we will also chart some sagas of achievement made possible by the leverage of the airline business—Southwest Airlines, for one, whose success formula has enabled it to earn fabulous profits from rock-bottom fares.

The union of devilish details and "godlike power," as Lindbergh found in the act of flying, makes commercial aviation compelling for yet another reason: the anthropology of the executive suite.

The men who run the airlines of America are an extreme type; calling them men of ego would be like calling Mount McKinley a rise in the landscape. Airlines demand a single strategic vision, lest the delicate choreography of airplanes, people, timetables, and finance break down. The airlines both attract and promote executives obsessed with control, who flourish at the center of all decision making.

The marginal economics of the industry—the proximity of success and failure to every decision—also breeds executives who love risk, who crave victory, and who are ruthlessly averse to defeat. The multitude of airline statistics causes chief executives to compete to the decimal point, as if they were comparing batting averages. Commercial aviation is, as Robert Crandall of American Airlines once told a Senate hearing, "intensely, vigorously, bitterly, savagely competitive." In the Darwinian process of the executive suite, the higher the rank of the executive, the greater his lust for the fight, and the greater the stakes. "Most executives," says Robert W. Baker, who grew up in an airline family and became a top executive at American, "don't have the stomach for this stuff."

At the highest level, at the airlines that matter, barely a dozen people have played this game in the past 25 years—a small group of white men who made the industry their sandlot from the late 1960s to the mid-1990s. Although it was through their efforts that flying became inexpensive and commonplace, they entered the industry at a time when flying was special and when the men in charge were looked upon as demigods of the industrial world. Thus it was that after leading the first voyage around the moon, astronaut Frank Borman turned down high-ranking job offers from the White House and elsewhere to become one of 43 vice presidents at Eastern Air Lines, in hopes of one day becoming its president.

For the most part these airline chieftains launched their careers at roughly the same starting point: early in the jet age, a time when flying conferred membership in the "jet set." Men still boarded airplanes in jackets and ties, while women (if they flew at all) wore white gloves and hats. As middle managers these executives worked with fabulously expensive machines, toy models of which they once played with. They supervised pilots steeped in the chain-of-command culture of the military—men who were trained to salute—and flight attendants chosen for their faces, their figures, and their servility. Conducting sensitive missions for the U.S. government and otherwise fulfilling the national interest, they had access to the power corridors of Washington. It was, in short, a career that went to one's head.

Through diverse paths these men rose to become only the third generation of management in the history of the airline industry. They were of an age and of a type. They knew each other well, variously forming alliances and making enemies of one another, all of them stricken with the same infatuation with aviation and all of them committed to achieving personal triumph.

As they began to reach the top—just as most of them were attaining their hard-fought ambition to "run something," as they often put it—the rules of the game were utterly transformed by Congress. More precisely, the rules were eliminated. In their heyday as a special industry, the airlines had carried on their business through a tedious, federally supervised process; it was as if the airlines were chess players required to clear their moves in advance with an arbiter committed to taking the contestants to a draw. In short order in 1978, for reasons that few fully understood at the time and that almost no one recognizes now, the airlines were loosed into a capitalistic free-for-all. The name given to this change was deregulation.

Although most of the airline chieftains resisted deregulation, it did, in fact, play squarely into their win-at-all-costs instincts as businesspeople. Fares plunged, and with them the surfeit of onboard service. It became fashionable (and remains so) to decry deregulation as misguided public policy, but the fact is that deregulation was inevitable. "But," the nostalgic persist in asking, "was it of net social benefit or detriment?" The answer is neither. Deregulation was a massive exercise in the redistribution of wealth, a zero-sum game in which not billions but trillions of dollars in money, assets, time, convenience, service, and pure human toil shifted among many groups of people, from one economic sector to another.

The most remarkable aspect of this upheaval is that so few men determined who won and who lost and in what proportions. This book tells the story of those men.

Each of them reacted differently to the same set of economic forces. Some, such as Bob Crandall of American, used technology to create new competitive weapons; others relied on more conventional weaponry, such as the 9 mm handgun that Frank Borman strapped to his ankle as labor strife mounted at Eastern. Some, such as Donald Burr of People Express, sought to manipulate their workers with promises of love and trust in the workplace; others, such as Richard Ferris of United Airlines, told his workers to do things his way or not at all. One, Frank Lorenzo, borrowed enough money to seize control of the greatest flying armada ever assembled to that time; another, Herbert Kelleher of Southwest Airlines, borrowed almost no money and procured as few planes as necessary. The globalization of the industry added another dimension to the range of strategic responses: Ed Acker of Pan American abandoned some of the most storied and valuable airline routes in the world, while Stephen Wolf of United Airlines and Sir Colin Marshall of British Airways created two of the world's first global megacarriers, defining the shape of the airline industry into the next century.

In the end most of these men were exiled from the executive suite. Though many had made themselves fabulously rich before departing, most were not in the game principally for the money.

The story of their entwined careers reveals many of the larger laws of the business world: that the same overweening ambition that drives so many executives to the top also assures their failure; that when executives form emotional attachments in business, whether to people, markets, or machinery, they deprive themselves of their best business judgment; that those who know an industry best are the most likely to take for granted, and ultimately ignore, its most inviolate principles; that although the rebuke may be slow in coming, greed, in the end, is almost always punished; that economics, in short, overpowers ego.

Just as they reflect the excesses of business in so many other respects, the airlines bespeak these lessons in spades.

HARD
LANDING

—

CHAPTER 1

TAKEOFF

In 1923, two decades after the Wright brothers' triumph at Kitty Hawk, flying remained a godlike act of derring-do. People in small towns across North America eagerly awaited visits by barnstorming pilots traveling in troupes called flying circuses. The barnstormers would draw people into an open field with a show of looping and wing walking, then work the crowd for paying passengers; the going rate was $5 for a 10-minute ride. Families traveled miles by oxcart to witness the display; the schools would let out. In the era of Grant Wood's *American Gothic,* the barnstormers introduced a generation of rural America to the modern age. The intrepid who actually went up for a ride experienced a thrill they never forgot.

Among the busiest of these aviation entrepreneurs was a quiet 21-year-old from Minnesota named Charles A. Lindbergh. Standing six foot two, he was known to his friends as Slim. Lindbergh was peculiar among the barnstormers. The others were mostly World War I air veterans who taunted death and lived high. Lindbergh, however, analyzed the risk of a stunt against its value in drawing a crowd. He resisted anything that might unsteady his hand or dull his reflexes, including the pilot stock-in-trade of liquor and coffee. Plainly, Lindbergh was in the game for something else. He studied the wind currents of the Rockies, the storm schedules of the Mississippi Valley, and the technical vagaries of his airfoils and engine. He scouted the countryside for well-drained fields where he imagined the airports of the future would rise, giving birth, as he enjoyed imagining, to "airlines radiating in every direction."

Intent on buying an airplane more advanced than his fabric-covered biplane, Lindbergh took unusual care to shepherd his expenses. He also worked diligently to maintain his income, particularly when other showmen began offering discounts. "I barnstormed over into Wisconsin but found that someone had been carrying passengers for half-price there," he wrote as a young man. "So I left southern Wisconsin and turned toward Illinois." Happily, Lindbergh soon landed steady pay, flying the airmail between St. Louis and Chicago.

His decision to undertake the fabled New York–to-Paris flight was financial, motivated by a $25,000 prize. Likewise did his backers have commerce in mind. A St. Louis banker, handing Lindbergh $15,000 in financing for his transatlantic airplane, used the occasion to ask, "What would you think of naming it the *Spirit of St. Louis*?" On another occasion the same banker made it plain that men of finance, not pilots, had the larger role in the capital-intensive world of aviation. "You've only a life to lose, Slim," he told Lindbergh. "I've got a reputation to lose."

The success of Lindbergh's 1927 flight to Paris—"Well, I made it," he announced, before being absorbed by the throng—sparked the Beatlemania of its time, except that it was much bigger. Major league baseball games came to a halt. Radio announcers sobbed. A skywriter emblazoned the Manhattan horizon with the words "Hail Lindy." The *New York Evening World* nominated the flight for "the greatest feat of a solitary man in the records of the human race." A new dance called the Lindy hop was born. Such a crowd followed Lindbergh into an elevator that his jacket sleeve was ripped off by the human pressure. By some estimates half of the population of the United States would physically lay eyes on him at one time or another. *Time* magazine, naming him its Man of the Year for 1927, declared, "Lindbergh is the most cherished citizen since Theodore Roosevelt."

A relationship that would alter the course of commercial aviation took off less than one month after the Paris flight. On that day nearly four million New Yorkers, more than half the population of the city, were thronged from the Battery to Central Park for Lindbergh's ticker-tape parade. At the uptown end of the parade, taking in the spectacle through a window in the Union Club at 51st Street and Fifth Avenue, was Juan Trippe, a wealthy 28-year-old aviation enthusiast. Trippe resolved to see Lindbergh that very day.

Their paths were already loosely entwined, for Lindbergh owed his job as an airmail pilot to Trippe. Born in 1899 and graduated from Yale in 1921, Trippe was a large man who radiated charm. He forged enduring friendships with the scions of some of America's great family fortunes—Sonny Whitney and Bill Rockefeller, to name two. Two years before the Lindbergh flight, Trippe had prevailed on one of his fraternity brothers, who had married into the Mellon family of Pittsburgh, to arrange a meeting with the congressman from that city, who was chairman of the House Post Office Committee. Trippe promoted a plan to shift the responsibility for carrying the airmail away from the United States Army to hired contractors. Trippe's scheme was soon adopted, an early display of a practice later called privatization.

When bids were solicited for the first airmail routes, more than 5,000 fortune seekers inundated the Post Office, but only 12 emerged victorious. A timber magnate in Seattle named William E. Boeing, bidding low because he built his own airplanes, won the line from Chicago to San Francisco, giving birth to what would become United Airlines. Florida Airways, created by World War I flying ace Eddie Rickenbacker, picked up the Atlanta-Miami run; it later became part of Eastern Air Lines. It was also thanks to Trippe's action that a company called Robertson Aviation received the St. Louis–Chicago airmail route, on which Charles Lindbergh served as chief pilot.

For Trippe himself, the airmail plan was fraught with unhappy irony. Though his company, Colonial Aviation, won the prized route between New York and Boston, Trippe wanted more: to bid for the route between New York and Chicago. But the cautious financiers on his board of directors feared overextension. Trippe narrowly lost a proxy fight and was thrown out of his own company.

It was only a week later, in June 1927, that Trippe found himself watching Lindbergh's riotous welcome from the comforts of the

Union Club. Despite his defeat in the boardroom, Trippe was already thinking bigger than ever. He wanted to recruit Lindbergh to his new plan, involving a company called Pan American World Airways.

Trippe broke a date with his fiancée and went to the Hotel Commodore, where 4,000 guests were attending a private party for Lindbergh following the ticker-tape parade. The young hero was already besieged with employment and endorsement invitations, eventually to total 7,000 offers. Trippe, miraculously wangling a few private moments with Lindbergh, distinguished himself from other opportunists by urging the 25-year-old aviator to accept no offers—not even from Trippe himself—until Lindbergh had hired a lawyer. Lindbergh, grateful at the display of gallantry, ultimately signed on as Pan Am's "technical advisor" at a rather modest retainer of $10,000 a year, plus stock options.

Trippe's fiancée, Betty Stettinius, nearly broke off the engagement after being stood up that night, but they were soon reconciled. When they married a short time later, Trippe became the brother-in-law of Edward Stettinius, a politically prominent steel executive on his way to becoming the U.S. secretary of state. Trippe had cemented his position in the three power structures that controlled success or failure in commercial flying: politics, public opinion, and finance. All he needed now were the places to fly and the payloads to carry.

Banished from his pioneering airmail company, Trippe forswore any postal contracts within the United States. If he could not get in on the ground floor, he would fly elsewhere: he would fly the U.S. mail *outside* U.S. borders. Ultimately he had the choice of three destinations: Latin America, Asia, or Europe. With Lindbergh at his side, Trippe resolved to conquer all three, like three great arms stretching from America.

First came the pioneering flights to the south. In seeking the first international airmail route, from Miami to Havana, Pan Am had to bid against a more experienced aviation company, but listing Lindbergh as a participant in the project guaranteed the contract for Trippe. Lindbergh was at the controls for the maiden flight to Havana, causing a mile-long traffic jam on every road radiating from Miami Airport.

The venture was hardly lucrative, alas. Even with generous payments from the Post Office, Pan Am could not cover the extraordinary cost of buying and flying its airplanes. Though never one to brood over accounting intricacies, Trippe studied the problem and realized that he could dramatically improve the economics of airmail by coaxing a few paying passengers onto each flight. Pan Am installed wicker chairs in the rear of the airmail plane, posted a $100 fare, and promoted the Prohibition-era flight as the passage to a legal drink. "Fly with us to Havana," went the pitch, "and you can bathe in Bacardi rum four hours from now."

Trippe had discovered what might be called the First Rule of Airline Economics: If a plane is going to take off anyway—once the fuel is purchased and the pilot paid and the interest rendered on the money borrowed to buy the plane in the first place—any paying passenger or payload recruited to the flight is almost pure profit. The fare paid by the last passenger taken on board represents a fabulously lucrative rate of return. But in Pan Am's case, Trippe had proved ahead of his time. Though Pan Am sold a Havana ticket to Al Capone, the wicker chairs flew mostly empty.

More interested in power than profit, Trippe remained undeterred. He continued flying the airmail to Cuba and, with Lindbergh, departed Miami in September 1929 to blaze a trail more deeply into Latin America. The commercial imperative was strong: U.S. investment was surging in South America, Wall Street was racking up bond underwriting fees there, and Washington was anxiously noting an outbreak of German influence on the continent (thanks partly to the birth of European air service to South America, via West Africa). Along the Pacific coast of South America Trippe and Lindbergh flew accompanied by their brides—the hemisphere's most romantic celebrity newlyweds. Wearing elegant civilian clothes instead of flying breeches, they drew torch-bearing and flag-waving crowds so great that at one point Lindbergh could not find enough clearing to land. Local political figures welcomed them not only as dignitaries but as saviors: Pan Am's service would enable much of South America to skip past the costly development of a railroad industry. (Neither did it hurt that Trippe's first name, taken from an aunt named Juanita, gave him a vaguely Latin air.)

At every stop on the South American journey Trippe dispatched a report to a public relations operative in Miami, whose florid press releases would help fix Pan Am in the public mind as the most important airline in the world.

While Trippe pursued his lofty ambitions overseas, the mail contractors operating inside the United States absorbed themselves in the more worldly concern of making a buck. The Post Office paid the airlines by the ounce but charged the customer by the envelope. Thus Eastern Air Lines found it profitable to stuff envelopes with wet blotters and send them by airmail; the shipping fees from the Post Office exceeded the cost of buying the stamps. Similarly did Varney Speed Lines (later Continental Airlines) introduce a line of Christmas cards weighing a full ounce in its principal hub city of Boise. Other airlines began conducting internal correspondence by registered airmail, as regulations required the Post Office to secure even a single registered letter in a sack with a 16-ounce lock.

Though costly to the government, airmail soon became smashingly popular, fostered in part by the spread of telephones and other instant communication devices, which pressured businesses to speed up their paperwork. A 23¢ airmail stamp made it possible to post a document in Peoria on Thursday afternoon and have it on someone's desk in New York Friday morning. As the economy of the late 1920s swelled on a tide of credit, banks realized that airmail paid for itself many times over when shipping money drafts and other interest-sensitive instruments. Manufacturers and distributors found that sending samples by airmail drew more attention to their products.

And businesspeople themselves began flying. The world's busiest airport in 1930 was in the oil boomtown of Tulsa, Oklahoma, which served more airline passengers than London, Paris, and Berlin combined. Gary Cooper, Clark Gable, and Sonja Henie were early fliers, as much for the publicity value as for the time saved in transit. But instead of demystifying air travel, its use by public figures only added to its mystique. Mary Pickford once stepped from a transcontinental flight in Kansas City, telephoned her astrologer in New York, and announced to the assembled press that the "stars weren't right" for her continued travel.

Airplane travel still seemed an unnatural act, and it wasn't a good bet statistically either. People flying in 1930 were roughly 200 times more likely to be killed than the passengers of forty years later. Navigation aids were rudimentary: pilots often followed railroad tracks, until one too many of them failed to notice the approaching tunnels. The death of the beloved Notre Dame football coach Knute Rockne in a 1931 TWA crash in Kansas was a devastating setback in public confidence. There were hazards on the ground as well as in the air: before 1930 at least a dozen people were killed by walking too close to whirling propellers.

The airlines did their best to relieve the anxieties—the terrors, perhaps—and other discomforts of flying. Passengers riding alongside the mail from San Francisco to Chicago on Bill Boeing's infant United Airlines got a parachute, a helmet, and goggles. Carriers distributed cotton balls to dull the earsplitting roar of the piston engines. Motion sickness was frightful, afflicting about half of all passengers; American gave passengers ammonia as a tonic for nausea, and some airlines hosed down their cabins between flights. Research showed that gaily colored interiors only intensified the anxiety of passengers; for decades aircraft cabins were therefore decorated in gray and other discreet tones.

No one better appreciated the challenges—and the virtues—of drawing passengers into the mail planes than Walter Folger Brown, a powerful Republican Party leader and confidant of Herbert Hoover. Brown was nothing if not an organizer. A Harvard-trained lawyer, he had headed a presidential commission that recommended creating two Cabinet agencies—the Defense Department and the Department of Health and Education—from a hodgepodge of other far-flung departments. He wore a top hat so high that his limousine required a specially outfitted roof. Brown sought and received an appointment from President Hoover as postmaster general, a position that made him czar of the airmail system.

Increasing passenger traffic, Brown reasoned, was the one sure way to wean the airlines from postal subsidies. But public confidence could be inspired only by big, financially secure carriers committed to safety, maintenance, and training, not by the fly-by-night operators abounding at the time. Brown changed the rules so that the airlines received payments based not on the weight they carried, but on the distance they flew and the volume of space they maintained in reserve for the mail. This system guaranteed the airlines a minimum payment every time a mail plane left the ground, and the bigger the

plane, the greater the payment. Though an outright gift to the airlines, Brown's scheme gave them the incentive to order the sturdier
and more costly planes then in development—planes, he hoped, that
would help convince a wary public that it was at last safe to fly.
Brown had codified the First Rule of Airline Economics into government policy: Once the flight was paid for, any additional payload
was pure gravy. Letter carriers soon began distributing promotional
handbills for select airlines. "Fly with the airmail! . . . Fly with American Airways," one read, promising a 10 percent discount on round
trips.

Having revolutionized the economics of the industry, Brown in
1930 turned his attention to its geographical structure. An outpouring of capital, loosed by the long-booming stock market and the
Lindbergh hysteria, had turned the airmail routes by the early 1930s
into an inefficient and illogical labyrinth. Brown's compulsion for
order was offended. Instead of a crazy quilt of routes, he imagined
clean lines running east and west, eliminating the circuitous zigzag of
connecting flights by which one airline handed off mail to the next.
To effect his plan, Brown went to Congress for the power to award
postal contracts regardless of the amount bid. Then he called the
principal airline operators to Washington and ordered them into a
conference room with a map of the United States. For two weeks he
cajoled them to swap routes, trade shares of stock in each other, and
do whatever else it took to eliminate duplication, irrationality, and
competition—in short, to divide the market to the exclusion of
everyone who had not been invited to the meeting. A United official
at one point turned to a lawyer and asked whether this activity might
violate the Sherman Antitrust Act. "If we were holding this meeting
across the street in the Raleigh Hotel, it would be an improper meeting," the lawyer answered. "But because we are holding it at the invitation of a member of the Cabinet, and in the office of the Post
Office Department, it is perfectly all right." The Post Office, in fact,
issued daily press releases about the conduct of the conference, to
which no one paid much attention.

Guided by Brown at each turn, the operators emerged from their
meetings with 90 percent of the nation's airways laced into three un-
broken lines running from New York to California. United Aircraft
& Transport controlled the northernmost route, via Chicago.

Transcontinental & Western Air, or TWA, had the center route, via St. Louis. American Airways was given the southern line, via Dallas. A fourth company, Eastern Air Transport, emerged with the routes running north and south along the Eastern seaboard.

The Big Four were born.

Everything was fine until an enterprising Democratic senator, Hugo Black (one day to become a Supreme Court justice), decided to hold hearings into the status of the airmail and learned of the postmaster general's activities three years earlier. The meetings at the Post Office Department were now cast as a grand conspiracy, dubbed the "spoils conference." Meanwhile the Democrats, led by Franklin Roosevelt, had seized the White House. So at 9:13 A.M. one morning in 1933 federal agents wearing synchronized watches stormed 100 airline offices around the country and carted away boxes of evidence. Roosevelt with great fanfare fired the private airlines and restored the mail routes to the army.

Roosevelt's move to embarrass the Republicans quickly turned into a bloody spectacle, for the military pilots no longer had the equipment or training to carry out the job. Within weeks 12 army fliers perished, five in the first week alone. The demure Charles Lindbergh took time from his trailblazing on behalf of Pan Am to harangue Roosevelt publicly, setting the nation's two most beloved public figures against one another in a conflict that would last their lifetimes. An editorial cartoon showed FDR hiding from a dozen skeletons wearing goggles and flying caps. Stricken by the first political crisis of his presidency, Roosevelt soon relented, restoring the airmail to private contractors. To save face, Roosevelt decreed that none of the previous contractors could hold any new routes—a thoroughly impractical requirement, since so much of the industry had been swallowed by the Big Four or driven from business in the wake of the spoils conference. Roosevelt therefore looked the other way when American Airways changed its name to American Airlines, Eastern Air Transport became Eastern Air Lines, and TWA added "Incorporated" to its name—all to qualify themselves as different companies. (United did not have to alter its corporate identity because subsidiaries had held the offending contracts.) The incumbent airlines preserved virtually everything they already had, although in this round of bidding two scrappy regional airlines managed to sneak into the airmail business. One, named Braniff, snared the Dallas-Chicago route. The other, named Delta, grabbed Atlanta-Chicago. It was, at least, a foot in the door.

Lawful or not, the manipulations of Walter Folger Brown prepared the airlines to handle an onslaught of paying passengers. But the public still needed convincing. It needed comforting—and a strong dose of marketing. It would get both from Cyrus Rowland Smith, the president of American Airlines.

Like Trippe, Smith was born in 1899. Like Trippe, he had learned to fly. But where Trippe flourished by uniting technology and politics, Smith, a drawling and hard-drinking Texan known to all as C.R., did so through a combination of technology and salesmanship.

With backing from Wall Street, American had gobbled up dozens of failing airlines around the country, including the airmail contractor that had employed Charles Lindbergh as chief pilot a few years earlier. In doing so American had built itself into the largest airline holding company in the United States, but the operation was far from seamless. When he became president in 1934, Smith's biggest challenge was the ragtag fleet, which included practically every species of airplane flying at the time. Smith vowed to move toward a single aircraft type.

The state-of-the-art passenger airplane was the DC-2, with seven window seats on either side of the aisle (in addition to an airmail compartment). It was a perfectly good airplane except that it never seemed to make money. Smith, an accountant by training, determined that with a few more seats installed (or with berths on night flights, as a "sleeper" plane) the DC-2 could operate in the black. On Smith's demand Douglas Aircraft in 1935 worked feverishly to make the plane wide enough to accommodate berths or 21 seats—three seats abreast instead of two. The additional seven seats made all the difference. They increased the cost of operating the plane only about 10 percent but increased the seating capacity by 50 percent. An instant moneymaker, the craft was called the DC-3 (the acronym stood for "Douglas Commercial").

It was a sleek, futuristic airplane, a flying work of art deco with rounded edges and mirrored aluminum. It looked sturdy and was—"relatively stronger than the Brooklyn Bridge," American boasted.

The use of sleeper berths on night flights helped to demonstrate the tranquillity of the ride. American sold its first sleeper ticket to little Shirley Temple, shaming adults who remained afraid to fly. On top of everything else the DC-3, at a breathtaking *180* mph, was fast. American at one point promoted the speed of DC-3 service with a magazine ad depicting a woman in her nightgown swooning, "He still loves me! He'll be home tonight, via American Airlines."

By 1938 there were 250 commercial airplanes plying the skies of the United States, and their paying passengers, thanks to Smith's DC-3, provided as much business as the mail sacks.

A new airplane was also enabling Juan Trippe and Charles Lindbergh to conduct the second phase of their three-way global thrust, this the most far-reaching of all. Pan Am was headed for China.

As soon as they brought home their first baby in 1930 (very possibly conceived during the South American trip), Charles and Anne Lindbergh began elaborate preparations to blaze the best route to the Orient. They chose "the great circle route," from the U.S. mainland to Alaska, to Russia, and south to Japan and then China—a route mostly over land. Flying in thermal suits under the midnight sun, the Lindberghs took weeks getting to China. Treacherous fog shrouded the killer mountain peaks along the way. The route, they judged, was impractical.

Pan Am would have to fly to Asia by the South Pacific instead. The distance might as well have been to the moon.

From San Francisco, China lay nearly 9,000 miles away, with only some sandbars, coral reefs, and volcanic outcroppings along the way. The longest ocean air route in the world at the time was being flown by a predecessor of Air France over the South Atlantic from French West Africa to Brazil, and that route was one quarter the distance facing Trippe and Lindbergh. Lindbergh threw himself into the design of a new airplane capable of the flight; when Lindbergh's son was tragically kidnapped, Trippe's engineers completed the job. What emerged was a massive water plane with four great engines, pontoons the size of fishing boats, and ample room for airmail and passengers alike. Trippe christened the new model the China Clipper, introducing the nautical theme in commercial aviation. From that point forward, chief pilots were captains and copilots were second officers, trading in their helmets and leather jackets for officers' hats and greatcoats bearing stripes at the end of each sleeve. Humphrey Bogart would soon star in a movie called *China Clipper*. And the plane itself would become a symbol for the inexorable spread of Yankee interests across the globe.

The long-range airplane solved only part of the problem. How would the clippers refuel en route? Where would the crews sleep, to say nothing of any passengers who might eventually be brought along? How would they eat? Where would they get fresh water?

In 1935, with no mail contract yet in hand, Trippe chartered a mammoth merchant ship in San Francisco and loaded it with the people and supplies necessary to create a chain of fully functioning colonies along the atolls of the Pacific. There were 74 construction workers, 44 airplane technicians, a quarter-million gallons of airplane fuel, food and fresh water to last for months, and five entire air bases, assembly required. Blasting away the reefs at Wake Island consumed five tons of dynamite. Tons of topsoil were brought to the barren outposts for vegetable gardens. A second expedition delivered pillows, lightbulbs, lounge furniture, beach umbrellas, teaspoons, and everything else needed for the new layover stations that Trippe was constructing; these outposts were the beginning of the Inter-Continental Hotels chain.

The postal contracts on which Trippe had gambled were soon forthcoming; the threat of Japanese hegemony in the Pacific made the United States government eager to foster the development of such strategically located islands as Midway and Wake. At the same moment in 1935 that C. R. Smith was preparing to roll out the first DC-3 at American Airlines, Juan Trippe watched a China Clipper soar past the half-completed Golden Gate on its maiden flight to China. In the dedication speech, the postmaster general said the achievement "rivals the vivid imagination of a Jules Verne."

The third arm of the Pan Am empire would extend across the Atlantic, to Europe; once again Lindbergh was there to help blaze the trail. The North Atlantic was a mere puddle jump compared with the Pacific, but in this case the challenge involved political instead of geographical barriers. Unlike the undeveloped continents to the south and west, Europe had a bustling airline industry of its own. For the first time the specter of economic protectionism cast a shadow over international aviation. It would take years for Trippe to break into Europe.

But meanwhile his strategy had bifurcated the airline industry in America. While grabbing every route outside the United States, Trippe had renounced any claim to fly within it. What happened inside the borders of the United States was somebody else's problem— nobody's more so than C. R. Smith's.

A moment of panic, if sufficiently frightening, can cloud the judgment of the best executive. Unfortunately, these misjudgments can have lasting consequences, as happened to C. R. Smith and a few of his colleagues when circumstances conspired to create America's first great fare war.

The outrage generated by exposure of the spoils conference had caused Congress to institute a radical reform: contracts would go to the lowest bidder, regardless of other considerations. Quickly bids plunged.

In one case, when the Roosevelt administration offered an airmail contract between Houston and San Antonio, Eddie Rickenbacker, eager to push west in order to diversify Eastern's north-south service, vowed to get the route even at a steep loss. Texas-based Braniff, intent on defending its territory against the Big Four, caught wind that Eastern was planning to bid less than a cent a mile. When the postmaster general opened Braniff's bid, he stunned the room by reading the figure of $0.00001907378 a mile. As everyone shook his head, he opened another envelope. "Eastern," he said, "bids zero-zero-zero cents."

"That's illegal!" cried Tom Braniff.

"The hell it is!" cried Eddie Rickenbacker.

Because Congress had put a time limit on every airmail contract, the incumbent airlines were forced continually to defend their routes against the encroachment of upstarts, intensifying the downward spiral of rates. On occasion C. R. Smith had to gamble in the commodity markets with his meager postal payments in order to make the payroll at American Airlines.

The major airlines were trapped in a conundrum. How could they buy more of the DC-3s that had so captivated the public (at a cost of nearly $100,000 per plane) unless they were assured of protection from rate wars? Yet how could they avoid rate wars when buying these costly new machines required them to defend their routes from upstarts and interlopers? The only answer, C. R. Smith and his colleagues insisted, was government administration of rates and routes. The irony of their pleading for protection from their own behavior did not deter them. Without regulation, industry's chief lobbyist declared, "There is nothing to prevent the entire air-carrier system from crashing to earth under the impact of cutthroat and destructive practices."

The timing of their plea was propitious. Roosevelt was in the throes of erecting government regulation on a scale unseen in American history. Congress had just been stricken with grief and outrage over the death of a beloved member, Sen. Bronson Cutter, in a plane crash and was eager to intensify safety regulation. Riding this momentum, the airlines got precisely what they wanted. The Civil Aeronautics Act of 1938 was readily adopted; it preserved all existing airmail contracts in perpetuity. The airlines had turned themselves into public utilities.

The price paid for this sinecure was the involvement of the federal government in every financial aspect of the industry's business—every route, every rate—through a new bureaucracy, eventually to be called the Civil Aeronautics Board. The Big Four had exposed themselves to the full weight of an old-fashioned statist controller, which established its headquarters in a pillared edifice directly across Constitution Avenue from the Washington Monument. C. R. Smith and his peers had yielded this authority precisely when their businesses were poised to take off in an exciting new direction, with passengers at last beginning to overtake airmail as the majority of the business. In their panic they had traded the future against the past.

In the name of blocking "destructive competition," the CAB simply prevented competition. Charter operators were whacked down. Regional airlines, known as "local service operators," were allowed to serve small locales in carefully circumscribed regions, all in the interest of delivering "feeder" traffic from outlying cities to connecting flights on the major airlines. Price competition vanished; any fare change required a tedious administrative and judicial review—a process derived from the principles framing the Interstate Commerce Act of 1887, which itself had been largely cribbed from the British

Railway Act of 1845. The bureaucratic compulsion for consensus caused CAB proceedings to drag on endlessly and yield random results. The role of presidential appointment in filling the five-member board heaped political pressures on top of whimsy and laboriousness.

At one point Louis J. Hector, a young lawyer from Florida, arrived at the CAB as a newly appointed board member and was immediately engulfed in a case involving the selection of a few small Midwestern towns for new air service. When the hearing examiner assembled the documents over which the board would deliberate, they stood nine feet tall. The reports were ordered condensed, after which the material spanned a mere 658 pages. Hearings were held, at which 38 members of Congress and 68 mayors and local boosters spoke. When they were over, the individual commissioners threw out the staff reports and gathered in a room with a map and some colored pencils to settle the matter. Purely to see what would happen, Hector insisted that the commission order air service to his father's home town of Clarinda, Iowa—a town that had not been mentioned anywhere in those nine feet of documents, whose mayor had not testified, and whose citizenry had not requested air service.

No problem, the other board members said. Clarinda was immediately added. (Hector had the gumption to explain that he was joking.)

As one would expect of strong-willed American business executives, the airline chieftains began to complain about bureaucratic delays and decisions that went against them individually, but they found the system to be addictingly comfortable. Though denying the airlines significant profits, regulation at least protected them against loss, regardless of economic conditions. Airline shareholders never had to fret over bankruptcy; failure was impossible. The system freed the airlines from worrying about the cost of doing business. The airlines, creating vast internal bureaucracies of their own, told the CAB how much money they required to run their businesses, while the CAB, using the airlines' numbers, merrily calculated the fares necessary to cover those costs, plus a modest profit.

With so little incentive to control costs, fares, predictably, remained beyond the reach of anyone but the expense account traveler or the well-to-do vacationer. International fares, regulated not only by the CAB but by a monstrous apparatus of foreign regulation, were likewise prohibitive. For the would-be passengers of the middle class, Pan Am introduced a marketing program called "Fly Now, Pay Later," in which the Household Finance Corporation provided an installment loan contract. Flying, in short, was like purchasing a car.

Even amid a tremendous postwar passenger boom, the airlines were still carrying just a million passengers a year, barely 1 percent of the population of the United States. As a group of Cabinet agencies dryly concluded in a 1947 report to President Truman, "Present rates remain a limiting factor on the growth of traffic."

But why should the airlines have cared? They could continue to grow simply by stimulating the huge, untapped market of people who had the means to fly and had not yet done so. Advances in aviation technology brought these people out in droves. The speed of the four-engine aircraft introduced after World War II—the Lockheed Constellation and the McDonnell Douglas DC-7—cut in half the time spent crossing the continent and the ocean. People abandoned ocean liners in droves to fly on Pan Am, and trains in even greater numbers to fly on American and other domestic airlines. The innovation of pressurized cabins enabled planes to fly over most inclement weather, encouraging more among the faint of heart to board. (Pressurized planes also made it possible to cook meat onboard without the fat oozing to the surface, widening airline menus.) These postwar planes were big—60 seats, as against the 21 in the DC-3—but there were still only a few hundred airplanes aloft in the entire country, all of them nearly full of men in suits and women in hats and white gloves.

The system of cost-based pricing had another salutary effect for the airline chieftains. Relieved of the worldly miseries that consumed executives in other industries, they could devote their energies to the infinitely more exciting pursuits of further improving passenger comforts, lobbying for more and bigger airports, hobnobbing with political and entertainment celebrities who flew in great numbers, and above all—the activity they cherished most—designing and buying even bigger, faster, and more exciting airplanes.

Thus in 1959 did the jet age come to the airlines. Travel times were cut in half yet again. C. R. Smith, introducing the Boeing 707, made the cover of *Time*. C.R. told *Forbes*, "We're going to make the best impression on the traveling public, and we're going to make a pile of extra dough just from being first." Internationally the first jets went into service for Juán Trippe at Pan Am. "This is the most important aviation development since Lindbergh's flight," Trippe declared. "In one fell swoop, we have shrunken the earth."

In 1968, approaching age 70, Juan Trippe stood before the annual meeting of Pan Am shareholders and announced his retirement. The lines of the Pan Am route map now reached to some 60 countries— a living network that would convey more people among more lands than anything in history. Just one Pan Am route, from San Juan to New York, accounted for the vast majority of the five million Puerto Ricans who moved to the United States in the postwar years, roughly equaling, by way of comparison, the number of African Americans who migrated from the southern United States to the North in the same period. Second only to Coca-Cola in worldwide recognition, the Pan Am trademark had become a fixture of popular culture, symbolizing the exotic. James Bond flew on Pan Am in *From Russia with Love*. A spaceship bore the Pan Am trademark in *2001: A Space Odyssey*. When the Beatles first landed on American soil, they held a press conference with the Pan Am logo conspicuously hanging behind them. Pan Am built the largest commercial office building in the world, a hulking structure defiantly set perpendicular to every other building in midtown Manhattan; Yves Montand, his arms stretched wide, serenaded midtown Manhattan from the roof of that familiar landmark in *On a Clear Day You Can See Forever*.

In the same year that Trippe announced his retirement C. R. Smith, also approaching 70, left American Airlines to become Lyndon Johnson's secretary of commerce. Smith retired at a time when his company no longer had bragging rights as the biggest airline in the free world. That distinction had passed to United Airlines, which was building itself into a colossus on the strength of acquisitions and the most successful marketing jingle in transportation history: "Fly the friendly skies."

Smith and Trippe did not know it at the time of their retirements in 1968, but after coming so far in only 30 years, their great companies were now on the edge of an abyss. The lockstep march of technology and economic progress was about to break formation. And the regulatory system they had created to guide this march would now suffocate the airlines instead.

On January 15, 1970, First Lady Patricia Nixon stepped on the frozen, windswept tarmac at Dulles International Airport near Washington and peered up. "My goodness!" she exclaimed. "Look how high it is!" Towering before her stood a bulb-headed 747 jumbo jet, trimmed in the trademark sky blue of Pan American World Airways—"the ark," as the dignitaries on hand pronounced it. "The potential impact of the 747 upon the future of mankind is so great," said a CAB official, "that it is difficult to identify another incident with which it may be compared in the entire history of transportation."

Climbing the dedication platform in a belted blue coat and white leather gloves, Mrs. Nixon came nose to nose with the leviathan jet. Because a sophisticated radar system was tucked into the tip of the plane, there was no way she could be permitted to heave a magnum of Dom Perignon against it. So instead Mrs. Nixon pulled a lever intended to release a spray of red, white, and blue water against the jet. The lever, unfortunately, got stuck, and the intended spangle did not materialize.

A few days later in New York, with the plane fueled and ready for its first commercial flight, a small clutch of picketers thronged the terminal at Kennedy Airport. "No more dirty planes!" "Clean air now!" "You can't get to heaven on a 747!" Tourists and gawkers further crowded the gate area. The delicate operation of ticketing and boarding several hundred people broke down in the pandemonium. Just as bad, mechanics could not shut the rear door of the plane. The maiden voyage of *Clipper Young America* was already hopelessly late.

Finally, as the London-bound 747 pulled away from the gate, Capt. Robert Weeks watched a cockpit thermometer cross the red line at 1,000 degrees. Engine number four was overheating. Back to the gate the aircraft rolled and ingloriously disgorged all the passengers and baggage loaded into her with such difficulty. "It's marvelous," the wife of TV producer David Susskind, one of the unlucky passengers, muttered sarcastically. "A dozen bathrooms—and no engines." By the time an alternate 747 had been loaded, the orchids pinned to the flight attendants were dead.

The Boeing 747—and to a lesser degree its brethren widebodies, the McDonnell Douglas DC-10 and the Lockheed L-1011—would devastate the airline industry, bringing it as close to disaster as the government had ever permitted. The planes were simply too big. Although there had been airplane gluts in the past, each generation of new and bigger planes was always ultimately filled with newly converted passengers coaxed into the air by the latest breakthrough in speed or comfort. This time it was different. Most everyone who had the means to fly was already doing so. A threefold increase in airplane size was too much airplane by a factor of at least two.

The financial stakes too had increased by orders of magnitude. Pan Am's $550 million order of 747s in 1965 ranked as the largest single commercial purchase ever conducted by a private corporation; other airlines' orders for 747s and other jumbos were nearly as large. It might not have been quite so bad except that the first 747s were delivered smack in the face of the deepest recession to hit the United States since World War II. Soon the Arab oil embargo made the gas-guzzling jumbo jets all the more uneconomical. National Airlines got rid of its first two 747s within a year. At least one airline parked a 747 and rented it out for business meetings, on the ground. Pan Am tried to borrow money from the Shah of Iran.

And it began to dawn on the executives of aviation that so long as all those mammoth aluminum vessels were being hoisted into the air with empty seats, it might pay—they just might be money ahead—if they offered a few of those empty seats at . . . a discount. They were as keenly aware of the First Rule as Trippe was when he installed wicker chairs in his early mail planes to Cuba: Every additional paying passenger puts more money on the bottom line.

To the extent the CAB permitted, which was not much, the airlines experimented with special discounts, mostly on a standby basis to assure that they would be used only by discretionary, last-minute passengers—customers who otherwise wouldn't be flying. "Youth fares" came into vogue, although they caused a backlash from middle-aged passengers who presumed the youthful passengers to be draft dodgers and drug abusers; for a time, in 1969, United opposed youth fares because it had a policy of providing transportation only to people who "look, act, and smell normal." "Family fares" were introduced, although in an early display of political correctness such programs were usually judged by the CAB to be "discriminatory."

Most such discounts succeeded in filling a few empty seats, which made them worthwhile, but still the jumbo jets flew half empty. Financially 1970 was the worst year in the history of the airline industry, with losses totaling $150 million.

The airlines might have eased their financial plight by flying their planes on additional routes, but the CAB denied them this opportunity as well. Additional routes, the CAB reasoned, would only cause the airlines to order still more planes, which would only worsen the capacity surplus. No, the agency decreed, it was better to let the airlines increase fares to cover their losses. This solution, of course, only drove more potential passengers away. Perversely, it further worsened the capacity excess by enabling the airlines to buy even more new airplanes—which, in turn, required even more fare increases.

The glut worsening, their fares scrupulously identical, the airlines began competing on service and amenities to a level unseen before or since. American installed a 64-key Wurlitzer piano in its jumbo jet lounges, with Frank Sinatra, Jr., at the keyboard on the inaugural flight. United staged "happenings" in its 747 lounges, featuring caricaturists, guitarists, and wine tastings. Taking product segmentation to the extreme, Continental's Hawaii flights featured the Diamond Head Lounge in first class, the Polynesia Pub in coach, and the Ponape Lounge in economy. Intent on enlivening the lounges even further, Continental scheduled appearances of a "folk-rock-pop" band called the Pineapple Splits.

The lounge wars gave way to the food wars, which in turn led to the booze wars. Northeast Air proclaimed itself "the all-steak airline to Florida." Delta introduced steak with a champagne accompaniment. National Airlines came back with free drinks of any kind. Eastern, though it had initially attacked free liquor flights as "unconscionable," immediately matched the policy. Continental began serving free Chivas Regal in coach, supplementing its famous "Dagwood" sandwich cart. American wound up pouring so many Bloody Marys that it made millionaires of the people who bottled Mr & Mrs T Bloody Mary mix. American's aircraft mechanics noticed that in some jumbo jets the bulkhead wall in the back of the plane was freshly gouged every day; it turned out that the flight attendants were required to get the liquor cart out at such an early stage in the ascent of the flight that they could stop the carts rolling backward only by ramming them into the wall.

Each new gimmick also added a layer of regulatory absurdity in Washington. The price of every drink, the rental cost of every movie headset, the number of seats installed abreast, the square footage of the lounges—every last detail required the approval of the CAB.

The CAB reached its low point when President Nixon appointed a new chairman, Robert D. Timm, a wheat farmer and GOP stalwart from the state of Washington. Timm abandoned even the pretense of trying to balance the airlines' interests against those of everyone else. He vowed to increase fares even more, to double the industry's rate of return, to crack down anew on the charter operators. He permitted the carriers to meet among themselves to decide which routes to cut back—a reduced-scale replay of the spoils conference 40 years earlier.

Before long the barons of the industry, grateful for Timm's sensitivity to their interests, invited him along for an exclusive golf junket in Bermuda. The press caught wind of the junket, and Timm was soon ousted as chairman.

In a burst of reform he was replaced by John E. Robson, a career Washington bureaucrat unknown to the airline industry. Robson was a short and small-boned man with a deep, loud voice and a cocksure manner. He was not the typical patronage appointment: Robson was a Harvard lawyer with an undergraduate degree from Yale. He had been around the Beltway a few times, working as a staffer in Lyndon Johnson's White House and as a Transportation Department undersecretary in the Nixon administration. Robson did not particularly care about the GOP. He did not, in fact, harbor any passions about the airline industry, much less about airline regulation. Robson came to work every day hoping to have some fun.

Robson was shocked at how deep the agency had sunk. Staff morale was shot. The other four commissioners were so consumed with consensus building and political back-scratching that each new decision seemed to have no effect except to ratify the previous one. It reminded him of something out of *The Last Hurrah*. As if to reflect its more dubious status, the CAB had been moved out of the grand old building facing the Washington Monument into an eyesore of an office building on a rise along Connecticut Avenue, just above the hangouts and hookers of Dupont Circle.

Robson brought in another career political bureaucrat, Howard Cohen, a former White House personnel officer. During the evening the two of them sat in Robson's corner office, with its panoramic view of the rush hour commuter traffic clogging Dupont Circle, and wondered aloud how it had come to this. An industry managed by intelligent, seemingly capable executives—why did they so freely delegate their affairs to an agency of government? Those executives—they were the ones with the jobs and the capital at risk; why didn't they make their own decisions about how best to nurture them? What did a couple of Beltway careerists know about the airline industry anyway?

Robson resolved to shake things up, if only for the entertainment value. He encouraged the staffers who were questioning the agency's role to bring their misgivings to the forefront of the agency's deliberations. He brought in consultants to examine the foundations of CAB policy. Robson also began publicly posting his daily appointment calendar, a list that the trade press often published. Suddenly, the airline chieftains who had always formed a line outside the office of the CAB chairman were nowhere in evidence on Connecticut Avenue.

Robson was intent on learning the basics of the industry. If the executives would not come to him, he would visit them, to find out how the airline industry really worked. Where his investigations would lead, Robson had absolutely no idea.

Robson scheduled a fact-finding trip to Texas; some interesting things were happening there, he was told.

CHAPTER 2

CHEAP THRILLS, LOW FARES

This was why Herb Kelleher had left New Jersey.
Kelleher was a lawyer in San Antonio. He had moved there in 1961, at the age of 30, because he could not stand the idea of spending another slushy winter in Newark—and because he was desperate to find a little excitement in the practice of the law. He had been an appellate lawyer, as worthy a specialty as existed in the bar but entirely derivative. It was nothing but hand-me-down cases. There was no action, and to Kelleher that was as bad as sidewalk slush. Kelleher was a card, a party boy, a drinker, a smoker. He liked a good time and he loved politics. All these traits had drawn him to Texas, where his in-laws resided.

Now, five years later, Kelleher knew he had made the right move.

He was shooting the breeze over cocktails with his friend Rollin King, a client in whom Kelleher had a special interest. King was a pilot, and Kelleher had been infatuated with flying ever since he had hitchhiked his way to Newark Airport as a college student and climbed aboard a DC-3. But in addition to his pilot's license Rollin King had an M.B.A. from Harvard. He had turned his love of flying into a business: ferrying hunting parties and business executives around Texas by air. King called his little charter company Air Southwest.

On this particular day, as the drinks flowed, King was bubbling with enthusiasm. A friend of his, a banker, had just returned from California. During his trip there, the banker had flown on an outfit called Pacific Southwest Airlines. PSA was strictly a California airline, plying the dense corridor between Los Angeles and San Francisco with old, inexpensive airplanes at the unheard-of low price of about $10 a ticket. Because it did not fly over state lines, PSA could fly on any schedule it chose, with whatever airplanes it desired, charging any price it wished. The federal government had no jurisdiction over it.

If California could support an airline within its borders, King told Kelleher, then Texas certainly could. Like California, Texas had big cities separated by long distances. Reaching for a cocktail napkin, King scratched three dots, representing Dallas, Houston, and San Antonio. Connecting the dots, he formed a nearly perfect triangle. On such a route structure, Air Southwest, King said, could be turned from a little charter service into a real commercial airline.

King recognized that two airlines, Braniff and Trans-Texas Airways, were deeply entrenched in the region, but their schedules were inadequate and their service poor. And so long as Air Southwest never stepped outside Texas, it could get a foot in the door by undercutting the established airlines, setting a fare below the official price established by the czars in Washington. A new airline could afford to do this, moreover, by flying inexpensive turboprop airplanes where the established airlines flew jets. A jet was a waste on a 200-mile flight.

Kelleher was delirious with excitement. He had been waiting and hoping for precisely this—the chance to combine his law practice with a plunge into the business world, and best of all in aviation. It wouldn't be easy, of course. People simply didn't start airlines in the 1960s. But the challenge only excited Kelleher further.

"Rollin, you're crazy," he said. "Let's do it."

King and Kelleher launched the new Air Southwest Company without the slightest idea of the horrors awaiting them. Had it been almost anyone else at the controls, Air Southwest would have never gotten off the napkin, much less off the ground.

Herbert David Kelleher, born on March 12, 1931, was an accidental baby. His mother became pregnant at age 38, a rarity for the time, particularly for a woman who already had a house full of schoolkids. Kelleher's father urged her to consider an abortion. Her pregnancy was difficult, confining her to the hospital for six weeks, and the labor was traumatic. Herb learned his humility early in life. "She would look at me and say, 'I wonder whether you were worth it,' " Kelleher would recall. One assumes she was joking.

As Depression families went, the Kellehers lived comfortably in the Philadelphia suburb of Haddon Heights, New Jersey; Herb's father worked for Campbell Soup, one of the few businesses flourishing in the era of the soup kitchen. But the Kelleher household was striking in other, less conventional ways. Herb's mother was Irish Catholic and his father was Irish Protestant, and they insisted that their children make their own choices about religion. The four Kelleher kids split evenly, Herb choosing on the basis of the basketball court at a nearby Protestant church.

While still a kid Herb watched World War II consume his entire family in one way or another, except for himself and his mother. His brother was killed in a U-boat attack at the war's outbreak. His sister moved away to a wartime production job at RCA while his other brother was in the navy. His father soon died of a heart attack, when Herb was 12. Herb and his mother, left at home with a radio and a war raging in Europe, would sit up half the night discussing religion, business, morality, and ethics.

His mother had drilled so much humility into her youngest son that when he had scored 29 points for the Haddon Heights Garnets and was on the threshold of breaking the basketball scoring record, he refused to take the shot lest he draw too much attention to himself from the team. The crowd cheered, his teammates egged him on, but still Kelleher kept passing the ball away. The coach finally called a time-out. "Dammit, would you shoot the ball?" he yelled, and with that encouragement Herb finally took his record-breaking shot.

He headed for Wesleyan University in Middletown, Connecticut. He was voted the outstanding athlete. He was student body president. He was a frat rat. He wrote the yearbook and published a humor column in the Wesleyan *Cardinal*. Tall and wiry, he excelled at the shot put, an event that demanded speed more than strength. He was invited to try out with the Philadelphia Eagles of the National Football League but instead went to New York University Law School on a scholarship, ultimately landing a two-year clerkship with the New Jersey Supreme Court and, finally, a position at a prominent New Jersey law firm. Along the way he got married.

It was on a winter day in 1961 that he left his office on Broad Street in Newark, stepped from the curb ankle-deep into icy slush, and resolved to reach Texas before the next winter. After arriving he had six months to kill while waiting for his Texas bar exam results (he ranked third in the state), so Kelleher joined his brother-in-law in backing President Kennedy's navy secretary, a little-known Texan named John Connally, in a dark-horse race for governor. Though he began the race with polls giving him 4 percent of the vote, Connally won, principally on the strength of a massive outpouring in San Antonio. Kelleher had delivered the city's North Side.

Five years later, with a law practice devoted to pipeline cases and property disputes, Kelleher was watching Rollin King sketch the Texas Triangle on a cocktail napkin. Kelleher wasted no time incorporating Air Southwest as a commercial airline and readily obtained an operating certificate from the state. He drained his savings and borrowed more to put up the first $20,000 invested in the new Air Southwest.

Then, he smacked headlong into the juggernaut of Braniff and Trans-Texas, "demonstrating the ancient truth," as *Texas Monthly* noted at the time, "that with enough money to pay for enough good lawyers, a dedicated opponent can keep almost anything from happening for years and years." Lawyers for the incumbent carriers chased Southwest from one Texas court to the next, mounting every argument they could muster against the state's operating certificate. Kelleher won in the Texas Supreme Court in 1970 and the United States Supreme Court declined to hear the matter—yet the fighting had only begun.

Braniff and Trans-Texas rushed to the CAB in Washington with the inventive claim that Southwest would, in fact, engage in interstate commerce even if its planes never left Texas airspace. After all, some Southwest passengers would no doubt buy tickets on connecting flights on other airlines that *did* fly outside the state. Kelleher was speechless. He had designed the legal architecture of Southwest Airlines specifically around the boundaries of federal jurisdiction, and suddenly he was being told that perhaps he was subject to federal jurisdiction after all. Kelleher stepped from CAB headquarters along

Connecticut Avenue and clenched his jaw in such fury that he split four molars at once, which drove him to his knees in pain.

The CAB refused to protect the entrenched airlines. When the case went before the Court of Appeals for the District of Columbia, a judge wrote, "This litigation should have been terminated long ago; its undue prolongation approaches harassment."

Kelleher's law partners, meanwhile, thought he was off his rocker. He had been devoting three quarters of his time to battling for Southwest. All of the seed money raised to launch the company had long ago been burned up in legal and consulting costs; Kelleher was now representing Southwest for free, to be compensated only if the company ever actually went into business and earned the money to pay his fee. He had to keep fighting if he had any hopes of getting paid—not to mention recovering any of the $20,000 he had put up in the beginning.

And there was more than money involved. Kelleher was outraged. He would show those bastards at Braniff. He would show those ya-hoos at Trans-Texas.

Air Southwest renamed itself Southwest Airlines and seemed ready at last to take to the skies. Veteran pilots were hired from a charter operation that was shutting down. Some of the stewardesses came from American Airlines, which had a policy of dismissing any over age 32. Unfortunately, in the years after Southwest had filed its original application for service in Texas, a couple of Lockheed Electras had lost their wings due to a severe vibration problem. Southwest, left with little choice but to go into business with the jet aircraft now in common use throughout the industry, bought three 737s and soon a fourth, all still in their coats of factory-white paint. In June 1971, with the maiden flight scheduled for the following day, Braniff and Trans-Texas once again got a court order halting operations on grounds that Southwest had departed from the plan on which its flying authority had been granted by the state.

Kelleher jumped into a Southwest plane conducting its final proving flight and was dropped off at the Texas capital of Austin, where the members of the Texas Supreme Court were attending a cocktail party. They consented to hear his appeal the first thing the following morning. That night the Texas attorney general gave Kelleher the use of his library; all night Kelleher stayed up researching and writing.

He went before the Supreme Court without a change of clothes, made his case, and won. The battle, for the time being, was over.

"What do I do if the sheriff shows up tomorrow with another restraining order?" a Southwest executive asked when Kelleher assured him the company's first flight with paying passengers could proceed.

"Leave tire marks in his back," Kelleher shot back.

Kelleher was a born slob. En route to a speech before a church congregation in San Antonio he once spilled an entire Bloody Mary on his suit. (He made the speech anyway.) On another occasion, driving to a bank to plead for more money to keep Southwest alive, he accelerated too quickly in reverse and spilled a full cup of coffee on his clothes. (He still got the loan.) He could not bear to evict loiterers from his office. Ultimately his legal assistant, Colleen Barrett, made it her mission to impose a semblance of order on Kelleher's life, taking control of his calendar, traveling with him, saying no to people to whom he would otherwise say yes. She once told him she intended to fill a fogger with stain remover to spray him when he returned from lunch.

Southwest's operation was born in similar chaos. The airplane hangar at its home base in Dallas was so encrusted with grit that it took two days to get the doors open the first time. The company had to borrow a jack to change aircraft tires, and its mechanics had to pump the air by hand. When a wing flap was damaged in a collision with a bird, Southwest's mechanics broke through a locked fence protecting a 737 owned by LTV Corporation, stole the corresponding flap, and installed it on their own plane.

Such resourcefulness came naturally to an upstart company whose culture consisted principally of the survival instinct. Employees were painfully aware that Braniff and Trans-Texas—the latter now having changed its name to Texas International—had done everything possible to keep the people at Southwest from ever starting their jobs. They knew that Herb Kelleher had been working largely gratis to keep the dream alive.

From the beginning Southwest had another competitor as well: the automobile. Texans thought nothing of jumping into their cars or pickups for the 250-mile drive from Houston to Dallas, say, or a drive of roughly the same distance from Dallas to San Antonio.

Southwest promoted its new service as an alternative to driving, showing a weary businessman yawning behind the wheel while another enjoyed a quick and relaxing flight aboard Southwest.

But therein resided another of Southwest's many legal travails—the matter of which airport it should serve in its headquarters city. As the company was fighting for its life, the U.S. government was filling a cow pasture with the world's largest expanse of concrete to create Dallas–Fort Worth International Airport—DFW, by its federal airport code. The nearly 18,000 acres of airport property was as big as the island of Manhattan—big enough, certainly, to provide a home for a new airline with just three jets. The problem for Southwest was that DFW, in the interest of perfect compromise, was under construction in the middle of nowhere, precisely equidistant from the far-flung metropolises of Dallas and Fort Worth. Southwest's reason for being would evaporate at DFW; how could it ever coax people from their cars for a 45-minute flight when the trip to the airport took at least that long? No, thank you, Kelleher said. While all the other airlines moved to the gleaming new DFW, Southwest would remain at the broken-down Dallas Love Field, which, though obsolescent, was conveniently situated on the perimeter of downtown Dallas.

Once again the incumbent airlines saw an opportunity to torpedo Southwest. The municipal bonds used to finance the construction of DFW, it turned out, contained some fine print requiring all airlines to abandon Love Field. The Dallas City Council, reminded of these provisions, announced that Southwest would be thrown out and Love Field put in mothballs. Southwest could serve Dallas from DFW or not at all. The decision was a death sentence.

Kelleher stared at the fatal provision in the bond issue. Then it hit him: The language specified that all "certificated" airlines had to leave Love Field. The only meaningful certificates in the legal world of the airlines were those once handed out by the CAB, and Southwest had never gotten that piece of paper because it was never subject to CAB jurisdiction. Southwest was an airline—no point in fooling anyone there—but not a *certificated* airline. Kelleher went all the way through the court system again, and once again he won.

Remaining at Dallas Love Field was vital in another respect. It enabled Southwest Airlines to establish its marketing identity on a double entendre, to position itself around the eminently marketable concept of "love" and everything that the word might imply to a good-old-boy Texas businessman in the early 1970s.

In-flight almonds were called "love bites." The company's stock symbol was LUV. Eventually the automatic ticket dispenser was called a "quickie machine." But most conspicuously, flight attendants were made to dress in orange hot pants, clinging tops, white belts, and vinyl knee-high boots. "Our love service means having things around to make you happy," a Southwest flight attendant cheerfully promised in a television ad, "like me!"

Southwest offered no apologies for making sex so vital to its public image. This was, after all, 1971. To recruit flight attendants it ran advertisements seeking "Raquel Welch look-alikes." Another television commercial, shot from behind and below, showed flight attendants in hot pants climbing a set of boarding stairs. A third promoted Southwest's frequent service with a leggy flight attendant seated in an overstuffed chair asking, "How do we love you? Let us count the ways: eight-thirty . . . eleven o'clock . . . one-thirty . . . four o'clock . . . ." And as her voice and image began to fade, an airplane slowly moved across the screen, its fuselage suggestively pointed into her lap. The approach was crude, but the passengers followed.

The Southwest flight attendants were part of a long tradition, for the first women ever to work in an aircraft cabin were hired as part of a marketing gimmick. In 1930, a time when the public was still largely terrified of flying, a nurse named Ellen Church was denied a job as a pilot at Boeing Air Transport (within a year of Boeing's affiliating with United Air Lines). But a shrewd official of the airline saw in her the potential for something else. "It strikes me," he wrote in a memo to his boss, "that there would be a great psychological punch to having young women stewardesses. . . . Imagine the national publicity we could get from it." He recommended hiring nurses, because they were trained to attend to the frightened and infirm and would undoubtedly be sufficiently mature besides. "I am not suggesting at all the flapper type of girl, or one that would go haywire. You know nurses as well as I do, and you know that they are not given to flightiness." Nurses, he pointed out, have seen enough of men "not to be inclined to chase them around the block at every opportunity." His four-page guidebook for flight attendants urged them to be "good girls." It would be one of the last times that anyone would worry about the flight attendants making passes at the passengers rather than the other way around.

As the years progressed, the ostensible reasons for hiring only women as flight attendants ranged from their purported comforting properties to the belief that they simply had a greater toleration for abuse. A report compiled at American in the early 1960s asserted that flight attendants married so quickly because "they learn a great deal of patience and tact in handling people—assets that prove invaluable in the give-and-take of marriage." The average stewardess kept her job only two years, perhaps a few months longer. The airlines could have reduced the turnover rate by employing married women, but they steadfastly maintained no-marriage rules into the 1960s and beyond. It was claimed that the rigors of family life presented too many restrictions on the go-anywhere, go-anytime career of the stewardess. But one of the real reasons for the no-marriage policy emerged in a class action suit against United that dragged on for decades. In a deposition a company executive admitted that the policy was partly intended to create the impression that in the abstract, at least, male passengers had a chance with any flight attendant.

The sexual chemistry in the crucible of the airplane cabin worked not only because all the flight attendants were female but also because virtually all the passengers were male. Wives sometimes accompanied men as passengers, but it was certainly rare for a woman to fly alone, on business, even in the 1960s and early 1970s. "If you're interested in meeting a man en route, consider flying first class—at least one way," an American promotional document read in 1972. "Since most businessmen, and very few women, travel this way, you'll find it easier to see, and be seen." United in 1970 was still flying a men-only flight between Chicago and New York, complete with free cigars and golf balls.

For the most part the airlines over the years made the sexual culture of the passenger cabin only an implicit part of their marketing. Though trained to serve and to display themselves as physical specimens, stewardesses were a protected and patronized lot. Once booze began flowing in airplane cabins, C. R. Smith decreed that on American Airlines it would be given away, not sold. "Would you want your daughter to be an airline hostess if she sold whiskey?" he asked. In 1957, when American opened its Stewardess College, it established rigorous curfews and installed an elaborate protective alarm system around the perimeter of the school. Stewardess uniforms were proper—tailored, if anything, and a bit on the military side. Even at Continental Airlines, where Chairman Robert Six unabashedly demanded comeliness in his flight attendants, the outfits were classy rather than sexy. In 1963 Six's wife, the actress Audrey Meadows of *Honeymooners* fame, was responsible for adding an elegant string of pearls to the uniform.

This polite reticence began to crack in Texas, not with the birth of Southwest but several years earlier. In 1965 Braniff Airways introduced a ritual called the "air strip," in which stewardesses peeled away layers of their designer uniforms during the course of a flight, down to their blouses and skirts. ("Does your wife know you're flying with us?" Braniff's ads asked.) For the first time body language was an explicit part of airline marketing. By the early 1970s the sexual revolution was in full swing (with the feminist movement trailing slightly behind). Continental adopted the degrading motto, "We really move our tails for you!" Perhaps most infamously, National Airlines launched its "Fly Me" campaign, as in "I'm Debbie! Fly me!"

Where sexiness in the seventies was concerned, however, nobody pushed it to the extreme of Southwest Airlines. The positioning of Southwest as the love airline was one of the most smashingly successful campaigns in airline history, even if almost no one outside Texas ever saw it. Sexiness got Southwest Airlines off the ground. But it would not keep it aloft forever.

After a year in business Southwest had still not established a ridership sufficient to sustain itself. When people phoned in reservations, there was no need to bother making a record of them. "Fine, sir, we've got you down!" a passenger would be told, leaving him blissfully unaware that Southwest didn't even have a reservations system. By mid-1972 Southwest was in financial jeopardy. There was no choice but to sell a plane. In a fleet of four jets, that meant a 25 percent reduction in capacity. That, in turn, meant layoffs. Or did it?

The employees of Southwest—many of them having been let go

by other airlines, all of them thoroughly steeped in the company's early fight against the odds—were willing to do just about anything to avoid layoffs. Some of them went to management with an extraordinary proposal: to maintain the existing four-airplane schedule with only three airplanes.

The company was incredulous. The only way to accomplish that would be to get the planes in the air after they'd been on the ground only 10 minutes—an unheard-of feat. Fine, some of the employees said. We'll turn them around in 10 minutes.

Pilots and management supervisors were soon helping with baggage. Tickets were collected on board rather than at the gate. Each airplane was restocked with beer, booze, and soft drinks through the rear door while passengers were still deplaning through the front. Flight attendants worked their way to the front of the cabin as passengers exited the planes, picking up newspapers and crossing seat belts row by row, rather than waiting for ground handlers to come aboard. Once the last passenger had deplaned, the remaining flight attendants began performing the same tasks from front to back. "When they meet, they have time to brush their hair," a trade publication, *Aviation Week & Space Technology,* would incredulously report. And as the next cargo of passengers came aboard, they did so with no seat assignments, which meant that people simply stepped into one seat and then the next and then the next, in a nice, orderly, rapid sequence.

Everyone's job had been saved. Braniff and Texas International watched in horror as Southwest gave birth to the airline industry's first 10-minute turnaround.

Herb Kelleher was the master strategist of Southwest Airlines and continued to rank among its largest stockholders. He was also the courtroom tactician and the chief schmoozer with the political establishment. His legal assistant, Colleen Barrett, was immersed in critical personnel and administrative matters. Kelleher was a member of the board of directors. But Kelleher had no executive position with Southwest—no title, office, or salary. Even if Southwest was his principal client, Kelleher remained a lawyer in private practice.

The man hired actually to manage Southwest Airlines—someone who, it was hoped, actually knew something about running an airline—was an irascible coot named Lamar Muse. Muse had been given up by others as a has-been, but one with an extraordinary record to recommend him. He had spent the early postwar years at Trans-Texas, making it the most profitable local-service operator by means of an uncommon business strategy: negotiating fixed price rather than variable cost contracts from the Post Office Department, which meant that by flying the mail cheaper, he could swell his bottom line. This success won him a high-ranking executive job at American, but he had quit out of protest when the company added linen-and-china food service in its short hops along the East Coast (an amenity that was eventually scuttled because it exhausted the flight attendants). Muse ultimately wound up in Detroit at a cargo airline called Universal, where he introduced to the airline industry the practice of bringing everything into a single airport—a "hub"—and sending it back out to its ultimate destinations along "spokes." Muse quit that airline too, because it insisted on ordering a Boeing 747, which he considered a costly frill.

Now, as the president of the marginal, newly founded Southwest, Lamar Muse was vitally concerned with cost and profitability. It bothered him that in its three-cornered route system one of the company's planes was flying empty each night back to the maintenance base in Dallas. Muse decided to offer seats aboard the late-night maintenance flight to the public. Having no idea what to charge for the flight, he settled on $10, a nice round number, about equal to the bus fare between the cities—an off-peak fare, one might say, well below the regular fare of $26.

Southwest purchased exactly one radio ad to promote the $10 flight. To everyone's amazement, the departure gate was swamped with would-be passengers.

It was obvious that they weren't the businesspeople to whom Southwest had been pitching itself. They were college kids, old folks, middle-class families—people who weren't flying somewhere to spud an oil well or to sell a railcar full of industrial coatings. So Southwest decided to charge one fare during the day (a peak price) and a much reduced fare on every flight after business hours and on weekends.

Off-peak flights were soon jammed with new, first-time passengers; a state official in Texas would later comment that whenever he observed Southwest boarding a flight, he expected to see a "chicken coop on top of the airplane." The combination of surging revenue and declining costs on the quick-turn, three-plane operation enabled Southwest to cut its regular daytime fares still further below the prices of the established carriers. Soon these flights too were performing well.

Braniff and Texas International were jolted into action. Having failed to kill Southwest in the courts, Braniff moved to snuff it out once and for all in the marketplace by offering a $13 fare on flights in the state—a 50 percent discount from Southwest's daytime fare. So thinly capitalized a company as Southwest, Braniff reasoned, could never last long matching that fare.

Indeed it could not, but Kelleher and Muse resolved to see just how long they could last. Southwest's ad agency rushed out a new series of ads that proclaimed, "No one's going to shoot us out of the sky for a lousy thirteen bucks!" In addition to matching the $13 price, Southwest offered an alternative: anyone choosing to travel at the full $26 fare would receive either an ice bucket or a free fifth of liquor. Since most business passengers were flying on expense accounts, they naturally chose the $26 flight and the free gift, and it was not usually the ice bucket they requested. For a time in 1973 Southwest was the largest Chivas Regal distributor in Texas. Southwest had discovered another lesson in airline marketing: giving the expense-account customer something for free that he could take home instead of to the office—in short, a kickback—won his undying loyalty.

The combination of in-flight titillation, 10-minute turnarounds, off-peak pricing, and free bottles of booze had at last firmly established Southwest among the incumbent airlines. After the books had closed on 1973, Southwest actually had a profit; it totaled only a few hundred thousand dollars, but it was a profit. And soon the company was skimming those profits and plowing money back into Southwest Airlines stock for the benefit of employees. The industry's first employee-owned airline was born.

It was still only a Texas operation, for the CAB remained inalterably opposed to any new airlines in the interstate market. Just the same, Southwest's influence would very quickly extend well past the boundaries of the Lone Star State, thanks, ironically, to Texas International—and thanks, above all, to a kid from New York named Frank Lorenzo.

· · ·

Born May 19, 1940, the son of Spanish immigrants, Francisco Anthony Lorenzo grew up around his father's beauty parlor on Third Avenue just south of midtown Manhattan, one of the toughest places in the world to own a retail business. The family made its home in the Rego Park section of Queens, on the periphery of LaGuardia Airport, where American Airlines and Eastern Air Lines were landing their Douglas DC-3s and Lockheed Electras practically by the minute, even in the 1950s. Lorenzo loved airplanes and would hang pictures of them on the walls of his bedroom. Yet even at a tender age Lorenzo had a peculiar ambition in aviation: he aspired to *own* airplanes every bit as much as to fly them. Taking a lesson from his father, who dabbled in the stock market, Lorenzo began buying airline shares at age 15 after taking a flight to Europe with his parents. His first purchase was TWA, then controlled by a Lorenzo role model, Howard Hughes, one of the world's richest men.

Sporting a perfect pompadour, Lorenzo wore a stern look for his photo in the 1958 yearbook at Forest Hills High School. He intended to become an engineer but abandoned the notion at Columbia University. Lorenzo had a glib, charming affect—Frankie Smooth Talk, classmates called him. As a freshman he threw himself into campus politics, assuming a leadership position in a student government faction aligned with a group of gentile fraternities. According to an account later published in the *Columbia Daily Spectator,* Lorenzo's political organization was concerned it would get cheated out of votes in the sophomore class elections. To fight back, "They discussed the possibility of voting twice."

The group came up with a list of students who had dropped out but whose names had not yet been removed from the university enrollment lists. Lorenzo and his fellow conspirators could vote more than once using these names. As the campus paper reported it,

> Frank Lorenzo was the first—and only—one actually apprehended in the act of double-balloting. . . . At first he denied everything and . . . claimed that he had tried it as a "stunt" in order to test the Elections Commission and see if anyone could actually get away with voting twice.
>
> His political cohorts at that time decided Lorenzo was on his own and that they would deny knowing anything about it.

Lorenzo soon cracked under the pressure of the Board's questioning and admitted to voting twice.

Academically, however, Lorenzo performed well enough to go on to Harvard Business School, where he became vice president of the Finance Club and immersed himself in studies of the great wealth builders. He read biographies of Andrew Carnegie, Averell Harriman, and other giants of fortune. And then it was back to New York for a real job, for a career in the industry with which he had developed a fascination by age 15. He accepted a position in the treasurer's office at TWA.

But TWA was not to be Lorenzo's final home. Before long he moved a few blocks to the New York headquarters of Eastern Air Lines, where he worked as a financial analyst. Eastern's hold, too, was tenuous; Lorenzo wanted to find his own fortune instead of helping his bosses make theirs.

Bob Carney, a Harvard friend and classmate who was working in New York as an assistant to Siegmund Warburg, the great financier, agreed to strike out with Lorenzo. In August 1966 they each put $1,000 into Lorenzo, Carney & Company. They resolved to act as consultants, as experts in aviation finance, with a specialty in assisting companies in troubled situations.

The partnership combined Carney's golden contacts in the banking community and his gift for financial analysis with Lorenzo's salesmanship and savoir faire. They began modestly, using the New York Public Library as their office, scouting amid the stacks for prospects who might need their combination of financial and airline expertise. Before long they landed a consulting contract at Zantop Air Transport, a cargo operation that ferried parts among the automaking regions of the Great Lakes. They studied the finances of a publication called *Aviation Daily,* whose publisher gave Lorenzo a tremendous break by taking him as a guest to a meeting of the exclusive Conquistadores del Cielo, a club of industry leaders who got together periodically for fast-gun competitions, knife throwing, high-stakes gambling, and other such manly pursuits. Showing up at a Conquistadores meeting conferred legitimacy in the clubby world of commercial aviation. Lorenzo, it appeared, was on his way.

In the summer of 1969 Lorenzo flew to New Orleans for a con-

vention of the nation's local-service airlines hours after Hurricane
Camille had devastated South Louisiana. Lorenzo had services to
sell, and the delegates flying in for the meeting were among the ripest
of his prospects.

A great bull market was under way on Wall Street, with airline
stocks among the highest-flying performers. Like Lorenzo, the investment community had taken notice of the little regional airlines.
By the late 1960s the local airlines needed vast sums of money to replace their aging war-surplus planes with jets. Wall Street was eager
to assist with financial offerings and underwritings. Another young
man from New York had therefore also braved the aftermath of the
hurricane—Donald C. Burr, the chief stock picker at a mutual fund
called National Aviation. Burr had lately pulled off some of the
smartest guesses on Wall Street, making him a bona fide star of aviation finance.

The local-service operators enjoyed sumptuous feasts at their conventions, with the major vendors of airplanes, engines, and spare
parts outdoing themselves to sponsor lavish bars and buffets. Burr
was standing by a vast hors d'oeuvre table holding a drink when he
was approached by Bob Carney.

"Are you Don Burr?" Carney asked.

"Yes," Burr answered heartily, feeling every bit the celebrity.

"Frank Lorenzo would like to meet you," Carney intoned.

Like I'm supposed to know who that is, Burr thought. "Who's
Frank Lorenzo?" he asked.

Carney, acting very much the consigliere, motioned across the
room, where Burr observed a dark, elegant fellow working the
crowd—someone, Burr thought, making an effort to appear important. Burr made his way across the room, where he was introduced
to Frank Lorenzo.

Their liking for each other was instantaneous. They were both up-
and-comers on Wall Street, specialists in aviation finance. Born precisely a year apart, Lorenzo in May 1940, Burr in May 1941, they
were both under 30, much younger than the crusty airline veterans
who surrounded them. And they quickly discovered they had something even deeper in common: a passion—a lust, really—for aviation.

As a boy growing up near Hartford, Burr became giddy with excitement when his parents took him to the airport to see planes conducting their final approach over a dike in the Connecticut River. Often the plane was a silvery Lockheed Constellation, blowing a peacock tail of flame and sparks from each of its four piston engines—great fire machines, through Burr's eyes, appearing almost out of control, ready to crash. Years later, while in college at Stanford, he joined the campus flying club and resolved to fly over Mount Whitney, all 13,000 feet of her. (Burr's mother was a Whitney.) Burr did not trifle himself with the fact that the club's airplane was rated to fly no higher than 10,000 feet. As he climbed toward the peak, the air grew thin. Burr was seized with hypoxia, acute oxygen deprivation. But instead of losing consciousness he began to laugh out loud at the mountain, convinced that he could do anything, even reach out and touch the peak. The plane stalled and stalled again, and each time Burr ground the engine harder and resumed his climb until finally he had coaxed the craft over the top. Having nearly drained the fuel tank, he followed his conquest by an emergency landing at Paso Robles.

Newly infatuated, Lorenzo and Burr soon ditched the local-service operators' convention and headed into the bayous of South Louisiana, driving their rental car from one Cajun bar to another in search of oysters and booze, marveling at all the boats blown ashore and blocking the parish streets in the aftermath of Hurricane Camille. Not long after, when Lorenzo and his business partner, Bob Carney, won a consulting contract from British West Indian Airways, they took Burr along on a gin-and-cigar junket to Trinidad and Tobago. In the worst way Lorenzo wanted Burr to join their consulting business, but Burr declined, determined to become president of the mutual fund company where he worked. After that, he said, perhaps he would go into business with Lorenzo.

Before long Lorenzo and Carney had accumulated enough in fees to afford a prestigious business address, in a small office on one of the top floors of the Pan Am Building. In February 1969 they had incorporated a new outfit, called Jet Capital Corporation, and made plans to sell stock in a public offering. The stock sale went forward in January 1970, landing $1.5 million, just before the great bull market of the 1960s began crashing to its end.

The shares of Jet Capital had been sold to the public at $10 each. But before the sale, Lorenzo and Carney had sold shares to a few of their friends at just $3.50 each. Before *that,* Lorenzo and Carney had sold shares to themselves at 12¢ each—and not just a few shares. The total of $44,700 that Lorenzo and Carney had personally invested put about three quarters of the stock of Jet Capital in the hands of Lorenzo and Carney. Members of the public, having invested $1.5 million, wound up with one quarter of the shares. On the strength of a well-written prospectus, Lorenzo and Carney controlled most of that $1.5 million, having spent less than $45,000 to get it. It seemed like magic.

Lorenzo and Carney had planned to use this money, in turn, as equity—as flash money to borrow more money, with which they would buy jets, which, in turn, they would lease to the airlines at a profit. The leasing market, however, collapsed at about the same time as the stock market, dashing their plans—but leaving $1.5 million at their disposal, waiting for a new purpose to present itself.

Then one day, while packing for a European vacation, Lorenzo grabbed a pile of annual reports on small airlines—pleasure reading. Paging through them after his arrival in Spain, he decided that he and Carney could do a lot more than simply render advice to financially troubled airlines. They could use the money from the Jet Capital offering to participate in whatever financial turnaround they prescribed for their client. They could position themselves as financial advisors and the advice could be, Sell to us.

Sitting in Utica, New York, lay their first target, Mohawk Airlines, a local-service operator launched, like so many others, on the back of the DC-3. Mohawk linked Buffalo, Albany, and Syracuse, among other upstate towns, with New York City. Mohawk had management with vision. It was the first airline in the world to dedicate a newfangled device called a computer to the onerous task of managing reservations. It had also become, in 1957, the first airline in America to hire a black stewardess. It was the first of the little regional airlines to enter the jet age, but it had gone overboard. Mohawk by the early 1970s was suffocating under a pile of debt.

Lorenzo met with Robert Peach, Mohawk's leader, a tempestuous and flamboyant former World War II aviator. Before long, with a contract to provide consulting advice to Mohawk, Lorenzo began putting in place a restructuring plan by which he would emerge in control. But Mohawk's board grew apprehensive about the young, smartly dressed 30-year-old from Wall Street. With the company's fortunes sinking fast, the directors arranged instead for Mohawk to be taken over by Allegheny Airlines, another local-service airline operating in the East. The purchase would help catapult Allegheny into becoming USAir, but Lorenzo and Carney left with $1.5 million still burning a hole in their pockets.

Bob Peach, for his part, had lunch with Frank Lorenzo shortly after the company had slipped from his grasp. Afterward Peach went home to prepare to present a speech to the Rotary Club. He walked into his closet to get dressed, grabbed a gun, and killed himself.

As Lorenzo was trying to acquire an operating airline, Don Burr was still managing mutual fund investments. One of the many holdings that the fund maintained was a package of securities in a little airline hardly anyone in New York had ever heard of. The company was Trans-Texas Airways.

For years the family owners of Trans-Texas had made a comfortable living by flying oil prospectors, rig salesmen, and cattle traders among the small towns of the Southwest. Still operating a fleet of unpressurized, 1930s-era DC-3s, the company in the 1960s made a small killing in the Vietnam troop buildup, collecting draftees from across Texas and delivering them to an induction center in Louisiana. Later, as South Texas became a kind of poor man's Florida for retirees from the Midwest, Trans-Texas also did a lucrative trade shipping the remains of winter "snowbirds" in caskets back to their hometowns for burial. Among U.S. airlines, it ranked about 20th in size.

It was in 1969 that Trans-Texas, also variously known as Tree-Top or Tinker Toy Airlines, changed its name to Texas International Airlines, an aggrandizement it justified by its service to a few sunbaked destinations on the southern side of the Rio Grande. But the company had problems that no name change could cure. Like Mohawk, Texas International had overwhelmed itself with debt in the transition from propeller planes to jets, and creditors were beginning to close in. Perhaps worst of all, after years of coexisting with Braniff Airways in a cozy oligopoly over the air routes of Texas and neighboring states, Texas International had unsuccessfully assisted Braniff in its legal assault on the encroaching Southwest Airlines. Its courthouse remedies exhausted, Texas International was left to adopt the unfamiliar practice of competing to defend its routes.

Don Burr had an idea that his friend Frank Lorenzo could come in as a consultant and develop a plan to help save Texas International. With his standing as a mutual fund investor in the airline, Burr convinced Texas International to pay Lorenzo and Carney $15,000 a month to evaluate the company and recommend a regimen for recovery. The prescription ultimately urged by Lorenzo and Carney was to sell the company to Lorenzo and Carney.

They looked on the plan as the failed Mohawk bid redux. Lorenzo told the Texas International directors that he would convince the company's creditors to refinance the airline's mountain of debt on new, easier terms. And he, Lorenzo, would persuade them of the company's worthy prospects by raising $5 million in needed new equity—including most of that $1.5 million still accumulating T-bill interest in the accounts of Jet Capital. Don Burr took the vital step of arranging for his fund to inject some of the fresh equity as well.

The board of Texas International, like the board of Mohawk a short time earlier, looked warily upon Lorenzo. As the directors debated, Herb Kelleher caught wind of the Lorenzo plan and immediately swung into action in behalf of Southwest Airlines. Kelleher had been sure that Texas International was doomed; now, even if Lorenzo's refinancing plan ultimately flopped, it would indefinitely prolong Texas International's death throes. That would hardly be in Southwest's interests.

Kelleher showed up at a Texas International board meeting offering to reorganize the company on the same terms that Lorenzo was proposing. But when Kelleher walked into the boardroom, he noticed that Lorenzo was seated with the Texas International directors, awaiting Southwest's presentation. Lorenzo had one of the company's major investors, Don Burr, already in his corner. Kelleher was too late.

As it turned out, a third would-be buyer of Texas International had also made the scene: none other than Howard Hughes. A decade earlier Hughes had been ousted from TWA by the company's lenders. He now appeared intent on recreating the kind of vast, coast-to-coast route network that he had once controlled at TWA. The great recluse had recently grabbed control of a company called Air West. Integrating Texas International and Air West would, essentially, put Hughes two thirds of the way toward creating another transcontinental airline.

Howard Hughes's aides marched to the CAB and demanded disapproval of the Lorenzo deal. They argued that Lorenzo had hogtied Texas International with conflicts of interest—conflicts mostly involving Frank Lorenzo and Bob Carney. Lorenzo fought back, arguing that his plan represented the last best hope of saving the airline. In the end, at a point when the creditors were preparing to pull the plug, the Texas International board decided to back the Lorenzo plan. The CAB, too, ultimately approved.

It was a proud moment: with a big boost from his friend Don Burr, Lorenzo had vanquished both Herb Kelleher of Southwest and Howard Hughes himself. His personal holding company, Jet Capital, soon owned 24 percent of Texas International's stock, using money raised from other investors. And having acted as the airline's financial advisor, Lorenzo had structured the transaction so that his one-quarter ownership gave him 58 percent voting control.

In an industry rife with overachievers, Frank Lorenzo, 32 years old, had just become the youngest president in the history of commercial aviation since Juan Trippe had entered the industry more than 40 years earlier. Now he needed help in running his new airline.

From boyhood Donald Burr had passion—passion and glibness, the attributes of an evangelist. As a grammar school pupil he became a proselytizer for his church, chauffeured from town to town to recruit other youngsters into an organization called Pilgrim Youth Fellowship. He seemed destined for a career in the ministry until, as a sophomore in high school, he was thrown into a ferocious statewide election contest for the leadership of the fellowship. The adults took over the campaigning, and the electioneering grew ugly and dirty. Burr broke with religion in disgust, never again to set foot in a church except for the occasional ceremony.

Growing up in blue-blood Connecticut, in a house with Revolution-era bullet holes in the shutters, Burr was one of those maddening kids who seem perfect in all ways. He played piano and

saxophone; sang professionally; was a class officer, championship
soccer player, and one of the leading scorers on the Ellsworth High
School basketball team. His grades, however, were excruciatingly average.

He fell in love with a cheerleader named Bridget. One day, after
making his way across country to attend Stanford University, Burr
decided that he just *had* to see her, he *needed* to see her, he couldn't
wait *another* day, so he got on a motorcycle and drove all the way
back to Connecticut, the last two days without sleep, his face wind-
burned and splattered with bugs and mud, until he got home, took a
shower, set out in search of Bridget, and found her. Approximately
forty weeks later he became a father. Along the way, they married.

Burr had wanted to become an English professor—anything but
a businessman. His father, who was sclerotic and infirm even in his
30s, was an engineer whose career never really got off the ground.
Business is dirty and bad, his parents had told him. *You'll certainly
not be a businessman.* But after a while in college, Burr decided that
the anguish of writing was too great for him to consider a career in
literature, and he had a family to think of besides. At Stanford he
met David Packard, who was catapulting Hewlett-Packard into the
ranks of big business. Judging Packard to be of impeccable integrity,
Burr decided it was okay after all to become a businessman, and he
switched into the business curriculum, ultimately arriving in the
M.B.A. program at Harvard about the time Frank Lorenzo was leaving.

Burr ultimately succeeded in his quest to become president of National Aviation, the mutual fund operator. His office at 111 Broadway looked down on the Trinity Church graveyard, where one of the
soot-blackened headstones belonged to Alexander Hamilton, killed
in a duel by one of Donald Burr's distant forebears, Aaron Burr. But
after becoming president, Donald Burr began to fight with the conservative men who served on his board. Tired of buying a little
United Airlines stock here and selling a little Boeing there, Burr
wanted to run something, the way his friend Frank Lorenzo, with
Burr's help, had firmly taken charge at Texas International. Burr
grew passionate, arguing with his board so strenuously that his arms
flailed.

Burr's frustration became dangerous. He owned a small single-

engine plane called a Mooney, known for speed—a hot-rod plane, as
Burr thought of it. The plane was his escape vehicle for the weekend.
One weekend Burr climbed into the Mooney with his wife, then nine
months pregnant, and his two children in the back seat, bound for a
weekend of skiing in Vermont. Though the weather was threatening,
Burr took off. Soon the plane was caught in a snow squall. It pitched
and dove. His children began to vomit all over the back seat. He
couldn't make sense of his instruments. Airports were closing; he
could not find a place to land. Soon he was running low on fuel. A
controller finally talked him through a landing in the blinding storm.
Never again would Burr pilot an airplane.

Burr left Wall Street in 1973 to work at Texas International, headquartered near Hobby Airport in Houston. Texas International
made its home in a windowless building constructed of galvanized
metal whose azure hue caused employees to call it the Blue Barn.
Figuratively the Blue Barn resembled Peyton Place, with Byzantine
intrigue and office politics that eyewitnesses would later describe as
Kafkaesque.

Burr accepted Lorenzo's job offer, making it clear he wanted a full
partnership: the same pay, stock options, and responsibilities that
Lorenzo had. They would become co–chief executive officers of
Texas International, as Burr understood it. But when Burr arrived in
Houston, he found Lorenzo had made him chairman of the executive committee, whatever that was. Then, when the two of them paid
a visit to Alvin Feldman, the head of Frontier Airlines in Denver,
Feldman looked at Burr's business card and remarked that at some
companies, the most powerful executive carried that title. Lorenzo
soon made Burr an executive vice president instead.

Once Burr was on the scene, Lorenzo's longtime partner, Bob
Carney, was all but yesterday's news. Though Carney continued his
probing financial investigations and maintained vital contacts in the
banking community, it was Burr who became Lorenzo's soul mate.
Despite their misunderstanding over Burr's titles, they worked, ate,
and drank together—and always the conversation was airlines, their
airline. When Lorenzo married, Don was his best man. When Burr's
son Cameron was born, Frank was the godfather. But they also
fought. Burr would grow emotional, yelling and gesticulating, until
Lorenzo would cut him down, elliptically targeting some vulnerabil-

ity, playing a "conversational crossword puzzle," as Burr called it, to keep him and others off balance.

How come our on-time performance was so bad last month?

Frank, you may remember that we had a hurricane!

Well, then, why didn't you have the planes tied down?

"He would make you feel despicable," Burr later said.

Yet still they grew closer. They began jogging together, eventually competing in the New York Marathon, skiing together, spending holidays together, and always, it seemed, quarreling.

On one issue, though, they were in complete agreement. With Southwest Airlines having replaced its fourth airplane, it was soon bringing in its fifth and sixth 737s. Texas International had an edge over Southwest since it had many connecting routes outside of Texas on which Southwest was prohibited from competing. But Lorenzo and Burr would have to cut costs if they had any hope of competing inside Texas.

Burr and his operating aides therefore hung tough when a labor contract for the airline's ground employees came up for renegotiation. Finally Burr went to Lorenzo for approval of a final offer that everybody at the bargaining table had resolved to live with. Burr, hearing no objection from Lorenzo, then gave the go-ahead to the company's chief negotiator. The negotiator, bargaining late into the night, at last closed the deal, and Burr once again called Lorenzo.

"Frank, great news," Burr said. "We got the deal."

"What deal?" Lorenzo asked.

"You know, the deal we discussed!"

"I didn't agree to that."

Burr was stunned. Of course Lorenzo had approved the deal, he thought. But now the company's negotiators had to go back to the bargaining table and take it all back. The union, outraged, promptly launched a strike, the first in Texas International's history. The strike, one of the longest in the industry in years, lasted some four months, but it was no financial calamity for Texas International. The industry had a program known as "mutual aid," in which all airlines subsidized the losses incurred by any one of them that took a strike. It was the airlines' way of assuring that wages never got disproportionately high at any one employer—that they would all remain in the same boat, so far as wages were concerned. During his long strike, Lorenzo raked in more than $10 million in mutual aid from the rest of the airline industry. He had turned adversity into gain. As he later confided to Burr, "We needed the strike."

The strike was a blessing for Lorenzo in another respect: it forced him to come to terms with Southwest, in a way that would revolutionize the airline industry.

The showdown came over service to the unlikely locale of Harlingen, Texas. Harlingen was a dusty border town in the southernmost tip of Texas, a Hispanic-settled agricultural center that seemed as much a part of Mexico as America. Texas International had served Harlingen for years. Although the city never seemed to produce more than a handful of passengers, the fare was always high. A remote six or eight hours by car from just about anywhere, Harlingen was vitally dependent on that air route. When the strike shut down Texas International's service, the townsfolk of Harlingen felt betrayed.

Southwest's operating chief, Lamar Muse, saw Harlingen as the perfect place for Southwest to take its next step; Harlingen was only a few minutes by car from the coastal resort of South Padre Island, which Muse recognized as an up-and-coming tourist spot. But Harlingen was among Texas International's most dearly held destinations, a monopoly route with high fares. Lorenzo vowed to block Southwest from Harlingen, sparing nothing in the effort.

Lorenzo's aides launched an advertising campaign depicting Southwest as a Trojan horse with wings, claiming that if Texas International were forced to abandon service from Harlingen, the city would lose its vital route connections to destinations all across America. Texas International, after all, could pick up business passengers and cargo in Harlingen and arrange their shipment to any region of America, if not on its own system, then on Braniff or another airline. Southwest, by contrast, was strictly a point-to-point carrier. Southwest did not write connecting tickets. It did not "interline" baggage or freight to other airlines. Southwest didn't even carry U.S. mail. (Doing so caused too many late departures.)

In defending his monopoly, Lorenzo hired a new general counsel named Sam Coats, a former Texas state representative who had grown up in Harlingen. Charged with rallying the hometown folks against Southwest, Coats failed to deliver anywhere near the support

Lorenzo required. When dozens of Harlingen residents made the long trek to Austin for a public hearing on Southwest's application (by bus, because Texas International was still on strike), virtually all of them promoted, rather than opposed, the new service by Southwest. The best that Sam Coats could do in Texas International's behalf was to have a funeral director from Harlingen testify that he relied on Texas International's connecting flights to ship snowbird caskets outside Texas for burial.

Southwest's new intrastate route was readily approved, and suddenly, at the nice round figure of $25 each way, Southwest was carrying close to a thousand people a day where Texas International had been lucky to carry a few hundred at $40. Before long, passengers from Mexico were coming over International Bridge in droves to seize the low fares. Harlingen Airport was teeming with such business that the dirt parking lot had to be paved over.

Lorenzo, Burr, and everyone else at Texas International watched as Southwest launched one jam-packed plane after another. Texas International had to do something drastic, fast. Its executives launched themselves on a crash course in discount pricing economics, with Lorenzo joking that they were now enrolled at Southwest University.

The duty to develop a response fell principally to two of Don Burr's subordinates. One was Gerald Gitner, who had been hired as Texas International's marketing head a few years earlier at the age of 29. Gitner was one of the true prodigies of commercial aviation, an industry in which, everywhere outside of Texas International, the old fogies held sway. Hired at TWA in 1968, Gitner had soon become the youngest vice president in the industry. He was, among other things, one of the first people in the industry to discover the "portable" electronic calculator—a device the size of a salesman's case that Gitner hauled around to route swaps and other complex bargaining proceedings among the airlines. Gitner reeled off numbers and analysis with such speed and intensity that his coworkers called him Gatling Gun Gitner. Eager for the chance to earn some equity, tiring of the dinosaurs who didn't "get it," Gitner abandoned his 40th-floor corner office at TWA, with its view of the harbor and Kennedy Airport in the distance, to work in the windowless confines of the Blue Barn in Houston. One of Gitner's principal aides, in turn, was James O'Donnell, who had started his career conducting sales calls on pharmacies for the maker of Vicks Vaporub. O'Donnell had gone on to Mohawk Airlines, where he had become acquainted with Lorenzo, and later to Texas International.

Burr and his aides began their counterattack by trying to pack more seats into each airplane. Most of the industry in recent years had been going in the opposite direction, ripping out interiors and installing ever wider seats with more room between rows. One of Burr's planners, however, read about the crash of an Aeromexico DC-9 in which some 90 people were killed, and exclaimed "Ninety? Shit! We're only carrying 70 on a DC-9!" Burr began studying ways of packing seats more tightly, a complex undertaking that demanded reconfiguring the ballast of the planes, recalibrating takeoff speeds, and installing altogether different tires.

As they studied ways to answer Southwest's advancements, Lorenzo's boys quickly realized the virtue in working for one of the smallest airlines in America. With all departments under a single roof, they could analyze boarding patterns by walking down the hall to the revenue processing department and flipping through the ticket stubs for any flight. While bigger companies compiled and collated their operating data according to the reporting requirements of the CAB, Lorenzo's people worked up their own spreadsheets by hand, according to their own curiosity, a task made infinitely simpler by Gitner's experience in operating an electronic calculator.

It soon became evident to all of them that Texas International could not compete head-to-head with Southwest. The company could replace the business it had lost to Southwest only by raiding the bigger, more established carriers of passengers. But with its Tree Tops image, how could Texas International ever hope to distinguish itself from the bigger airlines? With a price discount—if they could ever convince the government to allow it.

Lorenzo's former Harvard classmate, Bob Carney, urged caution; a price cut on the order of 15 percent, he argued, would be radical enough. The junior men in the group, Gitner and O'Donnell, pushed for something simple, something nobody could forget, something like half off. It reminded O'Donnell of his days selling Vicks Vaporub—*half off if you order today!* "A bargain isn't a bargain unless it's perceived as a bargain," Gitner argued.

The arithmetic was obvious: flying a plane completely full at one half the fare was better than flying it one-third full at full fare. Lorenzo, though eager for the acceptance of his fellow airline chieftains and reluctant to break their pricing stricture, began to appreciate the logic of slashing prices. He told people how busy his father's Third Avenue beauty salon became when a sign went into the window promoting a special on permanents.

Lorenzo gave his approval.

On November 2, 1976, Jimmy Carter defeated Gerald Ford. The following day, only a block north of the White House, Gerald Gitner of Texas International stood behind a lectern at the Hay-Adams Hotel to announce that the company was going to the CAB for permission to cut fares by 50 percent in a few markets—interstate markets. Texas International dubbed the new prices "peanuts fares." It was a pleasant coincidence that peanuts were the airline snack of choice and that the newly elected president of the United States was a peanut farmer. Flying back to Houston aboard Braniff (Texas International did not serve Washington), Lorenzo's staffers were delighted to overhear passengers marveling over the *Washington Star* account of that morning's announcement. "Jesus Christ! Did you see this?" one man exclaimed. "You can fly half-price!"

These were not charter fares. They weren't holiday specials. They were price cuts, pure and simple, of the kind for which the CAB was fully empowered to send people to jail, except that these fares would soon have the official blessing of John Robson and the other radicals who had moved into the CAB. For the first time in nearly 40 years, an airline flying people across state lines was allowed to institute an across-the-board price cut in response to market conditions.

Back in Texas it was off to the races. On the first day of peanuts fares, Texas International's passenger loads doubled. They doubled again on the second day, then hit an increase of as much as 600 percent by the end of the first week—with no advertising except by word-of-mouth and the free publicity generated by the peanuts angle. A product that many people had never even contemplated buying was now, at half off, well within their reach. The notion of value, seldom explicitly applied as a marketing concept in those days, was in full flower. Now confinement to a middle income bracket no longer automatically denied one the excitement and convenience of flight (if one happened to live in a town served by Texas International, that is). Surveys showed that 25 percent of the people flying on "peanuts fares" would have otherwise made their trip in a car; an additional 30 percent otherwise would have stayed home. Some of these new, first-time fliers began to think about doing it a second time, and a third.

To consumer advocates, Frank Lorenzo was a hero. Better still, Texas International's profit-and-loss statement, once dependent on handouts from the government and strike payments from the rest of the airline industry, began to glow. More flights were added, and the more Lorenzo's people went to the CAB, the more John Robson's people said yes. A number of other airlines offered their own versions of peanuts fares; Continental, for instance, introduced "chickenfeed fares," which the wags at Texas International quickly dubbed "chickenshit fares."

There was one drawback. The very success of peanuts fares strongly suggested that the airlines could manage their own affairs—that they could stimulate their own markets, widen the population of people who had shared in the privilege of flying, even create jobs and demand for new airplanes. But as delighted as he was at the outcome of peanuts pricing, Lorenzo did not want John Robson or anyone else in Washington getting the wrong idea about his intentions. Lorenzo went out of his way to say that peanuts fares were a limited, isolated demonstration of the virtues of flexibility in government regulation. They were *not,* he emphasized, an argument for doing away with it.

Lorenzo figured that Texas International would be annihilated in five minutes without the CAB. He could barely handle a single upstart such as Southwest Airlines, let alone survive being surrounded by them. Just as ominously, up the road a piece, in Dallas, American Airlines and Braniff had hundreds of airplanes between them. They sat there like caged gorillas. And United Airlines, the biggest in the United States, flew planes to all 50 states. It could suffocate a little carrier like Texas International if it ever had the freedom to do so.

Even to an innovator, even to Frank Lorenzo, the system was fine just as it was.

CHAPTER 3

NETWORK WARRIORS

Among the personality types reigning in American corporations, the aggressor is commonplace. He has an instinct for the jugular. He wishes to dominate. He enjoys the battle as well as the conquest. He breathes inspiration into his subordinates. He seizes on the unexpected. A vastly different species, the bureaucrat, is just as frequently found, and in his own way is as essential to corporate success. He thrives on detail. He revels in systems and processes. He emphasizes reaction over action. On occasion these divergent traits combine in a single executive. One such individual was C. R. Smith, who built American Airlines. Another was the executive who would later follow Smith to the top of American. His name was Robert Crandall.

Crandall would ultimately become the most feared and powerful man in the global airline industry. His very appearance intimidated people. He had thick lips, a hard, lean body, and blue eyes that flashed intensity, all bearing him a resemblance to the rock star Mick Jagger. He slicked back his hair with "greasy kid stuff," his part so perfect it looked as if you could cut your wrists on it. Crandall's canine teeth hung lower than the surrounding teeth. "Fang," some people called him, though not often in his presence.

Appearance alone did not account for Crandall's sobriquet. Crandall simply loved to triumph over his adversaries, to vanquish them utterly, to run up points on the scoreboard. "Go ahead," he told a marketing group. "Be ruthless. Be driven. Don't let anything get in your way." Though no fan of professional sports, he went out of his way to invoke Vince Lombardi, Lou Holtz, and other coaches whose teams he rarely watched but whose ruthlessness he admired. At a company dinner dance Crandall once cried, "We'll crunch our competitors so hard even Lombardi will hear it, and nobody will need a hearing aid to know we knocked them off their feet!" And with that he commanded everyone to the dance floor.

He pounded his desk, sputtered when he shouted, and spit out the vilest curse words—not merely the *hell!* and *son of a bitch!* typical of the executive vocabulary but caustic and abrasive words like *fucker* and *cocksucker,* with a plume of blue cigarette smoke trailing behind or gathering overhead. Crandall was aware that he inspired fear in many of the people who worked for him. He once joked that when turning to the mirror while shaving, he expected to see black wings.

But while seized with such emotion, Crandall also had a passion for logic and analysis—for hierarchies, systems, and structures. Let the other guys play poker; Crandall loved bridge, the logician's game. Crandall settled in a region where country and western and rock and roll reigned supreme, but he brooded to the rational scales of Mozart. Typographical errors, word misuse, and grammatical lapses hit him like strikes to the brow; they signaled untrustworthiness. Order was everything. At home his shop tools hung precisely, even if he was seldom there to use them. In later years, he ordered the placement of four custom-made podiums at strategic locations, for quick shipment wherever he happened to be giving a speech; Crandall refused to speak from any lectern failing to meet his specifications. If he noticed his wife's purse sitting on the kitchen counter, he might pry it open for inspection; finding it in the same condition as any purse, he would dump it out and reorganize it, throwing away the bits of grit that had accumulated in the creases at the bottom. "It drives her batshit," he would remark with a raspy nicotine cackle.

Above all, Bob Crandall was stricken with personal ambition. Was there a moment, he was once asked, when he realized that he wanted to run American Airlines? "Yeah," he answered. "When I was born."

• • •

Robert Lloyd Crandall came into the world at the midpoint of the Great Depression, on December 6, 1935. His father was rescued from unemployment by Franklin Delano Roosevelt's Civilian Conservation Corps, which caused the family to abandon its Rhode Island roots and travel to wherever the work was. Later his father sold life insurance from territory to territory. In his 12 years of public education, Crandall attended 13 schools.

He would later say that his peripatetic youth taught him how to meet and relate to new people. But it also taught him to fight. As a youngster Bob Crandall was a fat boy with quick fists. Every time he got to a new school, he felt an intense urge to get into a scrap. A decent fistfight was the only way to break in, he thought, the truest path to acceptance. Bob Crandall also studied, working hard to get good grades. Report cards, after all, were a kind of scoreboard in a competition of peers, a way of ranking oneself against another. Forty years after his graduation, an interviewer began to inquire about his academic record. "What kind of grades did you—?"

"Straight A's," he snapped, as if he were reliving the thrill of a championship ball game.

And he worked, and loved doing so, from the moment of his first job—digging out a basement for a new home, a boy and his shovel, blistering his hands and sweltering in the heat of a North Carolina summer; he was not yet an eighth grader. In later years Crandall found himself working in grocery stores. Because such stores opened early and closed late, he could get in a lot of hours before and after school. As a checkout clerk he enjoyed seeing how fast he could ring up a pile of groceries. His high school annual for his graduation year of 1957 said he was most likely to be found at the grocery store. His "pet peeve" was listed as "Democrats." The yearbook editors also observed that he was "noted for arguments."

A slimmed-down Bob Crandall worked his way through the University of Rhode Island, where he loved staying up until all hours debating—religion, current events, anything that could set off a round of intellectual jousting. With a scholarship to the Wharton School, he earned his M.B.A. while holding a job that allowed him time to study: the 5 P.M.-to-2 A.M. shift as a supervisor at WFIL-TV in Philadelphia. Before long he landed at Eastman Kodak, in the credit department, collecting money from film processors around the country.

But it was not photography, and certainly not bill collecting, that most captivated Crandall's interest. It was computers. Kodak had installed a state-of-the-art electronic system for tracking the money it had coming in. In 1960 Bob Crandall found himself one of the few executives in the country—in the world, really—with responsibilities in a new field of management called data processing.

He moved on to Hallmark Cards in Kansas City, which operated a computer system that monitored the sales of individual illustrations and inscriptions on a store-by-store basis: a four-line happygram with a rose might be going briskly in Sheboygan, for instance, while a five-line message with a violet was doing well in Los Angeles. The system alerted Hallmark's marketers when a price change was called for; if a particular package of 25¢ cards sold out faster than predicted, the next package might be shipped with 35¢ price tags.

Crandall was in awe of Hallmark's system. As he once explained, "They sold the shit out of greeting cards." But Crandall knew that Hallmark would not keep him forever. An urgent need for massive computer systems, the biggest ever built, was emerging in another industry.

An airline seat is like fresh food—a grapefruit, say—in that it spoils after so much time on the shelf. Every empty seat taking off on every flight is a spoiled grapefruit and exactly as valueless. Both required time, effort, and money to create, and both came to a wasteful, meaningless end. And on an exceedingly large number of flights, the sale of one last seat, according to the First Rule of Airline Economics, could easily decide whether the plane flew the entire distance in the red or the black.

As the builder of American Airlines, C. R. Smith had agonized continually over the problem of matching passengers with seats before the latter perished upon departure. The trick was to balance reservations against inventory, a far greater task than it might seem. At first, in the early 1930s, a single ledger had passed from hand to hand as agents in a central office recorded reservations and erased those that were canceled. With the advent of the DC-3, as the fleets and schedules of the airlines swelled and as the seating capacity of each plane increased, a single book became impractical, so multiple books were maintained. These had to be reconciled frequently—a massively time-consuming process—and even so, each book was inherently out-of-date at all times. Books gave way to chalk and slate boards and eventually to electric light boards. More and more agents were crammed into the reservations offices, with the line of sight to the blackboard limited by the space between structural support columns—22 feet in most buildings of the time. Some agents peered through opera glasses. Teletypes clattered. Clerks known as "card boys" scurried from desk to desk, eventually to be replaced by mechanical conveyors. One blackboard gave rise to multiple blackboards, which quickly encountered the same problems that multiple ledgers had caused. A science called "reservations theory" was born to cope with the exponentially worsening challenge, but to little avail; as with so much else in the airline business, there was no economy of scale in handling reservations. The more the airlines grew, the less efficient they became.

The need to coordinate reservations among multiple cities—indeed, among multiple airlines—added still another dimension of complexity. For most of their history the airlines had been scheduled like railroads: numerous stops along a single line, with passengers boarding and disembarking at each stop, sometimes to board a second flight on a different airline flying in a roughly perpendicular direction. Confirming the itinerary for a single passenger traveling on two connecting airlines required no fewer than 20 separate communications, making the airlines, even in the 1940s, among the world's biggest users of leased telephone lines.

But what if the entire process could be automated?

In the early 1940s the technical people at American contacted the major makers of adding machines and other computational equipment. American wanted a machine that could tell reservationists when particular flights were sold out and, just as important, when cancellations had once again made seats available. Not a single contractor would touch the job. There were too many variables, and the data changed too quickly. Although it was 20 years before the expression "real time" came into use, that, in a nutshell, was the realm in which American needed to operate—with a machine that could simultaneously receive and deliver information to and from hundreds of remote terminals, giving each location the benefit of the latest data entered into the system from any other location.

So American's technical people undertook the effort on their own, creating a grand contraption of tall cylinders, each representing a different flight on a different day. The cylinders were filled with marbles, one for every unsold seat. With each reservation a button was pressed and an electrical signal sent, opening a hatch at the bottom of the cylinder through which one marble was emptied. Conversely, the cancellation of any reservation caused a marble to be electrically released into the top of the cylinder, restoring the seat to the unsold inventory of the flight. The machine was ungainly and impractical, but it vividly demonstrated a potential solution.

After some additional experimentation, American convinced the Teleregister Corporation to join in. Together the companies developed a phalanx of switches, relays, and plugs, which they called "the brain." This room-sized device in turn was hooked to hundreds of little terminals that looked like adding machines. Reservationists were issued stacks of notched metal plates, which they inserted into their terminals as a way of notifying the brain which flight they were inquiring about. The brain responded with a signal that illuminated a green light, when seats were available, or an amber light, if the flight was sold out. A few years later, in 1952, the ganglia of wires and relays were replaced by a crude, homemade memory device—a giant grinding wheel, covered in aluminum and sprayed with an oxide, on which millions of tiny electrical charges could be deposited. American's Magnetronic Reservisor was nicknamed Girlie, because, it was said, she "told all."

The Reservisor, installed at American's LaGuardia Airport reservations center, was a technological marvel but still only a marginal improvement over books and blackboards. There was no way to attach an individual's name or phone number to a particular reservation; reconciling the passenger manifest with the electronic seat inventory remained a laborious manual process.

The advent of jets in the late 1950s made efficiency in record keeping even more essential while also making it more onerous. The speed of jet travel encouraged more business and leisure travelers to fly on impulse, demanding even more up-to-date inventory records and faster communication. American tried to keep up by adding more terminals and more reservationists, but this only slowed the process more while creating, according to an internal company report, a cost problem of "alarmingly unfavorable proportions." C. R. Smith was despondent.

Meanwhile IBM was absorbed in a Cold War project for the federal government called SAGE—Semi-Automatic Ground Environment, a rather innocuous name for the system that controlled the giant luminous screens used to monitor incoming nuclear bombers. SAGE enabled war planners to sit in a semicircle and play nuclear simulation games. It was one of the first real-time applications of computer technology.

One day in 1953 an IBM sales representative named Blair Smith, finding himself on an American flight sitting next to C. R. Smith, discovered that their surnames were only the first coincidence. Smith of American explained his frustration in managing reservations while Smith of IBM betrayed his eagerness to make a sale. Before long IBM had a contract to apply the war-making technology of SAGE to American's computer reservations problems. IBM called the project SABER, for Semi-Automatic Business Environment Research. For nearly a decade the project engineers toiled. Along the way, in 1959, an American executive flipping through a magazine stopped at an ad for the 1960 Buick LeSabre; he transposed the last two letters of the acronym and called the system Sabre. It would become, in every respect, the weapon that its name implied.

Sabre came to life in an office in suburban Westchester County, New York, late in 1962. At the time only 14,000 or so commercial computers of any kind were operating in the United States, nearly all of them issuing payrolls, compiling financial data, or solving massive scientific equations. None was engaged in computing in real time. Overnight American's reservation system was transformed from an adding machine to an instantly updated list of seats sold and available on each flight, including the name of every reservation holder and his or her phone number, special meal requests, and rental car or hotel information. Sabre was hailed as the world's most complex commercial computer, a "space age brain."

With airlines competing on the basis of Polynesian pubs and all-steak flights to Florida—competing, in short, on the basis of anything but price—American Airlines achieved a marketing triumph with its instantaneous and reliable telephone reservation system. Almost immediately American began gaining market share on the other airlines, including its archrival, United Airlines.

American's employees did not exactly greet Sabre with joy. The Transport Workers Union expressed concern that employees would be "slaughtered by the new mechanical monsters." C. R. Smith deflated such anxieties by promising that not a single reservationist would lose a job upon the arrival of Sabre. It was an easy promise to keep because, as Smith knew, those jobs were occupied almost exclusively by women and turnover was so high that the rate of natural attrition would almost perfectly match the pace at which the new computer system would be connected.

There was one additional value inherent in the Sabre system. As a company technical report dryly noted, Sabre "will be extremely useful in supplying management with abundant information on day-to-day operations." It was an understatement. From its first day of operation Sabre began accumulating reels of information, the most detailed information ever compiled on the travel patterns emanating from every major city—by destination, by month, by season, by day of the week, by hour of the day—information that in the right hands would become exceedingly valuable in the industry that American sought to dominate.

Those airlines that ignored the computer revolution did so at tremendous peril. One was Trans World Airlines. In 1966, four years after American was on-line with Sabre, clerks at TWA were still taking reservations by hand, on index cards. It was in that year that TWA hired a 30-year-old Bob Crandall from Hallmark Cards as its manager of credit and collections, though he would not stay in that position for long.

TWA had contracted with Burroughs Corporation to develop a massive airline reservations system called George, as in, "Let George do it." Yet even after $75 million had been spent, a staggering sum in the late 1960s, George was way behind schedule, and TWA continued lagging badly in the race to fill empty airplane seats. Finally Crandall was given the job of whipping George into shape.

Crandall impatiently listened to the excuses from the Burroughs people. George, they insisted, was almost ready. Just six more months! they begged. But Crandall recognized that massive computer systems reach a point at which they have either sprung to life or never will. There was no evolutionism or gradualism, no such thing as "almost ready." So in the spring of 1970 Crandall ordered a wall erected through the middle of TWA's computer center in suburban New Jersey. To one side he confined the Burroughs engineers, with their beloved if moribund George. "You've got six months," he told them. On the other side of the wall IBM was brought in to begin work on a new system. After precisely six months George was still not working. Crandall and his people went to the Burroughs side of the computer room, turned off the power, and told everyone to go home.

Crandall was summoned to a meeting with the chairman of Burroughs. The jilted executive glared at the smart-aleck young executive who had brought such loss and embarrassment to his company. "Young man," the Burroughs chief told Crandall, "your career is over."

Well, not quite—although within two years, by 1972, Crandall had hit one of those career plateaus that nearly every executive encounters while climbing the pyramid of corporate power. Passed over when a new chief financial officer was appointed, he grew angry and disillusioned. Convinced that TWA had lost its way, he decided to quit.

He was drawn to Bloomingdale's with the siren promise that he would succeed the incumbent president, Marvin Traub, as chieftain of the retailing giant. But Crandall found retailing exquisitely boring. Inventory automation didn't begin to approach the intellectual challenge of airline reservations. Nor did he particularly like managing low-wage, low-skill workers. And he perceived a caste system in retailing in which merchants were Brahmans and everybody in the back office was scum.

Bob Crandall had to get back to the airline business. It had everything he wanted from a career. Later on he would observe that "the airline business is fast-paced, high-risk, and highly leveraged. It puts a premium on things I like to do. I think I communicate well. And I am very good at detail. I love detail."

Happily an offer came quickly, from American Airlines. In April 1973 Crandall began work as the chief financial officer in American headquarters on Third Avenue in midtown Manhattan, practically next door to TWA. The headquarters staffers fully expected to see the new finance man, late of Bloomingdale's, strolling into American outfitted in the height of fashion—a wide tie, no doubt, and wide lapels. They were surprised, and a little disappointed, to see that their new colleague wore a skinny tie and narrow lapels. Very little of the fashion culture, it appeared, had worn off on Bob Crandall.

By coincidence, within days of Crandall's arrival American sank into a leadership crisis. Improbably, the enabling event was Watergate.

When C. R. Smith had left American to become Lyndon Johnson's secretary of commerce, he had been succeeded by George Spater, a melancholy-looking lawyer with wire-rimmed glasses. Whereas C.R. was famous for firing off memos from his own typewriter, Spater kept his office door closed because he could not abide the clatter of typing. Smith, recognizing the value of celebrities in consumer marketing, had hobnobbed with Clark Gable and Carole Lombard at the opening of *Gone With the Wind* in 1939; Spater, probably the most erudite man ever to run an airline, spent his free time immersed in the writings of Virginia Woolf and the arcana of medieval plainsong.

In 1971, three years into the job as chairman, Spater was anxiously watching American stumble. His insular management style had bred executive infighting below him. The great Sabre computer reservations system had begun to atrophy; in a standoff between the finance and marketing departments over who controlled Sabre's budget, much of the budget simply went unfilled. Worse, the widebodies were still flying half-empty. American's east-west route system was old and stale, denying American any meaningful participation in the one great growth market of the era—the north-south vacation traffic stimulated by the development of Florida and other warm-weather climes. American Airlines needed a bold stroke, a merger perhaps, or a big new series of routes.

Spater developed a strategy to compete, but he could fulfill his plans only at the sufferance of the federal government. Moreover, any doubt about the government's continued dominion over the airlines had been very recently lain to rest when Richard Nixon, in his first few days in office, personally interposed himself in the intricacies of a long-simmering CAB case over which airlines would receive new routes over the Pacific. Nixon had made himself lord and master over the airlines' growth.

In the fall of 1971, with American's problems weighing heavily on his shoulders, George Spater was contemplating a dinner invitation from Herbert Kalmbach, the personal lawyer of President Nixon. Spater knew that Kalmbach was handling much of the fund-raising for Nixon's 1972 reelection drive and that in addition to representing President Nixon, Kalmbach did legal work for archrival United. Spater agreed to meet Kalmbach at the 21 Club in New York. Over dinner Kalmbach told him that anyone giving $100,000 to the Committee to Reelect the President (later known as CREEP) would be regarded as being in a "special class."

Spater brooded. Though he wanted no favors from the Nixon White House, he worried that failing to contribute would expose American to the risk of unexpected action. It was terra incognita, Spater would later explain. "I think sometimes the fear of the unknown may be more terrifying than the fear of the known." Corporate campaign contributions were (and are) illegal, and Spater was not the type to break the law lightly. He was known as a man of sensitivity and integrity. He had written articles on morality and ethics.

While wrestling with his dilemma, Spater received a hauntingly strange nudge from C. R. Smith, the venerated former chairman. In an envelope Smith had placed four checks written on his personal account, each for $5,000, dated about one month apart and payable in cash. In a note accompanying the checks, Smith cryptically wrote that he figured that Spater might be needing some extra funds about then.

Spater knew precisely what Smith meant. He wasted no time in having a trusted aide cash the checks and pay a visit to CREEP headquarters, a block from the White House. "Here's five in cash," the American operative told Hugh Sloan, the campaign finance chief, turning over an envelope full of $100 bills. "There will be more." One by one the remainder of C. R.'s checks were likewise cashed into $100 bills, each a few weeks after the next, followed by another trip to campaign headquarters.

Because the contributions involved Smith's personal funds rather than American's corporate funds, no laws had been broken. But the Nixon people reminded Spater that American remained well short of its quota. Having already taken one step down the icy slope, Spater then slipped into outright illegality, authorizing the payment of an additional $55,000 through a series of off-the-books transactions involving a Middle Eastern business agent and a safe at American's headquarters in New York. That money too went to CREEP as a pile of $100 bills.

A few months after Nixon had been handily reelected, a list of unlawful donors to CREEP was obtained through a lawsuit by Common Cause. George Spater immediately went public, making American Airlines the first of a dozen major American corporations to confess to campaign finance illegalities; as a consequence of exposing himself to the first flash of publicity, Spater was spared from criminal charges by Archibald Cox, the Watergate special prosecutor. The role of the $20,000 in checks from the beloved founder C. R. Smith in priming the pump at CREEP was never publicly revealed; it was a secret kept even from most of the top officers at American. George Spater alone took the fall for American on Watergate. Sacked by American's board of directors, he moved to England, immersed himself in literature, and died a few years later.

C. R. Smith, his reputation unblemished in the affair, returned to the chairman's suite at American until a new successor could be found. There was no one fit for the job inside the company; Bob Crandall and the other senior officers were too green, particularly for the top job at so troubled a company. In an unusual move the board chose Albert V. Casey, an outsider though a well-rounded executive of stellar reputation. He had served as president of Times Mirror Company and publisher of the *Los Angeles Times,* and had worked in the railroad industry as well.

Crandall, suddenly, had a new boss to impress if he wished eventually to become the president of American. He received a boost from no less than C. R. Smith, who, in retiring from the chairman's position for a second time, left behind one of his trademark typed missives. It contained a thumbnail evaluation of each of American's senior officers. Though he had worked with him only briefly, the old man wrote of Crandall, "One of the brightest young financial men I've ever met. Formerly with TWA. Entirely competent."

Casey had the opportunity to learn this for himself even before his appointment was publicly announced. Crandall made a point of visiting Casey's temporary apartment in New York with a big, thick binder under his arm. In the book Crandall had organized all the particulars of American Airlines—its routes, financial results, fleet, fares. He and the new boss sat down and turned the pages together, one by one.

Crandall had made himself a valued advisor. Soon Casey was looking for a new senior vice president of marketing, a powerful position, a first among equals in the ranks of American's senior vice presidents. Casey asked Crandall to help him evaluate candidates for the job, only to find that during the interviews Crandall displayed a more impressive grasp of airline marketing than any of the people under consideration. Casey readily gave the marketing job to Crandall. After only one year at American, Crandall had become the most powerful of the company's senior vice presidents, one step away from the post held by Casey himself.

To Crandall airline marketing was a planning exercise, a numbers game, a two-sided exercise in maximizing revenues while minimizing costs. He set out to attack both aspects relentlessly and in unconventional ways.

As Crandall saw it, 35 years of government-sponsored fare increases had created a spendthrift culture at American. He began weeklong sessions in New York in which individual managers were required to present their budgets. Line by line Crandall would demand to know precisely where every dollar was going and why the expense could not be eliminated or controlled. *A security guard in St. Thomas? Why not a barking dog instead? Hell, why not a tape recording of a barking dog?* From 7 A.M. until midnight, day after day, the sessions dragged on. Crandall was purposefully contentious, yelling, screaming, glowering. Managers who displayed ignorance of their costs were terminated within days or even hours of their presentations. Each of these meetings, each of these confrontations, was designed by Crandall to teach a lesson to the manager sitting on the other side of the table.

Costs, however, were only half the battle, and probably the less important half. Marketing also meant selling, which in the airline industry traditionally meant big advertising budgets, celebrity endorsements, golf tournaments, destination promotions, and the comforts and titillations provided by stewardesses. But to Crandall, sales hinged on the intricacies of timetables and schedules. With his computers grinding away, Crandall began to study the degree to which even subtleties could make a huge difference in selling one more seat.

Airline schedules were published in a book called the *Official Airline Guide.* The *OAG* listed flights by city pairs—including connecting or "through" flights, as in Philadelphia to Buffalo through New York. Flights with the shortest travel time between any two points were listed first. This was a valuable display position, as years of history proved that the first flight listed between any two cities received the greatest number of bookings by far. Here, Crandall recognized, was a marketing opportunity.

In one of his first presentations to the American board of directors, Crandall said he was establishing the tightest possible connections on through flights—not only as a way of getting people to their destinations sooner, but as a way of endowing more of American's flights with listing bias in the *OAG.* Crandall even put limits on the move to save fuel by flying at slower speeds; the sale of additional seats attained through the preferred listing position in the *OAG* more than paid for the greater fuel consumption.

As valuable as Crandall found such studies, he knew that computers held the potential to perform much more valuable functions for American. Computers, as he had learned at Hallmark Cards, could sharpen to pinpoint precision a company's actions in the marketplace. They could be used as offensive weapons.

But Crandall quickly learned how deeply Sabre had slipped during the Spater years. On his first visit to Sabre headquarters, which had been moved to Tulsa, he was led to a basement and shown 1,000 cathode ray tubes sitting in their packing crates. The video screens had been ordered, paid for, shipped—and never so much as taken out of the boxes. They had sat collecting dust, held hostage for more than a year in a petty bureaucratic battle in which no one would release the funds to have them installed on the reservationists' desks. While the computer revolution was raging throughout American industry, reservationists at American Airlines were still absorbed in the machine-gun clatter of their IBM Selectric typewriters, used as terminals connected to the Sabre mainframe.

Staring at the sea of unopened boxes, Crandall could not believe his eyes. He immediately went to New York, pushed out American's top data processing executive, and brought in an old friend from TWA.

Crandall resolved to restore Sabre to its lost glory. There was no time to waste. The onslaught of technology was about to thrust Crandall into history's first computer war—with the industry leader, United Airlines.

From the time of the postal scandal in 1934, United had been the personal dominion of William A. Patterson, a short and cherubic man who had a marvelous touch with employees. To the extent that C. R. Smith had made American what it was, so too had Patterson built United. For most of his career Patterson unhappily watched American display its trophy as the nation's largest airline, but in 1961, with the blessing of the Civil Aeronautics Board, Patterson catapulted United far ahead of American by purchasing Capital Airlines. Before long United adopted the "friendly skies" appellation not only as a jingle but as an operating philosophy. Under Patterson United had breeding and culture and class. People wanted to work for it, which, in an era of competition based on service rather than price, made people want to fly it as well.

The mood changed almost overnight in 1966 when Patterson was succeeded by George Keck, an engineer. Although skilled at managing United's complex flight operations, Keck was alternately remote and confrontational as a manager. Stewardesses complained that he would plunk down in an airline seat without addressing them. He came to loggerheads with United's pilots over their demand to have a third man—a nonflying flight engineer, someone who looked at maps and instruments—in the cockpit of the newly introduced 737 jet. Keck, spurning his board of directors, agreed to have the matter submitted to arbitration, a proceeding that United lost. United would be saddled with three men in the cockpit for years, a decision that cost the company hundreds of millions of dollars in needless labor costs. The United board was furious. United's relations with the CAB grew uncharacteristically contentious. The onslaught of the jumbo jets worsened the company's financial performance. By 1970 United was deeply in the red.

Keck's standing sank even lower when United ran aground in the race to automate its reservations. The company was absorbed in a

$56 million project with Sperry Rand's Univac division to create the world's most powerful airline computer system, intended to exceed even American's Sabre. The software package alone was consuming the full-time attention of 200 technicians. A $5 million computer building had been erected in the most visible possible location: adjacent to United corporate headquarters in Elk Grove Village, near O'Hare Airport in suburban Chicago. Keck assured the board that he was personally supervising the program, that the system was almost ready. But when a team of independent consultants came in to make an evaluation, they pronounced the system a nonstarter. United, they said, should cut its losses and start from scratch.

By December 1970, the directors of United were unanimous: Keck had to go. He was fired at a board meeting the next day.

United was in trouble. Some of the directors actually worried that the company might be going down the drain. To some it bordered on a national security issue. United needed a savior, but who?

Charles Luce, the chairman of Consolidated Edison Company in New York, was still a newcomer to the United Airlines board of directors when Keck was fired, but he sensed a hidden agenda at work. Thomas Gleed, a prominent Seattle banker, had led the board against Keck. At about the same time Gleed had successfully championed United's purchase of the Western International hotel chain, headquartered in Seattle. Western's chairman, Edward E. Carlson, had been one of Gleed's close friends for more than 30 years.

And now, Luce noted, Gleed was suggesting that a new chairman to replace Keck was right in their midst: Eddie Carlson. It appeared that Gleed had pushed the purchase of Western partly as a kind of executive-recruiting maneuver.

But Luce could see that Carlson was fresh blood, a proven manager who was wonderful with people, someone who could begin patching things up with United's disaffected employee groups. In addition, weren't hotels the first cousins to airlines? A hotel room was every bit the ripe grapefruit that an airline seat was; left unfilled, it spoiled the instant that the front desk checked in the last guest of the evening. An airline, when one cut through the romance and the technical vagaries of flight, was nothing more than a marketing company, selling its product to a customer base nearly identical to that of a hotel chain.

Moving into the chairman's suite, Eddie Carlson had no particular loyalty to United Airlines. So with the company choking on its jumbo jets and with three men crammed into the cockpits of the smaller jets, Carlson promptly canceled flights left and right. He got rid of 5,000 of United's 52,000 employees. Other costs were cut, and United's financial performance quickly improved.

But some expenditures were sacrosanct. A lifelong golfer and self-described hero-worshiper, Carlson found himself unable to fire the golfer Arnold Palmer from his $50,000-a-year endorsement contract with United. Nor could he discontinue the company's sponsorship of the Hawaiian Open; the association of United with a daylong television broadcast featuring waving palms, island girls in grass skirts, and lush golf greens, all displayed on the rapidly spreading color television sets of America and broadcast during the depths of winter back on the mainland, was the kind of marketing, it was thought, that wrested business from the competition at a time when Washington was denying the airlines the opportunity to do so on price.

Moreover, Carlson began putting the image back into United's product, even where it cost some money. The subdued hues of the airplane cabins, anachronistic now that the public fear of flying had largely abated, were replaced with bright cabin upholsteries, some in Thai silk. He bedecked the fleet in a new paint job, adding a touch of orange to the company's traditional red and blue and a contemporary-looking *U* to the tail. Even the company name was administered a small face-lifting, changed from United Air Lines to the sleeker United Airlines. (Delta and Eastern would cling to the quaint "Air Lines" appellation, however.)

Most important, Carlson was listening to employees. After boarding a United flight, he would change into a cardigan sweater and then work the cabin of an airplane, asking pilots and flight attendants whether they were happy and what the airline could be doing better. Hearing any criticism or suggestion, he reached into his pocket for an index card and passed a note to an aide traveling with him. The card was delivered to the desk of the appropriate department head, who was required to take action and report back to the chairman. Eddie Carlson's index cards—"Ready Eddies," people called them—became a symbol of management's willingness to listen. In 1971 alone Carlson logged 186,366 miles on United, half of them in coach.

This was, after all, a service business, so Carlson considered the views and attitudes of stewardesses of particular importance. United had an official limit of two drinks per passenger, but Carlson told them it was all right if they selectively broke the rule. Just use good judgment, he said. When they told him they didn't think it was right to charge a dollar for a beer, Carlson readily rolled back the price to 50¢. When he told a group of stewardesses that the company would put them up at the Waldorf instead of the St. Moritz, he drew a room full of gasps, followed by an entire minute of applause.

While cutting back operations and improving service, Carlson also looked for new ways to make money, and his background caused him to look at United's flight kitchens. Hotels' kitchens made money, didn't they? Why couldn't an airline's? For this task he needed Richard J. Ferris, a rising young star in the hotel business.

Dick Ferris displayed all the caveman aggression that gripped Bob Crandall—the impatience for victory, the compulsion for control, the desire to dominate. But there were two important differences. For one, technology held no thrill for Ferris. And as one would expect of someone who had spent his career working in first-class hotels, Ferris had a touch of refinement.

Richard J. Ferris was born with verve and personality. He was a cheerleader at Berkeley High School in Berkeley, California, where he also played the lead in the spring play, *The Man Who Came to Dinner.* He was handsome in a fraternity house way, with a square jaw, dark hair, bright eyes, and a chiseled physique. He had a sly smile and a sideward glance. He was a relentless flirt. When school let out, he always found his way to Lake Tahoe for a summer of water-skiing and whatever job he could find to support himself. One summer he was a grocery-store stock clerk. Another summer he worked in construction. And in his first job waiting on people, he worked as a houseboy at the Ojibwa Resort at Tahoe.

He was not, however, an academic standout. Although his father had scraped for his boys to attend college, Dick Ferris's mediocre grades ruled out that possibility in his case. So he had enlisted in the army, in Japan, working as a lifeguard. Being good at relationships, Ferris hit it off with the son of a colonel in the First Cavalry Division. Through him Ferris in 1957 landed an assignment as the man-

ager of a club in Tokyo for noncommissioned officers—not just any
NCO club but the Rocker Four Club, one of the biggest in the world,
with two great ballrooms, slot machines, a mammoth kitchen, wall-
to-wall bars, and space enough for a 16-piece orchestra—filled with
American servicemen escaping from Korea for R&R in Japan. Cor-
poral Ferris suddenly had 150 people working under him, including
enlisted men with more stripes than he. He was 20 years old.

A few years later Ferris was at the Cornell University School of
Hotel Management, the most famous school of its kind in the country, applying himself as he hadn't in high school and performing at
the top of his class. He worked as a sommelier, and spent a glorious
summer as a transatlantic cabin steward for Pan Am. ("What a job,"
he would later say. "Me and six flight attendants.") In 1962, as the
chairman of a senior honors project, Ferris used the occasion to
write a letter to the hotelier he most admired in the world—the legendary Dan London of San Francisco's St. Francis Hotel, where
President Eisenhower had stayed, where MacArthur had stayed
when returning from the Far East—"Mr. San Francisco," as he was
locally known. Ferris asked London to serve as the toastmaster for
the banquet held in conjunction with the honors project and seized
the chance to make a job pitch for himself.

London could not have avoided recognizing Ferris as a stunningly
turned out and ambitious young man, more mature and worldly
than the average college senior. But London had a better idea for
Ferris than working at the St. Francis, only one hotel in a big chain
operated by Western International. Western maintained its corporate headquarters on the top floor of the Olympic Hotel, in Seattle.

"Go to work at the Olympic Hotel," London told Ferris. "If you
do well, they'll notice you."

Ferris followed the advice, writing a disarmingly brash letter to
Eddie Carlson, then still the chairman of Western Hotels. "I believe
that the financial structure of the industry is becoming more complex each year," wrote the graduating senior. "There seems to be a
special need for men who know the hotel business from the bottom
up, and who are also expertly trained in finance and taxation." Carlson was so startled by Ferris's presumptuousness that Ferris soon
had a job.

Ferris began work as a manager of the Olympic Grille, studying food and wine and wage levels, all the while going to graduate school and falling in love with and marrying a staff member. And precisely as London had predicted, Eddie Carlson soon took notice.

Ferris found himself on the fast track, transferred in higher positions to bigger and more important hotels year by year. Over a decade he would serve Western in six cities—Seattle, New York, Anchorage, Chicago, Johannesburg, Seattle again, Kansas City, and Chicago again. The high point was rising to manager of the massive and prestigious Continental Plaza, operated by Western along North Michigan Avenue in Chicago, next to the site where the towering John Hancock Center was under construction.

Hotels were everything to Dick Ferris. "In a way it's show business," he once explained, an image business, bright and exciting and important, yet small enough that a hotel manager could have complete profit-and-loss responsibility: his own people, his own budget, his own little corporation. Hotels gave an ambitious young executive the chance to run something at an unusually early stage in his business career, and Ferris left little doubt about his eagerness to be in charge. He was cocksure, always ready with an order, convinced that management consisted of leadership and that he had it. "Boy, was I full of myself," he later remarked.

Ferris, in any case, had paid his dues. With each move he had uprooted his wife and three children, reckoning that each new assignment was another step following the footsteps of Eddie Carlson himself, perhaps even to the top.

Then suddenly in late 1970 Ferris and other executives were summoned to an urgent meeting with Carlson. Western Hotels, the chairman told them, was being sold to United Airlines. Ferris was sick to his stomach.

A few weeks later Ferris was further crestfallen when Carlson took him aside at a company Christmas party to share the news that he, Carlson, was leaving his Western post to become the chairman of United itself. Before long, Carlson asked him to take charge of the food service operation at United.

As unsettling as it was, the offer was undeniably attractive. United's food operation was a fabled enterprise, launched in 1937— the first "flight kitchen" in the industry, pioneering the use of standardized trays aboard the newly introduced DC-3s and serving up

French pastries, finger sandwiches, and fried chicken, all in further-ance of its market-share battle against American. By the summer of 1971 United's food service operation was nearly large enough to qualify in its own right for membership in the Fortune 500, cooking up something like $200 million in meals a year—enough food to feed the city of Saratoga Springs, New York, three meals a day. The kitchens provided meals not only for United but under contract for other airlines as well. Ferris would have full profit-and-loss responsi-bility at the food service operation, just as he did at the Crown Cen-ter in Kansas City or any other hotel he might manage, only the food kitchens at United constituted a business many times bigger than even a large hotel. Ferris, confident and brash and hugely ambitious, agreed to take the job.

He annoyed and outraged people all over the system, jabbing his finger at the chest of anyone who didn't get the message that he was in charge, and he performed brilliantly. He cut costs by reducing the use of steak and chicken, but passengers didn't particularly miss it when he replaced them with something novel in the way of airline food—Chinese, for instance, and pasta, which were uncustomary of-ferings in the meat-and-potatoes era. Fish was affordable; he con-cocted ways to make it seem elegant, such as sole bonne femme and sweet-and-sour halibut and cioppino. To cultivate sales to other air-lines he went on the road, making elaborate—and successful—sales presentations. Before long, Ferris was promoted to the top market-ing job for the entire airline.

In November 1974 Eddie Carlson could tell the board of directors that United expected to report the highest profits in its history. At the same board meeting Carlson also shared his thinking about his own succession. Although he had spent only four years at United, Carl-son was now 63. Now was the time to anoint a successor who could grow into the position of chairman while Carlson was still on the scene. An orderly transition was essential; after the ill-starred reign of George Keck, United could not tolerate another traumatic change in management.

Carlson had spent weeks agonizing over the succession, isolating himself on his 40-foot ketch with a yellow legal pad and an evalua-tion checklist that a banker friend had developed in choosing his own successor. United, he knew, would need an aggressive competitor as well as an excellent manager at the top. Once again, he thought of Dick Ferris. True, Ferris was only 38 years old, much less experienced than other worthy contenders. But Ferris, he believed, could grow into the job.

When Carlson nominated Ferris as his successor, the United board kept him waiting for two hours while deliberating over the choice. Finally Director Justin Dart, a California industrialist serving in Gov. Ronald Reagan's "kitchen cabinet," emerged from the boardroom. "Some of the fellows have some reservations about Ferris," Dart said. "We like his drive. . . . We just wish he were a little older." In the end the directors decided to go along with Carlson's choice. While Carlson would remain head of the holding company, known as UAL, Inc., Dick Ferris would become president of United Airlines itself, assuming responsibility for the task of preserving United's hard-won trophy as the biggest carrier in America.

"So far," the *Chicago Tribune* noted at one point, "Ferris has kept on course, and his story of 'boy wonder' success seems destined for a happy ending. But in the airline industry even a smooth flight can run into unexpected turbulence."

While Ferris was taking the controls at United, Bob Crandall was burrowing more deeply into the bowels of the computer system at American Airlines. Though the company remained in perilous financial condition, he demanded the funds to resuscitate the Sabre system. With all airlines charging identical prices on competing routes, a fast and reliable reservations operation remained critical in the battle for passengers, nowhere more so than in American's continuing battles with United. United, for its part, had bounced back from its early missteps in its own effort to automate. Under Carlson and Ferris, United's in-house computer reservation system, called Apollo, had quickly become the jewel of the airline industry.

While warily watching United's efforts, Crandall was jarred by the disturbing news that the travel agents of the United States were taking steps to build a giant computer network, like nothing ever seen, a mechanism to display flight schedules and reserve seats on the airlines of the United States from any travel agency location in the country.

The travel agents' motive was plain enough. By the mid-1970s travel agents sold nearly half of all airline tickets. (The airlines sold the rest directly to corporate accounts and individual passengers—by phone, by mail, at airports, and at downtown ticket offices.) Travel agents had been multiplying like delis in Brooklyn, and in some cases they were assuming the same mom-and-pop look. Entrepreneurs, retired couples, wives of the wealthy—almost anyone could start a travel agency merely by stocking the *Official Airline Guide* and leasing some storefront space or a cubbyhole in a suburban shopping strip. Some people went into the business simply because they enjoyed traveling themselves.

The romance of travel was one thing, making a living from it another. Owning a travel agency was a tedious, detail-ridden vocation in which the profit margins were minuscule, particularly on air travel. Making an airline reservation required a travel agent to thumb through the *OAG*, which by now, 15 years into the jet age, was the size of the Manhattan phone book, with tissue-thin pages. Having identified the most appropriate flight for a customer, the agent would then telephone the airline—or multiple airlines, perhaps, in the case of connecting flights—and make the appropriate reservations. The agent wrote each ticket by hand or wheeled it through a typewriter, compiled a written itinerary, collected the fare, and sent the money (less the commission, then fixed by the CAB at 5 percent) to a central clearinghouse, which in turn disbursed it to the airlines. Travel agents had to maintain a bundle of phone lines and a stable of clerks, typists, and reservationists while managing a library of travel literature to advise clients on vacation destinations and business arrangements. But what if the travel agents could go on-line? With a few keystrokes they would have instant electronic access to the schedules, eliminating the need to turn all those pages in the *OAG*. With a few more keystrokes perhaps they could actually place and confirm a reservation, eliminating unproductive telephone talk time.

The agents' proposal struck terror in the heart of Bob Crandall. In addition to losing control of the distribution system, the airlines, Crandall feared, would undoubtedly have to pay a transaction fee for every reservation they received through an independent computer network—on top of the commissions they already paid to travel agents. That was how any such network was bound to work; the electronic age presented profitable and exciting new ways to distribute products, but the unwary were sure to wind up on the losing end of the fee structure. Crandall vowed that in this case the losers would not be the airlines; with more than 200 million tickets written each year in the mid-1970s, a small fee could quickly add up to hundreds of millions of dollars in expenses for the airlines. The agents' project, Crandall decided, had to be stopped. A big meeting of the American Society of Travel Agents, scheduled to begin only a few days later in Rio de Janiero, was the place to start.

Arriving in Rio, Crandall proposed to turn the travel agents' plan on its head. Instead of their establishing a reservations network, Crandall said, they should allow the airlines to create one—a single giant communication system reaching into the office of any travel agent anywhere, owned and operated by a consortium of the major airlines.

In a perfect world Crandall would never have pushed for a system jointly owned by all airlines. He would instead have made his own system, Sabre, available to individual travel agents for subscription. But Sabre was still recovering from its years of neglect, and American's finances remained lackluster at best. Moreover, if American began hooking travel agencies up to Sabre, United undoubtedly would begin doing the same, but with its more powerful system and financial resources that Crandall could only dream about. By urging the creation of an industrywide network, Crandall would score two victories, blocking the travel agents from establishing their own system while preventing United from forging a proprietary link with them. And for good measure, in the creation of a single system, United, as the largest airline in the industry by far, could be expected to shoulder the greatest share of the development expense.

Of course many of the expenses incurred in the use of this system—ticket printers, for instance, and computer screens—would be borne by the travel agents. But, Crandall argued, the agents would receive tremendous benefits from the network, not only in making reservations and issuing tickets but in printing itineraries and maintaining their books. Crandall managed to convince the agents that at least a joint study should go forward.

At United, Dick Ferris shared Crandall's view that the travel agents should never be permitted to establish their own computer reservations network. But Ferris had figured out Bob Crandall's game, and looked warily on the idea of creating a single system owned by the airlines. The airline business, Ferris knew, was a game of controlling the passenger. These computers were unspeakably powerful—that much was already clear, even in the mid-1970s. If United could begin installing its own computer terminals in travel agencies, it could garner untold additional passengers. United, of course, would have to display all airline flights, not just its own, on the agents' terminals; otherwise, the system would be of little value to the agents and their clients. But the presence of an Apollo terminal on their desktops was bound to put any travel agent in the habit of choosing United over its competitors.

Ferris and his aides spent months studying the issues. We've got a competitive advantage, Ferris thought. Why throw it away so everyone else can benefit? Why, he wondered, should United play the patsy by shouldering the greatest cost of a solution that would benefit all of its competitors—including American? Finally, at a daylong meeting, Ferris decided to quit dilly-dallying with the rest of the industry. On January 28, 1976, United announced that it would not join in any collective efforts. Instead it would in the months ahead begin making its Apollo system widely available to travel agents.

Without the participation of America's largest airline, the industrywide effort led by Bob Crandall was doomed. Now, it was every man for himself, a contest to see which airline could hard-wire its reservation system into the most travel agencies. Ferris and United Airlines had just launched history's first computer war. The computer reservations network, the greatest back-office tool ever created by the airlines, was now a weapon as well.

Bob Crandall was furious that Ferris had foiled his plans, but he had been bracing for the outbreak of battle. Crandall had ordered his field managers to listen for "competitive intelligence," demanding that they pass along anything they might hear about what United was telling travel agents. Max Hopper, one of Crandall's top data processing executives, had learned that United was warning agents away from an industrywide system, vaguely promising that it would soon have something better to offer them. So while they were publicly promoting the industrywide alliance, Crandall and Hopper were privately developing plan B, a strategy for having Sabre terminals, rather than a jointly owned system, installed in any travel agencies willing to pay for the equipment. The development costs would be huge, but Crandall would come up with the money somehow. This was the future. American, he believed, had no choice.

Shortly after Ferris had fired the first shot, Crandall flew to Dallas–Fort Worth Airport to address a meeting of American Airlines managers. "Where do we go from here?" he asked. "There is only one place we can go, ladies and gentlemen, and that's to battle. . . . American is going to fight on the agency automation front, and fight hard!"

While Ferris's forces at United were just beginning to plan their effort, American dispatched a wave of salespeople to the agencies that gave it the greatest business. The smooth talkers in the sales force were joined by technical people—"guys in short white socks," as they became known inside the company. They opened up big notebooks showing that a travel agent working on a Sabre terminal could book $800,000 worth of flights a year instead of $350,000 by flipping through the *OAG* and spending all day on the telephone to the airlines. American also paid consulting fees to a few of the country's largest travel agencies, ostensibly for their ideas about what the system should do; the promise of fees assured that these agents would choose Sabre, helping to create a groundswell that discouraged other agents from signing with United's Apollo.

On the rare occasions that United got the better of American, Crandall blew his stack and demanded immediate countermeasures. At one point United obtained an exclusive software license from a Florida company for a series of bookkeeping and other programs that could be made available to travel agents over the Apollo network. Crandall ordered his people to jump on the next flight to Florida, where they arranged to buy the very company that had sold the software license to United. American gained the benefit not only of owning the technology but of employing all the people who had developed it.

Sabre was not only a way of making fees, of course, but also a distribution system for American's own flights. Although agents could book flights on nearly any airline through Sabre, Crandall began enticing agents to skew their bookings toward American with an addictive new financial arrangement. The greater the dollar value of an agency's business with American, the greater the percentage the agency received on the entire sum. The standard 5 percent commission might be increased to 6 percent, say, on ticket sales over $1 million, or 7 percent on sales over $3 million. (American could easily pay the higher rate, since each additional passenger put so much money on the bottom line.) The more American flights an agency booked through Sabre, the greater its incentive to buy still more flights on American.

Most agents did not, of course, choose less convenient flights for their customers for the sake of the bonus rate. But "override" commissions, as they became known, certainly created the incentive for an agent to resolve close calls in American's favor. The whole matter, in any case, was considered highly sensitive. At an American Airlines management meeting, one of Crandall's top sales executives remarked that the incentive programs were "highly confidential" and that among the biggest and best travel agency accounts, "It takes constant attention, better cooperative programs, and in some cases a *big bag of money* to solidify and retain these relationships."

United had no idea what hit it. Convinced that he had started out with an advantage over the rest of the industry, Ferris immediately found himself a distant second in the race to hard-wire the travel agents. American had coordinated its Sabre sales effort from the top; United had allowed regional managers to handle the sales efforts in their individual territories, and some had pushed much less aggressively than others. United had established a policy of signing up only financially healthy travel agencies; American took anybody who could pay the equipment rental. And when United caught wind of the special commission structure that American had introduced to Sabre subscribers, it judged the scheme to be a questionable business practice. United then quickly adopted the same policy for itself.

The two remaining members of the Big Four, Eastern and TWA, would also push their in-house computer systems into travel agencies, but they would never overcome the early lead of American and United. Between the two leaders American remained way out in front. Even if American didn't have the most planes in the industry, it had the most distributors.

· · ·

Crandall's moves as American's marketing chief, though radical, did not test the limits of federal regulation. The steps he took to muscle in on the preferred listing positions in the flight guide, or even to create his massive electronic network, required either perfunctory approval by the CAB or no approval at all. It was in the far more critical areas of routes and rates that the CAB served as the airlines' Big Brother.

One of the agency's most persistent missions was to whack down the pesky breed of flying operation known as the charter airline. Charterers flew planes for hire, but they could not fly on a regularly scheduled basis; only the incumbent airlines with their congressional sinecure had that privilege. Once every decade or so, when the established airlines rushed out to buy the newest and biggest airplanes, another generation of charterers would spring up on the used airplanes that the majors were dumping. Offering deep discounts to the most popular tourist destinations (Las Vegas was always a leader), the charterers gave rank-and-file Americans the opportunity to taste what the established airlines priced for the well-heeled. The charterers could afford to offer such low rates not only because they flew inexpensive old aircraft, but because they scheduled only as many flights as they had sold all the seats for; a customer often had to purchase a seat weeks or months in advance. So long as the charterers functioned solely as a poor man's airline industry, carrying passengers who would otherwise never fly, the CAB largely left them alone. But in each cycle of rebirth, it seemed, the charterers would get bigger and bigger, serving more destinations with more frequent service, ultimately stealing passengers from the half-empty planes of the major airlines. At that point the established airlines would cry, the CAB would lower the boom, and the charterers would go away.

To the dismay of Bob Crandall, yet another generation of charter operators was cropping up in the mid-1970s as the major airlines cast off their first round of jets to make room for the jumbos and other second-generation jet planes. By all practice and tradition, the CAB had a duty to impose onerous new operating restrictions on these charterers as well. But there was a new chairman at the CAB, John Robson, a man with no background in the airline industry. He was a loose cannon; the CAB had even approved a 50-percent-off sale— "peanuts fares"—on a couple of Texas International's routes. Instead of slamming the charterers, Robson, unbelievably, had taken steps to *loosen* their operating restrictions.

As American's marketing chief, Crandall was beside himself. American had planes sitting on the ground for lack of passengers, and the charterers were flying full. They were bleeding the leisure business from the airlines' regular operations. The kind of simple, straight-off-the-top fare cut that Frank Lorenzo's people had come up with was no solution for Crandall; American's most important customers were business travelers, who did not care about price. There was no point in offering to fly business travelers for half off. Instead American and the other majors had gone to the hypocritical step of using some of their remaining excess airplanes to start their own advance-booking charter operations, engaging in the very practice of which they complained. But for Crandall, having an in-house charter operation was no panacea either; American was soon losing charter business not only to the upstart operators but also to United Airlines, where Dick Ferris's people had built up the biggest charter operation in the industry. United, in fact, was landing jet charters in Las Vegas every few hours.

Crandall finally decided that if Robson and the CAB would not crush the charterers—all of them—he would do the job himself.

Crandall had a kind of informal brain trust that gathered most mornings by 6 A.M., often long before sunrise in Manhattan, to talk through the major marketing issues facing the airline. On one such occasion, when the executives were discussing American's own in-house charter operation, someone had doodled an airplane on a chalkboard. Crandall stared at the drawing. Why, he asked out loud, should American fly a separate charter airline when its regular flights were half empty? He went on: "Why don't we pretend the empty part of our plane is a charter?"

Someone walked up to the blackboard (it might have been Crandall, but no one would recall for sure) and drew a line through the airplane. Part of the airplane could be reserved for regular airline service, with traditional, last-minute reservations and the usual high fares. The rest of the airplane could be treated as a charter plane. American could estimate how many seats would be flying empty on any regularly scheduled flight and sell those seats at cheap charter rates—better still, sell them below charter rates, squeezing the other charterers out of business.

The idea of charging two prices on the same flight wasn't by itself original. As early as the 1940s, with CAB approval, airlines began offering a few seats (at the front of the cabin, initially) at discounted "coach" prices; the remainder of the passengers flew first-class. Over the years the price spread widened, with the result that coach seats overwhelmed the cabin, squeezing first class into a small section at the front of the fuselage. By the time that most people were flying coach, there was no pretense that they were doing so at a discount; coach had become the standard fare, and a prohibitively expensive one at that. First class, at one time the standard product, had become a premium brand instead.

Crandall was not proposing to segment the plane into additional classes of service, but to discount—severely discount—a share of seats throughout the airplane. The great challenge, of course, was finding a way to sell the cheap seats only to discretionary, price-sensitive travelers—people who wouldn't otherwise be flying—while holding as many full-price seats as possible in reserve for people who traveled no matter what. How, in other words, could the company enable the middle-class John Q. Public to fly on a low fare, while assuring that business travelers still paid the full freight?

Crandall's group studied the problem and began coming up with answers. Vacationers, as the charterers had proved, usually made their plans weeks in advance; businesspeople didn't. Moreover, vacationers (in those days) usually remained a week or longer at a destination; business travelers almost never did. American could require people traveling on discount tickets to buy their tickets weeks in advance and to remain a week or longer at their destinations, just as the charterers did.

Crandall turned his attention to an even more vexing question: How should the company decide how many discount seats to sell in advance? If it sold too many, it would risk shutting out full-fare business passengers making plans at the last minute. Yet if the airline cut off discount sales too early, planes would still be departing with empty seats—spoiled grapefruits. There were some obvious guidelines. On weekdays, in the early morning and late in the afternoon, it made sense to hold back a greater number of full-fare seats for the business traveler. But even this was pure guesswork; the mix of passengers was unique for every flight. The patterns were shaped by trade shows and industry conventions, by Super Bowls and weather aberrations. Perfecting the estimations could add millions to American's bottom line, but it would require data processing power on an almost unimaginable scale. While Crandall worked on the refinements, rudimentary guesses would have to suffice.

Crandall's plan to offer charter discounts on regular airline flights was every bit as heretical as peanuts fares. At any other time in its history the CAB would have sent Crandall packing. But the CAB, after all, had started the whole thing by loosening the charter rules. How could it now deny Crandall the right to formulate his own competitive response?

In March 1977, under the reform-minded John Robson, the CAB gave Crandall the go-ahead. The name given by Crandall to the advance purchase discount was "super savers." Suddenly it was possible to fly on a regularly scheduled American flight from coast to coast for $227 instead of $412—not quite the 50 percent discount that Frank Lorenzo was offering at Texas International but an unheard-of price cut for such a major player as American. The scheme had the drawback of putting discount travelers in the same section of the aircraft as full-fare passengers, but that was a long-term problem. For the time being, Crandall's super savers were spreading throughout the airline industry and accomplishing their intended purpose. Within months the charterers were dead. Bob Crandall had killed them off.

Gathered with his top marketing aides at American headquarters on Third Avenue, Bob Crandall glared through a window at the TWA offices, where only a few years earlier he had been derailed in his rise to the top. Crandall listened as one of his people described a competitive move by TWA. As the discussion wore on, Crandall continued to stare outside, while slowly wrapping the cord from the open venetian blind around his hand.

Then suddenly he exploded, blurting out invective and jerking his arm away from the window. The blinds came crashing down. The marketing staffers looked on in horror as blood ran down the forehead of their enraged boss.

"Bob! Your head!"

"The hell with my head!" he shouted back. "What are we going to do about these sons of bitches?"

Crandall wanted a way to punish TWA. All of TWA's flights, as well as nearly every commercial flight in the United States, were visible in the Sabre terminals now being installed in travel agencies across the country. Crandall ordered one of his people to design a set of computer instructions enabling American, if it ever chose, to eradicate all traces of TWA from the listings in Sabre. Crandall wanted a single "transaction" designed, something that could punish TWA instantly, with a few keystrokes.

The program was duly created. It would prove of great value, although not against the enemy that Crandall had intended.

CHAPTER 4

"IN THE PUBLIC INTEREST"

Airline deregulation is encrusted with myth and misconception. One widely repeated account holds that a group of academic theorists, led by Prof. Alfred Kahn of Cornell University, romanced a naive political establishment with the promise of low airfares if only Washington would force the airlines to compete. The airlines, by this account, were dragged kicking and screaming into the coliseum of competition, where, like clumsy gladiators, they aimlessly slugged each other senseless. Only when it was too late did Congress grasp its folly.

Except for the part about the airlines slugging each other senseless, nothing could be further from the truth.

Few realized it at the time, but "deregulation" was well under way before anyone had even uttered the word. As Herb Kelleher and Lamar Muse were demonstrating with girls in hot pants, as Frank Lorenzo showed with peanuts fares, as Bob Crandall and Dick Ferris were proving in the computer wars, the men who ran the airlines competed no differently from managers in any American industry. Nearly forty years of federal regulation had stifled competition but not dulled the impulse to compete. Regulation had only forced airline executives to engage in mutated forms of competition. As a feat of legislation, deregulation only legitimized behavior that was already taking place.

To call deregulation a mistake—as many people would, for at least the dozen years to follow—was a waste of breath. Whether wise or misguided as a piece of public policy, deregulation had to happen. Government protection had its place in helping to establish the modern airline industry; certainly this protection fostered the technical development of the industry, particularly the birth of the jet age. But by the 1970s, if not sooner, airline regulation was as unnatural and anachronistic as Prohibition had been in the 1920s and poll taxes in the 1960s: each resisted the onslaught of common sense only through the political wiles of an entrenched constituency, and each crumbled only when the constituency was overwhelmed with political force. What distinguishes deregulation is that it triumphed even though it was opposed most strenuously by those who in practice had already embraced it—except one, as it would turn out.

Though historically and economically inevitable, deregulation became law at the moment it did as much by accident as by necessity. For while the airlines themselves were in the throes of change, a few unlikely individuals were crossing paths in Washington. One was a Harvard law professor eager to become a U.S. Supreme Court justice. Another was a U.S. senator who wanted to become president. A third critically important player was a partially reconstructed hippie intent on conducting his own rendezvous with history.

Among the paths guiding them into the affairs of the airlines was Watergate.

Phil Bakes would never forget packing for Washington. It was a brilliant day in Chicago, late in the spring, and he was barefoot in a pair of cutoff shorts. Straddling a Suzuki 500 along the curb in front of his parents' house, he rolled his right wrist forward and throttled the motorcycle up a ramp into the back of a U-Haul van destined for Washington.

At that moment a black sedan pulled up. A man in a dark suit stepped from the car and turned to the house.

"May I help you?" Bakes called out.

"FBI," he answered. He was calling on the family home, he explained, as part of a background check on Phil Bakes himself.

Bakes loved this. At age 27, with hair dangling on his shoulders, he was about to become part of the establishment, part of the solution, bound for the kind of good-government career one dreamed about after spending one's formative years in the late sixties. Bakes was about to join the most visible law enforcement organization in the nation: the Watergate Special Prosecution Force, which his old law professor Archibald Cox was putting together. The FBI was knocking on his parents' door and it wasn't a bust!

Bakes grew up a hellion. He liked to play hooky, especially to watch the Cubs play at Wrigley Field—heresy for a kid from White Sox country on Chicago's South Side. While a student at the all-male Brother Rice High School, he got into a fistfight over a girl and was discovered to have been drinking. Bakes refused to give the names of anyone else who had been drinking. His principal, Brother Rowan, in turn expelled him, permanently. Even worse, the school withdrew its sponsorship of his application to Notre Dame, the only college he had ever wanted to attend. Bakes was as ruined as any high school senior could be.

The humiliation brought out a greater rage than the young pugilist had yet experienced, a rage he secretly directed toward Brother Rowan. He enrolled in the local public school and studied relentlessly, bringing home nothing but A's. He got the lead role (as the boxer) in the school production of *Heaven Can Wait*. His stellar grades continued after he entered Loyola University (despite his dormitory expulsion for drinking there too). In 1968 he landed at Harvard Law School.

It was at the pinnacle of the antiwar movement, and Harvard was one of the great battlegrounds. Always happy for an audience, Bakes went on the lecture circuit, addressing community groups against the war. When he graduated in 1971 Bakes bought a 1959 Chevy school bus, painted the body red and the roof silver (the latter to reflect the sun), stocked it with head music, and took to the road with several pals; they spent a year of peace, love, and bodysurfing near Acapulco, on a fellowship courtesy of Harvard.

When Bakes finally settled down in a small Chicago law firm, he found himself bored stiff, but he bolted upright coming home on the train one afternoon when he read that Archibald Cox was leaving Harvard to become special prosecutor in the Watergate affair. After a few phone calls to Washington, Bakes was thrust into some of the most exciting and politically significant prosecutions in American legal history, presenting the case against Nixon aide John Erlichman to a federal grand jury, for instance, and winning his indictment.

At one point while serving on Cox's staff, Bakes was joined by a close friend who served on the faculty at Harvard Law. He was Stephen Breyer, a brilliant young professor who had worked with Bakes on the *Harvard Law Review* and recruited him to antiwar speaking engagements. Breyer had a yearning for the judiciary and a strong interest in politics, so he made a point of scheduling frequent sabbaticals in Washington, including one on the Watergate Special Prosecution Force.

Breyer, whose academic interests resided in the commercial side of the law, delved into the corporate aspect of Watergate. Among the dozen U.S. corporations drawn into the affair, the case of American Airlines drew Breyer's attention. Breyer wondered what would cause George Spater, an executive of seemingly unimpeachable integrity, to so flagrantly breach the nation's campaign laws. Investigating further, Breyer saw the answer clearly: the government had vested life-or-death authority over the airlines in the Civil Aeronautics Board. Though credited with nurturing the world's greatest air transportation system, the CAB had obviously lost its way. It was coddling the industry it was supposed to regulate, thereby pushing airfares so high that only a select class could travel.

The following year Breyer was back in Washington on another sabbatical, this one working on the staff of Sen. Edward Kennedy of Massachusetts. Kennedy was well acquainted with many faculty members at Harvard, and he and Breyer had both crusaded against the war in Vietnam. Kennedy wanted to run for president as soon as 1976, then just two years away, but the unwinding of the war was taking away the one issue on which Kennedy succeeded in appearing substantive. Without Vietnam Kennedy had little left but his name.

One thing Kennedy did have was a Senate chairmanship that gave him license to roam just about anywhere he wished; he headed a sub-unit of the Judiciary Committee with a distinctly ambiguous name: the Subcommittee on Administrative Practice and Procedure. If he picked his shots carefully, Kennedy could use the subcommittee to assert jurisdiction over almost anything inside the Beltway. But over what, precisely? Kennedy needed an issue.

Breyer told Kennedy that the subcommittee could resurrect the Watergate scandal, perhaps by holding hearings on the creation of a permanent special prosecutor's office. Or, Breyer said, the subcommittee could conduct hearings on one isolated corner of the Watergate case that had previously piqued Breyer's attention: the Civil Aeronautics Board.

It was a time of galloping, 12 percent inflation, which polls identified as the nation's most vexing problem. Gerald Ford, having just succeeded President Nixon, was on a campaign to "Whip Inflation Now." Yet at the very same time the CAB was merrily letting the airline industry gouge the traveling public with higher and higher fares. In the days prior to the arrival of John Robson, the CAB wasn't just the handmaiden of the airline industry, it was its concubine. This, Breyer told Kennedy, was a chance to take a vague and overbroad committee assignment and focus it like a laser beam on an easy target.

For an officeholder of Kennedy's aspirations, the political logic was overwhelming. An attack on the CAB would have a wonderful populist ring, while exposing the labyrinth of federal airline regulation would give Kennedy at least a narrow conservative stripe; he could be seen as a champion of the growing movement to curb the size of big government. And even if CAB wasn't a household acronym like EPA or USDA, Kennedy's subcommittee could get credit for taking on a complex, serious issue—"a nonglamorous, detailed, intricate, 'good government' job," as Breyer would later describe it.

Taking on an entrenched federal agency would set off a fierce, inside-the-Beltway political brawl, and Breyer needed help. He needed a troublemaker, a bomb thrower. He needed youthful idealism and enthusiasm. Breyer placed a call to his friend Phil Bakes.

For the restless Bakes, even the Watergate prosecution had, after two years, begun to lose its excitement. The special prosecutor's office was down to such second-rate intrigues as the financial entanglements of Nixon's personal friend Bebe Rebozo. As far as Bakes was concerned, he had hit the bottom of the Watergate barrel; he was ripe for a change.

"Phil," Breyer said, "let's get rid of the CAB."

The Civil Aeronautics Board—Bakes had barely even heard of it. But putting a federal agency out of business? Turning an entire industry upside down? Now that, he thought, sounded like fun.

There was one small problem, Breyer and Bakes discovered. Airline issues fell on the turf of Sen. Howard Cannon, a senior Nevada Democrat who was chairman of the Subcommittee on Aviation. Cannon was vitally interested in airline issues; airlines were as essential to the development of Las Vegas as air conditioning and dice. Cannon was doing everything he could to protect Vegas-bound charter operators from getting walloped by the CAB. If Kennedy provoked a turf war, there was little doubt that Cannon could lay claim to jurisdiction ahead of Kennedy's subcommittee. Cannon, in fact, could settle the matter single-handedly if he chose because he was also chairman of the Rules Committee, which, in addition to settling turf disputes, controlled the budgets of all Senate subcommittees, including Kennedy's.

As a consequence, Kennedy began to bow and scrape before Cannon. Kennedy invited Cannon's staff members to work alongside Bakes and Breyer, and he notified Cannon in advance before making any public pronouncements about the CAB. Kennedy went out of his way to praise Cannon's leadership in aviation issues—and conspicuously understated at each step the assault that he and his young staffers were planning.

Even if Cannon were neutralized, Bakes, for one, knew that the campaign against the CAB was doomed as long as the airline industry itself remained a monolith of opposition. The airlines had some of the most powerful Washington lobbyists on retainer. They had operations in all 50 states and in hundreds of congressional districts. And the airlines could count on the support of big labor in fighting anything that threatened high fares because high fares meant high wages.

Bakes and Breyer could only hope that the airline industry would crack.

In the late sixties and early seventies, a few soul-searching CAB staffers were regularly going to lunch to debate whether they were discharging vital federal duties or playing roles in a fantastic farce. Soon this small band was boring into the writings of the academic theorists who specialized in the narrow field of commercial regulation, writings heretofore widely ignored. There was a seminal 1951 book by economist Lucile Keyes, who attacked "the inherent tendency of regulation to favor existing carriers" as opposed to newcomers. There was a 1965 article in the *Yale Law Journal* by a young professor named Michael Levine, who stated that CAB policies "fostered unnecessarily high fares, encouraged uneconomic practices, and limited the variety of services available to the public." There were extensive writings by Cornell's Alfred Kahn, who argued that the policies of the CAB "tended to raise cost to the level of price," a phenomenon that benefited neither the airlines nor the public.

Monte Lazarus, the highest-ranking careerist at the CAB, was among the staffers most deeply questioning the agency's role. Lazarus finally decided he had had enough when he picked up the CAB legal brief in a case involving tariffs on cargo shipments of live animals and birds. "For purposes of this case," he read, "a rat is a bird." In 1973 Lazarus walked out to take a position with United Airlines.

In his new job Lazarus's duties included briefing top management of the airline on the latest public policy issues. It was precisely when the issue of regulatory reform had burst onto the Beltway in 1975 that Lazarus found himself with a newly appointed president to brief, Richard Ferris. Lazarus was surprised to learn that Ferris had an open mind on the subject. Ferris, in fact, demanded to hear the arguments on both sides. Having come from the hotel industry barely five years earlier, Ferris was not steeped in the culture of protecting "the world's finest air transportation system" from "ruinous competition." What was the matter with competition? Ferris wanted to know. Competition certainly had not ruined the hotel business.

What benefits had United received from government protection? Ferris asked. True, the CAB had blocked troublesome, price-cutting newcomers from the industry, but the agency had also restricted United's own ability to grow. Whenever United applied for a new route, the CAB either turned it down flat or, if finding the route worthwhile, awarded it to a smaller company instead.

In August 1976, four months after becoming chief executive, Ferris presented the United directors with a long report saying that legislation reforming regulation at least in some limited way was inevitable. By making itself part of the debate—by taking a stand, one way or the other—United could influence the outcome to its benefit. The bottom line, Ferris said, was this: However the airlines fared as a group under regulatory reform, United would fare better than others. United was the biggest airline, the proverbial 800-pound gorilla. It had more than 300 airplanes. It was sitting on a cash hoard approaching $1 billion. As in a game of marbles, whoever had the most planes and the biggest route system and the most money at the beginning of the game was bound to be the winner.

"United has little to fear from numerous small competitors," Ferris assured the board in his presentation. "We should be able to compete effectively by advertising our size, dependability, and experience, and by matching or beating their promotional tactics. . . . In a free environment, we would be able to flex our marketing muscles a bit and should not fear the threat of being nibbled to death by little operators." There was no need yet for formal action by the United board; Dick Ferris and Monte Lazarus would watch the situation further as it unfolded on Capitol Hill.

But as the next few weeks passed, it became obvious to some of the people around him that Dick Ferris was growing enamored of the notion of deregulation. Unshackling the airlines would give United—and Dick Ferris—the opportunity to compete, not just with jingles and champagne flights but with fares and routes. Bob Crandall had bested Ferris in the computer wars, there was no doubt of that. But when the contest came to airplanes, Ferris was sure he would win.

Ferris ordered his staff to continue studying the situation in Washington. There was no point in taking a public stand yet.

As a crusader for regulatory reform, Bakes felt the same kind of win-at-all-costs compulsion that motivated him following his expulsion from Brother Rice High School. We're gonna win this one, he told himself. We're gonna deregulate an industry. Bakes threw himself into a manic research effort. There were details and intricacies to nail down. Everything had to be perfect. No one was asking to abolish the CAB, other than a few academics in Cambridge and Ithaca. *Deregulation*—the word itself was just being born. It was a concept without a constituency. Nobody had ever written his congressman asking for it. This was policy making from whole cloth. Every small advantage had to be seized, every tiny argument mustered.

For instance, had the CAB *formally* declared a route moratorium, or had it simply discontinued approving route requests? Bakes had to know; it would make a difference in how villainous the CAB could be portrayed at the hearings. Monte Lazarus would know, Bakes suddenly realized.

It was late at night when Bakes tracked Lazarus down at the Continental Plaza Hotel in Chicago. Lazarus picked up the phone just as the hotel fire alarm began blaring.

"Monte, was there a formal route moratorium or not?" Bakes demanded. Bakes was the kind of person who talked loudly, in exclamation points, when he was charged up.

"Phil, I can't talk now! I think I smell smoke!"

"If there's a fire you might as well stay in your room!" Bakes snapped impatiently, demanding more details of the route moratorium.

When the Subcommittee on Administrative Practice and Procedure finally came to order in the Dirksen Senate Office Building on February 6, 1975, Senator Kennedy made himself the lead-off witness. "Regulation," he began, "has gone astray. . . . Either because they have become captives of regulated industries or captains of outmoded administrative agencies, regulators all too often encourage or approve unreasonably high prices, inadequate service, and anticompetitive behavior. The cost of this regulation is always passed on to the consumer. And that cost is astronomical."

For eight days, spread over the months of February and March 1975, a parade of witnesses came forth, carefully arranged by Breyer and Bakes to cast the regulators and the industry as evildoers. Proponents of deregulation generally got the chance to make their case first, putting the beneficiaries of the status quo on the defensive. Ralph Nader, an ardent deregulation advocate, was sworn in to lend his populist imprimatur to the cause. Ford administration officials were carefully chosen to make sure they personally favored and fully understood deregulation, even if their agencies had taken no official position. Among the academic theorists, Alfred Kahn of Cornell was chosen to testify because of his rapier intellect. ("I have been asked to hold my testimony to ten minutes," he began, "which means that I will have to talk terribly fast.") Computer studies and other evidence were introduced establishing how lack of regulation had created low fares within Texas (thanks to Southwest Airlines) and California (thanks mainly to Pacific Southwest Airlines).

As the hearings continued, Bakes felt that something was missing. There was too much emphasis on routes and rates and such inaccessible concepts as price elasticity. "We've got to find a scandal!" he said.

Watergate—perhaps it provided an opening. From their work on the staff of the special prosecutor, Bakes and Breyer probably knew more than anyone else on Capitol Hill about the airline angle in Watergate. American's off-the-books contribution to the Nixon campaign had violated not only federal election laws, they knew, but possibly CAB regulations as well—in particular, a law requiring the airlines to notify the agency when they paid fees or gave gifts to anyone. If American had violated this regulation, then the CAB was obliged to investigate. Had it done so, or had the Republican-controlled agency swept the case under the rug?

With the subcommittee hearings still under way, the Kennedy staffers launched a muckraking expedition. Sure enough, they discovered, a few CAB officials had begun looking into the matter. But the internal investigation had been scuttled; the investigation files of the CAB staffers had even been taken away and locked in a safe. "The only word that was flashing through my mind was *cover-up*," a CAB lawyer named Stephen Alterman would later say. Bakes was ecstatic. Here at last was a handle on a scandal.

The subcommittee immediately called on William Gingery, the head of the CAB's enforcement division, to appear as a witness. Gingery had nothing to hide; on the contrary, he was among the CAB staffers who had been trying to get to the bottom of the industry's Watergate role. But Gingery was humiliated at having been duped by his bosses and frightened at having to appear publicly. He wrote a long, rambling letter to Bakes and other Kennedy staffers, expressing dread at earning "the dishonor of the fool." A short time later, a few days before he was scheduled to testify, William Gingery shot himself dead.

Though Breyer and Bakes had succeeded in drawing the Beltway's attention to regulatory reform, there seemed little hope that the airline industry would crack. "Total deregulation would allow anyone to fly any route," *The New York Times* pointed out after the Kennedy hearings had concluded, "a situation that is unlikely ever to occur."

Taking no chances, the airlines were soon dispatching troops of lobbyists to stomp on the embers of deregulation. One after another they called on Bakes, who, following the end of Breyer's sabbatical, found himself leading the subcommittee crusade on his own. Every airline executive who walked into Bakes's office spouted the same rhetoric about preserving the world's finest air transportation system, often to the word, as if they were cribbing from the same briefing book.

A few of the airlines distinguished themselves for originality, however. Eastern Air Lines dispatched 47 flight attendants to Washington for a lobbying excursion. They all descended on blue-eyed Phil Bakes, who felt like a rooster, relentlessly flirting while holding forth on the virtues of deregulation.

Bakes was also taken with Frank Lorenzo, the chief executive of Texas International. Lorenzo, for one thing, was natty in a way people seldom saw on Capitol Hill—New York fashionable, almost *too* well dressed. More substantively, Lorenzo was one of the few executives who called on Bakes without an aide in tow, the only one who stayed longer than 20 minutes, and the only one who did not sloganeer about the world's finest air transport system. Though adversarial, it was a notably professional and stimulating encounter.

Bakes also had a memorable rendezvous with Al Casey, the man brought in to rescue American in the wake of George Spater's Watergate-hastened demise. Bakes knew that Casey was a glad-handing, backslapping Bostonian whose élan could fill a room, so he resolved in advance to overpower Casey with the force of his logic and the passion of his arguments—and above all with his cool demeanor.

As Casey and his aides entered the office, Bakes made a point of putting his feet on his desk to appear relaxed and unimpressed. He listened calmly as Casey argued against deregulation and dropped names at every chance—"I was talking with Eunice and Sarge the other day . . ."—and before Bakes knew it Casey and his entourage had waved and departed, without ever letting Bakes put forward a case of his own. Casey had gotten the better of him.

"Son of a bitch!" Bakes shouted, kicking his heel and shattering the sheet of glass on his desk.

• • •

When a president-elect prepares to assume the White House, the first real clues about his policies, as opposed to his campaign promises, are revealed in the appointments to his transition committees. A transition committee on regulatory policy might ordinarily draw little notice, but two weeks after Jimmy Carter defeated Gerald Ford in November 1976, the airline industry could not ignore the appointment of a 26-year-old lawyer named Mary Schuman to Carter's transition team for transportation matters. She came from the office of Nevada's Senator Cannon.

Even after Carter had denied Kennedy the Democratic nomination, the rivalry of the two men had persisted. Nevertheless, Bakes of the Kennedy staff and Schuman of the White House staff maintained a personal alliance in behalf of deregulation. As the White House and subcommittee staffers began working more closely together, Schuman would even begin dating one of Bakes's colleagues on the Kennedy staff, a Yale lawyer named David Boies, who was preparing to push the deregulation campaign to the trucking industry. Before long, Boies and Schuman would be married.

Within a month of her appointment, Schuman and a few associates wrote a paper for Carter on airline deregulation. Airlines, the paper said, were "naturally competitive." Regulation was "inappropriate." The policies of the CAB had brought about "inflated fares" and "half-empty planes." Airlines were "heading the way of the railroads," the memo said. Ted Kennedy, looming as a potential Carter rival in the next presidential election, was out in front on the issue.

There were five bills for airline deregulation already pending in Congress, Schuman told the president. But Carter, the memo added, might be able to turn all the action in Congress to his own political advantage. "Existing Congressional support," she wrote, "makes this issue one on which you may be able to score a relatively 'quick hit.' "

A quick hit. Every new president could use one.

While Schuman and her colleagues were preparing Carter's position paper, the airline industry was tying itself in knots attempting to forge a unified front against deregulation. For several months in early 1977 the airline industry enjoyed the best of two worlds, preserving its protection from upstart airlines while gaining some pricing freedom from the new CAB chairman, John Robson. But the

galloping success of Frank Lorenzo's peanuts fares and Bob Crandall's super savers had only strengthened the call for complete deregulation. If the airlines had the freedom to lower prices selectively, it
was only a matter of time, people realized, before the CAB would
allow them to increase prices as well. And the surest way to control
price increases was to unleash the full power of the free market—by
allowing newcomers into the business.

This is where the airline industry drew the line. Although few of
them had the nerve to say so publicly, the airline chieftains harbored
a deep fear that new competitors would start out as nonunion rivals;
what chance would an established old company with entrenched
unions have against a competitor like that?

The major airlines conducted their Washington lobbying through
a group called the Air Transport Association. The ATA operated on
consensus, essentially giving any major airline veto power on any
major issue. Vetoes, of course, were practically unheard-of. Higher
fares, lower airport taxes, accelerated tax write-offs—there was
rarely a dispute among the airlines over the usual Washington fare.
But as the ATA desperately tried to craft some meaningful opposition to the growing threat of deregulation, United held back, coyly
refusing to declare its position.

The situation became urgent as another round of Senate hearings
approached, and this time the host would be not the upstart
Kennedy but the all-powerful Cannon, who was reasserting his dominion over aviation matters as a way of telling Kennedy to quit frolicking on his turf. Unless United stopped equivocating, the airlines'
trade group would be forced to go into the hearings fractured, with
no position, abstaining from the most significant legislative debate in
airline history.

United had studied every angle. Ferris and his aides recognized the
risk that deregulation would provoke a tumultuous and uncertain
phase, with would-be airlines cropping up everywhere and zany pricing taking hold, but this phase would last only three to four years at
most. Deregulation was a safe bet for United.

When United's board of directors had assembled for their January 1977 meeting, Ferris called on Monte Lazarus to make the presentation. "Properly written, new legislation can unlock regulatory

shackles, open the way for new market opportunities for United and others, all without destroying the system, and all in the public interest, as well as United's. . . ."

Lazaraus declared, "We must report that the industry is sharply and, we think, hopelessly split. . . . We shall have to pursue our interests ourselves." He did not mention that United itself was responsible for the fissure.

With Ferris watching for the board's reaction, Lazarus concluded the presentation. "If you agree with these recommendations . . . we shall implement our action program immediately." There was silence. Then in the back of the room a single director slowly and deliberately began to applaud. Everyone turned to look. It was Justin Dart, the wealthy California industrialist, one of the best friends Gov. Ronald Reagan ever had.

At one of his earliest press conferences as president, Jimmy Carter announced that airlines represented the "first question" his administration would take up in his mission to reform government. The move was counterintuitive—a Democrat proposing to dismantle regulation. But as when President Nixon went to Red China five years earlier, partisanship was in retreat. Airline deregulation was transcending party lines, which vastly increased its chance of adoption. On March 4, 1977, Carter sent a message to Capitol Hill. "As a first step toward our shared goal of a more efficient, less burdensome federal government," he began, "I urge the Congress to reduce Federal regulation of the domestic commercial airline industry."

The president had just scored his quick hit.

Nine days later Ferris made his own announcement in a speech at the Commonwealth Club of San Francisco, saying that United backed the "general philosophy" of deregulation. Deregulation, he later added, would become "the greatest thing to happen to the airlines since the jet engine."

Though he was immediately the goat of the industry, Ferris was the hero of Capitol Hill. Phil Bakes of Kennedy's staff and Monte Lazarus of United immediately went to work scheduling their bosses together, knowing that despite some powerful differences in political ideology the two young, handsome, up-and-coming leaders would hit it off, which they did. Ferris also scheduled a fund-raiser for Sen.

Charles Percy from United's home state of Illinois; Percy, for his part, would take position papers from United and have them inserted whole into the *Congressional Record*. Ferris also recognized that United looked a little conspicuous backing deregulation all by itself, so he turned to Al Feldman, who was running Frontier Airlines in Denver, with whom he had become close friends. As the 14th largest airline in the country, Frontier was big enough to count as a national player but small enough to present some political balance when paired with United. Frontier was locked in a vicious battle for market share in Denver, and Feldman was eager to expand. Southwest Airlines, confined to the four corners of Texas by federal regulation, also joined the deregulation bandwagon.

The president was on board, and the industry had been divided. Labor still had the power to block, or severely dilute, any deregulation bill, but Bakes and the other crusaders found a way to buy off the unions: by assuring that any deregulation bill would outlaw "mutual aid," the program in which the airlines subsidized each other whenever one of them was forced to take a strike. Receiving that promise, the unions stepped out of the way. They might as well have sold Manhattan for $24.

The last obstacle to adoption of a bill was the formidable Senator Cannon, whose hearings were scheduled to begin within a week of Ferris's speech. The leadoff witness would be John Robson, the chairman of the CAB, who had already approved peanuts fares and super savers but whose agency had taken no formal position on its own survival.

"Once it is fully established, bureaucracy is among those social structures which are the hardest to destroy," the German sociologist Max Weber wrote. "The individual bureaucrat cannot squirm out of the apparatus in which he is harnessed."

Max Weber never met John Robson, however. In his two years as chairman, Robson had taken delight in shaking up the old order at the CAB. He had never gotten over his astonishment at the airline industry's eagerness to have the CAB—to have *him,* John Robson—make decisions for it. Now, with an invitation to testify before Senator Cannon's aviation subcommittee, Robson knew that the only sensible course was to cast the agency's lot with deregulation.

Robson recognized that he would be like a police chief standing before the city council to argue for the abolition of the city ordinances. If he went before the CAB stating only John Robson's radical position, his testimony would be meaningless. Robson had to get the other commissioners behind him. He and his assistant, Howard Cohen, furiously lobbied them for a consensus. Where the commissioners refused to come on board, Robson and Cohen lobbied their staffers, and then they got other staffers to lobby the staffers. Robson exhausted everyone inside the big blue building on Connecticut, so much so that in the end none of the other commissioners, it appeared, wanted to take on the onerous task of writing a dissent. Robson would go before Cannon to speak for a unanimous regulatory body, arguing, stunningly, to gut his own agency.

Cannon was visibly startled when Robson had concluded his testimony. Once Kennedy's rival on matters of aviation, Cannon immediately took a new tack, ordering his staff to begin working with Bakes of Kennedy's office. The writing of the Kennedy-Cannon deregulation bill was under way.

Senator Cannon did give the industry an opportunity to present its case. A few days after Robson's testimony, Albert Casey of American Airlines flew to Washington to present an elaborately documented argument against deregulation, complete with a pile of charts and graphs. Casey told Cannon's aviation subcommittee,

> Some supporters of deregulation seem mesmerized by computer models, created by academics without airline management experience, that tell them what they want to hear. Others are interested in a "quick hit," a phrase that I believe does no one any credit.
>
> Deregulating the airline business is a dangerous step. I say that because once the step is taken, there will be little opportunity to turn back. If deregulation doesn't work, you will see the finest air transportation system in the world begin to disintegrate before your eyes.

As Casey spoke, Phil Bakes, sitting with the Cannon staffers at the front of the hearing chamber, noticed a member of the American delegation, a mean-looking fellow with pointed teeth and slicked-back hair who was turning the pages of Casey's flip chart. At a distance the man struck Bakes as the kind of hoodlum he had always been instructed to stay away from growing up on the South Side of Chicago. A bodyguard, perhaps, Bakes thought.

When the day's testimony was concluded and the hearing room began to clear, Bakes noticed the mean-looking guy stalking toward him with a scowl, as if he were getting ready to throw a punch. The man stopped in front of him, scowling.

"You fucking academic eggheads! You're going to wreck this industry!" The man turned and left.

Who was that? Bakes asked.

It was Bob Crandall, someone said, the head of marketing at American.

While working on the Kennedy-Cannon bill, Bakes and his allies had to move into action on another front as well. Because a Democrat had moved into the White House, John Robson, a Ford appointee, was preparing to leave the CAB. The crusade for deregulation needed a successor at the CAB who was committed to the cause, not only to nurture the pending legislation but in the meantime to push the existing law to its limits, to continue the process of "administrative deregulation." Somebody had to make sure that peanuts fares and super savers and the like received approval while Congress parried.

In contemplating candidates for the CAB job, Bakes realized how important the media were becoming to the deregulation campaign. *The New York Times* had given the issue momentum by covering the Kennedy hearings on the front page. Columnists and editorial writers from *The Wall Street Journal* to *The Washington Post* were flogging the issue. The new CAB chairman had to be someone who drew good press, besides being smart and thick-skinned.

Bingo. Alfred Kahn.

During the Kennedy hearings two years earlier Kahn had performed brilliantly and humorously, getting much of the best ink. He was an academic, unfamiliar with the political rigors of Washington, but outsiders were in vogue at the moment, and Kahn had some political experience as chairman of the New York State Public Service Commission. Bakes and Mary Schuman of the White House staff maneuvered to ensure Kahn's appointment.

Once he had moved into the CAB, Kahn for his part needed an insider among his allies, someone who knew not only the law and the legislation but the politics. Thus did Phil Bakes, having engineered Kahn's appointment as CAB chairman, become the general counsel of Kahn's CAB.

There was no stopping the CAB now. An order was issued granting airlines the authority to cut fares 50 percent without government approval—a "free-fire zone," it was called. Before long the zone's boundary was raised to 70 percent.

As the Kennedy-Cannon deregulation bill cascaded through the committees of the Senate, Dick Ferris and Frank Lorenzo one day found themselves thrown together in the small quarters of a private airplane, which the owner of Beechcraft, the plane manufacturer, had dispatched as a courtesy to them both. The two were heading for a meeting of Los Conquistadores del Cielo.

Ferris, the head of the nation's largest airline, was intrigued by Lorenzo, who headed the smallest of the national airlines. Lorenzo struck Ferris as thoughtful and well-spoken on the subject of deregulation. Lorenzo exhibited no ill will toward Ferris for having torpedoed the united industry front against deregulation. Lorenzo seemed to grasp the inevitability of it, Ferris thought, and he expressed strong preference for the market economy.

Still, Lorenzo told Ferris, the small airlines would get squeezed in a deregulated world. In order to survive, Lorenzo said, little Texas International would have to "get big quick."

On April 12, 1978, Lorenzo made a trip to Wall Street with a public offering that raised $27 million. He was building his war chest.

The death of the senior senator from Arkansas, John McClellan, created a sudden shift in a number of Senate chairmanships, causing a void at the top of the Commerce Committee, of which the aviation subcommittee was a part. Into the position went Howard Cannon, making him chairman of both the subcommittee and its parent full committee—the two principal units of the Senate that would handle the deregulation bill.

The legislation reached the floor of the Senate on April 19, 1978. It passed by a vote of 83 to 9.

But to the dismay of the White House and the delight of nearly everyone in the airline industry, deregulation soon ran aground in the House of Representatives. The House Aviation Subcommittee actually torpedoed the bill, leaving the matter deadlocked for six weeks.

One of the most visible members of the subcommittee was Norman Mineta, a former mayor of San Jose, California, who in only two terms had become one of the leading lights in the House—a member of the post-Watergate class swept into office on the promise of integrity and reform. Bakes, though by this time the general counsel of the CAB, used a return trip to Capitol Hill to lobby Mineta.

"I'd really like some help raising some money," Mineta said, as Bakes would later recall it. "You think Senator Kennedy would come to the West Coast to do a fund-raiser for me?"

Bakes traipsed to the Senate side of the Capitol, where he called Kennedy from the floor.

"I think we have Mr. Mineta on board if you'd be willing to do a fund-raiser," Bakes reported. He deliberately withheld the fact that the fund-raiser would be in California.

"Why don't you tell him we'd be glad to help him out?" Kennedy cheerfully answered.

Before long Kennedy was on the phone. "Bakes! You never told me the fund-raiser was in San Jose!" But Kennedy lived up to his end of the bargain, as did Mineta.

Victory was so close that the proponents of deregulation were now willing to roll just about anybody's log. Frontier Airlines, headed by Dick Ferris's friend Al Feldman, felt it had a $433,000 tax reimbursement coming from the federal government and decided that the deregulation bill was as good a place as any to have the reimbursement written into law. Bakes considered the payment tantamount to a bribe, but Frontier's backing of deregulation was essential, and what was a little bit of taxpayers' money in the context of a massive shift in public policy?

Finally the aviation subcommittee approved the House deregulation bill. When the bill hit the House floor, a beaming Monte Lazarus watched from the gallery as the tote board rolled up the lopsided tally of 363 to 8. He caught the eye of Norm Mineta, who flashed the United lobbyist a thumbs-up salute.

A short time later Phil Bakes and Ted Kennedy pressed themselves into the West Wing elevator at the White House with a crew of Secret Service agents. There stood President Carter. He immediately struck Bakes as uncomfortable in the presence of Ted Kennedy, his avowed rival. Kennedy, who was nothing if not gracious when the situation demanded, immediately called attention to the significance of this day.

"Mr. President, I want you to meet Phil Bakes," Kennedy said. "He and Mary Schuman are the people responsible for this." Carter's lips grew tighter as the group exited.

But by the time he signed the Airline Deregulation Act of 1978, Carter was beaming with pride. Flanking him were Kennedy and Cannon, Monte Lazarus from United, Alfred Kahn, and even the former CAB chief, John Robson. "For the first time in decades," Carter said, "we have deregulated a major industry."

A mile to the north, as Carter spoke, a line had already begun forming outside CAB headquarters. Once the bill was law, more than 2,000 dormant airline routes would be instantly up for grabs. The CAB intended to dole out the unused routes on a first-come, first-served basis. So a spectacle ensued in which corporate representatives lined up along the Connecticut Avenue entrance to the CAB like rock fans waiting to buy concert tickets. Three days before President Carter had even signed the bill they began showing up, with thermos bottles, walkie-talkies, sleeping bags, folding chairs. Over the next two days the line grew, to 30 long by the time the bill was actually signed. The neighborhood was far from Washington's safest at night; one delegate was carrying a gun.

Curiously, however, one airline, Texas International, had no one holding a place in line. Frank Lorenzo, it appeared, had something else in mind.

CHAPTER 5

START-UPS AND UPSTARTS

When the deregulation bill was rushing toward adoption, the government of the United States committed an act that it had not performed in many years: it allowed Texas International Airlines to add service to a new destination. The lucky metropolis was Kansas City.

Frank Lorenzo and his associates marked the occasion with a circus parade to promote the arrival of peanuts fares to the city. A man dressed in a seven-foot Mister Peanut costume waved to the crowd from a little wagon pulled by a baby elephant rented for the occasion. In the midst of the festivities the baby elephant defecated, forcing Mister Peanut to dive out of the way.

Though the new route was a success, Lorenzo knew he could not survive the deregulation age on cheesy publicity stunts alone. Deregulation, in his view, had left room for only two kinds of airlines: very small ones and very large ones. Texas International was neither. On the marketing strength of peanuts fares the company had grown significantly, yes—to four million passengers in 1978. Yet it had ascended by only two positions on the Top 20 chart, to number 16. Texas International could either be crushed by the behemoth likes of United and American, on the one hand, or nibbled to death by the nimble, low-cost Southwest on the other, becoming, as Lorenzo liked to put it, "the ham in somebody else's sandwich."

But how to respond? Everyone in the airline industry seemed to be heading in a different direction. Texas International was even divided against itself, as much as any two airlines might be. Indeed, when the bracing wave of competition washed over the airline industry, Texas International, strangely, became the fount of several radically different airline companies, each representing a different response to the same set of economic forces—each, in its own way, springing from the ambivalent relationship between Don Burr and Frank Lorenzo.

Burr all but worshiped him. Burr would accompany Lorenzo to lobbying sessions, industry functions, and private meetings with top executives, and he would marvel at Lorenzo's earnest manner, his probing questions, his quick mind. Burr had never met a better thinker. He was also impressed with Lorenzo's good looks and his accomplishments as a marathoner. Lorenzo even skied passably. Frank, for his part, though circumspect in describing his feelings, would later tell people that he considered Burr a true soul mate and that he was deeply impressed by Burr's ability to pick himself up when the chips were down.

But just as in their first days together in the Blue Barn, Burr's awe and admiration were accompanied by fear and resentment. While he was Frankie Smooth Talk to the outside world, Lorenzo, in Burr's view, was Idi Amin to the people closest to him. Lorenzo picked away at people, trashing their work, identifying their weak spot and making it hurt, Burr thought, almost as if he were a Third World dictator in a torture chamber. Although he could raise his voice, Lorenzo did not particularly fit the screamer profile; he was too controlled. But the glare would intensify, the face would grow red, and the veins in his temples would begin to bulge, particularly as he assumed over the years the gauntness of a marathoner. When the officers of Texas International lined up for the Monday staff meeting, Lorenzo's secretary would watch them march in as if they were going to Bataan. Who's going to get it today? they would ask each other. One staffer walked into the office one day with a puncture wound in his hand and a streak of blood along his arm; he had stabbed himself with a pen during a three-hour plane trip with Frank.

Burr—Frank's best man, best friend, and top aide—thought he got the worst treatment of all. Burr periodically scheduled management retreats at a conference center in the woods north of Houston, to which Burr and Lorenzo would drive together. On the way back Burr, while behind the wheel, had to listen to Lorenzo rail about how poorly Burr had put together the meeting.

Burr did everything possible to commandeer the day-to-day control of the airline from Lorenzo, a maneuver Lorenzo himself facilitated by moving his personal office out of the Blue Barn and into a new suite of executive offices in the steel-and-glass shimmer of downtown Houston. Burr, left back at Hobby Airport with the operating staff, was convinced that Lorenzo had no sense of how an airline actually operated, of how the pieces fit together. As Burr later put it, "I didn't think Frank could run a lawn mower." But nobody else had Lorenzo's skill at schmoozing creditors, to the point of repeatedly postponing their claims. Lorenzo, to his credit, had also quickly grasped the potential of peanuts fares and had made them the cornerstone of the company's marketing.

But however vital Lorenzo's financial hijinks, Burr thought the future of the airline would be decided on other issues. With deregulation becoming law, any airline could offer peanuts fares or the equivalent without bowing and scraping before the CAB. Texas International had to find a new way to distinguish itself. The solution, Burr decided, was to transform the culture of the company.

In his youth Burr had been wrapped up in a book called *The Greatest Thing in the World,* in which a 19th-century Scottish clergyman named Henry Drummond called on people to establish love at the foundation of every activity in their lives. Burr still adored the book and kept it within reach. The same principle, he decided, could apply in the workplace—by trusting people, eliminating time clocks, reducing supervision, and giving employees the freedom to do the best job possible. Working with Texas International's chief of service, a man named Edwin Cathell, Jr., Burr spent months analyzing everything from Abraham H. Maslow's theory of the hierarchy of needs to the personnel policies at Bank of America, a company known for progressive employee relations.

The result was a "people's program" for Texas International, compiled in a set of black three-ring binders distributed to the officers of the company. A meeting on the plan was scheduled for a morning in April 1978, the week after the Senate had passed the Deregulation Act.

To soften up Lorenzo, Burr made a point of leavening the presentation with windy tributes to the financial turnaround for which Lorenzo was principally responsible. "We are a highly financially successful airline, and the focus of the entire airline industry, the public, and the legislators in Washington," the presentation read. "Maximization of the financial (e.g., cost cutting, marketing, peanuts fares, debt structure, etc.) was historically correct and absolutely essential for this company's survival at one time in our history.

"But when low fares become universal," the report went on, "we will be left in large part with the 'people' equation as the chief component of competitive leverage." Success and failure in the airline business, the report said, would be decided on customer service.

Happily, Burr went on, the workforce at Texas International abounded with "friendly, Southern types," but relying on regional characteristics alone would be insufficient. Texas International had to begin taking account of "every emotional and psychological need of the human animal." There were many variables in managing a successful airline, the report noted, but "manipulation of this variable can make it the most productive."

The black binders laid out a program of "leadership and love," which Burr proposed to effect through psychological indoctrination, open work spaces, jogging trails, and other steps to persuade employees that they were not only cared about but trusted. The Blue Barn would be abandoned in favor of a headquarters campus Burr proposed to construct in the woods north of Houston. The scheme would cost money, yes—that was where Frank would no doubt object—but every 1 percent increase in business attributable to newly happy and productive employees, Burr determined, would be worth $1,441,660 of additional revenue to the company. "All in all, those bucks buy a lot of people's programs," Burr's report concluded.

Having distributed the big black books in advance, Burr trooped from the Blue Barn to Lorenzo's newly established downtown executive offices to present the people's program to Lorenzo and other officers of the company. Burr was petrified. The plan meant everything to him. He had been thinking about these issues for years. He desperately wanted Lorenzo's approval.

After about 10 minutes Lorenzo interrupted the presentation.

"Don, come here a minute," he said. The meeting ground to a halt as Burr walked out with Lorenzo. The two men entered Lorenzo's office.

"This is complete bullshit!" Lorenzo snarled, slamming the book on his desk.

The fact was that Lorenzo at that moment was involved in an altogether different strategy with Bob Carney, his most tenured associate.

Carney, although thrown over by Lorenzo when Burr had made the scene, remained part of the action at Texas International. Carney was still a partner in Jet Capital, the company that he and Lorenzo had established nearly a decade earlier, in 1969, and Jet Capital in turn continued to control Texas International. Some people thought that even Lorenzo did not share Carney's gift for numbers. Nobody could pick apart a set of financial statements with greater insight. "Carney rolls the spitballs," Sam Coats, the general counsel of Texas International, liked to tell people, "and Frank shoots them."

Shortly after rejecting Don Burr's people program, Lorenzo traveled with Carney to Cambridge for the 15th reunion of the Harvard M.B.A. class in which they had first become friends. The time away from the office enabled them to discuss the future in earnest. They knew that Texas International had to get big fast, and that meant buying another airline. But which one?

The process of elimination narrowed the field quickly. Taking over any of the Big Four—United, American, TWA, or Eastern—would require leverage on a scale that even Lorenzo and Carney could not muster, for the moment. The next four—Delta, Pan Am, Western, and Braniff—were also too large by orders of magnitude. But the remaining two of the Top 10 were something different. Number nine was Continental. Ten was National. Though each did well over a half-billion dollars in business a year, they were a mere four times the size of Texas International. That put them well within striking distance.

Between them National was the more obvious target, the proverbial bird on the ground. Financially National was as conservatively managed an airline as one could find, a fact that appalled Lorenzo and Carney while whetting their appetites. National, they readily discovered, had practically no debt, meaning that it failed to tap fully the earning power of its assets. If National was not going to exploit the leverage inherent in the company, then Lorenzo and Carney would. Texas International, they determined, could seize National and borrow enough money against National's own assets to pay for the entire acquisition. Lorenzo and Carney could essentially buy another company for free. The phrase "leveraged buyout" had not yet come into common usage by Wall Street, but that was precisely what Lorenzo and Carney had in mind.

Going after National would be radical in another respect. In the 40 years of regulation by the CAB, there had never been a hostile takeover in the airline industry.

Lorenzo and Carney had secretly studied the possibility for weeks. Then, in their old stomping grounds of Cambridge, they decided to make their move.

Slowly and imperceptibly, at Lorenzo's direction, Texas International began buying National Airlines stock in the open market in trades as small as 100 shares. In four weeks Lorenzo picked up 9.2 percent of National's stock outstanding. Then, as he prepared a public announcement of his intentions, Lorenzo decided to give the head of National the courtesy of letting him know that he was about to lose his company. As he reached for the telephone, Lorenzo's hands were trembling.

Shortly after Juan Trippe had retired in 1968, a breathtaking route map was mounted in the 46th-floor executive offices of the Pan Am Building. In gold lines the map displayed Pan Am's tentacles across the world, not just to such great capitals as Tokyo and London but to such exotic climes as Karachi, Cartagena, and Pago Pago.

Inside the borders of the United States, however, the map was utterly blank.

As the chosen instrument of international aviation policy, Pan Am traditionally had little need for domestic routes. The other major airlines could carry passengers as far as the borders of America, where anyone continuing overseas would transfer to Pan Am (or to a foreign airline with reciprocal landing rights in the United States). In Trippe's view Pan Am did not have to stoop to the banality of carrying passengers within U.S. borders.

Everything was fine until President Truman began to weaken Pan Am's monopolies in the immediate postwar years. Northwest Orient became the second U.S. airline with authority to fly passengers over the Pacific. Braniff won a few routes into the Pan Am stronghold of Latin America. TWA under the wily Howard Hughes became an additional U.S. carrier over the Atlantic. Further deterioration occurred in the Nixon years, when several additional airlines won the right to fly the Pacific. One of Trippe's successors, Najeeb Halaby, tried gamely to plead against further encroachment, but as a former Federal Aviation Administration official in the Kennedy administration, he was wearing the wrong colors to help Pan Am in the Nixon years. "Switch over to our side," Nixon aide H. R. Haldeman told him, "and we may be able to help you."

The Carter administration was soon making things worse than ever. With his hands-across-the-water inclinations, Carter was allowing new foreign airlines to serve the United States, skimming even more passengers from Pan Am: KLM into Los Angeles, Lufthansa in Miami and Atlanta, and British Caledonian in Houston, for instance. Where Pan Am had once conducted 100 percent of the flights into and out of the United States, it now had less than 10 percent.

Pan Am might have coped with the competition—except for the empty space in the middle of its route map. The approach of deregulation awakened the company to the need to collect its own passengers within the United States, but by that time Pan Am had so alienated every branch of the U.S. government that no one in Washington was willing to say yes. Pan Am, as one historian noted, was "the only airline in the world without a country of its own." Finally, when deregulation became law, Pan Am's beleaguered management resolved to fill the hole in the route map as quickly as possible.

The first chance came when Frank Lorenzo put National Airlines in play. Pan Am would have been wiser not to bite at National, an airline whose fleet, route system, and corporate culture were almost wholly incompatible with theirs, but Pan Am was panicking. Though its predicament was decades in the making, it wanted a solution overnight. In competition with Texas International, Pan Am jumped into the bidding for National Airlines.

The companies tussled for weeks, trading charges and counter-charges, trying to outrace one another's stock purchases, and enlisting high-powered legal and lobbying aid. Pan Am deployed Sol Linowitz, the noted lawyer, corporate executive, and diplomat who had just negotiated the Panama Canal treaties for the United States. Lorenzo hired Leon Jaworski, a former Watergate special prosecutor. Lorenzo also borrowed from the underdog strategy that Herb Kelleher of Southwest Airlines had used against him, showing up at hearings and local community meetings with only one or two executives in tow, in contrast to the platoon that Pan Am always dispatched.

As he watched the takeover drama play out from the distance of the Blue Barn, Don Burr realized that his friend Lorenzo had once again maneuvered himself into a position of indifference, in line to score a victory no matter which way the action unfolded. If he won the battle, Lorenzo would catapult Texas International well into the ranks of the Top 10. But if Pan Am outbid Lorenzo, then Pan Am would have to buy the shares of National that Lorenzo had already purchased—at a much higher price than Lorenzo had paid. Lorenzo would reap such a windfall, a Pan Am official observed, that "it would put him in a position to gobble up United Airlines."

In the fall of 1979 Lorenzo capitulated, crying all the way to the bank. Pan Am bought 100 percent of the shares of National Airlines for $374 million. Of that amount $108 million went to Texas International, and when the accounting was over, more than one third of that was pure after-tax profit. Lorenzo, who had turned $44,700 into $1.5 million a few years earlier, had just multiplied that sum into $35 million. And immediately the money was burning a hole in his pocket.

Within several days of toting up his winnings, on an autumn Saturday night in Los Angeles, Lorenzo arrived at the house of Continental Airlines chairman Bob Six and his wife, former *Honeymooners* star Audrey Meadows. Lorenzo rang the bell. Six came to the door.

Lorenzo was expecting dinner and a serious conversation about a merger between Texas International and Continental. It all made so much sense, Lorenzo believed. Continental flew a small fleet out of Houston. So did Texas International. If Lorenzo could convince Bob Six to combine his company with Lorenzo's, they would have a large fleet, enough to compete with Southwest or American or just about anybody who came their way.

At that moment in 1979, with C. R. Smith long departed from American, Rickenbacker gone from Eastern, Patterson long gone from United, and Howard Hughes out of TWA—at that moment, with Lorenzo standing on his front stoop, Bob Six was the greatest living figure in the airline industry. Swept up in the leather-helmet hysteria following the Lindbergh flight, Six had been fired from his job as a utility company executive for taking flying lessons on company time. He bought part of an airline called Varney Speed Lines in 1937 and changed its name to Continental, eventually making it one of the Top 10 airlines in the country.

Six foot four, with thick lips and beefy hands, he seemed larger than life. Before Audrey Meadows he had been married to Ethel Merman. He hunted grizzlies, owned a pet jaguar, and talked in a stream of put-downs, invectives, and profanity. He left a pile of cigarette ashes on the floor alongside his desk, too distracted to think of reaching for the ashtray. He was friendly with presidents, employed some of the best lobbyists in Washington, and did a land-office business hauling military personnel and matériel in and out of Vietnam. He also conducted covert operations for the CIA in Laos. Six had the experience and the connections to turn Continental into a small player in the Pacific when the U.S. government began chipping away at Pan Am's dominion there in the 1960s.

On this Saturday night, however, the 72-year-old Six had apparently confused the date of his dinner meeting with Lorenzo—either that or he had forgotten it altogether. Like Dorothy at the gates of the Emerald City, Lorenzo was instructed to depart and come back another time.

At about the same time he met with Six, the newly flush Frank Lorenzo sat down for breakfast at the Hotel Carlyle on the Upper East Side of New York with Edwin Smart, the head of TWA. Whereas most men in this situation might offer to buy breakfast, Lorenzo offered to buy TWA. Smart, stunned, walked out before the eggs arrived.

Everywhere he turned, it seemed, Frank Lorenzo was being shown the door. Though he had been a leading spokesman in the failed battle against deregulation, Lorenzo remained an outsider in his own industry. Maybe it was those peanuts fares; they had certainly annoyed the big players. Or perhaps it was his Latin ancestry; the airline industry was as WASP as they came. Or maybe it had something to do with Lorenzo's refusal to accept the hand he had been dealt. Deregulation had just changed the nature of the game and Lorenzo wanted the cards to be dealt again.

So what if he had to take on the big boys to save his company? Lorenzo was smarter. He knew how to leverage a balance sheet. He had once defeated the mighty Howard Hughes. He had extracted $35 million in net trading profits from Pan Am. The prejudice of the industry's titans—whether directed at him, his parentage, his company, or his response to deregulation—would represent no obstacle once the right opportunity presented itself.

But Lorenzo had a crisis to deal with first, a crisis both personal and professional. The president of his company—the best man at his wedding, the father of his godson—was walking out.

Saying "I quit" to Frank Lorenzo had become a kind of ritual for Don Burr. There was, for instance, the occasion when Texas International began service to Las Vegas, a destination known for its well-established sensitivity to bargain-priced travel. Burr convinced Lorenzo that the fare from Dallas should be $39, but Lorenzo, not entirely free of his ambivalence about low fares, soon changed his mind, insisting on $45.

"Thirty-nine!" Burr cried.

"Forty-five," Lorenzo answered.

"Thirty-nine!" Burr cried again.

"Forty-five," Lorenzo answered again.

"I quit!" Burr said, and before walking out he took aside Jim O'Donnell of the Texas International marketing staff and said that even though he was quitting and heading for Martha's Vineyard, he was counting on O'Donnell to see that the price remained at $39. "Don't yield one dollar!" Burr commanded him.

After a good pout, however, Burr had always come back, if only to endure more anguish. The memory of Lorenzo slamming down his people program a year earlier still stuck painfully in his craw.

Thankfully, so far as Burr was concerned, Lorenzo had abandoned the idea of taking over National Airlines. Now, Burr noted,

Pan Am, not Texas International, faced the daunting task of trying to absorb that airline. But it was clear to Burr that the outcome of the National bidding had only postponed—and enlarged—the inevitable. With more flash money than ever sitting in the bank, Lorenzo was bound to attack an even bigger rival. And Burr knew that once Lorenzo had bought another airline, it would be his job, Don Burr's job, to put the pieces together. Burr began to fantasize anew about quitting.

He recognized that it wasn't a great time to walk out. In the year following adoption of the Deregulation Act the airline industry had been almost stagnant. A suffocating recession was under way, triggered by the second great oil shock, due to the revolution in Iran. The Federal Reserve had pushed interest rates into the stratosphere as an antidote for rampant inflation.

But if anybody could land on his feet, Don Burr thought, it was Don Burr. He had earned a reputation in the airline industry, thanks to the transformation of Texas International into a vibrant, profitable airline. "We had turned around an atrocious piece of shit," Burr later insisted. "The world knew about us." Above all, Burr knew that only by leaving Lorenzo could he ever hope to put his people plan, with its emphasis on trust and love and manipulating the psychology of the workforce, into action.

From his office in the Blue Barn, Burr called his friend and mentor at the new executive offices in downtown Houston.

"I resign," Burr said.

"Ha," Lorenzo answered. "Fine." He snickered, having heard this spiel a hundred times. "It's about time."

Burr hung up. Then he called Melrose Dawsey, Lorenzo's secretary and Burr's personal friend, and invited her to join him in leaving to look for a new opportunity. She readily agreed. Then he called Gerry Gitner, who had become one of the most important cogs in the Lorenzo machine but who had tired of working at Lorenzo's beck and call. On the eighth day of the decade of the 1980s, Burr, Gitner, and Dawsey walked out of Texas International, eager to see what the new world of aviation had to offer—equally eager, in Burr's case, to prove something to Frank Lorenzo, unaware that in leaving Lorenzo, he had only entwined their fates more closely than ever.

Leasing a small office in northwest Houston, they put out word that they were available for hire as a management team, ready to right any listing airline, but they also harbored the fantasy of starting their own airline. Burr knew from competing against Southwest that it was possible to start an airline from scratch and succeed against the established competitors, so long as the service was priced at the level necessary to tap the latent demand for air travel. Best of all, by starting from nothing Burr would have the best chance to create the kind of culture he had so eagerly wanted and failed to instill at Texas International.

Starting an airline from nothing—how did one do it? The first and most important thing, Burr decided, was to maintain absolute secrecy from Lorenzo. "We figured Frank would do whatever he could to kill us," Burr later explained. "We'd judged him to be vindictive and pissed off."

They needed to raise money, but to do so they first needed equity. Burr sold a car; a house; two ski condos in Park City, Utah; and his Texas International stock. He wiped out his savings, raising a total of $350,000. Gitner scraped together $175,000. Dawsey chipped in $20,000.

But they also needed something to sell—an idea, a concept. What kind of airline should it be?

During one of Texas International's management retreats in the late 1970s Gerry Gitner had talked up the idea of trying to transplant the Southwest-style low-cost, high-frequency operation to an altogether different part of the country—the Northeast, say. It was a bold notion, invading an area where the major airlines had for so long held dominion. But lately, with the economy plunging and the price of jet fuel soaring, the major airlines had been cutting back in the region. The Northeast had become the Rust Belt, deemed unworthy of the teeming airline service it had once enjoyed. High energy costs were killing off the old mills. Workers were moving to the oil-enriched job meccas of Texas and Colorado. With their newly endowed freedoms under the Deregulation Act, American Airlines and United Airlines, in particular, were pulling planes out of the Northeast and either grounding them or dispatching them to stronger markets—the West, to be sure, and transcontinental service. The airlines remaining behind in the Northeast region were vulnerable. USAir, one of the leading short-haul airlines there, had breathtakingly high costs.

Burr and his partners recognized that they would have some special advantages that no incumbent airline could overcome. First, a new airline would have no unions, at least not to begin with—not ever, if Burr had anything to say about it. Second, with an all-new workforce, no one would have any seniority, meaning that everyone would be starting at rock-bottom pay. Third, their new airline could serve the Northeast from an inexpensive and largely ignored terminal at Newark Airport, away from the congestion and high costs of Kennedy and LaGuardia.

Burr was happy to hear that Newark's North Terminal was wide open—though horrified at what he found on his first visit. Owned by the Port Authority of New York and New Jersey, the terminal had been built to handle a couple of DC-3s a day. After the Newark riots of late 1960s, New Yorkers got in the habit of using LaGuardia and JFK instead, even though for many Newark remained by far the most convenient airport. The North Terminal, long abandoned, was a disaster area, strewn with garbage, teeming with rats, and reeking of urine. The ceiling was all but falling down. The windows were opaque with grime.

The idea of putting down an airline in the North Terminal had occurred to other people since the signing of the Deregulation Act, but each previous tenant had quickly come and gone. "No one has ever made it here," one of the Port Authority people told Burr. "Why would you want to move in?" One aspiring airline founder had even moved some furniture into one of the terminal's office suites; in his haste to depart ahead of his creditors, he had never moved the furniture out. It would become the first office furniture at Burr's airline.

Burr knew the place would clean up and that there were some wide-open markets to hit from Newark. American had cut back service to Buffalo and had gate space available there. Columbus was wide open; American had pulled back there as well. United had retrenched at Norfolk. It was true that none of those cities was booming like the oil towns that Southwest was serving in Texas, but they all three had healthy economies. And new passengers, first-time passengers, might flock to a new airline, assuming that the fares were low enough—below the cost of driving or taking Greyhound.

Burr and his cohorts traveled to Boston to meet with a venture capitalist. They arrived early to prepare in advance over an ice-cold weekend in February of 1980. One of Burr's friends gave them the use of his office, but with the oil crisis raging, the heat was turned off for the weekend. Dawsey sat at a typewriter and Burr and Gitner stood over her shoulders, all three of them in their overcoats, as she typed a final draft of their business plan.

The venture capitalist committed no money, but he did pose a critical question. "What are you going to call this company?"

Burr was sure that some brilliant name would naturally suggest itself. "The name will flow from the design," he answered smugly.

The venture capitalist admonished them to think hard about a name, to come up with something that as closely as possible described the kind of business they intended. "Name it for what it's going to be," he said.

A day or two later it hit Burr. We're a people company, he thought. We're people with a people program, working to move people. That was it: the company would be called People Express.

In deciding on New York for his operating base, Burr had an additional reason to choose Newark: there was no room left at either La-Guardia or Kennedy Airport. The problem was too many airplanes.

Just as it took man millions of years to learn that there was a limit to how much soot and smoke he could pump into the atmosphere, so too did it take a while to grasp that the sky could accommodate only so many planes at once. "The plain truth," a congressman from Delaware warned, "is that near collisions in mid-air, of disastrous proportions, are being narrowly averted every day only by the emergency action of skilled pilots—or by Providence." The year was 1956.

Technology (radar and computers) and public works (more airports and more runways) increased in stages the number of planes that the system could safely accommodate at any time. But from the time of the DC-3 the government consistently and severely underestimated the burden of managing the airspace, with the result that it never caught up. In 1956 public awareness was heightened by the collision of a TWA Constellation with a United DC-7 over the vastness of the Grand Canyon, killing 128 passengers. Then, with Christmas approaching in 1960, in the midst of the transition to the jet age, a United DC-8 bound for JFK (then Idlewild Airport) smashed at 400

mph into a TWA Constellation conducting an approach to La-
Guardia. The collision, over Staten Island, rained wreckage and remains into the streets of Brooklyn.

The limitations of the system were most evident at hours of peak
operation or when bad weather restricted takeoffs and landings. The
FAA could cope only by stacking up airplanes en route to their destinations. By the late 1960s the practice of circling had reached ab-
surd proportions, particularly on flights to New York, as Jack
Lemmon and Sandy Dennis lampooned by endlessly waiting to land
in *The Out-of-Towners.* Planes bound for New York were sometimes
stuck in holding patterns as far west as Denver.

At various times from 1968 forward the government would nu-
merically limit takeoffs and landings at many of the nation's airports,
but these restrictions would remain permanent at only four locations: Chicago O'Hare, the world's busiest airport; Washington National, which shared airspace with the military; and the New York
City airports, except Newark. Landing assignments—slots, as they
were called—had turned out to be a finite natural resource: Oregon
had the redwood forests, Texas had oil, and New York had slots.

By 1980 the vicissitudes of the air traffic control system were of
concern to no one more than Frank Lorenzo. Not content merely to
run Texas International, Lorenzo, following Don Burr's lead, resolved to start a new airline of his own, also in New York.

Lorenzo had attended the same management meetings at which
Gerry Gitner, before quitting Texas International, had talked up the
idea of moving into the East Coast. Lorenzo knew as well as anyone
that there were vacuums forming on the East Coast, an area safely
distant from Southwest Airlines. Moreover, even if the major airlines
still controlled the slots, they were not actually using all of them.
American, in fact, had acres of hangar space sitting empty in New
York, Lorenzo learned.

But while his ex-colleague Don Burr planned to apply the low-fare
formula at second-tier destinations from New York, Lorenzo was
looking to do the same on some of the most heavily traveled routes
in the world—in the corridor that linked New York with Boston and
Washington, D.C. These were routes long dominated by Eastern's
Air-Shuttle, an operation that Lorenzo came to know from the inside
during his brief time as a financial analyst at Eastern. Lorenzo be-

lieved that Eastern had allowed the shuttle markets to turn cold. Service stank. Performance was spotty at best. The shuttle was a veritable cattle car. The best proof to Lorenzo was the anachronistic success of train service between New York and Washington. Who would have thought that passenger trains could flourish in 1980?

But why should Lorenzo, controlling the 17th largest airline in the United States, choose to start an altogether new airline? Why not simply expand his existing airline under its own colors, on a route-by-route basis?

For one thing, Texas International, though profitable, had a reputation as a difficult debtor, thanks partly to Lorenzo's unremitting renegotiation of repayment terms. Starting a new airline would allow Lorenzo to tap the airline spigot on Wall Street unencumbered by Texas International's balance sheet. In addition, Lorenzo knew that expanding Texas International's existing base of operations would only throw more planes in the path of Southwest, with its ultrahigh productivity and low fares, and in front of American, with a massive fleet in Dallas and a growing computer reservation system with which to direct passengers.

Finally there was the matter of the unions. Every new arc added to the Texas International route map would be governed by the same onerous union contracts. Any newly hired pilots would have to be paid union wages and scheduled according to the work rules of the Air Line Pilots Association (ALPA). This reality was anathema to Lorenzo; how could he hope to take business from the entrenched Eastern shuttle unless he could undercut its price, and how could he do that unless his costs were much lower? Establishing a new airline would solve all these problems.

Lorenzo chartered a new entity called Texas Air Corporation. Texas Air, in turn, created an operating subsidiary, which began hiring pilots at $30,000 a year, two thirds the average union rate of $45,000 at Texas International. Used DC-9s purchased from Swissair—airplanes, ironically, that Don Burr had ordered for Texas International shortly before quitting—were assigned to the new subsidiary. The planes were painted fire-truck red, with a giant apple design adorning the tail. The name given the new airline was New York Air.

The $35 million in cash left from the abortive National Airlines takeover was "upstreamed" from Texas International to Texas Air, giving it all the money it could ever spend in starting up an airline. But Lorenzo decided to use the occasion of New York Air's formation to raise more cash anyway, scheduling a $40 million stock offering by Texas Air. Although Texas Air had no track record whatsoever, not so much as an earnings statement, the stock analysts on Wall Street greeted the offering enthusiastically; New York Air, they explained, was bound to succeed because it was so closely patterned after Southwest Airlines.

But if New York Air was to be a New York airline, it needed landing slots—and quite a few, if it was to compete with the hourly service of the Eastern shuttle. To wangle the necessary slots from the FAA, Lorenzo needed a Washington-wise insider on the Texas Air team. Having spent time in Washington lobbying against deregulation, he knew just whom to call.

When President Carter signed the Deregulation Act, Phil Bakes felt his mission was complete. He had intended to leave Washington immediately to accept an attractive job offer from Cummins Engine Company, an Indiana manufacturer noted for its progressive management policies, but Kennedy beseeched him to serve as deputy manager of his campaign to become president in 1980. It was a depressing affair, particularly following the infamous interview in which anchorman Roger Mudd asked the candidate why he wanted to be president; Kennedy was unable to put together a coherent answer.

Shortly before the Democratic National Convention the call came from Frank Lorenzo. Bakes agreed to meet him for breakfast in the Jockey Club at the Fairfax Hotel (later to become the Ritz-Carlton), one block west of Dupont Circle.

Bakes was fearful that Lorenzo was looking for a lawyer or a Washington lobbyist, or someone who acted as both, and Bakes was determined to act as neither. He had been trying to avoid the ennui of law ever since he had fled Chicago to join the Watergate prosecution. He was convinced he had a calling to manage people, and he fervently wanted to run something.

Lorenzo explained that he needed someone to get the slots on which to launch New York Air—a lawyer's role, just as Bakes had feared. But Bakes's anxiety began to melt. Lorenzo related, at great length and in detail that surprised Bakes, the story of his failed relationship with Don Burr. Lorenzo said he had been devastated by Burr's departure from Texas International, that he had not slept well in the four or five months since Burr had quit. Lorenzo's old Harvard pal, Bob Carney, was still around, but Lorenzo said Carney was not the soul mate that Burr had been. Lorenzo confessed to Bakes that he sometimes felt insecure around strong personalities, and there was no doubting that Burr was one of those.

Lorenzo went out of his way to assure Bakes he had changed. He said he knew that some people needed more freedom than others; he seemed to be saying that he hadn't given Burr enough room. That wouldn't happen again, Lorenzo assured Bakes. This was music to the ears of Phil Bakes. He told Lorenzo he was willing to go to work as a lawyer, a Washington lawyer, no less, so long as he could be sure that doing so was a step toward one day really running something. Lorenzo assured him it was.

Before long, as Bakes served out his final days in the doomed Kennedy candidacy, he and his wife, Priscilla, had dinner with Lorenzo and his wife, Sharon. It was a wonderful evening, full of mirth and camaraderie. Later that night Priscilla turned to Phil. Lorenzo, she said, was looking not only for a partner but for a brother.

Whatever the emotional component, the commercial virtue of hiring Bakes was readily apparent. Bakes knew the Deregulation Act better than anyone else on the planet. Rules had been established supposedly assuring that "new entrants" would not be denied the chance to compete simply because the incumbent airlines already had the slots tied up. The law provided no assurance, however, that a "new entrant" could instantly establish itself as one of the biggest airlines in one of the world's largest aviation markets, as Lorenzo envisioned New York Air. To offer an hourly schedule of service to Boston and Washington, Lorenzo needed dozens of slots at La-Guardia (as well as some in D.C.). Each and every one had to be gotten from somewhere—mostly from the incumbent airlines.

To Bakes, the assignment to cajole the landing slots was another campaign, no different from the campaign for deregulation, or the Kennedy-for-President campaign, or, for that matter, his campaign to avenge his expulsion from Brother Rice High School. He used his insider's knowledge of the law and the regulatory infrastructure to work every angle possible at the Transportation Department. He got his old boss Ted Kennedy to insert a speech into the *Congressional Record* endorsing New York Air's efforts. He got his friend Stephen Breyer to use some of his influence on the Hill as well.

A short time later Bakes and Lorenzo were sitting in an ad agency office in New York and watching some fashion models display the freshly designed uniforms for New York Air's flight attendants. This, Bakes told himself, is why I am in this job. In the midst of the display, Bakes was called away to the phone. The slots matter, he was informed, had been settled.

"Shit!" Bakes cried, rejoining Lorenzo.

What was wrong? Lorenzo wanted to know.

When Bakes explained that the government was granting New York Air two fewer slots than it had requested, Lorenzo was gleeful. New York Air had been given virtually everything it had asked for. And suddenly Phil Bakes was saying yeah, it was great news. Bakes thought that New York Air might become to him and Lorenzo what Love Field was to Herb Kelleher and Southwest Airlines: a cash cow, a larder from which all manner of expansion could be financed. Texas Air was on a roll.

Don Burr was also on a roll. On his 39th birthday a venture capital affiliate of Citibank agreed to invest $200,000 in People Express. Burr purposely kept the sum small so that no single investor would be able to exercise much control. Burr wanted to retain control to assure that nothing, no one, stood in the way of the great experiment he was planning—an airline built around Maslow's hierarchy of needs, in which employees would not receive much money but would enjoy more love and trust than they had ever experienced on the job.

The only way to avoid giving control to any one investor was to go public. Ever since Lindbergh's time, in periods of economic contraction as well as expansion, investors were willing to put money into airplanes. "Maybe it's sex appeal," Alfred Kahn once quipped, "but there's something about an airplane that drives investors crazy." But it had been seven years since Burr had worked on Wall Street. When Burr was at Texas International, Lorenzo and Carney had handled all the finance. Where should Burr turn?

It occurred to him that starting an airline had such novelty value—like gene splicing, say, or personal computers—that the investment bankers of the high-technology world might have an interest. Burr landed a luncheon date at the University Club in New York with William Hambrecht, whose Hambrecht & Quist in San Francisco had become one of the leading financiers in the newly emerging industrial hotbed known as Silicon Valley. For about 45 minutes they made small talk. Then Hambrecht began to excuse himself to catch a plane to Martha's Vineyard.

Burr was hit with panic. *This fucking guy is not going to give me my shot!* he told himself. Burr began blurting his spiel: low costs, low fares, regular service from Newark, fast turnaround . . . As Hambrecht finally got up to go, he assured Burr that he had already researched Burr's plan. Hambrecht had only wanted to see what Burr was like. Hambrecht & Quist, he said, would act as underwriters for the initial public offering of People Express. As Hambrecht dashed away, Burr gripped his chair to keep from falling.

Burr then had to find the airplanes with which to launch People Express. Lufthansa, it turned out, was getting rid of the 737s in its fleet and agreed to refurbish them in the colors and logo of People Express. The tail of each plane would be emblazoned with two squiggly lines representing two faces in profile. The design reminded Burr of two human forms making love.

A week before the People Express stock offering was scheduled for market, Burr noticed that the Lufthansa people were not returning his calls. The deal had been negotiated, but the closing hadn't occurred. Burr began snooping around. Boeing, it appeared, was offering Lufthansa top dollar to buy back the same planes, which it intended to turn over to American Airlines as loaners against a major purchase of new aircraft.

Burr, still working out of the little office he had set up in Houston, boarded the next flight to the West Coast, where he confronted a Boeing executive. "What's going on with these Lufthansa planes?" Burr demanded.

The Boeing man demurred and stonewalled.

"You're a bunch of whores and bastards!" Burr screamed. "I didn't think Boeing could operate this way. This is outrageous! If you won't tell us what's going on, we'll buy DC-9s [from McDonnell Douglas] and never buy a Boeing product again!" Burr stalked away.

With the stock offering a few days away, People Express still had no airplanes to its name. Burr heard that Ansett Airlines of Australia, controlled by financier Rupert Murdoch, might have some planes available. He flew to New York and begged his way into an appointment with Murdoch, owner of the *New York Post*. Burr was shown into an office so expansive he could barely tell that the man at the other end was Murdoch himself. It seemed to take Murdoch half the afternoon to walk across the office to greet him. This being election day in 1980, all that Murdoch could talk about was the apparent landslide victory in the making for Ronald Reagan over Jimmy Carter—the last thing in the world Burr cared about or wanted to discuss at the moment.

Those planes . . . what about those planes?

Murdoch, it turned out, had no idea whether he had planes on the market or not. "Come to Australia next month," he cheerfully instructed him.

Burr arrived back in Houston, dejected. Walking into the office, however, he noticed a message from Lufthansa. Boeing had backed down. The 737s would be painted with People Express faces on their tails after all.

People Express went to market a few days later at $8.50 a share. Burr had purchased 710,000 founder's shares six months earlier at 50¢ each; they had just increased in value 1,700 percent. Frank Lorenzo, it appeared, wasn't the only one who could engineer a killing on a stock sale.

On New Year's Eve in 1980 Burr and his fellow People Express executives held their last meeting in Houston before moving their office and their families to Newark. They met at their principal conference location, a Tex-Mex place called Ninfa's on the edge of the city's exclusive River Oaks neighborhood. Within a few days they were in Newark for good. Burr wound up in a corner room on the top floor of the Howard Johnson Motor Lodge across the highway from the airport, where he had a clear view of the runways. Burr would enjoy watching the planes taking off and landing from the privacy of his bedroom. Soon he would be watching his own planes.

Lorenzo and Bakes were thrilled to announce that Alfred Kahn would become a member of the New York Air board of directors.

Kahn, however misleadingly identified as the father of deregulation, was nonetheless good copy and a bona fide media darling. He enthusiastically backed New York Air, itself the very embodiment of deregulation. Plus Kahn was a New Yorker. Bakes liked that: a brash New Yorker for a brash new airline. To further strengthen the New York marketing theme, one of the planes, with great fanfare, was rechristened *The Little Flower,* the nickname of the great former mayor, Fiorello La Guardia.

But among the union pilots of America, New York Air overnight transformed Frank Lorenzo into public enemy number one. "Runaway shop!" the pilots' union cried. "Rotten to the core," said *Air Line Pilot* magazine. The pilots' outrage was understandable: here were a half-dozen airplanes, with many more to arrive in the months ahead, representing dozens of opportunities for copilots at Texas International to step up to the captain's seat, to earn a fourth stripe on their sleeves, to get a significant raise in pay—all being switched to a subsidiary where their wage rates, work rules, and seniority provisions did not apply.

The pilots would launch a $1-million publicity campaign to vilify Lorenzo. They rented a billboard near the Blue Barn at Hobby Airport showing a Texas International jet transforming itself into the colors of New York Air, with a devilish caricature of Lorenzo in a cowboy hat tearing a union contract in half. Union leaders threatened a boycott of Pepsi products because a Pepsi bottler happened to sit on the Texas Air board. They persuaded the widow of Fiorello La Guardia to boycott the festivities commemorating the first flight; the late mayor, it turned out, had been a champion of the pilots' union, once marching at the head of the New York State Labor Day parade alongside Air Line Pilots Association founder Dave Behncke at a time, in the early 1930s, when the union was battling a hated nonunion operator.

The pilots' union would litigate and threaten and cajole, and none of it would hurt New York Air in the slightest. Lorenzo had vanquished them. If anything, the more loudly the pilots' union railed against New York Air, the more successful the airline became. The public was increasingly fed up with labor unions and was drifting to the right, a fact most evident at this moment in the Reagan landslide. ALPA's boisterous campaign only made people take notice that there was a new airline in New York that offered halfway decent service at a low price. It was free publicity, just like the pooping baby elephant in Kansas City. Even in an old-line union town like New York, people couldn't have cared less about the whinings of a few union pilots down in Texas—particularly when New York Air was offering Gotham one of the best bargains in air travel it had ever seen.

Service to Washington was inaugurated at $49 ($29 on weekends), compared with Eastern's $60, plus a passenger got a free drink on New York Air, and, for a time, a free bottle of champagne, borrowing from the Southwest Airline liquor giveaway of seven years earlier. Texas Air drove home its message in newspaper ads showing people drowning themselves in champagne. "Celebrate, New York!" they said. "You'll never have to fly the Eastern shuttle again."

Eastern fought back valiantly, handing out 50-percent-off coupons to anyone flying the shuttle; Lorenzo responded by offering $15 to anyone who turned in one of the Eastern coupons to New York Air. (A rash of counterfeit coupons came into circulation.) Before long New York Air was flying close to 100,000 people a month. Practically overnight New York Air had captured one quarter of the market held by Eastern's shuttle in one of the world's busiest and most important airline markets. New York Air was the most successful airline start-up in history.

Don Burr had at last secured four planes from Lufthansa, with at least a dozen scheduled to come in. Hiring the people to staff People Express turned out to be much easier than finding the airplanes.

A hard recession was still on, with 8 million Americans unemployed and new college graduates among the hardest hit. An ad for flight personnel in Buffalo drew 12,000 eager applicants. The pay was meager—about $17,000 to start, except for pilots, who received twice that—and everyone had to buy stock, even if doing so required borrowing money from the company. Anyone who came into People Express, Burr decreed, would have to invest a substantial portion of his or her net worth in the company. That way if the company failed, they would all go down with it.

Candidates were administered a variety of tests to assure they were compatible with the culture Burr had in mind. The employment rolls swelled, mostly with people from marginal colleges; in profiling recruits, some of the company's executives considered an IQ of 105 to be ideal. Certainly Burr had his standards—very specific ones. His employees had to be friendly, and passionate about serving the customer. In the interest of low fares People Express passengers would be asked to carry their bags on board or pay three dollars. Anyone who wanted coffee would pay fifty cents. Burr was linking the ticket price to the lowest common denominator of service demanded by the customer—pure transportation. The ticket price had to be lower than the cost of driving, or forget it. ("There's no potholes up here," one of the company's early ads would observe.) But even if the company could not provide extensive service, Burr thought, it could offer warm service. Southwest Airlines had proved the everlasting value of that. Warm service cost nothing to provide, but it made a deep impression on the customer. So what if People Express was a no-frills airline? The friendly attitudes of his employees, Burr decided, would be the ultimate frill.

Burr also wanted employees who were something to look at. People Express was going to introduce the radical notion of cross-employment, in which everyone would have a secondary job. (Lorenzo resolved to attempt the same at New York Air.) Every single employee of People Express would be required to put in time at a job with customer contacts; many, including the chief financial officer of the company, would hold second jobs as flight attendants. Everybody would have to be good-looking. Burr told his personnel people that although he didn't demand Rock Hudson looks, every employee at least had to have a "quality of attractiveness." Burr, in fact, made it the policy to train everyone as a flight attendant, even if many would never actually perform the role, meaning that no one with a disability could be hired. No one would be coming to work in the North Terminal in a wheelchair.

The idea of job rotation had another virtue: it would prevent the pilots of People Express from becoming aloof and independent, as they were at every other airline. Burr, at bottom, mistrusted pilots. "Pilots have a character flaw," he once explained. "They have an innate sense of superiority and entitlement. Aggressive males are drawn to piloting. . . . It's heavily left-brain dominant, very well toilet trained." Rotating pilots into other jobs—accounting, customer service, scheduling, whatever—would keep them focused on the company as well as the cockpit. "It's very disruptive to have them only fly planes. It doesn't fully use their talents. Therefore, they get unhappy. . . . They become bad employees." It went without saying that engaging pilots in the affairs of the company would also make them less prone to unionization.

The recruits received unremitting hours of indoctrination, in which Burr himself conducted much of the training. His tie pulled low, his arms flailing, his feet madly scurrying around the classroom, Burr went on for hours. He would fill the chalkboard with diagrams that looked like football plays. "The guy thinks he's John Madden!" one of the skeptics in his class told himself. Drawings of dragons and dragon slayers hung at the front of the class. Business, Burr explained, involved a struggle between good and evil, in which People Express was cast by destiny as a force of good against the evildoers of the airline industry—such as Frank Lorenzo of Texas Air. "Be Luke Skywalker," he told them, "not Darth Vader. Ultimately love is stronger than evil." His training concepts swung from Spielberg to Freud. He would tell people about the glow he felt as a boy walking from his mother's kitchen after she had said something approving. "When your mother gave *you* that unconditional love," he would ask managers, "did it make you want to do more, or less?"

They all worked ungodly hours, seventy or eighty a week, to get the airline started. Burr actively promoted office romances. "The greatest thing that can happen to you is to fall in love at work," he told them. Some employees thought that Burr, a married father of four, wanted people to conduct extramarital affairs at work in order to loosen their connections to the distraction of home life. He told people that wasn't what he meant, but office romance became so commonplace that people ultimately began calling People Express the Love Boat.

The company threw a party in a ballroom at the nearby Newark Sheraton the night that the FAA finally awarded People Express its operating certificate, removing the last obstacle to the commencement of operations. It was a raucous event. The alcohol flowed freely. People sneaked off to the second floor of the hotel to find dark spots to have sex. Others wept with joy. "It was just a huge emotional release," Burr would recall of the occasion. And in the midst of it, Don Burr presided like their king, hoisted over the crowd and carried around on their shoulders. They were his followers. They were his flock. They were almost his disciples.

On August 3, 1981, three months after People Express had conducted its maiden flight, 13,000 of the nation's air traffic controllers walked off the job.

Under federal law the strike was illegal. President Ronald Reagan ordered the controllers' union, PATCO, to call off the walkout. The union refused. He ordered the strikers, as individuals, back to work. They refused. Two days later the president fired every last one of them. Reagan's action would utterly transform relations between organized labor and managements in the United States. Hollywood would take a hard new line against its unionized writers, professional football against its players. Trucking and other gritty industries would take their most aggressive stands ever against workers. On the day that President Reagan fired the controllers, organized labor began to lose its fangs, and in no industry would that become more apparent than in aviation.

The more immediate effect of the PATCO walkout, however, was disarray, undoubtedly the worst turbulence to hit the airways of America since FDR canceled the postal contracts fifty years earlier. Travel ground to a halt. The government began planning measures to ration airspace—slots—as never before. The government said things would return to normal in a few weeks; then it said the damage would take months to repair. In truth, the airways would never return to normal, not any time in the 20th century.

At the moment the controllers went out, Don Burr and Gerry Gitner, the president of People Express, were in Germany with their wives, closing the purchase of their second round of refurbished Lufthansa 737s. Burr remained in Germany with his wife while Gitner and his wife boarded one of the newly purchased planes and headed for Newark, the only passengers on board. "Come up with a new plan," Burr told him, "or we're dead."

Newark was closed due to the strike when the plane arrived; the plane was permitted to land only because it was a ferry flight. The next day, a Sunday, 35-year-old Gitner cleared off the dining room table at his home in Morristown, New Jersey, and with a few other executives began to consider a way out of the disaster. In addition to coping with a cutback of their already meager, four-plane operation at Newark, he had to find a way to deal with the new incoming airplanes. Refusing the airplane deliveries was no option; People Express had a $7-million letter of credit in Lufthansa's hands, serving as a performance bond; if the planes were not received on schedule, People Express would have to make good for the full amount. In that case a bankruptcy filing would not be out of the question.

There was only one solution, Gitner realized: "bypass routes," as he called them, flying not into Newark but to altogether different cities where slot restrictions had not taken hold. But where?

Gitner wanted to fly to places that fit the People Express formula: markets that could be stimulated by low fares. Florida, the ultimate discretionary destination, as price-sensitive a market as existed anywhere, was as good a place as any to try—not Miami, obviously, because it was a busy airport suffering along with the other major airports in the country. But what about Jacksonville? Sarasota?

Where to fly from? Buffalo, Gitner declared; Canadians loved Florida, and People Express could capture Toronto traffic from there. And why not Columbus? No airline had ever flown nonstop from Columbus to Florida.

There were a few small technical problems with Gitner's bypass scheme. For one thing it was August, not exactly the height of the tourist season in Florida. For another the incoming airplanes were configured all wrong for the flights. Florida was a three-hour trip, not the one-hour jaunt the planes had been ordered for. The ratio of lavatories to seats was inadequate. The People Express no-free-food formula didn't work nearly so well on a flight three times longer than the founders had planned.

But those were details, and this was a desperate case. The plan went into action—and worked, like a miracle. The people of Columbus and Buffalo and Toronto loved the idea of an ultracheap nonstop flight to Florida, even if it wasn't Miami, even if the sun was at its most unbearable intensity of the year. It was still Florida. Gitner had saved the day. And even though Newark service was gradually restored, Don Burr quickly learned, to the everlasting chagrin of a few other airlines, that Florida was a People Express kind of market.

• • •

People Express promoted itself as the way to "fly smart," taking some inspiration from the Volkswagen as the car with cachet. It worked. Ted Kennedy and his niece Caroline, the daughter of John Kennedy, flew People Express. Actor Christopher Reeve, at the height of his Superman fame, was another conspicuous customer. The masses followed.

In Columbus, Ohio, the company drew so many baggage-laden passengers—because there was no free baggage checking on People Express—that they actually wore the airport carpet threadbare. When service was added to Burlington, Vermont, thousands of Montreal residents, balking at the prohibitive fares charged by heavily regulated Canadian airlines, began driving the 100 miles to Burlington in order to catch People Express to Newark or Florida. People Express was consistently filling its planes and doing so without the benefit of a computer reservations system, a stunning feat. Burr, in fact, stubbornly eschewed such technology, relegating it to the category of high-cost indulgences. If someone wanted to make a reservation on People Express, he or she could call People Express, bypassing travel agents and computer reservation systems altogether.

Burr's people genuflected at his every command—except for the president of People Express. Gerry Gitner was soon chafing badly under Burr. Gitner began to fear the company was growing too fast. He thought that fares were too low. The two men fought, "for hours, days, and weeks," as Burr later described it.

Gitner's discomfort was evident when Burr attempted to establish rules for the unorthodoxy ruling People Express. Burr wanted to record a simple list of powerful rules—guidelines against which every employee of People Express would be required to judge his or her decisions. These were to be called the Precepts. They would, Burr declared, become the gospel of People Express. People Express would create a better world. People Express would bring happiness to passengers—correction, make that *customers*. It was devoted to profit making, yes, but only as a consequence of doing good works. So far as Burr cared, the pilots could fly the planes upside down, so long as they followed the Precepts.

Surrounded by his top executives, Burr excitedly scrawled out the Precepts on big sheets of paper, which he taped to the walls.

One: Service—Commitment to the growth and development of our
        people.
Two: To be the best provider of air transportation.
Three: To provide the highest quality of leadership.
Four: To serve as a role model for others.
Five: Simplicity.
Six: Maximization of profits.

The Precepts, in and of themselves, all made perfect sense. But it was
the way in which Burr compiled them, the way he handed them
down, that so irritated Gitner. It was almost as if he were chiseling
into stone tablets, almost as if he were handing down command-
ments, except that his numbered six rather than ten. Gitner watched
incredulously as the day wore on, Burr becoming more animated,
gesturing widely. Within weeks, Gitner had quit.

Anxiety hung heavily over the resignation of the founding president, but Burr assured his flock that they should not read anything
untoward in Gitner's departure. "Gerry loves planning," Burr explained, "and that's already done at People Express."

In times of regulation and not, there have always been three ways to
expand an airline.

The most direct means is acquisition, as Frank Lorenzo had attempted, unsuccessfully, with National, Continental, and TWA. Because they are built on unique economic foundations and strong
internal cultures, however, any two airlines may mix poorly. Pan Am,
the victor in the National takeover drama, quickly found it had committed one of history's most disastrous mergers. Pan Am employees
looked down their noses at the National people; the National people
thought the Pan Am veterans were conceited. In the back-office accounting operation, Pan Am people simply threw National ticket
stubs on the floor, to be swept up at the end of the day. National people resented wearing Pan Am uniforms. Both groups spent so much
time scowling at each other that they forgot to smile for their passengers. On-time performance plunged. In the interests of equality,
Pan Am had to increase pay and benefits for the former National
workers, making the acquisition more costly than ever. On top of
everything else, National's north-south routes were running in the

wrong direction to give Pan Am the passenger feed it needed to Asia and Europe.

The second avenue of expansion involves creating altogether new markets. Texas International, Southwest, and American with its super saver fares had each succeeded in using low prices to stimulate new business and to do so profitably, though only on a few routes, or only within a single state, or only on a selected number of seats per airplane. People Express was now putting the concept to its fullest test, although it too was beginning from a small base. As successful as these experiments were, they were vastly overwhelmed by the intractable recession of the early 1980s. In 1980, the year that the upstarts came into being, the airlines of the United States carried 297 million people—a decline from 317 million the year before. In 1981 the total fell even further, to 286 million.

The shrinking national airline market added value to the third method of expanding an airline: taking territory by force. Here too, as New York Air was proving against the Eastern shuttle, the means involved price. Though that battle was raging in only a single market (between New York and Washington) the moral was clear: the entrenched carriers of commercial aviation, even the Big Four, were not immune to the upstarts.

New York Air and People Express, fraternal twins, were the first progeny of deregulation. They were thriving, but it was still early. There would be deaths as well.

CHAPTER 6

THE EMPIRE STRIKES BACK

Deciding where airplanes should fly, and at what hours of the day, requires four-dimensional thinking, an affinity for solving puzzles in which the pieces are continually moving. The scheduler analyzes passenger traffic patterns, economic trends, maintenance timetables, fueling requirements, flight times, loading and unloading intervals, noise rules, slot availability, airport curfews, labor costs, fuel prices, and fare levels, among a few dozen other factors, at every location where the airline conducts business. From these variables the scheduler produces a flight plan, from which the airline in turn establishes its financing, staffing, food and beverage requirements, sales strategy, and a series of contingency plans for bad weather, mechanical failure, and every other misery that can befall an airline. The permutations increase arithmetically according to the number of aircraft and geometrically according to the number of aircraft types in any given fleet—another of the reverse economies of scale that plague airlines as they grow.

Even in the era of regulation, when these decisions were made with the unwavering oversight of the federal government, scheduling was an arduous planning exercise. In the deregulated era, it involved the additional complexity of anticipating how one's competitors were conducting the same calculations.

In the early days of deregulation, as now, only one person in any major airline had a wider command of the operation than the scheduler, and that was the president. Among those parameters subject to human manipulation, the scheduler worked within boundaries established by the president. If the scheduling department was the nervous system of the airline, then the president's office was the brain. It was an office well suited to someone who liked to be in control.

By the beginning of 1980, seven years after he had joined the company, 45-year-old Bob Crandall was still not the president of American Airlines. This meant, among other frustrations, that he lacked dominion over the vital scheduling function, a frustration that was all the more galling because on the organization chart of American Airlines, the scheduling department reported to him. Despite the chain of command, Crandall was forced to battle endlessly with Robert Norris, American's senior vice president of finance, who insisted on maintaining veto power over the flying schedules. These apocalyptic flare-ups ultimately landed in the office of Albert Casey, American's chairman and president, who finally took Crandall's side. Norris soon left American Airlines.

Vanquishing that rival, however, did not bring Crandall any closer to the presidency he coveted. Crandall was in a horse race with yet another of American's senior vice presidents—a brilliant Ph.D. named Donald Lloyd-Jones, the head of operations. Though neither the radical thinker nor the strong personality that Crandall was, Lloyd-Jones had spent more than twenty years at American. He was popular among employees, who could easily spot him walking the halls of American's Third Avenue offices with a pipe clenched in his teeth. Crandall's own relationship with Lloyd-Jones, though outwardly collegial, was imbued with rivalry. Crandall had once ordered the firing of a public relations executive who scheduled a media interview with Lloyd-Jones that Crandall thought he was more suited to handle; Lloyd-Jones intervened and got the PR man reassigned instead.

Crandall's problem was resolved when Frank Lorenzo, looking for legitimacy and experience to match his outsized ambitions, called to ask Crandall to come to work for him, not at Texas International but at a major airline befitting Crandall's standing—another takeover target, now in Lorenzo's sights. Rumors swept Texas International that Lorenzo had offered Crandall a $3 million signing bonus.

With the company's brilliant marketing chief a hot commodity, the board of American saw fit to elect Crandall president in July 1980, with Casey remaining as chairman. Bob Crandall had at last defeated Donald Lloyd-Jones. "Each of us wanted to be president of the company," Crandall would later remark. "I was successful and he wasn't." Notably, Crandall saw to it that the scheduling function continued to report to him instead of to his successor as marketing chief, making Crandall's control of the operation unassailable.

His promotion made Crandall the equal of Dick Ferris at United, except that United remained a much larger airline, with 369 airplanes to American's 253. In the minor scheduling realignments of the Big Four following deregulation, American, in fact, soon slipped behind Eastern airlines, becoming the third-ranked domestic airline not only in fleet size but by the most widely accepted yardstick, the total mileage its paying passengers flew. In his first speech as president to American's top marketing executives, in February 1981, Crandall demanded unwavering commitment to a renewal of the company's success.

"The game we are playing," Crandall told them, "is closest to the old game of Christians and lions." He demanded "that every one of your players knows the game plan, that every one of your players knows the stakes, that every one of your players has pride in himself or herself, and that every one of your players is committed to the victory that we simply must have." Crandall asked, "I wonder if all of your people feel so strongly about American that they bleed American red, white, and blue?"

Despite the enthusiasm of his halftime speeches, they were not the primary reason Crandall had aspired so urgently to the presidency of American. "I've always been a person of ideas," Crandall would later explain. "As a leader you have a lot of latitude to test your ideas." And Bob Crandall had quite a few of those.

Crandall began every week with a staff meeting in the boardroom at American Airlines headquarters on Third Avenue, a windowless room filled with the latest audiovisual gadgetry. Any aspect of an airline's operations could be reduced to numbers, and those numbers could be reduced to charts and graphs, and they, in turn, could be burned into a slide or an overhead transparency. Hour by hour the numbers were projected against the wall as Crandall and his inner circle remained assembled around the massive conference table. A blizzard of paperwork went around—long reports written in excruciating detail. "Let's turn the pages," Crandall liked to say.

This planning session would go on most of the day, occasionally late into the night, the ceiling literally disappearing above a cloud of cigarette smoke. Only two or three nonsmokers sat at the table, each sinking deeper in his seat as the accumulating haze inched lower and lower. Tom Plaskett, Crandall's successor as American's head of marketing, had to change his clothes the minute he returned to his home every Monday night, so overpowering was the nicotine odor to the rest of his family.

Bob Crandall loved meetings, the longer the better. He once scheduled a meeting for 5 A.M., and one of the participants showed up in his pajamas. During staff meetings there was never a bathroom break, ever. The participants either waited for lunch or dinner or excused themselves when duty called. Crandall, for his part, never did have to get up. His subordinates on occasion would slyly pour him cup after cup of coffee just to see if they could force him to take an unscheduled break, but they never succeeded. They credited Crandall's stamina to "mankind's biggest bladder."

As many as three pens clasped in his shirt pocket, his gold-rimmed glasses glistening under the harsh lights of the meeting room, Crandall maintained his concentration for hours at a time. In later years, in a new headquarters building, Crandall's aides would gather around a massive conference table with a surface so white it made one squint. Crandall and his people used croupier sticks to push computer runs and internal reports across the vast surface. Junior executives assigned to make presentations would work all weekend, perhaps staying up half the night on Sunday. They would walk into the meeting with knots in their stomachs, for it was an unforgivable sin at American Airlines to appear in a meeting before Bob Crandall without having every fact at one's command. He would cut you to ribbons. Some executives endlessly tracked Crandall's moods, timing their approaches accordingly. Others simply accustomed themselves to Crandall's temper—the screaming, the swearing, the sarcasm, the sputtering through those thick lips and pointed teeth. Some even found they could dish it right back to him, *they* could bully *him,* particularly if they had the wits to hit him fast with a compelling intellectual argument. Logic, in the end, could snap Crandall from a rage.

Nothing held greater interest for Crandall than the company's progress against other airlines—mainly against United—in hard-wiring travel agencies to the Sabre network. By the time he had become president, some 2,000 travel agencies around the country had been signed on as subscribers, in many cases after a pitched battle with United. Sabre had invaded the point of sale like no other distribution system in history, and the travel agents using Sabre had little idea of the extent to which they were being controlled. American accomplished this feat through a practice that Crandall's people called "screen science."

A travel agent sat before a terminal with a telephone headset strapped across his or (usually) her head. She took the customer's query—What have you got from LaGuardia to LAX tomorrow morning?—and typed in the relevant cities, dates, and times of day. Sabre then culled through its database, which included the schedules at every airport on the planet, going out some 300 days into the future. It then displayed a screen full of flight suggestions ranked according to how closely they matched the query—usually several screens, in fact, if the agent chose to view them all.

Years of relying on the *OAG* had conditioned travel agents to expect to see the fastest flight listed first. Crandall's people found that in more than half of all reservations travel agents now selected the flight appearing on the first line of the Sabre terminal. In about 92 percent of all cases, the reservation was made from the choices listed on the first screen.

But how did Sabre, with its many mainframes and its millions of lines of programming, actually choose which flights to list on the first screen? The first *line*? How did Sabre decide which flights were most "convenient"? The answer depended on how one defined "convenient."

Sabre was programmed to score flights according to a formula based on the elapsed time of the flight, the proximity of the departure hour to the time requested by the agent, whether the flight involved a connection, and whether the connection involved a switch in airlines. The formula left great room for judgment, however, in the weighing of these factors. American promised travel agents that the best service based on these criteria would always be displayed on the first screen, regardless of the airline providing the service. But American made no such promise with respect to the all-critical first line, where, if it happened to serve those cities, the American flight invariably appeared.

American's salespeople promoted the virtues of selling from the first screen and the first line. "Trust the machine," they told the travel agents, and the agents did, causing American's share of the business in the local market to increase vastly. One study found that although American flew 42 percent of the seats between New York and Los Angeles, it got 60 percent of the business booked by travel agencies subscribing to Sabre. Between Baltimore and Chicago American had 25 percent of the total flying capacity but 44 percent of the bookings made through Sabre. In an industry in which a single market share point could make a huge difference in profitability, the marketing power of Sabre was explosive. "I would suggest we limit the results of this research to a need-to-know basis, since it could create some heat from our subscribers," one of Crandall's top aides wrote in a memo.

Crandall's people searched for ways to assure American top billing wherever it went head-to-head with another airline, regardless of who offered better service. "We must achieve first screen, first line in every competitive situation," one of Crandall's lieutenants wrote in an internal memo. When American introduced service from Dallas to Honolulu, for instance, Sabre, left to its own devices, listed the competing Braniff flight first. Braniff's flight, after all, was nonstop, while American's service involved a layover in Los Angeles. There was no way that a mere tweaking of the algorithms could overcome the fact that Braniff arrived in Honolulu two hours faster than the American flight; Sabre's flight-scoring algorithms would have to be corrupted outright.

One of Crandall's top sales people demanded just such a cheat in a memo to Richard Murray, one of Sabre's handlers. "I would like to adjust our Sabre display on our service to HNL out of DFW," he wrote. "What do we need to do to provide the necessary bias to give American the preferred display?" Another request came to add 57 minutes of bias in favor of American's service from Chicago to Honolulu. In that case, a memo noted, "The bulk of the displacement would be at United's expense."

Murray, though initially a willing participant in the practice of screen science, soon thought the top brass were getting greedy. We've got a good thing going here, Murray told them. Let's not call too much attention to it. He pleaded to penalize other airlines' flights only in tiny increments, in hopes that the travel agents and the other airlines might not notice. But people in the company were soon making snide remarks to Murray, questioning his loyalty. Didn't he bleed American red, white, and blue?

Murray's unease turned to panic when American mounted a major marketing study of DFW. In some cases the information that Sabre was accumulating was confidential, data that American had pledged never to use in furtherance of its own operations. Murray had been asked by Max Hopper, Bob Crandall's data processing guru, to ask Lorenzo's people for permission to use some confidential Texas International data in American's marketing study. In return American would share the results of its analysis with Texas International. While awaiting reply from Texas International, Murray was watching a slide presentation at a marketing meeting and was stunned to see the very same data—Texas International's booking figures at DFW—projected for all to see.

The two men would later disagree over whether the data in question were the confidential property of Texas International. In any event, when Murray confronted him about American's use of the numbers, Hopper answered that he thought Murray was getting Texas International's approval.

"I haven't gotten the authorization!" Murray explained.

"Well, it's too late now," Hopper said.

Within American there was no stopping Sabre. One after another requests went up the hierarchy for tens of millions of dollars to add more tentacles to the network, all intended, as Crandall's people wrote in a budget request, to "enhance American's control over its key distribution channel, the travel agency market." The rate of return projected in each of the expansion proposals was listed at "500 percent plus"—surely among the greatest payoffs ever promised by a management to a corporate board. Within a year of Crandall's becoming president, American had enlisted 3,500 travel agencies, and there were tens of thousands left to conquer. Crandall's network, as the marketing staff wrote in a memo, had done nothing less than reshape "the flow of passengers through the air transportation network, in a manner most beneficial to American."

The "Robert L. Crandall Factory of Ideas," as a company historian would call it, also discovered a way to turn Sabre terminals into cash registers, ringing up a few bucks for American Airlines whenever a travel agent booked a ticket on another airline through the Sabre system. It happened because of Frank Lorenzo.

Late in 1981 Lorenzo added a new spoke to the New York Air network: LaGuardia to Detroit, a direct incursion into some of American's most dearly held territory. American's Detroit run was part of the C. R. Smith legacy, dating back nearly 50 years, the kind of route that distinguished American as the "businessman's airline."

The galling thing, in Crandall's view, was that he had to list New York Air's flights in American's computer system. Travel agents by now were wise enough to realize that American and United played games with their computers, but withholding an entire block of flights was something that Crandall knew the travel agents would never stand for. So while New York Air was invading American's territory, American was forced to facilitate the onslaught.

Worse still, New York Air, in pursuit of its low-cost strategy, was refusing to perform many of the favors and courtesies that had long been taken for granted among the airlines—for instance, accepting baggage from the connecting flights of other airlines. It was the same story with People Express, and Southwest, for that matter. The upstart carriers were a "breed apart," as Crandall put it. They were not contributing members of the air transport system. They were in it for themselves.

After Lorenzo announced New York Air's invasion of Detroit, Crandall angrily ordered that all such upstarts—New York Air, People Express, and Southwest—would have to begin paying a fee to American for every sale transacted through Sabre—as much as three dollars for each booking, a sum that exceeded the entire profit margin on many flights. Predictably the upstarts did not react well to the fee plan, neither when first proposed by Crandall nor when matched by all the other airlines rich enough to have built such systems. They simply refused to pay the fees. As long as the computer networks listed the upstarts' flights, a travel agent could always call the airline directly for a reservation and a ticket, avoiding any transaction through Sabre.

American had a counterpunch for that as well. New York Air's flights to Detroit, and everywhere else, were suddenly appearing at the bottom of the screen in thousands of travel agency computers across America. New York Air's reservations began to dry up. Soon Lorenzo was forced to cut back from eight Detroit flights a day to four, then from four to none.

In the space of several weeks, Bob Crandall's computer network had pushed a competitor out of one of the busiest and most important business markets in the world.

Crandall knew that the computer battles were only tactical skirmishes in a war with the upstart airlines. American also needed a strategy, a grand design. Though still well contained, the new airlines, Crandall thought, presented nothing less than a mortal threat. The upstart airlines had junior, often entry-level, staffs, paid accordingly, while at American the average employee had nearly 12 years' seniority. The new airlines also had no unions or, in the case of Southwest, unions that did not try to prop up wages through featherbedding. It appeared that success and failure in the airline business was suddenly being defined within the personnel budget, and in American's case those costs were nearly as high as any in the industry.

One member of Crandall's brain trust, a young, Canadian-born executive named Donald Carty, had been wrestling with the problem from the moment that People Express had gotten aloft. Among the options he studied was starting a new airline outside the existing American Airlines, as Lorenzo had done by starting New York Air outside Texas International. As much as Lorenzo's westward expansion annoyed the people at American, they had to admit that the whole New York Air gambit was brash and brilliant. Crandall, however, believed that a proud and seasoned workforce was part of American's franchise in the marketplace. Expanding the existing airline would be preferable to starting an altogether new one, and yet . . .

Crandall brainstormed endlessly over this challenge with Carty and other members of his inner circle. Creating a new airline versus expanding the old airline; hiring new, low-cost employees versus maintaining high salaries for veteran employees—these permutations eventually began to suggest an altogether different concept. "If we can't create a new airline outside of American," Crandall said, "we'll create one inside American."

Yes, that was it: two airlines, or more precisely, two separate and distinct workforces, each flying the same airplanes and the same routes. If you already worked for American Airlines, your job and salary were secure; indeed, you would continue getting salary increases. But for every person hired in the future—every flight attendant, pilot, baggage handler, ticket agent, and mechanic—the story would be different. Each would come in at lower starting wages and in some cases at reduced benefits as well. Through the years, as they gained seniority, this second category of workers would receive raises, of course, but they would remain on a lower scale than the older, more established employees, those lucky enough to have been hired by the early 1980s. In fact the new hires would never catch up. They would be perpetually confined to a second-tier status that the unions would come to call the "b-scale."

The faster American grew—a worthy strategy in any case, in the newly deregulated world—the more new people it would be able to hire at b-scale rates, and the lower its *average* labor costs would go. The bigger American became, the closer its costs would approach the levels enjoyed by New York Air and People Express.

Bob Crandall christened his newfound strategy with the pretentious name "the Growth Plan," although there was no disputing that the plan was something extraordinary. It was, to begin with, a major change in strategy for a corporation that had so far responded to deregulation by cutting back on its traditional route structure and getting rid of airplanes. In order for the Growth Plan to work—in order to hire enough new employees to drag down American's overall labor costs quickly—Crandall would have to launch the biggest expansion in airline history. And he would have to do this as airport capacity was tightening and as new competitors were continuing to flood the market, all in the face of higher fuel prices, stratospheric interest rates, and an uncertain market. But Crandall believed it had to be done: the top people at American were convinced that now, in the early 1980s, with upstarts popping up all over, the winners and losers were being permanently decided in the airline industry.

Part of the Growth Plan's genius lay in how diabolical it was. The one controlling obstacle to the plan, of course, were the unions at American. The very concept of a two-tier wage system ran 180 degrees counter to the fundamental all-for-one, one-for-all principles of unionism. But the Growth Plan was conspicuously structured to benefit *existing* union members, who in an expanding airline would enjoy vastly greater promotion opportunities, meaning that their salaries would increase even more than otherwise. The incumbent employees would reap this windfall on the backs of future employees, but what did it matter when the winners under this strategy were the only ones able to vote on the proposal?

After months of careful preparation Crandall and his people began presenting the b-scale proposal to employees as their labor contracts approached expiration. Through the sale of stock and other means, American had accumulated a massive war chest, the means to win a war of attrition should the unions refuse to approve the two-tier wage scheme.

The first union contract to come up for renewal was that of the Transport Workers Union, whose 10,000 members represented mechanics and other ground employees. Nonunion replacement workers—scabs, in union parlance—were standing by around the country, collecting $25 a day just for waiting. Crandall and other company officials, often in the face of a booing and hissing crowd, were on the stump, pointing out that existing employees would benefit tremendously under the growth that would follow. Finally, with a strike imminent, the TWU relented. B-scales were born.

Members of the pilots' union were even less difficult to convince. A huge proportion of the pilots at American had been hired at one time, in the explosion of flying that accompanied the onset of jets in the mid-1960s. By the early 1980s many of the members of that bulging pilot class were still stuck in the copilot's seat. Crandall and his aides demonstrated that as American bought more planes—a fleet expansion made possible by hiring new employees at cheap wage scales—these veteran pilots would finally be thrust into the captains' seats, getting a big raise in the process. Crandall's task was made even easier by the fact that the pilots at American, though unionized, were not part of the Air Line Pilots Association, which represented pilots at all other union airlines. Dealing with a distant national leadership in Washington would have made b-scales a much harder sell.

The flight attendants required more convincing. The job of persuading them fell to Tom Plaskett, American's marketing chief. Seeking to neutralize the union's leadership, which was more outspoken than the membership, Plaskett met with flight attendants in small numbers, reasoning that it would be easier to intimidate the rabble-rousers from making speeches in a small room than in an auditorium. Altogether Plaskett held 145 meetings with flight attendants, and he drew an ocean of tears in those meetings, by his later account. "Flight attendants deal with everything on a more emotional, visible level," Plaskett would explain. And as they cried still more, "It dawned on me: What was coming to the fore in their minds was, 'I'm not worth what I'm paid.' . . . We're telling them, 'There's someone out there who's willing to do your job at half the price.' " In the end, as they watched the company training every secretary in corporate headquarters to act as a strikebreaker, flight attendants making $30,000 a year decided that they would stay on the job and allow American to hire future flight attendants at about $15,000 a year.

With his b-scales firmly in place, Crandall in early 1984 began unleashing orders for hundreds of new airplanes. Pilots, mechanics, and flight attendants flooded into American. The Dallas hub added new spokes. Still more planes and more employees came aboard. Despite the intractable recession, earnings soon reached record levels, enabling the airline to buy even more planes and hire even more people. Within a few years American was bringing in planes at the rate of nearly one per week and hiring as many as 1,000 new employees a month. At an industry meeting in Washington, Herb Kelleher of Southwest Airlines would one day remark that being headquartered in Dallas with American made him feel like Finland in the shadow of Russia. With perestroika at its height, Crandall shot back, "There's one important difference: I ain't reducing troops."

The one nagging problem with an expansion fueled by b-scalers, of course, was that the low-paid newcomers quickly came to realize that they were receiving distinctly unequal pay for equal work. This presented Crandall with a labor relations problem in the short term and in the years ahead with a significant strategic challenge: maintaining b-scales past the point at which the b-scalers themselves attained the majorities in the unions that represented them. The whole thing would have to be managed delicately. "I don't want to hear anybody ever say, 'We beat the union with this,' " Crandall instructed his managers. Crandall even tried to stifle use of the derisive epithet "b-scale," coined by union leaders, in favor of the benign-sounding "market rate" scale.

At the height of the expansion Crandall sat under the bright lights of a recording studio to tape an orientation message for the legions of new employees streaming through the front gates. He rendered a stirring account of American's origins on the mail routes that Charles Lindbergh flew. He gave a pep talk on the competitiveness of the post-deregulation world of aviation—"the nearest thing to legalized warfare" he told his new employees. As for American's split workforce, he said,

> After you go to work, you will become aware of the fact that people hired some years ago, during the years of regulation, are paid what we call the "existing employee" pay scales, while you and most of your coworkers are paid at "market rate" scales. Some people have suggested that our new employees may feel some resentment towards those with more seniority. That's very unrealistic, and I hope you won't let it happen to you. Keep in mind that the more senior employees worked for the company during the years of regulation. They helped build American into the great company it is. In effect, they built the legacy that promises a good future for all of us.

Alas for Crandall, the historical precedent wasn't entirely encouraging. In the year 217 A.D. the expansion-minded Roman Emperor Caracalla introduced history's first known two-tier pay system, with lower rates of pay for some soldiers. Although it was not the only morale problem that the emperor faced, it most certainly fueled the plot by which eventually he was assassinated by his own troops.

While conceiving of the b-scale plan and tweaking its computer network against the upstart airlines, American was conducting a third major post-deregulation move. It was quitting Manhattan.

In addition to cutting costs, the move, as Chairman Al Casey reckoned it, meant laying to rest the regulated past. American had been reducing flights in the Northeast and moving its planes westward. American, he declared, would make its new home in the grassy prairies along the edge of Dallas–Fort Worth International Airport.

Though American had been a major operator in Dallas since the days of the 1930 spoils conference, it was always viewed as an out-of-town corporation. Even little Southwest Airlines readily established a more visible corporate presence in Dallas than American ever had. But among them all the most powerful airline in Dallas was Braniff Airways, not only a beloved local institution but the biggest airline by far at DFW.

If American Airlines was to become the king of the hill in its newly adopted operating center, then Bob Crandall would first have to dislodge Braniff—a company going through some puzzling and extraordinary changes just as American was moving to town.

For much of its history, Braniff had been notorious for poor operations and indifferent service. Then, in 1964, a 35-year-old financial analyst in Dallas named C. Edward Acker persuaded the directors of a local insurance company to buy a controlling interest in Braniff and put him in charge of shaking things up.

Eddie Acker stood out in two respects: he was basketball tall (well over six feet) and demonstrably intelligent (he had skipped two grades, second and eighth, on his way to Southern Methodist University). With a soft chin, a bemused smirk, and spectacles that made him a ringer for the network anchor John Chancellor, Acker also had a bearing that reassured older, more established men, such as the insurance company directors who entrusted Braniff to his care.

Acker hired the advertising agency Jack Tinker & Partners, fresh from the triumph of a breakthrough for Alka-Seltzer ("No matter what shape your stomach's in . . ."). Mary Wells, the account executive, had Braniff's planes painted in seven different jelly-bean colors. She brought in Emilio Pucci from Milan to design the exotic flight attendant uniforms used in the "air strip." Meanwhile, Acker had recruited the tempestuous Harding Lawrence to help whip Braniff's operations into shape. Mary Wells and Harding Lawrence proceeded to conduct America's most celebrated interoffice romance.

Under Acker and Lawrence, Braniff reorganized its route struc-

ture around the infrequently used system called hubbing. Braniff's
hub was born of necessity when Braniff took the lone 747 in its fleet
(painted orange, it became known as the Great Pumpkin) and scheduled it between Dallas and Honolulu. The naysayers of the industry
said that no airline could ever collect enough passengers to fill a
jumbo jet to Hawaii except on the West Coast or East Coast, or perhaps in Chicago. But because Braniff had resisted the pell-mell rush
to buy whole fleets of 747s, the company could afford to buy a great
number of smaller "feeder" jets, such as 727s. Thus DFW was fairly
teeming with Braniff's jelly-bean planes, all zipping in and out from
as far east as New York and as far west as California, and from
dozens of smaller cities in Texas and up and down the Tornado Alley
that ran through Oklahoma and Kansas. These small planes, in turn,
were feeding passengers not only into the Great Pumpkin but into
each other. The 727s were both arriving and departing full of passengers. When Braniff failed to snuff out Southwest Airlines in the
courts, it added still more small planes to compete against Southwest.

Braniff's powerful hub vividly demonstrated another inviolate
rule of the airline business: Whoever has the most flights from a city
gets a disproportionate share of the passengers. Frequency enhanced
convenience—the convenience of flying the day of your meeting, not
the night before; the convenience of arriving just an hour before your
business was scheduled to begin. Frequency also preserved valuable
flexibility: a business traveler could catch a later flight if his meeting
ran over, or surprise the family by grabbing an early flight home. The
marketing benefit of frequent service was so ironclad that it was expressed in its own mathematical representation, called the S-curve, a
graph that showed that by maintaining 60 percent of the flights from
a city, for instance, an airline invariably drew much more than 60 percent of the passengers.

Though Braniff's was among the earliest and most brilliant
demonstrations of hub power, the company's glory days were not to
last. The beginning of the end, improbably enough, had begun with
the Watergate scandal.

With their gaily painted airplanes and smartly robed flight attendants, Acker and Lawrence in the early 1970s eagerly wanted more
destinations to serve, but the government was making none available,

except overseas, as part of the slow dissolution of Pan Am's monopoly. The White House played a prominent role in these foreign route awards. Just as American had, Braniff felt the hot breath of the Committee to Reelect the President. Before long Acker and Lawrence went to Washington to deliver personally an envelope bearing $40,000 in hundred-dollar bills to the Nixon people.

After the illegal contribution was made known, the Securities and Exchange Commission launched an investigation of the internal money-laundering maneuvers conducted to generate the cash off the books. A story began to circulate in the industry that Braniff was being pressured to offer up a human sacrifice, just as American had ousted George Spater. Acker, meanwhile, had also been called before a grand jury investigating whether Braniff used illegal dirty tricks in its effort to block Southwest from going into business.

In the midst of all these controversies Acker announced he was quitting Braniff. Acker told people he yearned to escape from the shadow of Harding Lawrence, who had become the more visible figure in Braniff's success. Throughout the airline industry, however, people were convinced that Acker had another motive in leaving: to protect Lawrence, and Braniff itself, from the long arm of the law.

With Acker departed, Braniff was without its ballast. Previously a Spartan, cost-conscious operation, Braniff soon opened a massive new headquarters campus at DFW, with a pair of olive trees flown in from Greece for the courtyard. (They died the following winter.) Having already hired Alexander Calder to paint the exteriors of some of the company's airplanes in garish designs, Lawrence now commissioned Calder to produce dozens of works for the walls of corporate offices. Lawrence installed his 32-year-old son in a high-visibility vice president's job. The company chose an advertising slogan that reflected the image of the chairman as much as the image of the airline: "When you've got it, flaunt it!"

Lawrence was convinced that deregulation would be a disaster and that Congress would quickly reverse it. Not one to waste an expansion opportunity, Lawrence in the hours before deregulation became law instructed his man in line outside the CAB to apply for every new route he could lay his hands on. Lawrence got his wish, winning dozens of routes. But under the government's use-it-or-lose-it policy, Braniff had to begin flying the new routes almost immediately. Lawrence dispersed many of the planes from his hub in Dallas to such far-flung destinations as Albany, Birmingham, and Cleveland. He borrowed massively in a crash campaign to bring in still more planes. On one day alone at the peak of the expansion Braniff commenced service to 16 additional cities, a feat that no airline had ever come close to achieving. Lawrence had also added service to London and other cities overseas. As the expansion ran amok, Braniff's newly hired flight attendants literally lost track of where they were landing as they announced the arrival of their flights. From 1975, when Acker had left, to 1980, when American was moving to town, Braniff nearly doubled in size, from the tenth largest U.S. airline to the eighth.

Bob Crandall was practically rubbing his hands together as he watched Harding Lawrence disassemble Braniff's beautiful hub at DFW. Just then the perfect plan popped out of the Crandall idea factory.

Tom Plaskett, Crandall's successor in the marketing department, had been brooding sternly over ways to cut costs. In the delicate dance of planes, employees, and passengers at DFW, American, it appeared, was inefficiently matching ground crews with flight schedules. As it switched more planes into Dallas, American was clustering arrivals and departures around peak times of day, helping passengers to make connections without forcing them to idle away hours in the molded plastic chairs of the airport. (Frozen yogurt was not yet a commonplace diversion.) But while it convenienced passengers to bunch arrivals and departures, the practice also created long stretches in which baggage handlers and other members of the ground crew had little to do. By spacing flights more evenly, it would seem, American could avoid scheduling work crews at the level dictated by the peak of operations.

Nothing might have pleased Plaskett more than to race to Crandall with his plan to cut manpower costs at DFW, but Plaskett had to do his homework first. The issue was delicate because American's head scheduler was close to Crandall and resisted reporting to Plaskett. So Plaskett went to Melvin E. Olsen, a more junior executive in the scheduling department. Mel Olsen had started out as a baggage handler for Western Airlines, chasing laboratory mice around the cargo hold whenever a box bound for the University of California at San Diego broke open. Olsen had been displaying computer expertise long before he had so much as touched one. After becoming a schedule analyst at Western in the 1960s he had kept track of the fleet by running an ice pick through a series of hand-punched cards in which the holes matched up according to aircraft types.

"Should we de-peak DFW?" Plaskett asked Olsen.

Instinctively Olsen knew the answer was no; if anything, he thought, American should move in the opposite direction. It was all a question of elementary mathematics.

Every single airline market involved an origin and destination—a city pair. Airlines traditionally served these markets by flying "point to point" with convenient, nonstop service. But by requiring passengers to change planes at a hub airport, an airline could vastly increase the number of city pairs it served. In its effort to ensnare passengers from Eastern in the southeastern United States, Delta, for instance, had long followed this practice in Atlanta, giving rise to the often-repeated Dixie complaint that whether flying to heaven or hell, you had to change planes in Atlanta. Braniff, and later American itself, was conducting the same sort of schedules in and out of Dallas.

Olsen realized that in a mathematically perfect world the number of markets an airline could serve from a hub increased exponentially as the number of cities from the hub increased arithmetically. This presupposed, however, that every passenger on every arriving flight had the opportunity to get aboard any one of the departing flights, all of which required the airline to schedule the arrivals as closely together as possible, and the departures as well. Olsen knew that to gain the full geometrical advantages of a hub, flights would have to be precisely timed to arrive and depart in "complexes" or "banks."

The beauty of complexing appeared even greater when Olsen ran computer simulations on the costs involved. As the number of cities was increased around a hub, the number of passengers flying through it increased exponentially, but the number of people on the ground required to service the flights rose only arithmetically. Using American's cost and travel-pattern data at DFW, he found that each city added to an existing bank of flights brought in 73 new passengers a day, at an average fare of $180—a total of $13,140 in additional revenue. But the incremental cost of servicing those additional passengers totaled only $560. American shouldn't be de-peaking DFW, Olsen realized. American should be adding as many flights as possible and scheduling them in bunches as tight as possible.

Olsen presented the results to Plaskett, who immediately grasped their significance. "Mel," Plaskett said, "I want to show this to Mr. Crandall."

Crandall had several good reasons to latch on to Olsen's findings. For one, this was leverage you had to love—a program that would increase costs, yes, but would increase revenues by a much greater factor. For another, Crandall knew that deregulation, reduced to its essence, meant grabbing and keeping airline passengers—controlling them for their entire journey. Olsen's plan would help American avoid handing off connecting passengers to competing airlines. Third, the expansion would also help American seize more of the business in Dallas from which Braniff now appeared to be walking away.

Finally, it was evident that a third party was now planning to make the scene at DFW: Delta Air Lines. Gravely for American, Delta was threatening to make DFW its next proving ground for the hub concept it was applying so successfully against Eastern in Atlanta. There was no way Bob Crandall was going to let Delta get the jump on American at DFW. Crandall ordered the airline to plan for peaking DFW beginning with its summer schedule in June 1981.

But which new cities should American serve from Dallas? Crandall began reviewing a list of destinations that could be added to the flight schedules; as it happened, he chose cities that the weakened Braniff already served—Austin, Amarillo, Corpus Christi, Midland, Lubbock, and others.

The big day was barely four months away, and the local managers at DFW were beside themselves with anxiety. It can't be done. . . . That's too many flights! . . . We need more belt loaders! But Crandall would tolerate no such treason. Hearing of any obstacle to the hub plan, he immediately blew it away.

While gearing up for the big hub buildup, Crandall's people were also putting the finishing touches on a secret project that had been years in the making—a device they recognized would have even greater value as a way of addicting passengers to American's big new hub.

The project dated to Crandall's years as the marketing chief. When policy makers began using the word "deregulation," Crandall began asking how American could maintain the loyalty of its long-standing customers, to say nothing of preventing new competitors from grabbing any first-time travelers. Crandall wanted some way of building brand loyalty for airline seats, which were essentially commodity products.

Meanwhile the endless computer studies at American had turned up another fascinating fact. Although American carried 25 million passengers a year, something like 40 percent of its business came from about 5 percent of its customers. There were that many repeat customers—"frequent fliers," one might call them. Any incremental customer was welcome, of course, but every incremental *frequent* flier was, on average, nearly 10 times more valuable.

The idea of targeting repeat customers was an old one in the airline business, and as with so many marketing innovations it began at American under C. R. Smith. About the time he was introducing the DC-3 in 1936, Smith was made an honorary Texas Ranger. Couldn't American, he asked, issue membership plaques in a club for good customers? Marketing its DC-3s as "Flagships," American expanded on the nautical theme by naming this new organization the Admirals Club.

More than 40 years later Crandall's people were looking for ways to reawaken such brand loyalty. "Do we even know who our frequent customers are?" they asked. The answer was not really. Before the great travel agent onslaught of the 1970s, back when business-people (and their secretaries) made most of the airline reservations, Sabre was programmed to search for multiple appearances of the same telephone number and periodically compile a list of the names associated with those numbers. (Surnames were too common and misspelled too frequently to be of much value in searching electronically.) The telephone area code located the individual in a particular state; American then searched driver's license records for addresses. Through this laborious and expensive process American was able to maintain a mailing list of repeat customers totaling about 150,000.

But in the early 1980s the same phone numbers were showing up over and over, by the hundreds and thousands—the phone numbers of travel agencies making reservations on behalf of their clients. American no longer had a reliable way of identifying repeat passengers. Travel agents were standing in the way of American's contact with its customers. The wizards of Sabre were ordered to find a way of assigning a number to every frequent passenger, whether the reservation came through a travel agent or not.

Tom Plaskett had been supervising the brand loyalty project that Crandall had started but failed to complete as head of marketing. Plaskett at one point was reminded of the original brand loyalty scheme in the retailing trade—S & H Green Stamps. Plaskett recalled his boyhood experience of licking the stamps that had accumulated in a kitchen drawer and fastening them in redemption books when the family needed a new toaster or some such, a ritual repeated in millions of postwar households across the country.

Plaskett's Green Stamps reverie triggered a more recent memory. In a round of sales calls on major travel agencies and corporate accounts, Plaskett had been surprised to observe an old Admirals Club plaque hanging on a customer's wall.

"What is that?" Plaskett asked.

The Admirals Club had long ago been discontinued in a cost-cutting move. The CAB also helped to push it out of existence by forcing airlines to open their airport lounges to anyone willing to pay an annual fee, eliminating the invitation-only exclusivity that gave the clubs cachet. Yet years later, Plaskett noted, here was this man still proudly displaying his Admirals Club membership. And on that plaque were affixed little gold stars that had been provided by American Airlines, one for every 100,000 miles the man had flown.

That was it. American could have its customers accumulate mileage instead of Green Stamps, earning free travel instead of household appliances.

The concept was not unheard-of among the airlines. Southwest Airlines already had a program in which secretaries got free travel after booking so many trips for their bosses. Lorenzo had been passing out scrip in $10 denominations to passengers at DFW—coupons good for future travel on Texas International. On the hotly competitive Los Angeles–to–San Francisco run, Western Airlines distributed punch cards to passengers good for a $50 discount after five validations, following a promotion long in use by West Coast car washes.

Still, the notion was controversial when broached inside American. This would be a frequent-flier program on a scale unseen in the airline industry. Some of the American people warned that it might be seen as a breach of a long-standing taboo against corporate discounting. Because frequent fliers tended to be business travelers on expense accounts, corporations could legitimately claim the free travel awards as their property. In that case American would be seen as rebating to major corporations, which could touch off a scramble by other airlines to begin cutting prices outright for their major corporate customers. The idea filled some of Crandall's people with dread.

Plaskett and his supporters countered that individual customers would never allow their employers to take away their free travel awards. Although conducted in the open, this program in every respect would be nothing more than a kickback—the payment of something valuable to an individual in order to influence his decision in spending somebody else's money. "It's based on individual greed," Plaskett would later comment.

While also gearing up for the big expansion at DFW, Crandall, Plaskett, and their underlings began putting the frequent-flier program in place. The element of surprise was critical. Other major airlines would have no choice but to match the program, but it would take them months to catch up, months in which American would have the entire field to itself. By having all the necessary Sabre programming written and debugged in advance, American would allow passengers to start accumulating mileage on the very day that it announced the program.

Everyone assigned to the project signed an oath of secrecy. One of Crandall's top salespeople, Michael W. Gunn, was reminded of growing up near the Rose Bowl in Pasadena. Whenever Michigan came to play, giant screens went up around the sidelines to keep stadium visitors from watching the team practice that year's Secret Play. This frequent-flier thing—it was just like the Secret Play, Gunn thought.

. . .

On June 11, 1981, at DFW, American Airlines conducted the biggest
overnight expansion in airline history. The evening sky hanging over
Dallas and Fort Worth suddenly resembled a suburban backyard
teeming with fireflies. There were airplanes everywhere.

The noise, however, was less benign. DFW had been built with
two parallel landing strips running north and south. Jets landed and
took off over the pastures, lakes, and ghettos of light industry lying
between Dallas and Fort Worth. But American's mammoth expansion required the airport to make use of a third runway—an alternate, diagonal ribbon of concrete known as Runway 13L, intended
mainly for use during heavy crosswinds. At the end of the diagonal
runway lay the drywall subdivisions of Irving, population 105,000.

The roar of an old 727 accelerating on takeoff could crack the sky
and split the ears, often approaching the threshold of pain at up-
wards of a mile away. Beyond Runway 13L, in the middle of an area
that local boosters called the Metroplex, the jet din was radiating repeatedly, on a schedule like Chinese water torture for the eardrums.
Tom Plaskett, who had been intimately involved in planning the
flight expansion, happened to live 2.3 miles from the end of the runway. "My God," he said, "what have I done?"

The ensuing community uproar was almost as loud. Overnight,
pressure mounted on the FAA, the airport authority, and American itself to cut way back. Crandall thrust himself into battle mode. The
whole Dallas expansion was suddenly in jeopardy. Crandall bought
local TV time and recruited employees as lobbyists, telling them their
jobs were in jeopardy. American wasn't to blame for the noise problem
at DFW, Crandall said. The culprit, he said, was Southwest Airlines.

Crandall's allegation involved at least a small leap of logic. It had
been 10 years virtually to the day that Southwest had been in business, during which time Southwest had never once landed a flight at
DFW. Southwest still made its home at the old Love Field, a few
minutes from downtown Dallas. Moreover, even after a decade in
business, Southwest counted barely 30 small airplanes to its name. It
was less than one tenth the size of American. Crandall argued that
the noise could be abated by letting American's planes make a hard
left turn after leaving Runway 13L, but they could not do so, he said,
without intruding upon the airspace around Love Field, where
Southwest operated all by itself.

Crandall was outraged that Southwest was permitted to keep the close-in Love Field open at all. "DFW, not Love Field, is the region's gateway," Crandall said. "It is DFW that gives residents of the Metroplex access to the nation and the world, and it is DFW which has provided the economic impetus for the development of the Metroplex, including Irving." The solution to the noise problem was not to curb American's expansion, he said, but to cut back on Southwest's "unbridled growth."

To Herb Kelleher, Crandall's rantings were just one more attack from another self-interested competitor who wanted to put his little company out of business.

In the decade since Southwest had gotten its financial footing, the company had never stopped making money. Southwest didn't have a hub and didn't want one. It didn't want to add new cities except slowly and deliberately. It mainly wanted to fly full airplanes from point A to point B at a low cost with as many flights as possible per day—preferably by the hour. Its success was evident in its growing number of imitators, principally People Express, New York Air, and a company called Air Florida, which had recently burst on the scene.

Deregulation, it appeared, had finally opened the boundaries confining Southwest to the four corners of Texas. Kelleher—the spiritual leader of the company, though still not a company manager—hosted a meeting to urge the company's managers to prepare to break out of the state. Southwest, he said, had run its course in Texas. On top of the original three cities of the Texas triangle it had added Harlingen, Corpus Christi, Lubbock, Midland, Amarillo, El Paso, and Austin, lacing the Lone Star State with dozens of flights a day—each one bringing new, first-time fliers into the market as well as stealing business from the sputtering Braniff and in some cases from American. Southwest's frequent, low-fare service had altered the character of Texas itself; among the 10 largest cities in the state, no two were more than 55 minutes and about $25 apart on Southwest. El Paso, for one, separated from the rest of Texas by hundreds of miles of tumbleweed and sand, became more fully absorbed in the state's affairs. Children torn between parents in the prosperous divorce capitals of Dallas and Houston became regular commuters aboard Southwest flights. Long-distance romances and marriages survived thanks to

Southwest, including Kelleher's own; his family home and his law practice remained in San Antonio while his business affairs were increasingly conducted in Dallas. When deregulation hit, Southwest was at last approaching membership on the airline industry's Top 20 list. It was time, Kelleher told the company's executives, to reach outside Texas as well.

Some of Southwest's leaders, panicked with aviation agoraphobia, resisted Kelleher's urgings, but he soon prevailed. Southwest announced that it would offer service out of Texas, beginning with New Orleans.

Between Houston and New Orleans lay the principal oil route of the era, as the federal waters off the Texas and Louisiana coasts were opening to a new wave of offshore drilling for natural gas. New Orleans was also an exceedingly popular tourist destination among Texans, just within a day's drive from Houston; with Southwest's fares there would no longer be any reason to drive. For Southwest the new route would be a gusher.

Southwest's enemies quickly went on the counterattack, led by House Majority Leader Jim Wright of Fort Worth (later Speaker of the House). Wright had been among the greatest champions of DFW and had therefore opposed allowing Southwest to drain off passengers to Love Field. Now, in addition to defending Braniff's operations at DFW, Jim Wright had the interests of a new corporate constituent, American Airlines, to protect as well. Wright demanded hearings on whether "automatic entry," as used in the Deregulation Act, was meant literally. Did Southwest automatically have the right to begin service to a new city, or did the government have the standing to make it defend its wish to do so, to hamstring it with more hearings and pleadings? Kelleher, still handling the legal chores for Southwest, organized a massive signature drive and hired Mayflower movers to deliver scores of petition-laden boxes to Washington. Southwest won; regulators determined that "automatic" indeed meant automatic. Southwest had the right to fly to New Orleans.

Jim Wright in 1979 finally resolved to remedy the failings of the regulatory system with the fiat of legislation. Wright pushed a new law that would simply ban any airline operating from Love Field from ever flying outside Texas. There would be no deregulation for Southwest Airlines.

Kelleher headed for Washington with his legal assistant and ever-present advisor, Colleen Barrett. He called on his old pal from New York University Law School, Bob Packwood, now a senator from Oregon and soon to be the chairman of the all-powerful Senate Finance Committee. No one could understand why the senator from Oregon was suddenly attending drafting sessions on obscure legislation involving an airline that nobody outside Texas ever heard of. But Packwood saved the day. Although not entirely defeated, Jim Wright was forced into a compromise. Southwest, the parties agreed, would be permitted to fly from Love Field only to any of the contiguous states—Louisiana, Arkansas, Oklahoma, and New Mexico. American and Braniff signed off on the compromise, codified as the Wright Amendment.

It was the best Kelleher could get. He had exhausted his remedies, had wrung out every redress that the legal and political systems afforded. "The Wright Amendment is a pain in the ass," he would explain, "but not every pain in the ass is a constitutional infringement."

It did not remotely bother Kelleher that as Southwest slowly expanded, the airline unions had sprung up almost everywhere on company property. Neither did Kelleher have any problem paying market-rate wages to pilots, flight attendants, and other workers. As one of its biggest shareholders, he simply wanted the company to deploy its workforce in the most efficient manner possible.

To help accomplish this Kelleher, wearing his lawyer's hat, insisted that department heads participate in the contract negotiations involving the employees in their jurisdiction, a practice far from routine in labor relations. More commonly the entire affair of collective bargaining was turned over to lawyers and negotiating specialists. But professional negotiators were principally interested in controlling wages, and wages, so far as Southwest was concerned, were not the main issue. Only the middle managers understood the fine points of a 10-minute airplane turnaround, which was why Kelleher insisted on their presence at the bargaining table.

This was labor strife at Southwest Airlines: Kelleher was out for dinner and drinks with a group of pilots. The drinks had been numerous enough to dull Kelleher's wits, so when the pilots offered to fetch his brand-new car from the hotel parking lot and meet him at the front door, he saw no reason to decline their kindness. As he emerged from the hotel, there were four pilots standing at the corners of his 12-cylinder S-class Jaguar, each one relieving himself on a wire wheel.

There had, however, been a few genuine traumas within the ranks of senior management. Lamar Muse, the white-haired and mustachioed airline veteran so gifted at making the planes run on time, had grown a little too uppity for some of Southwest's directors. For one thing Muse had appointed his young son as a senior vice president.

In addition Muse pushed a scheme to bring in a bunch of new airplanes and start an altogether new operation based outside Texas, much as Frank Lorenzo had accomplished with New York Air. Muse proposed to establish this second operating base in Chicago, at the dilapidated old Midway Airport. Muse's plan would roughly double the size of the company overnight. Muse wanted what most airline chieftains wanted—more. But overnight expansion was not part of the Southwest formula. Adding too many employees too quickly would dilute the underdog spirit by which Southwest was still flourishing. It would mean taking on unaccustomed debt. As the feuding worsened, Muse finally slapped his keys on a desk and left Southwest Airlines, never to return.

Kelleher was concluding some legal business in Houston when he was notified that the board of Southwest Airlines now wished to make him its chairman. Boarding a flight for Dallas with Colleen Barrett, he had only one suit in his garment bag and knew it would be several days before he could get home to San Antonio. To spare the suit a wrinkling in the overhead bin, Kelleher discreetly went to the back of the plane and hung the garment bag in the crew closet.

A flight attendant politely told him that the closet was not for passengers. "That's okay," he whispered. "I'm the president of Southwest."

"Yeah," she answered, "and I'm the king of Siam."

Kelleher did not, however, consider himself competent to run the day-to-day affairs of an airline. He needed an experienced executive to fill the void left by Lamar Muse. With Southwest spreading its wings, with Braniff flying willy-nilly, and with American building a powerful machine, someone new was headed to Dallas.

· · ·

Growing up in Iowa, Howard Putnam learned to fly when he was nine; his father strapped blocks of wood to the foot pedals of the family's little Piper Cub. Putnam went on to aeronautical school and put in time as a baggage handler, but he was a sharp kid with a stout personality. Putnam wound up on the fast track at United Airlines, where he became one of the top marketing executives under Eddie Carlson and later under Dick Ferris.

That was the problem—Dick Ferris. He and Putnam were about the same age, but Ferris was one long step ahead of Putnam on the organization chart. Putnam wanted to run something, but he would never have the chance at United so long as Ferris remained. His big chance came with the recruiting call from Herb Kelleher.

Hired as the president of Southwest, Putnam saw it as his mission to guide the company from a quaint and quirky organization into the billion-dollar airline it seemed destined under deregulation to become. Putnam installed new financial controls, personnel policies, and planning procedures. But he also recognized that the company's culture accounted for much of its commercial success. To avoid smothering the family feeling, Putnam engaged an industrial psychologist to help keep check on the reforms.

Awash in profits, Southwest eventually began to plan a huge order of airplanes, something like $1 billion worth. Other airlines, ordering whatever happened to be the new or sexy or cool plane of the moment, invariably wound up with many species of aircraft in their fleets. Southwest, by contrast, flew only 737s, requiring it to stockpile parts and train pilots and mechanics for only one kind of plane. The efficiencies were huge. Now, instead of rushing out to buy something altogether new, Southwest persuaded Boeing simply to update the old reliable 737.

The Southwest board, unaccustomed to dealing in the 10-figure range, asked Putnam to engage an independent expert to evaluate the order. Putnam called a retired maintenance executive he had known at United, where hundreds of people might work for months evaluating a new aircraft design. For a $600 fee and a few free flying passes, the consultant spent two weeks studying the matter, then filed a handwritten three-page report. The plane was just fine, he had concluded; Southwest's order was economically sound. Before long, on the basis of this analysis, Southwest had a new generation of 737s on the way, with many more to follow.

On another front, Southwest's female-only flight attendant policy was getting the company into trouble. When the issue came before the courts, one judge acknowledged that Southwest had a "unique, feminized image" that "continues to play an important role" in the airline's success. But he struck down the ban on male flight attendants by noting that "Southwest is not in a business where vicarious sex entertainment is the primary service provided." Uniforms also became an issue. It was 1981, for Pete's sake, and flight attendants were still required to wear hot pants, which had become not only demeaning but appallingly out of fashion. Nevertheless Howard Putnam held firm in contract talks, arguing that hot pants were a trademark of sorts. (A Southwest TV ad showed rows of passengers flashing Olympic scorecards as a scantily clad flight attendant passed through the aisle.) Putnam also looked at Southwest's dress code as a kind of employment screening device, which assured that women who "felt good" about themselves in revealing costumes, such as cheerleaders and baton twirlers, would number among those seeking to become flight attendants on Southwest. Putnam came dangerously close to provoking war with the flight attendants.

Kelleher, the corporate chairman, intervened. Hot pants became optional.

Putnam's tenure at Southwest was to be brief. Another Dallas airline soon found itself in need of a new chief executive. With losses swelling, with creditors panicking, and with the American juggernaut advancing, Braniff had fired Harding Lawrence. In the final showdown between Braniff and American, it would be Howard Putnam facing Bob Crandall.

As for Southwest, the board of directors decided enough was enough. It was time for Herb Kelleher, still the titular head of the company, to quit his law practice, move into the corporate headquarters full-time, and assume complete control of Southwest Airlines.

"No one expects Braniff to go broke," *The Wall Street Journal* remarked. "No major U.S. carrier ever has."

Howard Putnam, then 44, certainly had no reason to think otherwise when he left Southwest and walked through the doors at Braniff in September 1981. He personally moved his belongings in a pickup truck in order to dramatize the need to control costs. He walked into the Braniff headquarters and saw works by Calder from one wall to the next. He ceremoniously removed one such painting from his own office and replaced it with something to inspire him in his new job: a photograph of a Southwest 737 christened *The Herbert D. Kelleher.*

What Putnam did not realize, until he took his first close look at the company's books, was that Braniff had precisely 10 days' worth of cash remaining. Harsh measures alone were insufficient: Braniff required desperate measures. Putnam fell back on the success formula with which he was most familiar. He went before the board and declared that although Braniff was four times larger, he would in short order transform the company into the transcontinental equivalent of Southwest Airlines.

Putnam immediately ripped out the first-class section from every airplane in Braniff's domestic fleet and made the entire cabin coach class, just like Southwest. Appealing to Braniff's hometown popularity, he called it "Texas class." As Don Burr was doing at People Express, Putnam installed extra-large overhead racks so people were less inclined to check luggage. He began eliminating jobs and bureaucracy and simplifying work rules, and even the hard-nosed unions, taken in by his enthusiasm, went along.

Most significantly, Putnam decided that Braniff would allow no more passengers to switch to American's newly swollen service from DFW. He was drawing the line. Almost immediately after becoming chairman, Putnam stood up at a press conference and announced that on every competing flight, Braniff would undercut American by 50 percent. Instead of bleeding red, white, and blue, as Crandall demanded of his employees, American would simply bleed red.

Bob Crandall flew into a rage over Putnam's fare slashing. So carefully, so gingerly had Crandall been nurturing American back to health that in barely a year of Crandall's presidency the airline had finally amounted to something. Now Braniff was ruining everything. American, of course, would match those fares even though doing so would wipe $7 million from its bottom line every month, just like that.

Yes, American would match Braniff dollar for dollar and passenger by passenger, and it would do much more than that. It would swamp Braniff's routes with still more new flights, to the extent it had the planes to serve them. The bias built into the Sabre system, already such a powerful marketing tool, would be supplemented with instructions prompting American reservationists to steer people away from Braniff.

The mission was clear. Years later Tom Plaskett, Crandall's highest-ranking associate, would remember the kind of admonition that went around the executive offices. "We've got to maximize the economic pressure," the executives said to each other. "We've got to make them go away." As Plaskett would recall, "It was not good-spirited competition."

There were strange things happening at Braniff. Flights to Dallas would be booked full right to the last minute, then dozens of passengers would no-show; Braniff was turning away reservations, only to find its planes unexpectedly flying half-empty. Top officials at American swore that these tales were exaggerated and that if anyone at American ever used any such dirty tricks against Braniff, they were lower-level employees acting out of overzealousness. If so, perhaps they were employees who had been told, from the lips of Crandall himself, that American had to "steal" passengers from Braniff, that nothing must stand in the way of "the victory that we simply must have." American's scheduling department was also doing its part, adding service to still more of Braniff's destinations. It was as if American were overlaying a whole new route system on top of Braniff's, Putnam thought.

Putnam tried a new tack. Radio spots were prepared to convince passengers that any virtue in flying American existed only because of Braniff. "Normally American only gives you low, unrestricted fares when they face low-fare competition," one of the ads declared, "and it's usually competition from Braniff."

The anti-American campaign spread to print advertising with an ad claiming that Braniff had a better on-time record than American. Crandall, just returned from his early morning run, saw the ad during breakfast and blew his stack. He raced to American headquarters, stormed into Plaskett's office, and reached for the phone. It was time to give Howard Putnam a piece of his mind.

• • •

About five years earlier, when he was still the marketing chief at United, Putnam had received a telephone call from Bob Crandall, then in the marketing job at American. The conversation was never made public.

"Howard," Crandall told him, "if you raise your drink prices, we'll raise ours tomorrow."

Putnam couldn't believe his ears. Crandall went on, "If you raise your movie price, I'll raise ours."

"Bob!" Putnam said. "We can't talk about that!"

Putnam went to inform United chief Dick Ferris. Ferris too was dismayed at Crandall's suggestion.

Putnam flashed back to that conversation on the February morning in 1982 when he stared at a telephone message from Bob Crandall. Putnam checked with Braniff's in-house counsel. The fight with American had grown very ugly. For Braniff's protection Putnam, the lawyer thought, might be wise to return the call with a tape recorder running. Putnam did.

"I think it's dumb as hell, for Christ's sake all right, to sit here and pound the shit out of each other and neither one of us making a fucking dime," Crandall said.

"Well—"

"I mean, goddamn! What the fuck is the point of it?"

"Nobody asked American to serve Harlingen," Putnam shot back. "Nobody asked American to serve Kansas City. . . . If you're going to overlay every route of American's on top of every route that Braniff has, I can't just sit here and allow you to bury us without giving you our best effort."

"Oh, sure, but Eastern and Delta do the same thing in Atlanta and have for years."

Putnam could sense what was coming. "Do you have a suggestion for me?" he asked.

"Yes, I have a suggestion for you," Crandall answered. "Raise your goddamn fares twenty percent. I'll raise mine the next morning. You'll make more money and I will too."

"Robert, we can't talk about pricing."

"Oh, bullshit, Howard. We can talk about any goddamn thing we want to talk about."

The conversation ended. Putnam's lawyer popped the tape from the recorder and filed it away.

Putnam tried other desperation moves. A two-for-one sale. The Great Escape sale. Anything to get a few more people into Braniff's Easter-colored airplanes. But each promotion was less successful than the last.

And then, just as Braniff appeared to be breathing its last, all of Dallas, it seemed, rallied to resuscitate it. Putnam, weary, haggard, yet perpetually smiling for the television cameras, was becoming a local celebrity, a role he played to the hilt. He began appearing in powerful television spots, displaying a firm and earnest manner. "Texas, we need your support," he pleaded. "Fly Braniff now!" Tom Landry, the beloved coach of the Cowboys, filmed another television spot. "Fly Braniff," Landry begged. "The Cowboys do!" And suddenly the M.B.A.s and computer programmers and sales executives who had transferred from New York with American a few years earlier were the outsiders, the upstarts. They were Yankees—carpetbaggers. Presenting their employee IDs to write checks, some were sneered at by salesclerks. Bob Crandall's children were harassed at school. A local media war intensified newspaper and broadcast coverage of the fight, with the coverage heavily tilted, as it invariably is in such cases, toward the underdog. American's shareholders were exposed to the spectacle of television cameras chasing executives around a ballroom at the annual meeting.

Crandall himself was responsible for drawing the worst PR. He casually remarked within earshot of the press that he would be perfectly happy to see Braniff "go out of business." That way, he explained, American would be up against "healthier airlines" less inclined to slash fares out of "desperation." The Dallas business establishment was appalled.

Later a Braniff official said publicly that he thought American was using Sabre to cancel Braniff reservations outright—something that almost certainly never happened. But truth didn't matter anymore. People in Dallas now believed American to be capable of any ruthlessness. The power of Sabre had taken on mythically monstrous proportions. As a consequence of Braniff's exaggerated allegations, the U.S. Justice Department commenced its first look at the potentially disruptive powers of computer reservation systems.

The local outpouring in Braniff's behalf was touchingly evident on a Sunday night at Billy Bob's, a barnlike country dancing place that hosted a free party to buck up the morale of the Braniff workforce. The band members sank to their knees and bowed as Putnam came up on the stage and took the microphone, and heartfelt applause went up from the Braniff employees who filled the dance floor. But Putnam was muted and the crowd sullen too. People knew. Travel agents were now treating Braniff like the plague. A rumor swept the dance floor that a Braniff flight from Miami had just landed at DFW with only six passengers aboard.

"We're gonna do it," Putnam told the crowd with strained enthusiasm and a limp wave of his fist, and no one, including him, believed it.

The dust-up at DFW caused the Justice Department to empanel a grand jury. Crandall was uncomfortable with the whole situation. "I get nervous when I get a parking ticket," he was quoted as saying in *Business Week.* "I don't like the notion that some 'authority' is interested in anything I did."

In no mood to take chances, Crandall and one of his lawyers climbed aboard an American flight for Los Angeles for consultations at the law firm representing American in the federal investigation. But the flight was stuck on the tarmac. A torrential spring thunderstorm had moved into the area and remained squarely over DFW. Lightning filled the sky. Tornadoes were sighted. Crandall and the lawyer sat in their seats and waited.

Then a pilot emerged from the cockpit and approached Crandall. He bent over, whispered something in the president's ear, and departed.

"We're getting off," Crandall told his companion, rising from his seat. "Braniff has just shut down."

Crandall led the lawyer to the rear stairs, which were lowered to allow the two men to deplane. In the great expanse of concrete, ankle-deep in water, the rain pounding and the wind swirling, Bob Crandall and his lawyer, soaked to the bone, stood with their briefcases, waiting for an American Airlines vehicle to pick them up.

Putnam had ordered a Chapter 11 bankruptcy filing, a move that in his judgment demanded the strictest secrecy in advance. Braniff's assets, principally its airplanes, were scattered all over the world. Anyone owed money by Braniff, including foreign governments or lending institutions, might well seize any Braniff airplanes within their jurisdiction if they knew a bankruptcy filing was imminent. Putnam wanted every last plane back in Dallas before the papers were filed.

Preserving the element of surprise before the shutdown meant that thousands were severely inconvenienced. At DFW people stared at the TV monitors. "Newark: canceled . . . Lubbock: canceled . . . Houston . . . San Antonio . . . San Francisco . . . Orlando . . . Los Angeles . . . Toronto . . ." all canceled. Initially passengers assumed the violent weather was to blame, but later they began to notice that the doors to Braniff's premises in the airport were strapped and bolted shut. The Braniff planes began parking, forming long conga lines in lime, cranberry, and other festive colors.

Howard Putnam, dabbing his eyes, his voice cracking, finally went public before a forest of microphones with the announcement that Braniff would fly no more. "The checks that are out there now will not go through," he said. "There's no cash to support them."

Deregulation had claimed its first victim.

The stock prices of other airlines went through the roof, none more so than American. People were suddenly thronging American's ticket counters. All those new routes laid over Braniff's system were in place to pick up the slack. American was soon carrying 64.7 percent of the passengers at DFW, up from 45.7 percent before Braniff failed. Some 96 percent of all the connecting passengers who arrived at DFW on American flights were soon also leaving on American flights, up from 65 percent two years before.

But in the hours following Braniff's failure there was a small technical problem for American to contend with. At Sabre headquarters officials realized that thousands of Braniff flights were still listed as available for sale in travel agents' computers across the country. Braniff's schedule had to be removed immediately, but such a major revision required something on the order of a system restart, a kind of rebooting operation. A major airline had never failed. There was evidently no easy way to eradicate its flights from the computers.

Actually, it turned out, there was. Somebody remembered the incident a few years earlier at American's old headquarters in New York, when Bob Crandall had pulled the venetian blinds down on his head while staring angrily at TWA headquarters across the street. Crandall had ordered his aides to design a series of instructions that would enable American to blow every TWA flight out of Sabre instantly. Although the instructions were never used, they remained on the shelf.

With the clouds billowing and the lightning still striking, the program was quickly modified; TWA's designator codes were replaced with Braniff's. And with a few keystrokes every trace of Braniff Airways evaporated from the computer reservation mainframes of American Airlines.

CHAPTER 7

WORKINGMAN'S BLUES

It is the curse of the airline chieftains: though fleets and schedules respond readily to the manipulations of management, airline finances do not.

To a degree unusual in business, the costs of running an airline are outside management's control. Fuel, for instance, accounts for roughly 20 percent of the cost of doing business—sometimes much more, depending upon the machinations occurring in the Middle East and the state of balance in the delicate global petroleum markets. Landing fees and airport rentals are another huge and mostly nonnegotiable expense. The cost of borrowing money, set principally by the Federal Reserve Board, is still another significant item, controllable only to the degree that management resists buying the newest and hottest airplanes. In the history of commercial aviation, only Southwest Airlines and one or two others have ever displayed such self-control.

Travel agency commissions became another huge item of expense. For years they had been fixed at 5 percent of the ticket price, but in the deregulation era, with the airlines courting the affections of travel agents both to steal and to protect market share, commissions were spiraling higher, eventually to reach 10 percent, with agents writing an ever larger proportion of the airlines' tickets.

That left only one big-ticket item under management's control, and at most airlines it was the biggest of all: labor represented as much as 40 percent of the expense in running an airline.

Airline employees had been in fat city for years. Although a few airlines took brave stands against big wage increases, most agreed to pay their union workers whatever it took to preserve peace on the flight line. The airline bosses were pushovers because they knew that the contracts each of them signed were always quickly matched by every other airline, fixing costs on an equal footing. It was no concern to the airlines that these costs marched higher and higher, as long as the regulators in Washington simply waved through the fare increases necessary to cover them.

When the starting gun of deregulation launched the race to cut costs, the fun was over. A few airlines, such as Delta, held out against the pressure, reasoning that a motivated and experienced workforce was more important to the marketing mix than a reduction in costs. American, and eventually some imitators, tried to lower costs by flooding the flight lines with newly hired b-scale employees, protecting tenured employees from the trauma of a wage cut. But every airline came to feel the same pressure: cut costs in order to cut fares or say good-bye to a franchise that had taken decades to build.

Nowhere was this change more painful than at Eastern Air Lines. Eastern's labor costs to begin with were slightly higher than average, owing in part to the company's high proportion of takeoffs and landings to miles flown. Another source of trouble was the fact that Eastern's bundle of north-south routes made it a vacation airline, with price-sensitive markets that low-cost upstarts were bound to attack. Eastern could defend its market share only by reducing the living standards of its workforce.

But ultimately the labor upheavals at Eastern became violent because this struggle became a contest between two men, each of whom, alas for Eastern, was singularly unsuited to accommodating the other.

One was Col. Frank Borman, who as a former fighter pilot and astronaut knew better than anyone the sensitivity of an aircraft to one's hands. As a corporate leader also, Borman needed to feel the instant response of the people under his control. The "command approach to management" was how one of his most loyal aides would describe his style. Borman—the Colonel, to his subordinates—referred to Eastern's operations center as "mission control." His column in the employee newsletter was titled "View from the Top." He used a rubber stamp to brand documents with instructions to RUSH.

His adversary, Charles E. Bryan of the International Association of Machinists and Aerospace Workers, would not be rushed. Bryan delighted in resisting authority. A short, square-shouldered man with a pug face not unlike Edward G. Robinson's, Bryan in a way suffered from Frank Borman's disease: he too had a need to be in charge. Bryan drew his power from a local union organization 13,000 strong, representing nearly everyone who touched an Eastern airplane without flying in it, from the lowliest cabin cleaners to the most skilled engine mechanics.

At issue between the men was the control of the company that carried more passengers than any other airline in America.

Like United, which began life as an affiliate of Boeing, Eastern came into the world as the progeny of an aircraft manufacturer. With eight open-cockpit biplanes called Mailwings, the company won one of the earliest postal contracts, in 1928. By the early 1930s it was conducting the first passenger service between New York and Washington, as well as a vacation flight to Florida. ("From frost to flowers in 14 hours!" Eastern promised.) Flying to Florida via Atlanta broadened Eastern's reach into the interior of the Southeast.

Eastern before long came under the control of General Motors Corporation, which installed a new take-charge potentate. He was Capt. Eddie Rickenbacker, a race car driver who had once owned the Indianapolis Speedway but who was best known as the greatest of America's flying aces in the dogfights of World War I. When General Motors put Eastern on the block a few years later, in 1938, Rickenbacker stopped at nothing to get control, once even getting GM chairman Alfred P. Sloan, Jr., out of bed for a late-night bargaining session.

Rickenbacker won and handily raised the $3.5 million in necessary capital. Rickenbacker was held in awe by the generation of boys who had grown up in the years following World War I to become stockbrokers and investment bankers. One of Rickenbacker's idolaters was the young Laurance Rockefeller, grandson of the Standard

Oil magnate. Laurance became Rickenbacker's principal financial backer, playing a vital though largely unseen role in Eastern's affairs for more than 50 years, practically to the bitter end.

In keeping the company of Wall Street's leading financiers, Rickenbacker became determined to extract the maximum amount of revenue possible from every airplane in Eastern's fleet. The airline business was a matter of "putting bums on seats," as Rickenbacker described it, and he saw it as his mission to keep as many of those backsides in the air for the greatest number of hours feasible per day. Restricted by the CAB largely (though not entirely) to the East Coast, Eastern connected the nation's densest population areas with short-haul flights, principally to Boston, New York, and Washington, along with the Atlanta and Florida routes. It was these populous markets, combined with Rickenbacker's commitment to his bum count, that distinguished Eastern for much of its history not as the airline that flew the most miles or made the most money, but as the one that carried the greatest number of people.

Keeping planes in the air demanded quick turnarounds and many flights per day. In the late 1930s these principles moved Rickenbacker to establish a service called the Merry-Go-Round, with 20 round trips a day between New York and Washington. (It was aboard the Merry-Go-Round that regular passengers qualified for the Eighty Minute Man Club, a precursor of the frequent-flier programs of the 1980s.) The Merry-Go-Round operated successfully for years, but by the early 1960s Eastern needed something extra, a new gimmick. There was a recession on, and while benefiting from the constant use of its planes, Eastern also paid dearly in fuel, airport fees, and maintenance for its high proportion of takeoffs and landings. Eastern needed a higher load factor—a higher ratio of backsides to seats— to remain viable.

An Eastern executive named Frank Sharpe, newly hired from American, proposed a *no-reservation* Merry-Go-Round service with a guaranteed seat for anyone who showed up. Any passenger could race to LaGuardia and step on a plane bound for Boston or Washington, any hour on the hour. The trick was that Eastern would have to keep planes standing by at all times to make certain that everyone showing up for a flight got a seat. In exchange for the freedom to fly so spontaneously, the customer, it was reckoned, would gladly save

Eastern money by sacrificing his cocktails, his chicken divan, and his "social calls by the stewardess," as noted in one account.

The idea was a winner, and on April 30, 1961, the Eastern Air-Shuttle was born. *The New York Times,* rarely so prone to overstatement, hailed the shuttle's birth as "the greatest advance in aviation since the Wright brothers." On the few occasions that Eastern actually had to put a backup plane into service, such as when the entire Boston Symphony showed up for a shuttle flight one evening after a performance in New York, the resulting goodwill and publicity more than compensated for the cost. As the fastest link between the nation's political and financial capitals, the shuttle became the highway of the highbrow, a fabled celebrity-spotting venue: Henry Kissinger! Felix Rohatyn! It became a storied enabler of intercity romance; Carl Bernstein of *Washington Post* Watergate fame and his wife, writer Nora Ephron, developed a script concept called *Eastern Shuttle.*

Notwithstanding the shuttle's instant success, Rickenbacker in his time was no genius of passenger marketing, as became painfully obvious during the transition to jets. Mistrustful of jets and resentful of their tremendous expense, Rickenbacker was hopelessly late in ordering them. His procrastination enabled the up-and-coming Delta Air Lines, which competed in much of Eastern's territory around Atlanta, to seize the moment. Delta ordered some of the same jets of which Rickenbacker had declined to take delivery, making inroads that Eastern would never reclaim. Rickenbacker also dismissed Jetways as frills. Worse still, he was notoriously cheap with the spare parts inventory, which meant that Eastern experienced an exceptional number of mechanical delays. Service aboard the East Coast shuttle, never luxurious, became downright obnoxious. A club called W.H.E.A.L.—We Hate Eastern Air Lines—began to flourish, a kind of frequent-flier support group that thousands of Eastern customers actually took the trouble to join. Eastern's motto, "The Great Silver Fleet," was twisted by many into "The Great Stingy Fleet."

The forced retirement of the 73-year-old Rickenbacker from active management in 1963 was no panacea, however. Like the hapless George Spater, who followed C. R. Smith into the chairman's suite at American, the second generation of management at Eastern fell short, in no small measure because the first generation of management couldn't resist meddling. Rickenbacker's immediate successor, a former air force undersecretary named Malcolm MacIntyre, was driven to drowning himself in martinis at lunch by the indomitable Rickenbacker, who remained a company director and who mercilessly second-guessed all of MacIntyre's moves. MacIntyre finally departed, and Rickenbacker, nipping quite a bit himself in his later years, was at long last pushed out of the boardroom altogether. He died a few years later at age 82.

In came another new chief executive, Floyd Hall, a man whose look and style embodied the era of the Organization Man. He had been a pilot over at TWA—a captain, ultimately—who had earned an M.B.A. in his free time. An intensely intellectual man with a dashing thin mustache, he arrived at Eastern at the apogee of the postwar obsession with industrialism, committed as no airline chief executive before him to the principles of what was then called "scientific management."

Hall crowded Eastern's offices at Rockefeller Center with a small army of whiz kid executives. Within a few years Eastern's executive ranks swelled to include 43 officers at the vice presidential level alone. Nervously watching passenger defections to Delta, Hall with abandon ordered the jets that Rickenbacker had eschewed. He devoted himself to repairing Eastern's soiled image with passengers, ordering Rosenthal china and Reed & Barton silverware to coax business travelers back into first class and paying a big licensing fee to become the official airline of a new family vacation destination, called Walt Disney World, that was under construction in Orlando in the late 1960s.

Hall's actions pulled Eastern from the edge, but his management practices began to cause more problems than they solved. Eastern's legion of vice presidents began fighting among themselves, and its marketing began to assume the pretensions of its management style when, with the race to the moon in full swing, Hall added a stripe to the color scheme of Eastern's aircraft in a hue he called "ionosphere blue." Eastern adopted "The Wings of Man" as its new motto. It was only natural that Hall would try to extend the outer space theme by hiring the best-known orbital adventurer of the day.

Within a few weeks of Eastern's first flight and within a few months of Lindbergh's Atlantic crossing, Frank Frederick Borman II was born in Gary, Indiana, on March 14, 1928. Lindbergh's triumph defined Borman's childhood. As a five-year-old he traveled with his family to Dayton, the home of the Wright brothers, where he got a ride with a barnstormer, an experience he was thrilled to recall for the rest of his life. He read and reread *The Red Eagle,* a children's novel about airplanes. He developed a passion for building model airplanes from balsa, silk span, and dope on a card table unfolded in the living room. The happiest moments of his life, he would recall 50 years later, involved working with his hands—not just building models but hunting in the deserts around Tucson, where his family had moved to help him escape his boyhood allergies. As a youth there Borman financed his ammunition purchases by catching Gila monsters, which he sold for experimental use to the University of Arizona. His mother was once told by a teacher that Frank, a lonely boy, had trouble getting along with classmates because he was so bossy.

He began flying at age 15, financing his lessons with money he earned by pumping gasoline and sweeping out Steinfeld's Department Store ("Tucson's best," he would proudly note). Flying was everything. An airplane responded so beautifully, so precisely, to one's hands. One day as a teenager Borman was caught in a violent thunderstorm, the plane knocked in all directions by turbulence. When he finally came in for a landing, a powerful crosswind nearly swept his plane off the runway. It was then that Borman realized that he operated at his best in a crisis.

Achievement—winning—was also vital to Borman. Though small in stature, Borman became the first-string quarterback of his high school football team as an underclassman, leading it to the Arizona state championship in 1945. He had an unusually large head for his size, and his friends called him Squarehead.

Destined for a career in the military, Borman won an appointment to West Point through the sponsorship of a judge with whose son Borman built model airplanes. As a cadet Borman distinguished himself with his bullheaded pride. When an upperclassman once ground his heel into the toe of Borman's shoe, West Point hazing tradition demanded that Borman, a lowly plebe, bear the torture silently. Instead he called the upperclassman a son of a bitch and threatened to kill him. Borman graduated in 1950, eighth in a class of 670, marched in Harry Truman's inaugural parade, and launched into fighter pilot training as a true believer in the unofficial air force motto, "Every man a tiger." At one point he ruptured an eardrum practicing dive-bombing with a head cold. He was dismayed to receive orders back to West Point as an aeronautical instructor, but made the most of the assignment. Any unlucky cadets who happened to nod off in Professor Borman's class got erasers thrown at their heads.

Borman's combination of fighter pilot flying and scientific training (not to mention his proven ability to withstand physical torment) won him an appointment as an astronaut in the Gemini program. In two weeks aboard Gemini 7 in 1965 Borman established an endurance record for space flight and helped to conduct the first docking in space. Borman would later describe the "magic feeling" he experienced from the responsiveness of the Gemini spacecraft to his controls. It was the same glorious sensation Borman always felt piloting the swept-wing F-86 Sabre, one of the principal weapons in America's Cold War arsenal—a jet fighter whose builders happened to include an aircraft mechanic in Columbus, Ohio, named Charles E. Bryan.

Bryan's father was an alcoholic, a seldom-seen figure as young Charlie was growing up in the coal-mining hollows of West Virginia. From the time of his earliest memory Charlie Bryan had to work. As a first grader he sold newspapers on a street corner in a grimy coal-dust town, shouting "Extra!" on the day Japan attacked Pearl Harbor.

The postwar years were a time of great northerly migration, not just among blacks but among Appalachian whites. For many the promised land—the first big city to the north—was Columbus, Ohio, a city just beginning a Cold War boom in the aerospace and technology industries. At the same time that Frank Borman was immersed in the duty-honor-country culture of West Point, Charlie Bryan was a tenth grader working at a drive-in theater in the Whitehall section of Columbus, a few miles east of Ohio State University. When his mother moved to a different part of town, Charlie could not bear to leave his job and his paycheck, so, barely old enough to hold a driver's license, he began living alone in a shack beneath the movie screen, sleeping on an army cot and showering at a nearby trailer park.

Charlie Bryan had an intense manner and a stubbornness that always seemed to get him what he wanted, and his classmates recognized it. He was forever being recruited to run for elected positions in his church groups and other organizations, and he never seemed to lose. But despite his rising to a variety of leadership positions, Charlie Bryan was not social. He did not mingle easily. He felt close to groups but distant from individuals. Though later married (and divorced) twice, Bryan would spend much of the rest of his life living alone, which was how he preferred it.

By the time he was graduated from high school, Bryan realized that he cared deeply about money and in particular the possessions money bought. His years of working as a teenager gave him the savings to buy a Buick Riviera with a blue body and a white hardtop, a car that people couldn't help noticing in 1952, particularly when the driver was barely shaving. On the same day he wore his cap and gown he began a mechanic's job at North American Aviation (later part of Rockwell International) and was soon working side jobs as well— night jobs doing freelance aircraft maintenance and working in a grocery store, all to make extra money. Charlie Bryan wanted a house with two bathrooms where everyone else of his economic station had a single bath—and maybe even a little extra to wager in the stock market.

When a recruiter from Eastern Air Lines turned up in Columbus one winter day in 1956, Bryan eagerly showed up for an interview. As a teenager Bryan had traveled to Florida with his mother and had vowed one day to live there. It was not just the warm weather that he found so attractive. It was also the romance, the beaches, the palms—"like a deserted island," as he would explain. He took a mechanic's job at Eastern in an instant.

Aircraft mechanics is a solitary craft and a profession of precision, two attributes that brought out the best in Charlie Bryan. He rebuilt wings and changed gears on old Lockheed Constellations and ultimately earned a reputation as a top engine-change mechanic, the most demanding job in any maintenance hangar.

Decades earlier, in a fateful turn of events, the International Association of Machinists had received an engraved invitation to unionize the hangars at Eastern from Eddie Rickenbacker himself. The IAM was an establishment union with rock-solid American values, and Rickenbacker was petrified that some Communist-affiliated union might otherwise organize his mechanics. (In later years, the union headquarters in Washington would come under the leadership of an avowed socialist.) Charlie Bryan, the loner mechanic, began turning out to hear speeches by one of the IAM's great leaders, a fiery orator named George Brown. Bryan discovered himself to be a hero-worshiper, and Brown's stirring addresses caused him to throw himself into the affairs of the union. He soon became a shop steward.

A seminal event in Bryan's union career occurred in 1961 in the midst of a crisis, after the wings broke off two Lockheed Electras in quick succession. The problem was ultimately attributed to a vibration-inducing design flaw, which could be remedied by removing the engines and remounting them with altered connections. Eastern, with one of the world's biggest Electra fleets, launched a crash effort to complete the makeover as quickly as possible, including round-the-clock shifts in the maintenance hangar.

Some of the mechanics, resentful of working a midnight shift, approached Charlie Bryan to complain. Bryan studied the engine overhaul scheme, diagramming the process on a few sheets of graph paper. He analyzed the staffing required to perform the individual tasks involved in each overhaul. He pondered the schedule by which each Electra was intended to enter and leave the hangar. Ultimately he calculated that with a few minor adjustments in the process the midnight shift could be eliminated while actually increasing the speed of the changeover. Eastern's management, stunned, readily adopted Bryan's plan. The event suggested to Bryan that a union official—that he, Charlie Bryan—might know as much or more about running an airline as the people paid big salaries to do so.

As for his own work schedule, however, Bryan preferred the solitude of the midnight shift. He quoted from Eastern mystics. He steeped himself in Kahlil Gibran. He became absorbed in the work of faith healer Edgar Cayce. But as aloof, as downright weird, as Bryan struck some of his fellow mechanics, he continued relating brilliantly to groups. He exuded intelligence. His demagoguery was skillful. He studied, and aspired to, the style of John Kennedy. His telephone number appeared in the Miami phone book under a pseudonym: Charles Leader.

Once, after hearing the word "extemporaneous" used in conversation, he rushed home to look it up. While paging toward the word in his dictionary, he noticed a conspicuous entry for the Latin expression *ex aequo et bono,* "according to what is fair and good." He fell in love with the expression, adopting it as his personal motto and later having it printed on union business cards and stationery.

As time passed Bryan seemed to know more and more about the operations and management of Eastern Air Lines. Discerning an unfailing trading pattern in the stock price of Eastern shares, he began buying and selling on cue, raking in enough profits to buy a '65 Austin Healy 3000 convertible. Management did little to disabuse him of his self-importance when the payroll department began using Bryan's ever-precise overtime records as a check against its own. Later in his career his say-so over corporate affairs—the control he could exercise from his position of union leadership—reminded him of his days running engine tune-ups, a power trip if ever there was one. "It was an awesome experience being right next to that engine, running it at high power settings, sometimes even takeoff power," he would tell an interviewer years later. "It was like standing right next to a volcano. You could actually feel the bones in your body vibrating from all that power right there in front of you that you were actually adjusting, and had control over."

On Christmas Eve in 1968, in mankind's first voyage around the moon, Frank Borman and his crewmates raised a wave of goose bumps the world over while reading aloud from Genesis. "Merry Christmas, and God bless all of you," Borman had said, closing a television broadcast observed by 1 billion people, "all of you on the good earth." Despite a number of harrowing moments unseen by the civilian world, the Apollo 8 mission, commanded by Borman, had been a triumph, no one's more than Borman's. Less than a month later he and his wife were seated conspicuously close to Richard Nixon during his inauguration ceremonies. Borman addressed a joint session of Congress and appeared before the College of Cardinals in Rome, speaking from the identical spot where Galileo in 1616 had been found guilty of heresy.

Despite his celebrity as a space explorer, Borman by 1969 was ready to abandon NASA. He was spending more than 200 days a year away from home, and his wife, Susan, was feeling all the stress and anxiety that Borman took pride in sloughing. During the Apollo mission, with its untested entry and exit from the gravitational field of another celestial body, Susan Borman displayed a bittersweet image to the nation as she nervously ran her pearls between her lips. No one, including her husband, realized at the time that she was also dousing her fears with alcohol.

Leaving NASA, Borman was the most sought-after executive material in America. Nixon aide H. R. Haldeman tried to recruit him for a high-level White House appointment. Ross Perot, the wealthy Texas computer magnate and crusader in behalf of Vietnam POWs, nearly landed Borman as the head of a new political organization to conduct "town hall" broadcasts. Many corporations called, but Borman refused to hire on as a trick pony. He wanted a real job, doing real work—a chance to prove himself in the world outside the military and the space program. In this respect none of the other invitations Borman received matched the appeal of the offer from Eastern Air Lines.

It was a job the title of which bespoke genuine responsibilities: vice president of operations. The position paid only $60,000 a year, a fraction of what a retiring astronaut might pull down elsewhere, but working at Eastern meant working with airplanes, and Borman still loved airplanes as much as ever. Even after a trip to the moon, Frank Borman was still building model airplanes. He began working full-time at Eastern in July 1970. "I figured right then and there, if I didn't blow it, I'd be president," he later commented.

But Borman stumbled within weeks of entering Eastern's nondescript, poured-concrete headquarters on the perimeter of Miami International Airport. The pilots who flew for Eastern were different from the pilots who flew for the U.S. military. Borman discovered that they actually wanted to make money. Before he knew what hit him, the pilots' union rolled him in a critical series of negotiations, saddling Eastern with one of the most punitive labor contracts in the airline industry. The top management was furious. In his official performance review Frank Borman received a "below average" rating.

But Borman, soon much wiser, recovered. He worked compul-

sively, spending day after day on the road despite his intention to
remedy the absences of his NASA years. Unwittingly he was worsening his wife's drinking and emotional problems, which finally re-
sulted in her lengthy convalescence in a treatment center. (Her
valiant recovery was poignantly detailed in Borman's memoirs, published under the title *Countdown.*)

There was treachery along Borman's path to the top, which hard
work alone would not overcome. By the time Borman arrived, the
power struggle among the many vice presidents in Hall's organization had split the top leadership of the company into two warring
camps. One group, led by Hall himself, consisted of the corporate
leadership in New York, the platoon of bright young analysts he had
brought aboard. The other faction was based at Eastern's operating
headquarters in Miami, where Sam Higginbottom, Eastern's president, ran a fiefdom of his own. Though he had seen plenty of internal politics in the military, Borman was shocked at the extent of the
divisiveness gripping Eastern: the rival camps not only had their own
staffs and headquarters but even separate public relations executives,
each of whom leaked negative gossip about the other faction to the
press. The finger-pointing worsened as Eastern was inundated with
Lockheed L-1011 widebodies that had been ordered in earlier years.
The new jets afflicted Eastern with excess capacity. Other airlines had
similar problems—too many 747s and DC-10s. The L-1011s, however, were shipped with troublesome engines, worsening Eastern's
image for poor service.

In his first several years Borman—hired and championed by Hall,
but reporting to Higginbottom—walked a tightrope between the two
factions. The situation was resolved when the Eastern board finally
intervened on the side of Hall, the chairman. Higginbottom, the
president, was forced out. Borman, however, would never forget one
of Higginbottom's admonitions to him. "Frank," Higginbottom
told him, "this company is almost impossible to manage."

Borman had an ally in 65-year-old Laurance Rockefeller, who remained one of Eastern's principal shareholders. Rockefeller saw in
Colonel Borman many of the same qualities that he had revered as a
boy in Captain Rickenbacker. "Frank is like the Captain in modern
dress," Rockefeller once remarked. "The virtues are the same—guts,
drive, energy, leadership." Rickenbacker, however, had been capable

of letting down his guard every now and then and relaxing. Borman, in Rockefeller's view, was "unremitting."

Acting at the board's request, the company named one of its directors, a former *Reader's Digest* president, to a senior vice president's post in the marketing department. None of the company's officers—not even Hall—was informed of the true role of the man from *Reader's Digest:* to act as an investigator, nothing less than a spy, for Laurance Rockefeller. Rockefeller's mole discreetly interviewed the senior officers about the company's problems, and when the fingers swung around to Floyd Hall, Borman was among those doing the pointing. He inveighed against his mentor's Harvard-inspired management techniques, he reported that Hall was protecting deadwood in the executive ranks, and he informed Rockefeller's man that the factionalism between New York and Miami was still crippling the company, even long after the ouster of Sam Higginbottom as president.

Eastern had been losing money for years; the bankers were threatening to pull the plug. "Frank Borman is the only man in the United States who can save this company," Rockefeller now declared to his fellow board members. In May 1975 Borman was informed that he was being appointed president of Eastern Air Lines. "Thank you," he answered. "I'll do my best."

Borman had one foot in the door, but Hall still had two years remaining as chairman and chief executive. The two men began quarreling. Hall attacked Borman's orders to outfit passenger service agents in bright red jackets (as Delta had done) so they could be easily identified by deplaning passengers. Hall, suffering from health and marital problems, was moving further into left field, in Borman's view. So Borman decided to confront the man who had brought him to Eastern in the first place.

He told Hall to step down. Hall protested that he had two more years to go. In that case, said Borman, the board would have to decide between the the two of them.

Thus was Floyd Hall—like MacIntyre and Rickenbacker before him—forced from the executive suite. Two years ahead of schedule, Borman, 47 years old, became the chief executive officer of Eastern just before Christmas in 1975.

He would sink or swim not on the buoyancy of his triumphs in space but on his capabilities as a corporate executive. Eastern's fortunes would rise or fall with him as well, and with them in turn the livelihoods of 33,000 employees. There was, Borman declared, no place for living in the past. "There has always been a certain romanticism associated with the airline business," he warned his senior executives in a memo after becoming chairman. "We must avoid its perpetuation at Eastern at all costs."

Still at his fighter pilot weight of 168 pounds, the new chairman of Eastern assumed command from a headquarters office known as Building 16. It might as well have been Stalag 17. Located on the perimeter of the airfield at Miami International Airport, it was a nine-story structure of poured concrete and skinny windows with all the aesthetic appeal of a shoe box standing upright. In an effort to dress up the ninth-floor executive offices, arched doorways and other Moorish touches had been added, along with a sweeping cantilevered stairwell. The walls were done in a plastic wallpaper of orange stripes. Into Borman's office went air force fighter-plane paintings and photographs of his two sons, both in uniform; they too had attended West Point. On his desk sat a paperweight that read, "Press on. Nothing in the world can take the place of persistence."

The atmosphere swung between the barracks and the locker room. People who trifled with insignificant business matters were dismissed as "dipshits." Once, getting briefed on the grounding of yet another L-1011, Borman barked, "Have you fixed it yet, or are you going to make a diner out of it?" During a meeting of officers he once asked a female vice president to fetch him a cup of coffee. (She refused.)

Whatever his macho mind-set, there was not a trace of ostentation about the Colonel. He drove Chevrolets—at one point an early-model Camaro convertible that he had rebuilt with his own hands. His musical tastes ran to Merle Haggard. He ordered every officer in the company (himself included) to pitch in as baggage handlers during the busiest periods, explaining, "Everyone whose mission is not critical to the peak period goes out to help." He scrapped the "Wings of Man" slogan as a pretension. Long before the idea ever occurred to Lee Iacocca's people at Chrysler, Borman reluctantly agreed to take to the airwaves as Eastern's advertising spokesman in a memorable series of television advertisements. "Don't make me sell Tang," he protested.

Though he craved leadership roles, Borman was no joiner. He accepted an invitation to become a member of the secretive and exclusive Conquistadores del Cielo but came to hate the club. The idea of grown men gathering at an isolated ranch struck him as weird, like a bunch of adult Boy Scouts hanging out in the woods. "If you quit this organization," he was told by Paul Thayer, a legendary aerospace executive, "you'll never go anywhere in this industry." Borman quit anyway.

Aloof, analytical, characterizing his management challenge as a "mission," Borman set about to restore discipline and profitability to Eastern. Within months of becoming president he fired or demoted 24 vice presidents. He drew attention to costs by walking from office to office flipping off light switches. Fresh from his wife's alcoholism recovery (and his own newborn life as a teetotaler) Borman banned drinking during company hours (including lunch), a not unreasonable policy for a company whose executive offices were located at the edge of the airport tarmac.

Executive perquisites came under severe attack. Eastern had a policy of allowing officers to lease company cars, including Mercedes Benzes, which the company depreciated practically overnight and then sold to the officers at the reduced value; Borman wiped out company cars. An executive jet, used by executives for personal as well as business travel, was jettisoned; Borman required Eastern executives to begin conducting their travel by commercial airline instead. He curtly fired a longtime Eastern spokesman, golfer Jack Nicklaus, calculating that the company maintained the costly endorsement contract principally because the executives enjoyed the opportunity to golf with him occasionally. Borman, for his part, hated golf; it was too slow a game. "You're not selling enough tickets," he said. "Good-bye."

Though Borman, like most airline chief executives, had a weakness for new planes, he did succeed in negotiating perhaps the most lucrative airplane deal in history. He agreed to make Eastern the proving customer for the A-300, assembled in Toulouse, France, by the Airbus Industrie consortium from parts made throughout Europe. Desperate to break the hold of Boeing and McDonnell Doug-las in the United States, Airbus agreed to lease a number of planes to Eastern for six months free of charge. Borman told an employee meeting, "If you don't kiss the French flag every time you see it, at least salute it."

Then Borman turned his attention to the most vital yet delicate matter of all: the livelihoods of his employees. They owed it to the future, Borman told them, to cut back their wages.

Like a politician on the stump, Borman launched a never-ending round-robin of trips through the Eastern system; even employees working in the middle of the night on the loneliest airport shifts got a dose of give-it-up religion. He began a letter-writing campaign to his employees, drumming them with the need for sacrifice. "One of the great joys in life," he told them, "is found in subordinating one's personal desires and efforts to the success of a group." He alternated from the velvet glove to the iron fist, between bended knee and thrusting chest, depending on the circumstances. There was always a crisis, it seemed—a mission, dangerously close to failure—for the sake of which Borman would convince employees to give up wages they were scheduled to receive. "We could be unable to meet our pay-roll," he warned at one point. Sen. Edward Kennedy's deregulation proposals became the bogeyman, constituting "a very serious threat to the continuation of Eastern Air Lines as we know it." Finally, in November 1978, he wrote, "The President has signed the deregula-tion bill. . . . It's quite clear that we do not have the [necessary] re-sources—airplanes, cash." And with each letter came another plea to forgo something that employees otherwise had coming. "God bless you all," he added in the last paragraph of nearly every letter.

While some of these programs involved outright concessions by employees, the most creative and long-lasting was more complex and certainly more innovative: employees agreed to wager a percentage of their salaries on the company's profitability. If earnings totaled less than a stipulated level, employees received less than full pay—96.5 percent of what they were otherwise entitled at that time, to be precise. If profits exceeded the agreed-upon benchmark, wages too would swell—to 103.5 percent of the baseline level. Borman called this the "variable earnings plan," or VEP.

In so cyclical an industry as aviation, in which tiny changes in in-

terest rates and fuel prices and macroeconomic conditions have a
huge effect on the bottom line, VEP gave Borman a stunning management advantage. It turned his employees, in essence, into Eastern's bankers, enabling him to borrow tens of millions of dollars
from them—unsecured, not so incidentally, and without interest—
and to repay them only if the money happened to be available at a
later time, which, as the years progressed, it increasingly was not.

In the profit and loss column, Borman's first five years running
Eastern were pages from an executive storybook. Borman turned the
losses of the Hall regime into the greatest profits Eastern had ever (or
would ever) report. There were problems, grave problems, but they
only increased the challenge—and the heroism of his triumphs. "His
associates," *The Miami Herald* crowed, "say that he alone resuscitated a dying airline." Added *Time* magazine: "Borman has accomplished a remarkable turnaround." Borman celebrated Eastern's
profitability by placing some of the largest airplane orders in history,
and this time the airplanes were not free. Already a ward of its
bankers, Eastern went even more deeply into hock.

Then Charlie Bryan became president of Eastern's largest union.

Bryan did not initially consider himself an enemy of Frank Borman.
On the contrary, as Bryan was coming into prominence in District
100 of the International Association of Machinists, he sat with Borman at a company dinner party and thrilled to hear Borman describe
the mission of Apollo 8. Bryan could feel the goose bumps on his
arms as Borman spoke. "I'm sitting here with the Magellan of our
time," he told himself.

Political reality soon brought Bryan down to earth. By the early
1980s, with interest rates swelling and fare wars spreading, Borman's
variable earnings plan was varying in the company's direction much
more frequently than in the employees'. Borman's hero status with
employees began to wear thin: in one anti-VEP protest employees
carried signs saying, "Earth to Frank: No More VEP." But Borman
cried that Eastern needed VEP more than ever. New York Air had recently invaded the Eastern shuttle's market, and People Express was
running cut-rate flights in Eastern's mainstay market to Florida.

Bryan won the IAM presidency on a promise to eliminate VEP,
which he dubbed the "veritable extortion plan." Bryan, who had

worked so many odd jobs in his life, who cared so deeply about the kind of car he drove and the number of bathrooms in his house, knew how much a few dollars a week meant to a union worker.

Bryan indeed was the living embodiment of the principles of the machinists' union, an organization devoted like few others to the dollar value of a paycheck. When Lyndon Johnson laid down a 3.5 percent limit on wage increases throughout the United States, the IAM struck five airlines for 39 days and walked away with a 5.5 percent wage increase. The IAM made a mockery of President Nixon's wage and price freeze. When Jimmy Carter's wage "guidelines" became law, an IAM settlement at Eureka Vacuum Company was declared illegal by the Council on Wage and Price Stability.

Charlie Bryan's zeal for that tradition was evident the instant he assumed office. The outgoing district president, in a gracious newsletter offering congratulations to Bryan, added a sincere if awkwardly written farewell: "Mr. Frank Borman, whom I have the utmost respect for, was the company official, in my opinion, that did the most for Eastern Air Lines in the 31 years I have had an employee-employer relationship." Twelve days later Bryan, now in control, distributed a newsletter of his own, which, if nothing else, was grammatically written. "The Gestapo tactics of Martin Ludwig Borman and his Nazi scorched earth policy," Bryan wrote, "will not work with this union leadership."

A few months later Bryan showed up at Eastern's 1980 annual meeting of shareholders with a briefcase full of proxies, about 100,000 shares' worth, and nominated himself to serve on the Eastern board. He knew of course that he had no chance to win, but that was beside the point. As he later explained, "I did it just to get attention." At the annual meeting the following year, Bryan showed up with even more proxies, this time on the order of a half-million. It was still only a fraction of what the election of a director required, but he managed to use the meeting as a public platform for dressing down the Colonel. "You made history with Apollo 8," Bryan said. "Why do you *ignore* the history lesson the British learned regarding 'taxation without representation' by continuing to ask our employees to give, contribute, and sacrifice, but [telling them] 'don't get involved at the top'?"

Bryan's penchant for grandstanding was equaled by his talent with the media. He equipped District 100 with fax technology, then in its infancy, and began distributing his bulletins to the press as well as to his membership. He understood, as few union people ever have, that he could use publicity to help fulfill his purposes only by delivering a compelling story. When the company began forcing machinists to take their coffee breaks at the same time of day, the long lines at the canteen caused some workers to return to their posts a few minutes late. Wages were docked. Bryan called Borman and barked, "Quit fucking with people just because I got elected!" Bryan then planted the suggestion that a strike, or at least a work slowdown, could erupt over the issue. Before long a big headline asked, "Will Coffee Ground Eastern?" In the glare of the publicity Eastern backed down.

Another round, however, went to Eastern. Borman had been smarting ever since another airline executive had teased him about one of the featherbedding work rules that the machinists maintained at Eastern. The rule required Eastern to keep three union members on hand when a plane pushed back from the gate—one to drive the tractor and two to walk along the wings. Borman established new procedures when in 1981 Eastern was preparing to open a new terminal at Atlanta's Hartsfield Airport, a terminal for which Borman had borrowed heavily to help Eastern block the inroads that Atlanta-based Delta was continuing to make on Eastern territory. Eastern calculated that the machinists' push-back rule would force it to employ 44 machinists that the company otherwise would not require at the expanded operation. No, Borman ordered, from that point forward Eastern would use the reverse thrust capability of its engines, not a push-car operator with his union wing walkers.

Bryan would cotton to none of this. He raced to Atlanta and stood behind the wheels of the first plane to push back with reverse thrust. The showdown was at hand. In one corner, weighing in at about 160 pounds, from West Virginia, the frowning and square-shouldered Charlie Bryan. In the other corner, tipping the scales at 100,000 pounds, from Seattle, Washington, a Boeing 727. The plane lurched. All eyes were cast to Charlie. And with those big tires slowly revolving in his direction, Charlie Bryan flinched. He dove out of the way to avoid getting rolled over by the aluminum beast (later saying he had been knocked away by the blast of an engine).

Borman and Bryan shared a notable face-off in Caesars Palace, where the IAM was holding a national convention. Borman, friendly with the union's international leadership, had been invited to address the group. Bryan had just published a newsletter suggesting that Eastern was deliberately understating its profits in order to pressure employees into more sacrifice.

Bryan was at a slot machine when he heard himself being paged. The hell with it, he said, continuing to play. Suddenly Borman was stalking purposefully toward him. "Bryan," he barked. "Why didn't you answer my page?"

"I've got a cup full of coins!" Bryan cried.

Ignoring the protest, Borman grabbed Bryan by the arm and pulled him into the coffee shop. The men sat down.

"What the hell are you trying to do?" Borman demanded. "Make us look like a bunch of crooks?"

Bryan peered back quizzically. He had no idea what Borman meant.

"Look at this!" Borman commanded, shoving Bryan's accusatory newsletter in front of him.

Bryan peered down. "I can't read this," he said. "I don't have my glasses."

"Here. Take mine."

And for the next several minutes the renowned astronaut and the little-known unionist swapped the same pair of glasses over a coffee shop table, locked in combat over a union newsletter.

On the bottom line, Borman's fairy-tale success at Eastern lasted from 1975 to the early 1980s, when a variety of forces converged to plunge the company headlong into reality.

With its price-sensitive "frost-to-flowers" markets, Eastern was more vulnerable to attack from the upstarts than any other established airline. People Express was already cutting in; others would follow. On Eastern's business routes, New York Air was still taking a huge bite.

Worse still, Eastern was losing passengers just as it was being inundated with new airplanes. Borman had ordered the planes amid the fuel shortages of the 1970s, moving aggressively to replace his old gas-guzzlers with modern, fuel-efficient aircraft. But the price of jet fuel by 1983 at last was plunging. While People Express and New York Air were happily flying against Eastern with old gas-guzzlers that had been purchased used for a song, Eastern was flying new, fuel-efficient aircraft—just when fuel efficiency mattered much less. At the same time interest rates remained at stubbornly high levels. Borman was on the wrong side of both markets. Further compounding the disadvantage, Borman's new planes were big 757s; the upstarts, by contrast, were flying much smaller planes, enabling them to offer greater frequencies against Eastern than they otherwise might.

Borman courageously tried to break the mold by which Eastern had operated since the Rickenbacker days. At a retreat with his top managers in the Florida Keys, Borman approved a plan to thrust Eastern into the transcontinental markets, from New York to California—the routes endowed upon American, United, and TWA but denied to Eastern from the time of the postmaster general's spoils conference in 1930. The incumbent airlines reacted as if Borman were trying to kidnap their firstborns. "You'll have to take me out of that market feet first!" Dick Ferris of United publicly declared. "We'll protect it to our dying breath." Eventually Eastern washed out of the transcontinental market.

In another, even bolder, restructuring move, however, the Colonel triumphed. He made Eastern into an international airline.

In 1982, gasping for its final breath, Braniff had put its most valuable asset up for sale: its routes into South America, a prize steeped in history.

In the Lindbergh era Pan Am had established two great route systems deep into South America, like two long, slender fingers. The first ran from Miami through the eastern Caribbean and on to Venezuela, then along the Atlantic coast, at the eastern edge of the continent. The second route ran through the isthmus of Central America to Colombia, then along the Pacific coast through Ecuador, Peru, and Chile, with a leap across Argentina to Buenos Aires. In 1966, shortly after taking control of Braniff, Eddie Acker spent several days in Juan Trippe's office in the Pan Am building persuading Trippe to sell the routes along the Pacific side of South America to Braniff. Trippe ultimately relented.

The routes were like a mint for Braniff, burgeoning as the

economies of Latin America swelled in the 1970s on oil exploration and a tide of money borrowed from the banks of the industrialized world. Latin America was the best moneymaker in the Braniff system and in later years, alas, one of the few moneymakers it had.

When Braniff put out word that it was willing to part with the Latin routes, Borman snapped to attention. He raced to New York on a Sunday night in April 1982 and holed up with a delegation from Braniff, bargaining without interruption until a deal was struck at 2:30 A.M. Braniff agreed to sell the routes to Eastern for the pittance of $30 million. After settling on the terms, Borman told his underlings back at corporate headquarters in Miami that if anything prevented the deal from closing, he would fire the guilty party. They did not disappoint him. Within hours the historic routes were safely Eastern's. The company considered the operation so exotic that the employee newsletter featured a pronunciation guide for the new destinations: "LEE-mah," "SAN-tee-AH-go," and "Bway-nos-I-rays" among them.

It was perhaps Borman's most brilliant stroke in nearly 12 years as an airline chief executive, but one would not have known it the following day. When Borman arrived at a ballroom in New York for the annual meeting of Eastern shareholders, hundreds of Eastern mechanics and ground workers were noisily demonstrating outside. At one point 150 of the protesting mechanics crowded into the meeting room wearing anti-Borman buttons. Charlie Bryan was at it again.

And with good reason. The machinists' contract was about to expire.

Borman's pleadings for more concessions had not let up during Charlie Bryan's first few years in office. The pilots, still enraptured with their astronaut chairman, assented to just about any concession that Borman requested, but the machinists were different. So calloused had they become to Borman's continual demands that restroom walls and daily conversation were soon sprinkled with the acronym BOHICA, as in "Bend over, here it comes again."

Borman had not done himself any good by committing a huge gaffe in one of his BOHICA demands. In a videotaped plea for concessions he noted that the wages involved were trifling—no more than "the cost of a few six-packs of beer" from each paycheck. The machinists, sensitive to their Joe Six-Pack image, took deep offense and began sporting lapel pins saying NO DEPOSIT, NO RETURN. Eastern for its part distributed buttons to employees that said, I LOVE MY JOB. THANKS, EASTERN.

With his contract up for renewal in early 1983 Charlie Bryan was eager to lock in a big wage increase after all those years of BOHICA. Colonel Borman recognized that he had to offer a decent settlement, but he said the company simply couldn't withstand the kind of numbers Bryan was throwing around. The union set a strike date for March 1983. Fine, Borman said. Unless Bryan moderated his demands, the Colonel declared, Eastern would take a strike by the IAM.

Borman's aides were jubilant. At last Eastern was going to stage an epochal confrontation with the International Association of Machinists, a fight for which the officer corps of Eastern had been itching for some time. Some of Borman's board members had likewise been urging a major confrontation. The pilots' union had also grown resentful of the machinists, and the flight attendants as well. Both groups indicated that if the machinists struck, they would cross Charlie Bryan's picket lines. In a stunning display of cooperation, the pilots even agreed to yet another wage concession, although a temporary one—a 14 percent wage deferral. All Eastern needed to fly through a machinists' strike was a corps of strikebreaking mechanics. "We can kill these guys!" Borman's people told each other.

The machinists' membership meanwhile remained squarely behind Bryan. When Borman appealed directly to the membership with another "God bless you" letter, a fuel-tank cleaner and aircraft polisher in Miami named Barbara Mungovan mailed a poem to Borman explaining why the membership of the machinists' union was fed up.

> *In good faith I took a wage freeze, and gave you my 3.5.*
> *You said you had to have it, to help Eastern survive.*
> *I gave up things I needed, I gave up a new car*
> *Then you spent my money on a "union bustin' " seminar.*
>
> *I gave up my vacation, and my skiing trip*
> *And all you gave to me was more gloom and doom lip.*

I gave up eating steak—cost of livin', I'm not able.
I'm sure your family thinks of us, when it's on your dinner table.

You feel now you don't need us, after we supported you.
Explain this to my son—it's a hard thing to do.
You say you can fly without us, that it's easy to do.
Frank, if you really think you can, then God bless you.

Management presented a final offer—a 32 percent increase over 30 months. "If you turn down this contract," Borman told the rank and file, "it will mean the end of Eastern as we know it." He added, "If the union doesn't accept, we'll have a strike," and further, "Eastern cannot and will not improve this offer."

Borman was offering a substantial sum, yes, but most of the increase came at the end of the contract. The machinists, having fallen behind their peers at other old-line carriers, wanted more up front. Charlie Bryan would get it for them, they were sure. The machinists rejected Borman's final offer three to one. But just to make sure he wasn't leading his membership down the path to oblivion, Bryan discreetly had decided to take his measure of Eastern one last time.

In the years ahead, no one would hold greater influence over Charlie Bryan than Randy Barber. Though barely in his thirties, Barber had already become a high priest of economic organizing, a self-taught financial analyst with a strong leftist bent. Frank Borman would come to refer to Barber derisively as Charlie Bryan's "personal guru."

Barber came by his ideological pretensions honestly. Born in Wyoming and reared in Colorado, he was the son of a Methodist minister who had been one of the earliest leaders of the civil rights movement. Randy Barber himself, attending Dartmouth in the late 1960s, would later say that he majored in antiwar activism. After college Barber wound up a teacher in Bourges, France.

While there Barber became fascinated with a labor strike at a watchmaking factory in Besançon, France, where the workers had taken the unusual step of seizing the plant and resuming production on their own, without benefit of management. It was Marxism in action, with the workers seizing the means of production. Barber absorbed himself in supporting the strikers by selling "wildcat" watches.

Once back in the United States Barber joined a radical writer named Jeremy Rifkind in a counterculture organization they called the People's Bicentennial Commission. While combing the writings of Jefferson, Paine, and other Colonial intellectuals for quotes and comments with modern revolutionary relevance, Barber and Rifkind also threw themselves into real-life socialism, helping to establish a women's chicken processing cooperative in Connecticut and supporting the worker boycott under way against the antiunion textile giant J. P. Stevens & Company.

As his labor activism intensified, Barber observed that one of the largest sources of capital in the world resided in the pension funds of America, funds that were created and managed to benefit workers. By 1978 he and Rifkind had written a manifesto for worker exploitation of the funds, called *The North Will Rise Again: Pensions, Politics and Power in the 1980s.* Rifkind ultimately drifted into other causes, but Barber became the toast of the lecture circuit in labor circles, pulling down grants and eventually landing a teaching post at Florida International University in Miami.

It was there that he was introduced to Charlie Bryan of the IAM's District 100.

Bryan needed someone like Randy Barber, not only a bona fide lefty, in keeping with the increasingly liberal leanings of the machinists' union, but also an intellectual and one, as it happened, with an aptitude for numbers. Thus did Barber find himself on Bryan's payroll as a financial consultant.

In trying to convince the union that Eastern could not meet its 1983 wage demands, Borman took the remarkable step of offering to open the company's confidential books to an independent review. Borman suggested that this review should be conducted by independent business school professors. Bryan refused the offer. "In business schools they don't teach trade unionism," he explained. "I'm not interested in having someone who runs a business school determine the destiny of my membership." If anyone were to examine Eastern's books in behalf of the IAM, Bryan determined, it would be the long-haired, thirty-something Randy Barber.

Barber brought in some pals who had honed their analytical skills in the union campaign against J. P. Stevens. Together they traveled to Miami with a huge, padded suitcase in which Barber carried an Osborne One, one of the earliest desktop personal computers. Borman, true to his word, threw open the company's ledgers, and Barber and his friends began running the numbers.

Among the records before them were Eastern's most up-to-the-minute reports to its bankers. To Barber's astonishment a few calculations showed that Eastern was professing its willingness to take a strike with just 12 days' worth of cash in the till. It appeared to Barber that unless Borman came up with a lot of cash quickly, Eastern would be dead—in bankruptcy—in as little as two weeks if the machinists mounted an effective strike.

Hearing his consultants' findings, Charlie Bryan decided to call Frank Borman's bluff.

With the strike deadline looming, Borman received a call from a slight acquaintance whose in-laws included a member of the mob. The acquaintance told Borman his life was in danger; someone had put out a contract to kill him.

Borman called the FBI, which obtained some information deemed to be corroborative. The FBI urged Borman to begin wearing a bulletproof vest. Borman also took a crash course in the use of a 9 mm semi-automatic pistol and strapped one to his ankle.

Borman took an additional security precaution. The original tipster had urged him to hire one of his relatives, a young man, and said that Borman should keep the fellow conspicuously in his company. The young man would be recognized by the mob as someone with an indirect link to the Genovese family. So for a few days there was a stranger accompanying Borman and hanging around his office, a talisman against a mob hit.

Meanwhile Borman and his aides were looking at the same cash figures that the machinists were privately celebrating. Borman's underlings, undeterred by the low cash balances, wanted the strike more fervently than ever. They conducted a fact-finding mission to the headquarters of Northwest Airlines in Minneapolis, one of the few carriers with any experience in taking strikes. Borman's people had also lined up the necessary replacement workers. Many of Borman's 18,000 nonunion employees were ready to toss luggage, clean toilets, and perform the other tasks that the IAM members handled in addition to the more sophisticated crafts represented in the union.

Borman was ready too, but he wanted more cash in the bank. Even if the pilots and flight attendants marched through Charlie Bryan's picket lines, Eastern would still undoubtedly experience a drought in revenue, at least for a while. Even a slight disruption could have a huge financial effect. Borman did not take on missions he expected to fail. He needed a cushion to help absorb the financial blow.

Borman scheduled a breakfast meeting with Willard C. Butcher, the chairman and chief executive of Chase Manhattan Bank. Chase was Eastern's lead bank—the Rockefeller bank, long managed in past years by Laurance Rockefeller's younger brother, David. Now, however, there was new management at the top in the person of Willard Butcher. The banking group led by Chase maintained a $200 million line of credit for Eastern. Borman requested $110 million— enough, it would seem, for Eastern to take the strike.

There was one small technical problem. Tapping the remainder of the credit line would put Eastern in default on some of its borrowing covenants, the minimum financial standards that the banks required Eastern to maintain as a condition for lending it any money at all. All Borman needed was a simple waiver of the bankers' covenants.

Borman explained the urgency of the situation to Butcher. His answer, to Borman's astonishment, was no. "We're not going to waive the covenants," Butcher said flatly. He was a banker, not a strikebreaker.

Seldom in his life had Borman been so depressed. He knew that caving in to the machinists would devastate his credibility, not only with them but with all of Eastern's employees. Indeed, the pilots had even agreed to a wage deferral to fortify Borman's financial preparations for a strike. Settling with Bryan would make it appear that Eastern was using the pilots' generosity to subsidize the machinists' big wage increase. But taking a strike with so little cash meant not only bankruptcy but liquidation—an outright seizure of Eastern's assets. It would be an abject failure of the mission.

A short time later at the bargaining table, Charlie Bryan won everything he asked for.

In Miami, Atlanta, New York, Houston, and everywhere else that Eastern operated, Frank Borman's managers were disconsolate, as if they had spent weeks practicing for the big game only to be sent home from the locker room. The pilots' union ordered the ballots recounted on their wage deferral vote. Mechanics, baggage handlers, and other members of the machinists' union arrived for the night shift in droves to enjoy lording their victory over their managers. Some of them produced the lapel buttons that management had previously distributed—I LOVE MY JOB. THANKS, EASTERN—but altered them with tape to read, THANKS, CHARLIE.

As the machinists' merrymaking swelled, Borman slouched to his home in Miami. While he was relating the depressing events of the preceding days to his wife, a reporter for a Miami television station came to the door.

"Colonel, what happened?" she asked.

"We were raped!" he snapped, closing the door.

CHAPTER 8

STORMY WEATHER

Regardless of how skillfully acquired or how cleverly deployed, airplanes do not fly on the talents of corporate management. How does it happen? What makes an airplane fly?

Lindbergh once made an instructive analogy from his boyhood in Minnesota. He and his young friends enjoyed racing across the log-jams floating listlessly in the northern reaches of the Mississippi River. Some of the logs were too short and narrow to support the weight of an average-size boy. Lindbergh discovered that he had to race quickly over these logs, stepping from each to the next before any one of them had the chance to sink. The same principle applied to flight. "Safety," Lindbergh learned, "lay in speed."

Airplanes do not take off or remain in the air through the pressure of the oncoming air against the bottom of the wing, as commonly thought. This pressure contributes to aircraft flight but hardly accounts for it.

In addition to being pushed from below, an airplane's wings are pulled from above, as if on a marionette's string. This happens because the top of a wing is contoured and the bottom is flat. As the wing slices through the atmosphere, the air slipping along the top must travel a greater distance than the air passing on the bottom. The air on top therefore moves faster.

This condition causes lift through the combination of two immutable properties of physics, each taken for granted in everyday living. The first principle is that as air moves faster, it exerts less pressure downward—just as tornadoes and other windy storms coincide with regions of low air pressure on the weather map. The second principle is that air always moves from areas of high pressure to low pressure, as the cigarette smoke in the still air of an automobile rushes through a window crack toward the fast-moving, low-pressure area outside the window. Thus, as air cascades along the bottom of a wing, it is also being sucked, as if from a vacuum cleaner, toward the top of the wing. The faster the wing travels laterally, the greater the pressure differential above and below. The greater the differential, the greater the lift generated. Safety lay in speed.

The combination of speed and surface area created by a modern jet engine and wing is truly prodigious. Each square foot of wing surface can support about 100 pounds, which is why a 747, with a wingspan encompassing 5,000 square feet, can hoist a half-million pounds.

Because of those tremendous speeds and surface areas, the angle at which the wing is attached to the plane and the angle at which the plane itself rises into the air are acutely critical variables. So too is the smoothness of the path taken by the air over the wing—the aerodynamics, that is. If air fails to adhere evenly to the contours on the top of the wing, buffeting occurs. If the airflow departs completely from the surface, lift vanishes, causing the airplane to "stall," as if the marionette string had snapped or the vacuum cleaner were switched off.

So long as the wing is of proper design and in working order, only one thing can corrupt the flow of air over the surface, and that is ice, such as the ice that was forming on the wings of Air Florida Flight 90 sitting at snowy National Airport in Washington on January 13, 1982.

That an airplane flying for a company called Air Florida should be stuck in a blizzard was richly ironic. Some months after leaving Braniff in 1975 under the cloud of Watergate, the indefatigable Eddie Acker had had occasion to fly on Air Florida, then a three-year-old airline that operated three propeller-driven Lockheed Electras and a single 707 jet. Air Florida reminded Acker of the South-west Airlines he had battled back in his Braniff days. Deregulation, though imminent, had not yet taken hold when Acker discovered Air Florida; like Southwest, it was still confined to the boundaries of a single state.

Acker realized he was desperate to take control of another airline. "Once you get hooked on the airline business," he explained, "it's worse than dope." With the backing of some friends, Acker purchased a controlling interest in the airline for just $1.5 million.

As he had demonstrated back at Braniff, Acker was incapable of small-scale management. He began picking up used jets all over North America, tapping some of his oldest and best connections for financing. He changed Air Florida's markings from a rusty orange to blue and green. "We operate in a warm climate, so our jets had better look cool," Acker explained. Passengers on morning flights got orange juice spiked with champagne—"sunshine sparklers." And Acker began applying the Southwest Airlines pricing formula: severe discounts, especially at off-peak hours, with fares below the cost of driving. As more planes came in, boardings rose by 100 percent over the previous year, then by 200 percent, and in some months by 300 percent.

Once deregulation had hit, Acker applied the same principles in the interstate market. When United announced its withdrawal of service from Toledo, Acker backed in with flights to Florida at ultralow fares. When National Airlines was purchased by Pan Am, he grabbed National's old route from Miami to London, offering first-class seats upholstered in sheepskin and a free ride from the airport in London aboard a Rolls-Royce limousine. Acker launched a new route from Miami to Dallas by offering "free flights for a kiss," by which a certain number of customers would fly free simply for smooching an Air Florida "kiss miss" stationed at the airport.

At age 50 Ed Acker was having the time of his life at Air Florida. He literally ran between offices, going the entire day without sitting. Reaching for a dog-eared copy of the *OAG* in his pocket, Acker flipped from page to page calling out new destinations: Tallahassee, Port-au-Prince, Honduras—essentially, whatever tickled his interest.

In much the way that air rushes into areas of low pressure, airlines look for opportunities to thrust their airplanes into locations where their competitors are withdrawing. In July 1981 Pan Am, still fum-

bling over its acquisition of National Airlines nearly two years ear-
lier, cut back severely on the New York–to–Florida routes for which
National had been principally known. Grabbing at opportunity,
Acker threw nearly half of his planes into the void, making Air
Florida overnight the second most dominant carrier along the East
Coast, exceeded only by Eastern Air Lines. (A few weeks later, after
President Reagan had fired the striking air-traffic controllers, People
Express would join the fray.)

The New York Times labeled Acker "the darling of deregulation."
Fortune magazine suggested that Acker was "the ablest of the entrepreneurs catapulted to prominence by airline deregulation." Air
Florida, said The Wall Street Journal, had become "one of the great
American corporate success stories." It did not particularly concern
the investment community that Air Florida's debt had ballooned at
a time when interest rates were in the stratosphere or that the company's profits were subsidized by Acker's maneuverings in the foreign currency and stock markets. If anybody could keep on top of
the numbers, Wall Street figured, it was a genius like Ed Acker.

A few weeks after he had dispatched all those planes from Florida
to the Northeast, the research analysts of Wall Street turned out in
force for a luncheon presentation by Acker. But when he rose to the
podium, Acker said he was not able to discuss the affairs of Air
Florida with them, for a reason he knew they would all understand.

"I talked to Cunard Lines," he said, "and told them I was interested in a job as captain of the Titanic. They informed me that I was
fifty years too late."

Having thoroughly confused his audience, Acker went on. "Not
having that challenge available, I decided to try to find one comparable to that. And so I am accepting the chairmanship of a company
called Pan American World Airways." As the analysts recovered
from their shock, Acker turned over the podium to someone from
Air Florida and left.

Within days of arriving at Pan Am, Acker took the extraordinary
step of reversing the flight cutbacks along the East Coast that the
previous management had just made—the service that Acker himself
had rushed with Air Florida to fill. Having enjoyed the excitement of
building Air Florida, Ed Acker, it appeared, was now bent on destroying it.

• • •

It was at the height of the conflict that Flight 90 found itself delayed at Washington National that January afternoon in 1982.

The snowstorm had begun around noon, causing people to head home early. Barely two miles from the airport, in between the Washington Monument and the Pentagon, the 14th Street Bridge was clogged with cars and cabs. Bound for Tampa, Flight 90 was nearly full with passengers enjoying the low prices of the Pan Am–Air Florida fare war. Seventy-one passengers were aboard, plus three infants, three flight attendants, and two pilots.

In the captain's seat Larry Wheaton took in the snowy scene around him and cursed the afternoon of delays. Wheaton, 34 years old, had taken off or landed in ice only eight times in his career as a 737 captain. Before joining Air Florida, he had flown for a little commuter airline in the Florida Keys called Air Sunshine, whose fleet included old DC-3s and whose chief executive officer doubled as a dentist in Key West. Acker, then at Air Florida, had purchased Air Sunshine as a way of gaining airport access in the Keys. For Larry Wheaton and his fellow Air Sunshine pilots, the takeover was a windfall of career opportunity. Suddenly they had the chance to step up from propeller planes to jets and from first-officer rank to captain. At other airlines pilots spent 14 years on average to reach a captain's position on the seniority list; Wheaton had done it in barely one quarter of that time in flying for Air Florida.

Sitting next to Captain Wheaton was his first officer, Roger Pettit, who surveyed the snow and thought about school being canceled the next morning. "I'll bet all the schoolkids are just crapping in their pants here," he said to his captain at one point. "Yahoo!" As an Air Florida pilot Pettit had conducted only two takeoffs or landings in ice; on the final rollout today he would be at the controls.

The two men knew enough about cold weather flying to have the wings deiced. Air Florida's ground operations were handled at National under a contract with American Airlines, which brought the deicing equipment into position. But a replacement nozzle had been installed on the deicing hose, causing water and deicing chemicals to be applied in improper proportions.

When the Jetway was reeled in and Flight 90 finally cleared to push back from the gate, Captain Wheaton didn't want to delay. Unfortunately, the tug that American brought in for the push-back didn't have chains on the tires; instead of pushing the big 737, it simply spun its wheels on the ice. Wheaton told the tug operator that he would use reverse thrust from his engines to back up. The American mechanic on the ramp replied that reverse thrust was not a proper procedure at this time; hot exhaust could melt snow and create ice in any number of locations on the plane, including along the leading edge of the wings. Wheaton cranked up the engines anyway. After more than a minute of reverse thrust, the plane had still not pulled away. A tug fit for the job was finally found.

Flight 90 was ordered into a taxi line behind an apple-red DC-9 flying for New York Air, another new carrier serving National Airport. Captain Wheaton, noting that he still had snow or ice on the wings, pulled as closely as he could behind the New York Air plane to bask in the heat of its engines. He apparently had not read the section of the operating manual that stated that in cold weather pilots must keep even greater distances from the engines of other planes— again, so that snow is not melted and turned to ice.

Flight 90 could have received another shower of deicing fluid, but the flight was now already nearly two hours behind schedule. "Boy, this is a losing battle here on trying to deice those things," said Copilot Pettit. He and the captain could take some comfort from observing that other planes were taking off with a little ice or snow. Even if the men had little experience with these conditions, they were journeyman pilots. They could handle this.

The copilot prepared to take the controls. "Slushy runway," he said to the captain. "Do you want me to do anything special for this or just go for it?"

No, Wheaton said, "unless you got anything special you'd like to do."

The FAA control tower, meanwhile, was bubbling like a coffeepot in an old Maxwell House commercial. It had been only five months since President Reagan had fired the striking controllers, and the tower was severely understaffed. The airport having been closed for part of the day, the controllers had to cram as many planes down as possible, while also relieving the backlog of tardy departures. At the moment an Eastern flight, barely two miles away, was being directed to a landing on the same runway. The controllers were cutting it close.

"Palm 90," crackled the control tower. (Air Florida flights were addressed as Palm, New York Air as Apple.) "Palm 90, taxi into position and hold. Be ready for an immediate." That meant taking off as quickly as possible to clear the runway. "No delay on departure, if you will," the controller emphasized.

"Ladies and gentlemen, we have just been cleared on the runway for takeoff," the cockpit announced. "Flight attendants, please be seated."

The captain released the cockpit controls to his copilot. "Your throttles," he said.

"Okay."

With no time to lose, the copilot throttled the engines even before he had completed his hard turn into the runway. Flight 90 rolled down the runway . . . and rolled, and rolled. It was having trouble getting speed. The 737 seemed sluggish, heavy.

The engine settings were at the highest level deemed prudent, yet still the plane was rolling listlessly. Neither pilot was aware that ice had formed in the engine sensors.

Pettit noticed that the gauges on the cockpit control panel were suddenly haywire. "God, look at that thing!" he cried. "That don't seem right, does it?" The airplane continued lumbering beneath him, like wounded game trying to make a break.

"That's not right!" the copilot again said.

It was up to Captain Wheaton to decide to abort the takeoff. There was still time. But he sat silently as the copilot prepared to pull back on the stick to get the 737 off the runway. Aborting the takeoff in this kind of slush would be risky, particularly with airplanes coming in behind them to land. Indeed, as Wheaton and Pettit tried to make sense of their senseless gauges and their stubbornly slow speed, they heard the Eastern flight behind them acknowledging that it was "over the lights."

At that moment, perilously close to the end of the runway, Air Florida Flight 90 reached the intended takeoff speed of 138 knots. But the speed had been calculated on the presumption that the engines would be performing properly; the engines in reality were severely underperforming, even though the cockpit controls showed them to be at full power.

As Flight 90 lifted laboriously from the runway, the nose pitched up. Had the engines been cranked high enough, it probably wouldn't have mattered, since safety, after all, lay in speed. By the same token, had the wings been free of ice, the improper engine settings wouldn't have been such a problem.

Flight 90 was doomed.

The stall warning sounded. Below lay the ice-covered Potomac, ahead the 14th Street Bridge, clogged with commuters bound for the suburbs of Virginia.

"Larry!" the copilot cried. "We're going down, Larry!"

"I know it."

Twenty-four seconds after leaving the runway, Flight 90 slammed into the bridge. All but five aboard died, most from fractured heads, necks, and chests.

The icy rescue effort, in which one heroic bystander dove into the chilled waters to attempt a rescue, created some of the most dramatic footage seen in the history of prime-time news. The country was left with an unshakable image of a tail fin emblazoned AIR FLORIDA poking through the icy surface of the Potomac.

In the days ahead an estimated 100,000 reservations evaporated.

A few months later the company's chairman suffered a stroke. Donald Lloyd-Jones, who had been nosed out by Bob Crandall in the horse race for the presidency of American two years earlier, was brought in to try to save the company. It was too late. Debt levels were too high for Air Florida to tolerate such a decline in patronage on top of all the damage inflicted by Pan Am. In droves, passengers that Acker had once coaxed from Pan Am to Air Florida were now being coaxed back to Pan Am. In a matter of several weeks some $14 million in revenue vanished from Air Florida, and now there was no stock or futures-trading profit to cushion the blow. Lenders moved to seize the company's assets. The IRS slapped on a tax lien. Air Florida, the Cinderella story of airline deregulation, filed for bankruptcy.

Filling the service void, once again, was Eddie Acker.

Acker had settled quickly into the corner office on the 46th floor of the Pan Am building, the same suite where once, as a Braniff executive, he had negotiated the purchase of the Latin American routes from Juan Trippe. The 46th floor was an extraordinary place, not only for its great, gold-lined route map but for its burled walnut furniture and the commanding southerly view of Manhattan, with the Empire State Building in the foreground and the Hudson River cutting a ribbon in the distance. The various chairmen of Pan Am—not just Trippe and Acker, but also the four hapless chief executives who had served in between—sat so high over New York City that not a single distraction from outside could be heard, other than the occasional roar of a jet airplane.

Though Pan Am was losing $1 million a day, Acker saw no merit in continuing the flight cutbacks that the preceding management had instituted. The alternative was for Pan Am to grow its way out of its problems, which among other advantages was fun. In addition to restoring the East Coast service that helped push Air Florida over the edge, Acker soon added more cities to the route map. Still waving his copy of the *OAG*, he added one after another—Warsaw, Kansas City, Pittsburgh, and others. Before long he was flying a new Pan Am flight to his home in Bermuda. Newly remarried, Acker was urged by his wife to launch service to the French Riviera; when he encountered some internal opposition to the idea, she was incredulous. "Why don't you just *tell* them to do it?" she demanded. (Service to Nice was launched.) Pan Am swarmed into the Caribbean, putting Frank Borman and Eastern on the defensive.

To pay for all this new service, including the new airplanes, Acker simply heaped on additional financial obligations. Acker could always get a plane deal financed. Thus to the liabilities and fixed costs Pan Am had already accumulated—in buying the 747s, then in buying National Airlines, and then in covering the losses generated by both moves—Acker heaved on still more.

For all his impulsiveness—even if he managed Pan Am as a kind of multibillion-dollar amusement—Acker had a guileless and unpretentious quality that made him extremely popular. He would stoop over to pick up cigarette butts on the concourse of Pan Am's Worldport terminal at JFK. He counted his chauffeur among his closest confidants on corporate matters. If he mistrusted the data he was getting from the revenue department, Acker would call his limousine and head off to the administrative offices in suburban New Jersey to flip through hundreds of ticket stubs, returning to Manhattan with his fingertips reddened from the carbon-copied tickets. Moving to improve on-time performance following the purchase of

National Airlines, Acker demanded that airplanes push away from the gate even when passengers were still standing in the aisles. When his critics at one point attacked him for managing by intuition, Acker refused to deny it.

"Intuition is a powerful force," he responded.

Among the surprises greeting Acker when he arrived at Pan Am was the dearth of experienced executives. Years of purges had driven away dozens of top officials. Many of these executives had received absurdly generous severance packages in which they retained not only their salaries but their membership in the Sky Club, high atop the Pan Am building. Luncheons and happy hours at the Sky Club looked like reunions of the departed.

As part of his effort to rebuild management, Acker hired Stephen Wolf, who had spent 15 years at American. Wolf, age 40, had been through the star chamber of Bob Crandall's budget reviews and had seen American brought back from the edge of financial collapse on the strength of relentless cost cutting. Literally within hours of joining Pan Am as a senior vice president, Wolf began boring into budgets and personnel records, looking for ways to stem the red ink.

A few days after Wolf's arrival, Acker was leading him around the Sky Club, making introductions.

"Ed, does he work for us?" Wolf asked after one such introduction.

"No," Acker replied matter-of-factly. "He's gone."

He's gone?

"Ed," Wolf whispered. "I think he's still on the payroll."

But that was Pan Am, a company practically frozen by the inertia of grandeur and tradition, as was evident to another of Acker's recruits, 37-year-old Gerry Gitner, who became a top officer of Pan Am after resigning as the president of People Express. Gitner walked into the Pan Am boardroom to meet the vice presidents reporting to him and was so startled to see them rise from their chairs that he turned around to see who was walking in behind him. After eliminating every cargo airplane in Pan Am's fleet in order to get more passenger planes, Gitner was puzzled to see a few pieces of cargo-handling equipment still remaining at Pan Am's operation in Frankfurt, Germany. "What's that doing here?" Gitner asked. The local manager explained that the equipment was being maintained so it would be ready whenever Pan Am brought back the cargo planes.

Wisely Acker did not rely on outsiders alone to bolster the ranks of senior management. He also promoted Martin R. Shugrue, Jr., a 41-year-old Pan Am lifer, into his inner circle. Shugrue, a former navy fighter pilot, had coincidentally flown the search plane that located the bobbing Gemini 8 capsule with Frank Borman aboard in 1965. A short time later Shugrue became a 707 flight engineer for Pan Am, a position from which he climbed into top management.

Under Acker the three of them—Wolf, Gitner, and Shugrue—worked mightily to restore even a modicum of profitability to Pan Am's operations. When the paperwork crossed Wolf's desk for his own company-sponsored membership in the Sky Club, Wolf refused it; Pan Am veterans were offended by Wolf's display of sanctimony. Gitner, having spent much of his career at Texas International, knew well the value of free advertising; he ordered a new paint job for the fleet, replacing the delicate Bodoni lettering that said "Pan American" with a giant "PAN AM" that stretched the entire height of the fuselage. Shugrue, who had once worked as a hat salesman, became famous for taking key customers out for raucous nights on the town.

But none of Acker's turnaround moves drew more attention than his prices.

Acker began walking into offices literally issuing orders to cut prices, the same way he added new cities to the route map. At one point he walked into a meeting of executives agonizing over whether to match a price cut that Eastern had just instituted and was stunned that they would belabor the issue. "You have no choice!" Acker snapped. Failing to meet a price cut meant losing business, even if only a few passengers. Acker wanted to fly full airplanes even if the flights lost money; he wanted momentum. He wanted people talking about Pan Am's comeback. He wanted to steal back every single bit of business that the previous management had given up, in the United States and overseas.

Even better than matching a price cut was initiating one, offering the customer, as he once told a management group, "the most terrific travel bargain that he has ever probably seen in his life."

Acker also declared a new policy toward Freddie Laker, a cut-rate British charter operator expanding into the scheduled airline busi-

ness over the North Atlantic. Laker, declaring it his mission to provide low-fare international service for "the forgotten man," spent five
years trying to get approval to conduct low-fare flights to the United
States, and finally in 1977 had won the U.S. government's approval,
thanks to the burst of consumerism sweeping Washington. Before
Acker arrived in 1981, Pan Am had arrogantly turned up its nose at
Laker, uninterested in trying to capture the backpacking bargain
customer. Acker, however, harbored no such contempt. Didn't it
make sense, he asked, for Pan Am to go for some of that business?
One of Pan Am's top analysts threw himself into the issue and
quickly concluded that Pan Am could indeed benefit. The analyst
handed over a 16-page report to Acker, who flipped the pages for a
few seconds and promptly ordered prices to London slashed by
nearly 60 percent.

In short order Laker's operation was dead. "I didn't do it to put
him out of business," Ed Acker would later say, "although I didn't
mind if it had that effect."

And then, most outrageous of all, was the "ninety-niner," as
Acker called it—a $99 fare to anywhere in the United States, offered
in the winter of 1982–83. No Saturday stay, no advance purchase restriction—just walk up to the ticket counter and go. Even a coast-to-
coast flight plunged to $99, for the first time on any airline in years.
Every other airline, unwilling to lose a single passenger to Pan Am,
matched the ninety-niner, and although prices climbed back a few
weeks later, profits had been devastated across the industry. In the
first quarter of 1983 the U.S. airline industry racked up the deepest
quarterly deficit in its history, $640 million.

To an extent Acker's sell-at-any-price philosophy was accomplishing its intended effect, pumping blood into Pan Am's sclerotic
arteries and infecting the organization with the spirit of rebuilding.
Lapel buttons popped out saying, I'M AN ACKER BACKER. Acker
began holding massive meetings of managers and eventually com-
panywide meetings, using high-technology satellite linkups that were
still rare for the time. Although no one would ever confuse Acker, a
man of no small elegance and savoir faire, with the abrasive Bob
Crandall, Acker took to giving the same kind of locker-room pep
talks. After Frank Borman of Eastern had snatched Braniff's Latin
American routes—a prize Acker made no secret of coveting for him-

self—Acker wrote a letter to Pan Am employees declaring, "We should all dedicate ourselves to making sure that Eastern regrets that they ever obtained those routes." Speaking to a management group in Miami he vowed, "We are going to be leaders in the future. We are not going to take a back seat to anybody because of their pricing! We are not going to let Eastern Air Lines run us out of any more markets. We are going to start running *them* out of markets! . . . We will survive and Pan American will become the finest, most respected airline in the world today, just as it was 15 or 20 years ago when it introduced 747s."

Despite its palliative effect on morale, there were some grave problems with Acker's strategy. As Bob Crandall had taught the industry a few years earlier, in the late 1970s, slashing prices was a worthwhile strategy so long as some seats were still sold at full price. The First Rule of Airline Economics demanded selling otherwise empty seats at any price—but not every seat on the airplane. Marginal pricing was a worthy strategy for the last seat sold but not for the first. Selling everything so cheap not only reduced the total revenue attainable for any flight but also debased the value of the product in the mind of the consuming public. Pan Am was flying more seats and taking in less per seat. It could not survive by cutting back limousines and Sky Club memberships. Something major had to give—and that meant asking employees to give back some of what they had won in the regulated era.

Acker did not have the time or the capital to cut average costs with b-scales, as American was doing. Nor was there time for an imaginative "variable earnings plan," such as Borman had used successfully for so many years at Eastern. Pan Am, Acker resolved, had to whack hard immediately: 10 percent had to be cut from everyone's wages, he determined, to avert Pan Am's failure.

For the delicate job of negotiating with the unions, Acker chose Marty Shugrue. Shugrue already had plenty of experience dealing with organized labor at Pan Am, which was no mean task. Pan Am's workers had never been the highest paid, thanks to Juan Trippe's view that working for such an institution was reward in itself. As a consequence Pan Am became the most heavily unionized airline in America. Even the secretaries were members of the Teamsters. Featherbedding was legion. Because only Teamsters could operate forklifts and only members of the Transport Workers Union could operate belt loaders, the act of horizontally removing an aircraft part from an overhead shelf and then vertically lowering it to the ground required two people and two machines. The merger with National Airlines only heaped on a new layer of work-rule complexity.

If anybody could go to the unions for concessions and come out alive, however, it was Shugrue. He was the son of a union beat cop in Providence, Rhode Island, and had been a Pan Am union member himself in his flying days. He was still on drinking terms with some of the most powerful labor leaders in the industry; one, the head of the Transport Workers Union, was a close family friend.

Ten percent, Shugrue begged—a 10 percent cut to save Pan Am. The unions answered that they would rather strike.

Shugrue knew a strike would be curtains. Although Pan Am would save on fuel and salaries in a strike, there would be no relief on the interest expense. If a strike shut down the company, Shugrue knew, Pan Am would be dead in a matter of days.

The unions finally said they would come to terms—on one big condition. Pan Am had to promise to restore the 10 percent cut by the first day of 1985, now less than three years away, with no bargaining required. An automatic "snapback" would have to occur.

Acker and his aides were in a serious bind. Would the fare wars abate within three years? Who could tell? But it was clear that the next three years promised no relief from upstart airlines, particularly on Pan Am's price-sensitive leisure routes. Acker and Shugrue knew there was no way the company could reasonably hope to restore those pay cuts three years out. Yet Pan Am needed the 10 percent concessions now in order to survive.

Shugrue felt as if he had a gun to his head, so he did what any desperate person does. He lied.

Snapback? Sure, he told the unions. Absolutely. It's in the bag.

With the concessions in place Acker went back to the things he loved: cutting fares, adding new destinations, and acquiring airplanes. The snapbacks were a couple of long years away. He would worry about them then, he decided—unaware that a violent conflict elsewhere in the industry would by then reach Pan Am's doorstep as well.

CHAPTER 9

CONTINENTAL DIVIDE

Frank Lorenzo was a restless man. He imagined himself a builder, a creator, perhaps to airlines what Carnegie was to steel or Rockefeller to oil. By the early 1980s he had, in fact, come much further than anyone would have expected of someone growing up the child of Spanish immigrants in Queens. He had taken control of Texas International and had more than tripled its size. He had created New York Air; though struggling for landing slots and pushed to the bottom of the screen on American's Sabre network, New York Air was still flying and still stealing passengers. Lorenzo had established a new holding company, Texas Air, which was flush with the winnings from his takeover attempt against National Airlines.

Yet all he had built was still no empire by airline standards. Texas International, for all its growth, had risen from the 19th largest airline in the industry only to the 15th. New York Air was a savvy niche operator but no powerhouse. Altogether Lorenzo had a measly 37 jets. He was still the ham in somebody else's sandwich. It was time again to go shopping for an airline. The target this time was Continental Airlines.

Lorenzo had approached Continental previously only to get the cold shoulder from the aging founder, Bob Six. This time Lorenzo would not give him such an opportunity. This time Lorenzo would go into the open market and simply buy a chunk of Continental's stock, then get a tender offer rolling. Although he'd be able to buy virtually every share in the company, Lorenzo resolved to limit his ownership to just under 51 percent, enough to give him control of the entire company. On February 6, 1981, he stepped into the open market and purchased nearly a million of Continental's shares. Then he called Bob Six.

Once again the legendary Six, semiretired now, sent Lorenzo packing. Lorenzo, he said, should be talking to the newly appointed president of Continental Airlines, a man whose name made him appear destined for success in aviation: Alvin Lindbergh Feldman.

Though born in the year of Lindbergh's Paris flight, Al Feldman did not make airlines or flying his first choice in careers. Feldman was an engineer from Akron, a whiz kid who worked for Aerojet General Corporation, a subsidiary of General Tire & Rubber Company, whose controlling shareholders in turn had long held a major interest in Denver-based Frontier Airlines. One of the many local-service operators that had sprung up after World War II, Frontier served dozens of small communities smack in the middle of the Middle West from Denver Stapleton Airport; it had been slowly slipping for years. Aerojet General had finally dispatched Feldman to Denver in 1971 with orders to liquidate the airline. Feldman, however, quickly grew smitten with the airline business and asked for the chance to resuscitate Frontier instead. His bosses back in Akron agreed.

Feldman stepped up passenger amenities (including smoked almonds, which caused people to order more drinks) and rebuilt Frontier around a hub system. He also inspired Frontier's employees to greater heights of performance with a mixture of aggression, bluntness, and sincerity. Feldman hung an ugly picture of a purple vulture in the company's boardroom bearing the inscription, "Don't just sit there—go kill something!" He structured the company so that every employee was involved in either sales or operations, explaining, "If you're not doing one, you must be doing the other." Under Feldman, Frontier was one of the nation's most consistently profitable airlines.

When he jumped to Continental in 1980 to assume the management chores from Bob Six, Feldman threw himself into his work, all the more so after his wife died of cancer. Fifty-two years old, six foot three, handsomely graying at the temples, he remained at his desk during lunch, eating a coach-class meal prepared on the Continental flightline. Feldman, thoroughly absorbed, was in love with Continental Airlines.

But Lorenzo's maneuvers, it would appear, were about to take the company away from Al Feldman. The tender offer was like a magnet around iron filings: within days Lorenzo owned 48.5 percent of Continental's stock, with money he borrowed in part by pledging Continental's airplanes as collateral. Al Feldman observed dejectedly, "It's the first time in my life I've ever lost."

Noted for the Frontier turnaround and for a noteworthy if brief tenure at Continental, Feldman suddenly became the hottest free agent around. Marvin Davis, having recently acquired Twentieth Century–Fox, discussed bringing him aboard as chief executive. The directors of Pan Am were looking for a new chief executive officer (to fill the job ultimately given to Ed Acker) and asked Feldman if he would be interested.

Feldman, however, soon had reason to say no to his suitors: the employees of Continental had come forward with a plan to mount a rival takeover attempt, with Feldman as their leader.

Continental's employees were wearing lapel buttons that said, FRANK WHO?, but in fact they knew only too well. Lorenzo had been vilified in the union campaign against the creation of New York Air. It was also common knowledge to union people that Lorenzo in his early days at Texas International had taken one of the longest strikes in airline history. Ominously, Lorenzo had filed a legal statement in connection with the proposed takeover saying that if he established control of Continental, "it will be necessary to renegotiate existing collective bargaining agreements." By this time "renegotiate" was an often-used word in the Lorenzo lexicon—a word whose first five letters made it a cousin of the less dignified "renege." The employees of Continental were beside themselves at the idea. They had *contracts,* after all.

A group of Continental pilots came up with the ingenious idea of using an employee stock ownership plan, or ESOP, to block Lorenzo. Continental would issue enough new shares to the employees' group to dilute Lorenzo's position safely below the level of control. The employees began to search for financing, while Feldman penned a letter to Lorenzo. "I must tell you," Feldman wrote, "that each day more of our employees come forward to manifest their resolve to reject your bid for control of Continental. They are determined to oppose you with every means at their disposal. In the face of their determination, it may not be possible to merge our two airlines."

Together, Feldman thought, he and the employees of Continental just might have a chance of beating Lorenzo.

Lorenzo was bothered by the FRANK WHO? buttons. "When you own 48.5 percent of a company, it means certain things," he said. "It means you get certain rights." He was offended to see Continental employees turn "goggle-eyed," as he put it, when he stepped on a Continental flight. "Listen, I've checked my horns with my luggage," he told them.

Lorenzo needed a point man to carry out his takeover moves, and the assignment went to Phil Bakes. Once more Bakes assumed his crusade mind-set, just as when he had campaigned for deregulation or had lobbied for the slots with which to launch New York Air. To Bakes victory was all the more important because Lorenzo had given him so much responsibility and authority in the wake of Don Burr's resignation. Bakes resolved to prove himself worthy of Lorenzo's trust.

Bakes's opportunity came when Continental's annual shareholders meeting occurred in the midst of the takeover battle. As Bakes entered the ballroom in Denver's fabulous Brown Palace Hotel, a throng of angry Continental employees was noisily demonstrating with picket signs: "Don't bank on Frank. . . . You can't buy pride for peanuts." The throng marched into the ballroom, many in their flight uniforms, looking like the military, and Bakes was suddenly filled with dread. He was the personal embodiment of the enemy that had brought these hundreds of people together. It was a mob scene. What if they lose control? he wondered.

Feldman, who was chairing the meeting, knew that he had to give Bakes the opportunity to speak. Bakes, after all, was carrying proxies for as many shares as everyone else in the room put together. Bakes stifled his fear, rose, and asked to be recognized.

"I am the authorized representative of Texas International Airlines," he declared. Bakes then placed a motion on the floor to block the employee takeover.

Silently the crowd around him looked on with contempt. "Thank you, Mr. Bakes," Feldman said evenly. "The chair rules your motion out of order." A thunderous, jeering ovation went up from the crowd.

Bakes stood stoically. "Mr. Chairman, I move to appeal the ruling . . ."

"The chair's rulings are not appealable."

Bakes vainly invoked *Roberts Rules of Order.* "Point of order . . ."

"The chair's rulings are not appealable."

After further fruitless protests Bakes finally sat down.

Up to the microphone went a short, beefy man with a mustache. It was Dennis Higgins, who had been a pilot for Texas International since the time it was flying DC-3s as Trans-Texas. Higgins had no standing to speak at the meeting—this was a Continental shareholders' meeting, and he made no claim to owning any Continental shares—but the fix was in, and Higgins was warmly received by the partisan, anti-Lorenzo crowd. After introducing himself, Higgins put on his glasses and read his speech, written out on a single sheet of paper.

> We, the pilots of Texas International, have come to this meeting at personal risk to tell you some hard truths about dealing with Frank Lorenzo. The truth is this: Mr. Lorenzo *is* a brilliant man, perhaps a market manipulator without peer. We are here, however, to tell you that he is also a man who has done nothing to show that he cares one whit for the 3,400 Texas International employees who work for him. An airline is a service business, only as good as the people who make the service work. . . . We are compelled to report that Mr. Lorenzo's current employees are a dispirited group.

When, mercifully for Bakes, the meeting ended, he was thronged by microphones and television cameras. Once the interviewing ordeal was over, he approached Continental founder Bob Six, who had been seated in the ballroom with his wife, Audrey Meadows. Bakes simply wanted to shake Six's hand. Six, though gruff, was not ungentlemanly. His actress wife, however, cast a chilling glare at Bakes through the entire encounter.

• • •

Lorenzo and Bakes were much more worried than they could publicly let on. If successful, the takeover by Continental employees would be a showstopper for Texas Air. If Texas Air acquired more shares on the open market, Continental could simply create additional shares in itself and sell them to employees, diluting Lorenzo to a level below majority control. Texas Air had about $100 million already invested in Continental stock. If the employee buyout went through, Texas Air would be a minority shareholder in a company that was majority-controlled by employees who were openly hostile to Frank Lorenzo.

Then, when Lorenzo and Bakes least expected it, victory came from Continental's own home state of California. The state's chief securities regulator ruled that Continental could not issue millions of new shares to employees without the approval of all *existing* shareholders. Texas Air controlled virtually half of all existing shares and could doubtless get the few additional shares necessary to checkmate the plan. Al Feldman and the employees were doomed unless they could get the California legislature to override the state securities commissioner.

Bakes flew to Sacramento and swung into action. He thought he had seen it all in politics—the lobbying, the logrolling, the trade-offs, the quid pro quos—but he had never seen anything like this. "It made you feel dirty," he later explained. Someone representing a state assemblyman came to Bakes's hotel room and requested stock options in exchange for his vote. "Get the fuck out of here," Bakes said. In this sea of influence peddling Bakes tapped one of his old Kennedy connections, getting an assemblywoman named Maxine Waters (later to become a leading member of the U.S. House of Representatives) to give an impassioned floor speech against the employee takeover effort.

Bakes's campaign succeeded. The measure to override the state securities commissioner died. Continental, it appeared, was nearly in the bag.

Then late one night in Washington about two weeks later an associate in one of Lorenzo's law firms was hanging around the Senate chambers as Congress debated President Reagan's massive tax-cut legislation. Standing in a hallway, the young lawyer overheard someone say that Sen. Dennis DeConcini of Arizona had discreetly slipped a rider into the Reagan tax bill that would allow the Continental ESOP to go forward. Senator DeConcini, it turned out, had a brother-in-law who was a Continental pilot.

Bakes returned to action, only this time on the familiar turf of Capitol Hill. The employee takeover had become a cause célèbre, and Bakes faced an even greater battle than that in California two weeks earlier. Capitol Hill was teeming with uniformed Continental pilots promoting the virtues of employee ownership and the evils of Frank Lorenzo, adding to the lobbying confusion surrounding the major tax bill.

Both sides zeroed in on the House and Senate members serving on the conference committee pounding the final tax bill into shape, but the most important target was Dan Rostenkowski. The chairman of the House Ways and Means Committee, Rostenkowski was also heading the conference committee, as befitted him on a major piece of tax legislation. Lorenzo, having hired the Washington law firm of Robert Strauss, the former Democratic Party chairman, was one of the few people who got in to see Rostenkowski. Lorenzo was also seen huddling in the Senate cafeteria with Sen. Lloyd Bentsen (later to become treasury secretary under President Clinton), causing the pilots' hearts to sink.

All day and night it went on. At 2:30 A.M. on the final night, outside the conference committee room, Bakes and Lorenzo collapsed next to each other at the bottom of a marble staircase. They would know shortly whether they had blown $100 million or were on the verge of finally bringing off the first hostile takeover of an airline in modern times. They were frightened. They locked gazes. Bakes had never felt closer to Lorenzo.

About a half hour later it was over. The DeConcini rider was defeated: Texas Air had won again. Although it was theoretically still possible for the employees' buyout to succeed so long as the financing remained in place, Lorenzo and Bakes had the upper hand now.

Al Feldman was part of a small group of high-level executives and professionals who enjoyed adventurous two-week vacations with their families out west each summer, often at a remote and exclusive fishing camp in Idaho. The vacationers were Feldman's dearest friends. One was Dick Ferris, the president of United, who had grown close to Feldman as they battled jointly in favor of airline deregulation. Another was Travis Reed, an aircraft broker and deal maker who had served as undersecretary of commerce in the Ford administration. Both Feldman, newly widowed, and Reed, then unmarried, were living in Los Angeles; they began spending many of their evenings together.

Over dinner, night after night, Feldman told Travis Reed how much he disliked Lorenzo and his tactics and how desperately he wanted to save Continental. "He was emotionally 100 percent immersed in it," Reed would recall years later. "It was a battle to the death." As the battle dragged on, Reed watched Feldman go from his usual two drinks or so to five—"big drinks," as Reed would later describe them. Feldman became obsessed with fending off Lorenzo. But strangely, in the period when the employee takeover received its devastating setbacks in Sacramento and Washington, Reed observed a conspicuous change in Feldman's attitude. His intensity had diminished. His anxiety had melted away.

Then President Reagan fired the air traffic controllers. Four days later, a Sunday, while everyone else in the airline industry scrambled over their flight cutbacks, more bad news arrived at Continental headquarters. The nine banks that had agreed to finance the employee takeover were withdrawing their commitment. The airline industry, the banks said, was in too much turmoil.

A group of employee leaders met with Feldman in his office. They were planning a trip to Sacramento—one last-ditch effort to lobby for reversal of the fatal ruling by the securities commission a few weeks earlier. Feldman told the takeover leaders not to bother; all hope was lost. The employees decided to go anyway.

Feldman reviewed a press release announcing the collapse of the financing. He then left his office, only to return later that evening carrying a package. Shortly before 6 P.M. a security guard stepped into Feldman's office, asking how long he planned to work. "A few hours," Feldman answered.

Phil Bakes decided that if the Continental employees were going to drag him back to Sacramento for one more round, then Frank Lorenzo could show up this time. Although Lorenzo had joined in the lobbying in Washington, he had resisted participating in the nastier and much lengthier legislative battle in California. Bakes felt strongly that Lorenzo needed to appear at a press conference in the California capital. Continental was headquartered in Los Angeles, after all. Lorenzo's name had achieved too much prominence for him to miss out on this, the last political skirmish in the long battle to vanquish the employee takeover. Lorenzo flew into Sacramento late on the same Sunday that the employees' financing had fallen through.

The next morning Bakes arrived first for breakfast and sat down to await Lorenzo. A group of the Continental pilots, making the trip from Los Angeles over the discouragement of Al Feldman, were having a breakfast meeting in the same hotel. One of the pilot leaders approached Bakes with a look of devastation on his face.

"I've just gotten word," he told Bakes earnestly. "Al Feldman has killed himself."

Bakes stood in disbelief.

The other members of the Continental group were filing in from their conference room. Another one of the pilot leaders saw Bakes. He thrust his finger in the air.

"You killed him!" the pilot cried. "You killed him!"

Bakes was still in a state of shock when Lorenzo arrived for breakfast a moment later.

"Frank," Bakes said. "Al Feldman's dead. He killed himself."

Bakes watched the color vanish from Lorenzo's face. Lorenzo, it suddenly appeared, was losing his breath. He had to sit down. Then "Frank was on the next plane out of Sacramento," Bakes would later say.

Alvin Lindbergh Feldman had shot himself with a Smith & Wesson .38 special purchased two weeks earlier, on the same night that his friend Travis Reed had noticed an easing of his countenance. Feldman had not been able to pick up the gun until California's 14-day waiting period had lapsed. According to the coroner's report, Feldman had been "despondent since the death of his wife" and "concerned over attempts by Texas International to take over Continental."

Al Feldman was buried near San Diego, with the members of his summer fishing group serving among his pallbearers. As they carried the remains of their friend, Travis Reed heard an anguished cry behind him. He turned to see Dick Ferris of United Airlines striking the top of the casket with a fist, tears streaming down his cheeks. "Damn you, Al!" Ferris cried. "Why did you have to do this?"

In all the attention that Feldman's death received, few were aware that the former head of Mohawk Airlines had likewise taken his own life nearly a decade earlier, also in the midst of a takeover encounter with Francisco Lorenzo.

Lorenzo had purchased just enough stock, 50.9 percent, to assume majority control of Continental. He named himself and two others to the company's board of directors. One was Phil Bakes. The other was John Robson, who, as CAB chairman, had played such a prominent role in bringing Lorenzo's peanuts fares to fruition. With Alfred Kahn also sitting on the board of New York Air, Lorenzo now counted two former CAB chairmen among his trophies.

The Texas Air representatives attended their first meeting of the Continental board in December 1981, giving Lorenzo his first opportunity to look closely under the hood of the company he had acquired. The senior managers of Continental, still shell-shocked from the takeover fight, conducted a presentation. Continental, they projected, would lose $60 million in 1982—twice the loss Lorenzo had expected. It got worse: Continental, it turned out, was in imminent jeopardy of defaulting on its borrowing agreements. Amid the distraction and expense of the takeover battle, it appeared, all financial discipline had been lost.

At one point during the meeting John Robson observed that there was no cash flow forecast, a projection commonly shared with directors. Robson, however, could piece together the data from the other reports the directors had before them. "Judging from these projections," Robson finally said, "the company is running out of cash."

"Yes," one of the Continental executives answered matter-of-factly. "The company will probably be out of cash in February." That was two months away.

It was time, as Bakes would later recall, to go into "action mode." Fifteen percent of Continental's workforce was fired. A banking group was told that they would have to relax their repayment terms. Unions were called to emergency meetings and were informed that they would have to make concessions quickly; though the machinists and flight attendants balked, the most costly employees—the pilots—agreed to fly more hours and give up $90 million in wages they had already been promised over the following two years.

In addition to retreating on Continental's labor contracts, Lorenzo began to back away from some of the explicit promises made in the heat of the takeover battle. He had, for instance, assured Continental employees that their operations would not be dissolved into Texas International's. He put the same promise in writing in a letter to a member of the California Assembly: "The fact is," Lorenzo had written, "we do not even intend to merge the two companies, but rather plan to operate Continental as a separate airline." Now that he controlled the company, Lorenzo ordered it enmeshed with Texas International after all, causing still more layoffs.

Lorenzo knew he had a good reason to risk the dangers inherent in the merger of any two airlines, a reason he often described with the phrase "critical mass." An airline didn't necessarily have to be big in overall terms (although that had its virtues), but it had to be big in its principal operating locations. It was on the same principle that Bob Crandall had pulled airplanes out of the Northeast to concentrate them in Dallas, where the Sabre computer system was directing more and more passengers into American's planes. Lorenzo was eager to pull Texas International's planes *out* of Dallas, where they stood in Crandall's path, and concentrate them elsewhere—namely Houston and Denver.

The entire fleet was painted in Continental's trademark white, eradicating the identity of Texas International Airlines forever. Lorenzo now commanded the nation's seventh largest domestic airline, behind only the Big Four, Delta, and Northwest. As ingeniously as he had financed and assembled it, actually operating it exceeded Lorenzo's ken. He needed to find a new president; Crandall had already turned him down.

It was the moment Phil Bakes had been waiting for. In his two years with Lorenzo, Bakes had procured the landing slots with which to establish New York Air and had succeeded in bringing the seizure of Continental to closure. Now 36 years old, Bakes thought he at last had an opportunity to run something.

But on a flight to a fund-raising expedition in Boston, Lorenzo broke the bad news to Bakes. "We're going to be announcing a new president and chief operating officer of Continental," Lorenzo said, and the choice was not Bakes.

Bakes was devastated. Who could be more worthy? he wondered. The choice, Lorenzo said, was Steve Wolf, a senior vice president of Pan Am.

Steve Wolf? From a loser company like that? Bakes was unable to contain his anger. His face was ashen.

"You're just not ready yet," Lorenzo said.

Stephen Michael Wolf was considered a peculiar personality in airline circles—aloof, formal, even stiff—but he was also known as hyperattentive to the details of running an airline. Growing up in East Oakland in the 1940s, he displayed an uncommonly precocious compulsion for order: his mother would later tell people that when she put food on the tray of his high chair, the toddler Stephen would instruct her precisely where he wanted each dish served. "Put it here!" he would command, jabbing his finger against the tray. "Put it here!"

Wolf played football as a kid, sprouting on his way to six foot six. But his career in athletics was cut short by a family trauma when he was 15. His father walked out, leaving Stephen to provide for his mother and two younger sisters. An awesome sense of responsibility had struck him at a most vulnerable age. The boy was suddenly the man of the house.

He arranged a special school schedule of four hours a day so he could work full-time at Davidson & Licht, the jewelry store on Broadway in Oakland. He swept up, ran errands, wrapped gifts, and polished silver—working with, and around, tiny things.

Wolf moved on to much tougher, higher-paying jobs, which invariably had something to do with the transportation of things. He landed on a loading dock at United Parcel Service, soon becoming a supervisor even though he was a part-time employee, going to a city junior college and later to San Francisco State on the side. During the summer months he spent four hours a day in school, then six hours at UPS, and then another four hours working a second job: unloading railroad boxcars at a Fisher Body plant, packing trailers at a trucking firm, or handling cargo along the docks. Over the course of a few summers Wolf worked as a member of the Teamsters, the Stevedores, and the Auto Workers' unions.

A career in cargo might not have been the first choice for most graduates in the mid-1960s, but Wolf was thrilled to take a trainee position at American Airlines' cargo operation in San Francisco. Expected to reach a supervisory position in 12 months, he made it in 12 weeks. From there he moved to Cleveland and then to New York, where in a hangar at JFK he caught the attention of American's newly appointed chairman, Al Casey, whose own background included working in railroad freight. At the time that Casey was propelling Bob Crandall along the fast track at American, he also took Wolf under his wing. Soon Wolf was working on the passenger side of the business, doing the same with people that he had been doing with boxes and crates.

A conspicuous individual to begin with because of his towering height, Wolf took great care in his personal appearance. He had a thick, immaculately trimmed mustache and wore bright red suspenders, which only exaggerated his height. When American produced a sensitivity training film for flight attendants in the late 1960s, Wolf was shown walking down a New York City street wearing a trenchcoat, head and shoulders over the crowd, in a scene intended to depict the hustle and bustle of modern life. Years later Wolf would take delight in recalling that the soundtrack music behind his appearance on the film was the romantic theme from the movie *Midnight Cowboy.*

Though intensely methodical and results-oriented, Wolf began to lose steam professionally at American, and his rapid ascent began to slow. Some of his peers had moved ahead of him. He urgently wanted a promotion and a raise but was turned down for both. Wolf left to go to work for Ed Acker at Pan Am, where he was stung by the bug that bit so many in aviation. He wanted to run something.

An offer from Frank Lorenzo to become president of Continental Airlines was his opportunity, and Wolf leapt at it. A short time later, sitting down with a reporter from *Business Week,* Wolf boasted of what a brilliant team he and Lorenzo made. Lorenzo, said Wolf, "has very profound financial strengths, and I'm a very good operating guy. I think we balance each other superbly."

Once at Continental headquarters in Los Angeles, Wolf scheduled both the airline and himself to perfection. He conducted one-on-one meetings as he drove to the dry cleaner. People on the operating side of the airline, where details particularly mattered, were deeply impressed with Wolf's mastery of intricacy. But to others Wolf seemed so compulsively attentive to detail that he could not begin to see the scope of Continental's problems. With the financial crisis worsening, Lorenzo at one point rushed into Wolf's office for an emergency consultation, only to find the president sprawled on the floor studying upholstery samples. On another occasion a marketing executive looked on as Wolf tried to explain to someone else the exact shade of paper stock he desired for Continental's timetables. "I want it to be this color," Wolf barked, stabbing his finger against a beige telephone receiver. "*This* color, understand?"

The people around him thought Wolf was not above an occasional round of office politics. One Sunday night Lorenzo, at home in Houston, called corporate headquarters in Los Angeles as Wolf and his aides were immersed in making budget cuts for the year. Lorenzo was unhappy to learn that Bakes, now a senior vice president, was absent from the meeting. Lorenzo tracked down Bakes at home. "Why aren't you at the company?" he demanded. Bakes told Lorenzo that Wolf had not informed him of the meeting. It was a pure power play, Bakes thought. Wolf was cutting him out.

Wolf did not recognize that he slighted Bakes at some peril to himself. Though junior to Wolf on the organization chart, Bakes was a card-carrying member of Lorenzo's inner circle, which Wolf was not. Lorenzo, in fact, was regularly conducting end runs around Wolf, talking privately to Bakes about what was happening in the company. Because Wolf seemed to make a point of introducing himself as Stephen, Lorenzo made a point of calling him Steve, with a whiff of sarcasm.

Wolf before long could not avoid sensing that things were not entirely right for him at Continental. The issue came into focus when Lorenzo announced that Continental was moving its headquarters, notwithstanding his promises. "Contrary to what has been speculated," Lorenzo had said in a letter, "Texas International has no plans to move the headquarters of Continental out of the state of California." But months later he told executives in Los Angeles to start packing for Texas International's hometown of Houston. Wolf, preparing for the move, decided it would be wise to sign a month-to-month lease on an apartment in Houston. He even rented furniture. Wolf could sense trouble ahead.

And indeed enemies old and new alike, sensing Lorenzo's weaknesses, had begun to circle.

Sitting in his office overlooking Newark's North Terminal, Don Burr read aloud from *Business Week* to his companion and fellow People Express founder, Melrose Dawsey. Stephen Wolf was quoted as saying how well he and Lorenzo worked together. "That guy is gonna last a month," Burr cackled. "Frank will kill this guy."

The separate launchings of People Express and New York Air had only intensified Burr's rivalry with Lorenzo. When a fleet of 20 secondhand 727s came on the market through the liquidation of Braniff, Burr expressed interest in acquiring them, but Lorenzo, it turned out, was eagerly seeking the same planes. Burr was convinced that Lorenzo was making a play for the airplanes simply to be a spoiler, to drive up the price that People Express had to pay—"one more of Frank's deals to frustrate what we were doing," he would later claim. But Burr moved quickly and nailed down the 727s, some of which, he decided, would be scheduled to fly from Newark to Houston, piercing the heart of Lorenzo's new Continental hub.

Burr could not have chosen a more sensitive spot on which to inflict pain. Houston–New York was among the most vital routes in the Continental system and one that Lorenzo essentially had all to himself. Other airlines served the same pair of cities only with connecting service—Delta through Atlanta, for instance. The established airlines were lazily raking in as much as $320 for a one-way ticket.

In addition to the economic imperative for Burr to jump into Houston, there was also the emotional one. As Burr would say a decade later, "Maybe I thought it would be a wonderful way to jab Frank." He determined to swamp Lorenzo with low prices—$69 one way—and massive service: 727s jammed with seats, initially three flights a day, then up to eight flights a day . . . 1,600 seats every day, swarming into Lorenzo country, each in a plane bearing the double facial profile of People Express.

The confrontation was all the more pleasurable for being played

out in the old headquarters town of Texas International, where Burr
and Lorenzo had once been so fast. Many of the renegade Texas International employees now working at People Express still had connections to Houston. Melrose Dawsey, who had been Frank's
secretary back in the old Texas International days, had a child who
spent time in Houston with her ex-husband.

Delightedly Burr awarded Dawsey the privilege of traveling to
Houston to conduct the press conference announcing the invasion.
Lorenzo would learn from his former secretary, now with Burr in
Newark, that People Express was attacking Continental.

In Dallas Bob Crandall's people were taking "screen science" to a
new level of sophistication. And with Frank Lorenzo—Mr. Peanuts
Fares himself—taking control of Continental, they had a new target
in their sights.

This much was apparent to Dick Murray of the Sabre staff one
day when he took a phone call from Continental. Lorenzo's new airline had just posted discount fares in a number of cities. But the discounts on 49 particular routes were not showing up on Sabre
terminals in travel agencies across America.

That didn't seem possible to Murray. "There's been a screwup
somewhere," he told Continental. But when he investigated, Murray
learned that the discounts had been deliberately withheld from the
Sabre network on routes where American competed. Murray later
saw an internal memo that cited "suppression of all Continental
fares" at the discount level between the 49 city pairs.

Later a Sabre staffer sheepishly approached Murray and laid a file
on his desk. She said she had been directed to work on a program
that would automatically suppress any discount fares loaded into the
Sabre mainframes. The program would withhold the data from travel
agents long enough to give American time to study whether it wished
to match the fare cuts, thus blocking the competition from stealing a
march on American. "She had been sworn to secrecy," Murray
would later recall.

When he was denied a promotion and assigned to report to one of
his rivals, Murray decided it was time to leave American. He scheduled a meeting with Bob Crandall and informed him that he had an
offer from Lorenzo to join Continental. "Jesus Christ! Don't go to

Continental," Crandall said. "We're going to put them out of business!"

Lorenzo had hired Murray to try to make something of Continental's modest in-house computer reservation system. Lorenzo understood as well as anyone the power of massive computer reservations systems in the airline industry. With Dick Murray joining his team, Lorenzo could at least begin to investigate the potential of expanding the Continental system into a more meaningful force—a counterweight, perhaps, to the passenger-gathering power of Sabre and Apollo (and to a much lesser extent the networks that TWA and Eastern were also installing in travel agencies). Above all Lorenzo wanted to join in the practice of collecting fees from other airlines for electronically processing reservations made in their behalf; he bitterly resented having to pay the tax that Bob Crandall and Dick Ferris collected for every reservation that their networks handled for his airlines.

After Murray had joined Continental, a subpoena arrived in connection with a federal investigation of computer reservations systems. Murray came forward, regaling Lorenzo with tales of tweaking and bias and fare suppression and stolen data at Bob Crandall's American—some of the tricks having been directed against Lorenzo's airlines. Lorenzo suddenly thought he had a smoking gun with Bob Crandall's fingerprints all over it.

The next thing he knew, Murray was in a room full of Justice Department lawyers, with a stenographer taking down every word.

While Dick Murray toiled over computer problems and Steve Wolf moved to consolidate the hub operations in Houston and Denver, Frank Lorenzo was busy trying to keep Continental's finances from collapsing. Continental by 1983 was losing money faster than ever. Though the recession had lifted and fuel prices were beginning to abate, a new fare war had erupted, much bigger than anything yet to hit the airline industry, triggered by Ed Acker's "ninety-niner" at Pan Am. Matching the Pan Am fares creamed Continental. Thankfully for Continental, Lorenzo had not lost his touch on Wall Street; he funded the losses with underwritings. In addition a major insurance company in Houston, American General Corporation, invested $40 million in options on Continental stock, declaring that it believed the company, and the industry, to be strong turnaround bets. "Frank laid on all the charm he knew how to lay on," Phil Bakes would recall.

But even Lorenzo could not continue funding Continental's losses forever. The only way to reverse the tide of red ink was to attack the single largest controllable area of costs: labor. That was now Phil Bakes's department.

Though still resentful that Wolf had been given the presidency, Bakes was delighted that Lorenzo gave him the responsibility for attacking Continental's labor costs. That, Bakes was sure, was where the company's future would be decided. Indeed, in a series of meetings after the July 4th weekend in 1983, Continental's bankers agreed to relax further the terms of the company's debt, but only if the company cut back severely on its labor rates. Flying in for those meetings on a clear night over New York City, Bakes had a breathtaking view of all the Independence Day pyrotechnics below—a fitting metaphor, he thought, for the fireworks doubtless to come.

The average Continental pilot was earning about $90,000 a year, including benefits—not a king's ransom in 1982 and 1983, perhaps, except that he received that pay for an average of about 11 days' duty per month. The pilots had already agreed to significant cutbacks, but in Bakes's view their concessions had bought the company only a little more time. The pilots would have to be pressured to give up much more, along with the other union groups.

Continental's flight attendants earned salaries and benefits averaging $37,300 and enjoyed work rules that Bakes considered reprehensible—large hotel rooms with double beds on overnight trips, for instance.

But the most immediate labor-cost issue involved Continental's mechanics, who pulled down nearly $40,000 a year. Bakes had had some acquaintance with their union, the IAM, during his Kennedy years. The IAM was so enamored of Teddy Kennedy and his pro-labor stance that it donated the use of a private airplane for the ill-fated Kennedy presidential campaign. Such loyalties didn't mean a thing now, of course.

The Continental machinists were working under an expired contract, which made them the first targets for deep cuts. The talks on a new contract were proceeding perfectly rationally, with the prospect of some give-and-take. But the atmosphere at Continental changed overnight when Charlie Bryan and the machinists' union at Eastern crushed Frank Borman, walking away with a 32 percent increase. After Bryan's triumph in Miami the Continental machinists didn't want to hear a word about the financial problems of Continental. They wanted the same contract from Lorenzo that Bryan had won from Borman.

Without bothering to consult Steve Wolf, who was still his boss, Bakes called together his own subordinates and declared that Continental would take on the machinists. "We've got to prepare for a strike!" Bakes announced.

There was indeed virtue in taking a strike. Under the peculiarities of airline labor law, if the machinists went on strike, the company could replace them immediately with scab workers—and do so on whatever terms the company chose. A strike would cure Continental's cost problem, at least insofar as it involved the machinists.

On August 12, 1983, Frank Lorenzo took the machinists strike that Frank Borman had refused to accept. It was, for Lorenzo and Bakes, far from a disaster. The pilots traipsed through the machinists' picket lines. The middle management groups at Continental and Texas International, not yet fully comfortable with one another, galvanized into a unified group in the interests of keeping the airplanes aloft. Within days Continental was back flying at full strength, having cut its labor costs in the process—a big step on the long path toward reversing the company's fortunes.

While Lorenzo and Bakes were rejoicing, they knew they had yet to take on the flight attendants and pilots in order to lock in the easier debt terms the bankers were willing to provide, and there was a huge payment coming due in a few weeks. And although the machinists' strike had been utterly broken, it *had* driven away some business and burned up a lot of cash in the pell-mell effort to recruit and train scab workers.

Five days after the machinists had walked out, Hurricane Alicia swept through the center of Houston, shuttering businesses for days and driving anyone who could afford it into air-conditioned hotel rooms. Bakes and his family checked into a Guest Quarters Suite Hotel, where Bakes began crafting a mighty speech, one that Lorenzo would deliver in the days ahead to convince employees to consent to wage cutbacks or accept the consequences.

But what exactly were the consequences?

· · ·

A few months earlier Bakes had been interested to read about an appellate court decision in Philadelphia. A New Jersey building supply company called Bildisco had filed for bankruptcy protection, and in doing so had repudiated its labor contracts along with its financial obligations, as if its work rules and wage rates were accounts payable. The court ruled that if collective bargaining agreements threatened the claims of other creditors, they could, in fact, be unilaterally abrogated—wiped out, kaput, while the company continued about its business. Bakes passed out copies of the case to some of his fellow executives.

Bankruptcy. The notion was so . . . intriguing: a perfectly solvent company, with a valuable franchise and assets of tremendous value, nevertheless using bankruptcy as a way of escaping from wage agreements it no longer wished to honor. It would be a provocative measure, certainly far less preferable than a negotiated settlement with the unions, but among some of Lorenzo's senior executives a negotiated solution appeared less likely all the time. Continental's senior vice president of flight operations, Richard Adams, jotted down some notes at one point in which he observed, "I don't believe we can get these concessions on a voluntary, persuasive basis. . . . We must get an awfully big stick. . . . Most effective stick may be Chapter 11." In August 1983 Harvey Miller of Weil, Gotshal & Manges, the dean of the bankruptcy bar, traveled to Houston from New York for his first consultation with Lorenzo and his aides.

Bankruptcy remained a fallback position. No airline had ever gone into bankruptcy and emerged to fly again. Braniff provided a harrowing precedent. No one knew whether the public would ever trust a bankrupt airline. Lorenzo, Wolf, and Bakes launched one last campaign to talk the unions into a deal.

They met with Continental's pilots in the air-conditioned chill of a hotel ballroom near Houston Intercontinental Airport as a fog of humidity blanketed the city and the cleanup from Hurricane Alicia continued. Lorenzo had flown in from New York just in time to give the speech. Wolf and Bakes flanked him at the front of the room. It was obvious to Bakes that Lorenzo was nervous—nervous in a situation that demanded Lorenzo be at his calmest and most deliberate. The pilots stared angrily at Lorenzo and his confederates, wondering why, after agreeing to grant concessions a year earlier—why, after agreeing to cross the machinists' picket lines—they were being singled out again to give more.

What Lorenzo wanted, in brief, was to cut their wages nearly in half, immediately, even though the existing pilots' contract had 13 months left to run.

"The company," Lorenzo told them, "is losing money at an alarming rate." Just as bad, American and United were bearing down with "biased travel agent computer reservation systems that distort traffic patterns and competitive market shares." People Express, he noted, was also closing in, attacking Continental's home base of Houston. Bob Crandall was hiring b-scale pilots to expand the American fleet at a terrifying rate just 250 miles away in Dallas.

It was all perfectly true, but Lorenzo's voice lacked conviction. His tone lacked sincerity. He was speaking in clipped sentences. Good Lord, Bakes thought, the veins were popping out in his forehead!

Lorenzo stuck with the script and pressed ahead, reminding the pilots of how vigorously he had fought deregulation. But that was history. "Today," Lorenzo said,

I philosophically believe in deregulation. Although it is tough on all of us and on the company we work for—and Continental could perish because of it—I much prefer over the long term to be subject to the rule of the marketplace, rather than the bureaucrat. . . .

The People Expresses, the Southwests . . . are drastically altering Continental's marketplace. Unless we change with the marketplace, we will perish.

Lorenzo's message was plain enough: You, veteran pilots, are not worth what you are paid.

I am sure that this will be the most difficult decision of your professional life. I suspect some may propose that we call it quits and not attempt to go forward. But I ask each of you to step back, emotionally and intellectually, from that precipice. If the pilots cannot do what is necessary, thousands of jobs may be lost, perhaps forever. Even pensions could be in jeopardy. . . . I say this not to be mean, not to be confrontational; not to appeal to your emotions; and certainly not to bluff. I and the company do not like to take on the unions or risk brutalizing our workforce. Rather, the economic imperative of survival at this company is to reduce our costs dramatically. Nothing can change that fact.

The pilots who had been with Continental since before the Lorenzo takeover—the majority of those present that evening— heard an awkward speech by a frightened-looking man with an unconvincing bluff. The much smaller group of pilots who had come to the company from Texas International saw something different. Lorenzo, they knew, meant every word. Their spokesman was Dennis Higgins, who had stood up on the floor at the Brown Palace Hotel in Denver two years earlier to tell the shareholders of Continental Airlines that Lorenzo did not care "one whit" for his employees.

"Frank's going to press the test here, fellows," Higgins now told the Continental pilots.

"What do you mean?" he was asked.

"You've got a bad man you're dealing with. You're going to wake up one morning and feel like a truck drove through your living room."

"Aw, you're making too much out of this." The Continental pilots had fended well for themselves under the blustery Bob Six and the cost-minded Al Feldman. The head of the union group at Continental, Larry Baxter, fancied himself a master strategist. "We can take care of Frank," he told Higgins.

Though the president of Continental—Lorenzo's number two executive, at least on paper—Stephen Wolf did not like all the head banging. It was not his style, and if there was anything Wolf had, it was style.

When he abandoned his aloof manner, Wolf could hold an audience rapt. He was such a big man, towering in those suspenders, with tremendous hands, like those of a basketball forward. His perfectly modulated voice, his entire manner, was earnest, particularly through a microphone. His voice sounded intimate, almost whispering, although at the right moment he could display flashes of intensity as well. Some of the pilots thought his style was all a put-on, but many others were convinced that Wolf was sincere. Those who worked closely with him suspected that Wolf put so much faith in his powers of persuasion because he didn't have the stomach for direct confrontation.

Wolf set out on his own to try to win the concessions from the pilots peaceably. More time, Wolf pleaded. Lorenzo was watching his beloved cash balances shrink by the minute. More time, Wolf pleaded. "I'm trying to do it in a cooperative situation," Wolf would recall years later, "and Frank is bashing them." Bakes, for his part, began to think that Wolf was downright naive to think he could reason with a bunch of pilots.

Continental, in Lorenzo's judgment, finally passed the point where Wolf could have more time. The issue was almost academic. The finances had grown so desperate that in only a matter of days practically no amount of concessions from the pilots would be sufficient to save the company.

At seven o'clock on a Tuesday night in September 1983, after another day of crisis and with the bankers asking why there were still no concessions, Lorenzo sat Wolf down.

"I want to be more involved in the basic direction of the company," Lorenzo said. "I just don't think it's going to work."

Wolf had never heard such words from a boss. Lorenzo was giving Wolf a severance check.

"I've never been . . . let go," Wolf said. "Can't we work something out?"

The answer was no. Wolf had to go.

The following morning Wolf approached Larry Baxter of ALPA with a warning about Lorenzo. "You need to take him very seriously," Wolf intoned. Wolf then telephoned each of his fellow Continental officers to thank them and bid them adieu, thus taking his leave on a warm note.

Wolf then departed Houston for Dallas to see his longtime girlfriend, Delores E. Wallace, a former flight attendant instructor who was on the fast track at American. Instead of hopping a plane, Wolf folded himself into his BMW sedan and made the 250-mile trip alone, as committed as ever to his career, wondering where he would land next.

· · ·

On a Saturday morning three days after Wolf's departure Phil Bakes sat behind the desk that Wolf had occupied and felt as if he were walking on somebody's grave. The hastily cleaned-out office now belonged to Bakes; the title of president, he hoped, would follow before long.

Lorenzo and other officers joined Bakes to review the latest cash report. There was about $35 million in the till, not enough to cover Continental's obligations past the following week. The next payroll was approaching. More ominously, Continental's bankers were coming to Houston in a few days—on the same day that the huge debt payment was due.

Texas Air, as Continental's parent company, could easily have floated another underwriting to keep Continental aloft. Lorenzo, however, refused. "We're not running a welfare agency," he explained at one point. He was tired of dickering with the unions. The coup de grâce occurred when the flight attendants, on the same morning that Lorenzo and Bakes were studying the cash report, refused to show up for a meeting in which the company intended to make one final appeal for concessions.

Lorenzo gave the nod to Harvey Miller, the bankruptcy specialist from Weil, Gotshal. It was time to file for Chapter 11 protection. The date was September 24, 1983, a Saturday. The press was notified that Continental would have a major statement later that day.

This was no Braniff-style liquidation, however. Lorenzo and Bakes now had the chance to create a brand-new company, except that they didn't have to round up airplanes and terminals, as Don Burr had in establishing People Express. They didn't have to fight a legal battle for an operating certificate, as Herb Kelleher had at Southwest Airlines. They didn't have to beg and plead for slots, as their own formation of New York Air had required. Continental now had the right to tell everyone to go home, to not bother coming in for their last paychecks: Don't call us, we'll call you. And it could invite people back—as few or as many as it cared to—on whatever terms it wished.

What wages should be paid? Bakes's aides quickly produced a copy of the pay scales being established by a new group of owners and managers trying to build a new airline from the ashes of what had been Braniff. The wages at the new Braniff—Braniff II, people would call it—were on average just about half of what Continental had been paying.

That was it. The Braniff II rates would be applied at the resurrected Continental. Cockpit captains, previously paid close to $90,000—men who may have entered into alimony settlements or investment partnerships based on the expectation that a contract was a contract—would be invited back to work at $43,000 a year, if they happened to be among the lucky. Flight attendants making $35,700—women who had entered into mortgages and who had car payments and who had enrolled their children in parochial schools, perhaps, on the same expectation—would have to adjust to $15,000. Top mechanics, their fate already handed to them when they walked off the job the previous month, would, if invited back to work, receive $20,800 instead of $33,280. Bakes was marshaling the arguments he would present to the bankruptcy court: if this didn't seem fair, it was because years of government regulation had coddled these employees and punished the consumers of the nation. Bankruptcy, Bakes would tell the court, was the only way to redress this imbalance in accordance with the wishes of Congress and the forces of the marketplace.

As the press conference grew closer, Bakes and Lorenzo feverishly contemplated their other rebuilding moves. Where would Continental, once reborn, fly? It obviously could not resume its full schedule of service to 78 cities. But maybe, just maybe, it could get back in the air quickly with service to two dozen or so of its most important destinations.

What fare would it charge? It had to be low, Bakes believed, a "blow-your-mind number." It had to be lower than Southwest's fares and it certainly had to be lower than People Express's. Whether the fare was profitable by any conventional method of accounting didn't remotely matter at this point: Continental no longer owed anyone a dime. The fare had to be low enough to get blood back in the arteries of Continental. The decision was $49, to anywhere.

When would they resume flying? How about Tuesday? Launching an airline on that schedule was a ridiculous goal, this being Saturday. But it was part of the imperative for momentum—to get off the ground fast. Tuesday it was.

Bakes reviewed a draft copy of the news release that would be distributed to the press already assembling a short distance away. Before each appearance of the name "Continental" Bakes inserted "The New," as in "The New Continental." It was hokey, he realized, but he was already launched on another campaign, another attempt at the near-impossible, partly for the sake of seeing whether it could be done. If Continental had a chance to make it in the marketplace, it had to position itself as something radical and new. Bakes did not want people looking on Continental as the "Proud Bird" of yore, struggling to regain a fraction of its former glory. He wanted people to look on it as a small airline expanding from a small base, an airline with a great future, not simply a great past.

Before long Lorenzo and Bakes made the short drive along Buffalo Bayou to the Allen Park Inn, a glorified roadside motel, where they released to the world the news of the New Continental, and to Continental employees the news of what had just happened to them and to their jobs. When they returned to their offices, Lorenzo was deeply depressed. It dawned on him that no matter how ingenious a business strategy, the bankruptcy filing was an admission of failure—the failure to persuade employees and lenders to come to terms voluntarily. Even for someone of Lorenzo's commitment to the means that justified the ends, it was not a happy feeling. Lorenzo suddenly struck Bakes as burned-out and dejected.

The following day, Continental's top officers would be summoned to headquarters for the grim task of deciding which operations and which people would be eliminated. "It's your baby," Lorenzo told Bakes.

Lorenzo did not, as critics came to believe, slash and burn with relish. What he did was, if anything, even lower. He walked away and let someone else do it for him.

The officers of Continental Airlines assembled in the boardroom, capable journeymen, for the most part, with decades in aviation behind them. Bakes—37 years old, a lawyer with three years' experience in the airline industry—was awed by the experience arrayed before him. There were men like Dick Murray, who went all the way back to Mohawk Airlines in upstate New York, where he had helped refine the first computer reservation system in the airline industry, earlier even than American's Sabre; who had helped to build Bob

Crandall's Sabre into one of the world's most sophisticated marketing tools; and who had come to work for Lorenzo to begin accomplishing the same for him. As Bakes looked at the long faces of
Murray and the others, he wondered for a moment whether he could
really do this: order each of them to eliminate two thirds of his operation, two thirds of his budget, two thirds of his people or more.
Bakes realized he couldn't trust himself to negotiate the nitty-gritty
of it. This exercise, he suddenly realized, was painful enough without
having to hear about individual cases of hardship or need and to ar-
bitrate the close calls. So he assumed the bearing of a dictator. Just
cut, he told the assembled managers. "You do it or I'll do it for you."

The older and wiser men shook their heads.

"We've been through a merger," Bakes reminded them. "We've
been through a strike. *You* got us through it. You can do this too."

The men left, soon to begin returning one at a time, with their lists.
Hour by hour, department by department, the red lines went
through the payroll lists. About 8 P.M. Dick Murray came in, protesting the arbitrariness of Bakes's order. Murray carried a ream of
computer printouts showing that his people, the reservation people,
added revenue to the company rather than draining it. Bakes refused
to listen.

"Give me your roster!" Bakes bellowed. And through one name
after another he indiscriminately draw lines, then shoved the list
back to Murray. "Here," Bakes said. "Here's your plan!"

"If that's the way you want it," Murray said, walking out. And
Bakes had no idea whether he would ever see Lorenzo's computer
man again.

In Newark news of Continental's Chapter 11 reached Donald Burr,
who, instantly joyous, scheduled a party to celebrate. Lorenzo's tumble into the abyss of bankruptcy tingled the Calvinist core of Donald Calvin Burr. Burr had long told people that "what Frank sows he
will reap." Now Burr said, "He's gotten what he deserved!"

On top of the thrill of seeing justice done, Burr felt he could claim
much of the credit for the victory. Those ultralow fares on the Continental bread-and-butter route from Houston to New York—they
had pushed Frank over the edge. "We took credit," Burr later said.

Burr, more expansion-minded than ever, began recruiting pilots among the victims of Continental's Chapter 11, emphasizing that by taking a job with People Express, they could cast their lot with the forces of good—and go to war against Frank Lorenzo.

The great plan for the New Continental quickly encountered an unlikely obstacle. As Bakes cried in a meeting, "What if we don't have enough fucking pilots?"

Just before the intended relaunching, Bakes began picking up rumblings that the pilots might actually strike. A strike against a bankrupt airline—nobody had even thought to worry about it, it seemed such a non sequitur. But the pilots and the flight attendants were preparing for one just the same. And although union pilots regularly crossed the picket lines of other airline unions, their own picket lines were sacrosanct. A scab pilot—there had been very few in the history of the Air Line Pilots Association—marked himself as a professional pariah. "The vilest enemy of the morale of aeronautics," David Behncke, the founder of ALPA, had declared, "is a scab."

Fortunately for Bakes a surfeit of pilots was on the market, the result of route cutbacks by the major airlines in the recessionary years following deregulation. Bakes established a phone bank to begin recruiting replacement pilots, one by one. It was not an easy task. When a recruiter found a willing pilot, a cheer went up in the room.

By Tuesday morning, just three days after the bankruptcy filing, Continental had just barely enough pilots to get aloft on Bakes's schedule. Anyone who thought that people would never fly a bankrupt airline got an instant lesson in consumer elasticity: passengers were lining up 50 deep in Houston for Continental's $49 fares. But the unwillingness of Continental's pilots to accept positions with the New Continental quickly began to crimp Bakes's rebuilding plan. The press began a deathwatch. "The threat of a strike," said *The Wall Street Journal,* "might be enough to doom the airline's attempts to reorganize and survive."

Bakes refused to give the press any ammunition with which to speculate. He instructed the company's principal spokesman, Bruce Hicks, to attribute canceled flights to mechanical delays rather than to the lack of pilots. "Tell them anything," Bakes barked. Regardless of what the truth was, Bakes said, "we're *not* cutting our schedule."

The days passed with a few more flights here and there but still too few pilots. Two of Continental's operating executives approached Bakes with a reduced schedule. "We're out of pilots," one of the schedulers glumly reported.

Bakes's jaw went tight. "We're not going to announce any cutbacks!" he shouted at the schedulers. One by one more pilots were drawn in, although in a number of cases they were put to work before they had received the requisite training in Continental's aircraft. Anonymous callers harassed the strikebreakers at home and on the road, particularly at night, when they were trying to sleep between flights. Bakes instructed scabs to register in hotel rooms under fictitious corporate names, and each night Bakes and his aides, and finally Lorenzo himself, telephoned the pilots to offer encouragement.

The inchoate Continental wasn't a pretty sight, but it worked. After weeks of fits and starts, it was aloft, apparently for good. And Phil Bakes, at long last, was made Continental's president.

A few weeks into Chapter 11 hundreds of Continental and former Texas International pilots crowded into a hotel meeting room near Intercontinental Airport in Houston. Larry Baxter, the head of the union at Continental, took the podium.

Baxter struck many as a somewhat peculiar individual. He had a habit of darting from subject to subject in midsentence—"kind of like wind shear," another ALPA leader would later comment. Baxter often seemed to look past the person he was talking to. In the maelstrom of the Continental bankruptcy his eccentricity was in full bloom.

"Everything will be all right," he assured the confused and angry pilot group. Baxter explained that he had been having a recurring dream in which a herd of cattle were charging toward him, their heads lowered. Then, in his dream, guitar music filled the air, and the animals slowed, and soon they were milling peacefully about him . . . and the man playing the guitar was Frank Lorenzo. The Continental pilots could not believe the bizarre words passing from the mouth of their leader. Something like 50 pilots at that moment rose from their chairs, walked out of the meeting, and decided to cross the picket lines, returning to work for Bakes and Lorenzo.

A few days later Baxter was in Washington for a union strategy session. He was convinced that Frank Lorenzo was nearby, and he wasn't playing a guitar this time. Baxter said Lorenzo was out to kill him. Soon Baxter was recalled from office.

Into the job came Dennis Higgins, the former Texas International pilot. Under him the pilots' union fought back gamely—in court, where it was convinced it could reverse the abrogation of its contracts, and in the corridors of Houston Intercontinental Airport, where striking pilots paraded with placards trying to discourage strikebreakers from flying. The picketing pilots received extensive written instructions for use in conversations with scab pilots: "Use Frank's past lies against him. . . . Ask what the future under Frank will be like. . . . How can they now believe him after all the lies and half-truths? . . . Convince them we want to rebuild a profitable company as much as he does. . . . We all want to fly. . . . Under Lorenzo, Continental will ultimately fail."

But everything went against the striking pilots, even under their newly invigorated leadership. The early court cases, in which the pilots tried to reverse the bankruptcy filing as an act of bad faith, were discouraging; the litigation would drag on for years. Over the months more and more pilots crossed the picket lines. Picket duty became a pathetic, solitary sojourn by downcast, out-of-work pilots, holding out on principle, silently walking up and down the airport hallways in uniform as passengers clambered past them to fly on the ultracheap fares that Phil Bakes had put in place.

In their frustration some pilots adopted goon tactics. The putrefied head of an elk was thrown through the picture window at the home of one strikebreaker. A firebomb was later pitched at the home of a scab pilot in Boulder, Colorado. A Continental pilot was arrested outside a Continental office in El Segundo wearing camouflage clothing and carrying bolt cutters and acid. Stink bombs went off in the Continental corridors in the hubs of Houston and Denver.

In November 1983, two months after the Chapter 11 filing, two striking Continental captains made a U-turn while driving in San Antonio and were pulled over by a state trooper. While the men were being questioned, another motorist pulled up with a bag she had seen the pilots ditch from their car. The bag contained two pipe bombs. Searching the car, the trooper found binoculars, a wig, a drill, maps—and photographs of houses belonging to three scab pilots, including one that was just a few blocks distant. The would-be bombers were sent to prison for eight years.

ALPA, though never linked to the bomb plot or any other acts of violence, was consumed with loathing for Lorenzo. In the pilots' anthology of familiar quotations, one achieved new currency at ALPA headquarters: "Nobody ever lands with the gear up twice." ALPA had learned its lesson. The world of deregulation was a cruel one, filled with vicious adversaries. The pilots vowed never again to be caught unawares. They would lay plans to exact revenge on Lorenzo. And in the meantime they would force other airlines, one in particular, to atone for his sins.

CHAPTER 10

BREAKING RANKS

As employees, pilots are a difficult lot. By convention and necessity they are the masters of their vessels, answerable to no one for as long as the engines are running. Airline presidents have the power to control entire fleets, to decide where and when every plane shall fly. But once those decisions are made, no one tells the pilot how, or even whether, to fly.

From its origins flying was touted as a libidinal experience for men, or at the very least something that intensified their masculinity, in the manner of sports and soldiering. A 1920s-era ad for a flying school appeared under the headline "The Aviator—The Superman of Now," to which it added, "Flying is the greatest sport of red-blooded, virile manhood." The official history of the pilots' union notes that men had always been drawn to piloting in part for "the looks they got from attractive young women."

To the extent that flying was deemed a masculine endeavor, it was all but forbidden for women. The writer Antoine de Saint-Exupéry, who spent years flying for a predecessor company of Air France, once declared, "Flying is a man's job and its worries are a man's worries." Amelia Earhart had to be accompanied by her father on her first flight because of the pilot's conviction that women might become hysterical when flying. Earhart's fame was attributable in no small measure to the uncanny physical resemblance she bore to a notable male aviator: "Isn't she like Lindbergh!" one newsreel announcer proclaimed.

For most of airline history, and never more so than in the 1970s, the military served as the airlines' farm club, turning out three quarters of the pilots who entered commercial aviation each year. These men were selected, both by the military and the airlines, in part according to whether they fit a paradoxical psychological profile: capable of operating well within a rigorous, rule-bound system, but also given to extreme independence and self-assuredness of judgment when the situation demanded. It was precisely this combination of attributes that also made pilots prone to unionism.

The founder of their union, David Behncke, had been a barnstormer, rising to prominence by campaigning for the installation of hoods over cockpits in commercial airplanes; up to that point the cockpit was usually exposed to the wind and the elements, the better to give pilots the feel of the slipstream. Behncke got the Air Line Pilots Association off the ground by shrewdly ingratiating himself with Franklin Roosevelt, becoming the only prominent figure in the industry to defend Roosevelt's seizure of the airmail routes in the wake of the spoils conference. Roosevelt made a point of including the following language in the legislation that ultimately restored the routes to private contractors: "Public safety calls for pilots of high character and great skill. . . . Therefore the law should provide for a method to fix maximum hours and minimum pay." In other words, in order to get an airmail contract, an airline would have to allow ALPA on the premises.

It is safe to say that the power went to Behncke's head. He treated his own employees so abusively that they formed a union themselves, which he refused to recognize. In the late 1940s Behncke presided over the construction of a new union headquarters near Chicago's Midway Airport, demanding alignment of the screws and bolts along a precise north-south axis. Behncke was ultimately thrown out of ALPA after the entire organization had defected to a rival union and he had changed the locks to prevent any of the old members from sneaking into the building. He was dead of a heart attack six months later, at age 55, in 1953.

But his creation of ALPA was an enduring legacy, and a vital one as the industry underwent its rapid evolution. Paying pilots was a simple matter when they spent an entire shift flying at 175 miles an hour or less. But the advent of new technology—four-engine airplanes that nearly doubled the speed of flight, followed by jets that doubled it again—made the issue of pilot pay vastly more complex. Flight times were often shorter than the time spent waiting for the next leg of a journey or waiting to leave the gate in the first place. From the pilots' point of view, getting paid simply to fly was insufficient; they also wanted to be paid to wait. At the same time, while bigger and faster planes enabled the airlines to carry more passengers on a single flight, pilots demanded premium rates of pay according to the size and speed of the planes they flew. Over the years these demands created many rigorously formalized rules governing pilot pay.

The most precious asset of any pilot was his seniority. Seniority determined not only the size and speed of the aircraft a pilot could fly but also whether he flew with the stripes of a second officer, first officer, or captain. Dr. Ludwig Lederer, the corporate physician at American Airlines in the 1970s, remarked that "the pilot's life is founded on three things: sex, seniority, and salary, in that order."

If it is fair to stereotype people according to the profession they have chosen, doing so with pilots is easy. They are macho, chesty, often full of themselves, and sometimes downright overbearing; theirs, as Lindbergh once remarked, was an activity in which "man is more than man." At the same time pilots as a group top the scales in pure intelligence. They are decisive and usually passionately committed to an outcome.

Among them, no one displayed these traits more plainly than Dick Ferris.

Ferris's wife, Kelsey, worked hard to keep their three sons from knowing how important their father was becoming in the hierarchy of United Airlines. But after Ferris was named the president of United in 1974, their subdivision in suburban Northbrook, north of Chicago, was buzzing with gossip. Was it true, eight-year-old Andrew Ferris wanted to know, that his father had gotten a big promotion?

Kelsey Ferris decided it was time the boys knew. "Yes," she said.

"Oh! Is he finally getting to be a pilot?"

Andrew's question was entirely apt. A United 747 captain named Jack Starr told Ferris that the president of United Airlines ought to know how to fly and offered to make a pupil of Ferris. Ferris initially demurred, saying he was too busy. Then, on a flight from the West Coast with his boss Eddie Carlson, Ferris reached into his travel bag and pulled out some flying manuals that Starr had left in his office to whet his interest.

"What are you doing?" Carlson demanded.

Carlson was horrified that Ferris would even consider taking up flying. The presidency of United was too demanding, and there were risks in learning to fly. But the chairman's disapproval was like a starting flag waving in Ferris's face.

Ferris was a natural pilot, Starr would later comment. "He listens, cooperates, thinks, responds quickly, and is basically an aggressive personality." When *Fortune* magazine found out that the new president of United was learning to fly, it crowned him "fearless Dick Ferris." After only six hours of instruction Ferris was flying solo. Later he flew Learjets. Ultimately, when placing one of the biggest aircraft orders in history, Ferris made a side deal in which the head of Boeing agreed to schedule Ferris at the controls for one of the first test runs ever conducted for the big new Boeing 767 jet.

In addition to personal gratification there was practical virtue in Dick Ferris's new hobby. Ever since the bitter battle over the three-man cockpit, the pilots' union had been estranged from management at United. Even Eddie Carlson had failed to gain the full trust of the pilot workforce. Dick Ferris's becoming a pilot would begin to break the cycle of suspicion at United. Here at last, in the pilots' view, was a president who cared, who took such an interest in their work that he went to the extraordinary time and trouble to learn the job himself (even if doing so was as much fun as a fellow could have). Ferris, the pilots realized, would understand, even if he didn't fully agree with, the arcana of work rules. He would acquire a more profound appreciation than the average CEO for the delicacy of safety, for the infinitesimal tolerances of flying, for the skill necessary to save an airplane in a vulnerable position. Indeed Ferris in later years would experience firsthand the shock of losing an engine past the point of no return on a takeoff roll. He would once watch his instruments flicker into darkness due to an electrical malfunction. Ferris would know piloting and he would know pilots. The leadership of the pilots' union embraced Ferris and his management so totally that they awarded him a union seniority number. He was literally one of them.

When the pilots' contract was up for renewal in 1981, Ferris, in a radical departure from industry practice, personally involved himself in the nitty-gritty of the talks. His goals were to get the pilots to fly more hours per month and to break at last the three-man cockpit. Ferris gave money to the union to finance a series of weekly informational newsletters that reflected his point of view. He opened the company's books to union representatives. He schmoozed the rank and file at every opportunity. And grasping the power of the new, high-cost communications technology becoming available, he sent video messages by satellite and distributed videocassettes to the company's pilot "domiciles" around the country. Gathered around the big screen, the United pilots witnessed an act of male genius. "Some of your golf games are getting too good," Ferris scolded them. "I'll see you get 15 days off [a month] and that you are the best paid in the business. But the rest of the time your heart and your body and your soul are mine."

With Ferris's charismatic coaxing, the United pilots overwhelmingly assented. The new work agreement, with more flying per month and the abolition of the three-man cockpit on small jets, was such a departure from past practice that it became known as the "blue skies" contract, a name taken from the blue books in which contracts were published. Ferris, to be sure, made some concessions of his own. He promised never to establish a nonunion runaway shop, as Frank Lorenzo had with New York Air. He vowed to furlough no pilots. And he agreed to major increases in pay; a 747 captain in the early 1980s would pull down $161,000 a year, about twice what most of Ferris's middle managers earned.

"We just entered a new era of labor management relationships here," John F. Ferg, the union's chief negotiator, proclaimed.

Ferris was riding high. Before long, in April 1982, Eddie Carlson retired from his chairman's position with the parent company, UAL, Inc., leaving Ferris alone at the top—and more indomitable than ever. "Eighty to 90 percent of my time is spent working with people: getting them to do what I want them to do, when I want them to do it, and, most importantly, getting them to do it willingly," Ferris explained to a group of business school students at Purdue, without acknowledging a trace of irony. "That's my job."

He could not be still. Like an adolescent boy unconsciously bouncing his knee under his desk in algebra class, Ferris squirmed and fidgeted behind his massive desk, custom-built from granite, at United headquarters in Elk Grove Village. No matter how hard he was working, sitting at a desk made Ferris feel sedentary, so he outfitted his office with a podium so that he could work standing up.

He called together his station managers from around the country and sternly forced them to defend every dollar in their budgets (much as Bob Crandall did at American). One by one they gave their reports, in alphabetical order according to the cities they managed (except for the poor soul from Hawaii, who had to go first because his flight home left so early). Ferris listened intently, glowering at anything that displeased him. The sessions grew so confrontational that the managers awaited their turns with sweat running down their backs, nervously making face and finger gestures at each other while the boss was concentrating on somebody else.

In much the way that a pilot feels toward his aircraft, Ferris by 1984 was feeling proprietary toward United Airlines. The company at last was making real money. Meanwhile, however, the takeover mania sweeping the oil industry was showing signs that it might metastasize to commercial aviation. Ferris was panicked at the thought that his great airline—the airline that he was at last turning around—might fall prey to some raider.

In August 1984 Ferris convened an emergency meeting of his board of directors. Board meetings simply did not occur in August. "What the hell is this about?" the directors asked one another as they arrived.

Ferris told the directors of his takeover fears. "I've worked too hard and given too much of my life to this company to let that happen," he said.

Thus, he explained, he had taken steps to conduct a leveraged buyout of United in which he and a few other top members of management, and possibly the employees as well, would become the owners of the company. Ferris said he had already spoken to Goldman,

Sachs, the Tiffany of investment banks, which had expressed a willingness to arrange the billions of dollars in financing.

Ferris could see that he had stunned his board. "Our mouths were open," director Charles Luce would later recall.

The United board did not often stand up to Dick Ferris; no board lightly balked at the ambitions of a chief executive officer. And for the most part Ferris had always treated his directors with the proper deference, such as when he included them in the deliberations over whether United should support deregulation. But in this situation Ferris was making the directors anxious. "Well, Dick," said Walter A. Haas, Jr., the former chairman of Levi Strauss, "suppose the board doesn't *want* you to do this?"

By happenstance Luce, recently retired as chairman of Consolidated Edison in New York, had at that very meeting become the senior director of United, director Robert D. Stuart, Jr., having excused himself in the midst of the meeting to catch a flight to Norway to begin an appointment as ambassador in the Reagan State Department. The position of senior director was unofficial but critically important. More than a decade earlier Tom Gleed had acted as senior director in sacking George Keck from the chairman's position and bringing in his friend Eddie Carlson from Western Hotels (the chain had since been rechristened Westin).

In his capacity as senior director Luce asked Ferris to excuse himself from the room. Among the first to speak up was retired astronaut Neil Armstrong, one of the board's most venerated members. Armstrong was quiet but of stubbornly determined integrity. He had just been through the drama of a major takeover as a director of Marathon Oil, which U.S. Steel had rescued from Mobil. The United directors, Armstrong said, should not have their judgment clouded by the fact that it was their own chairman who was proposing the leveraged buyout.

"This is a takeover offer, fellows," Armstrong said. "We'll have to shop for a better offer."

A few hours after the board meeting the phone rang in Luce's hotel room. It was Dick Ferris. "Can I have dinner with you?" he asked.

Ferris sheepishly explained that he had spoken further to his contact at Goldman, Sachs, who informed Ferris that the firm would have trouble financing the deal if the United board wasn't squarely behind it. Ferris's fantasy had crumbled. He had succeeded in nothing more than agitating a board that considered him a little impulsive to begin with.

"Dick," Luce said, "you don't make many mistakes, but when you make one, it's a big one." Like a schoolteacher making someone write on the blackboard for misbehaving, Luce told Ferris to telephone each and every director to say the deal was off. The episode was never made public. But as Luce would later say, "This incident really shook the board."

The rejection of his LBO proposal was a small matter, in the eventual scheme of things, compared with another snubbing that Dick Ferris was receiving. The pilots' union was making Ferris the enemy.

In a sense he had brought it on himself. Ferris had failed to keep the pilots' union at arm's length. He was too chummy with its leaders; he had extracted too many concessions in the blue skies contract, and now he had a backlash on his hands. By a single vote of the local council the old slate of union officers was swept out. In came a new group whose leaders were still seething over the loss of the three-man cockpit. The new leaders vowed to restore distance between the union and management and to put the interests of pilots ahead of, rather than alongside, those of United Airlines.

The timing of the union shake-up could not have been worse. Negotiations were scheduled to begin on a new contract to replace the expiring blue skies deal. Suddenly the air was electrified with acrimony.

The timing was terrible in another respect: United operated the world's most valuable fleet of airplanes principally from two hubs, Denver and Chicago, and both were suddenly under intense attack. In the case of Denver the enemy was the resurgent Continental Airlines, a fact for which Ferris had himself partly to blame. When Lorenzo and Bakes had announced that Continental would fly its way out of bankruptcy with $49 fares to anywhere, they knew that United was the one airline that could checkmate their move. No airline had greater route overlap with Continental than United, principally in and out of Denver. By giving the order to match Continental's $49 fare, Ferris could have killed the company before it ever got back off the ground. But Ferris had decided that Lorenzo was already dead anyway, so after a furious internal debate he matched only selectively. He had miscalculated; Continental was now surging in Denver, in large part at United's expense.

Ferris's other enemy as he entered into negotiations with the pilots was far more worrisome. This was an old adversary—Bob Crandall.

Crandall had ordered billions of dollars' worth of airplanes after putting his b-scales in place, all as part of his vaunted Growth Plan for American Airlines. Having nearly saturated Dallas with planes, Crandall turned to O'Hare in what he called the Chicago Action Plan, grabbing every slot and gate on which he could lay his hands—every slot and gate, in any event, that Dick Ferris did not snatch first. Ultimately American alone would spend well over $100 million just on additional landing slots. Though there was little doubt that United would always be number one at O'Hare, it mattered immensely to both companies whether American was a close number two or a distant one. The unhappy position of being a weak number two was becoming painfully evident to other airlines at other hubs: Eastern, struggling against Delta at Atlanta; Delta in turn struggling against American at DFW; Frontier, God help it, slugging it out in Denver with United *and* Continental. Airline economics demanded that American come as close as possible to attaining parity with United at O'Hare. The same economics dictated that United try to prevent American from doing so.

Both companies launched costly local advertising campaigns. American threw a giant soiree to woo the affections of 1,000 Chicago-area travel agencies. Each of the two companies intensified its effort to convert travel agencies to its own computer reservation system. American snagged corporate business by offering free first-class upgrades to United accounts. Ferris ordered his top executives to begin a concerted effort to ingratiate themselves with the local establishment through civic activities.

Most of all United needed a lot of new airplanes, fast, to stay well ahead of American. United, however, could not simply add airplanes to its fleet. Ferris had to match the Crandall strategy of lowering his costs with each new airplane, and Ferris could do that only by convincing his pilots to accept b-scales. There was obviously no way Ferris could expand with pilots hired at twice the wages Bob Crandall was paying.

When Ferris had turned 21 years old in 1957, he had received a letter from his father conveying a piece of wisdom that had long been passed from one generation of Ferris men to another: "Get along peaceably if you can, forcibly if you must." No one could have given Ferris more perfect advice for his face-off with the new slate of pilot leaders. Ferris might have relied on his well-honed golf-course manners, on his charismatic powers of persuasion, but instead he went straight for force. He had been deeply hurt at the election of the ardently antimanagement union slate, and to the extent that the pilots' leaders presumed him to be the enemy, so did he judge them.

He involved himself deeply in the negotiations, as he had four years earlier, but this time with incendiary consequences. He displayed his strongest tough-guy bearing, even pounding on tables. And right from the beginning of the talks he laid down the conditions for a peaceful settlement: "You match the American contract," he said, "and we'll accept that."

For the new pilot leaders at United, however, matching American was out of the question. American's b-scales, in their view, were anathema to the pilots' profession—and irrelevant as a precedent besides. The pilots at American who had consented to Crandall's demands were not part of the Air Line Pilots Association. The American pilots in their infatuation with C. R. Smith had broken away from the more militant ALPA organization more than 20 years earlier, in 1963, establishing an in-house union.

No, ALPA declared, there would be no b-scales at United. To which Ferris declared there would be no new airplanes.

As the contract talks continued into 1985, Ferris's refusal to buy airplanes not only aroused resentment among his pilots but began to take its toll on United in the marketplace. Airline traffic was swelling on the continuing tide of low fares. Other airlines—People Express, Delta, even Continental, to say nothing of American—were buying all the planes in sight. Before long United was actually canceling flights because of a plane shortage.

Ferris's friends and associates, while they supported his strategy, began to worry about the passion with which he was pursuing it. Chuck Luce, the senior board member, was concerned that Ferris had "lost his balance," as he later put it. Ferris's mentor, the newly retired Eddie Carlson, concluded from a distance that Dick's toughness was making it easy for the leadership of ALPA to turn the

membership against management. To John Zeeman, Ferris's marketing chief, Ferris's relations with the pilots' union "was like a love
affair gone bad." If Ferris had only removed himself from the bargaining process, Zeeman would later say, "that emotion would have
stayed out."

There was an element in the escalating confrontation that was no
fault of Dick Ferris, however. It was purely bad luck that Dick Ferris happened to be the next in line after Frank Lorenzo and Phil
Bakes had heaped such failure and humiliation on the Air Line Pilots Association. ALPA was itching to take on Dick Ferris.

The union had conducted an extensive postmortem of its failure at
Continental and learned that it communicated poorly with members.
In part because pilots often lived hundreds of miles from the operating bases at which they reported to work, barely one fifth ever
showed up for union meetings. To overcome the estrangement ALPA
brought in experts to establish a video department in Washington.
Experts in telephone communication instructed the union in using
"cell block" meetings and "telephone trees" to keep members informed—and to keep pressure on the rank and file when the time
came to act with unity. In its studies of the failed Continental strike
ALPA had also discovered the critical role that wives played in the
decisions of their husbands in crossing picket lines. Thus United
pilot wives were soon being recruited to union "family awareness"
meetings.

The pilot leaders at United appointed a longtime 737 pilot named
Frederick "Rick" Dubinsky as the strike chairman. Dubinsky had
followed the standard path to flying, starting out building model airplanes and dropping out of college because he could not wait to get
his hands on the real thing. Dubinsky and his assistants recruited
fully 1,000 pilots as volunteers on the strike committee. Soon they
were putting in 10,000 hours a week preparing to strike against
b-scales. They were making more than 7,500 phone calls a day to
spread the anti-Ferris gospel. Reams of information were distributed, including household finance how-to tips for strikers and lists of
foods to avoid in times of stress. And everyone received indoctrination in the need for unity: we must fight b-scales; b-scales will de-
grade the pilots' profession; we must not give Dick Ferris what Bob

Crandall got from the American pilots; United must find other ways to compete with Continental and People Express.

When ALPA put the matter to a vote, 96 percent of the United pilots authorized a strike. Word came from the ALPA offices in Washington that the United pilots should not worry about financing the strike: the national union would provide all the strike funds necessary, to the point of mortgaging the eight-story ALPA headquarters building on Massachusetts Avenue.

While the showdown drew closer, some good would come to Dick Ferris as a result of the Continental bankruptcy. The anti-Lorenzo fallout was also raining on Pan American World Airways, in a way that would enable Ferris, and United, to bring off perhaps the most brilliant transaction in airline history.

At the beginning of 1985 the jig was up for Ed Acker. The unions had discovered the big lie. Pan Am did not have—and had known all along that it never would have—the financial strength to deliver the promised snapback on the wage concessions of three years earlier. Pan Am's finances were so precarious that it had even been using its pension programs as a piggy bank. The pension plans by 1984 were so dreadfully underfunded that Pan Am had been forced to freeze retirement benefits, intensifying the resentment of the rank and file. "Employees will not trust management until its word can be relied upon," Lazard Frères, the investment banking concern, wrote in a report to the Pan Am board on January 31, 1985.

Acker was in a dreadful fix. Fulfilling the company's snapback promise would bankrupt Pan Am. Yet the unions were already threatening to call a strike, which could bankrupt the company equally.

This painful conundrum was weighing on Acker when he took time out to attend a party aboard the yacht of publisher Malcolm Forbes. Dick Ferris happened to be attending the same event. "Ed," Ferris said, "I want to talk to you." The two men departed the yacht and began walking along the dock, deep in conversation. Would Pan Am be interested, Ferris wanted to know, in selling its routes to the Orient?

It was a preposterous and practically unthinkable idea. The Pacific routes were the jewels of Juan Trippe's crown, the most famous—and lucrative—international air routes in the world. But for

Ferris the routes represented a bold solution to a vexing strategic challenge. Ferris recognized that one day the United States would be saturated with airplanes and there would be no place left to grow—except overseas. Ferris had commissioned a study evaluating which of three continents made the most sense for United to establish as a major destination. On a scale of one to ten, South America scored a two. Europe was between six and seven. The Pacific was a ten.

United in fact had launched its first and only international route three years earlier, in 1982, from Seattle to Tokyo, but securing the necessary landing authorization had consumed 12 years; victory had come only through the personal intervention of President Reagan. Entering the Asian market to any meaningful degree would require landing rights in Singapore, China, Taiwan, Hong Kong, the Philippines, Thailand, and Korea, to say nothing of bargaining for expanded authority in Japan. It would take a lifetime to assemble that kind of operation from scratch. But by paying Pan Am, Ferris could perhaps accomplish the same result.

There was no telling for sure whether such a deal could go through. The legal questions were mind-boggling. The flying authorities and the landing rights—were they corporate assets, like factories or mines, that Pan Am was free to trade away? Or were they licenses that the respective governments conferred? Pan Am had never actually paid to acquire those operating rights; did it now have the right to sell them? If so, how could anyone begin to determine the price? Ferris was eager to find out.

The Forbes party, in fact, was not the first time that Ferris had broached the matter; three years earlier he had secretly met Acker at an off-brand motel near JFK to propose buying the Pacific routes. Acker had politely brushed him off. This time things were different. Pan Am, like United, was headed for a cataclysmic union showdown, but unlike United, Pan Am had no financial wherewithal.

"I'll think about it," Acker finally answered.

Neither man realized that at that moment an executive in the Forbes organization was leaning over the ship's deck above with a camera. He snapped a shot of the two men deep in conversation; he later sent a copy to each. Referring to an oily spot on the pier beneath them, the photographer added the caption: "That's Crandall down there, wondering what you're talking about."

• • •

Marty Shugrue of Pan Am, like Dick Ferris of United, was a pilot, but unlike Ferris he still had strong rapport with the pilots' union. With minutes to spare before a strike, Shugrue reached a settlement with the Pan Am pilots that provided for a phased restoration of their lost wages, a kind of partial snapback.

After the pilots came the Transport Workers Union, representing mechanics. A settlement appeared hopeless, but that was okay, Pan Am's management reasoned, because Pan Am could fly through a mechanics' strike. Pan Am could stay in business so long as it had pilots, and the pilots had signed.

The mechanics walked off the job at midnight on February 28, 1985. But to the astonishment of everyone else connected with the situation, the Pan Am pilots honored their picket line. Acker and Shugrue had completely miscalculated. Pan Am was all but shut down. Once again the sins of Frank Lorenzo were being visited on another airline. "The Continental situation, more than anything else, taught the pilots' union some religion," a union official was quoted as saying. "The pilots' union decided it was better to start honoring other unions' picket lines, at least for a while, or the unions weren't going to get anywhere."

Acker recognized that Pan Am was a victim of Lorenzo fallout, but it was cold comfort. Like any executive who had put in more than a few years in the airline business, he had a thing about maintaining a cushion of cash. In his mind Pan Am required a cushion of at least $300 million. Pan Am was practically down to that already, with no place to turn for more. The banks had cut Pan Am off. The entire fleet was already mortgaged to the wing slats. The landmark headquarters building in midtown Manhattan had long since been sold. Ditto the InterContinental Hotel chain. Only the routes, the circulatory system of Trippe's great beast, were left to sell.

Among the company's routes those over the Pacific, despite their high fares and storybook history, were the only logical ones to sell. Among the achievements for which they received insufficient credit, Acker and his aides had reoriented the U.S. route system to feed Europe-bound passengers into New York and Latin-bound passengers into Miami, but there was far less feed to the West Coast for Asia. It would take $3 billion worth of new planes and new routes to make that happen. The 747s Pan Am used from the West Coast to the Orient were also in need of replacement; in the easterly headwinds of the winter the planes often required fuel stops or had to fly with reduced loads, unlike the later-model 747s that other airlines were buying.

The rest of the airline industry, meanwhile, was eating Pan Am's lunch in the Pacific. Northwest, unlike Pan Am, had extensive routes running from the interior of the United States to the West Coast and thence to Asia, enabling it to collect transpacific passengers that Pan Am relied on other carriers to bring to it. Pan Am was also inundated with new competition from Asia itself. In addition to Japan Air Lines there were a number of national carriers from the booming Pacific Rim—Korean Air, Singapore Airlines, Cathay Pacific, and Thai Airways—that offered sumptuous onboard service with flight attendants paid a small fraction of what Pan Am paid.

With the kind of money they could get by selling the Pacific, Acker and Gitner could not only pare down Pan Am's oppressive debt burden but also build additional routes to the surviving Pan Am gateways of New York and Miami. Finally there was, in the case of the Pacific, a ready buyer in the person of Richard Ferris.

Acker tracked him down at the 1985 Hawaiian Open, the annual golf tournament that United used to beam images of putting greens and girls in grass skirts across America every winter. Ferris and his marketing chief, John Zeeman, were in a practice round on the 13th hole when Ferris was called to the phone. He caught up with the group on the 16th hole and casually asked Zeeman to join him privately after the round. The two walked to the hotel and closed the door of Ferris's room behind them.

"You can't fucking believe it!" Ferris exclaimed. "They want to do the Pacific deal!"

The following Saturday, on April 20, 1985, Eddie Acker and Gerry Gitner sat down with Dick Ferris and one of his aides in a suite at the Plaza Hotel (then owned by United) and named their price: three quarters of a billion dollars. Ferris, to their surprise, readily agreed. In one of the biggest commercial transactions in history there was no haggling over money.

Acker knew that the transaction would be emotionally wrenching for the Pan Am board, many of whom had served alongside Juan

Trippe. Acker answered to some of the most distinguished directors in corporate America: Donald M. Kendall, the chairman of Pepsico; Sol Linowitz, the former general counsel and chairman of Xerox Corporation, who had negotiated in behalf of President Carter in the Middle East and the Canal Zone; Akio Morita, the chairman of Sony Corporation; and other notables. Many of the directors had long delighted in hearing Lindbergh's tales of the early days.

But nobody played the relationship game better than Acker, and this was a situation that called on all of his skills. Acker needed to recruit a board member to join him in championing the deal. One way to lock up such loyalty, he thought, was to give a director a financial incentive in the outcome.

Acker turned to William T. Coleman, Jr., a noted civil rights attorney and power broker who had played a leading role in the landmark desegregation case *Brown* v. *Board of Education.* Coleman later stood out among civil right advocates for his Republican leanings, and had been transportation secretary in the administration of Gerald Ford. In that capacity he was among the Ford administration officials who gave momentum to the deregulation campaign that was completed during the Carter administration. Coleman's law firm, O'Melveny & Myers, was not Pan Am's usual counsel, but for this transaction Acker asked whether Coleman would have his firm do the legal work, which would be massive. There's no evidence that Coleman wouldn't have supported the sale in any case, but years later the great lawyer acknowledged the appearance of a conflict of interest. "One could always argue that when you have someone on a board whose firm did legal work, that affects you," Coleman explained years later. "I hope it didn't."

Approving the Pacific sale was, as Acker had expected, difficult for the board. But with Coleman in his corner and with $750 million in cash hanging in the balance, Acker won the board's approval.

In Dallas Bob Crandall was jealous and outraged to learn that United was buying the Pacific division of Pan Am—and that he had never been given the opportunity to bid on it. Crandall could not imagine why he had been entirely cut out.

In fact Acker and Gitner had considered shopping the routes to Crandall, whose interest in establishing foreign routes was well known. But Pan Am had previously conducted a major airplane swap with American, and they had found Crandall prickly and impossible to satisfy. The Pacific sale was an emergency transaction. A strike had been raging and cash dwindling. There was no time for dealing with a difficult personality. No one ever told Crandall that he was denied the chance to make the airline deal of the decade because he was just too tough.

Despite his jubilation, Ferris knew the timing could not have been more dreadful. He was writing one of the biggest checks in corporate history at the very moment he was telling the United pilots that he required b-scales to survive against American. Three days after the Pacific announcement, at United's 1985 annual meeting of shareholders, protesting pilots rained on Ferris's parade, inundating him with hours of questions and conducting picket duty outside the hotel. The pilots also fixed their strike date: May 17, 1985, less than a month away.

United's management went into high gear. The company drew down half of a $1.5 billion line of credit to bolster its cash position. Under heavy security it established an operating center, with dim lighting and Ferris's would-be flight schedules projected against the wall. Ferris continued to lobby individual pilots, hanging around dispatch rooms on weekends in his casual slacks and golf shirt. He also scheduled a major road show in a campaign to win them over with his salesmanship and charisma, talents that had proved so useful in his pilot dealings of the past. But at location after location attendance was virtually nil. The pilots were boycotting his meetings. Union people, he learned, were photographing any who dared to attend.

Ferris was furious. They are intimidating my pilots! he thought.

The union's massive unity campaign reached its peak on Sunday, May 5, 1985, in a satellite production involving dozens of technicians and weeks of planning—a rally broadcast live to pilot domiciles in Los Angeles, Denver, San Francisco, Seattle, Cleveland, Miami, New York, and Washington from Odeum Expo Center in Chicago. Strike chairman Rick Dubinsky, his gargantuan image projected on a huge screen over the podium, was like an oracle announcing the end of the earth. "We're now just 271 hours and 52 minutes away from the time when every United pilot must face the most difficult test of his life," he solemnly declared.

The rally was moderated by Paul Anthony, the studio announcer for the PBS show *Washington Week in Review.* The radio commentator Daniel Schorr reviewed the status of the issues in the talks. Retired anchorman Howard K. Smith spoke on the history of labor-management relations.

A tape was shown of Dubinsky interviewing a pilot who shamefacedly told the story of how he had crossed the picket lines at Continental—of how it had nearly ruined his life, making him a marked man, causing his copilots to refuse to engage in any conversation with him deeper than a cockpit checklist, a situation with potentially disastrous safety consequences. A pilot called in from Cleveland via satellite asking whether the union would have any way of knowing how many pilots were scabbing. "You, the pilots," Dubinsky said, "will not only know how many, but *who.*"

The high point of the conference came near the end as the podium was taken by the trial lawyer F. Lee Bailey. Bailey had been a marine fighter pilot who never quit flying; he averaged 40 hours a month at the controls of his Learjet. As it happened, he was engaged to a United flight attendant.

If any of the pilots felt misgivings about the strike—if any felt demeaned, or guilty, or low-class, or obstreperous at the idea of walking a picket line—Bailey went a long way toward salving their anxieties and endowing their intentions with legitimacy. Nothing, Bailey said gravely, would eradicate pilot professionalism faster than a two-tier wage system in the cockpit. Although everyone in the audience would remain in the a-scale, in future years a swelling crowd of b-scalers would be after their jobs, eyeing the veterans for slipups, making discreet comments to their supervisors in hopes of knocking them out of their captains' seats. "Won't that be great for teamwork?" he asked sarcastically. "Has technology made flying so much less difficult that we can put *half-valued* people up there?"

With the rain pounding the metal roof of the Expo Center, Bailey went on in the grandiloquent style of a lawyer giving a jury speech. Ferris, he said, had a debt to the rest of the industry—a debt incurred when he joined with the forces of deregulation.

This is a giant risk. Mr. Ferris has to take it, you understand, if there's any chance of success. You are *the* test case. There will never be another day like this. If United goes, TWA, Delta, Eastern, Northwest, Pan Am are gone. "Two-tier," or something equally as corrupt, will be in, and that will be history. And you will have the misfortune to live through the transition, which will be horrendous. . . . Mr. Ferris put them in the deregulation bucket and it is his job to cure their problems if he can, and he is the spearhead by designation. . . . And if they succeed, we will have pilots like the boy from Air Florida—and I mean "boy"—who . . . did not know what ice was and committed suicide with a bunch of passengers in a takeoff that I wouldn't have expected an astute *student* to even attempt. . . .

What you must do is simplicity itself. Look in the mirror and ask yourself, "Am I worth what I'm being paid? Or have I, for 20 years, conned the American public into thinking that there were demands in this job that really don't exist?"

It all came down to honoring the picket line, Bailey said. If none of the pilots crossed, he said, Ferris would have to crumble.

During the hours of speech making no one mentioned that the pilots' negotiators had already, in fact, agreed to b-scales, though only of a few years' duration, until the American pilots could be emboldened to shake loose the two-tier system. Ferris, however, was not content with the pilots' concession. An airplane lives for 20 years or longer; he wanted b-scale for a generation, not just a few years. Dick Ferris wanted what Bob Crandall had.

Ferris was aware that he could not count on all or even most of his pilots to stick by him. The cornerstone of his strategy to fly through a strike involved a corps of strikebreaking pilots, some 570 strong, who were now in Denver being trained in United's operations, aircraft, and procedure. They would keep the airline aloft at a level sufficient to keep the cash flowing. In the beginning United would fly at 50 percent of capacity, Ferris estimated. Then, if the pilots refused to relent, United could creep back to its full schedule of 1,550 flights a day over several months by hiring and training new pilots. By that time, if the strike had gone on that long, Ferris would have destroyed the union that had betrayed him.

The pilots' union too recognized that those 570 pilots controlled

The visionary Juan Trippe (*left*) launched Pan Am's airmail service to South America in 1929, with Charles Lindbergh in the cockpit. "We have shrunken the Earth." (*Smithsonian Institution*)

Marketing genius C. R. Smith of American Airlines introduced jet travel to America in 1959. "We're going to make a pile of extra dough just from being first." (*American Airlines*)

Herb Kelleher battled to launch Southwest Airlines in 1971. If the sheriff shows up with another injunction, he said, "leave tire marks in his back." (*Southwest Airlines*)

ABOVE: Dallas's Love Field gave Southwest an operating base as well as a marketing identity. "How do we love you? Let us count the ways . . ." (*Southwest Airlines*) LEFT: Taking control of Texas International in 1971, Frank Lorenzo soon became the industry's youngest president at age thirty-two. Calling it "our little airline," he would make it the nation's largest. (*AP/Wide World Photos*)

TOP: Robert Crandall roiled the industry after becoming American's marketing chief in 1973. "Be ruthless. Be driven. Don't let anything get in your way." (*American Airlines*) BOTTOM: Crandall's deft internal politicking helped him win the presidency of American from chairman Al Casey (*left*) in 1980. When did Crandall first covet the job? "When I was born." (*American Airlines*)

Within days of Continental's Chapter 11 in 1983, Phil Bakes excitedly details his rebuilding plans as a depressed Lorenzo looks on. "It's your baby," Lorenzo told him. (*AP/Wide World Photos*)

Lorenzo's 1980 creation of New York Air triggered a union hate campaign, including this billboard in Houston. "Runaway shop!"
(*Courtesy of Dennis Higgins*)

ABOVE: Ed Acker (*left*) announces that Pan Am will sell its historic Pacific routes to United in 1985, as Dick Ferris stifles his glee. "You can't fucking believe it!" Ferris told an associate. "They want to do the Pacific deal!" (*AP/Wide World Photos*) BELOW: Former astronaut Frank Borman announces the 1986 sale of Eastern to Lorenzo. "No one can run a company under these circumstances." (*AP/Wide World Photos*)

In 1986 Don Burr sold People Express to the rival of his life,
Frank Lorenzo, catapulting Texas Air to number one.
"Frank is capable of any kind of behavior to win."
(*AP/Wide World Photos*)

Charlie Bryan of the machinists' union at an Eastern
shareholders' meeting in 1986. He told his rank and file,
"Weapons formed against you will not prosper!"
(*AP/Wide World Photos*)

RIGHT: Phil Bakes presided over Eastern's demise in 1989. "It was as if the people who worked and managed were marionettes." (*Christopher Morris/Black Star*) BELOW: Crandall leads a counterdemonstration as striking flight attendants cripple American in 1993. Management, one official claimed, was victimized by the "gay and lesbian component [in the union membership]." (*AP/Wide World Photos*)

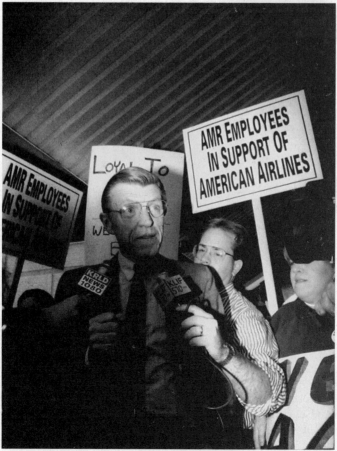

LEFT: Sir Colin Marshall celebrates his 1993 investment in USAir. Asked years earlier to name his dream job, he readily answered, "To be the chairman of British Airways."
(*AP/Wide World Photos*)

Two decades after its traumatic birth, Southwest hit the East Coast and Herb Kelleher was thrust into the spotlight. "Being a millionaire ain't what it was in the 1890s." (FORTUNE *is a registered trademark of Time Inc. Used by permission. All rights reserved.*)

everything. Shutting down only half of United was insufficient. If hundreds of scabs reported to work, the will of the strikers would erode almost instantly. Each of those intended scabs had to be convinced not to perform the job for which he had been hired.

United was lodging the strikebreakers at two hotels near the company's training center in Denver, where they had plenty of time on their hands. An ALPA leader named Jamie Lindsay (once described by ALPA's international president as "a nuclear reactor without enough water") led the countertraining effort. He ran union hospitality suites in the company's hotels, right under Ferris's nose. He arranged for carry-out pizza by the dozens and beer by the case for fraternal meetings with the intended scabs. Little was spared in the way of moral suasion and professional pressure.

There was another element, more discreet, in the campaign to keep the newly hired pilots from crossing. Some of the pilots who had been hired to train the strikebreakers were themselves on strike—at Continental Airlines. From the outside it appeared a case of union hypocrisy, strikers training strikebreakers. But Continental strikers were acting as double agents, a kind of fifth column within United. Some, when they weren't conducting sessions on flap settings and engine speeds, were making small talk—about what Lorenzo had done to the pilots at Continental, about the ideology of the confrontation at United, about the importance of refusing to fly the very equipment that the recruits were being trained to operate.

Ferris's advisors told him that everything was ready, the troops were at hand, United could break the strike. Ferris in turn gave the same report to his board of directors. In a vote of confidence they came squarely behind Ferris, with one exception. Wally Haas, the former chairman of Levi Strauss, expressed reservations about taking the strike; it would obviously create hard feelings, and hard feelings were the last thing management needed in a service business. Before long Haas would quietly leave the United board of directors.

Ferris was still at corporate headquarters at 11 P.M., the hour the strike had been scheduled to begin. At 11:01 he was told the pilots were walking. For only the second time in history and for the first time since 1951, the United pilots were on strike.

The dimly lit operations center had been geared up to operate the company at 50 percent of capacity. But as midnight passed, then the wee hours, the horror began to spread and then took hold.

Where were the replacement pilots? Five hundred and seventy had been trained. Six showed up.

The flight attendants also failed to show up for work.

Even about 30 management pilots refused to cross the picket lines.

United struggled to get what little in the air it could. Fifteen percent of the operation was all it could muster. Ferris was stunned and so were thousands of airline passengers. The world's finest air transport system was suddenly in one of its worst snarls ever. On a typical day United boarded about 130,000 passengers, more than one out of every six people flying in America. Its flights linked 157 cities in all 50 states. Hawaii might as well have been a wholly owned subsidiary of United. Now passengers who had been assured that United would be operating its most important flights found themselves high and dry.

American—the reason that Ferris was taking this strike—was the greatest beneficiary in dollar terms. Every American flight was departing O'Hare crammed from stem to stern. A day into the strike American carried a record 152,000 people, on a Sunday. The strike was a godsend to Bob Crandall's efforts to make American a powerhouse number two against United at O'Hare. To get long-lasting benefits from the United strike, American even set up folding tables at the airport to recruit United passengers as members of the American frequent-flier program.

Crandall's people were certain, in any case, that the strike would go on for some time. Crandall's analysts had sent the computers into overtime, running pro forma estimates of the financial effects of the strike not only on American but on United. The cost incurred by United in the first five minutes of the strike, Crandall's people determined, was so great that Ferris would have to hold out until he got what he wanted.

The emotionalism of the strike preparations did not let up once the pilots were picketing and the planes were grounded. Twenty-four-hour security went up around the Ferris home in the northern Chicago suburb of Northbrook. The strikebreaking pilots—what few there were—were horribly harassed. Some of their wives received threatening calls. Some of the working pilots found feces in their flight bags.

Some of the striking pilots would later claim that at various points Ferris went off the deep end himself. A pilot named John Vick testified that he ran into Ferris in Denver and was bowled over to hear Ferris explain, "I am the chairman. I have all the chips. I am a 1,300-pound gorilla!" Union leader Jamie Lindsay claimed that when he too came across Ferris in Denver, Ferris said, "Why don't you travel back to the Dumpster you live in?" (The comment caused ALPA to distribute lapel buttons picturing trash receptacles.) Ferris would later deny ever making such comments, but there was plenty of bravado in Ferris's stance. "ALPA can't win," the *Chicago Tribune* quoted him as saying. "There's no sympathy out there for the pilots."

But ultimately there arose the issue of cash, which can make even the sturdiest CEO weak in the knees. This affliction hit Dick Ferris on about the seventh day of the strike. Watching cash fly out the window at a dizzying pace, he called his senior managers together and said he was going to settle on the terms last agreed to by the union. B-scales would be established, but only for a brief period. Ferris had nowhere near the deal that Bob Crandall had.

Like Frank Borman's aides at Eastern in the similar circumstances there, Ferris's people were shocked and dismayed. We've come this far, some of them thought. Why not go 60 or 90 days? But Ferris was intent on settling.

In the end, Ferris got the worst of both worlds—a long strike *and* a lousy settlement. The circumstances of the walkout had created some thorny back-to-work issues, intensified all the more by the emotions running out of control on both sides. In a decision that seemed calculated principally for punishment, United said that those few pilots who had scabbed through the strike would get "super seniority," jumping ahead of those who had struck. In an equally insulting move the union demanded job protection for the nearly 570 strikebreakers who had snubbed the company that hired them.

For another three weeks the strike raged on, driving more passengers from the company, deepening further, if that was possible, the enmity between Ferris and his most important employee group. A number of board members were upset that after the divisive economic issues had been resolved, Ferris continued to irritate the pilots over back-to-work issues. "That was putting a match in a tank of gasoline," as senior director Chuck Luce later put it. The National Mediation Board ultimately proposed the Solomon-like solution of letting a court resolve the ancillary issues, but only after weeks' more hatred had accumulated.

On June 6, 1985, after not quite a month, United was back in business. It was a changed United, certainly from the vantage point of marketing chief John Zeeman. Though devoted to Ferris, Zeeman could see how grave the damage had been. "That was not a strike we won," he would say years after leaving United. "It was the worst thing to happen to the company in 50 years. Emotionally, we never came back. . . . Before the strike we were the greatest airline in the country, maybe the world. Afterward, we weren't."

One of the least welcome effects of the strike was its depressing influence on United's stock. This was the precise midpoint of the 1980s, when the takeover epidemic was intensifying. A low stock price on even the biggest corporations was like a blue light twirling in the ceiling of a dime store, an advertisement to the likes of Carl Icahn or Boone Pickens or Sir James Goldsmith or Ivan Boesky or Donald Trump or for that matter, Frank Lorenzo.

United was an inviting target in another respect. Unlike Pan Am, which had been raiding its pension plans to keep afloat, United had been overfunding its pension accounts—or so Dick Ferris was told by his advisors on Wall Street. Ferris, they thought, would be wise to deplete the retirement funds of excess cash so that a raider did not try to seize the company and use United's own cash to help pay for the deal.

But what could he do with the money?

Ferris placed a call to Frank A. Olson, the chairman of Hertz. Olson was a salesman's salesman and sports enthusiast; he had signed O. J. Simpson, in the 1970s, to one of the earliest and most productive sports celebrity endorsement contracts. Ferris too was a longtime acquaintance. Olson knew all the airline bosses because of the frequent marketing tie-ins between their industry and the rental car business. Olson and Eddie Carlson had been close for years, and all three men—Olson, Carlson, and Ferris—shared a passion for golf.

"We're sitting on a pile of cash," Ferris told him, cash that had to be spent. "I want to buy Hertz."

Hertz, however, was not at the moment Olson's company to sell, having become one of the far-flung subsidiaries in the portfolio of RCA Corporation. Soon Ferris was in contact with Thornton Bradshaw, the chairman of RCA, to make the pitch to him, and Bradshaw bit. For $587 million, Hertz, the world's leading rental car agency, was United's.

Although there was no shame or embarrassment in conducting defensive acquisitions in the 1980s, Ferris would forever refuse to acknowledge the Hertz purchase as an antitakeover measure, not even to the members of his inner circle. For everyone but Frank Olson, Ferris had a different explanation, one that Ferris pushed so hard it took on a life of its own, inside United and outside. Ultimately the cover story became the reality.

The acquisition placed United squarely into a third major sector of the travel and tourism business, on top of Westin Hotels and United Airlines itself. If properly stitched together, these three businesses, Ferris told his associates, could become something extraordinary—an integrated travel empire on a scale never before seen. The pièce de résistance, the glue that would bind it all together, would be Apollo, United's sprawling computer reservation network. Apollo could take the three separate businesses and assemble them into a single product, that product being a trip, a seamless travel experience, arranged in a single phone call and carried out with unheard-of efficiency and convenience. You could complete your rental car contract and check into your hotel at the United counter at the beginning of your journey. Your luggage could be delivered directly to your Hertz car. Apollo would know that you wanted an aisle seat in the smoking section (they still existed then) and a midsized sedan and a room on the concierge floor. And you could pay for everything on a single credit card imprint. Ferris's people threw themselves into the job of endowing Apollo with such intelligence.

But to legitimize his global travel empire Ferris needed two additional things. The first was a much bigger hotel operation, including hotels overseas—particularly in Asia, now that he controlled the vast Pan Am routes there. Ferris went shopping and quickly bought the Hilton chain in late 1986, for nearly $1 billion.

The other thing he needed was to reach into Europe, by tying in key United flights with those of a European airline while simultaneously extending the reach of the Apollo reservations network. That way passengers in Europe could be directed toward an airline friendly with United, which, in turn, would turn them over to United for their connecting flights in the United States, where they would drive in Hertz cars and lodge at Westin or Hilton hotels.

One night, in their search for strategic partners in Europe, Ferris boarded a British Airways flight to London with United marketing chief John Zeeman. When they landed in London they raced to a breakfast meeting with Colin Marshall, chief executive of British Air. Following breakfast they jumped into a chartered plane to Cologne, Germany, where they were whisked past German customs and into a luncheon meeting with Heinz Ruhnau, head of Lufthansa. Soon they took off again in the chartered plane, this time for Paris, where they held a dinner meeting with the people from Air France. And when their whirlwind tour was concluded, Zeeman and Ferris realized that by having breakfast with the British, lunch with the Germans, and dinner with the French, they at least had planned their meals well.

As Ferris moved to fulfill his vision there was grumbling inside United, and not just from the pilots. Ferris's own managers urgently wanted more planes to meet the attack from American in Chicago, more planes to fight Continental in Denver, more planes to throw against People Express, growing like a weed everywhere.

But Ferris, the pilot, was thinking less and less about airplanes. He still had the number one airline, and on top of that the number one car rental outfit and the number one hotel chain in the world. As he later put it, "We were ready to own the world."

CHAPTER 11

GLOOM OVER MIAMI

Processing and transmitting information along an electronic network is an almost wholly derivative activity. Whether a cable television system, a complex of automatic teller machines, or an airline computer reservation system, a network exists not as an end in itself but as a convenience to those who create and consume an underlying product: a Hollywood movie, a banking service, a seat on an airplane. The sociologist Marshall McLuhan's 1964 assertion that "the medium is the message" is by more recent standards a quaintly over-enthusiastic characterization of the Information Age. Even if the medium is the message, it is not the product. Though it may enhance value, it creates nothing. By themselves computers, networks, and systems can no more fly people between cities than they can print money or direct actors.

Yet in the mid-1980s it almost seemed otherwise to Frank Lorenzo. New York Air and the resurgent Continental Airlines, were, taken together, the largest airline operation in the country without a direct electronic tie-in to the travel agent community. Some 30,000 travel agencies, accounting for two thirds of all airline reservations, had been hard-wired, but the mainframes of only five airlines resided at the other end. American's Sabre system remained the leader by far, with 34 percent of the agencies devoted to its system.

United's Apollo system was still number two, with one quarter of the travel agencies. The remainder of the market was divided among systems operated by Eastern, TWA, and Delta.

When the government moved to crack down beginning in 1983—partly in response to the failure of Braniff and partly in response to the vocal complaints of Frank Lorenzo—Bob Crandall took the lead in defending the systems. "The preferential display of our flights, and the corresponding increase in our market share, is the competitive raison d'être for having created the system in the first place," Crandall told Congress. Crandall's protests were unheeded, however. His system was seen as too successful; he had pushed too far. In late 1984 the government outlawed screen bias.

Lorenzo remained unsatisfied, complaining that American and United still found ways to play games against him. In January 1985 both systems delayed loading a new round of Continental fare cuts into their systems, making the discounts invisible to travel agencies. (American blamed a power outage; United claimed that Continental had failed to pay the requisite $100 loading fee). Wherever the blame lay, computer reservation systems clearly remained devilishly effective marketing tools. Travel agents could get advance boarding passes on American flights, for instance, only if they were Sabre subscribers. Likewise, only Sabre subscribers could be assured of having the most reliable, last-minute seat availability information.

Even after these and other imbalances were ameliorated by regulation, travel agents sitting in front of terminals leased from American and serviced by American—and that American had trained them to operate—remained significantly more inclined to choose American over other airlines, even when the screen listings were scrupulously neutral. (The same was true of United and its Apollo system.) In study after study the statistics made it clear: a concentration of terminals in a given geographical area continued to produce a disproportionate amount of business for American (or United, or the other three airlines offering terminals) relative to the number of flights that the airline had in that market. The airlines referred to this phenomenon as the "halo" effect. "Whether bias exists or not," Mike Gunn, one of Crandall's top marketing people, told a sales meeting in 1984, "we know we can get more business from a Sabre-automated account."

In the minds of Lorenzo and many others the networks were the stuff of economic mythology: guarantees against failure for those who possessed them, assurances of slow death for the have-nots. Frank Lorenzo wanted a halo for himself.

In June of 1985, while the airline industry was transfixed by the bitter strike raging at United, Lorenzo made a deal to acquire Trans World Airlines—his second attempt to take over the first airline he had ever flown, the company whose stock was the first he had ever owned. There was widespread speculation that Lorenzo wanted TWA, with its routes across the Atlantic, to foster a low-fare revolution around the globe. But others knew better. Lorenzo, they could see, had an additional and probably greater motive: to lay his hands on TWA's computer reservation system, the same system that Bob Crandall had helped to create in the early 1970s, before joining American Airlines.

In the end, Lorenzo's reputation would cost him TWA. The company's unions were so mortified at the idea of having him on the property that they maneuvered the takeover artist Carl Icahn into a position to take control, failing to appreciate that he was no picnic either. There was something vague and off-center about Icahn; whereas Lorenzo was accused of forever backing out of his deals, Icahn would never quite come to closure on one. Lorenzo and Icahn tussled over TWA for weeks, the battle growing increasingly personal. In the end Icahn won TWA. The once-great airline of Howard Hughes became Icahn's newest cash cow. TWA was as good as dead.

Lorenzo walked away from the TWA contest with $51 million in trading profits and other payments, a consolation prize of the type he had become so practiced at obtaining. But he was still without a computer reservations network.

For Phil Bakes, watching Lorenzo tangle with Icahn was like watching two gypsies play cards.

Bakes followed the action, barely, from the distance of the Mediterranean. In the midst of the United strike Bakes had walked away from Continental Airlines for a few weeks for a road trip through his family's ancestral homelands in Italy. Bakes would later call the trip one of the high points of his life.

He could revel with his family knowing that back home he had made something of the godforsaken airline that Frank Lorenzo had turned over to him. With the summer schedules of 1985, Continental had not only reached but surpassed the level of operations it had suspended the day it went into Chapter 11 two years earlier. Along the way the company had scored one decisive legal victory after another. The federal judge overseeing the bankruptcy case embraced the company's move to wipe out its labor agreements, concluding, "There was no intent or motive to abuse the purpose of the Bankruptcy Code." (The judge would soon accept a $250,000-a-year position with one of Continental's law firms.) Congress, nevertheless, took it upon itself to reform the bankruptcy laws in order to prevent anyone from automatically wiping out wage contracts through bankruptcy, a kind of "Lorenzo Amendment" to the bankruptcy laws.

Bakes also took pride in the company's marketing triumphs; it was holding its own against United in Denver even without a reservation network. Continental fought back with price, a strategy financed in part by the free use of roughly $1 billion of creditors' money and labor costs that were only half what they had once been. But nobody could attribute Continental's success solely to the benefits of bankruptcy. Continental was an on-time airline with good service and a crop of eager and compliant young workers, strikebreakers all.

The traumas had been numerous. The pilots' union was maintaining its pathetic strike against Continental, as if a strike would reverse the rulings of the bankruptcy court. There had also been public relations setbacks, such as a full-page ad in *USA Today,* signed by Patty Duke, Tony Randall, Daniel J. Travanti, and some 30 other union actors, claiming that Continental cared "more about money than safety." And there were those pantywaist bankers, forever imploring Bakes to end the insane fare wars. Bakes would give them a courteous or patronizing brush-off, while thinking to himself, "What are you going to do? Sue us? We're in Chapter 11!"

Despite all the growth—the furious fleet expansion, the development of the hubs at Denver and Houston—Bakes had kept the lid on costs, in some cases no thanks to Frank Lorenzo. Lorenzo, it appeared to his associates, had an inferiority complex about abandoning the legacy of superior passenger service for which Continental, under Bob Six and later Al Feldman, had been so justly famous. Lorenzo was still sensitive about the Mr. Peanut image that stuck to him from the Texas International days. So the same Frank Lorenzo who was getting credit in the business schools as the cost cutter extraordinaire had jumped all over Bakes when hand-cut radishes and other frills were cut from Continental's menus.

Bakes was proud of himself. He had not blinked. And now he was on the verge of fostering a whole new round of changes at Continental, on many levels. He envisioned a radical series of marketing innovations making air travel even more affordable to more people. He assembled a full-time team of staffers into a study group he assigned to designing "the airport of the future": a paperless airline operation without tickets—an unheard-of concept in 1985. He imagined passengers boarding airplanes and paying for their seats by swiping credit cards through an electronic reader. They would use their credit cards even to get baggage tags and self-check their luggage. Lorenzo, however, did not appreciate Bakes's studies. "What are we wasting money on this shit for?" he asked at one point, almost as if he were slamming down Don Burr's "people plan" of six years earlier. Bakes kept the airport-of-the-future project alive anyway.

Bakes had not, however, become the media hero of Continental's recovery, or at least not the main hero. Just as the press had misleadingly identified Lorenzo alone as the bogeyman in the bankruptcy filing, so did it focus on him, not Bakes, as the ace of the comeback. With a self-satisfied smile on his face—he could look so handsome when he smiled—Lorenzo was pictured in *Business Week* under the headline "Continental Is Soaring Out of Chapter 11." Lorenzo took pains to foster the rehabilitation of his public image, even turning out for Continental Airlines Night at a Houston Astros game. "You get a real high with the employees," he told a reporter present for the game. "They are so happy."

Bakes, though he did not broadcast the fact, knew that if there was any such change in the attitude of Continental's employees, it was principally the result of *his* efforts, *his* plans, *his* programs. He was spending fully 30 percent of his time on the line, meeting with employees. He had installed a profit sharing program, and not only were there profits, but they were shared. He had launched a "gain sharing" program that rewarded employees—pilots who burned up less fuel, for instance—with cash payments. He began planning training programs for middle management intended to infuse the company with a new "participatory culture," as he liked to call it, and this stuff was selling.

On September 5, 1985, two years to the month after the proceedings had begun, Bakes and Lorenzo announced that Continental Airlines was emerging from Chapter 11. They proudly declared that creditors would get 100 cents on the dollar, which was literally true, except that in some cases the creditors would have to wait years to receive full payment. In other cases involving benefits for certain employees who went on strike, the payoff was zero cents on the dollar. In the same budget hotel from which they had shocked the world with their original announcement, Lorenzo and Bakes now proudly basked in the media floodlights. Bakes hailed "one of the most successful reorganizations of a billion-dollar company in the history of American industry." Lorenzo boasted that "Continental has come back from the brink in fighting form."

Few knew it at the time, but Lorenzo was also closing in on another computer reservation system—a system controlled by an executive who needed Lorenzo every bit as much as Lorenzo needed him.

Frank Borman was beside himself with anguish and frustration. He had spent his adult life operating within a chain of command, much of it with himself at or near the top. But the command structure of Eastern Air Lines had suddenly been inverted. Now the workers were in control, like "monkeys running the zoo," he thought.

The Colonel's misfortunes were rooted in the 32 percent settlement he had awarded the machinists to keep Charlie Bryan from leading a strike. Eastern's bankers, perceiving no irony in the situation, were so outraged at Borman's capitulation that they moved to restrict his credit lines even further, even though it was their refusal to release cash under those same credit lines that caused Borman to cave in the first place. The combination of swelling costs and tightening credit threw Eastern into a genuine cash flow crisis.

Borman was in the midst of this drama on the day that Frank Lorenzo put Continental into Chapter 11. Within hours Borman was in a video studio at company headquarters in Miami, peering into a lens and grimly demanding immediate pay cuts of 15 percent.

Without them, he warned, Eastern might very well file for bankruptcy, "à la Continental," or liquidate altogether, "à la Braniff." Eastern executives fanned out through the system, distributing Borman's videotaped bankruptcy threat.

Once reported by the press, the bankruptcy threat did less to intimidate Eastern's employees than to frighten its customers. The Continental Chapter 11 filing had burned thousands of passengers, travel agents, and tour operators, just as the Braniff bankruptcy had. Nobody was eager to be the third cigarette on the match. Practically overnight Eastern passengers redeemed some $2 million worth of individual tickets. Miami-based cruise lines that provided airline tickets to their customers abandoned Eastern. By threatening bankruptcy Borman had only worsened the cash flow crisis. At Eastern's hub in Atlanta, the machinists hired a skywriter who filled the air with the message "Frank Borman, Resign Now"—not as arresting as "Surrender Dorothy," perhaps, but a startling message just the same.

In this round of BOHICA—"Bend over, here it comes again"—the unions were in a better position than ever to demand something in exchange for their concessions. Randy Barber, who had once joined with a band of French unionists that had seized control of a watch factory, helped to structure an extraordinary range of ownership concessions by the company. Eastern employees received shares in Eastern Air Lines equivalent to 25 percent of the company's equity. Their unions won complete access to the company's internal financial reports any time they wished to examine them. Budgets, spending authorizations, fleet planning—the blizzard of confidential paperwork that drifted through any major corporation—all now passed through the hands of Charlie Bryan, his colleagues in the other unions, and all of their aides, minions, advisors, and hangers-on.

On top of all that the unions had been awarded three seats on the Eastern Air Lines board of directors, the fulfillment of a dream for Charlie Bryan. Joining him on the board was Robert V. Callaghan, president of the flight attendants' union at Eastern, and an outside lawyer representing the pilots.

Borman consented to these extraordinary concessions with the enthusiasm of an inmate on his way to the electric chair; he relented not just under the pressure from the unions but on the advice of some of his own aides. Something had to be done, they counseled him, to break the cycle of mistrust and confrontation that had become the way of life at Eastern Air Lines. There had been too many close calls, too many bluffs, too many brushes with bankruptcy. Some board members also viewed the company's concessions as an opportunity to teach some reason to Charlie Bryan, to impress him with the gravity of Eastern's problems and the awesome responsibility of managing the company's delicate affairs. Peter O. Crisp, who represented the Rockefeller interests on the board, made a point of cozying up to Bryan. John T. "Jack" Fallon, a Boston real estate maven, would take Bryan to football games or share stories about his good friends, the Kennedys, whom Bryan so admired. Bryan would later admit to delighting in the attention.

In the new participatory atmosphere, a program was established for employees to identify cost-saving ideas. Individual workers were appointed to operating committees. Time cards were ripped up. Employees began going the extra mile—delivering errant luggage to passengers on their way home, for instance. And suddenly Eastern Air Lines, that crucible of labor-management hatred, was a cause célèbre. Consultants, journalists, and academics descended on the company. *Washington Monthly* magazine called it "the largest experiment in labor-management cooperation in American history." One of Eastern's consultants told *The New York Times* that "Eastern has the most extensive employee participation system of any American corporation today." A study team from Harvard won a Department of Transportation contract to determine how Eastern could serve as a model for other companies. And Charlie Bryan was no longer just a labor leader. He was now a statesman, a shining example of union-management cooperation. He went on tour, giving speeches about codetermination.

Eastern tried to extract some small marketing advantage for its newly forged "partnership" with organized labor. Borman renewed his appearances in Eastern's television advertising, surrounded by mechanics, flight attendants, and pilots. "Who can serve you better than the owners?" he asked. Eastern extolled itself as the first employee-owned airline in America (causing Herb Kelleher of Southwest Airlines to write Borman a chiding letter. "You're off by 10 years," Kelleher said.)

But while Borman was outwardly proclaiming that "the war is over," he was dying inside. The warm-and-fuzzy act was a brave face, intended purely for public consumption. Privately he considered all the union involvement to be so much "crap." Borman cringed with each new accolade in the press. Where the newly born team spirit existed, it was confined largely to a single location—Kansas City, a newly established hub through which Borman was again struggling to break into the transcontinental market. It was true that an impressive harmony had taken hold there, but it was far from typical. Kansas City was a brand-new operation with many freshly hired employees. It was not crowded with embittered middle managers and die-hard unionists.

Through it all management was blind to the monster it was creating: an employee group, and a union leader in particular, hailed as exemplars of employee participation when in fact there was really no employee participation at all. All the unions had really received was access to Eastern's confidential internal documents and three out of sixteen votes on a board of directors, which might as well have been three in a million. Those concessions had established a détente in the cold war at Eastern, but no peace. And both sides remained sufficiently armed to fulfill the Cold War concept of mutually assured destruction.

If there was any doubt about the fragility of the peace, it was erased in April of 1985, when the machinists' contract once again came up for renewal. The Colonel wanted yet another BOHICA deal, preserving some of the concessions already in place. And amazingly Charlie Bryan, now playing the role of union statesman, urged his members to assent. They did not. Over the advice of their beloved leader, the aircraft mechanics and baggage handlers and fuel loaders who made up the IAM voted down the proposed new contract in a ratification vote. After few minor changes Charlie Bryan got the deal approved, but the incident had shaken him and his aides. It was apparent that however wild-eyed and radical Charlie Bryan might seem, he was actually a moderate next to the majority of his membership.

Borman, perhaps worst of all for him, had lost much of his standing with his pilots, a group for whom he had once walked on water. He appealed for their understanding on professional grounds. "To the best of my knowledge," he told their leadership during a meeting at the Miami Airport Ramada, "I am the only pilot running a major airline." He pleaded urgently for the pilots to adopt b-scales in their next contract. "I am not standing here like Ferris did and saying, 'Take this or nothing.' Maybe I made the [mistake of thinking] that we could act like adults and look at the numbers together and reach a conclusion." While waiting for b-scales Borman hit the brakes on hiring new pilots, but he soon found himself without enough pilots to fly his own schedule. In the last week of October 1985 alone he was forced to cancel more than 500 flights from crew shortages, only worsening Eastern's financial problems.

It was a testament to the Colonel's long-range vision that despite the intense, minute-to-minute financial pressures, he never wavered from his commitment to building up Eastern's computer reservation system. It had grown into the third largest system in the industry, with 17 percent of the travel agency market, significantly exceeding the TWA and Delta systems and beginning to close in on United's Apollo. Eastern's network, called System One Direct Access, was noted among travel agents for a number of outstanding features, in some respects exceeding even Sabre and Apollo. The growth of System One and the accompanying halo effect on Eastern's bookings was one of the things keeping Eastern alive.

But then it hit. The Big One—the one killer fare war that was capable at last of putting Eastern over the edge.

Ed Acker started it just as the winter tourist season was kicking off in the fall of 1985. Pan Am wanted cash. Acker wanted full airplanes. Still infatuated with $99 fares, he slashed prices to that level from New York to Florida. Eastern, of course, would have to match.

Don Burr would not be undersold on principle, and he needed cash besides. Before long People Express announced a $69 fare to Florida. Eastern, of course, would have to match.

The following day Lorenzo weighed in. New York Air, gravely damaged in the Northeast by the controllers' strike but alive and kicking and causing trouble elsewhere, would fly to Florida for $39. Eastern, of course, would have to match.

In the midst of the Florida pricing war, in rolled the massive machine of American Airlines, staking a huge new hub in San Juan, in the heart of Eastern's most profitable operation. Crandall's coterie could see that Eastern was wounded and reeling. American had adopted, as an explicit internal goal, the "domination of Caribbean marketing."

Only one thing could save Eastern. Yes, it was back to the well for more concessions, but it really, *really,* counted this time. Anybody could see that. Thirty-nine-dollar fares to Florida! The sky was falling, really and truly.

Borman wrote a letter to employees saying that all those concessions in the past, all those "temporary programs," were no longer sufficient. "We must look beyond Band-Aids." This time Borman wanted a straight 20 percent off the top. And this time there was no "God bless you" at the end.

Once again cries of "BOHICA!" went up from the locker rooms and dispatch centers of the airline. Like his insensitive comparison of an earlier wage giveback to a few six-packs of beer, Borman's characterization of years of concessions as mere "Band-Aids" outraged employees anew.

The three principal union groups—the machinists, pilots, and flight attendants—had never particularly gotten along, neither at the leadership nor at the membership level. That now changed. Combined rallies were staged at snowy locations in the north. Lawyers were jointly engaged—not some slouch Miami Beach outfit but Skadden, Arps, Slate, Meagher & Flom of Wall Street, the General Motors of the takeover bar. If Borman couldn't run Eastern, the unions would look into running it themselves. They already owned 25 percent of the company, after all. Charlie Bryan pleaded with his members to buy stock, noting that if each of Eastern's 40,000 employees bought just $3,000 in shares, the workers would control Eastern Air Lines.

Watching the spectacle from a distance, Eastern's bankers added more uncertainty still: unless Borman had the wage cuts in place by February 28, 1986, they told him, they would cut the company off for good. It would be curtains for Eastern, a certain bankruptcy filing.

In his career as a pilot and astronaut Borman had never flown a mission without three courses of action firmly planned. The first was to complete the mission, the second was to resort to an acceptable alternate mission, and the third was to bail out. Borman now reduced his goal at Eastern to three options. He would try to win over the unions; failing that, he would find a buyer for Eastern; failing that, he would file for Chapter 11 protection. In his dealings with his fellow officers, his board members, and the unions, he expressed his new strategy over and over, as if it were his mantra: "Fix it, sell it, or tank it."

Borman knew his credibility was shot. If he had any hope of completing the first mission, he needed a stalking-horse, a real warmonger.

No sooner had this realization hit Borman than a call came from Frank Lorenzo. He wanted a meeting. "I'd like to talk to you about System One," Lorenzo said.

They got together at a small office that Eastern maintained in New York, and it was immediately obvious to Borman that Lorenzo wanted System One very badly. They discussed the variety of ways a transaction could be structured, including a merger of System One and the in-house Continental reservations system. No deal was reached, but they agreed to revisit the matter soon. Borman took immediately to Lorenzo, who was direct, just like Borman, and who hated small talk, also just like Borman. Borman decided to unveil his hidden agenda tentatively, almost as if he were making a joke.

"I might get back to you [to sell] not just the reservation system but the whole airline," Borman said.

"I wouldn't be interested in doing anything unless it's a friendly arrangement," Lorenzo answered. "But if you want to talk further, just give me a call."

Borman flew back to Miami so excited he could hardly contain himself. "I regarded Texas Air as an ace in the hole," he later explained.

Borman quickly contacted Richard Magurno, a soft-spoken former Peace Corps volunteer who had risen through the ranks of the Eastern legal department to become the general counsel of the company. Magurno had grown close over the years to a number of Eastern's distinguished outside directors. Borman excitedly described his conversation with Lorenzo. He wanted to go to the board immediately, then to the unions, brandishing Lorenzo as his new bogeyman. Borman wanted the world to know that if the unions didn't deal, if

Charlie Bryan didn't cave this time, they'd have Frank Lorenzo to deal with.

Although he did not consider it his place to say so directly, Magurno thought the Colonel needed a cold shower. Acting impulsively would throw Eastern Air Lines into play, particularly in the frenzied takeover environment of December 1985. So Magurno placed a discreet call to his best contact on the board: Roswell Gilpatric, a retired 79-year-old partner in the New York law firm of Cravath, Swaine & Moore, who had served as deputy defense secretary in the Kennedy White House. Gilpatric in turn called Borman and urged him to move with caution.

Within a few weeks, with the crisis at Eastern mounting, Borman was having his second meeting with Lorenzo, during an industry function at the sprawling Marriott resort center in Fort Lauderdale. This time Lorenzo seemed wary. "I want to know if you're serious about selling Eastern, or are you just using me as a bargaining chip?" he demanded. Borman explained his strategy—to fix it, sell it, or tank it—and promised that if he failed in the first goal, he would deal with Texas Air in good faith.

Borman talked to other potential buyers. Northwest Airlines, financially strong, wasn't interested. He met in Washington with Don Burr of People Express to discuss a possible merger but dismissed Burr as a real-life Elmer Gantry. "He was loony tunes," Borman would later recall. Borman even sounded out some oil companies, which at the time were the biggest takeover players in the game. There too he drilled a dry hole. That left only Frank Lorenzo.

To that point Borman's dealings with Lorenzo had been strictly sub-rosa and totally informal. In the takeover culture that had developed in the mid-1980s, merger deals, regardless of the contact between willing principals, were not set into motion until the investment bankers from Wall Street had become involved, like ministers at a baptism. Borman contacted Eastern's investment bankers at Merrill Lynch. He was ready to play his ace in the hole.

"What do you think?"

It was the afternoon of Friday, February 21, 1986. The Presidents' Day weekend was about to begin, and Phil Bakes had plane tickets from Houston to Washington. Frank Lorenzo had just invited himself into Bakes's office, announcing that Frank Borman's investment bankers had telephoned. Eastern Air Lines, they had told Lorenzo, was officially available.

"What should we tell them?" Lorenzo asked Bakes.

Bakes could hear nothing but alarm bells. After dodging the airline unions with New York Air and destroying trade unionism at Continental, Texas Air was not exactly the ideal candidate for defusing the most volatile labor situation anywhere in the United States. As Bakes would later put it, "We were the wrong savior for this flock."

Bakes tried to be direct with Lorenzo: "I think it's a swamp from which we will never return."

But Lorenzo began to rhapsodize. Eastern, a company he had once worked for . . . Eastern, one of the original Big Four . . . One could never build anything like that today, he thought. "That franchise," Lorenzo said in Bakes's office. "That name . . ."

Of course, Lorenzo recognized, it was a damaged name; the labor wars were so unfortunate. And its routes—they were uniquely vulnerable to competitive attack, stuck in the world's single most competitive airline market, the East Coast. Eastern did not have a cozy position in some hub, Lorenzo thought, where it could hide a lot of high costs. But he had seen worse, had even been involved with worse—Continental, for instance. When he bought it, Continental had a lousier market position than Eastern at this point, Lorenzo thought.

And of course Eastern had System One, the jewel in its otherwise dull crown, a crucifix to wave in the path of the advancing Sabre and Apollo systems. Apart from its virtue as the third largest airline reservation network in the country, System One, as Lorenzo would explain, was the only computer reservation network in the United States the purchase of which was remotely plausible.

Bakes realized that Lorenzo, absorbed in a reverie, had already made up his mind, to which Bakes thought, "You tune me out, and I'm out of here." And 90 minutes later Bakes was on an airplane, on his way to a great weekend, leaving Lorenzo to deal alone for Eastern.

Frank Borman had known the international president of the machinists' union for years. He was William "Winpy" Winpisinger, rotund and irascible, full of bombast, with ideological leanings as far to the left as one could reach in mainstream politics. Winpisinger and Borman loved fast cars. The machinists sponsored an Indy-class race team, and the two men frequently sat together at the Indianapolis Speedway, the same racetrack once owned by the erstwhile Eastern chairman, Eddie Rickenbacker.

So Borman could confer with the union chief freely and confidentially when Winpisinger was in Miami for an AFL-CIO function on Friday, February 21, 1986. Although the pilots and flight attendants were also resisting Borman's plea for 20 percent pay cuts, it was Charlie Bryan who most worried the Colonel. Was there anything Winpy could do?

Winpisinger was in a desperate fix. To the extent that he admired his friend Borman he mistrusted his own local president. Winpisinger thought Bryan had made himself into a king, so much so that people sometimes mistook Bryan for the international president of the machinists' union.

"Charlie hears voices," Winpisinger told Borman.

But at the same time, Winpisinger was painfully aware that the rank-and-file resentment against Borman was powerful and still building. Borman had gone to the well once too often. And in any event, Winpisinger was mostly powerless under the union's constitution to control Bryan.

Winpisinger gave Borman a pep talk. Just keep bargaining, he said. Everything will work out. But in encouraging him to continue pressing, the international president left Borman with the indelible impression that he, the mighty William Winpisinger, would step in at the last minute and sit on Charlie Bryan if it was necessary for saving Eastern Air Lines.

Frank Borman left his meeting with Winpisinger heaving a sigh of relief. Maybe he could, after all, fix Eastern. Maybe, just maybe, he could checkmate Charlie Bryan.

That evening, word came back from Frank Lorenzo. He was willing to buy Eastern. He would pay only $600 million, however, peanuts for that great name, that great franchise, that jewel of a computer reservation system. In fact, under the proposal presented by Lorenzo, about $300 million of the purchase price would be paid to Eastern shareholders by extracting cash from Eastern itself; Eastern, in short, would be paying for half of its own acquisition. And regardless of the outcome, the offer was good only if Eastern agreed up front to pay $20 million to Lorenzo as a nonrefundable "inducement fee."

Lorenzo, moreover, would not keep the offer on the table for long. His lawyers still had all the draft contracts in their word processors from the recent attempt to buy TWA; all they had to do was switch the names and the numbers. There was no reason for delay. The takeover offer, Lorenzo said, was good only until midnight Sunday.

If Borman was going to use Lorenzo as a bogeyman with the unions, he had to work fast. He had barely a day to fix it. For good measure, with jealousy and hatred running so high on all sides, he was back to wearing his bulletproof vest.

The pilots' union and the flight attendants' union had been coaxed to the bargaining table, where Borman's aides were fervently trying to talk them into the 20 percent wage reduction. Charlie Bryan, however, was vomiting. After going years without a sniffle, he was now gripped by a debilitating flu. His fever shot up to 103 degrees. Shuddering with chills, he felt as if he were in a meat locker.

He had just returned from a Saturday afternoon board meeting with several of the directors, where he was put on notice that Eastern was ready to resort to plan B, selling it—and not to just anyone. Unless the machinists capitulated to the 20 percent cutback, Eastern would be sold to the most dreaded enemy of the airline unions, Frank Lorenzo. As the directors and investment bankers for Eastern importuned him to come to terms, he warned them off. "Watch out," he said. "I've got the flu."

That evening Bryan was back at the local union offices with his consultant Randy Barber. They pondered the variables, ran economic scenarios, pondered every what-if they could imagine. From all they could tell, Eastern had passed the financial fail-safe point. There was no hope for the company, certainly not with the current management and possibly not with any management. The 20 percent concession might prolong the company's life a few months, they reasoned, but it would only postpone failure. Moreover, Barber was convinced that the rank and file would never stand for more BO-HICA. Only 10 months earlier they had handed Charlie Bryan his head by voting down a concessionary contract that he himself had urged them to accept in the name of peace.

The Eastern board was scheduled to meet again the following day, Sunday, February 23, 1986, a few hours before Lorenzo's deadline. Bryan went to bed with his fever and nausea and no idea what the following day would bring.

On Sunday afternoon, the directors' limousines began pulling up to Building 16 alongside the mammoth expanse of Rickenbacker Fountain, where the image of the founding chairman was cast in bronze relief on a stone monument. The fountain itself, however, was dry, the water drained and the power cut off years earlier in a cost-saving move.

The front doors led to an expansive lobby with a great circular reception desk in the middle. The marble floor, like the fountain out front, bespoke the pretensions that Eastern had once harbored. To the left, as one entered the lobby, a great route map hung on the wall, with little lightbulbs dimly burning behind each of the cities served by Eastern, all the way to LEE-mah and Bway-nos-I-rays. The lobby also bore the telltale markings of previous efforts to redecorate on a tight budget—a section of wood paneling here, some wallpaper striped in green and orange there.

The directors strode through the lobby to a door next to the twinkling route map and entered a small auditorium outfitted with ionosphere blue carpeting. In the auditorium several rows of seats were arrayed theater-style before a small, elevated stage, where a large table sat. It was on that stage, with their advisors seated in the audience and the curious hanging around the lobby outside, that the directors sat down to decide the future of Eastern.

The directors assembled only briefly in the afternoon, long enough to hear that the documents for Lorenzo's purchase were nearing completion and that the pilots and flight attendants were negotiating in earnest over Borman's 20 percent demand. For the machinists, however, Bryan was still refusing to entertain the cutbacks. The offer from Lorenzo, due to expire at midnight, would be presented for a vote after dinner.

The directors adjourned and were driven the few blocks to the Airport Hilton, where they ate salads and sandwiches and desperately wondered what would happen next. Where, someone asked, was Bill Winpisinger? The machinists' international president had promised to bring Charlie Bryan under control if the threat of a sale to Lorenzo had been insufficient; it was now time to call on Winpisinger to do so. Jack Fallon, the old Kennedy family pal on the Eastern board, tried to track down someone on Ted Kennedy's Senate staff in Washington for help in locating Winpisinger. On Presidents' Day weekend it was an almost impossible endeavor.

Back to Building 16 trooped the directors, back into the auditorium, slamming shut the doors behind them at 7:30 P.M. and leaving an even larger crowd of bystanders and onlookers assembled in the main lobby of Building 16. Soon word arrived that the flight attendants had settled, consenting to the demand for a 20 percent cutback to save Eastern. During a recess Borman encountered Randy Barber, the machinists' advisor. "Well," the Colonel asked, "is Charlie going to change his mind?"

"You'll have to ask him yourself," Barber answered.

"I did," Borman answered. "He said no. It's too bad, but I'm through begging."

As adamantly as Bryan was continuing to stonewall, those who listened carefully were noticing a slight wavering on one point. There would be no more concessions from the machinists, he was saying, *for this management.* Was Bryan leaving the door open to concessions if Borman were out?

The fact was, in Bryan's view, that giving concessions to Frank Borman was like giving drugs to an addict, like passing a wine cork under the nose of a drunk. All it did was intensify his craving for more concessions. Implicit in Bryan's reasoning was the possibility that the machinists *would* cave to the demand for concessions if the management of Eastern were somehow changed to Bryan's liking. The union had made no secret of its wish to see Borman sacked. "Frank Borman—Resign Now!" the skywriters had written.

Of course the Eastern board could never sack Frank Borman on the motion of Charles Bryan; the directors of no major company would ever allow a union leader to dictate who occupied the office of chairman. But perhaps Bryan had shown them an opening. Perhaps there was a middle ground.

A recess was called. Borman pulled Bryan into an elevator in the lobby. They rose to the top of the building, to the executive offices, with the screaming-70s orange vinyl wallpaper and arched doorways. There Borman turned Bryan over to two of the board's most distinguished members: H. Hood Bassett, one of South Florida's leading bankers, and Peter Crisp, the Rockefeller representative. What if Eastern got a vice chairman to serve alongside Borman? the directors asked Bryan. Perhaps even someone of Bryan's choosing? Would he *then* consent to the 20 percent cutbacks?

No way, Bryan said.

The directors had made an extraordinary offer and had been refused. Now they were really mad.

Bryan offered a proposal of his own: instead of consenting to the 20 percent cutback, the union would commit to saving an equivalent sum through productivity improvements and other measures that didn't invade anyone's paycheck. Bryan would promise right then and there that if the union failed to save the company that sum of money, the 20 percent cutbacks would occur automatically in six months' time.

No way, the directors said.

Borman appeared from his office, announcing that he had reached Winpisinger in Washington—Winpisinger, who had promised to "handle" Charlie. Borman turned the receiver over to Bryan and left him alone with Randy Barber at his side.

"What's going on?" Winpy asked his local president.

"Well, we're going at it hot and heavy," Bryan answered. "They're threatening to sell the company to Lorenzo."

"What's your judgment?"

"The way they're trying to destroy this company, there's no way that I'm going to subsidize that," Bryan said.

Winpisinger anguished over his predicament. He wished he could take over the bargaining himself, but there were no grounds to fire Charlie Bryan. Yet something had to be done fast to prevent the sale to Lorenzo. One way or another, the machinists simply had to come to terms. And between the two unionists—the international president, on the phone in Washington, and the local president, sitting in Frank Borman's office on the ninth floor of Building 16—there was no disagreement about the price the rank and file would require for another BOHICA deal. That price was Frank Borman's head.

"Goddam it," Winpisinger said. "Get it done!" Bryan handed the telephone receiver back to Frank Borman and left the office.

Winpisinger then told his close friend that however much Borman might have been counting on him, he was powerless to rein in Bryan.

"You know this means the end of Eastern," Borman answered, his voice growing raspy.

Maybe, maybe not. But all Winpisinger could say was, "So be it."

It was 11:40 P.M. when the directors reassembled in the blue auditorium.Frank Lorenzo's deadline was rapidly approaching. Borman finally lost his composure. He was trembling. Pointing his finger at Bryan, he began to shout. "I'm going to tell the world that you destroyed this airline!"

"And I'm going to tell them *you* did!" Bryan answered. "So where does that leave us?"

In the lobby, a telephone rang on the circular reception desk. An Eastern public relations executive lifted the receiver. "Continental Airlines," he cheerfully answered.

The directors were both furious and frightened. Serving as an outside director in an earlier age accorded a bit of distinction and a little bit of money besides. It was so easy. A director showed up and got a check for a few thousand bucks. In the case of an airline board, a director and his wife also enjoyed free travel privileges, usually in first class. But the Eastern directors were now at risk for something they had never bargained for: the likelihood that they would be sued personally if they mishandled this delicate situation in any way.

Midnight had arrived. The directors had a bona fide offer from Frank Lorenzo on the table. Lorenzo, thank goodness, had just extended his deadline, although only to 4 A.M. Option number one—fix it—appeared to have failed. If the directors failed to act on option number two—sell it—that left only the final alternative, tank it. In that case the shareholders of the company would wind up with nothing. As creditors standing last in a long line of claimants, individual investors would find that their shares were worthless. If the directors passed up the opportunity to get *something* for the shareholders by selling to Frank Lorenzo, they would be giving depositions and answering interrogatories for years, to say nothing of the risk to their personal assets, which in some cases were considerable.

The board's lawyers, from the firm of Davis, Polk & Wardwell, tried to give their clients some comfort. Nothing was forcing the directors to act immediately. Salomon Brothers, the investment banking firm advising the directors, had still not rendered an opinion of the fairness of Lorenzo's terms to Eastern shareholders. In the absence of a fairness opinion, the board still had the cover necessary to take more time.

But what if Lorenzo went away? The board would have no choice then but to tank it.

Texas Air sent word into the boardroom that it would indemnify the directors up to $35 million if they were ever sued—*if,* that is, they agreed to sell the company to Texas Air. The whole rotten affair had gone on too long. The paperwork had just been completed. It was time to vote.

The senior director, Jack Fallon, was presiding. The sale to Texas Air was moved and seconded . . .

"Hold it!"

The meeting came to a halt as Charlie Bryan excused himself to the lobby outside. Soon, two other directors, Hood Basset and Peter Crisp, were called from the meeting room. With a gaggle of advisors in tow the directors and Bryan made their way to a small, private office on the other side of the lobby.

As the remaining directors waited, Borman left for a breath of fresh air. Under a nearly full moon he stood in front of Building 16. He rolled his tense shoulders and stared at the bronze image of Capt. Eddie Rickenbacker. He knew he had lost control of the situation. Eastern, he was sure, was going to be sold.

Returning to the lobby, Borman encountered the caucusing directors as they sped back to the boardroom.

"Well?" Borman asked Peter Crisp, the Rockefeller man. "What is it?"

"You'll hear in a minute," Crisp answered. With his proposal at issue, Charlie Bryan remained in the lobby.

When everyone else had been seated again at the directors' table, Hood Bassett, the senior director, announced that the machinists were prepared to assent to concessions—but only of 15 percent. Bryan, the director explained, felt the machinists had already contributed the equivalent of 5 percent through increased productivity.

Some of the people in the room were incredulous that Bryan would chisel at such a moment, but there was more.

"Mr. Bryan's offer," Bassett continued, the muscles of his face tightening, "is contingent upon the appointment of a board committee to search for a new chief executive officer."

Well, at least it's out in the open, Borman told himself.

Borman rose, struggling against another loss of composure. "Any allegation that the IAM has already given 5 percent is nonsense." Besides which, he said, the company had to have the full 20 percent in any case.

He turned to Wayne Yoeman, Eastern's chief financial officer, a retired brigadier general with a Harvard Ph.D. "Don't you agree we can't do this with 15 percent?" Borman asked from the stage.

"It would collapse the company!" Yoeman answered.

Borman continued. "If the IAM will give 20 percent like the other employees, I'll submit my resignation this evening."

Dick Magurno, the company's general counsel, watched the scene unfold with dismay. The 5 percent was meaningless. *Of course* the company could survive without it. The company could even make money without it. But the directors had boxed themselves in. Emotions had overwhelmed everyone, on all sides. Charlie Bryan couldn't give the board 20 percent, and the board couldn't give him 5 percent.

Borman once again had to depart the meeting room, since his job was now at issue. In the lobby he approached Bryan. "Just so you know, I'm volunteering to leave. No one can run a company under these circumstances."

Then one of Bryan's lawyers emerged from the auditorium. The directors would accept the 15 percent solution. They would allow Bryan to help pick a vice chairman, as previously offered—but they would not throw out Frank Borman.

"Their promises are no good!" Bryan snapped. "Only drastic action will do!"

The crowd in the lobby had become a throng. Though it was now well after 2 A.M., employees were showing up to find out for themselves whether Eastern Air had been fixed, sold, or tanked. Finally the auditorium door flew open. "They did it!" someone yelled. "They sold the airline!"

Joe Leonard, a top Eastern executive, emerged from the auditorium to grab Borman and haul him back inside. The directors gave him a standing ovation that rang into the lobby. When he reemerged, Borman was engulfed in the crowd of employees. They wanted to hear it from him. He began to speak softly, in a whisper.

"I'm sorry to tell you that as a result of our inability to reach agreement, the board did the only thing it could do and that was to sell." The buyer, he said, was Texas Air.

Borman paused.

"I'll think of something more to say tomorrow," he finally said, his voice cracking.

Following the board vote, the pilots were desperate to nail down their new contract. Giving up 20 percent was better than going to work for Lorenzo with wages still at issue. But some of Borman's people were refusing to sign, even on the company's hard-fought terms. Why should Eastern settle now? Why not let the new boss, Frank Lorenzo, bargain for himself?

Borman sensed he was on shaky ground legally, but turned to his aides. "Sign," he instructed them.

It was 3:30 A.M. when the pilot leaders went to him to offer their profuse thanks. They found him with tears streaming down his cheeks.

"I'm sorry," he said.

Charlie Bryan tried to put the best face on an unthinkably horrible situation largely of his own making. Lorenzo, he thought, was at least a businessman. It might be a pleasure to deal with a businessman instead of an astronaut, Bryan thought. "It might be surprising the relationship that could develop between Lorenzo and our organization," Bryan said publicly. "For all his faults Lorenzo is a businessman who has demonstrated that he knows how to run a successful company. I can work with Frank Lorenzo."

Within a few hours Bryan and his people had crafted a message to Lorenzo, which they sent by telegram.

In view of the actions of our board of directors at Eastern Air Lines, it appears you will be in control of the airline in the near future.

District 100 of the machinists union has been consistent in its pursuit

of service excellence with maximum productivity and efficiency. . . . It is
my sincere hope that we can succeed in developing a joint effort in pursuit of those goals. I believe that a cooperative relationship between us
would be a pleasant surprise to the flying public, Eastern employees, and
the entire financial community. I am at your disposal to schedule a meeting to begin exploring the challenges and opportunities that lie ahead.

Bryan would never receive an answer to his invitation.

A day later the two Franks, Lorenzo and Borman, sat behind a table
covered with white fabric and a forest of microphones. Although
Eastern Air Lines would remain a separate company until the
months of reviews and approvals and shareholder votes had been
completed, it was only appropriate that the two men appear together
before the media, whose representatives had crammed into the blue
auditorium of Building 16. It was the largest media turnout in Eastern's history, and as Lorenzo learned from the first question, they
were ready for blood.

"Mr. Lorenzo, you are known as a union buster. Are you proud of
that title?"

"No—"

"—and he stopped beating his wife yesterday," the Colonel
quickly snapped. "Why don't we take another question?"

Lorenzo tried to get back to the union busting issue, but the reporters couldn't hear him in the back.

"Mr. Lorenzo! Please speak up!"

Lorenzo did manage to convey his history as a union truck driver.
"You know," he said, "I remember the day when I carried a Teamsters card in my wallet and worked my way up through school. So
any talk of 'union busting' is absolute nonsense."

But what about Borman? What about his contract? the reporters
demanded.

"Will we be honoring Mr. Borman's contract? Absolutely!"
Lorenzo said.

"When the takeover is completed?"

"Of course we will," Lorenzo answered.

Yet it was only days later that Lorenzo stepped into Borman's office at the top of Building 16 with a different message. Borman still

felt he was in the middle of a crusade to make Eastern profitable. He believed he had a residue of rapport with the Eastern pilots. In truth the Colonel wanted very much to remain the head of Eastern, even if it was soon to become a wholly owned subsidiary of Texas Air.

No, Lorenzo said. As soon as the deal was concluded, Borman would have to leave. He would have to make room for someone else.

In the great game of executive musical chairs another seat was removed forever. Col. Frank Borman was out of the game, for good.

Phil Bakes stared at Frank Lorenzo over a dinner table at the sumptuous Inn on the Park in Houston.

"You've done a great job," Lorenzo told him, "but Continental is fixed now. We feel you're the guy to take on Texas Air's biggest asset, and biggest challenge." Eastern Air Lines.

Bakes was sick to his stomach. He had not held up his hand for Eastern. Eastern was a cesspool, he thought. He had opposed the acquisition to begin with. Continental—his baby!—had barely emerged from Chapter 11. He had battled at every turn to rebuild the market while keeping costs down. He had endured the slings and arrows of Frank Lorenzo.

And there was so much work left to be done. Bakes wanted to rehabilitate his image, to repair the damage his reputation had suffered in the dark days of Continental's failure. He wanted to complete his plan to create a "participatory culture" at Continental. Bakes was also now dreaming of a huge international expansion. He was contemplating a complete makeover of the company's tired logo and its worn aircraft interiors. His "airport of the future" project, with its ticketless operations and self-serve bag check, was well under way.

"Continental really *isn't* finished," Bakes corrected Lorenzo. He felt the knot in his stomach tightening.

And besides which, Miami? Who wanted to live in Miami? Bakes had settled in in Houston and loved it. His wife and son were comfortable there. They had a beautiful home in the exclusive Memorial section, near parks, near downtown.

"I really love where I'm at," Bakes went on.

"Somebody else can do that," Lorenzo said. "We need you for the really tough challenge."

Bakes said he wanted to think it over, but there was no point in trying to bluff Frank. "Obviously," he said forlornly, "what's best for the company, I'm going to do." About three weeks later Texas Air announced that Bakes, age 40, would become the president and chief executive officer of Eastern Air Lines.

The final act in the acquisition of Eastern was a vote of approval by Eastern's shareholders. There was not much mystery about the outcome of their vote, considering that as part of the merger agreement Texas Air had already locked up the majority of the shares. In fact there were probably good reasons not to have a meeting. Bakes, for one, saw nothing but the potential for disruption.

"But we've got to have a meeting!" one of the Eastern people said. "It's a legal requirement."

"Fine," Bakes said. "Have two lawyers sit in a room and sign some papers."

The truth was that some of the old directors wanted to have a final meeting, as a kind of send-off.

Fine, Bakes said reluctantly. "You better be prepared for what you get."

His fears were well-founded. Charlie Bryan, exercising his privileges as a shareholder, took a microphone and went on and on, haranguing about Borman and Lorenzo and other issues until finally a gadfly shareholder named Lewis Gilbert, who had made a career of attending annual meetings all over the country in the name of shareholder democracy, stood up, pointed his finger at Bryan, and shouted, "Get to the point!"

Bryan turned with a scowl to the distinguished if slightly eccentric older gentleman. "You wouldn't know a point if it hit you in the head!" he screamed.

Some people laughed and others simply shook their heads in silence as Bryan droned on, refusing to yield the floor. When the votes had been counted and the merger deemed effective, Bryan was still talking, refusing the entreaties of senior director Jack Fallon that he retake his seat. Finally the meeting was simply adjourned, and the people from the company began departing, but Bryan, undeterred, walked from his seat to the front of the auditorium, continuing his speech. Someone from the company had shut down the public address system, but Bryan simply raised his voice. And then they turned off the lights, leaving Charlie Bryan alone on the stage of the darkened auditorium, still talking.

Although Lorenzo had only begun to consolidate his control over Eastern, the management of the company went out of its way to include him in its deliberations, as was only right and proper. At one point a longtime Eastern planner and marketer named David Kunstler, one of the true brains of the organization, sat down with Lorenzo in New York to brief him on the company's competitive challenges and opportunities. Kunstler had a great deal of credibility with the Eastern organization for having opposed some of the more disastrous moves in the years after deregulation.

Kunstler felt Eastern should concentrate its resources rather than disperse them, and now, he told Lorenzo, was the perfect time for Eastern to put everything it could into Newark. There were strong indications that People Express, after making life so miserable for Eastern for so long, was vulnerable. Perhaps under Lorenzo a focused and revitalized Eastern could finish it off. And if People Express were gone, Eastern, by making the proper moves in advance, could position itself as a dominant carrier in Newark.

It was an eminent if dastardly proposal, but Kunstler would never get the chance to bring it off. Only days earlier, Frank Lorenzo had been talking to his old friend and old enemy, Don Burr. Lorenzo had something else in store for People Express.

CHAPTER 12

NOSEDIVE

It was a proud moment: the arrival of the first 747 in the People Express fleet. As the plane neared Newark Airport, Donald Burr, fascinated from adolescence with watching planes come in, excitedly climbed to the roof of the North Terminal for a better view.

The voice of a Port Authority police officer bellowed from below. "If you don't get off the roof right now," he shouted, "I'll shoot you!"

Burr would later tell the story as proof of the Port Authority's ingratitude. People Express, after all, had by 1984 transformed the godforsaken Newark Airport into the eighth largest airport in the country, bigger even than LaGuardia, handling 2 million passengers a month. Yet the Port Authority still treated People Express with contempt, refusing to allow Burr to install a People Express sign on the terminal, falling down in its commitment to keep the airport bathrooms clean. Burr, who had a compulsion about clean bathrooms, ordered his employees to clean them themselves.

But the story of Burr's gunpoint confrontation was much more revealing of Burr than of the Port Authority. To Burr aviation was romance. Managing people was variously an exercise in love and obedience instruction. Transporting passengers was like an act of New Testament good works. An airplane bearing the double profile of People Express was an object of genuine affection.

Burr had created a stunningly large airline—and a successful one—from nothing. After barely three years in operation, People Express was equivalent in size to Braniff before its demise. In the New York area People Express had become the number one airline, with more departures than even Eastern with all its shuttle flights. To an entire generation of backpacking students—kids who either lived on the East Coast, went to college there, or had girlfriends or boyfriends there—passage through the North Terminal had become a postadolescent ritual.

The melee at the North Terminal reached its height after Burr put his newly arrived 747 into service flying to London for $149 each way. Hundreds of passengers eagerly jammed into a corner of the terminal for the announcement listing the lucky passengers who had cleared the standby list. People leaned, crouched, sat, and laid themselves out dead asleep, some having been there for days, until the public address system crackled and the entire crowd snapped to attention, heads craning to hear each name. Screams of pleasure and anguish variously rang through the terminal as, passenger by passenger, the standbys were called.

Four years from its first dicey days in business, People Express was serving 50 cities, each of which, little by little, had stretched the niche formula upon which the company had been based. There were the Florida destinations added during the controllers' crisis, the major cities with big passenger markets (Boston and Baltimore), the personal favorites (such as Hartford, where Burr had grown up watching the fiery Lockheed Constellations land), and of course destinations that tweaked Frank Lorenzo (not only Continental's turf in Houston, but New York Air's in Washington). To his London destination Burr later added Brussels.

To that point Burr's expansion had brought him head-to-head with moderate competition at best. In Florida, for instance, he was up against the weakest sisters in the family of airlines: Pan Am and Eastern. Over the Atlantic to Europe, Burr was up against Pan Am and TWA, relics of the past struggling for breath, with punishingly high costs and a need for cash so desperate that they gave away their seats to wholesalers and tour operators.

To the pundits of commercial aviation it was an article of faith that People Express would remain profitable so long as Burr continued picking on the weaklings and the other upstarts—in other words, so long as he steered clear of the industry giants. Yet Burr knew that failing to grow in a market in which all your competitors *were* growing meant that he would soon fall behind. The whole airline industry had become a living expression of the S-curve of yore: he who has the most planes gets *more* than his proportion of the passengers.

Regardless of the economic imperative to continue growing, Burr did not know where or when to stop—or even how; whenever an airplane bared a little shoulder, Burr had to have it. He was soon bringing in planes at the rate of one every three weeks or less. Burr, it began to appear, knew how to manage only growth. People Express was like a Ponzi scheme of emotions, in which everything would remain fine so long as each day brought more thrills and chills than the last. "High growth is important to hotshot people," he told a reporter. "It's where you get your excitement and your learning. It makes for commitment and high levels of energy." People Express *needed* growth. Don Burr needed it.

In June 1984, with more 747s in the fleet, Burr attacked United and American in the transcontinental market, where Frank Borman had flamed out a few years earlier. Then in August 1984 he stunned the airline world by announcing a dozen flights a day from Newark to O'Hare Airport, not only the heart of the United operation but the secondary outpost (after Dallas) of American's huge Growth Plan expansion. "You have two bull elephants out there," Burr said publicly. "But we have built a powerful hub at Newark, we can carry people from cities all over the East through Newark to Chicago, and so nobody can drive us out of that market." Burr charged as little as $59 one way to Chicago, less than one quarter the prevailing fare. In addition he began offering a $6 connecting flight along his spokes into Newark—from Pittsburgh, say, or Hartford—for anyone flying on to Chicago.

Six days after Chicago it was Miami; no longer would People Express serve only the secondary markets in Florida. On the same day Burr announced service to Detroit, the same destination where an earlier invasion by New York Air had caused Bob Crandall of American such consternation. The following month, in September, it was a second transcontinental route, this time to San Francisco, a United stronghold. Days later Burr was off to Denver, where the three-way war was raging among United, Continental, and Frontier. And finally, in November 1984, in a departure from the Newark script, Burr launched direct service to several Florida cities from Minneapolis, Detroit, Chicago, and Cleveland, stealing passengers from just about everyone else in the industry as the height of the tourist season hit.

In every case the airline on the receiving end of Burr's attack tried to match his fare, but usually on just a fixed and small number of seats per plane, often for only a limited period, and invariably with a host of severe restrictions. People Express had no such complications in its pricing. It was the same fare, every day, every flight, varying only according to the old Southwest-style peak or off-peak pricing. Just as Burr and his associates had made a virtue of the simplicity of peanuts fares back at Texas International, so too did People Express promote the simplicity of its fare structure; one series of ads showed a reservationist for the fictitious "BS Airlines" double-talking through a series of ludicrously complex restrictions. Even where the major airlines bravely matched People Express dollar for dollar, Burr still benefited because the low fares brought so many passengers into the market that all airlines benefited.

As the passenger rolls swelled, however, service began to break down at the most vulnerable point: reservations. People Express was handling reservations like an airline of the 1950s, with crude mechanical and electronic equipment. A travel agent could not book a client on People Express through a computer reservation system because Burr was still refusing to pay transaction fees to Sabre and Apollo. To make a reservation someone—a passenger or a travel agent—had to phone People Express directly, which proved a maddening experience; the relentless busy signal at People Express accounted for the first acquaintance of many people with the redial button on their telephones. By 1984 some 6,000 potential passengers a day failed to connect by phone.

Burr also suffered uniquely from the age-old problem of over-booking. People Express permitted customers to buy their tickets after they had boarded the airplane, giving no passenger the slightest incentive to honor a reservation, much less to cancel one after his or her plans had changed. No-shows were so numerous that People

Express began overselling some flights by 100 percent. Often, of course, many of the expected no-shows actually materialized, leaving dozens of unhappy people with confirmed reservations stuck in the pandemonium of the North Terminal.

Burr, though initially dismissive of computer technology as a costly frill, finally got religion and contracted with NCR to develop an in-house reservations system for People Express. Burr demanded a crash effort, a "mini–Manhattan Project." Month by month the development team provided encouraging reports, but after a year the team leaders seemed to be waffling. Burr soon realized he had "a dry hole." Fired, NCR threatened to sue. "I don't give a shit!" Burr answered. He hired a small division of American Express to start from scratch. Burr, as 1984 drew to a close, was no closer to a computer reservation system than he had been in mid-1983.

There was also a kind of family stress taking hold in the company. Burr's goal was to have every employee think of himself as a manager, but there was too little management of the managers, too little rhyme and reason to everyone's activity. Burnout swept the organization at all levels, including the top. Burr feverishly tried to keep employees focused on the Big Picture—the vision of People Express as the fulfillment of a dream. An in-house television station was established—WPEX—with a rah-rah news format that enabled Burr to continue pumping people up. He drilled the Precepts into everyone's heads: "commitment to the growth and development of our people . . . to be the best provider of air transportation . . . to provide the highest quality of leadership . . ." Business plans and reports and decisions all had to be expressly evaluated against the Precepts. He read aloud to his managers from *The Greatest Thing in the World*—the chief executive of the fastest-growing company in the history of aviation, reading aloud from his boyhood treasure tome, his feet propped on a desk, his shoes and socks removed. He distributed rambling memos that read like something from the self-help section at a chain bookstore rather than like the work of someone who once contemplated a career as an English professor:

> I am personally and painfully aware that in a place known for its primary aspiration—an intense, unyielding and demanding commitment to people, ourselves and our customers: Precepts One and Two—June has

proven to be an extraordinarily difficult month for these same people. There have been tears of joy and sorrow as our heroes and champions have struggled to cope with the truly extraordinary demands of an historic month. . . . Our unique problem, if you could call it that, is because we are so inordinately productive, the demand for our product is outstripping our ability to produce it. In short, we are operating beyond our practical capacity.

Not to worry, Burr went on.

The intent of our effort, which we in fact accomplished, was to enhance our competitive survivability. This greatly ensures that we can build a place strong enough to allow us to aspire to enjoy the promise of our Precepts.

The People Express system, he believed, would soon spread to hospitals and schools. "This group," he solemnly told a meeting of senior managers, "has been brought together to help us lead the world into the next century." Burr's confidence was so strong that he signed a 25-year lease for a massive new terminal to be constructed at Newark—a new place to grow, to escape from the horrors of the North Terminal.

Three days later Bob Crandall, the Enforcer, finally lowered the boom.

Crandall had not forgotten his experience as the data processing manager at Hallmark Cards, where a 1960s-era mainframe tracked sales trends down to the individual display slot at each retail location—and adjusted every restocking shipment accordingly. Now Crandall would do the same with airline seats.

Experimentation with this concept had begun in the late 1970s, when Crandall wiped out the charter operators with his "super saver" prices. Setting aside a certain number of seats for sale at a discount began as an imprecise process, which Crandall and his people set about to refine. Their aim was to vary the proportion of discount and full-fare seats day by day and departure by departure, according to whether booking patterns were running ahead of or behind a predicted level.

In principle the concept was as old as the bazaar or the farmer's market, where prices varied by the minute according to the rules of supply and demand—and, in the case of grapefruits or other fresh food, how close to perishing the product was. A few years into Crandall's Growth Plan the number of individual seats for sale on American Airlines at any moment totaled roughly 110 million: nearly 1,500 departures a day, each with an average of 220 seats, any one of which could be reserved 330 days into the future. This number required data processing power, and more particularly software, on a scale unseen in most industries. Crandall's strategy of concentrating flights into hubs complicated the process by still another order of magnitude: in analyzing whether to sell a full-fare seat on a single flight segment, for instance, American had to take account of whether it might be displacing a discount passenger seeking reservations on *two* flight segments and which of the two sales at various fare levels would generate more revenue.

The Sabre system was overflowing with priceless historical data, years of bookings from which American could deduce how many days in advance vacationers tended to book to San Juan, how many days in advance business travelers booked to Detroit, in May as opposed to September, on Tuesday as opposed to Friday, in the morning versus the afternoon or evening. Every flight had a unique profile. Crandall wanted his staff to monitor the rate of actual bookings in various fare categories, compare them to the predicted rate, and then adjust the inventory of variously priced seats accordingly. To this tedious yet tremendously meaningful process Bob Crandall gave the leaden name of "yield management."

Responsibility for yield management was assigned to Barbara R. Amster, who had become one of the few women to attain a senior position in the boys' club of commercial aviation. She did so on pure genius, and a comfort level with computers born of having started out in the New York office as a telephone reservationist on the early Sabre machines. When she undertook the assignment in the late 1970s Amster had 30 clerks up to their chins in keypunch cards. Amster's people began gobbling up every new piece of data processing technology in an effort to refine the process ever more minutely.

When by 1984 Crandall and Amster had nearly perfected the process, it seemed like alchemy. If People Express were offering a $99 fare to the West Coast, for instance, American, in theory, could advertise the identical fare but sell only as many seats as the gigabytes of historical data in the Sabre system suggested it should sell at that price. The remaining seats on that particular flight—the number varying by the day or perhaps by the hour—would be held in reserve for full-fare passengers making their arrangements closer to the day of departure. So while both People Express and American might advertise $99 flights to Los Angeles, the *average* fare on the American plane might be $250, say, while the average on People Express, where every seat was the same price, could never be more than $99. Crandall, it appeared, had attained the ultimate fulfillment of the First Rule: Any incremental passenger is worthwhile, at virtually any price.

There were, however, a few drawbacks. For instance, more full-fare business travelers than ever found themselves next to passengers traveling at one half the price or less. That was a serious long-term marketing problem. Another, more immediate problem was that the marginal passengers who topped off the airplane made marginal reservations. As People Express was also discovering, the no-show problem was worse at lower fare levels. It made no sense to make 40 seats available for low-fare travelers if 20 of those people turned out to be no-shows.

Crandall's people set themselves to work urgently attacking the no-show problem. American needed to begin capturing the low end of the market if Crandall were to fill all those planes coming into his fleet—planes he needed to buy as a way of hiring more pilots, flight attendants, and mechanics at b-scale wages. Instead of merely reacting to the likes of People Express, Bob Crandall now had to use low fares to steal passengers from them as well as to create new markets to fill his new planes. Crandall, in short, had to take the fare wars to a new level.

It bothered Crandall that People Express and the new, low-cost Continental were conditioning people to think that only they offered discount fares. The notion had to be eradicated from the public consciousness, Crandall believed, before the upstarts had permanently segmented the market. Even the business traveler was no longer securely American's. Though one had to pay fifty cents for a cup of coffee on the typical People Express flight, Burr, in entering the long-haul transcontinental market, had finally added a first-class section—and the service was not horrible! Likewise, Southwest's service, though stripped down and basic, was impeccably consistent and iridescently friendly. Crandall was concerned to learn that some businesses had begun requiring employees to travel at the lowest fare available, regardless of the level of service it required them to endure.

Of all these low-cost carriers, People Express was, in early 1985, the greatest threat by far. But People Express was also perhaps the most vulnerable. Barbara Amster of the American pricing department considered People Express "the guys with the Southwest Airlines philosophy but without the brains of Southwest." More aptly, perhaps, Don Burr and People Express had all the great ideas of Herb Kelleher and Southwest Airlines but lacked their discipline. Either way, People Express had to die. As Crandall's planning chief, Donald Carty, would one day proudly explain, "We devised the fare structure that put them out of business."

On January 17, 1985, Crandall and his aides unveiled the new pricing strategy under study for so long. Passengers would have to go to the unusual length of paying for their seats when reserving them, just like buying a ticket to see *A Chorus Line* or the New York Yankees. You reserve it, you own it. You would not be a no-show. By selling nonrefundable tickets, American would avoid massive revenue losses. By bringing in more revenue, American could subsidize discounts to a level deeper than anyone had previously imagined possible for a major airline.

It took one's breath away: fare cuts of 70 percent, in some cases more. DFW to New York: cut each way from $344 to $99. Fort Wayne to Chicago: cut from $125 to $39. This wasn't just the odd route here or there to compete with Braniff or New York Air or People Express. This was almost everything. Crazy Eddie pricing had reached the major airlines. *Every seat must go!*

American had out–People Expressed People Express. Because he had no computer systems and no yield management, Don Burr would have to offer every seat on any given flight at the price Bob Crandall was offering on a fraction of his. Crandall was only too happy to let Burr sell a cheap seat to anyone that American had turned away for the sake of a passenger paying the full fare.

Within minutes of American's announcement, all airline stocks plunged; investors braced themselves for the bloodiest fare war ever.

People who had never dreamed of flying were now madly dialing American Airlines and before long all other major airlines, as the fares were quickly matched. United immediately canceled vacations for reservationists. Clients began lining up outside the doors and into the streets at local travel agencies. The Saturday-night stay restriction typical of the ultralow fares became such a commonplace feature in travel itineraries that hotels and rental car companies experienced a significant (and, as it would turn out, permanent) increase in week-end demand. Against all the great pricing leaders of airline history— Kelleher and Muse of Southwest; Lorenzo, Gitner, and O'Donnell of "peanuts fares" fame; Burr of People Express—Bob Crandall had seen their bets and had raised them. Or as Tom Plaskett later proudly explained in a meeting with American's bankers, "They threw down the price card, and we trumped it."

To Don Burr it was as if a bull's eye had been painted over his like-ness.

"This is it!" he cried, slamming the newspaper down on the desk of one of his marketing executives. "This is a shot across our bow! If we don't invent a way to deal with this, we're history! We're going to be dead meat!"

In his panic Burr wanted to know how many seats American was offering at these prices. Two seats on any plane, or 20, or 200 on a DC-10? There was no way of telling from American's ads or public comments. Burr began rounding up people to dial the phones like mad, posing as American customers and keeping track of which flights had sold out of discount seats and which still had low-fare seats available, but the answers kept changing. The advertising agency working for People Express was pressed into action; hun-dreds more calls went out. But the more they called, the less they knew. As the days progressed, calls went out by the thousands, even-tually to United as well, once it had matched American. The answers kept changing there too! Burr was beside himself. How could he compete with something he couldn't see? How could he fight the devil?

And—*whump!*—just like that, the losses mounted at People Ex-press. Twenty million dollars in a matter of weeks, a tide of red ink such as People Express had never experienced. The panic worsened.

What could Burr do? Like many executives in times of crisis, he listened to Wall Street, and following the admonitions of the stock analysts who had always criticized People Express's fares for being too low, Burr *raised* fares in the midst of everyone else's lowering them.

Soon Burr was shocked to realize that Continental and New York Air between them were making severe inroads against him in New York. Burr couldn't believe his complacency. He had allowed Frank Lorenzo to creep up on him.

Worst of all, Burr was dying at the thought that the mystique shrouding People Express was now evaporating. The red ink forced him to withhold profit sharing. The stock price was plunging. Soon there were union organizers at his doorstep. Burr imagined his employees turning on him, the pilots in particular. He heard that they were referring to the Precepts as "Kool-Aid," the poison-spiked beverage that the demonic cult leader Jim Jones had used to conduct a mass suicide a few years earlier in the jungles of Guyana. Burr imagined the pilots in their cockpits asking one another, "Have you had your Kool-Aid today?"

Burr was in the depths of this depression when the editor of *Inc.* magazine stopped in with a tape recorder one day in the summer of 1985. Burr complained of being surrounded by "bad forces." The love and trust, he said, were dissipating. People Express had become . . . corporate.

"But doesn't it give you an extraordinary sense of achievement?" the interviewer graciously asked. "A thrill?"

"You know," Burr answered, "it used to. When the first planes were delivered here, three whole planes—now that was a thrill. . . . Now when I look out there, I don't know, there are just so many damn planes out there. It's just not the same anymore."

Later Burr's mother called—the woman who had steeped him in the notion of public service, who had warned him against becoming just another money-grubbing businessman. She was planning a trip to visit Burr's brother. She had purchased her ticket, she said, on American Airlines.

But Burr was not finished yet—far from it. The team from American Express was madly working on the new in-house computer system, by which Burr hoped to adopt the same variable pricing that American, United, and even Continental were now using against him. And then another comeback opportunity emerged. While visiting an exclusive tennis club in Carmel, California, a guest of his investment bankers, Burr learned of a deal by which he might restore the market power of People Express—while also acting in the role of Frank Lorenzo's spoiler.

The final battle for the dominion of Denver was under way.

Frontier Airlines, once a regional powerhouse in Denver under the late Al Feldman, was struggling for survival, caught in the crossfire between United and Continental. In the unwritten rules of the post-deregulation era, three major airlines operating within a single hub city was at least one too many. As American had displayed in Dallas, operating a hub had become a contest to control the maximum number of passengers between the maximum number of city pairs. This strategy demanded a huge number of airplanes flying hundreds of hub landings and departures every day, like a hive of worker bees racing to and from their queen. It was only marginally economical for two big carriers to conduct service on this scale at a hub; where three airlines attempted to do so, planes flew empty, which meant that fares plunged, which meant that no one made any money on anything. Thus was Chicago sorting itself out as the sole domain of United and American, Atlanta the sole domain of Delta and Eastern, Dallas the sole domain of American and Delta, and so on.

The imperative to eliminate one of the three Denver carriers had reached the point of no return by the mid-1980s. As the third-ranked carrier, Frontier's principal value had become that of the kingmaker. In September 1985 Frank Lorenzo of Texas Air announced an offer to buy two thirds of Frontier for $20 a share in cash, a total of $250 million.

When word reached Burr on the tennis court in Carmel that his old boss had put Frontier Airlines in play, he was like a pyromaniac in a match store. He cut short the vacation and raced to Denver, formulating a new mission for People Express along the way.

It was obvious to Burr that the major airlines were winning the fare battle on the turf that he considered his own: the short-haul route. They could do so, Burr began to think, because they charged such high fares on their long-haul, transcontinental routes. Therein resided the kernel of a comeback strategy, Burr figured: if People Express could force the major airlines to cut their transcontinental fares, they would lose the profits with which they subsidized their short-haul flights. They could no longer afford to maintain such low fares in the mainstay markets of People Express. His company would be saved.

Burr realized, however, that he could never trash the prices for the entire transcontinental market just by flying a few jumbo jets between New York and California. Frontier, Burr determined, presented the solution. He imagined uniting Denver and Newark with massive service, an "air bridge" connecting two powerful hubs: 50 cities in the East feeding 50 cities in the West, and vice versa. People Express, overnight, would become a major transcontinental carrier.

Anyway, Burr thought, what choice did he have? The Reagan administration was letting the major airlines gobble everything in sight; he had to keep up. And the Precepts—Burr would extend them to a wider workplace, would prove that trust and love could work even in a unionized environment such as Frontier's. "Over time," Burr would publicly explain, "the fundamental ideas that give direction to People will find root at Frontier."

Don Burr did not realize that he was whistling "Dixie." The majors were not, as a matter of fact, using their transcontinental routes to subsidize their short-haul routes—at least not enough to account for their 70 percent discounts. The majors were offering low fares against People Express because they had computers that enabled them to offer rock-bottom prices to discretionary passengers and still keep as many seats as necessary in store for higher-paying passengers. *That* was the cross-subsidy that was killing People Express.

After reaching Denver, Burr approached not only the management of Frontier but the unions as well. Although Burr practically had to hold his nose at the mere mention of the word "union," he stifled his prejudice and earnestly told the union leaders that the employees of Frontier were much better off casting their lot with him than with his union-busting former partner Frank Lorenzo. Burr was then off to New York, where the Frontier board was scheduled to meet.

With the deal hanging in the balance, Burr stopped by a newsstand to pick up *The New York Times*. To his horror he read that Lorenzo had just increased his offer, from $20 a share to $22 a share.

The Frontier directors were keen on selling to Burr, so devoutly did the employees of Frontier fear Frank Lorenzo. All Burr had to do was match Lorenzo's $22-a-share offer, and Frontier was his.

Burr offered $24 a share.

Gerald O'Neil, the controlling shareholder of Frontier, smiled. "That's a remarkable offer," he said. The board agreed to lock up the deal for Burr. Burr flew back to the North Terminal and drew a standing ovation from his loyal employees.

Burr was not through yet. A major commuter airline named Britt Airways came on the market, an operation with nearly 50 planes zipping in and out of Chicago and St. Louis, feeding small-town passengers into connecting flights on United or American; Burr bought it on barely a day's notice. Then came the largest commuter airline in the country, Provincetown-Boston Airline, which scheduled a flock of airplanes among the little airports of the Cape and the Vineyard and Nantucket in the summer and then migrated them to Florida in the winter. It too went into the kit bag of Don Burr.

Burr believed he was buying time—simply grabbing passengers any way he could, even if he had to buy planes and terminals along with them, until his own computer reservation system came on line. But some people sensed a different motive. As the Frontier takeover generated headlines, Burr was having dinner at home with his children. "Dad," asked his 12-year-old, Kelsey, "what's this Frontier thing?"

"Dad is just doing what's popular," his 20-year-old son, Whitney, interjected. "The raider-type stuff."

Burr felt a stab in his heart. "It's exactly what I'm *not* doing!" he snapped.

Burr was able to finance his plunge into the takeover game thanks in part to the media's blindness to his struggles. In January 1986 Burr appeared on the cover of *Time,* joining a hall of fame that included Charles Lindbergh and C. R. Smith of American. *Business Week* had previously put Burr on the cover, calling him a "new wave capitalist," a "1980s business giant who may in time rank with Henry Ford."

Academia also continued to swoon over Burr and his unorthodoxy, holding them out—just as it had Eastern, in its short-lived pe-

riod of labor-management détente—as the American answer to the
Japanese economic challenge. At Harvard Business School students
viewed a videotape documentary about Burr on a 10-foot screen that
made him look like Mussolini. One Harvard professor held out People Express as "the most comprehensive and self-conscious effort to
fit a business to the capabilities and attitudes of today's workforce."
Even the venerable dean of the Harvard Business School, John H.
McArthur, who once had the young Don Burr as a student, joined
the board of directors of People Express.

Burr had vowed that he would not be taken in by his own press,
that he would not even read it. He knew he was vulnerable to the effects of that kind of adulation. With his survival in doubt, he knew
he had to stay focused, to keep his internal balance, to be like Herb
Kelleher at Southwest Airlines, whom Burr considered "innately
humble." Committed though he may have been to keeping his ego in
check, it was, after all, pretty tough to miss oneself on the cover of
Time. He couldn't help noticing all the academics and consultants
swarming through his organization. He told himself that no one—
not Lorenzo, not Crandall—had ever built a billion-dollar airline
from scratch.

And as the adulation continued, Burr's need for control intensified. Burr was increasingly surrounded by yes-men, people who
would tolerate his rages and do his bidding. Some pilots swore that a
few of Burr's aides actually began to emulate his walk—stooped
slightly forward, one hand behind the back, the other perhaps on the
chin, the face intense with concentration. Burr surrounded himself
with his people even on weekends. He bought a century-old home
facing the water on Martha's Vineyard and enlarged it into a 10-bed-
room mansion, a retreat for business, a place to continue preaching
love and trust and the Precepts to the people he often thought of as
children. The Vineyard home was his castle; "my moat," he would
later observe, "was people."

As he had planned, Burr grafted the systems and culture of People
Express onto Frontier; the disaster was monumental. Frontier had
always been considered a classy airline, and the years of warfare with
United and Continental had only brought out the best in service at
all three. Now longtime Frontier passengers were being charged 50¢

for a cup of coffee. To stuff more seats into Frontier's airplanes, Burr took out the galleys and began serving cold meals—three bucks for crackers, cheese, maybe some sausage. "Kibbles'N Bits," people called it. Ingeniously Continental positioned agents in Denver's Terminal D, where Frontier operated, and distributed 5,000 free boxed lunches to anyone showing a Frontier or People Express ticket.

Burr cut prices and cut them again, fervently trying to "boom" the market to cover his operating costs with an explosion of marginal passengers; Continental and United, however, matched him dollar for dollar and then some. Soon a passenger could fly anywhere from Denver for $89 and to many destinations for much less—to Colorado Springs, in fact, for a grand total of $9.

"My agenda was beat the shit out of Don Burr," Lorenzo's marketing chief, Jim O'Donnell, would later explain. "My agenda was to win." O'Donnell, the former Vaporub salesman who helped create peanuts fares, loved this kind of guerrilla sales war. Frontier had posted a billboard outside the Stapleton airport proclaiming that it had the lowest airfares in Denver and vowing to "change this board" if anyone proved otherwise. Because of a technicality involving the addition of an advance purchase requirement, a 14-day period occurred during which Frontier, in fact, did *not* have the lowest fares. O'Donnell procured a giant camper and parked it in the abandoned gas station lot underneath Frontier's billboard, hoisting a 30-foot banner that said, "We'll be here until you tell the truth." Frontier gamely sent some of its $3 Kibbles'N Bits boxes to the camping Continental executives as a kind of peace offering; they took a box apart and promptly announced that as a unit of People Express, Frontier was charging $3 for a snack box with only $1.26 worth of food inside.

Lorenzo's forces, meanwhile, also targeted Burr's sacrosanct home base of Newark, offering $99 fares to as far as the West Coast. Continental used a *New Yorker*-style cartoon in an ad depicting the huddled masses of the North Terminal milling about with stink lines rising from their hair. "Give me your tired, your poor," Continental's ads declared, "your huddled masses yearning to be free of People Express."

By May 1986 the media were at last on to Don Burr in a big way. Overbooking, always a problem, ran out of control as Burr's people tried to eradicate no-shows without computers to track reservation trends. *The Wall Street Journal* reported that an elderly woman had clunked a People Express agent over the head with a telephone. A frustrated man pushing his mother in a wheelchair had grabbed a sheaf of papers from behind a People Express counter, heaving them into the air in a flutter. People Express was now "People's Distress." The company grew tardy on some of its payables.

Burr himself could feel the end approaching as he walked the hallways at Newark. Where once there had been love! and trust! there was now panic and grief. In his mind's eye Burr saw the image of the heroes' planet in the movie *Star Wars* destroyed by a terrible beam of energy from Darth Vader's Death Star. "These were my children being slaughtered," he would later say. Then even the board of directors turned against him. Twice in the summer of 1986 William Hambrecht of Hambrecht & Quist, the investment banker who had been so important in getting the company off the ground, asked Burr to resign. "You guys are out of your fucking minds!" Burr snapped. "If I resign, this place will fall through the floor!"

But they were right about one thing, Burr realized. Something drastic had to happen. All that mattered now was how much could be salvaged of the People Express vision and how much the employees of People Express could get for their stock in the company. Among these employee shareholders, there was none bigger than Burr himself. Another major shareholder was his companion, Melrose Dawsey.

Burr knew what he had to do. There was no end to the number of people who would buy his planes and gates and slots and routes, but there was only one person, Burr figured, who would be willing to buy out the company in its entirety. And only he, Burr, could get him to do it.

"Don, I kept this," Lorenzo said to Burr. "I knew there would come a day when this would be appropriate."

In Lorenzo's hand was a small section of propeller blade, the customary gift presented to departing executives back at the old Texas International. The keepsake had been prepared for Burr when he had left in 1980 to start People Express, but Lorenzo had withheld the gift, saving it through all the gothic turns in their relationship over the following six years. Now, it appeared, the two of them might be getting together again.

The 1986 summer season on the Cape was just beginning. Burr was at his 10-bedroom "castle" on the Vineyard; Lorenzo was at his place on Nantucket. John McArthur, the Harvard business school dean who had joined the board of People Express, was acting as a go-between, helping to keep the negotiating process on track. As Lorenzo and Burr talked, they felt a little of that old warmth coming back. Don, the best man at Frank's wedding . . . Frank, the godfather to Don's child . . . their years of marathon training together . . . skiing together . . . the salad days back at Texas International, in the Blue Barn. They began to joke about their titanic egos. Maybe, at last, they thought, Texas Air—with Eastern and Continental and New York Air and People Express and Britt and Provincetown-Boston—maybe *that* was a company big enough for both of them. Maybe they could make it work this time.

There would in any case be a big role for Burr in the organization, of course! Burr was sure he heard the words pass Lorenzo's lips: Don, you can become the chief executive of Continental and the president of Texas Air; I can remain chairman of Continental and chairman and chief executive of Texas Air . . . Burr would have the chance to weave the culture of People Express into Continental. The Precepts would live on.

Only one person stood between the fulfillment of the reunion fantasy: Dick Ferris of United Airlines. For several weeks Ferris gamely played for Frontier, first for a substantial portion of its fleet and later for the company in its entirety. Frontier had been Al Feldman's airline, before Feldman had moved to Continental Airlines, where he took his own life. Ferris and his friend Travis Reed had a plan to put the Frontier fleet to work for United in Denver, "a final salute," as Reed would explain it years later, to their martyred friend.

Ferris reached an agreement with the board of People Express to buy Frontier, only to watch the deal slip through his fingers. The pilots of United Airlines, unable to contain their loathing and mistrust of Ferris, refused to agree on the terms by which the pilots of Frontier would be absorbed into United. The pilots' union at United had the de facto standing to veto Ferris's purchase of Frontier, and, unbelievably, it did.

When United was out of the picture it was Frank Lorenzo who took control of Frontier, along with everything else that had become a part of People Express.

"While this may be a bittersweet moment in personal terms," Burr said at a press conference, "the sweetness far outweighs the bitterness. . . . It doesn't matter if the faces aren't painted on the tails." The important thing, he insisted, was that People Express would still be around, as part of Texas Air, to fight "those fat cats, like United Airlines and American Airlines."

It was a notable day in another respect. For a year American Express had been working feverishly to complete the computer system intended to endow People Express with the sophisticated pricing and reservations management it needed to stay afloat in the turbulent new skies of commercial aviation. On the day he announced the merger agreement with Texas Air, Don Burr's computer was flipped on for the first time. Now it too was Frank Lorenzo's.

The reunion of Lorenzo and Burr was short-lived. When they went jogging together they argued about the executive titles Burr was convinced he had been promised. When they went skiing together Lorenzo turned out in a white jumpsuit and Burr laughed in his face. Before long Don Burr was gone, this time for good.

CHAPTER 13

THE SOUTHWEST SHUFFLE

The computer technology that wiped out People Express in the marketplace did for flying what the assembly line did for the automobile. It reduced it to the most common denominator.

Though discounted fares had been available for years, steep discounts had previously been the exception rather than the rule, available only regionally or seasonally. American's data processing breakthrough changed that, making the least expensive seats available throughout the year, in every region of the country. On some flights the cheap seats were few, but there were almost invariably *some*. An excursion for which the airlines once offered installment loan contracts could now be expressed in terms of the most prosaic and ubiquitous products and services: Boston to Miami for the cost of a new automobile battery, New York to Los Angeles for the equivalent of a few dental fillings.

The changing character of the passenger markets was evident to anyone who had previously spent time in airports and airplanes. For the first time the crowds walking through the Jetways began to resemble the same cross section of humanity one might find on a city street or in a suburban shopping mall. Flight attendants noticed that they were commanding unusually rapt attention during the preflight safety demonstration; millions of passengers had never observed the ritual. The airlines were unifying friends, families, and loved ones as no medium had since the advent of the Post Office, the telephone network, and the interstate highway system.

Though a novel experience for millions, flying did not long remain a glamorous one for most. As something sold cheaply, flying was no longer something most people felt the slightest compulsion to dress up for or otherwise regard with marvel. Where families of the 1950s and 1960s had scheduled excursions to the airport observation deck to watch the planes, they could now simply schedule reservations and fly on the planes.

The magic of "yield management" alone far from accounted for the widespread accessibility of air travel. For one, the ultralow fares were increasingly subsidized by much steeper fares charged of business travelers. For the airlines the net effect was salutary. While discount fares were plunging rapidly, the average of all fares was declining only slightly—to 11 cents a mile in 1986, from 12 cents a mile two years earlier. Even through the most relentless price cutting of the mid-1980s the airlines recorded their best operating profits in history.

There was one additional and important reason for those increased profits: lower costs for oil and, more significantly, for toil. Commercial aviation by 1986 directly employed well over 400,000 people. Among them the journeymen at the big, secure, and established airlines (United, American, Delta, and Northwest) enjoyed the grandfathered rewards of having started their careers in a time of government protection. The more junior employees at American and other airlines with b-scales had experienced no traumatic cutbacks but came into their jobs earning one half or less what their tenured colleagues were making. For the huge proportion of workers employed by struggling companies, living standards had plunged— whether gradually (as at Eastern, Pan Am, and TWA) or traumatically (as at Continental). In this respect as in so many others the airlines were among the leaders of the United States economy: wage cutbacks would soon sweep through other industries, particularly those that had succumbed, as the airlines also had, to the temptations of too much debt in the halcyon investment banking years of the 1980s.

In casting blame the losers in aviation's transformation could point to a variety of candidates. In the view of many, deregulation remained the principal enabling event. Others blamed the executives of the airlines—inexperienced at the rigors of the free market, congenitally unwilling to concede turf to their competitors, consumed in the gratification of their own considerable egos. Frank Lorenzo was a commonly cited villain (a "lightning rod," as he sometimes put it himself). Many placed the responsibility for labor's troubles in labor's own house, arguing that by so strenuously resisting change the unions had only heightened the need for it.

Regardless of who was most responsible, there was little doubt about how the process began. To find the principal agent of change one had to go back to the beginning, back through 14 years of airline history, for behind the birth of yield management and ultimate super savers was People Express and the low-cost Continental, and behind them was Texas International's lesson in peanuts pricing, and behind that lesson was Southwest Airlines.

It was a testament to the company's low profile that in 1986 most airline passengers had not even heard of Southwest Airlines. The company certainly had grown since its first breakout move after the signing of the Deregulation Act; it had increased its fleet nearly fourfold by 1986, to 63 airplanes. Even so it remained only the 14th largest of the 30 airlines in America. Southwest was still less than one tenth the size of United Airlines.

Inside the airline industry, however, everyone knew Southwest and only too well. It had never lost money, from the time it was fully established in business. And it had flourished while defying almost every success maxim of the post-deregulation world: it had no computer reservations system, offered no frequent-flier program, did not conduct yield management, and had never organized its flight schedules around anything remotely approaching a hub.

How did Southwest do it? Consultants and academics were forever crawling over the company, looking for an answer as if they were searching for the recipe for Coke. Through all the studies no one ever had a better explanation than Robert Baker, who as Bob Crandall's principal operating aide at American had come to know Southwest well. "That place," Baker would say, "runs on Herb Kelleher's bullshit."

· · ·

When Kelleher finally moved into Southwest as a full-time executive in 1981, the company still served only Texas, New Mexico, Oklahoma, and Louisiana—good places to do business at a time when oil prices were heading toward $40 a barrel. The unique federal rule limiting Southwest to Texas and the contiguous states remained in force, although it applied only to Southwest's service at Dallas. Kelleher resolved to strike west from other points, first to Phoenix, then to Los Angeles.

At the time, in the aftermath of the controllers' strike, the major airports in California still had a ceiling on landings and takeoffs, so Kelleher faced the same hurdle that Frank Lorenzo had to clear in establishing New York Air. Kelleher needed slots. He boned up on the special rules intended to advantage "new entrants." Though relatively young as airlines went, Southwest was no new entrant; it had been flying for seven years before deregulation became law. But Kelleher recalled that after the Deregulation Act had been signed, Southwest, in the midst of its big internal brouhaha over whether to begin service at Midway Airport in Chicago, had incorporated a subsidiary company. The new subsidiary had never gotten off the ground, but as a legal entity Midway Southwest was still very much alive.

Identifying his paper company as a "new entrant," Kelleher applied for and received the needed slots. He then simply traded them to Southwest.

Someone at the FAA soon wised up to the maneuver and moved to nullify it: slots, the agency decreed, could be traded away only by an operating airline, not a paper company. So Kelleher devised a new sleight of hand. He sold Midway Southwest to a charter company that owned a single Learjet. Then the charter company traded the slots to Southwest. This time Washington could not come up with a reason to disapprove the transaction. Southwest was suddenly serving Los Angeles.

When J. Lynn Helms, the FAA administrator, found out what had occurred at the levels below him, he summoned Kelleher to Washington. Southwest, he told Kelleher, had made a mockery of the rules intended to benefit new entrants. "Those were the rules," Helms said sternly. "We changed the rules, and you circumvented the changed rules."

Then Helms smiled, confessing that he loved Kelleher's fancy footwork. As he bid Kelleher farewell, Helms instructed him to exit the office with his most convincing hangdog look; Helms wanted his staff to think that Kelleher had been whipped in the woodshed. Kelleher walked out with his shoulders slumped and his head cast down, all the while grinning inside.

Along with California Kelleher added Las Vegas, Kansas City, Little Rock, St. Louis, and ultimately, in 1985, Chicago Midway Airport, Southwest's first strike east of the Mississippi River. (It had also entered Denver but soon quit; such cold and snow turned out to be enemies of the 10-minute turnaround.) After establishing itself at Midway, Southwest continued pressing east, to Detroit, Birmingham, and Nashville (a town that Kelleher decided to serve after visiting his daughter at Vanderbilt University). But Southwest did not go near the East Coast. The airports and airspace were too congested there for a 10- or 15-minute turnaround, especially in New York. Southwest therefore remained largely invisible in the East; although the business press covered the airlines as thoroughly as it did any industry, Southwest was still largely undiscovered by the national media.

In the markets that it did serve, however, Southwest instantly became popular. At each new city added to the system Kelleher scheduled flights to two, three, or maybe four destinations, usually cities at which the company had previously established itself. Most were only a few hundred miles distant, close enough that a community of interests, fostered by cars and the interstate highway system, already existed between them (Tulsa and Oklahoma City, Chicago and St. Louis, Dallas and Little Rock). As it spread in two directions from Texas—west to California and northeast to the Great Lakes—Southwest's route map came to resemble a haphazardly laced army boot.

Southwest typically did not commence service between any two cities until it could devote the planes and personnel necessary to running four, five, or six flights a day—even hourly flights where possible. In big cities (most notably Chicago) Southwest staked itself in secondary, usually close-in airports, just as it had founded itself at the convenient if bedraggled Dallas Love Field. Southwest then blitzed the local market with quirky television and display ads emphasizing its low, unrestricted fares and high frequency ("Just Say When"). Within a year of offering service Southwest often doubled the ridership of whatever circuitous or direct service existed previously and doubled it again within the second year.

It was unique among the airlines not only because it flew point to point instead of through hubs, but also because it built its markets almost entirely through a direct appeal to the public, bypassing travel agents. Southwest was happy to let other airlines fight for the loyalties of travel agents; doing so had pushed the commissions paid to travel agents to 10 percent of the ticket price, up from 5 percent in the regulated era. Southwest in fact did not particularly need travel agents. There were rarely any complicated itineraries involved in flying Southwest; the trip was usually just there and back, often in the same day. Southwest's fares were excruciatingly simple, generally just two prices (peak and off-peak) on any route. Travel agents, for their part, were only too happy to let passengers handle their own reservations on Southwest; at such low fares the commissions were hardly worth it, especially since for the most part travel agents had to book reservations on Southwest by phone. Southwest refused to pay transaction fees to the major computer reservation systems.

Such compulsive attention to costs was part of the reason that Southwest could offer low fares in the first place, while simultaneously recording the most consistent profitability in the airline industry. Ten-minute turnarounds (eventually stretched to 15 or 20 minutes, as airport congestion worsened and safety regulations tightened) and an uncomplicated back-and-forth, back-and-forth schedule kept the planes in the air an average of nearly 12 hours a day, far above the industry average. The company's continuing reliance on a single aircraft type—the Boeing 737—continued to save it vast sums in training and maintenance costs. Southwest also had incomparably small interest costs because Kelleher so assiduously eschewed debt; as it prepared for a big expansion in 1984, for example, Kelleher imposed a temporary austerity program so that it could be sure of paying for its next 21 jets (worth nearly a half-billion dollars) in cash.

But the most striking factor in the company's relentless success, and by some reckoning the most significant, was the way that Kelleher managed people.

Kelleher perpetuated the company's underdog spirit. He had

never fully recovered from the legal battle to get Southwest aloft and the trauma of its harrowing shoestring days, and neither had the earliest generation of employees. Maintaining the culture of martyrdom became so essential a strategy that it overpowered other corporate objectives; Southwest added cities and airplanes much more slowly than it could afford to, for instance, in large part to avoid an influx of new employees, which might dilute the purity of the "Southwest spirit."

At the company's frequent awards ceremonies, with a cigarette burning on the podium and a cocktail never far from reach, Herb solemnly presented sniffing, sobbing, or beaming employees with awards and certificates marking such milestones as a 10th anniversary with the company. (The earliest year in which employees could qualify for a 25-year pin would be 1996.) Kelleher told employees that when they served a cup of coffee or replaced an altimeter or conducted a takeoff roll or took a reservation by phone, they were not simply part of an airline. "You are involved in a crusade," he told them.

Like many crusades, Kelleher's flourished on an element of cultism, maintained not only around the aggrieved history of the company and the personality of the chairman but also through an eerily sophisticated screening procedure for new employees. There were no psychological tests, per se. But through a profiling procedure established for flight attendants and later adapted to other positions, Southwest rated applicants according to both their qualifications and their compatibility with the other employees in the same department. Job candidates might be required ("invited") to attend one of the company's many social functions so that they could be observed interacting with other employees.

Kelleher also took the risky step of actively fostering "fun" in the workplace—risky because employees can easily spot a fake when such efforts are structured to manipulate or offered as a substitute for pay or perquisites. Kelleher's intentions were indisputably commercial: happy employees are not only more productive but less apt to brood over setbacks and frustrations. More important, an ambiance of cheer—at the ticket counter, on the telephone, in the passenger cabin—was a critical component of Southwest's no-frills marketing formula. Warmth and mirth suggested a kind of resignation that told passengers, We're all crammed into this aluminum tube together, so we might as well make the most of it. The passenger was deemed paramount; every employee's paycheck bore the words, "From our customers."

At least two factors at Southwest rescued this culture from cynicism. For one, Southwest had always encouraged spontaneous acts of frolic, such as a flight attendant's conducting the preflight safety demonstrations to the tune of the *William Tell Overture* or the theme from *The Beverly Hillbillies,* or trying to see how many passengers would fit in a lavatory, or conducting a contest to see which passenger had the biggest hole in his sock. Instead of homogenizing the product (as no one did better than American, for instance), Southwest rewarded departures from the standard.

Southwest also succeeded in nurturing fun because Kelleher cast himself as the chief jester—and made himself the butt of the most jokes. No personal appearance was too demeaning, no crack too crass. Kelleher joined in the flight attendants' tradition of wearing leprechaun costumes on St. Patrick's Day and bunny costumes around Easter (when in-flight peanuts were served from colorful baskets). When a new corporate staffer named Ed Stewart was hired away from the buttoned-down American Airlines across town, he was invited to Herb's office for an official welcome and was startled to find Kelleher in his office wearing a black wig and sunglasses— Roy Orbison, of course. Without apology or explanation Kelleher introduced himself and welcomed Stewart to the company. When Stewart reached out his hand, Kelleher pulled him face to face and kissed him.

When the company filmed a welcome for new employees in rap, Kelleher was among the stars with a lip-synching solo:

> *My name is Herb—Big Daddy-O,*
> *You should all know me; I run this show.*
> *Without your help there'd be no love*
> *On the ground below or in the air above.*
> *Shuffle fun, shuffle shuffle fun,*
> *Shuffle fun fun, shuffle fun,*
> *Shuffle,*
> *Southwest!*
> *Fun fun.*

He began appearing in the company's television commercials, not in the hearty role of Lee Iacocca or the earnest role of Frank Borman, but as the clown. America West Airlines at one point ran a clever series of ads in Phoenix showing passengers hiding behind their sunglasses and pulling up their turtlenecks to avoid being seen on a low-rent, no-frills airline like Southwest; Kelleher countered as "the Unknown Flier," with a paper bag over his head. "If you're embarrassed to fly the airline with the lowest customer complaints in the country, Southwest will give you this bag," he said—with a pile of dollar bills flopping into the sack as he pulled it from his head. Though an exhibitionist, he shared in few of the usual gratifications of showmanship. He was unwaveringly self-deprecating. He talked incessantly about his unbridled consumption of Wild Turkey and cigarettes—four packs a day.

If Kelleher's man-of-the-people act was a put-on, none of his employees ever caught him wavering from it, and none of his competitors did either. Steve McGregor, then a public relations executive at American Airlines, once encountered Kelleher in the boarding area of an American flight in Detroit, introduced himself, and spent the next 90 minutes laughing and gossiping with Kelleher, a perfect stranger, in the first-class smoking section of a flight to Dallas. The encounter was a jarring contrast to one involving McGregor's own chairman, Bob Crandall, whom McGregor once accompanied on a flight to Los Angeles. Crandall, seated in the smoking section of first class, was approached by a passenger who introduced himself as a coworker of one of Crandall's children. "That's nice," Crandall grumbled, immediately turning back to his work. McGregor watched the humiliated young man slink away.

The sincerity of Kelleher's shtick, if it was nothing more than that, was never more evident than when Southwest began planning a new headquarters complex on the edge of Love Field in the late 1980s. The first thing anyone saw driving into the parking lot was a volleyball net stretched over a sand pit. The cafeteria was outfitted with a play area and an armada of toys for children visiting their parents at lunch hour. Employees mingled on a large rooftop patio overlooking the tarmac at Love Field, where Southwest's brown and red 737s took off every few minutes, the Dallas skyline looming in the background. Management would host its Friday afternoon beer blast and barbecue on that patio; every employee of Southwest Airlines was invited.

As for Kelleher's own office, the architect had received specific instructions: no windows. Once word had spread that he had a windowless office, Kelleher explained, how could anyone dare jockey for an office with a better view? To further control new-office politics, his executive assistant, Colleen Barrett, now a corporate officer, banned department heads from the committee planning the move; underlings, she and Herb reasoned, would be less absorbed in issues of office size and more committed to the merits of any space issue.

Kelleher decorated his nicotine-coated office with statues of wild turkeys and icons of his heroes: Harry Truman's signature, in a frame on the wall; a photo of Churchill and Roosevelt at Casablanca; a front page, encased in plastic and hanging by wire from the ceiling, dated the day that FDR died; an original bank check for $1.25, signed by Orville Wright and payable to the American Society of Mechanical Engineers. Kelleher was a hero-worshiper and a reader of history and literature who could reel off couplets from Wordsworth, aphorisms from Clausewitz, and exchanges from Nixon's 1950 debates with Helen Gahagan Douglas.

But the principal history on display in the new headquarters was the history of Southwest Airlines itself, all two decades of it. The corridors were specially designed as museum walls for the display of corporate memorabilia, some 2,000 framed items in all: newspaper and magazine clippings documenting Southwest's struggle to get off the ground, letters from mayors thanking Southwest for putting their cities on the map, snapshots taken at company banquets, photos of Herb in his bunny outfit. To assure that every office employee was exposed to the entire record, each item was mounted on a different wall as often as once per quarter.

In a long, skylit corridor of the new building the company created a gallery of mannequins dressed in Southwest flight attendant uniforms as they had evolved through the years. At the end of one hall stood one of the company's first automatic ticket machines, vintage 1979, displayed in a clear glass case as if it were the Hope diamond. Nearby sat a time capsule to be opened in the distant future, a kind of corporate hope chest filled with employees' own memorabilia (pass the tissues, please) from those years of struggle dating all the way back to 1971. Kelleher's personal contributions included a half-consumed bottle of Wild Turkey.

Many of the people who followed the airline industry—on Wall Street, say, or in the business press, and in some cases within the airlines themselves—did not grasp that Southwest was actually creating a separate airline industry in America. The bifurcation of the industry was a natural and probably inevitable result of a conflict also erupting within the American economy: a conflict between the demand for convenience and the demand for value.

A broad segment of the traveling public—vacationers and expense account passengers alike—had quickly become spoiled by the breadth and scope of the post-deregulation airline markets. The outbreak of hub scheduling made it possible to fly between nearly any two airports in America with one change of planes. It was possible to visit friends or family or conduct a sales call virtually anywhere within a day. Passengers by the late 1980s could fly with one stop between any of 48,860 pairs of cities in America.

For competitive reasons the Big Four airlines, as well as Delta, Continental, and Northwest, were furiously adding all the employees, airplanes, and infrastructure necessary to deliver the maximum number of passengers to the maximum number of destinations. Doing so, however, involved tremendous costs—forcing airplanes to wait for connecting passengers, paying crews to wait for airplanes, paying basic travel agent commissions plus extra "override" commissions, maintaining powerful computer systems, and creating vast management bureaucracies, to say nothing of the cost of buying so many airplanes. Ultimately the expense of establishing and maintaining these networks, however brilliantly managed, was borne by the ticket holder, through fares that regardless of the dollar amount were higher than they would have been otherwise. Anyone could fly through this network at extremely low fares, but only by making reservations far in advance and by complying with the airlines' restrictions. And all passengers, regardless of the price they were paying, had to endure the hassles and lost time caused by flying through a hub.

This is where Southwest came in. While the major airlines were frantically working to become all things to everyone, Southwest recognized that a huge number of people in any city would rarely want to fly anywhere except to a few other cities. The cost and complexity of the hub system was worthwhile for the 22 people a day on average who, according to Transportation Department data, flew between Kansas City and Norfolk. But how many people in Kansas City might fly to Oklahoma City—two cities linked by common industries, by family connections, by the Big Eight athletic conference, and by geographical proximity? Each day, it turned out, hundreds of people were eager to make that trip when they learned they could do so without changing planes, without making their plans far in advance, without scheduling a Saturday stay, and for a price of, say, $39 each way.

That Southwest operated largely in a market all its own was most evident in its headquarters town of Dallas. Southwest shared its operating center with the fastest growing and most ruthlessly powerful airline in the world, American Airlines. Yet even as both airlines grew, even as the airline industry became more competitive year by year, American and Southwest served increasingly divergent markets from their respective airports and actually became less competitive as time passed. Bob Crandall, who in 1981 had tried to bring down the weight of the local community and the federal government on Southwest's operation at Love Field, had by 1986 come to consider Kelleher a friend and perhaps even a bit of a role model. The two men collaborated on a video for a local roast, joked about their compulsive smoking habits, and looked for chances to needle and play practical jokes on one another. Kelleher in an astonishingly effective marketing move painted a Southwest 737 to look like Shamu the killer whale when Sea World opened a park in San Antonio. "Just one question," Crandall asked him. "What are you going to do with all the whale shit?"

"I'm going to turn it into chocolate mousse and spoon-feed it to Yankees from Rhode Island," Kelleher answered. The following Monday Crandall received a vat of chocolate pudding with a little Sea World spoon stuck in the middle.

Though Southwest was largely separate and distinct from the rest of the airline industry, there were unavoidably points at which they intersected, sometimes with a pyrotechnic result—never more so than when Bob Crandall unleashed the full power of his pricing computers with "ultimate super savers" in January 1985. Although American's principal target was People Express, Southwest was sure to be struck with some of the shrapnel. Analysts began to cut their recommendations on the company's stock. "Small carriers such as Southwest," *The New York Times* glumly remarked in March 1986, "will be at a growing disadvantage in an age of airline giants." As if beginning to fulfill the prophecy, Southwest's profits plunged in late 1985, though it did remain profitable.

One evening Kelleher was talking to a business executive at a cocktail reception in Dallas. "I see that American now has fares as low as yours," the man said.

"Yes," Kelleher admitted. But American, he patiently explained, required passengers to buy a ticket 30 days in advance. By contrast, Kelleher said cheerfully, anyone could walk right up to the airport gate and fly at those prices on Southwest.

"No, you can't."

"Yes, you can," Kelleher corrected him.

"You're full of shit," the man said.

The man refused to accept that he could avail himself of the lowest fare in the market without enduring a multitude of restrictions. American, Kelleher realized at that moment, had conditioned the flying public to believe that low fares were impossible without restrictions.

Kelleher decided to try playing the game Bob Crandall's way. Holding its corporate nose, Southwest made certain fares nonrefundable. Just as bad, it adopted advance purchase requirements. It would, alas, force itself to acquire computer technology to step up the sophistication of its pricing. (The annual report devoted barely a full sentence to the new computer system, under a black-and-white photo of a paltry-looking desktop video terminal.)

But Southwest quickly realized that by exposing itself to even the rudiments of yield management, it could take its low fares so much lower that they practically disappeared—while the flights themselves remained profitable. Suddenly a passenger could fly anywhere on Southwest Airlines for $19. After American had beaten People Express at its game, Southwest was beating American at its.

Nineteen dollars was so cheap that yet another new layer of travelers was drawn into the market—major league baseball fans attending away games for the day, the poor, and college kids on dates. Southwest promoted the new fares with television ads in which animated suitcases and overweight people in bathing suits jubilantly sang and danced to a Beach Boys melody: "And we'll have fun fun fun flying Southwest on a fun-fare today." The fun-fare concept quickly reached into the fabric of the company, as employees in planes and behind ticket counters were outfitted in surfer shorts, golf shirts, and tennis shoes. Kelleher wore his "fun uniform" to the office on Fridays.

Kelleher did harbor a flaw, however, one that was so obvious no one could appreciate it. He had made Southwest Airlines a one-man show.

In big business in America the life of the chief executive is considered a corporate asset. Companies carry insurance policies against the loss of a chief executive. At age 55 Kelleher was still a relatively young CEO, and as he had displayed in his remarkably athletic youth, he was a person of some strength and vigor. "I'm immortal," he would joke.

But he also had a family history of heart attacks. The man smoked four packs a day; he ate heartily and swilled Wild Turkey. His complexion was pallid. "I lost my color because of bourbon," he told people.

Kelleher certainly had a management team, including some of the sharpest people in the business. Any number of them could run the planes and the schedules and the finances as well or better than Herb—but not the people. For that Herb did not need merely a successor, he needed an understudy, an apprentice, someone who without adopting his shtick or even his style had an instinct for knowing how to make each of nearly 6,000 employees feel like one of the Three Musketeers. No such person existed.

There was one other respect in which Kelleher betrayed a selfish side, and not a trace of humor. Southwest, he declared, would never be anybody's takeover.

The opposition of top executives to hostile raiders was in the late 1980s so routine as to be an article of management faith. Kelleher, however, was not only management but ownership: he had been the first investor to put money into Southwest Airlines, and a takeover would put inestimable millions directly into Kelleher's pockets. But while Kelleher was different from most airline chieftains in owning a significant share of the enterprise he managed, he did not differ from them in his fervor for its independence. Southwest Airlines *was* Herb Kelleher. It was his platform, his podium—his stage. It was part of his psyche, and that was worth much more than mere millions.

While fighting the fun-fare wars against the majors, Kelleher also undertook a few discreet steps to assure that no one took his airline away from him. For the faster the airlines merged, the more conspicuous Herb's became. Southwest Airlines in 1986 was a sitting duck.

Twenty major airline mergers occurred in the first eight years of deregulation; of these, 11 occurred in 1986 alone. The sudden swell reflected the almost complete lack of antitrust enforcement by the Reagan administration, the surging tide of merger activity throughout American industry, and the economic maelstrom in which the airlines in particular found themselves: the compulsive drive for "critical mass" and the financial pressures brought on by fare wars and intolerable debt burdens. Counting Lorenzo's empire as one, the entire universe of airline holding companies operating nationally had been reduced to 10: Texas Air, United, American, Delta, Northwest, TWA, Pan Am, USAir, Piedmont, and, at number 10, Southwest Airlines. As a group these airlines controlled about 95 percent of the airline market of the United States. The consolidation had been so furious that one of the industry's leading technical and analytic services, Airline Economics, Inc., of Washington, D.C., issued a study in 1987 asserting there was nothing major left to merge with, nothing major left to fail. As the opening sentence of the study put it, "The airlines' intense battle to position themselves for long-run survival is essentially over."

Kelleher knew better. He installed a "poison pill" and the other standard takeover defenses of the time, but he also used the jungle drums of Wall Street. When people asked what he would do if a particular takeover artist made a move against Southwest, Kelleher, the funny man, would turn stone-cold serious and reply, "I will kill him."

An investment banker from Wall Street happened to visit—a whippersnapper, in Kelleher's view, the kind of person who brought out the curmudgeon in Kelleher. When the investment banker noted what a tempting takeover target Southwest remained, Kelleher cast his piercing blue eyes through the fellow's heart, rose from his seat, and began backing him against the wall.

"You're too young to know what scorched earth is," Kelleher said evenly, trying to control his temper. Stepping closer, he told the young man how the Russians had destroyed their own property rather than leave it in the path of the Nazi onslaught. The investment banker soon had his back against the wall. "Anybody who buys this company is going to have ashes, soot, and cinders!" Kelleher yelled. "Those who build something know best how to *destroy it*!" Kelleher had his hands clasped to the young man's shoulders.

The investment banker slipped from Kelleher's grasp. His glasses askew, he raced out of the office past Colleen Barrett, Kelleher's executive assistant.

"What happened?" she asked.

"I just sent a message to Wall Street," Kelleher answered.

In January 1987 Kelleher proudly reviewed the text for the company's soon-to-be-published 1986 annual report to shareholders. It told investors that the company was closing in on $1 billion a year in sales. It reported a record operating profit of $89 million. It enumerated a litany of operating accomplishments: "We breathed new life into Chicago's Midway Airport. . . . Nashville became our first foray into the promising Southeastern market. . . . For the sixth year in a row, we received the fewest complaints per customer carried of any airline serving the continental U.S."

As Kelleher studied the draft, he looked with satisfaction at the cover. It was, he thought, the perfect way to say "up yours" to the people on Wall Street and elsewhere who thought that Southwest had no future as an independent company. In bold yellow type against a black background the cover of the annual report read simply

In 1986
we didn't
merge.

Even if a kind of gentleman's agreement existed between them, it did somewhat unnerve Kelleher to see his friend Bob Crandall bringing so many airplanes and employees to Dallas. Crandall, of course, was temperamentally incapable of putting anyone at ease where his competitive intentions were concerned. But Kelleher knew to a degree that no one else seemed to appreciate that all those planes by themselves didn't mean a thing. Kelleher once had a visitor in his office while he was planning a skit to present at an industry conference. "Let's do a Dr. Ruth spoof!" Kelleher exclaimed. Then he pretended to be the sex therapist on the phone to Crandall.

"Remember, Bob," Kelleher said in a squeaky, accented voice, "size isn't everything."

CHAPTER 14

OPERATION STEALTHCO

For Dick Ferris even a day of fishing provided an opportunity to compete.

When he and his friend Travis Reed climbed into a boat together during one of their summer sojourns in the West, Ferris kept score. If he found himself with fewer fish at the end of the day, Ferris pleaded to stay out, even if they had already pulled in dozens of fish, even when Reed complained that his arm was killing him. "Being second is not something Ferris likes to do," Reed would later comment.

In 1987 it was obvious that Bob Crandall would soon have more fish in his boat than Dick Ferris. Airplanes were coming into the American Airlines fleet at the rate of nearly two per week. More meaningful to both men was the fact that Crandall was being hailed as the indisputable leader of the airline industry. Even if American was still not the biggest airline, by many outward appearances it was the best managed. With his spanking new planes and enthusiastic young recruits, Crandall was fielding a crisp and fresh-looking airline, while Ferris had older planes and pilots who were bitterly divided against him.

To some of his associates Ferris seemed to be anguished less by the inevitability of Crandall's ascent to number one than by Crandall's success in conceiving and implementing ingenious new ideas.

Ferris once had been the industry's leading young standout—a prodigy, president of the country's biggest airline at 38—but that was 13 years ago. Now it was Crandall who was the industry's most conspicuous leader of any age.

By 1987, however, Ferris was well on his way to completing a bold and imaginative strategy: his plan to build a three-sided travel empire around United Airlines. The idea of packaging plane trips, rental car contracts, and hotel stays into a single travel product terrified even some of Crandall's people in Dallas. With sufficiently aggressive management, they thought, the new United could overpower any of the marketing weapons American had yet conceived. Frequent-flier programs, the use of hubs to dominate geographic regions, sophisticated pricing—all could be crushed if Ferris began offering hotel discounts to lure airline customers, or first-class upgrades to entice rental car customers, or any such permutation.

The travel empire—it had become Dick Ferris's dream and vision, his path to greatness. "I will go to my grave," he would comment years later, "convinced that it was right."

But Travis Reed, for one, began to worry about Ferris's relations with the United board. The bitterness of the strike and the restiveness of Wall Street exposed Ferris to intense pressure at a time when he was also committing billions of dollars in shareholders' capital to his strategy. Over a glass of gin one day Reed decided to have a heart-to-heart talk with his friend. "Dick, you're doing some major things, and you've still got Eddie Carlson's board. You better get a few loyalists on there who will punch somebody in the nose when it comes time." Reed tried to be as explicit as he could. "You've got to get some buddies on the board, some guys who would go down with you."

Ferris, however, had no reason to doubt the loyalty of his board. His purchases of Hertz and Hilton were controversial, yes, but the board had unanimously—indeed, enthusiastically—backed each move. The confrontation with the pilots was hurtful and emotional, yes, but the board had been included in the process and, notwithstanding the lone dissent of director Wally Haas, had backed Ferris all the way. Ferris assured Reed he could handle his board.

Although Ferris was unaware of it, the fact was that some of the directors harbored great concerns.

Some felt that the presumptuousness Ferris had displayed three years earlier in his short-lived effort to buy the company through an LBO was only worsening. During one meeting Ferris informed the directors, "Now we're going to pass the dividend," as if he were ordering them to pass the butter. Declaring a quarterly dividend, though often a formality, is a happy event for the shareholders of a company and a ritual that directors take very seriously. William M. Jenkins, a retired banker who held one of the long-standing Seattle seats on the United board, complained to Chuck Luce, the senior director, "Since when does *management* pass the dividend?"

Then came the name game.

Shortly after the first of the year in 1987 Ferris informed his board that a new name would be established for the parent company. UAL, Inc., would no longer be UAL, Inc. A new corporate identity would help the company proclaim to the world that United wasn't just United Airlines anymore, that it was a seamless travel experience consisting of great names in hotels, cars, and yes, an airline as well. But while they listened to the merits of adopting a new corporate identity, the directors were dismayed to realize that Ferris was withholding the name itself, from his own board of directors. He said he could not reveal it so far in advance of the scheduled announcement date for security reasons! The board would eventually get briefed in advance, but only on the verge of the public announcement.

When the great day came, Ferris stepped behind a podium wearing a green tie—his favorite color, the color of a putting green, the color, as it turned out, that had been chosen for the new corporate logo. Linked by satellite from Australia to Hong Kong to Mexico City and points in between, the ladies and gentlemen of the press poised their pens and pencils on the surface of their notepads as Ferris said, "It's a name that you have not heard before, but most certainly will in the future . . .

"Allegis Corporation."

Ferris's design consultants explained that they had cobbled together *Allegis* from the root word for "allegiance" and from the Greek *aegis,* meaning protection. Never was a corporate name change so ridiculed, and among those who were already skeptical of Ferris's strategy the stupidity of the name only reinforced their views. Donald Trump, cruising on a wave of borrowed money and having just purchased a big chunk of UAL stock, said that Allegis sounded like "a world-class disease." Just as the airline was planting the flag in the Far East on the old Pan Am routes, Asian people had a particularly difficult time with the word (*Arregis?*). Employees of the airline itself began saying they were "allergic to Allegis." The day the new name was announced, UAL shares sank like a stone; the following day as Ferris tried to explain his travel service strategy to analysts, the share price only sank further. In a 24-hour period UAL shares dropped $3 to $56.50, erasing $150 million from the company's market value.

It was not the name change alone of course that accounted for the negativism on Wall Street. The continuing fare wars, particularly with Continental in Denver, were killing United's earnings. In addition Ferris's many and diverse travel companies were not yet producing huge dividends; there were not yet any synergies to speak of. Ferris warned Wall Street to be patient. It would be two years or so before all the pieces were in the right place, before the electronic "glue" of the Apollo system had cemented them. But two years was a long time to wait in the Roaring '80s—a period of fabulous stock profits, the greatest bull market in history—and United, UAL, Allegis, whatever the hell it was, was a laggard in the estimation of Wall Street. Among investment professionals Allegis Corporation was soon known as Egregious Corporation.

Wall Street did take note, however, that while Allegis did not exceed the sum of its parts, the parts themselves were performing beautifully. Dick Ferris had chosen his various businesses exceedingly well. He had bought Hertz and Hilton and had built up Westin at extremely favorable prices, and these assets had appreciated swiftly in the swelling economy. Far from solacing the traders on Wall Street, however, this fact only heightened their outrage. The individual pieces of Allegis, they realized, could be sold off piecemeal at tremendous profits. Allegis, it appeared, was worth more dead than alive.

As the computers on Wall Street calculated the soaring value of the pieces, savvy traders began snapping up shares at the parent company's depressed price. As the buying spread, the price of Allegis shares began creeping higher, causing individual investors to bail out with their profits and the professional speculators and money funds to jump in.

The buy-and-hold crowd was giving way to the get-rich-quick crowd. And the United pilots were getting nervous.

Rick Dubinsky, the strike committee chairman in the 1985 pilots' walkout, first discussed taking control of United Airlines over several glasses of wine on the night he had been elected chairman of the pilots' organization. The outgoing local chairman, Roger Hall, could see even through the alcohol haze that Dubinsky was instantly enthralled with the prospect. "He acted like a kid with a new toy," Hall would later remark.

Dubinsky immediately went into action. If the bitter strike had proved anything, in Dubinsky's view, it was that airline pilots were nothing more than hired help. "Airline pilots are simply a form of high-paid production workers," he would later declare in a speech at Harvard. "We produce revenue-passenger miles instead of widgets, TV sets, or shoes." Pilots, though long accustomed to thinking of themselves as "professionals," were not in fact professionals at all by the standard definition, Dubinsky realized: a professional could go into business for himself, could hang out his own shingle. Airline pilots could do none of that.

As Dubinsky saw it, buying United was the only way for the pilots to take control of their destiny—the only way to get the company out of the hotel business and the rental car business and to start rebuilding the *airline* again. United was once a premier carrier, he thought; under Ferris it was fast becoming an also-ran. The only strategy that made sense for the pilots was to bid for control of the entire airline; the Eastern unions, among others, had provided a painfully instructive example when they traded away hard-fought wages for a minority interest and a few board seats, which proved meaningless. At other places the unions gave up concessions strictly to keep their jobs. "We will not buy our jobs," Dubinsky declared. Buying jobs was indentured servitude. Instead, he said, "we will buy the company."

On a Saturday in April 1987, barely a month after Dick Ferris had rechristened the company as Allegis, some 40 United pilot leaders in civilian clothes arrived for a secret meeting at the Stouffer Hamilton Hotel in Itasca, Illinois, not far from O'Hare, where they voted to go forward with a project named Operation Stealthco—a takeover offer for their airline.

Ferris was on a Learjet flying to Des Moines the following day to give a speech as the newly appointed chairman of United Way when a call came from his office on the radio of the small jet. In his absence a three-page letter had arrived from the Air Line Pilots Association. They were proposing to take over United Airlines, they said, because they were fearful that someone else would do it first—and because they were resentful that Ferris was turning their airline into a car and hotel company as well.

They were offering $4.5 billion. They had $300 million in pension fund money under their control—flash money. They would stretch their equity by exploiting the tax advantages available to employee-owned corporations. They would cut back their own wages, making the company more attractive to lenders. They had spent time on Wall Street. They had conferred with Boone Pickens. They had consultants on the payroll. They were sure they knew what they were doing.

Ferris ordered the Learjet turned around. Immediately he was on his way back to Chicago, where United's head of flight operations prepared a telegram to the company's pilots. "Events have started a chain reaction," the telegram warned, "that may be very difficult to control."

On April 17, 1987, Dick Ferris began the day on a headline in *The Wall Street Journal* that defined the living nightmare of a corporate CEO: "Rising UAL Turmoil Threatens Ferris's Job as the Chief Executive."

"Even if the 50-year-old Mr. Ferris succeeds in fighting off the pilots," the article said, "his job may be in jeopardy, some people close to the UAL board suggest." The directors, the article explained, were upset that United—the airline, not the holding company—was performing poorly. Even more surprising, the article said that the board was putting Ferris's "whole business strategy under hasty review."

Senior Director Charles Luce was horrified. Although the article captured the sentiments that he and other United directors privately harbored, it was not the kind of publicity any of them wanted. The shareholders of United were now in a state of complete rebellion, Luce recognized, engulfing United in a three-way struggle for control among the management, the pilots, and Wall Street. Worse still, as the days wore on and as positions hardened among the combatants, a community of interests had begun to emerge between Wall

Street and the pilots. Both groups more than ever wanted to see Allegis busted up, and increasingly Wall Street and the pilots were unified in their judgment that Dick Ferris was the principal obstacle to the fulfillment of their wishes.

Under such incendiary circumstances, Luce thought, the board must not divide itself from management; just as important, it could not be *seen* as divided. A unified front was essential, even if it meant that some of the directors had to stifle their true feelings about Ferris. Regardless of what happened to the cars or hotel, the airline, Luce resolved, could not under any circumstances be allowed to fall into hands that might manage it clumsily or greedily.

The *Journal* article appeared on Good Friday in 1987. Over the weekend Luce drafted a response by hand and personally delivered it to the paper's office on Easter Sunday. The letter appeared in the next day's editions. Luce accused the *Journal* of publishing "inaccuracies and anti-management bias." He agreed with the article's conclusion that United's airline earnings were unsatisfactory but blamed nonunion competition from the likes of Continental Airlines, not Ferris.

"The UAL board," Luce's letter went on, "is four-square behind Mr. Ferris, his management team, and his long-range strategy." The *Journal,* it appeared, had the story all wrong. Ferris's job was safe.

Ferris himself, meanwhile, was arranging to protect Allegis even further, with the help of an old ally, Boeing.

In that one sector of the aviation business, life could not have been sweeter. There were no boardroom battles raging at Boeing, no rank-and-file rebellions, no ruinous fare wars, no bankruptcies. Boeing was riding a wave of aircraft orders unlike any ever, thanks in part to low fares and the greatest flying boom in history. In addition to expanding their fleets, the major airlines were also replacing their generation-old 727s, 737s, and 747s. These models were giving way to the 757 and the 767, with the two-engine, long-range 777 on the drawing board. Boeing now had two thirds of the worldwide aircraft market to itself.

But Boeing was concerned about a long-term threat on the horizon. It was Airbus Industrie, the European aircraft-manufacturing consortium. Nearly a decade earlier Airbus had broken into the

United States on the strength of the big order from Frank Borman at Eastern. Airbus, it turned out, built wonderful jets. With subsidies from the governments of Europe, it had priced these planes cheaply and was making further inroads. Boeing could not let Airbus gobble too much market share, and above all it could never permit it to move in on its best customer ever, United Airlines, which Boeing itself had once owned. United urgently needed planes. Everyone knew that United would soon have to place a massive order. So despite its booming production lines, Boeing was in a mood to do just about anything to clinch its standing with Ferris.

Agreeing to place a huge order with Boeing, Ferris simultaneously asked Boeing to provide $700 million to United through the purchase of notes. There was nothing unusual in an aircraft manufacturer providing financing to a customer, just as General Motors lent money to people to buy Chevrolets. But the $700 million in notes were convertible, at Boeing's option, into 16 percent of the common stock of Allegis. Boeing also received options to raise its interest in United to 30 percent and possibly higher. It was a preposterous transaction—a bald antitakeover move passed off as an investment. With the ability to shift a huge block of stock into friendly hands whenever the need arose, Ferris, it seemed, had stopped the pilots dead.

The stock speculators who had loaded up on Allegis stock on the expectation of a bust-up or takeover quickly bailed out. But in their wake was a ready buyer: a single investment partnership called Coniston, consisting of three bright young traders who had already made a killing in takeover stocks and had a few hundred million dollars with which to wager on United's shares.

Ferris would later recall dismissing this threat as "Coniston Schmoniston." But as he was preparing to announce the unveiling of the new Allegis Visa card, Ferris learned that Coniston had picked up 13 percent of his stock. There was more: Coniston announced that it was embracing the pilots' point of view. Coniston too believed that Allegis should be broken into pieces. Worst of all, Coniston announced that it would soon begin soliciting proxies from its fellow shareholders to have the Allegis board of directors thrown out.

A proxy fight was under way.

Ferris had been blindsided. Facing a genuine emergency, his people notified Boeing that it should start preparing to convert its notes into stock; Ferris and his board would need as many votes as possible to survive the proxy fight. But the people at Boeing, stung by criticism surrounding the white knight deal of only a few days earlier, answered that they would take his request under advisement. Ferris had been stiffed.

More bad news came in for Ferris. A poll conducted by a professional proxy solicitation firm predicted that Coniston would probably win a proxy fight. Ferris and the incumbent directors of United would lose.

Frank Olson of Hertz Corporation had been a friend of Dick Ferris's since long before United had purchased Hertz, and their relationship had grown much closer since then. As chairman of one of Allegis's principal operating subsidiaries and as a United director, Olson was either a participant in the events swirling around Ferris or a front-row observer. Increasingly he was also Ferris's confidant.

The two men grimly concluded that events had cascaded beyond Ferris's control. Wall Street's expectations had been raised; something was going to happen to the company, whether a takeover by the pilots, a takeover by a third party, the ouster of the company's board by Coniston, or some combination of such events. Wall Street was extorting Allegis, and Ferris had to find a way to make a payoff. The only way to do that, Olson told him, was to begin dismantling Allegis voluntarily and putting the proceeds in the hands of the shareholders. "Dick, we've got to sell something," Olson said. "This is ridiculous, to continue to hold on to it." Such were the ironies of corporate strategy in the 1980s: Ferris had taken the first steps in building his empire to help ward off a takeover, and now, just two years later, he had to take it apart to accomplish the same result.

What should Allegis sell? "Start with Westin and see if that satisfies them," Olson said. "If not, then let's sell Hertz."

Ferris gave Olson no argument. Too much had changed; it was time to relent. Ferris would begin making preparations to sell at least part of his empire and distribute the proceeds to shareholders.

Even if that satisfied Wall Street, Ferris still had the pilots to worry about. Dubinsky was more fervent than ever in his desire to take control of the airline. But the International Association of Machinists, an institution better known for slaying managements than for defending them, soon rose to Ferris's defense.

The machinists and the pilots at United had been like quarreling stepsiblings for years. The pilots had crossed the machinists' picket lines in a 1981 strike, and the machinists in retaliation had crossed the pilots' picket lines in the Great Strike of 1985. At the national level the machinists' union harbored grave philosophical misgivings about employee ownership. As Charlie Bryan of Eastern had proved, the IAM had become the vanguard of the American worker by bargaining over every nickel, every coffee break, every work rule, in the belief that such small things, cumulatively, would make a significant difference in the living standards of the membership. In order to get a little more here and there, the unions needed someone to bargain against. The union *needed* management. For that reason the machinists' leadership in Washington was unalterably opposed to workers becoming the bosses. John Peterpaul, international head of airline operations for the IAM, came down forcefully on Ferris's side. "If I own the company," Peterpaul would explain, "who am I going to strike?"

On April 14, 1987, Peterpaul sent a letter to Dubinsky of the pilots' union declaring the machinists' opposition to a takeover by the pilots, and he made sure that the letter became public. The machinists' action was a breakthrough for Ferris, who assured his directors that the pilots were on the run. "Don't worry about the machinists," Ferris told his board. "They're with us."

Unfortunately for Ferris, the machinists' work contract at United at that moment was up for renewal; alas, the talks were going badly. With the fires still building against Allegis on Wall Street, the contract talks between Ferris's people and the machinists fell apart on May 29, 1987, a Friday. The following Friday, June 5—with Coniston launching its proxy fight and the pilots pulling together the details of their takeover plan—the machinists' union jerked the rug out from under Ferris. In a letter to Ferris's board Peterpaul said that the contract negotiations were in a shambles and that a strike might begin at any time. "The management and the board has [sic] lost our confidence," Peterpaul wrote.

The directors were flabbergasted. Ferris had been so confident of the machinists' support, so cocky about it. Among the board mem-

bers most disturbed was Richard P. Cooley, one of the Seattle delegates on the United board. Cooley was the chairman of Seafirst Corporation, the huge banking enterprise. Though far from the senior
member, he commanded tremendous respect from his fellow directors. On Friday, June 5, 1987, Cooley telephoned Chuck Luce at his
home. Cooley said he and another director—William Jenkins, the retired chairman of Seafirst—agreed that "we ought to have a new
CEO." The two Seattle bankers would, of course, defer to Luce; as
senior director it was his job to decide whether the board should conduct a vote of confidence. "It's up to you," Cooley emphasized.

After brooding over the weekend Charles Luce polled the board, except for Ferris and the other officers of the company who sat on it.
The outside directors were unanimous that a special meeting should
be held in New York on Tuesday to decide the fate of Dick Ferris.

As the directors made their travel arrangements, Luce scheduled
a visit to the midtown Manhattan offices of Hertz. If the board decided to oust Ferris, Luce knew that Allegis would need a new chief
executive officer, and Frank Olson, he thought, was the ideal person
for the job. Olson had been singly identified with the tremendous
success of Hertz for more than a decade. He was a leading figure in
the international business community quite apart from United Airlines. Having joined the United family after the bitter pilots' strike
two years earlier, he was untainted by any involvement in that event.

"Frank, we've got to have an alternative to Dick," Luce said.
"You're the logical guy."

But to Olson it was as if Luce had come to his office bearing not
a job offer but 30 pieces of silver. The whole thing stank. Yes, Ferris
remained a lightning rod, but he had agreed to come to terms with
Wall Street by selling part of the Allegis empire; Olson himself had
helped convince Ferris of the need to compromise. The idea of becoming chairman of Allegis was horrifying. Olson could not bear
the thought that Ferris might see him as part of the plot. In addition
Olson did not want to leave his position as chairman of Hertz. Hertz
was his life. It was obvious, moreover, that Hertz was destined for the
auction block. The sale of any company was a delicate event and
could easily become a traumatic one; Olson wanted to devote his loy-

alties and energies first to the protection of Hertz. Every fiber in him told Olson to say no way.

Luce began a little pressure play. "If you don't do it," he said to Olson, "one of the other directors will."

Great, just great, Olson thought. While he was no airline person, Olson thought he knew more about the business than anyone else on the board. He had been doing business with airlines for most of his years at Hertz. He had been close to Eddie Carlson back when Carlson left the Westin chain to save United. Olson counted a number of the currently reigning CEOs—not just Ferris, but Crandall and others—among his friends. Olson, furthermore, had built his career in the rental car business around raising capital for high-cost assets, dispatching them according to rapidly changing economic conditions, pricing them as perishable products, and maintaining them mechanically for reliability and longevity—the essentials of airline management. He knew computer reservations systems. He had a large and geographically diverse labor force.

Olson began to soften. He told Luce that if the board unanimously determined to eject Ferris, he would serve as chairman, although only until a permanent successor could be found.

While Luce was meeting with Olson, the Securities and Exchange Commission in Washington approved the documents that Coniston Partners planned to use in the proxy fight against Allegis. The firm began preparing the mailings by which it would try to convince the shareholders to have all 16 directors of Allegis summarily removed.

The directors of Allegis gathered at Morgan Stanley in New York on Tuesday, June 9, 1987, exactly 50 days after they had declared themselves "four-square" behind Dick Ferris and his corporate strategy. These same men had voted to approve, in some cases with great enthusiasm, all the acquisitions they now wanted to shed. Only weeks earlier, in fact, they had signed Ferris to a five-year employment contract.

What had happened in 50 days that they now wanted to be rid of him?

For one, the stock speculators had accumulated the strength to replace this board. The board could not let that happen. Getting thrown out in a proxy fight would be a monumental humiliation.

Worse, resisting the proxy fight while defending the status quo would expose the directors to shareholder lawsuits, with the attendant personal liability, the same threat that had provoked the directors of Eastern Air Lines to consent to a takeover offer from Frank Lorenzo a year earlier.

Finally, the directors had a commitment to protecting the integrity of the airline—a commitment that some of them, including Chuck Luce, put even higher than their fiduciary duty to the company's shareholders. Back in 1970, when Eddie Carlson had been brought in as chairman during the last leadership crisis, Luce, then a new director, saw nothing less than the economic security of the nation in the balance. He took the airline, the biggest in the free world, very seriously, almost as if the free world itself were at stake.

"The principal motivation must be to keep the airline a viable enterprise serving the public," Luce was now saying. "Dick's program won't do that."

As for the directors' personal misgivings about Ferris, these had never previously been sufficient to act on, usually not troublesome enough even to mention to him. But in Luce's mind, at least, Ferris appeared to have lost his balance. "Dick was getting weird," he later said. Ferris, moreover, had come to symbolize everything that the dissident forces swirling around Allegis had come to resent. If Ferris stayed, the directors would be thrown out and he with them. If Ferris left, there was every chance that at least the directors would survive—to protect the airline, to find an orderly way of mollifying Wall Street and placating the pilots, and to protect their own necks.

Ferris arrived at the meeting prepared to bring the board up-to-date on a series of negotiations with Dubinsky of the pilots' union. But in a waiting area adjacent to the meeting room he was approached by Frank Olson. "Dick," he said, "you are my friend." And with that Olson told Ferris what the board was about to do to him.

Ferris was called into the boardroom, where Luce informed him it was the board's will to sell everything but the airline—hotels, cars, everything. And, Luce said, "It's in the best interests of the airline, and yourself, that we change management."

A vote had not yet been taken. Ferris was excused from the room as the directors each spoke one last time. John McGillicuddy of Manufacturers Hanover Bank suggested that Ferris had not been given a sufficient opportunity to state his case. So Luce and Andrew F. Brimmer, a former Federal Reserve economist who sat on the board, walked into the anteroom where Ferris waited, his heart pounding. They beckoned him to return to the boardroom, but by this time Ferris wouldn't have it.

"There's no point in my going back in there," Ferris answered. "You want my resignation. You got it."

The news of Ferris's ouster reached United's operating centers on the West Coast just as the bank of evening flights was getting ready to depart. Flight attendants spent that evening pouring drinks and passing out movie headsets for free. "We gave everything away," Kevin Lum, one of those flight attendants, would later say. "The big bad wolf was dead."

A few days later Chuck Luce, age 69, was riding his bicycle along South Broadway when he was hit by a bus. He suffered severe internal injuries. He would spend six months recuperating.

Fortunately for United, Luce had already appointed a search committee headed by board member Neil A. Armstrong, the former astronaut. Armstrong prepared a long, detailed, and fabulously lucrative job offer to the man who was already in the job on a temporary basis, Frank Olson. But Olson, while running the parent company, was also absorbed in the spin-off of Hertz, a transaction intended to help raise the money necessary to make a big cash payment to United's restive shareholders. Olson and a group of Hertz executives negotiated to buy Hertz for themselves for $1.3 billion with financing provided by Ford Motor Company. (The price received by United was more than twice what Ferris had paid.)

Olson declined Armstrong's offer, but he was not yet out of the soup. A permanent CEO still had to be found. Although Neil Armstrong remained the chairman of the board's search committee, Olson decided to take command of the search himself.

Although the candidates themselves would never realize the full scope of the search of which they were a part, Olson's mission would bring him into contact with the leading protagonists of the global airline world in the twilight of the 1980s. The search would last months longer than Olson had hoped. And no matter how it ended, it would have profound repercussions not just for United but for the global airline industry as well.

Immediately after leaving New York, Ferris had picked up his wife in Chicago and headed to the Teton Valley Lodge to meet their friend Travis Reed for some fishing. There were moments when Ferris had to be alone. On other occasions, reviewing the events with Reed, Ferris would turn beet red.

The airline industry had changed Dick Ferris. A chesty, aggressive, and ambitious man, he had gone too far in an effort to make the people in his organization behave with the same submissiveness as the airplanes. "Now you can become a human being," Travis Reed told him at one point. A severance package totaling more than $4 million would certainly be of help in making the transition.

In time an oil portrait of Ferris, in keeping with company tradition, would be hung in the United boardroom in Elk Grove Village. Along one wall, in the glare of recessed light against an expanse of rich rosewood paneling, the Ferris portrait became the fifth of the group, right next to Eddie Carlson's. But the style of the Ferris portrait was different. The others were traditional, earnest, distinguished—older gentlemen posed at ease. The image of youthful, square-jawed Ferris showed him smiling and leaning forward, as if ready to jump through the frame, with a Boeing 767 careening across the foreground, making the entire painting as extraordinary as Richard Ferris's years had been.

CHAPTER 15

FLY NOW, PAY LATER

Around the time of Dick Ferris's ouster, commercial aviation was settling into a state of equanimity for the first time since the advent of deregulation. The three-ring circus in Denver was over. Frank Borman and his hypercompetitive impulses had vanished. Braniff II was failing as surely as Braniff I had. Above all, People Express had been safely disposed of. Though the low-fare impulse lived on at Southwest Airlines, Herb Kelleher continued confining the company to short-haul niche markets that reached nowhere east of Michigan.

The airline industry had become a club of giants. Towering over them all was Francisco A. Lorenzo.

Takeovers had elevated Lorenzo into the aviation equivalent of John D. Rockefeller. Nearly 20 percent of the seats flying over America at any moment now belonged to him. In addition to owning Continental, Eastern, and the remnants of People Express and Frontier, he controlled 15 regional feeder airlines, many flying under his colors, each operating at the mercy of his schedules. He controlled the nation's third-largest computer reservations network, System One, hardwired into 17,000 travel agency terminals from coast to coast. No one could now dispute Lorenzo's oft-repeated claim, "We are airline builders."

The empire had been assembled with debt, rapidly approaching $5 billion worth. Frank Lorenzo treated the borrowing markets like a drive-up window; his publicly traded issues alone would soon number 24. At the height of Lorenzo's borrowing, the cash that Lorenzo laid out in interest alone—more than $600 million a year—exceeded the annual sales for nearly 100 members of the Fortune 500.

Alas for him, Lorenzo's size also made him more visible, and more inviting, as a target. For the moment United Airlines was not the grave threat it had once been. Recovering from the ouster of Dick Ferris, preoccupied with the search for a successor, shedding its various units in order to appease Wall Street, United at best was marching in place. The contest for survival at the top was therefore down to just two companies, and two men. Only one would last.

The ballroom chandeliers dimmed. The merrymakers fell silent, settling back to await the evening's presentation. On a projection screen at the front of the ballroom the film began.

Images of powerful bodybuilders filled the screen, their pectorals gleaming and biceps bulging. A deep, booming voice filled the ballroom.

"He is tough," the announcer said. "Mean . . . relentless . . ."

A United Airlines jet passed across the screen. "He is taking on the Big U!" the announcer exclaimed.

Another jet, this one in the markings of Delta Air Lines, appeared next. "He is fighting the Delta forces!"

Next appeared a Continental Airlines plane. "He looks the South Texas gang straight in the eye, ready to take them on—anytime, any place."

Who was this man?

"He is *Crando*!"

And at that moment on the screen appeared Robert Lloyd Crandall, the chairman, president, and chief executive officer of American Airlines, not in his usual broadcloth shirt, with his tie bar perfectly placed and his cuffs rolled precisely halfway up his forearm. No, for this little video presentation, to a meeting of company sales executives, Bob Crandall was in costume as Rambo, war paint on his 51-year-old face, a headband around his temples, a sleeveless tee shirt exposing his sinewy arms. He was stalking through a jungle set, a machine gun in his hands. The crowd went wild.

"He is *Crando!*"

As the lights came up, the live Bob Crandall took the stage in his civilian clothing, approaching the podium with a smirk on his face and the light glinting on his wire-rimmed glasses. When the cheering sales executives finally began to quiet for Crandall's speech—a serious speech, no doubt, for Crandall's speeches were always serious— Crandall leaned toward the microphone, threw his fists over his head, shook his arms, and roared.

"*G-R-R-R-R-R-R-AGH!*" And the crowd went wild again.

Crandall, in displaying his lighter side, had transformed himself into a parody of himself, like a Saturday morning superhero. Yet this was what his people had come to expect. It was what they *needed* in order to attain higher and higher operating results—which they were now delivering, like clockwork, year after year. Aided by the magnetism of its hubs and the passenger-collecting power of the Sabre network, American's torrent of red ink had turned into a stream of profits—$228 million in 1983, $234 million in 1984, and $346 million in 1985, by which time Crandall had well over $1 billion in cash on hand.

With the kind of leverage that Frank Lorenzo was employing, Crandall probably had the equity at his command to take over the entire U.S. airline industry. But Crandall had chosen a different course. By purchasing individual airplanes rather than whole companies, Crandall was able to hire his own people instead of taking on someone else's, and each new hire was another employee working at cut-rate, b-scale wages.

"We do not expect to join the great merger escapades of the 1980s," Crandall told his assembled managers at one point. "As far as I'm concerned, they can *all* merge into one giant airline. And we'll *still* beat them!"

Everyone in the audience knew that "merger escapades" was synonymous with Texas Air and Frank Lorenzo. It was a shock to people at American that after years of struggling to become number one against United Airlines, they had suddenly been eclipsed by such an outfit as Texas Air. But even if Texas Air was a joke by Crandall standards, he refused to let his people take Lorenzo frivolously. More than ever Texas Air was the enemy.

This much was evident when Crandall and his top aide, Tom Plaskett, took the rostrum at American's 1986 Fall Planning Conference

in Dallas to report on competitive conditions in the industry. "As
Chairman Bob likes to say," Plaskett noted, warming up the audience, "it's the nearest thing to legalized warfare."

Plaskett continued:

> When we think a minute about the new king of the hill, at least in
> terms of size, it should tell us that anything is possible. Some of you who
> grew up in this state will remember Trans-Texas Airlines, which flew its
> DC-3s to Waco, Abilene, and Beaumont. People said the "TTA" logo
> stood for Tree-Top Airlines, and they laughed. Then the airline got a
> route to a Mexican border town on the south bank of the Rio Grande
> and had the audacity to change its name to Texas International, and peo-
> ple laughed again. Next Frank Lorenzo took it over and tried to buy Na-
> tional and TWA, and everyone had still another good laugh.

"Well," Plaskett concluded, "no one is laughing anymore."

Miami International Airport, where Eastern was based, was known
to some as Cockroach Corner, not so much for the ubiquitousness of
the six-legged vermin (although that was reason enough) but for the
presence of so many dilapidated old airplanes. Nowhere else in
America could one see such a collection of ancient DC-3s and Boeing 707s, some of them broken-down and long ago raided for parts,
an engine missing from one, a tail section from another, like war veterans waiting to be fitted for prostheses. Many of the planes landing
at Cockroach Corner flew the colors of some obscure Latin American airline or freight operator.

Phil Bakes entered Eastern headquarters on the perimeter of
Miami International and felt as if he were walking into a mausoleum. The fountain at the front entrance was still dry. The bronze
Rickenbacker medallion was so oxidized that Bakes could not recognize the founder's image. Entering Frank Borman's old office on
the ninth floor of Building 16, Bakes was depressed to find dark,
paneled walls. There were even ashtrays in evidence.

But Bakes was constitutionally incapable of staying depressed for
long. Though he had resisted leaving Continental, he was now the
president of Eastern and thought he might as well make the most of
it. Almost immediately he ordered the fountain refilled and switched

back to life. The long-tarnished Rickenbacker medallion was freshly gilded and buffed. Bakes threw away the ashtrays in his office, had a fluorescent light installed, and had the walls painted white. Soon, Bakes was displaying his old swagger.

There was not much secret in Texas Air's official agenda at Eastern. Bakes's mission was to slash the costs of labor, furthering the effort on which Borman had never reached closure. After all those years of BOHICA, Borman had succeeded in reducing Eastern's labor costs to roughly the industry average. But by Texas Air standards, average was way too high. If Bakes could further gut Eastern's labor costs, Texas Air would have a new Continental Airlines, this one trimmed in ionosphere blue.

Bakes, however, purposely moderated his cost-cutting rhetoric. Although it was fine to put the unions a little off-balance, Bakes did not want to be seen marching into Building 16 with a club in one hand and a bankruptcy how-to manual in the other. He wanted to develop a full, well-rounded revitalization plan for Eastern to restore marketing strength, upgrade passenger service, and invigorate management at all levels. "We have to show we're not a one-trick pony," he told Lorenzo.

Lorenzo, though, kept asking, "When are you going to give your proposal to the unions?"

For a brief time Bakes resisted. He took the senior management away for the weekend to the Keys. He met with middle management incessantly. He began showing up for employee meetings—JFK, Atlanta, Miami, everywhere there were big operations—and people actually turned out, in some cases by the thousands. And they were listening! He told and retold the story of Continental's comeback; it did not hurt his credibility that as he was walking into Eastern, Continental was reporting its highest profits ever.

Eastern's employee newsletter, the *Falcon,* became Bakes's *Pravda.* In issue after issue Bakes appeared on the front page, variously looking thoughtful and sympathetic (his hand on his chin, his elbow resting on his knee) or confident and assertive (stabbing his finger in the air, chopping the top of a desk with the side of his hand).

"When are you going to give your proposal to the unions?" Lorenzo kept asking.

Finally, on January 21, 1987, Bakes did. "Our labor cost structure is a cancer," Bakes announced at a press conference. Pilots, despite having given Borman a 20 percent cutback only months earlier, were now asked to give up an additional 27 percent. Flight attendants, also having already cut their wages 20 percent, would now be expected to give up another 31 percent. As for Charlie Bryan's mechanics and maintenance workers, they had escaped the last round of cuts on the night that Borman had lost Eastern. Now Bakes targeted them for the steepest cuts of all: 47 percent. "The marketplace for people loading and unloading bags is not $43,000 a year on average," Bakes said.

Charlie Bryan just shrugged. With a full year left to run on the IAM contract, there was nothing to negotiate. "The issue of opening our contract is a nonissue," Bryan said. "We negotiate an agreement, and we don't go back and ask for more." When Bakes's aides hosted a meeting with the leaders of the unions, the IAM delegation walked out after 10 minutes, lest anyone interpret their attendance as an admission they were willing to deal.

On another occasion Bryan held an impromptu rally of machinists in an employee parking lot, crying out a passage from Isaiah inscribed on a medallion that his mother had once received from a television evangelist: "Weapons formed against you will not prosper!" He vowed to fight the new management of Eastern with the principles of passive resistance. "Martin Luther King was truly a great American," Bryan told the assembly, adding, "I don't care what your racial feelings might be." Company supervisors tried to break up the rally. They ordered Bryan to leave the parking lot. He refused. "We're going to prevail!" he cried to the throng. Five days later Bakes's aides ordered Bryan stripped of his company ID badge, banished him from Eastern Air Lines property, and ordered him, in writing, to desist from conducting any further "public soap operas."

Bryan befuddled Lorenzo's people. In a know-thy-enemy measure the Texas Air corporate office commissioned a confidential "white paper" on the IAM from a consultant (who confided in her cover letter that she had obtained information from union representatives "on false pretenses.") Members of the IAM, the report said, were "not overly intelligent." They were, it went on,

unsophisticated, chauvinistic, patriotic, unadventurous, in search of a secure and comfortable existence for themselves and their families. With

little but a time-clock job to aspire to, the Nobility of Work is an important element in their universe. . . .

The IAM is an insular, somewhat paranoid organization. Business is
the enemy. The Employer is always out to rape the worker. . . . The union
also appears to believe that maintaining the largest possible wage for its
members for the longest possible time is a greater service than maintaining their jobs.

But it was a union that was divisible, the report said, because it
bargained at once for so many unskilled trades along with the professionally licensed mechanics who maintained and repaired airplanes. "These are highly skilled workers," the consultant's report
said, "usually pretty bright guys, rather conservative. They don't like
being associated with the hot-headed bag-busters, [who are] less intelligent, of lemming mentality." But while the professional plane
fixers were the moderates of the IAM, the report said, "the unskilled
are the union's staunchest supporters as well as its biggest group nu-
merically. These are the guys with a psychic need for self-esteem."

A psychic need for self-esteem. Charlie Bryan could be accused of
many things, but pandering to the Freudian vulnerabilities of his
membership was probably not among them. Still, some of Lorenzo's
people were convinced that Bryan suffered from a complex of some
kind—and where it would lead, they could only fear. Bakes's aides
printed an anthology of Bryan's outrageous public pronouncements
in a booklet called *Charlie Says.* It looked like the *Little Red Book,*
by which Mao Zedong had led the mass insanity of the Cultural
Revolution.

Though Lorenzo lacked Bob Crandall's talent for operating detail,
he did have a genius for intrigue, as his top computer man, Richard
Murray, had observed for years. "He never tells one person everything about why he's asking a question," Murray once commented.
"He would tell an individual only enough to make them feel involved. Only he knew the total picture. He was very cryptic in his
conversation. He spoke in half-sentences. Conversations were difficult. You were left to try to interpret what he was saying, and if you
pressed it, you'd get him perturbed."

Lorenzo's oblique communication style was part of his mastery at preserving options, at imbuing his intentions with ambiguity. There was invariably a secondary level of operation running simultaneously with the primary one. As visible as Continental and Eastern were as airlines, for instance, Texas Air, the parent company, wasn't even listed on the building directory at its downtown Houston location.

Now Lorenzo would need his discretion more than ever before in his career. Though his control of Texas Air was unassailable, the individual components were full of fences and boundaries. Most of Lorenzo's companies had been built with publicly raised finances, which imposed a duty on him to manage those companies in the interests of those who had entrusted them with their capital. In Eastern's case, these investors included the employees. In many cases investors had liens or other security interests in the various assets under Lorenzo's control, down to the individual airplane. Thus any shuffling of the pieces around Lorenzo's chessboard had to be done with sensitivity to the other interests with whom he shared title to them. Lorenzo's companies could certainly conduct transactions with one another, even with Lorenzo calling the shots, so long as the terms were fair and the dealing conducted in the open.

This was where the intrigue came in.

To the extent that Eastern's employees continued holding out against Lorenzo's demands, its airplanes could be switched by degrees to Continental, where they would be flown by low-cost, nonunion crews. At one point Eastern's Toronto station manager returned from a meeting in Miami and wrote a memo explaining his understanding of the new strategy: "If we can't cut our costs, our aircraft will go to Continental." This might seem cold-blooded, the manager from Toronto noted, but it was evident to him that Lorenzo's people were capable of that. The new people at Eastern, he wrote, had "ice water in their veins."

In theory the interests of Eastern in such situations would be protected by the airline's board of directors, whose membership had remained largely intact after the Texas Air takeover (except that Charlie Bryan and the flight attendants' representative had been thrown off). But board meetings under Lorenzo were not what they had been under Borman. The long, detailed agendas and information packages the directors had once received in advance simply stopped coming. The voting seemed perfunctory. Two directors—

Jack Fallon, the old Kennedy family friend, and Roswell Gilpatric, the former Pentagon official and partner at Cravath, Swaine & Moore in New York—contacted Richard Magurno, the general counsel of Eastern, and asked him to pass along their concerns to Lorenzo. When Magurno did so, Lorenzo blew up. "They're going to come to understand that I own the company," he said. "It's a subsidiary of *my* company." Lorenzo then issued Magurno an order: "I don't want you to talk to the directors anymore."

"What do I do if they call me?" Magurno asked.

"Tell them you can't talk to them."

The Eastern directors left little record of any dissent, however, even when Lorenzo asked them to vote for measures that were arguably more in the interests of Texas Air than of Eastern itself. They approved the payment to Texas Air of a $6-million-a-year "management fee." Eastern soon began buying its fuel through a Texas Air brokerage subsidiary, paying a fee of a penny on every gallon—quite a sum over the course of a hundred million or so gallons a month. (The money raked in from Eastern—and Continental as well—was used among other things for trading in the commodity markets.) Eastern's large crew of salespeople were merged into Continental's much smaller sales organization, with the result that Continental enjoyed a vastly expanded sales presence while Eastern's was diluted.

Eastern became a kind of financial junkyard for Texas Air. In taking over People Express, Lorenzo had purchased a pile of People Express notes on the open market. A short time later Texas Air sold the same notes to Eastern at a profit of $4.4 million. This extraction of cash from cash-short Eastern, one of Lorenzo's top people explained, was simply a way of repaying Texas Air for having wiped out People Express as a competitor in Eastern's markets.

Lorenzo bought Texas Air a dozen gates at Newark from Eastern at $1 million each; the gates had been appraised at $2 million each. Texas Air switched a half-dozen widebody Airbus jets from Eastern to Continental, which turned around and sold them at a huge profit. Texas Air gave many reasons for the plane switch, but as one of Continental's top people later explained, "The thing that really flipped it was the message it would send to labor, especially the pilots." Some of Eastern's routes were also transferred to Continental—Miami–London, for instance.

And then there was System One, the jewel buried inside Eastern, the antidote to the unfair competition that American and United, in Lorenzo's view, had so long inflicted against him. By removing System One from Eastern, Continental could at last share in the passenger-gathering power of a reservations network. Meanwhile Eastern, which had received a fee for every reservation that System One processed for another airline, would now have to pay a fee, to Texas Air, for every one of *its* bookings made through System One.

Though System One had recently been appraised at $250 million by Merrill Lynch, Texas Air gave Eastern only $100 million for the network, none of it in cash. For the heart of Eastern Air Lines, Texas Air paid a note bearing a meager 6 percent interest rate.

On the more ambitious agenda of turning Eastern into another Continental, Texas Air was encountering nothing but frustration, not only because of union resistance, which Lorenzo had expected, but because of government inertia, which he had not. Phil Bakes and his associates might have deregulated the airline industry, but they had done nothing to deregulate an obscure agency in Washington called the National Mediation Board, which controlled the timetable for showdowns between labor and management. Established in 1926 after a crippling series of rail strikes, the Mediation Board administered a series of laborious and complex rules intended to keep the trains rolling and the planes flying amid labor strife.

The guiding principle was delay. To begin with, airline workers could not lawfully strike at the moment their wage agreements had expired, but neither could employers alter wages or working conditions. Both sides were required to honor the status quo and to bargain earnestly toward a settlement. Once the Mediation Board judged the situation to be hopeless, it started a 30-day clock ticking—a "cooling off" period during which, in reality, people tended to get hotter than ever. At the end of the 30 days management was at last free to impose new wages and working conditions on the employees. The workers for their part were free to walk off the job. In doing so, however, they faced the risk that management would replace them with strikebreakers to keep the planes aloft.

There was a certain historical beauty in the fact that the first contract expiring at Eastern under the Lorenzo-Bakes regime was the machinists'. It was the machinists, after all, who had walked off the job after Lorenzo had taken control of Continental in 1983. That strike had turned out to be the first step in creating the New Continental. Perhaps now a machinists' strike could become the first step in a turnaround at Eastern as well.

Bakes went out of his way to hasten the declaration of an impasse, busily revising his proposals, importuning Bryan to the bargaining table—even at one point offering to retrain those $40,000 baggage handlers so that they would one day make $40,000 as licensed mechanics. Bakes figured that if anything ever landed him on the cover of *Business Week,* it would be his retraining proposal.

To the extent that Bakes wished to make the situation appear hopelessly deadlocked for the benefit of the Mediation Board, Charlie Bryan obliged him. For months Bryan continued refusing even to attend meetings. "We don't acknowledge that they've given proposals," he said.

While Bakes parried with Bryan, Lorenzo, realizing he had his hands full at Continental, once again turned to an unlikely outsider for help.

It was more than four years earlier, in 1982, that a lawyer at Braniff had filed away a secret tape recording of a telephone conversation between Braniff chairman Howard Putnam and Bob Crandall of American Airlines. It was inevitable, perhaps, that the tape would not remain secret forever.

In the grand jury investigation following Braniff's failure, the airlines of Texas, including Braniff, had been blanketed with subpoenas. Braniff had turned over the recording, on which Crandall could be heard commanding his rival to "raise your goddamn fares twenty percent. I'll raise mine the next morning." The Justice Department went to court, accusing Crandall of attempting to fix prices and seeking an order to have him banished from the airline industry—as severe a punishment as Bob Crandall could ever have endured. (The fact that Crandall had telephoned Putnam at United Airlines years earlier, urging him to increase prices for drinks and movie headsets, was not made public.)

There was a problem with the federal case against Crandall, however. Even if one assumed the worst of Crandall's intentions—even if he had wished to importune a rival CEO into a price-fixing conspiracy—he had, after all, failed in the attempt. There is no such thing as a conspiracy of one. After more than two years of trying to make the case stick, Justice gave up, settling for a token sanction: Crandall would have to keep a written record of his discussions with other airline chieftains.

The more lasting effect of the Putnam affair was the damage to Crandall's reputation. Albert Casey, who was still chairman of American when the obscenity-studded tape transcript was made public, considered "very carefully" whether to fire Crandall. Crandall himself was mortified. To a group of gathered executives he once sighed, "That'll be in my obituary."

And yet wasn't life all about fighting? Wasn't it going from one schoolyard fistfight to another? Crandall pulled himself up. He threw himself more deeply into his grand Growth Plan. He launched an effort to soften his image. He went through a round of cosmetic dentistry to dull the points on his canine teeth. He deflated his pompadour in favor of a flatter, slicked-back look. "I rage less," he said publicly.

Crandall clung to all the top titles at American Airlines long past the point at which he might have begun to share them. Doing so made Crandall the sole leader through some of the greatest triumphs in American's history, solidifying his standing with a board of directors that had been jarred by the revelation of his intemperate conversation with Howard Putnam. Most conspicuously Crandall retained the title of president after becoming chairman, even though his predecessor, Al Casey, had readily shared the president's title with him.

Years later, while still serving under the same titles, Crandall would say that he refused to delegate the presidency for operating reasons. "I've never felt an airline should have a [separate] chairman and president, and as long as I'm here, there won't be," he explained. "The assets have to be managed centrally. You've got to have one boss. To have two is kind of wacko."

Publicly, however, Crandall had never been so explicit in his intentions. People in the organization were sure that he would one day anoint Tom Plaskett, his most senior associate, as American's president. Plaskett, the good soldier, remained outwardly solicitous of Crandall and by all appearances was content to wait as long as necessary. But by 1986 Plaskett was burning inside; he concluded unhappily that Crandall would never release the presidency.

It would have stunned people in the audience to know that when Bob Crandall and Tom Plaskett had stood before the entire management group of American Airlines poking fun at Frank Lorenzo, Plaskett at that very moment was discreetly negotiating to become president of Continental Airlines. A few weeks later, in November 1986, it became official: Lorenzo had stolen Crandall's top man—for the job that Crandall himself had turned down years earlier.

Plaskett assumed the presidency of Continental that Phil Bakes had vacated in going to Eastern. For Lorenzo, Plaskett was every bit the trophy that Bakes had once been. Even at 42 years of age, Plaskett was a ranking member of the aviation establishment, a full member of the club in which Lorenzo himself never felt fully tenured. *Fortune* had recently named Plaskett one of the 10 hottest executives in the country. *Forbes* said that Plaskett "plays a computer reservation system like a Stradivarius," noting, "His steady presence may be exactly what Lorenzo needs to convince skeptics that Texas Air can be an airline superpower instead of a bundle of debt."

But from the minute he walked into Continental headquarters in Houston, Plaskett found himself the odd man out, just as Stephen Wolf once had. If Plaskett ordered a slide show prepared, his new underlings would look at him as if he were from another planet. Lorenzo's people remarked that Plaskett always tried to go by the book, failing to recognize there was no book at Continental. People put in 12- and 14-hour days working for Lorenzo, but Plaskett liked to get in a round of golf now and then.

The cultural estrangement went both ways. In Plaskett's experience marketing was a highly sophisticated, computer-driven enterprise. Certainly Lorenzo's capture of the System One network from Eastern was a big step toward endowing Continental with that capability. But Lorenzo's team of madcap marketers—the same people who had staged the baby elephant stunt to promote peanuts fares in Kansas City and who camped out under the Frontier billboard in Denver—were now working for the fourth-largest individual airline in the country, and they had not lost their passion for the cute. When Continental became the largest airline in New York City, they announced the "biggest airline ticket giveaway ever": a free airline ticket to the first million comers. Lorenzo's people tried to stage the spectacle at Madison Square Garden, but the city obtained a court order blocking them. "They wanted a scene, a circus, and we don't want to put on a circus," a police spokesman said.

Plaskett may have been embarrassed by such brutish marketing tactics, but that embarrassment was nothing compared with the humiliation that followed his involvement in the biggest one-day merger in airline history.

On Lorenzo's orders Plaskett, on February 1, 1987, mashed together Continental, New York Air, People Express, Frontier, and all of their many subsidiaries into one giant airline operating under a single schedule. Only Eastern, with its poisonous labor problems, would remain a separate airline. Plaskett and others urged a go-slow approach, but as Plaskett would later comment, "Frank was adamant; it had to be done." Inside Lorenzo's shop some people called the merger the "big bang."

Suddenly Continental had 32 different galley configurations in its fleet. Continental meal trays wouldn't fit into Frontier warming carts. People with tickets on Continental found themselves boarding bright red New York Air planes. Passengers at Newark were herded from gate to gate as cancellations mounted. People Express employees were assigned to Continental flights with no idea how to operate Jetways. Golf bags, skis, and luggage of every shape and variety began to accumulate in a warehouse of lost bags in Houston. The entire system ran late all day long.

Lorenzo had not foreseen the worst problem of all: scheduling the newly swollen and far-flung workforce. As with so much else in airlines, crew scheduling creates a reverse economy of scale: the bigger the operation, the more difficult, costly, and inefficient it becomes. Pilots and flight attendants, calling in for new assignments as flight cancellations worsened, encountered busy signals, meaning they could not be reassigned, causing still more flights to be canceled. There's no such thing as a half-broken airline.

Morale plunged. People Express pilots accustomed to flying in the captain's seat—men who had flown for the original Braniff before *it* failed, for instance—found themselves junior to Continental pilots who were barely shaving. Continental could ill afford to make its pi-

lots so unhappy; every airline in the country was now trying to recruit pilots, to keep up with the surging demand caused by low fares
and to staff all those airplanes rolling off the assembly line in Seattle. As if eating seed corn, Continental began assigning training pilots to line flying, which meant that fewer new pilots could be
trained, which meant that the trainers had to fly that much more
often. Continental's pilot schedules began pushing federal safety
standards. As noted in one internal memo, "We never *intentionally*
overcommit on flying hours. Yes, we do push it to the maximum."
The memo chalked this practice up to "the axioms of operating in a
deregulated environment."

In April 1987, three months after the big bang, consumer complaints against the entire airline industry more than doubled, with
units of Texas Air accounting for more than half of all complaints
against all airlines. It was just a temporary public relations setback,
Lorenzo thought, and he could lick it, he was sure—just as Johnson
& Johnson through brilliant public posturing had overcome the marketing crisis following the Tylenol poisonings. In a letter Lorenzo appealed for understanding from the Continental pilots, expressing the
closest thing to contrition that he was capable of: "We have lived
through a lot together. We survived the bankruptcy, completed the
airline consolidations, saved thousands of jobs, and emerged as one
of the biggest airlines in America. . . . However, I know it has not
been easy for any of us, and we are still fine-tuning and continually
improving our operations, a fact which will continue to benefit you."

But in all the parsing of blame for the big bang debacle of 1987
there was only one president of Continental Airlines, and that was
Tom Plaskett. Vainly Plaskett tried to overcome the cataclysmic operating problems, but he had no capital: no money to tear out galleys, for instance, or to purchase the software by which to knit
together the various in-house computer systems of People Express,
Frontier, and Continental itself. So it was only a matter of time—
nine months was all it took—before Lorenzo unceremoniously
dumped Tom Plaskett. Plaskett's résumé would later put the best
face possible on his months at Continental, noting that he had introduced a measure of organization to "a complex cultural and operating environment."

And throughout those months of carnage, nobody followed the

disaster at Continental with more interest than Plaskett's former boss, Bob Crandall.

Doing all he could to compete with Frank Lorenzo on schedules and flights, Bob Crandall resolved to conduct a new tactic: he would make Lorenzo look bad.

Just as Continental was falling to pieces, Crandall's people went to the Department of Transportation and demanded a monthly public announcement of every airline's on-time performance—a policy they knew would hurt Continental disproportionately. As Crandall explained to his assembled managers: "I think it's entirely possible that we are confronted by a unique—and short-lived—window of opportunity. For eight long years, ever since deregulation, we have had to compete with our low-cost rivals on the basis of price and price alone. Today, thanks to growing public unhappiness, we have an opportunity to put quality back where it belongs: front and center. . . . It's going to be harder and harder for carriers to hide shoddy performance. The public is going to have an opportunity to know who's good and who's not."

Crandall also personalized the attack. When *Texas Monthly* published a scathing cover story on Lorenzo, Crandall ordered 15,000 reprints to assure even wider distribution. Crandall called on the government to deny international routes to Continental as punishment for "abusing employees." "They treat their people dreadfully," Crandall told *Business Week*.

Lorenzo's campaign to slash wages at Eastern moved Crandall to even greater histrionics. "The employees have no chance," Crandall said in *Airline Executive* magazine. "How do you think an employee will feel if you're 51 years old, you're a baggage handler, you've worked yourself up to $30,000 a year, and they come in and say, 'I'm going to cut your salary to $18,000. If you don't like it, you're fired.' They've deprived you of the ability to make a living."

"The cruel irony," Crandall said in a speech, "is that it wasn't success, it wasn't good management or a superior product that created the Texas Air empire. It was failure." One of Lorenzo's people offered a rejoinder that deliciously recalled Crandall's encounter with the tape recorder: "Since Crandall can't fix prices," a Continental spokesman told *Travel Weekly,* "he'll try to fix costs."

Lorenzo even provoked Crandall to abandon his declared policy against takeovers. The major airlines by late 1986 had largely recarved the route map of the United States, though the process was far from complete in California. Lorenzo had started a shuttlelike operation called Continental West and was scoring impressive early gains against United, the longtime market leader in California. American, by contrast, was a small player within the boundaries of California. Crandall had a problem. As more Californians accumulated frequent-flier miles flying on other airlines inside California, they were more likely to use those same airlines to travel across the United States.

Crandall might have painstakingly built up a major presence in California, as United and Continental had done. But Crandall learned that Lorenzo was preparing a possible bid for AirCal, the last surviving California independent. If Lorenzo succeeded, Crandall feared, the door would slam shut on California, with Lorenzo, of all people, doing the slamming. Crandall moved with dispatch, agreeing to pay a quarter-billion dollars for AirCal and adding yet another hub, in San Jose, to the American route map. Lorenzo, though bested, would sniff that Crandall had overpaid for AirCal.

California indeed became a battleground between Crandall and Lorenzo, not only over passengers but over travel agents. Lorenzo dispatched salespeople to persuade travel agents to abandon Sabre (and United's Apollo as well) and sign on with System One instead. Outraged, Crandall called the System One salespeople "Lorenzo's raiders" and chased Lorenzo from courthouse to courthouse trying to block Sabre agents from defecting to System One. Lorenzo in turn showered Sabre subscribers with cash, offering inducements and agreeing to pay any legal fees and damages they faced in switching networks. In time Lorenzo's raiders would spend the breathtaking sum of $250 million to entice travel agencies from rival reservation networks, an outlay that ultimately went down as more debt.

After buying AirCal and bringing in still more airplanes under the Growth Plan, American in November 1988 officially became the largest single airline in America, a position it had not held since 1961. Lorenzo still had more airplanes and more total market share than Bob Crandall, but his assets were divided between the two lobes of Texas Air. Crandall, by contrast, now controlled under a single brand nearly 17 percent of the airplane capacity in the United States. United was a close second. Delta, having recently acquired Western Airlines, was third. At the same time, American was reporting the highest profits in the history of commercial aviation.

Crandall proudly referred to American's industry-leading distinctions as "the trophy" during the annual conference of American's sales executives. "All winners hate to lose," he told them, "and one of the marks of a consistent winner is a sharp ear for the footsteps of those who envy the trophy."

He went on: "When do people feel good about their company and themselves? When they're winning. I'll tell you where low morale comes from. It comes from losing. How would you like to be working right now for Continental, or Pan Am, or TWA, or—God forbid—Eastern? Now *there's* low morale. Why? Because they are losing."

In fact the unions at Eastern cared much less about their position against American than about their position against their own sister company. Planes, people, routes, and a vital computer network had all been plucked from Eastern for Continental's benefit, reducing jobs, promotion opportunities, and the asset base on which Eastern might hope to earn a profit. It was these asset transfers that finally provoked the unions into launching counteroffensives against Texas Air.

The pilots established a program called "Max Safety," in which they flooded the flight line with brochures and stickers urging pilots to push to the limits of their discretion in holding back flights. "Better safe than sorry," "Fly by the book," "Take the time to be sure." The economic toll was tremendous. Delays due to requests for replacement altimeters increased 247 percent. Eastern's red ink flowed faster.

Before long, with a $2 million subsidy from ALPA headquarters in Washington, the pilots expanded their attack into the political arena. They carried preprinted cards addressed to the FAA and Department of Transportation on which they could detail individual safety problems observed on any aircraft. Washington was inundated with postcards listing complaints ranging from the horrific (a fire detection system left in "marginally acceptable condition" for more than three weeks) to the hilarious ("aircraft full of roaches").

Charlie Bryan's machinists, for their part, cast their lot with the flight attendants in a campaign to vilify Lorenzo in the public eye. As profound and emotional as the workers considered their fight, they recognized that the public might not easily be won over on issues of asset switching and wage cuts for $40,000-a-year baggage handlers. Thus, as detailed in a planning memo, the unions resolved to "make Frank Lorenzo the issue—personalize the conflict to one between him (i.e., the man who's the pillager of the American dream; the man who'd cut any corner to make a buck; the man who's a brutal, unscrupulous corporate autocrat)—and us (ordinary working people, fathers and mothers . . .)."

The memo outlined a campaign to investigate Lorenzo (including the use of a "pro-labor 'private eye' "), to pressure Merrill Lynch and other Lorenzo financial backers, and to whip up opposition in the Congress and through the media, all with the goal of ultimately forcing Lorenzo to sell Eastern either to its employees or to "an acceptable third party."

Lorenzo's likeness was printed on a poster behind the concentric circle of a gunnery target. "Stop Lorenzo" buttons and stickers spread like a virus. A Lorenzo "wanted" poster was printed. Jesse Jackson got into the act, leading a crowd of cheering anti-Lorenzo demonstrators at Lorenzo's 25-year reunion at Harvard Business School. The AFL-CIO organized a noisy demonstration against Merrill Lynch.

Before long the separate campaigns of the Eastern unions blended into a single orgy of hate against Lorenzo, and Congress began to take notice. Norman Mineta, the California Democrat who had provided a crucial swing vote in favor of airline deregulation partly at the behest of Phil Bakes, introduced a bill urging the Transportation Department "to conduct a full investigation into the management of Texas Air Corporation." The congressional opposition took on a bipartisan ring when the ranking Republican on the subcommittee, Newt Gingrich, also cast his lot with the union-backed legislative effort; his Georgia district encompassed Hartsfield Airport in Atlanta, around which lived a heavy concentration of Eastern union members.

For Lorenzo the far greater problem at Eastern remained the inertia of the federal agency that was still blocking wage cuts for the machinists. Eastern was devouring cash with losses. To keep Eastern alive long enough to conduct the final confrontation with Bryan, Lorenzo had to find some more furniture to throw into the fireplace. Eastern, he announced, would sell the venerable Eastern shuttle. The buyer, on extremely favorable terms, was Texas Air.

When the proposal to cleave the shuttle from Eastern landed at the Department of Transportation, it sent the agency's legal department into a stupor. The paperwork for the deal included a labyrinthine flowchart showing that Jet Capital, the personal holding company of Frank Lorenzo, was destined to receive 5 percent ownership of the shuttle, as a "fee" for having put the deal together. As they scratched their heads, the DOT people picked up *The Wall Street Journal* and read a page-one article about the financial "house of mirrors" at Texas Air, including an analysis of the cash that the parent company was "upstreaming" from its struggling airline subsidiaries. The following evening the DOT people tuned into ABC's *20/20* for a broadcast on alleged safety infractions at Texas Air.

The Transportation Department had finally seen enough. In April 1988 James Burnley, the secretary of transportation, announced that the FAA would swoop down on every airplane in the Texas Air fleet for a "white glove" inspection. Financial investigators, meanwhile, would pore over Lorenzo's records and take depositions from all his top aides, with the objective of deciding whether Texas Air was "fit" to operate an airline, let alone several of them. There had never been an investigation remotely approaching such a scale.

To Lorenzo it was all just "noise." With his entire empire under the microscope Lorenzo stood before the International Aviation Club in Washington and expressed thanks for the chance to discuss "the noise level that seems to surround Texas Air today."

> Ten years ago, this platform [at the Aviation Club] and many others around town were filled with industry officials and others debating deregulation. Some argued that with deregulation the consumer would be better served . . . others argued just the opposite. . . .
>
> It will surprise many of you, no doubt, that initially we opposed deregulation. I argued in Congressional hearings and in speeches that

deregulation would be very unfair to small airlines like Texas International . . . that it would pit us between the larger national carriers with substantial resources and the largely nonunion companies like Southwest. [Lorenzo did not mention that Southwest was now almost entirely unionized.] Little did we realize just how right we were. . . . So we set about the task of transforming our little airline.

Our little airline. Lorenzo went on to say that after taking control of Texas International in 1972 he built the number of jobs in his domain from 2,500 to nearly 70,000 and the annual revenue of his enterprises from $60 million to nearly $8 billion, all of it through "sound business strategy," he noted, "not 'corporate mirrors.' "

> While we don't harbor any beliefs that the noise surrounding us will disappear any time soon, nevertheless it is our hope that we will be better understood as we go forward. Texas Air has been on the cutting edge of positive change in this industry. We've saved 68,000 jobs and breathed life into several near-paralyzed airlines. Along the way we've angered some who have not appreciated our responsiveness to the consumer and the marketplace. I cannot offer them much solace, since we intend to continue to be responsive to consumer-driven market forces.

It took the government six weeks to conclude that Continental and Eastern were indeed safe and Texas Air indeed "fit" to run airlines. But while signing off on Texas Air's safety practices, investigators reacted with alarm to the strife gripping Eastern. In a memorandum to the transportation secretary, FAA administrator T. Allan McArtor noted that "the discord and complexity of the labor-management issues are deeper and more complex than at any other carrier. . . . Both sides have stated that they are 'at war.' "

Lorenzo and Bakes did soften their approach, though their efforts seemed intended less for peace than to get the Mediation Board off dead center and declare an impasse in the negotiations with Charlie Bryan. Bryan and Lorenzo eventually met face-to-face for the first time, over a three-hour dinner in Houston, during which Charlie Bryan proposed that they star together in a series of television ads for Eastern. "Nobody'd believe it!" Bryan said. Nothing substantive came of the dinner.

Finally the Mediation Board could put it off no longer. On February 1, 1989, more than a year after the machinists' contract had expired, the agency finally declared that an impasse indeed was at hand.

Tick . . . tick . . . tick. That glorious ticking of the 30-day clock.

It was now one month until the moment that Bakes's people had been referring to as "D-Day."

In Dallas Bob Crandall's people were also making plans.

For some time Crandall had been pressuring his scheduling genius, Mel Olsen. "What are you going to do when Eastern goes under?" Crandall ceaselessly asked. This was in fact a matter of some urgency, not because Eastern was in danger of imminent demise, but because American was continuing to choke on airplanes. Even after adding hubs in Raleigh-Durham, Nashville, San Jose, and San Juan—on top of Dallas and Chicago—American's internal studies showed that the airline needed more destinations for all of its incoming aircraft. Crandall needed new territory, and there was none more inviting than Eastern's.

But where? Crandall seemed intent on attacking Eastern's hub in Atlanta. Eastern had been slugging it out there with Delta for years, and Delta, strong but ponderous, did not intimidate Crandall.

Atlanta did not feel right to Olsen, however. He loaded every airline schedule in the United States into a forecasting model, including the Transportation Department's route-by-route passenger load figures. Then Eastern's schedules were removed entirely—eradicated from the data—allowing the forecasting models to run as if the airline industry suddenly existed without Eastern and its nearly 300 airplanes. The model projected a windfall of new business for Delta in Atlanta, business for which American could attempt to compete. But the analysis also showed a number of other routes—"hot spots," Olsen called them—that had nothing to do with Atlanta, routes on which there was no carrier around to pick up Eastern's business.

These routes all seemed to converge on Miami. Moreover there were international route authorities from Miami that were available immediately—to Guatemala City, Costa Rica, and elsewhere. "Bob, we should start positioning ourselves now," Olsen said. That way American could justify outbidding anyone else for Eastern's assets in

Miami, including its vital South American routes. Moving into Miami quickly would have the additional virtue of hastening Eastern's demise.

In August 1988, as Texas Air was announcing a quarterly loss of $256 million, American announced that it would establish a crew base in Miami. Publicly American insisted that the move was in no way related to the problems at Eastern, as mendacious a denial as a corporation could utter.

In Miami Phil Bakes had a strange, uneasy feeling—a sense of disconnect, as he later described it.

Soon, on March 3, 1989, the 8,500 remaining members of the machinists' union at Eastern would walk off the job. Elaborate preparations had been made to replace them with nonunion workers making a fraction of union wages. Bakes would then launch the rebuilding of Eastern. But as the great day approached, "I felt like I had nothing to do with it," Bakes would say. The battle had become fixed in almost everyone's mind as a personal confrontation between Frank Lorenzo and Charlie Bryan, as if Eastern itself did not matter. Bakes's old Washington friend Alfred Kahn had put it best when he was quoted in *The Wall Street Journal* calling Lorenzo and Bryan "two scorpions in a bottle." Bakes could not disagree, but couldn't people see that he and 32,000 other Eastern employees were in the bottom of that bottle as well? "It was as if the people who *worked* and *managed* were marionettes," Bakes later said, "carrying out the wishes of the unions and Texas Air."

Bakes could practically hear his credibility deflating. The dramatic rebuilding of Continental, the greatest airline turnaround in history, had endowed him with all the standing he had walking into Eastern. Now it was clear even to him that Continental was cratering. He could feel his miracle-worker image fading as he talked to employees and even his own managers about his goals and plans and programs for Eastern. Bakes had come in as a savior; now he felt like a bumbler.

The clearest barometer of the world's failing confidence was the price of Texas Air stock. When Bakes had left Continental to join Eastern more than two years earlier, in late 1986, the parent company's stock was rocketing on its way to $50. Bakes's wife had begged him to sell; practically their entire net worth was tied up in Texas Air. But Bakes thought that selling would signal a weakness of commitment. So as the big bang erupted at Continental and as the war escalated at Eastern, Bakes watched the stock sink like a stone to the single digits. Only later did he learn that Lorenzo, while preserving his control of Texas Air through Jet Capital, had cashed out his personal, direct holdings in Texas Air very nearly at the top, for about $10 million.

Although Lorenzo had rarely been accused of putting emotion ahead of money, the register tapes at Eastern suggested that he had let the campaign against the machinists get away from him. Apart from the plunge in Texas Air's stock, there was the debilitating cost (to Continental as well as Eastern) of the massive government investigation that the unions had brought down. There was the usurious price of the money Lorenzo was borrowing to fund his war chest against the machinists—an interest rate of 17 1/2 percent, more than two times the prime rate. The initial strike preparation had cost $70 million—recruiting and training scab mechanics, rounding up nonunion pilots in case they were needed, acquiring decoy cars for management, preparing more than 1.7 million Mailgrams to apologize in advance to frequent fliers, and so on. In the midst of Eastern's 30-day "cooling off" period, the combined airline operations of Texas Air reported a loss for 1988 totaling nearly three quarters of a billion dollars, the biggest loss in airline history, almost as much money as the entire industry had previously lost in its worst year ever. Moreover, Texas Air's staggering loss occurred as the rest of the industry was having its best year ever. How much of Texas Air's deficit represented financial fallout from Eastern no one could tell, but it surely exceeded by several times the $150 million a year that Lorenzo had been seeking to extract from Charlie Bryan's membership.

Bakes, for his part, could do nothing but lower his head and prepare for the collision. There was so much invested already. If it paid off, the returns could still be tremendous.

The most difficult preparations involved not the machinists but the pilots. The last time Bakes had been through this exercise, the pilots had walked through the machinists' picket lines at Continental like Schwartzkopf's forces crossing the Euphrates. Lorenzo was convinced that the pilots would never honor Charlie Bryan's picket lines.

Under Borman the pilots had sacrificed much more than the machinists had. In any case, why would any pilot walk away from a six-figure salary simply out of solidarity with the bag smashers?

A few dissenting voices were heard. James W. Arpey, who had spent 15 years with Lorenzo and who had personally driven scab workers through machinists' riotous picket lines at Continental, thought things were different this time. The Eastern pilots had already made so many concessions. "There's no way the pilots will let you do here what you did at Continental," Arpey warned.

"When push comes to shove," Lorenzo answered, "they will cross the picket line."

Sixteen days before D-Day the machinists took their official strike vote. The walkout was approved by 97 percent of the membership.

Nine days before the strike thousands of Eastern employees came to work wearing red tee shirts saying "Stop Lorenzo." Anti-Lorenzo signs were breaking out all over Miami.

Seven days before D-Day the federal mediators on the case asked President Bush to appoint a Presidential Emergency Board, as provided for under the airline labor law. The principal effect of such an appointment would be to delay the process for another 60 days. President Bush declined, saying, "The best answer is a head-on-head, man-to-man negotiation between the union and the airline," as if the idea had not yet occurred to anyone.

Five days before the strike Lorenzo appeared on the cover of *Fortune* for the special issue on "America's Toughest Bosses." (Among the six other bosses on the 1989 list, a second came from the airlines. It was Bob Crandall.) A new high school business textbook, published as the strike loomed, contained a page-long description of Lorenzo's fight with the machinists. Eastern was now immortalized as a textbook case of bad labor relations.

Two days before D-Day, on a Wednesday, the Eastern pilots individually received a mass-produced videotape showing Frank Lorenzo at his home, a pen in his hand, poised over a sheaf of papers. He was, he explained, signing a new contract for the Eastern pilots, one that would greatly increase their job security by maintaining the Eastern fleet at 222 airplanes. The offer was meaningless, however, unless the pilots crossed the machinists' picket lines.

The pilots were sorely tempted. Putting a fence around the fleet assured that there would always be aircraft to fly. The pilots could preserve their seniority status at Eastern, rather than risk starting out as second officers at other airlines. But the pilots' lawyers soon determined that the promise would be meaningless if Eastern ever went into Chapter 11, a prospect that seemed far from impossible. Lorenzo was offering protection that would disappear the minute it was most needed. The pilots' union told Lorenzo to get lost. ALPA would leave to individual pilots the decision whether to fly through the machinists' strike.

On Friday, March 3, 1989, with the strike scheduled to begin at midnight, Eastern's managers sent the machinists home at 10 A.M., 14 hours early, with pay. The workers scheduled for the next shift were contacted by telephone and telegram and given a paid day off. Eastern, terror-stricken about vandalism, did not want the machinists anywhere inside the fence at midnight. Manhole covers were welded in place to protect communication lines below.

At midnight Phil Bakes stepped onto a rooftop from the ninth floor of Building 16 and watched a group of strikers assemble on the perimeter of the company's property below. Minute by minute the crowd swelled, soon bulging against the chain-link fence. The strikers laced their fingers through the fence holes, shoving it in and pulling it out with the racket of determined rebels, as if they were storming the Bastille. Bakes felt sick inside.

The following morning he knew there was no point in rushing to work. When he arrived at 10 o'clock, there were plenty of scab mechanics but no pilots. That night at home, watching images of giddy strikers and stranded passengers on Cable News Network, Bakes wept for the first time since his mother had died five years earlier. The bold piece of economic engineering he had bulldozed through the Congress of the United States had just claimed another victim, and it was he.

Lorenzo had often dismissed the possibility of bankruptcy at Eastern. He couldn't "imagine a set of circumstances that would produce Chapter 11 for Eastern," as he once put it.

On March 9, 1989, within a week of the walkout, Eastern Air Lines, with a mountain of debt and hardly a trickle of revenue, was in bankruptcy.

But Lorenzo was not done yet. Though stripped to barely half its earlier size, Eastern still had the routes that Frank Borman had so proudly purchased for $30 million from the failing Braniff seven years earlier, in 1982. How much would they fetch now? How much, in particular, would Bob Crandall pay for those routes, after positioning American in Miami?

Perhaps by selling Latin America, Lorenzo could pull off a turnaround of Eastern after all—*facilitated* by Chapter 11. By selling South America at the right price, Lorenzo could pay off Eastern's creditors, recruit a cadre of strikebreaking pilots, and focus Eastern's resources on Atlanta, fighting a one-front war against Delta. Lorenzo was so confident of the plan that he dispatched Bakes to bankruptcy court with a complete reorganization proposal predicated on the sale of Latin America. In the meantime he began discussing the sale with Crandall.

For weeks in 1989, while the talks dragged on, Eastern ever so tentatively got itself back into the air, rebuilding operations with scab workers as the machinists, pilots, and flight attendants remained on strike. "If we have to build the company back with picket lines," Lorenzo said, "then that's how we will build it back." Bakes shook off his depression and threw himself into yet another campaign. By July, barely four months into the strike, Eastern was back in business, flying 30 percent of its flights, serving 77 cities (compared with 102 before the strike) with stripped-down service and low fares. It was a struggle, but it actually seemed to be working. The load factors quickly hit 67 percent. Lorenzo and Bakes, it appeared, were doing it again. Lorenzo had become the Richard Nixon of the airways!

Then suddenly Lorenzo had cold feet about selling a huge chunk of Eastern to Bob Crandall. Eastern was starting to look like Continental Airlines in the months following its bankruptcy, coaxing back the pilots little by little, a few more flights here and there, passengers clamoring for low fares . . . Lorenzo called a number of aides to a meeting in New York. Why, he asked, shouldn't Eastern *keep* Latin America instead of selling it to American? Why, he asked, shouldn't Eastern *build up* Miami instead of getting rid of it?

People in the room tried to remind Lorenzo that an entire bankruptcy reorganization plan had been predicated on the sale to American. The creditors had even been led to expect 100 cents on the dollar. But Lorenzo was undeterred. He was never a seller at heart anyway—least of all to Bob Crandall. So he backed out of negotiations to sell the South American routes, infuriating Crandall. With the Latin sale pulled from the table, Eastern's bankruptcy reorganization was off too.

Lorenzo's dream of a resurgent Eastern was in the end a death wish. Money that Lorenzo might otherwise have committed to creditors went down a rat hole. Before long Lorenzo would send Bakes back into bankruptcy court, only this time with a plan to repay creditors 10 cents on the dollar. By then Lorenzo had no choice; he *had* to sell Latin America. And the only company positioned to pay top dollar was, once again, American Airlines.

Crandall's people were soon rushing to buy their own copies of Rand McNally to locate Bway-nos-I-rays and the 19 other South American cities Eastern had served. With all the bilateral treaties and individual landing rights involved, the transaction required a courthouse of lawyers to complete. Over from Miami came some 70 boxes of documents that had been heaved into files over the years, each pertaining in some material way to the operation of those routes.

Once Crandall's people got their mitts into the operation itself, they were horrified at what they found. Eastern had not begun to keep up with the growth in the market. In city after city there were so few phone lines that each rang continually. When American installed more phone lines, they too rang incessantly. Further lines and phones were hooked up and they rang. "It was a complete shambles," Crandall would recall.

But it was a shambles with nothing but upside potential. Though Latin American travel still accounted for only a small fraction of total international travel by Americans, business relationships were blossoming between the continents. Talk was beginning to swirl about a new trading relationship that would ultimately take fruit as NAFTA—the North American Free Trade Agreement. Latin America was quickly coming to terms with its debt problems, once considered a time bomb that threatened to blow up the world financial system.

The arrival of American's Sabre system and the introduction of frequent-flier plans would sweep up even more traffic, leaving the

Third World airlines of the continent gasping for passengers. TACA, the national airline of El Salvador, say, or AeroPeru could not offer much diversity in their frequent-flier awards—no trips to Hawaii, for instance—nor could they be reasonably expected to crank up a computer system more powerful than anything existing in the Southern Hemisphere.

American's new South American system flourished all the more thanks to a shrewd trade by Crandall. He talked Lorenzo into tossing a small piece of Continental Airlines into the Eastern route deal: Continental's route between Miami and London. It was just a single route but a vital one, which Crandall could now use as a nexus to feed Europeans into his new South American flights.

Before long Latin America was the most profitable piece of American Airlines, just as it had been for Eastern, and before it for Braniff, and before it for Pan Am.

In the brief time he had served as the president of Continental Airlines, Tom Plaskett learned that aircraft suppliers made a point of keeping a little something in reserve in any negotiation with Lorenzo, even past the point of the handshakes, because Lorenzo would try to re-trade the deal. They called it the "Frank factor."

Phil Bakes would call this phenomenon the "last nickel" impulse. Bakes took a more charitable view than most, allowing for Lorenzo's upbringing in a nonaristocratic household. Lorenzo, in addition, simply changed his mind frequently, Bakes observed, without sufficient appreciation for how that affected his standing in the next deal.

Among the men who had served as Lorenzo's number two, Don Burr took the harshest view of all. "Frank is very simpleminded: you do whatever you have to do to make money," Burr would later claim. "Any means to any victory is okay. Frank is capable of any kind of behavior to win."

Regardless of the reasons, Lorenzo from the dawn of the 1970s to the dawn of the 1990s had established a pattern. When Jet Capital took over Texas International, it told the press that no major personnel changes were planned; several weeks later, the incumbent president was out. Three years after that he told his bargainers to make a deal with the union leadership at Texas International; he then refused to sign the deal. He had, at least in Burr's view, reneged not once but twice in promising titles to him. He had vowed, in writing, that he would not relocate the headquarters of Continental Airlines if he won control of the company, then proceeded to waste no time in moving the staff to Houston. When rising airfares caused an unexpected number of people to clamor for free Continental tickets in a big supermarket giveaway program, Continental simply canceled the promotion.

Reneging was such a routine of business with Lorenzo that when a middle-level executive once complained that Continental was failing to fulfill his employment contract, Lorenzo was quick to suggest a recourse: "If I were you," Lorenzo said with a straight face, "I'd probably sue me."

The pattern of reneging and re-trading was nowhere more obvious—or more excruciatingly documented—than in the New York bankruptcy proceedings of Eastern Air Lines. By the spring of 1990, a year into the proceedings, Texas Air had offered five separate repayment schemes, only to retreat from each and substitute a cheaper plan. A creditors' committee told the court it would "no longer tolerate Eastern's and Texas Air's inability to adhere to an agreement."

Amid the tussling over the terms of repayment, an independent Washington lawyer named David I. Shapiro had been investigating as a court-appointed examiner the financial affairs of Texas Air. Shapiro reconstructed the flow of funds in all directions through the Texas Air empire and determined that the parent company had plundered Eastern of as much as $403 million—funds in which other parties had a lawful interest, even if Eastern was Lorenzo's subsidiary.

The creditors demanded Lorenzo's head. Transactions so "smacking of fraud," they told the court, plainly justified throwing Lorenzo out. A hearing on the creditors' motion was held on April 18, 1990. Shapiro offered high marks to some of Lorenzo's line managers. "They, and particularly Mr. Bakes, have done an outstanding job in the face of impossible odds," Shapiro told the court. But he also said,

> The issue in reality—and I say this more in sadness than in anything else—is really Mr. Lorenzo. Can anyone blame the creditors for being outraged? I think this court knows from what it's seen, and I know from what I have seen, that Mr. Lorenzo only starts negotiating at the very last

minute . . . and once he makes a deal . . . he tries to renegotiate it. . . . He is just a tough guy to make a deal with.

After hearing the testimony and taking a 90-minute recess, Judge Burton Lifland climbed back to his bench at about 10 P.M. "The time has come," he declared, "to replace the pilot to captain Eastern's crew." Lorenzo was not fit to run Eastern. He was being thrown out "for cause," the judge said, "including incompetence." The judge noted that in the course of trying to reorganize Eastern, Lorenzo had burned up $1.2 billion that otherwise could have gone to the company's creditors, including its employees.

Lorenzo had stuck Bakes with the duty of remaining in the courtroom to hear the ruling. As the hearing broke up, Bakes and the Texas Air lawyers made their way uptown to the masculine, green-and-brass bastion of Smith & Wollensky steak house. Bakes called Lorenzo from a pay phone there. He found Lorenzo in bed and shared the news that they had been jettisoned from Eastern.

"Well," Lorenzo said to Bakes, "I guess it's not a surprise."

Bakes rejoined his party, and abandoning his compulsive attention not only to costs but to diet, ordered a New York strip steak, baked potato with sour cream, bleu cheese dressing for his salad, and a $100 bottle of Bordeaux, the last meal he ever charged on his Eastern Air Lines credit card.

Though it had outlasted Eastern, Continental was also in deep trouble, still suffering from the trauma of its amalgamation with People Express. In the late 1980s the growth in U.S. air travel had slowed while international travel surged, and Continental, still principally a domestic airline, bore much of the brunt of the slowdown as marginal passengers elected not to fly. Texas Air was faltering as well. Its debt burden now exceeded the entire output of goods and services of many Third World nations.

On the morning of August 9, 1990, the airline industry awoke to a stunning headline on the front page of *The Wall Street Journal:* "Bailing Out: Lorenzo Plans to Sell Continental Air Stake To Scandinavian Air."

The buyer was Jan Carlzon, the visionary leader of Scandinavian Airlines System, who was intent on establishing a foothold in the

U.S. market. Lorenzo agreed to sell the entire interest in Texas Air held by Jet Capital. The price paid by SAS to Lorenzo's personal holding company was $14 a share—more than three times the current market price of $4.50 a share. All told, Lorenzo wound up walking away with $30.5 million—a fraction of the $250 million that some of his aides had once reckoned his holdings to total, but a handy sum for a company verging on failure. On his way out Lorenzo had greenmailed his own company.

Four months after Lorenzo had safely gotten his money out, Texas Air joined Continental and Eastern in the bankruptcy hall of fame. Lorenzo had a hat trick. Everything had failed.

Bob Crandall rapidly filled the void left by Eastern in Miami. Before long American would control 85 percent of the airline seats going in and out of the vital gateway. Having so many seats at a single airport, as he once explained to a meeting of his pilots, gave Crandall control not only over the local aviation market but over the community's travel agents as well. "We can say to them, 'We need all your high-fare traffic. And if you don't give us your high-fare traffic, you don't get any seats at Christmastime. And you have to have seats from me at Christmastime, because *I* have 85 percent of the seats here in Miami!'

"That," Crandall went on, "is the way this game is played. This is a nasty, rotten business, and we've got to play to win."

CHAPTER 16

"TO FLY, TO SERVE"

The self-destruction of Continental Airlines vividly revealed a principle as old as passenger flight itself: people will tolerate many sacrifices to fly, but they will not tolerate surprise. They may sit with their knees to their chest for a low fare, but they will not stand for a lost bag. They may spend all night in the boarding area waiting to clear a standby list, but they will display no patience for a 30-minute rain delay. Predictability—the fulfillment of expectations—is the most important factor in whether an airplane flight is a pleasantly efficient experience or one of modern life's worst travails.

This principle is doubly important on international flights. They are longer, more costly, and generally involve less tolerant categories of humanity: business executives and tourists with money. Moreover, most transcontinental flights occur over water, great distances from the safe harbor of an airport, heightening at least slightly the anxiety of every passenger.

But over the Atlantic, on the world's busiest international routes, the airlines of the United States and Europe allowed their standards of excellence and uniformity to slip badly in the 1970s and early 1980s. Preoccupied with mergers, fare wars, and financial pressures, the three leading carriers—Pan Am, TWA, and British Airways—allowed their punctuality, their counter service, and their in-flight product to lapse. Though some of the small European airlines were noted for outstanding service (Swissair, for instance), transatlantic travel had been reduced nearly to the commodity status of a discount flight to Florida.

The problem was most evident at British Airways, an airline established under the name Imperial Airways on a route to Paris in 1924. Imperial, a state-owned enterprise with a charter to replicate by air the empire that Britain had once conquered by sea, reached India in 1929 and South Africa two years later. Even after evolving into British Overseas Air Corporation in 1939, the culture of the company remained decidedly imperial. At BOAC airplanes were said to take "voyages," not "flights." The pilots wore greatcoats, silk scarves, monocles, and kid gloves. Anyone so familiar as to address a crew member by his first name was rebuked: "This is an aircraft, not a barge!"

Passenger service, however, was always closer to barge standards. BOAC was operated like a railroad, for the sake of a schedule. Departure times were chosen for anything but the convenience of the passenger. The company was managed by engineers, not marketers. Its poor service became legendary even in popular culture when the Beatles detailed a horrific BOAC flight to Miami Beach in "Back in the U.S.S.R."

Anyone who thought the service couldn't get worse quickly learned otherwise. The British government had long divided the international routes leaving Britain between two companies: BOAC, which handled all the long-haul, intercontinental routes, and British European Airways, or BEA, a pugnacious airline with an eager young staff, which mainly hopped to destinations on the continent of Europe. In 1972 BOAC and BEA were mashed together in the name of efficiency, in part to atone for the sin of each developing a separate computer reservation system. The resulting company was called British Airways, and in the annals of aviation mergers there was to that point none worse. (Pan Am's acquisition of National a decade later would become a disaster on roughly the same scale.)

The culture gap was unbridgeable. The long-haul people at BOAC considered theirs a gentleman's airline and BEA a tradesman's airline. BEA people considered themselves true competitors and their brethren employees to be snobs. The respective staffs couldn't agree on logos or other rudiments of marketing. Service grew worse as every deficiency was deemed someone else's fault and someone else's responsibility to repair. Hot meals were served cold because the people from one side of the company wouldn't fix the food warmers belonging to the other side. Complaining passengers got a brusque brush-off if they happened to ask the wrong employee for a remedy. The top management of the airline, instead of knocking heads together, was absorbed in the trendy "management by consent" objectives of the 1970s. People regularly joked that the "BA" designator code, used in the airline's flight listings, stood not for British Airways but for "Bloody Awful."

British Airways survived in the marketplace thanks to artificial help. Her Majesty's Government merrily pumped in whatever capital the company required to fund its losses and keep its employment swollen to the levels worthy of statist patronage. British Air employed more people than any other airline in the world—55,000 at its peak in the early 1980s—while ranking seventh in terms of passengers carried, roughly the same as the old Braniff, which had one quarter as many employees.

In addition British Airways survived on a surge in postwar transatlantic travel that simply would not stop. The advent of the four-engine airplane in the mid-1940s and the jet in the late 1950s made a relic of the ocean liner. The ascent of the multinational corporation, beginning in the 1960s, caused a tremendous new wave of travel between the United States and Europe. The spread of electronic communications and the dismantling of fixed currency exchange rates in the 1970s began melding the financial systems of the world into a state of interdependency, while the slow dissolution of protectionist barriers further swelled global travel. The postindustrial maturation of the U.S. economy accelerated the process, as U.S. manufacturers increasingly turned overseas to find markets for their goods.

British Airways was assured its share of this market thanks to a third vital factor: politics.

Free trade has always been, and remains, an impossible dream in aviation. Though aviation has long fostered hopes for international peace, in diplomatic terms it has created nothing but jealousy and conflagration. Like bees, airlines pollinate the world's financial system with capital. They create, mobilize, and transport wealth in proportions vastly exceeding the fares paid by the passengers. Without the surge in transatlantic air travel the rebuilding postwar economies of Europe would never have accumulated the dollars necessary to begin purchasing American manufactured goods. In Britain BOAC was lovingly said to stand for "Bring Over American Cash." Deciding which airlines should carry the cash, cargo, and passengers between which points has been one of the most contentious ongoing debates in international diplomacy, a contest to determine which countries shall pay the toll for international travel and which shall collect it, and in what proportions.

On just one occasion—in Chicago, with peace approaching in 1944—the world's nations attempted to reach an omnibus agreement on how to apportion the spoils. The effort failed. Ever since, airline service between any two countries has required a treaty to assiduously balance the opportunities and costs between them. Because airlines often wish to fly from their home country to a second country and then on to a third, a complex series of interlocking arrangements has arisen, each of which narrows the options of the parties in coming to terms on the next.

Notably it was a conflict between the delegations from the United States and Britain that caused the Chicago convention to fail. That these two countries—the closest allies in the world, then and now—should become such bitter adversaries is a reflection of both the huge stakes at issue and an inescapable fact of geography: the United States is vast and Britain small, about the size of Oregon. There is no way that Britain could give the United States as much flying opportunity as the United States could give Britain.

Twice since World War II, meeting on both occasions in Bermuda, diplomats from the United States and United Kingdom have reached uneasy truces to regulate flights between their territories. Periodically there have been amendments to the Bermuda agreements, but enough restrictions on American service have always been maintained to ensure that British Airways was protected.

Then in the early 1980s, with deregulation taking hold in the United States, some extraordinary developments occurred on the British side of this relationship. The conservative government of Prime Minister Margaret Thatcher declared that Britain would cut loose its long-held industrial interests—British Gas, British Telecom, and British Airways among them. There would be no more free ride from Whitehall.

As "privatisation" drew near, British Airways—the "Bloody Awful" of yore—transformed itself into a real airline. Everything about the airline changed: its fleet, its pricing, its schedules, its advertising. This metamorphosis, moreover, had repercussions far beyond Britain. The rebirth of British Airways would send shudders throughout, and permanently alter, the airline markets of the world.

Perhaps most surprising of all, the changes would be introduced by an executive who had spent his life in the service business, without ever working for an airline.

His name rang with a distinctly Anglican tone: Colin Marsh Marshall. He was born in 1933 on the outskirts of London; his grammar school years were punctuated with the sounds of warfare. As a teenager he found the bombed-out city to be a drab, depressing place, so he ran away to sea, becoming a purser for the Orient Steam Navigation Company. In the next seven years he sailed 21 voyages between the United Kingdom and Australia.

At age 25 Marshall left the oceans but remained in the business of serving people, joining Hertz. Marshall washed cars and put in time behind the rental counters, not as a lowly entry-level employee, as he would later suggest, but as a management trainee, first in Chicago and then in Toronto. In barely a year he was Hertz's general manager in Mexico City, and within a year of that the assistant to the president in New York City. By 1961 he was general manager in London; the following year he had added much of Europe to his territory as well. He was not yet 30.

From London Marshall pondered a Europe undergoing a subtle yet significant change. The early 1960s witnessed the spread of multinational corporations every bit as much in Europe as in the United States, particularly with the birth of the European Common Market. Marshall observed that alongside these changes, a pan-European market was emerging for travel. An increasing number of business people renting cars in Paris, for instance, were from countries other than France. A British company that sent employees to France, moreover, might also have employees traveling to Geneva, say, or Brussels.

Although this phenomenon would be taken for granted in later

years, the transnational behavior of Europe's markets was not conspicuous to everyone in the business world of the early 1960s—not
to Colin Marshall's bosses, in any case. Hertz's European operation
was Balkanized into six divisions ("fiefdoms," as Marshall thought
of them), each reporting to New York. Each fiefdom had its own
country manager and its own sales organization. Every country
manager was out for himself.

Sitting in London, from which the greatest number of multinational customers traveled, Colin Marshall found this system mad-
deningly limiting. He thought Europe needed a czar to rule over the
lords—someone with the authority to make a deal for the wider benefit of Hertz. If Marshall himself became this czar, his career would
take another giant leap forward. In 1964 Marshall traveled to Hertz's
headquarters in New York to pitch his idea. He was thanked and
told nicely to get lost.

Marshall jumped ship to Hertz's mortal enemy, Avis. His boss
there was the legendary Winston "Bud" Morrow, a backslapping
salesman of the first order. Morrow popularized a 1960s corporate
fad known as "visible management," in which every executive in the
company spent at least part of the year working alongside the rank
and file, which in Avis's case meant behind the rental counters and
underneath the automobile hoods. Thus did Colin Marshall again
get the chance to learn customer service at ground level.

Morrow put Marshall in charge of Avis's European operation—a
scant empire, to be sure, with barely a dozen cars in London and the
same in Scotland. Marshall quickly built the operation, taking dead
aim at Hertz by offering corporations and major travel operators
special discounts across the continent. Transcending geographical
divisions, Marshall outfitted employees across Europe in matching
red blazers. More significantly he adapted the roaringly successful
advertising campaign that Doyle Dane Bernbach had developed for
Avis a few years earlier, in 1962—"We're No. 2. We Try Harder"—
and turned it into an expression of Avis's internationalism, translat-
ing "We Try Harder" into more than a dozen languages and listing
each in a single display advertisement. (*Nos esforzamos más . . . Nous
faisons plus pour vous satisfaire . . . Wir geben uns mehr Mühe . . .*)
Marshall thus announced to the world that Avis was a unified worldwide brand, asked for in many languages. The campaign flew in the

face of conventional multinational marketing, which held that a company distinguished its product for a local market, not an international one. But Marshall's strategy succeeded: by the early 1970s Marshall had overtaken Hertz in Europe and had done so with methods that Hertz itself had rejected.

Marshall was soon called to Avis world headquarters in Garden City, New York, to become the number two executive under Bud Morrow. Avis was a down-and-dirty organization, literally and figuratively. The corporate headquarters was filled with people who had started out with dirty knuckles, turning gaskets and replacing oil filters. Sales were still promoted according to the old-boy rules: politicians received free cars, competitors were railroaded out of airports in collusion with Hertz, illegal campaign contributions were made.

In the rough-and-tumble environment of the home office, Marshall was as conspicuous, as one of his subordinates would later remark, as "a paste jewel thrust upon the finger of society." He talked funny. He struck some people as arrogant. He displayed such an uncanny knack for remembering faces and names that people suspected him of maintaining a secret file. Some of his colleagues judged him zealously self-promotional. After Marshall had spent a few years as the number two man in New York, the company published a promotional booklet called *The Avis Story,* which attributed the company's international success to "a brilliant management team . . . beginning with Mr. Colin M. Marshall." (The next edition of *The Avis Story* referred instead to "a very capable management team.")

A story made the rounds that spoke volumes about Marshall's keen mind as well as his sometimes off-putting manner. After hiring one of the engineers who had created the original Sabre system at American Airlines, Avis in 1972 was preparing to roll out the first electronic computer reservation network anywhere outside of the airline industry. (It was touted as "The Wizard of Avis.") During a meeting of top Avis executives, a dummy sample of the system's statistical reporting power was distributed. As everyone marveled over the detail generated by the computer, Marshall looked at a long string of big numbers and spoke up. "Excuse me," he said. "That column doesn't add up."

"It doesn't have to," someone said.

"Why not?" Marshall demanded.

"Well, they're just nonsense numbers." This was a dry run, after all.

Marshall was gravely offended. "Why would you use 'nonsense numbers?' "

But people nearly always came to judge Marshall in the end as the perfect gentleman. Tough, yes; mean, no. And there was no disputing that Avis flourished under his tutelage; he deserved the credit. But who deserved the blame, when things went awry?

Avis, owned by International Telephone & Telegraph Corporation, was ordered sold when the Justice Department attacked the conglomerate on antitrust grounds in 1972. But because the gasoline-sensitive car rental industry promptly went into the tank following the Arab oil embargo, ITT had difficulty finding a buyer. While the search dragged on, a federal court put the control of Avis in the hands of an independent trustee. Bud Morrow, still chairman, opposed the trustee's appointment and came to swords' points with him. Suddenly, Morrow sensed that his number two executive had designs on the number one job. "I think Marshall's ambition was tickled," Morrow would later recall. Marshall, it seemed, was putting himself on friendly terms with the trustees. Morrow felt betrayed.

Then in November 1976 a committee of three outside directors revealed to the SEC that Avis had made "improper" or "otherwise questionable" payments totaling $425,000, including unlawful U.S. political contributions and payments to officials in foreign countries. Although Avis noted that none of its top executives had personally ordered any of the payments, it did take the trouble to add this one, measured sentence in one of its filings with the SEC: "Several members of senior United States management, including the then-two management directors, had knowledge of some of the foregoing payments and 'off book' cash funds at various times." The two management directors at the time were Bud Morrow and Colin Marshall.

There was another intriguing matter that drew the attention of the SEC. An Avis subsidiary had written a $470,958 check to a shell company in the tax haven of Jersey, one of the Channel Islands near France. Internal Avis records identified the sum as a consulting fee paid in Italy. Very shortly after making the payment, Avis won a lucrative tax ruling in Italy that added roughly $3.7 million to the company's bottom line over the course of two otherwise very lean years—a time when Avis urgently needed higher profits to make the company more attractive to potential buyers. In one filing with the SEC, Avis pointedly noted that it was unclear whether the $470,958 payment ultimately reached any government officials "for purposes of influencing official action"—whether, in short, Avis had paid a bribe.

Morrow left Avis under pressure in the wake of the disclosures, and Marshall ascended to the top position in the company. Ultimately Marshall was held entirely blameless in the affair. Indeed the court-appointed trustee issued a statement expressing "complete confidence in Mr. Marshall as chief executive officer of the company." The controversy was quickly forgotten, though not by Bud Morrow, who for years harbored resentment over how his protégé had emerged unscathed. "The thing had a very deep odor about it, frankly," Morrow said later of the Italian tax payment. "It was a very doubtful, doubtful transaction." When yet another edition of *The Avis Story* was published, virtually all mention of Bud Morrow's contributions had been eradicated.

In 1977 Avis finally was sold to Norton Simon, Incorporated, a conglomerate built up by the mercurial king of the consumer goods takeover, David Mahoney. Marshall was put in charge of a new division that included not only Avis but Hunt-Wesson Foods. Marshall devoted himself to the work of "refreshing" the prosaic brands of Wesson Oil and Hunts canned tomatoes—essentially taking the same goods and making them appear to be something altogether new and improved. But Marshall chafed under David Mahoney, complaining to others that he could not tolerate working under such autocratic and tempestuous leadership. Nor was Colin Marshall's heart in edible oils. Gravely unhappy after a short time at Norton Simon, Marshall journeyed back to London. And when yet another edition of *The Avis Story* rolled off the presses there would be virtually no mention of Colin Marshall anywhere in its pages.

As they were leaving New York, Marshall's wife asked him what job he would most like in the world. "I would like to be the chairman of British Airways," he answered. A short time later, as if the management gods had been eavesdropping, the call came. In January 1983 Marshall joined British Airways as chief executive, though not as chairman.

. . .

Marshall came to British Airways knowing as much about airlines as anybody could without ever having worked for one. For nearly two decades, ever since the mid-1960s, he had spent 65 percent of his time traveling internationally, flying into every nook and cranny of the globe to plant the flag of Avis Rent A Car. In addition to being one of the world's most frequent fliers, Marshall negotiated contracts with the airlines—"fly-drive" deals in which an airline and a rental car company, within the boundaries of a particular country, would try to increase their respective sales by promoting the other's products.

When his old boss at Avis, Bud Morrow, heard the news that Marshall was joining British Airways as the number two man, his first thought was that the number one man had better watch out. But the chairman of British Airways was entirely capable, it appeared, of taking care of himself. He was Sir John King, soon to become Lord King. He was vaguely noble, the result of his having married the daughter of the 8th Viscount Galway (if anyone was counting). He hunted in Leicestershire, fished in Scotland, and painted in oils. He was acerbic and sarcastic.

Lord King was also active in Conservative Party politics and was close to Prime Minister Margaret Thatcher, who wanted British Airways primped for sale to private investors, assuming that it could ever be made attractive enough for anyone to want. This was where King came in. Thatcher instructed her friend to shake the airline to its very foundations to endow it with a semblance of efficiency and marketing.

In the two years before Marshall arrived, King attacked British Airways with abandon. He sold a million square feet of office space in London, got rid of 80 superfluous airplanes and wiped out dozens of routes. With the more than $500 million in cash generated by these moves, King offered early retirement and severance to a veritable legion of employees—nearly 20,000 in all—thereby reducing employment to 36,000 in the course of two years. Soon the bleeding had stopped. King's turnaround moves did little, however, for the biggest challenge: filling the company's mostly empty airplanes.

Marshall felt like an archaeologist arriving at British Airways, shovel and brush in hand, clearing away decades of bad attitude in search of a treasure. The hidden treasure was the world's most extensive route system (Marshall himself had flown on most of it) and an operating base at Heathrow, the world's richest multinational gateway. Although he knew firsthand about the grubby aircraft, curmudgeonly employees, and poor schedules of British Airways, Marshall now had an insider's view. He could see that internal politics had corrupted the organization and that morale remained in ruins, and nothing, he knew from his Hertz and Avis years, was more essential in a service business than morale. In Marshall's view customers had the memories of elephants for bad experiences. And worse, they talked, and talked, and talked, about poor service, particularly when it involved so conversation-worthy a topic as air travel. "In war," Marshall began telling people, paraphrasing Napoleon, "morale outweighs matériel by three to one."

Marshall's first step, anachronistically enough, was sensitivity training—a regimen of classes with the agonizingly off-putting name "Putting People First." In groups of 150, employees were dragged groaning and shrugging into classes for a few days at a time, but as one would predict with any expensive and well-designed mass-indoctrination program, they emerged from the experience saying that it was, well, *okay* . . . pretty interesting, in fact. Employees were guided through role playing and exercises in imagination, all to educate them in how the customer felt and how to accept responsibility for solving a passenger's problems. They were trained to think of themselves as "emotional laborers," no different from nurses or welfare workers, for among the 450 passengers checking in for a fully loaded 747 flight, they were told,

> there will be a businessman, tired and obsessed by a particular problem; a woman with two children joining her husband abroad, anxious about going to a new country, perhaps worried about the house, schools, and so on. There will be a granny who has never flown before. . . . Every human or emotional state you can think of will be there: euphoric, depressed, anxious, happy, excited. And all will be suffused by a level of preflight anxiety.

While the courses were under way, Marshall began distributing lapel buttons that said, I FLY THE WORLD'S FAVOURITE AIRLINE, as if repeating the phrase often enough might actually begin to make it true. (Having learned visible management at the foot of a master at Avis, Marshall naturally wore one of the lapel buttons himself, even if it was a little conspicuous on his immaculate British tailoring.)

British Airways's poor service was evident not only over the North Atlantic but within the United Kingdom itself, where a much smaller airline named British Caledonian was making severe inroads. "BCal" hired flight attendants for appearance and outfitted them in tartan skirts, airing commercials that showed a chorus of male passengers singing, "We wish they all could be Caledonian girls." British Airways was under pressure to put not only spit and polish but also sensuality into its rusty, surly product.

An emphasis was placed on youth in hiring, facilitated by age discrimination statutes that were far less onerous in Europe than in the United States. At the same time educational requirements for flight attendants were reduced. Marketing executives used the word "sparkly" to describe the kind of personality they wanted employees to project. The employee newsletter promoted a "grooming room," conveniently located in Terminal One at Heathrow, where employees were urged to schedule a consultation if they suffered from "a weight problem," or "difficult hair," or "ugly hands," or "spotty skin." Even electrolysis was available for unsightly hairs. Any uniformed employee who did not "look right" would be "taken away from the job."

Before long, British Air's in-flight magazine was calling attention to the new look, in case anyone had missed it: "Passengers checking in at the airport can't fail to have noticed the warmth of the welcome from the smiling BA girls behind the desks, and the freshness of their looks, their complexions smooth, their make-up alive with colour and gloss."

Marshall also demanded a makeover for the airplanes. He hired the same design firm he had used at Avis, causing a hue and cry over the use of a foreign firm by the state-owned airline, but this was only the beginning of Marshall's refusal to play by old rules. (He would, for instance, place some of the biggest airplane orders in history with America's Boeing instead of the state-supported European Airbus.) Many expected the Yankee design contractor to come up with a horrible and garish new paint scheme, but to their surprise the look was elegance itself: an angular, high-tech arrow that conveyed precision, accompanied on the tail by a classic coat of arms fit for Pall Mall. Under the insignia was a ribbon bearing a four-word inscription that summarized Marshall's marketing philosophy: "To Fly, To Serve."

Relentlessly Marshall's people began to survey passenger attitudes, down to what they thought of each individual flight and each individual check-in agent, eventually accumulating a massive database on what people wanted when flying and what they were willing to pay for. Surveying passenger preferences enabled the company to estimate whether adding $4 in perfumes or candies to an amenities kit or a meal tray would enable the company to charge an additional $5 for the ticket. Marshall instructed his people to run a complete profit-and-loss analysis on every element of service, as if it were a capital construction project. Almost invariably the research showed that any modest improvement in service registered as a major breakthrough with the customer.

To address the problem of full-fare business travelers flying alongside tourists on discounts, Marshall invented something called "business class." There would be three classes of service aboard a single airplane (coach, business, and first), each of which, Marshall decreed, should become a product, a "brand," all by itself. Marshall brought in brand specialists from Mars candies and other consumer product companies to explore ways of distinguishing and promoting each class of service, knowing that as the airline placed a larger proportion of passengers into the premium classes, its revenues would swell on only a slight increase in cost. His first- and business-class sales soaring, Marshall was delighted to leave the low-fare tourists to fly on Pan Am and TWA.

By 1986 British Airways was in fat city, ready to fulfill Prime Minister Thatcher's goal of privatization. As the preparations were being made in the spring of 1986, however, financial disaster struck in the North Atlantic.

A U.S. Navy diver had been shot by Lebanese extremists who had hijacked a TWA flight from Athens. Palestinian terrorists had seized the Italian cruise ship *Achille Lauro*. Fifteen people were gunned down at an airport ticket counter in Rome. A bomb exploded on a TWA flight from Rome to Athens, killing four. After President Reagan had ordered the bombing of Libya, few passengers wanted to take the chance of flying on whichever transatlantic flight Col.

Muammar Qaddafi would happen to choose as a target for reprisal. The nuclear accident at Chernobyl only elevated the apprehension of flying anywhere near Europe.

British Airways suffered the most severe plunge in business in the company's long history. In the week after the Libyan bombing—a week in which it could have expected 50,000 reservations in any remotely normal market—the airline recorded only 20,000. Colin Marshall's people had to come up with something fast or simply accept that their most important and profitable route would be moribund.

Marshall had immersed himself in the intricacies of American behavior in his years with Avis and Hunt-Wesson. He knew something about what made American consumers tick. He knew that Americans were suckers for freebies and that the American media were suckers for a story. Since it was a media event that had chilled transatlantic travel, Marshall determined that British Airways would stage a media event to bring it back.

After a crash study British Airways announced that it would *give away* every one of its seats over the Atlantic for a day, a total of 5,000 free seats. "Go for It, America!" the promotional headlines trumpeted. The seats would be awarded in a drawing; a few of the lucky 5,000 would be chosen for the additional prize of tea with Prime Minister Margaret Thatcher at No. 10 Downing Street. British Airways was suddenly a news story in which thousands of people were seen shedding the dread of terrorism to clamor for an airline seat over the North Atlantic. An instantaneous surge in reservations occurred.

While catching the publicity wave, Marshall and his people moved to sustain the recovery; investors would balk at buying British Air's shares unless they were convinced that the revenue stream had stabilized. So Marshall and his people kept the sweepstakes spirit alive by scheduling an additional series of contests and prizes through the summer months of 1986. They lowered themselves even to scratch-off prize coupons, with prizes carefully chosen to appeal to the Anglophile in every American. Scratch and win a free Rolls-Royce! Win a £100,000 shopping spree at Harrods!

The scheme worked. While no barn burner, the summer was at least salvaged. A few months later, in February 1987, Her Majesty's

Government sold British Airways for a total of $1.4 billion. Before the year was out Queen Elizabeth II had rewarded Colin Marshall with knighthood.

Every passenger flying on British Airways represented an empty seat on Pan Am or TWA. Though no one competed as aggressively on price as the Americans, Marshall would always need a certain number of low-fare passengers to fill up his airplanes, so he would always try to meet the lowest coach price in the market. As time passed, however, an increasing portion of British Airways passenger cabins were given over to premium classes, at huge price markups. Soon British Airways was bringing in 15 percent more revenue than the average airline on the same number of passengers—money that went almost entirely to the bottom line.

Marshall was delighted to watch Pan Am and TWA chase each other's tails for the marginal passenger, while driving business travelers and the well-to-do into the arms of British Airways. But Marshall was also aware that he would not always have it so easy against the Americans. Bob Crandall, alas, was taking baby steps into Europe.

It was the failure of Braniff in 1982 that put American into Europe, when American picked up Braniff's route authority from Dallas to London's Gatwick Airport. It was the sole international route in American's empire then, but it was a lucrative one—the "oilman's route," linking the oilpatch of Texas with the burgeoning fields of the North Sea. In time Crandall's planners began studying whether American should do more, including, typically, whether American might kill off some other player to benefit itself. In this case the target was not a company but an airplane: the 747, that lumbering leviathan.

The 747 was the workhorse of the transatlantic, and even in the early 1980s it was too much airplane for the job. Pan Am and TWA could fill their eastbound 747s only by forcing airline passengers from cities all across America to fly to the East Coast, most often to JFK, where a jumbo jet hungrily awaited its fill of connecting passengers.

In stepping into the market, American had the advantages of the newcomer. Instead of using 747s, it would fly over the Atlantic with the newer, smaller, and vastly more economical 767, which had two engines instead of four and two pilots instead of three. American as a result did not have to fly through New York or any of the other traditional, high-cost East Coast gateways. Using the power of the hub, American could assemble all the passengers it needed to fill a 767 in the middle of the United States—in Dallas or Chicago.

"We can fragment the market," Crandall's brainy scheduler, Mel Olsen, told his colleagues. "We can make the 747s die." Crandall instantly grasped the beauty of the strategy.

What's more, Crandall's people realized, they could apply the same strategy on the other side of the ocean by landing in a heartland airport. The British were extremely prickly about letting anyone fly into London, but surely, Crandall's people thought, they would allow a new foreign airline to serve an outlying city—Manchester, say.

They were right. The British were only too happy to let American gamble on a flight between two secondary cities like Chicago and Manchester. A flight like that couldn't begin to hurt British Airways, could it?

Before long American applied the same strategy with the French. Though no less protective than Britain, France was only too happy to let American fly from a two-bit city such as Dallas to Orly, the secondary airport serving Paris. Next American sought authority to serve the industrial city of Lyon. The same strategy was applied to Germany.

These moves were slow and tentative, limited by the rate at which Crandall's lobbyists could persuade U.S. diplomats to bargain for the new landing rights and by the rate at which the diplomats, in turn, succeeded in winning those rights. As the end of the 1980s approached, with Crandall's Growth Plan at its peak, American had still more incentive to look overseas. "We were betting on the come," one of Crandall's top analysts, Gerard Arpey, would later recall. "We ordered a lot of airplanes in the mid-1980s, and we had to have a place to put them." Cumulatively, city by city, the strategy worked. By 1988, when Crandall and his people were also plotting their assault on Eastern's territory in South America, American Airlines was serving 13 cities in Europe. In passenger terms it was still way behind British Airways, Pan Am, and TWA. Crandall was a long way from killing the 747. But it was a start.

. . .

Through the years British Airways had flown to the United States under frequently shifting terms and conditions. For all the landing authorizations it won from the U.S. government, one restriction had never loosened: once a British Airways plane landed in the United States, it could fly nowhere except back out. It was unlawful for any foreign airline to fly passengers (or cargo) between any two U.S. cities. British Airways could pick up transatlantic passengers in 18 "gateway" cities in America, but it still relied on United States carriers to deliver nearly half its passengers to those gateways.

Therein lay the problem. Increasingly those same U.S. carriers were flying over the Atlantic themselves. Where American might have once flown a passenger from Phoenix to New York so he could board a British Airways flight to London, American was now flying that passenger into Dallas to connect on its own flight over the Atlantic. Delta, too, had also been slowly building up its presence over the Atlantic.

As Marshall pondered his predicament, he realized that there was a clever, almost cute, solution. He would make himself a partner of United Airlines.

Though a major player in the Pacific after 1985, United had never flown a flight to Europe and had no intention of doing so. United, in short, was no competitor of British Airways. So why couldn't United function as a surrogate for British Airways between the cities of the United States? United could try to recruit Europe-bound passengers onto its flights, then dedicate itself to turning them over to British Airways for the rest of their journey. British Airways, in turn, could find a way of steering *its* passengers arriving in the United States into connecting flights aboard United. Both airlines would win.

Preliminary discussions began in the months before Dick Ferris was ousted as United's chairman. Negotiating in utmost secrecy, Ferris and Marshall saw so much merit in such a joint operation that they even discussed United's buying a 20 percent ownership interest in British Airways, with British Airways doing the same in United. Together the two companies would establish the world's first Anglo-American airline. When Frank Olson of Hertz took over as interim chairman after Ferris was removed, he found the entire issue suddenly in his lap. Facing him across the bargaining table was one of his fastest friends in the business world, Colin Marshall. Marshall had once worked at Hertz himself. Later, as the chief executive of Avis, Marshall had competed vigorously with Olson, but in the aristocracy of the executive suite the two men had only grown closer.

Looking on American, and Crandall, as a common enemy, Olson and Marshall ultimately approved an arrangement known as "code sharing." Code sharing was created to evade another of the immutable rules of airline marketing: passengers, though never eager to change planes, harbor an even more powerful aversion to changing *airlines.* The odds of a missed connection multiply. Luggage is more apt to become errant. The marathon race between airport gates is elongated. In the years before computers dominated, the airlines came up with a practice that tricked travelers (and travel agents) by hiding the fact that they would have to change airlines on certain connecting flights. The *Official Airline Guide* would list a number of flights, particularly to such faraway destinations as Alaska, under the two-letter designator code of a single airline even though the service involved one airline meeting a connecting flight with another. The government felt justified in permitting this deception because the flight crews in such cases switched planes with the passengers. Usually the return flight reversed the same arrangements. The combination of airline deregulation and computer reservation networks facilitated this practice.

In Europe code sharing, considered an outright subterfuge, was a violation of the law. Indeed British Airways, invited by the U.S. government in 1984 to comment on the practice, responded without equivocation. "British Airways," the company said, "believes that it is intrinsically deceptive for two carriers to share a designator code."

But in 1987, as the practice came into even more widespread use, British Airways and United announced the most sweeping code-sharing arrangement yet undertaken in the world—"the ultimate global airbridge," as they called it. When a travel agent summoned a list of flights from Denver, say, to London, she would now observe a British Airways flight going the entire distance—as well as a United flight leaving and arriving at the same time. The appearance of the same flight twice gave the partnered airlines twice the opportunity to sell the same service. And in either case the customer would be buying a ticket on which it appeared that he or she would be flying a single flight on the same airline for the entire journey, when in fact the passenger would discover that the itinerary actually involved not only a change of airplane but a change of airline. It was a new kind of screen science, only in this case Bob Crandall was the target rather than the inventor.

British Airways and American were hardly the only combatants over the North Atlantic. There was also Pan Am, reeling in the cross-fire. But Pan Am was about to get a new boss intent on reversing the company's fortunes.

From the ashes of Braniff Airways had risen a new airline, flying under the Braniff name but known throughout the airline industry as Braniff II. It was controlled by Jay Pritzker of Chicago, a former naval aviator whose family owned the Hyatt Hotels chain. By 1987, alas, the new Braniff was struggling just as its progenitor had. Pritzker resolved to merge with a larger airline.

Pritzker was friendly with Pan Am's Ed Acker; Braniff II in fact employed Acker's son. Acker reacted enthusiastically when Pritzker discussed the possible purchase of Pan Am by Braniff—the company that Acker himself, in an earlier age, had built into a powerhouse.

At the time of Pritzker's overture Pan Am was again in desperate straits. It had largely burned up the $750 million it had received from United two years earlier as payment for the Pacific routes. Its position had worsened not only against American, a new rival, but against British Airways, a long-standing one. The directors of Pan Am were pressuring Acker to extract still more wage concessions, a confrontation for which Acker displayed little enthusiasm. A board meeting to vote on a sale to Pritzker was set for December 1, 1987.

To the extent that Acker was delighted by Pritzker's emergence as a rescuer, Marty Shugrue, now the vice chairman of Pan Am, was beside himself. Pan Am, *sold*? Shugrue considered it unthinkable. Unlike Acker, Shugrue was a Pan Am man from the start. He went into overdrive, rounding up his pals in the union leadership to plead for new concessions from employees, arguing that if he could deliver wage cuts to the directors of Pan Am, then the board would have no reason to sell to Pritzker. "The clock is ticking!" Shugrue cried to the bargainers on both sides. Literally minutes before the board meeting began, letters, signatures, and handshakes were exchanged. Shugrue triumphantly entered the oval-shaped boardroom of Pan Am announcing that there was no need to sell. The concessions were in hand.

That was impossible, Acker said.

And with that the directors of Pan Am were treated to the spectacle of the chairman of the board and the vice chairman at war before their eyes. The argument dragged on for three days of meetings and adjournments as Acker and Shugrue each attempted to torpedo the other's deal. Pritzker walked away from the entire mess, once again leaving Pan Am on the precipice of failure.

Pan Am in reality had few problems that could not be cured with fuller airplanes and higher fares, especially over the Atlantic. But among the Pan Am directors—and particularly in the view of Bill Coleman, among the most senior of them—the main problem was sky-high wages. With the company's two top executives feuding, Coleman took matters into his own hands, approaching the company's union leaders to establish their price for the concessions he thought the company so urgently required. Two days before Christmas in 1987 he got his answer: their price was Acker's head. Coleman obliged. While he was at it, Coleman resolved to make a clean sweep; he fired Shugrue as well.

Acker, who had an employment contract with Pan Am, walked away with a settlement on the order of $1 million. Shugrue got 90 days' pay.

A committee of the board—the same committee that had recruited Acker when *his* predecessor had been fired seven years earlier, in 1981—readily found a new chief executive. The new man at Pan Am was Tom Plaskett, freshly fired from Continental Airlines. Shugrue, for his part, landed on his feet as well. He accepted an offer to become president of, ironically, Continental Airlines. Plaskett and Shugrue had essentially exchanged jobs. Miraculously, in this round of executive musical chairs nobody had taken away any of the chairs.

Plaskett rode the elevator to the 46th floor of the Pan Am building and turned toward the chairman's office, the room in which Juan Trippe had presided over the world's greatest airline, in which a succession of followers, culminating with Ed Acker, had presided over its demise. Plaskett could see the rendering of the Pan Am network hanging at the end of the hallway, those gold lines delicately painted over the mahogany map of the world, lines to places like Tokyo and Hong Kong—places that Pan Am had long since abandoned. It broke Plaskett's heart to see that map; before long he ordered it stripped from the wall.

Happily, though, for him, Tom Plaskett was at last running something. Denied the opportunity at American by Crandall's unwillingness to delegate, again denied at Continental because of what he considered Lorenzo's meddlesomeness, Plaskett now had an entire company to himself. But what a mess it was, so much worse than he had been led to believe in agreeing to take the job. "When I arrived at Pan Am in January," he told a group of employees later in 1988, "I found a company that was not just weak and foundering. I found a company in utter chaos."

He asked, for instance, to see the marketing plan.

The marketing plan?

Yes, the marketing plan. Where is the marketing plan?

Huh?

There was no marketing plan, he was told.

Pan Am, Plaskett discovered, was selling seats by the bucket to wholesalers and consolidators—outfits that then resold them to the public at a markup with those small ads and fetching prices that appear in the travel section of the newspaper. Pan Am was practically giving those seats to the wholesalers and letting *them* make the profits, while the company itself was failing even to cover the costs of putting its planes in the air. Pan Am did not have the computer power to perform yield management. Indeed its reservations department was not even a part of the marketing department.

Plaskett looked with foreboding at the newly announced linkup between United and British Airways. Though Plaskett was offended by code sharing, which he considered misleading to the flying public, he tried to break into the game himself. Pan Am established a code-sharing deal with Malev, the Hungarian national carrier. Under this arrangement Malev's flight from Budapest to Frankfurt would appear under the same flight number as a connecting Pan Am flight from Frankfurt to New York. It was the best arrangement of its kind that anyone would make with Pan Am.

Eagerly, almost desperately, Plaskett tried to break into a new European computer reservations network, called Galileo, that British Airways and several other airlines were establishing to fend off American's Sabre in Europe. The Galileo partners said no, they did not want to have a bankrupt among them.

But the battle would be won or lost, Plaskett decided, not with the big systems and big financial moves, but with the individual customer. This was where Colin Marshall had succeeded in saving British Airways, and this was where Pan Am had its most severe problems to overcome.

Plaskett was shocked to walk into the Worldport terminal and see two long, snaking lines of customers: after checking bags passengers had to stand in another line for a boarding pass. "The minute they walked in our door, we inconvenienced them!" Plaskett told his employees. The airplanes themselves were deplorable and filthy, with outdated bathrooms and upholstery and side panels and lighting and carpeting. Plaskett scrounged the cash to have them all ripped out, telling people that without new interiors there would be no passengers, and without passengers there would be no Pan Am. Furthermore, he ordered those airplane exteriors polished every 45 days.

Pan Am had been staffing jumbo jet flights with four or five fewer flight attendants than the competition, making the passengers angry and the flight attendants angrier still, which in turn only made the passengers all the angrier. More flight attendants! Plaskett decreed.

Plaskett installed yield management programs and took back much of the sales effort from wholesalers. He went on the stump, as he had five years earlier at American when he had won the first b-scale contracts in the airline industry. He resolved to communicate, to prove that he was different from the previous failed managements of Pan Am. "I am a believer!" he announced to a group of employees.

Plaskett, who had long thought of himself as cool and detached, as a "professional manager," was soon becoming emotionally vested in the turnaround at Pan Am. In his second day on the job, as he deplaned from a Pan Am flight, he had been moved when a flight attendant waved good-bye, then called after him earnestly, "We're counting on you." Some 24,000 jobs were hanging in the balance, some 24,000 livelihoods.

"Ladies and gentlemen," Plaskett told his employees in a big meeting, "I *can't* do it alone. I don't have all the answers. I need your help. We have to do it together. The time has come to put the past behind us . . . to bury our prejudices, and to challenge the old ways of doing things. . . . It is time for Pan Am to move beyond the legend."

And as surely as Plaskett's commitment deepened, so too did things begin to turn around, ever so tentatively. Blessed with a robust economy and a sudden strengthening of transatlantic travel, Pan Am recorded a profit in the third quarter of 1988, a stunning recovery from a year earlier. Moreover the revenue figure for the quarter was a record, better than any in the company's history, even when it had the Pacific routes! Cost-cutting labor agreements were finally being ratified and put in place. Seats once occupied by passengers on wholesale tickets were now gradually being taken over by customers paying a profit margin to Pan Am. Although British Airways was coming on strong and Plaskett's old pals at American were making inroads, Pan Am itself was gaining ground.

Pan Am, Plaskett thought, was going to make it.

In the labor wars that had raged for years at Pan Am Capt. James MacQuarrie of the Air Line Pilots Association was a voice of reason among the union leadership. It was he who had led the pilots off the job in 1985, forcing Pan Am to sell the Pacific—but he had also brought them back to work quickly. MacQuarrie appreciated grandeur and tradition. He lovingly maintained a 200-year-old home in New Hampshire. He tinkered with vintage automobiles. No one in labor or management cared more deeply about the survival of Pan Am, which made it all the more ironic that MacQuarrie, age 55, happened to be the captain of Pan Am Flight 103 departing Heathrow Airport for New York four days before Christmas in 1988.

Flight 103 that day bore evidence of the comeback for which Plaskett had been so desperately working. For one, the 747 jet, christened *Clipper Maid of the Seas,* had 259 people aboard—a healthy load, with plenty of the high-class travelers Plaskett was trying to woo back. There was a U.S. Justice Department lawyer, returning from a Nazi-hunting mission in Austria; a high-ranking government official from the newly established African state of Namibia; an engineer who had served as the sound man for the rock group Pink Floyd; five officials of the Central Intelligence Agency.

Its passenger compartment loaded with Christmas gifts and luggage, the plane was topped off with fuel for the long trip into the headwinds of the jet stream. At 6:25 P.M. MacQuarrie taxied to his runway and took off to the north, toward Scotland. There, heading toward 31,000 feet, Flight 103 banked to the west to make a straight shot over Scotland toward Kennedy Airport.

It was after two in the afternoon in New York. Plaskett was nearly ready to leave the office for the holidays when Pan Am's senior vice president of operations rang him on the phone. An air traffic controller in Scotland had reported that Flight 103 had disappeared from his screen—actually, that the dot had broken into five dots, each of which had quickly evaporated. At the same instant an earthquake had registered on the Richter scale in Scotland, with the epicenter at the village of Lockerbie.

"Why, God," Plaskett said.

What had registered as an earthquake was actually the impact of the *Clipper Maid of the Seas* striking the earth. Eleven citizens of Lockerbie were also killed.

There has never, of course, been an airplane disaster that was not shocking, not tragic in the extreme. But never before this one had the carnage been so horrific. Some victims were vaporized in the midair explosion. Other passengers, falling for miles, their clothes and skin torn from their bodies by the friction of the rushing air, struck the rain-softened fields of Lockerbie and sank inches into the ground. It was like Bosch's vision of hell, such was the combination of horror and surrealism.

At JFK relatives arriving to meet their loved ones collapsed in anguish. In the Pan Am building cries of sorrow rang through the hallways. And then, on the reservations line, there was silence. In a matter of hours the airline lost half its transatlantic bookings. In the days ahead more reservations disappeared. Nearly a half-billion dollars' worth of business went away, and there were no new reservations to replace them.

The public was quickly forgiving of most aviation disasters, but not this one. This was a terrorist bombing, executed with cold-blooded, pinpoint precision. There was nothing random about it; it was plainly an anti-American act. Suddenly anyone contemplating an international flight on Pan Am—Pan Am, that symbol of American influence across the globe—found himself weighing the odds of survival en route.

Tom Plaskett knew the war was over. His job now, his new job, was to obtain the most favorable terms possible for the surrender. Within barely a month of Lockerbie, Plaskett stood up at an aviation conference in New York and acknowledged what everyone in the world already knew: Pan Am had to be sold or merged. One way or another Pan Am, Plaskett declared, was officially for sale.

Practically overnight Plaskett's enthusiasm, his I'm-a-believer rhetoric, had been drained away. Much of what he saw elsewhere in the airline industry now filled him with resentment and outrage—including some of the innovations for which he himself had once claimed a measure of credit, such as frequent-flier programs and sophisticated computer reservations systems.

"It used to be enough just to be a megacarrier," he would later tell an audience, "but not anymore. Now," he went on,

> you have to be a *global* megacarrier to really be taken seriously. If you and your equity partners or marketing partners or code-sharing partners or commuter partners don't have stations in Perth and Peoria, in Beijing and Bangor, in São Paulo and Santa Fe, in Hamburg and Hannibal— along with a global computer reservations system to tie it all together and control your capacity, manage your yield, add up your frequent-flier miles . . . well, then, buddy, you just don't count anymore.

But Plaskett had his pride. If Pan Am was going to be sold, it would be in one piece. There would be no liquidation, no death by inches, no selling of assets and leaving the people behind without jobs. There were careers at stake—livelihoods, families. Two hundred and seventy lives had been lost during Plaskett's tenure; he refused to be responsible for the loss of 24,000 jobs as well.

Selling a company was rarely the path to heroism in corporate America, but in Pan Am's case it was the best anyone could hope for. Tom Plaskett still had a chance to be the hero.

CHAPTER 17

THE GILDED COCKPIT

The men of commercial aviation were sometimes like actors in a long-running soap opera. From time to time one of them would disappear, only to reemerge in a new role. From one incarnation to the next their roles often grew more fantastic. Marty Shugrue, to pick just one example, had been kicked out of Pan Am, only to become the president of Continental Airlines. In barely a year's time he was removed from that position by Frank Lorenzo, who in turn was soon ousted from Eastern. The trustee subsequently appointed to manage Eastern in bankruptcy—to deal away its many pieces to the surviving airlines of America—was Marty Shugrue.

In the late 1980s one of the biggest roles in the industry was still not cast: the position of chairman, president, and chief executive officer of United Airlines.

Perhaps never before had an executive search been more crucial or challenging to a major company. United needed a builder as well as a liquidator, someone to reclaim United's lost glory while disposing of the last remnants of Allegis; a healer as well as a battler, who could repair the fissures within United while regaining the ground lost to American and other airlines.

In searching for candidates, interim chairman Frank Olson was vitally concerned with the company's need to cast an audience pleaser, someone who could enrapture United's skeptical employees. If the firing of Ferris was not sufficient proof, then the fates of Frank Borman and Ed Acker had been: in an industry demanding so many financial sacrifices, the workers would have some say-so over who held the leading roles.

Olson's first recruiting call had gone to his close friend Colin Marshall, whom Olson viewed as the most qualified man in the world to lead United, taking account of United's delicate culture. "Could I interest you in returning to the United States and becoming chief executive officer of United Airlines?" Olson asked. Marshall thanked Olson but said, "No. I'm committed."

Olson had to go to his fallback position: to recruit the man whom he considered simply the most qualified CEO, regardless of suitability to the culture of United. That was Bob Crandall.

Part of Olson's motivation in approaching Crandall involved the obvious benefit to United of eliminating Crandall as a competitor. Crandall was judged to be so essential to American's success that plucking him from the company would be like removing the general from an army whose next officer was a lieutenant. But that was the smaller part of it. Olson principally was awed by Crandall's achievements and abilities. Having no illusions about Crandall's intense and abrasive personal manner, Olson wrestled with the question of whether United could tolerate Fang; he was anxious enough about the risks that he asked the United board for its blessing to approach Crandall. The board assented. Crandall would be asked to name his price.

Crandall was such a workaholic—and so relished victory as its own reward—that people sometimes failed to recognize that he also cared deeply about his personal wealth. The talks between the two men culminated over a dinner in the Carlton House in New York, where American owned an apartment. Olson was sure he had Crandall on his hook when the two men came to terms on a signing bonus exceeding $12 million.

But the job switch of the decade was not to be. Maurice Segall, the chairman of Zayre Corporation, who served as chairman of the compensation committee on American's board, proposed to bind Crandall to American with a set of golden handcuffs. Crandall was granted 355,000 shares of American stock, with a guarantee that if the share price fell below $33.20 the company would make up the difference in cash. It was, essentially, a put option worth a minimum of $11.8 million, but Crandall would become vested in the shares only at the rate of 12 percent a year. In order to receive the entire award, he would have to remain at American until January 1, 1996, when he would be 60 years old.

The counteroffer from American was less money, by Crandall's reckoning, than the bonus United had put on the table, but he accepted it anyway. "I thought very seriously about it," he would say of Olson's offer. "But I thought it would be very difficult to transfer my allegiance [from American]. I'd been here a long time."

Disappointed and eager to restore his full attention to Hertz, Olson threw the search for a new United chairman back into the lap of fellow board member Neil Armstrong. They would go the conventional route of using an executive-search consultant. But, really, how many candidates existed for the job of saving United from Bob Crandall?

Few executives in aviation had played a greater diversity of roles than Stephen Wolf. Fifteen years at American, followed by one at Pan Am—followed by a traumatic year under Frank Lorenzo as the president of Continental. Wolf always refused to discuss publicly his departure on the eve of Continental's Chapter 11 filing, other than to call the entire situation "very unusual," a phrase that he often used to describe something unpleasant. Wolf's silence about his forced ouster helped preserve his anti-Lorenzo aura, perpetuating the impression that he had resigned out of protest over Lorenzo's plans to ditch the union contracts. Wolf was lionized in labor circles, helping to launch him on a spectacular—and lucrative—career odyssey.

In early 1984 Wolf landed as president of Republic Airlines in Minneapolis, the 10th largest airline in the country and a failure waiting to happen. Formed by haphazardly stitching together three regional airlines after deregulation, Republic, amazingly, served more cities than any other airline in the United States. "An *unusual* route structure, to say the least," Wolf would comment. Republic's marketing innovations at one point, in 1982, included a free ticket in exchange for five box tops from Chex cereal. Its logo was a blue goose. More significantly its employees had not yet been put through the wringer of wage concessions. Wolf thought it would not look proper to be sucking a huge cash salary from so troubled a company, so instead he negotiated for options to buy 95,000 shares of Republic stock. Stock options by contrast were "tasteful," as he would later put it. Wolf determined to make something of Republic.

Wolf's ideas, and his sincere if aloof manner, went over well with employees. "I can't put my finger on it, but Wolf seemed to hit it off better with us than other Republic executives," one pilot official said. A trade magazine marveled at how in a time of such industry strife, "the employees of Republic appear to have welcomed him into their fold." With scarcely any of the turmoil afflicting other airlines, Wolf clinched the needed concessions by trading company stock for wage cuts.

Consumed, as he had been at Continental, with all things pertaining to appearance and design, Wolf laid to rest the blue goose logo and emblazoned the Republic name across his airplanes in letters more than a yard high. He redrew the route map, making Republic a powerhouse in hub cities where it faced only a single competitor. Analysts began recommending purchase of Republic's shares, from which everyone had once fled. The stock price soared, and with it the value of Wolf's options. Soon came Republic's first profits in five years, and then record profits and a still higher stock price—and then, in 1985, the United strike. Although American was the biggest winner overall from the United strike, no carrier reaped a greater windfall relative to its size than Republic. Its planes packed, its fares holding strong, Republic, though at the bottom of the airline industry's Top 10 list, recorded the second highest profits in the airline industry in 1985.

It was the perfect moment, Wolf decided, to get out. Such profits would never last. Republic would soon have to borrow tremendous sums to update its fleet. The labor agreements would also be expiring, and as Pan Am and others had discovered, the second round of labor-cost concessions could be even more traumatic than the first. Even with 17 million passengers a year, he considered Republic too small to survive in an industry in which the giants were still getting bigger.

It went without saying, of course, that selling Republic would give the stock price one last kick upward, and few shareholders would benefit from that kick more than Stephen M. Wolf, whose number of options had grown to nearly 163,000 shares. To the extent that anyone cared, which was not much at this point, Wolf would also look better cashing out along with all the shareholders of the company, including the employees for whom he had arranged grants of stock.

The potential buyer to whom Wolf turned was an obvious choice: the crosstown rival, Northwest Airlines, which competed head-to-head with Republic.

Northwest, long the industry's most conservatively managed and financially successful company, was then headed by a 38-year-old bodybuilder and Vietnam veteran named Steven G. Rothmeier. Rothmeier was no more famous for personal warmth than Wolf; running a couple of the largest airlines in America from the same city, the two men had never met. One evening they agreed to talk over dinner at a family steak house in St. Paul.

Wolf was so intent on selling Republic that he met with junk-bond impresario Michael Milken to plan a hostile takeover of Northwest, should it prove necessary to provoke Northwest into making a defensive acquisition. But Rothmeier, it turned out, was actively searching for a way to secure more passenger feed within the United States for Northwest's vital routes over the Pacific, where United had lately become a powerful new competitor. Republic, Rothmeier recognized, was the perfect acquisition candidate. A meeting of the minds had occurred before the two men had ordered their steaks.

Northwest paid nearly $1 billion for Republic. The price per share was $17, for a stock that Wolf had options to buy for as little as $3.75. In the end the boy who started his transportation career on the loading docks of Oakland walked away from Republic with $2 million in option profits and $1 million in severance.

The other Steve, Steve Rothmeier, was not so fortunate. Once Wolf had departed the scene, Rothmeier was left to put together 14 union groups, two incompatible fleets, and two vastly different cultures. Republic's flight attendants, accustomed to the freer spirit of a smaller airline, bristled at a dress code requiring high heels and "acceptable" earrings only. Some protested by wearing their lapel wings upside down. Republic employees came into the merger already having made deep wage concessions for Wolf; even though they had been paid in stock for these concessions, they resented making less than their counterparts from Northwest. The former Republic pilots launched a work slowdown, posting signs that said, "Zero pay increase, zero airspeed." Northwest's in-house Sperry computer system gave the cold shoulder to Republic's IBM system.

Northwest's operations began to break down. "The results of the discontent are pushing us dangerously close to self-destruction," a middle manager wrote in a memo.

Shortly after Republic was gone, Wolf found himself eating a lunch of organically grown tomatoes at a health ranch in Arizona with Saul Steinberg, a wealthy (and portly) New York investor and takeover maven. Steinberg controlled Tiger International, which owned the Flying Tiger Line, an all-cargo airline famous in its day for introducing the nation to year-round fruits from California and for transporting Roy Rogers's Trigger and other famous animals. Its slogan was "Anything, Anytime, Anywhere." In 1977, a year before adoption of the Deregulation Act, Phil Bakes and his associates conducted a kind of legislative dress rehearsal by pushing through a bill that deregulated air cargo only. This move opened the way for Federal Express, UPS, and other freight forwarders to buy their own airplanes, which proved disastrous for Tiger's business. Compounding its financial problems, Tiger had an unusually generous pilot contract. Steinberg's investment in the company was withering. Would Wolf, he asked, try his magic hand?

Wolf anguished over the consequences of attempting a turnaround and failing, balanced against the triumph of pulling off a long shot. Ultimately he accepted an offer from Steinberg, once again with a massive award of stock options.

His reputation with labor still very much intact, Wolf entered his first meeting with the Tiger pilot leadership and was surprised to see the men stand and remove their jackets: they were all dressed in red suspenders, the Wolf sartorial trademark. The real moment of truth came after midnight a few months later, in November 1986, when Wolf met with union leaders in a hotel near LAX and warned them that unless the pilots renounced 30 percent of their wages, the company would simply be liquidated. In the wee hours, after caucusing, the pilots declined.

At that moment Wolf stunned everyone in the room by pushing

himself away from the table, leaping to his feet, and shouting, "It's over!"

He turned to the company's general counsel, Lawrence M. Nagin. "Larry," he said, "we're going. It's over, it's over, it's *over*." And they walked out the door—so far as the pilots could tell, in order to commence the liquidation of Tiger International. The next day another union chieftain called to entreat Wolf into further bargaining. "It's over," Wolf responded, "it's over, it's *over*." When the union's international leaders called from Washington, they got the same message.

Days later the pilots signed a contract on Wolf's terms. They too received some stock in exchange for their concessions.

Wolf gave the Tiger fleet a fresh new design and decided that it was time to sell this company as well. Federal Express came in as the buyer. But before he even had the opportunity to cash in his options, Wolf found himself under pressure to decide on another job offer, this one from United Airlines.

It might have dismayed Wolf to know that he was the third person contacted for the United job and, above all, that he had been approached behind his old boss, Bob Crandall. But Wolf had the enthusiastic backing of Neil Armstrong, the search committee chairman. Wolf would have to walk away from a fabulous fortune in Tiger options to accept the position with United, but Armstrong resolved the matter by awarding Wolf options on 250,000 United shares. That meant that every $4 price increase would put another $1 million in Stephen Wolf's pockets, and, with the stock having traded at more than $100 a share, such a price change was not uncommon.

For a boy who grew up poor, Wolf acclimated himself easily to the badges of fortune. He purchased a sprawling apartment on the 63rd floor of a skyscraper towering over Chicago's North Michigan Avenue, just as Wolf himself towered over all who stood near him. He outfitted the residence with antiques juxtaposed with ultramodern decorator touches: stark white walls, a cantilevered staircase, and window blinds that could be raised and lowered at the touch of a button. But the dominant feature was the view, through windows some 20 feet high: Lake Michigan to the east, the Sears Tower to the south. Wolf could watch air shows along the shore of Lake Michigan by glancing downward at the aerial acrobatics.

The move to Chicago also occasioned a change in Wolf's marital status. He and his girlfriend, Delores Wallace, had maintained their relationship after Wolf had left American Airlines seven years earlier, in 1981. Wallace had remained at American, where she had risen from flight attendant instructor to membership in Crandall's inner circle as the vice president of personnel resources. Crandall, for all his ruthlessness as a taskmaster, was perhaps the best boss in the airline industry for female executives; a number had attained top positions in Crandall's organization. If Crandall harbored any of the sexist bias so prevalent in the airline industry, it was snuffed out by his obsession with performance. Crandall had tolerated Wallace's romance when Wolf was at Republic and Tiger, but United was a different story. "If Stephen ends up at United," Crandall warned her, "we've got a problem here."

So once Wolf had accepted the United offer, Delores Wallace quit American, quit Bob Crandall, and walked away from one of the highest positions ever attained by a woman in commercial aviation. She married Wolf and threw herself into studying French. She and Wolf loved France and everything about it. They visited regularly. Wolf loved French cooking and wines, especially Burgundies.

United, unfortunately, did not fly to Paris, nor anywhere near Europe. United's new code-sharing deal with British Airways would feed transatlantic passengers into United's domestic flights, but that was a poor substitute for United's flying to Europe itself.

Wolf saw four compelling business reasons for United to alter its strategy. The U.S. market, as most carriers realized, was reaching maturity. Second, Europe was a place where labor costs made U.S. carriers competitive: United was paying coolie wages compared with Lufthansa and Air France and other state-subsidized European carriers. Third, adding another continent to United's portfolio diversified its geographic risk. (Latin America, another continent outside the United route map, looked attractive to Wolf for the same reason. In fact Wolf had recently paid a courtesy call on President Carlos Salinas de Gortari in Mexico City.)

Finally, Wolf could see that the long-standing U.S. carriers to Europe—Pan Am and TWA—were on the ropes. Either could fail. As unthinkable as it might seem, *both* could fail, and if so, Bob Crandall would undoubtedly push American Airlines into the vacuum.

Thus, from the moment he was introduced to Sir Colin Marshall, Wolf took pains to point out that United's code-sharing deal with British Airways was a legacy of the previous management. "I want to keep our arrangement in place," Wolf said, "but you specifically need to know that if I can ever find a way for United to fly to London, I will." Marshall had no problem with that. He was sure that any such service by United would be small. If British Airways ever had to compete directly with United over the Atlantic, he thought, it would be on only one or two routes.

As Wolf was uprooting himself to Chicago, he flew frequently on a United flight regularly staffed by Bobbie Pilkington, an official of the Association of Flight Attendants. Wolf, she would comment, was as delightful as passengers came, until the briefcase was unsnapped. "It was the most bizarre thing. Everything about his countenance changes when he gets involved with his work. He gets cold, hard. His color changes. Everything about that man changes. He goes to gunmetal gray steel." Wolf, thrown as an adolescent into full-time work to support a family, had never learned how *not* to work.

Plainly, though, Wolf's challenges—and opportunities—provided plenty of motivation. Overtaken in 1988 as the nation's largest airline, United needed airplanes badly, but it remained a deeply troubled company with disaffected employees and pilot salaries that were out of line with the rest of the industry. "It was," as he later put it, "unusual, if not strange." Reversing those problems could make Wolf not only a fabulously wealthy man but a celebrity besides. He could become, as *The Wall Street Journal* said, the "Iacocca of the Airways."

Wolf had walked into United expecting at least the recognition by United's pilots that he was a bona fide "airline guy," not a "car guy" as Olson was or a "hotel guy" such as Ferris. But even if he was the kind of chairman they had been clamoring for—indeed, *because* he was that kind of chairman—the leaders of the pilots' union were fretful over Wolf's arrival. The pilots' leadership, still infatuated with the idea of taking over United, were not eager to see their members co-opted by a new CEO with a sterling image. The ALPA leaders in Chicago told the top union brass in Washington that they intended to cast Wolf as the bad guy. Although some of the headquarters people were troubled by this, they were powerless under the ALPA constitution to interfere.

The tar and feathers were waiting when Wolf, shortly after assuming the United job, traveled to Hawaii to make a presentation to the United pilot leaders. This time the pilots were not waiting in red suspenders. Wolf stepped to the front of the room and took the microphone. As he began to speak, he found that the microphone cord seemed to be stuck on something. He looked down. The cord disappeared under a curtain. Wolf tried to jerk it loose, but it remained stuck. The cord, it appeared, had been fastened to the floor! Wolf, all six foot six of him, went through his presentation fussing with the cord and stooping at the waist, humiliated, deprived of the stature that he had always used so effectively in trying to win the support of his adversaries.

Wolf told the United pilots that he wanted to make the airline grow, that he wanted to swell the fleet—but that he first wanted to cut still further United's costs. This gave the pilot leadership all the ammunition it needed in the character assassination campaign that followed. Anti-Wolf stickers were passed into cockpits. Because it was not specifically accounted for in their contract, pilots refused to fly two newly delivered Boeing 747s in the 400 series, the newest and best jumbo jet model ever built; the cost to United of leaving the two planes on the ground totaled $200,000 a day. Taking a page from the Max Safety playbook at Eastern Air Lines, the United pilots adopted a strategy they called "Sweet Sixteen"—delaying one minute past the 15-minute grace period that the government gave the airlines before counting any flight as late. In one month only 62 percent of United's flights were scored as on time, a shockingly poor showing at a time when passengers were closely comparing the percentages. The pilots also insisted on topping off their fuel tanks, weighing down their vessels so that they consumed more fuel.

Then, a curious thing happened. While publicly pillorying Wolf, the pilots actually invited him to join them in their effort to mount an employee takeover. His involvement would clearly lend respectability to the marginal prospects for such a monumental takeover. Wolf considered himself something of a pioneer in the whole area of employee ownership in the airline industry (although he, like others, often failed to appreciate that Southwest had initiated the trend), but he wanted no part of a buyout. He did not want to load up the balance sheet with debt; he wanted to buy airplanes and make United grow. He wanted to launch United into Europe and Latin America. He wanted to match and beat back the thrusts and parries of Bob Crandall.

Wolf wanted nothing to do with the employee takeover scheme.

In the spring of 1989 the airline industry was transfixed by a new drama seizing Northwest Airlines, a drama that would ultimately reach the stage at United.

After buying Republic from Wolf, Northwest's internal strife and service had plunged to the same cataclysmic lows that followed the National–Pan Am merger and the union of BOAC and British European Airlines. In one month only 25 percent of Northwest's flights were on time. Marvin Davis, a 300-pound Beverly Hills billionaire and an airline deal waiting to happen, was suddenly on the scene. "When I was a boy, I liked to play with toys," he would later tell an ALPA official. "I still like toys. They've just gotten more expensive." Davis offered to buy Northwest for $2.7 billion.

Another bidder for Northwest soon emerged, however—a partnership of three wealthy investors who had once worked together at Marriott Corporation. The Marriott men had backing from KLM Royal Dutch Airlines, which was eager to become the second foreign airline to buy into a U.S. carrier (following SAS's move into Continental). Supplementing KLM's money with funds borrowed in Japan, the Marriott men were able to outbid Marvin Davis handily.

The last had not been heard of Marvin Davis, however. The Northwest siege was barely concluded when he offered $5.4 billion for United Airlines. United shares climbed $46 in a single day—and with them the net worth of Stephen Wolf. A takeover of United that gave all shareholders that chance to cash out would put $42 million into Wolf's pockets!

The United board gathered in Elk Grove Village, the portraits of United's five previous chairmen looking down from the dark rosewood walls. "The board has concluded Davis will be successful," director John McGillicuddy said at one point. "If this is going to happen, Steve, would you consider joining forces with the employees in a bid for the company?"

Wolf turned the question over in his head. He knew that if a raider took over the company, he could hand over the keys and walk away wealthier than he had ever dreamed possible. On the other hand, if Wolf became part of an insider group taking over the company, he would keep his job *and* he would get his $42 million in stock proceeds—a happy combination of events, to be sure. But in that case Wolf would be seen handing $42 million of the company's money to himself. It wouldn't *look* good. People, he thought, would consider him a "greedy son of a bitch." He told himself, "There is not an inch of upside here."

"This is a very serious decision for me because I have a very large stock option," he told the directors.

And yet what of the airline? What of the employees? If Marvin Davis took it over, he would doubtless extract wage concessions to help pay for the deal. If the employees took it over, they would have to make concessions in that case as well—there was no doubt about that—but at least they would receive an ownership interest in exchange. Wolf agreed to join forces with the pilots, and to begin recruiting other employee groups to the plan.

The orders hurriedly went out to ALPA members across the United system: remove all the anti-Wolf buttons and stickers from the cockpits and locker rooms. "We must now demonstrate that employee ownership means cooperation and employee-management peace," a union official explained. The flight attendants were invited into the ownership group, the price of admission being a 10 percent cut in their pay. They told Wolf and the pilots to get lost. The machinists, unalterably opposed to the deal because it would so severely leverage the company, played the spoiler at every chance—through lawsuits, lobbying, and repeated threats of a strike. Brian Freeman, a witty and acerbic consultant to the machinists, said that no one should be fooled into thinking that this was the pilots taking over United Airlines. It's "just a Wolf in pilots' clothing," he said. Wolf and the pilots had to better Marvin Davis's terms, of course, if they hoped to win the company; the price they offered was $300 a share— which, by happenstance, raised Steve Wolf's take as a shareholder to $54 million.

To buy a company for something like $7 billion, the employees would need a partner with deep pockets. Wolf knew just whom to call: Colin Marshall of British Airways. The two men had grown closer, despite Wolf's warnings that United would someday seek to invade British Air's territory in Europe. Marshall had arranged for the British Airways board to host the United board in London, wining and dining Wolf and his fellow directors. Wolf was planning to reciprocate the gesture by having the British Airways directors to dinner in his chic 63rd-floor apartment.

Marshall wanted a piece of the U.S. airline industry more urgently than ever—and something stronger than joint marketing arrangements and code sharing. He told Wolf to count British Airways in, for $750 million.

Since 1926 U.S. law had restricted the voting control of foreign interests in a U.S. carrier to 25 percent. Therefore, Wolf's group said, British Airways would receive only 15 percent voting control, safely within the statutory limits. This figure, however, significantly understated the financial influence that British Airways would wield in the newly constituted company. It was the twilight of the eighties, and the deal was practically all debt. The would-be buyers of United— Wolf, his fellow top executives, the legions of pilots, plus British Airways—were putting up a mere $1 billion in cash in a deal worth almost $7 billion. Anyone could see that British Air's $750 million represented 75 percent of the equity. With voting control or not, British Airways was all but proposing to make a wholly owned subsidiary of United Airlines.

When the documents for the takeover were released publicly, there in black and white was the shocking truth of the monumental fortune that Wolf had riding on completion of the deal. Wolf knew in advance that the publicity would be ugly, but as he later put it, "I underestimated by 4,000 percent how unpleasant it would be." The facts were no different than if Marvin Davis were taking over the company, he thought; the value of his stock options was the same either way. Wolf kept telling himself that he was simply acting as the front man in a deal that enabled the pilots to walk away with a voice in United's affairs—a greater voice, for sure, than Davis would offer them. But the media, Wolf was mortified to conclude, were more interested in the "greedy son of a bitch."

On September 14, 1989, a Thursday, the United board gave its final approval to the takeover by Stephen Wolf and the pilots of United, with British Airways acting as Daddy Warbucks. On Friday

Marvin Davis withdrew his offer. All that remained was to nail down the financing.

The following week in Washington, Transportation Secretary Sam Skinner sat down for breakfast with Al Checchi, one of the former Marriott people now putting the finishing touches on the takeover of Northwest. Skinner was suddenly saying that he had a problem with one important aspect of the deal. The voting interest of KLM Royal Dutch Airlines in Northwest was to total only 5 percent, well within the statutory guideline, but there was a second test of control, Skinner noted, not a statutory limitation, but a policy of long standing that allowed foreign airlines to hold no more than 49 percent of the equity of a U.S. carrier. By this test the debt-ridden Northwest takeover failed, because KLM was providing $400 million of the $700 million in equity. Their entire deal at stake, the former Marriott executives readily agreed to restructure the terms of the investment by KLM. But all eyes quickly turned to Elk Grove Village, Illinois, where British Airways was preparing to provide *three quarters* of the equity necessary to bring off Stephen Wolf's takeover of United. Fears quickly spread that the United States government would scuttle the deal.

About then a top official of the machinists' union was talking to an official of Mitsubishi Bank when he happened to mention that the machinists would begin contract talks with United the following month. Regardless of who owned the company, the union man said, the machinists wanted a big pay increase and they were going to get one. . . .

At about the same time an official in Japan's ministry of finance was publicly expressing the first doubts raised in Tokyo about all that Japanese money feeding America's LBO craze. . . .

And the bankers who were expected to finance the takeover began studying the breathtaking personal profits that Wolf stood to gain—money, they realized, that they would be indirectly providing. . . .

And USAir announced that it was expecting lower earnings, causing people to wonder how United could justify its rosy financial projections. . . .

And soon, one by one, the banks were saying no thanks. The employee takeover of United was dead.

It was as if the door had slammed shut on the 1980s. On Friday the 13th of October, 1989, as word spread that for the first time in the LBO era a big deal was falling apart for lack of financing, the Dow Jones Industrial Average plummeted 190 points in less than two hours.

Sir Colin Marshall had not been warned about the imminent collapse of the deal. Stunned, he quickly washed his hands of the entire mess. Within so cautious and distinguished a company as British Airways, it mattered urgently to some people just who was to blame for the company's embarrassment. In particular the PR people who worked for Lord King, still the titular head of British Airways, were intent on protecting their boss from the tarnish. Word went out to the British press on a hush-hush basis: This was Colin's deal.

But no one's reputation suffered as much Stephen Wolf's. His credibility with employees lay in ruins. He had allowed himself to be diverted from his real job. Wolf resolved to recover—to restore his reputation and put the nightmare behind him. Although the pilots were already investigating how to resuscitate their deal yet again, Wolf tried to snap everyone's attention back to the airline itself—the need to improve quality, the need to grow. There were planes to order, destinations beckoning around the globe. He was planning a new color scheme for United's fleet.

And on so many fronts, there was a war to fight with Bob Crandall.

Almost from the minute Wolf had walked into the executive suite at United, the people around him, and around Bob Crandall at American, began to look on the competition of the companies as a battle of two chief executives, a battle on the order of Godzilla versus the Thing. Both men would forever deny any personal motivations in their corporate warfare, yet both would consistently take actions and make comments in the presence of others that betrayed an intense personal rivalry. Although the competition lacked the emotional intensity of the Lorenzo-Burr dispute, it *was* tinged with personal history. Wolf's career had hit dead calm at American, so he quit, and his career had thereafter blossomed. Crandall privately expressed annoyance and a touch of jealousy at the wealth Wolf was in line to accumulate at United. Although Crandall had shaken loose a bonus worth at least $12 million after turning down United's job offer,

Wolf, having accepted that offer, was now in a position to profit by that much in a good week—assuming another graceful opportunity presented itself for him to begin cashing in his options. Wolf, moreover, was not the only American Airlines exile working at United headquarters; Jack Pope, long Crandall's top finance man, had also recently quit American to go to work for United.

"Need I remind you," Crandall told a group of his managers at one point,

> there are several former AA employees sitting up there in Elk Grove Village, Illinois, making a lot of noise? Just last week the big guy up there was quoted as saying, "Quality comes first. Growth will follow." Now, where do you suppose he got *that*? He was reading the inscription on *our* trophy! Our job is to make sure that's as close as he ever gets.

The fight raged on many fronts, from 1989 through 1991. United laid out $72 million to buy Air Wisconsin, a large feeder airline at O'Hare, principally as a way of scooping up more landing slots in the market-share battle with American. It was a perfectly straightforward transaction; United simply happened to beat American to the prize. But Crandall sought to reverse the deal in the federal courts, mounting every imaginative antitrust claim he could muster. United finally agreed to part with a dozen of the Air Wisconsin slots, although in the bargaining Crandall agreed to pay nearly $3 million for each. It was all part of a pattern of singling out United for harsh treatment, Wolf believed. "Very unusual corporate behavior," he would call it.

Wolf took his own steps to keep the authorities abreast of Crandall's mischief. Wolf had made a point of getting to know Sam Skinner, who before becoming transportation secretary was a well-known lawyer in United's hometown of Chicago. Skinner was widely thought to have political ambitions in Illinois, and it went without saying that the support of one of the state's biggest employers would be of no small value. Wolf and Skinner had become pen pals of a sort—"Dear Sam," "Dear Steve"—to the point that Wolf felt comfortable sending the transportation secretary the text he had obtained of a Wings Club speech given by Crandall. In the speech Crandall derided political leaders for mishandling international aviation negotiations and accused Skinner's agency of suffering from a "leadership problem" and "diplomatic dithering." Wolf transmitted the speech to Washington with a cover letter that noted, "Bashing of this type is simply not constructive." Skinner answered with a friendly thank-you.

But nothing compared with the battle royal over one of the great questions of U.S. aviation policy in the early 1990s: which of the two airlines, American or United, should win the authority to fly between Chicago and Tokyo?

For years only a single U.S. carrier, Northwest, had enjoyed the privilege of carrying passengers between the two great cities, but a new round of multilateral bargaining had opened up the route to a second carrier of the U.S. government's choosing. With Wolf and Crandall battling for every last passenger at O'Hare, the Tokyo route would become a vital source of passenger feed—at full-fare and first-class prices to boot. The route was worth an estimated $300 million a year in business. The profit margin was projected at 18 percent, the kind of return available in the cosmetics business maybe, but nowhere else in aviation.

It was a battle destined for decision as much on influence as on economics. United won the support of Chicago Mayor Richard Daley and Illinois Governor James Thompson, leading Crandall to accuse the company of playing political games. American meanwhile was conducting a massive local advertising campaign—"American means business in Chicago"—on which it was rumored to be spending some $6 million in the first half of 1990.

In the end United won, a decision that Crandall took so bitterly that he personally fired the Washington representative who had been handling the lobbying. Of all the government decisions that ever went against American, Crandall would say, "the worst screwing we got was Chicago–Tokyo."

By 1990 Stephen Wolf and Bob Crandall were each separately convinced that they had very little time left to align their companies as "global megacarriers" for the next century. They feared that Europe, never particularly welcoming to the Americans, would slam shut by the end of 1992, when the European Community would be fully constituted. Crandall and no less Wolf were especially keen to stake a major claim in the vital gateway of London. American's existing flights mostly flew over London to the heartland of Europe, while United still had only the data-processing artifice of service to London through its code-sharing relationship with British Airways.

Domestic political uncertainty intensified the pressure to act quickly. President Bush had largely maintained the hands-off antitrust policy of the Reagan years, but as Crandall aide Bob Baker would explain, "There was a sense that if we wanted to get some of this shit, we'd better get it while we could, we'd better not do this too many times or the government's going to shut us down. The fact is we're getting bigger and bigger and United is getting bigger and bigger and the smaller carriers are falling by the wayside, and the music would stop soon."

As eagerly as the two rivals wanted to act, their opportunities were limited. Whether "diplomatic dithering" played a role or not, opening up new overseas routes was an agonizingly slow process. And there were precious few airlines left to be taken over—except, most notably, Pan Am, still out there with a For Sale sign hanging around its corporate neck.

Crandall and Wolf looked covetously at Pan Am, now in the hands of Tom Plaskett. The three of them, all once colleagues in the marketing operation at American Airlines, were now aligned in a triangle, each with an eye on the other two. The standoff would be readily resolved if only Wolf or Crandall would move to seize Pan Am. But there would be no frontal attacks, no bidding wars. For as eagerly as Plaskett wanted to sell and Wolf and Crandall wanted to buy, a vast chasm of strategy and expectation existed in the middle of that triangle. Would Pan Am, one of the greatest names in the history of commerce, survive as an affiliate of a rescuer? Or would it, like Eastern, be shredded, with its people, to pieces?

CHAPTER 18

LONDON CALLING

Chicago has the world's busiest airport, Dallas the biggest, Denver the newest. But in the world of international flight, none of them comes close to matching the importance of Heathrow Airport in London.

Much more than an airport, Heathrow is a crossroads that links the Middle East with North America, Africa with South America, Europe with Asia and every other continent. Heathrow is to the planet Earth what Chicago, Dallas, or Denver is to the United States. In terms of handling international passengers, no U.S. airport—not JFK, Dulles, or O'Hare—ranks even in the world's Top 10. But the whole world changes planes at Heathrow.

Along with being vital, Heathrow is inaccessible.

Like the New York airports, Heathrow has long been governed by slots, every last one of them long ago spoken for. Europe is a crazy quilt of air traffic control; a flight to Heathrow from Athens, say, may encroach on the sovereign airspace of Albania, Bosnia, Italy, Liechtenstein, Germany, France, Belgium, the United Kingdom, and possibly a few others, including NATO, depending on the route. European air traffic control is a tower of Babel involving 55 control centers, 18 varieties of computer hardware, nearly two dozen operating systems, and something like 70 programming languages. No one, therefore, can be positive when an inbound flight from the continent might reach Heathrow. In determining how many takeoffs and landings can be permitted and at what times of day, Her Majesty's Government and the slot planners must allow for any number of flights arriving at nowhere near the correct time. Landing capacity also has to take account of the unpredictable London fog.

On top of everything else, Heathrow is hemmed in by the suburban sprawl of London. There are two runways at Heathrow. In the interest of diluting the noise over the surrounding communities, the authorities restrict one runway to departures and the other to arrivals, instead of allowing each to handle both.

Heathrow is a closed shop, and that fact alone has helped to solidify British Air's position as the self-proclaimed "world's favourite airline." That Heathrow is British Airways territory is evident to anyone driving through the main entrance, where a giant scale model of the supersonic Concorde, painted in the colors of British Airways, is on display. As a result of takeovers, mergers, government grants, and the company's influence with the British Airports Authority, British Airways controls about 38 percent of the slots at Heathrow, while the remaining airlines of the world each have trifling operations in comparison. British Airways also enjoys the finest indoor quarters in the airport; it received its own sprawling new terminal in the late 1980s. The new facility, Terminal Four, is trimmed in British Air's colors, with dozens of huge screens identifying the check-in points for the world's most exotic destinations. Check-in service is supreme: a bank of video cameras monitors the queues by destination, with computers guaranteeing the most efficient deployment of check-in personnel.

The sinecure of British Airways at Heathrow was assured for perpetuity in 1977, when the government declared that no newcomer would be allowed to land there. Pan Am and TWA were grandfathered at Heathrow, but all latecomers—Braniff, Delta, People Express, and eventually American Airlines—were forced to land at the newer and much less convenient Gatwick Airport. Not that the British discriminated against foreign airlines alone: the Briton Freddie Laker's SkyTrain service to Newark was in its time also banished to Gatwick. Gatwick was fine for shuttling low-fare tourists between the United States and the United Kingdom, but no full-fare business traveler was eager to spend six hours on a flight to England only to endure an interminable cab ride, much less a bus trip, upon arrival. Airlines flying to Gatwick were also disadvantaged because they received only a small part of the traffic bound for the Continent or elsewhere: oil sheiks could not fly nonstop to Abu Dhabi through Gatwick; finance ministers could not reach Nairobi. Heathrow, not Gatwick, was the turnstile through which passed the richest and most important travelers in the world.

In a fateful step in 1980 the United States, at the behest of Sen. Edward Kennedy and House Speaker Thomas "Tip" O'Neill, demanded some amendments to the treaty known as Bermuda II in order to allow Pan Am to fly from Boston to Heathrow. Britain agreed, though at a price: the United States had to agree that only two U.S. airlines could ever serve Heathrow at the same time, even if space became available for more. If not Pan Am or TWA, the amendment read, only their "corporate successors" could land at Heathrow—whatever that meant.

Los Conquistadores del Cielo—what a bizarre organization it was. The top executives of commercial aviation, only a few dozen in number, competed to the point of annihilation 51 weeks a year and then spent the week after Labor Day together on a spread of more than 15,000 acres in Wyoming called the A Bar A Ranch. They would turn out in cowboy hats and boots—Stephen Wolf in an elegant knitted sweater, perhaps, and Bob Crandall in a leather vest and bolo tie. They would feast on prime rib, buffalo burgers, trout pâté, and bacon smoked on applewood. Their poker stakes regularly surpassed $10,000. Though city slickers all, they would throw themselves into fast-draw competitions, trapshooting, fly fishing, and horseback riding. The tradition of the games included a race on horseback in which the contestants stopped at the halfway point to pull on pink frocks; as the aviation men galloped to the finish line, their dresses waved in the wind.

Although a welcome diversion, the 1990 gathering was clouded by a new and tremendous stress: the imminence of war in the Persian Gulf. One month earlier Iraq's lightning-quick invasion of Kuwait had thrown the global airline industry into a hard depression, devastating the airlines as no event had since the firing of the air traffic controllers nine years earlier. The price of oil, after mercifully plunging from the heights of the early 1980s, once again spiked upward. The greatest military buildup since World War II—the allied operation known as Desert Shield—reactivated thousands of reserve pilots, pulling them from the cockpits of their commercial airliners. Civilian U.S. aircraft were also diverted to the Persian Gulf. American Airlines conducted so much flying for the U.S. government that the pilots' union attempted to negotiate a special set of work rules, provoking a bitter labor-management conflagration and accusations of a lack of patriotism. After its most sustained period of profitability since deregulation, the U.S. airline industry was bathed in red ink.

Unlike the controllers' strike, the invasion of Kuwait and the military escalation that followed afflicted airlines outside the United States as well. The European airlines suffered disproportionately due to their proximity to the terrorist threat, and in this respect Pan Am might as well have been a European airline; whatever small recovery Pan Am had mounted after the bombing of Flight 103 was wiped out by the new hostilities in the Gulf. Chairman Tom Plaskett considered putting Pan Am into bankruptcy, but that was thinking the unthinkable; instead he would press on in the search for a rescuer, and the Conquistadores meeting, he knew, would be an excellent place to look.

One evening after everyone had reached the A Bar A Ranch, Plaskett approached Stephen Wolf. It was an ironic occasion for Plaskett. A decade earlier Plaskett had been two steps above Wolf in the marketing department at American Airlines. Plaskett would never forget the elaborately detailed presentation that Wolf made putting forward his case for a promotion and a raise. Plaskett had told Wolf he was not yet ready for the promotion, and before long Wolf had quit American. (Plaskett and Wolf also shared the experience of having each served less than one year as the president of Continental under Frank Lorenzo.)

Plaskett told Wolf he was eager to hear an acquisition proposal from United, and was encouraged when Wolf agreed to give the matter some thought overnight. Wolf, of course, was as eager as ever to put United into Europe, but not at the cost of swallowing Pan Am and all its problems.

The next morning, as the breakfast dishes were being cleared, the two men sat down over coffee in the rustic mess hall at the ranch. Wolf had scratched out a cryptic proposal on a single sheet of paper, with the words "United" and "Pan Am" evident nowhere. The paper listed two Pan Am routes to London: one from Los Angeles, one from San Francisco, and the figure $75 million. Plaskett was crestfallen. Pan Am was dying by the day. What Wolf was proposing was a Band-Aid, a palliative, not a cure. Plaskett went back to New York to resume the task of fighting off Pan Am's creditors.

Within days, however, Plaskett sensed an opportunity to make another approach. Wolf unveiled the largest airplane order in history— $22 billion—making United the U.S. launch customer for the new Boeing 777. Looking on from Pan Am, it was evident to Plaskett that Wolf was trying to stage a series of blockbuster announcements to snap United back from the distraction of the employee takeover. Perhaps, Plaskett thought, a merger with Pan Am could become part of the new momentum.

This time Plaskett decided to resort to the tease. He would entice Wolf by offering to sell just a piece of Pan Am—the airline equivalent of an ankle, perhaps, or some cleavage. Then, once it had a few hundred million dollars of life-saving cash in hand, Pan Am would have the time to coax United into going all the way.

But what enticement to use? The Pacific was long since gone, to United, in fact. The Latin American routes were a possibility; United was under pressure to make a big move there now that American was operating the Eastern routes in the region. But Latin America alone would not provide Pan Am with the cash it needed to survive in the short term. That left London.

The delicacy of aviation relations between the United States and Britain had turned Pan Am's routes to London into a seemingly priceless asset. The amendments to the Bermuda II treaty, after all, restricted Heathrow to Pan Am and TWA, or to their "corporate successors." Pan Am, in other words, could not sell half or any fraction of its operation at Heathrow to anyone. Doing so would introduce a forbidden third U.S. carrier into Heathrow. Selling the operation in London was an all-or-nothing proposition.

Wolf had only to hear Plaskett say "Heathrow" to grasp the significance of the overture. Wolf had just begun attempting to pick his way into Europe on the usual tedious, route-by-route basis. If he came to terms with Plaskett, in just this one transaction United would win the right to land at Heathrow from five U.S. gateways (New York, Washington, Los Angeles, San Francisco, and Seattle). Overnight United would control 15 percent of the entire transatlantic airline passenger market, three times the share that Bob Crandall had established for American after nearly a decade of painstaking effort.

The deal would also give United the rare and in some cases valuable authorities that Pan Am in the Trippe era had won beyond Heathrow to Europe—to Amsterdam, Berlin, Brussels, Hamburg, Helsinki, and Munich. And quite apart from London, Plaskett was willing to toss in a route from Washington to Wolf's beloved Paris. It would be the same kind of bold stroke by which Wolf's predecessor, Dick Ferris, had propelled United into the Pacific five years earlier, in 1985 (also by cleaving routes from Pan Am). It was the kind of breakthrough that could get United moving again.

The message was by no means wasted on Wolf when Plaskett said he wanted to consider any deal for Heathrow only the first step toward a possible takeover of the whole enchilada—or more aptly the whole Blue Meatball, as Pan Am, with its big blue logo, had long been known. "That's interesting," Wolf answered. "I'll get back to you."

As urgently as he wanted to buy Heathrow, Wolf from the git-go had absolutely no interest in eating the entire Blue Meatball. Wolf knew Pan Am well; he had served there a decade earlier, under Ed Acker, and he knew that Pan Am's problems had only worsened. When companies cut back, Wolf thought, they lose both their youth and their best, most seasoned people. Everyone left behind had been through a decade of hell with the company. There was no way Wolf was going to put United through that kind of merger, particularly after all that United had been through. Wolf would prod Plaskett into closure on the Heathrow deal and that alone.

The companies came to terms at $400 million. Plaskett, almost everyone in the industry thought, had given Heathrow away. The U.S. government's pension watchdogs, who had an interest in any large movements of cash or assets out of Pan Am, even argued that the U.S. taxpayer had an interest in a higher price. Plaskett was undeterred. The world failed to appreciate the hidden value in the

deal—an implicit promise that Stephen Wolf would at least attempt
to come to terms on the purchase of Pan Am in its entirety and the
rescue of all its jobs. Plaskett remained unaware that Wolf had already made up his mind to the contrary.

Crandall was apoplectic that Wolf had stolen the march into
Heathrow, but he made a quick recovery. There was a second Amer-
ican company with precious landing rights at Heathrow. It was
TWA, and TWA was in nearly as sorry a condition as Pan Am.

In the rarefied atmosphere of the race to London, Carl Icahn of
TWA could force Crandall to pay top dollar. For six routes to
Heathrow Crandall forked over $445 million; Wolf had paid less for
more from Pan Am. Icahn, for additional millions, agreed to throw
in 40 slots at O'Hare. With this purchase Crandall scored a double,
because many of those slots had been on lease from TWA to United.

In the megacarrier race United was the runaway leader over the
Pacific, although American certainly had designs there. American
was the leader in Latin America, although United likewise was moving to follow. Over the Atlantic they were in a close heat—so long as
their respective purchases closed as planned. But the lineup at
Heathrow was about to change in another way, and the politics were
huge.

Nearly seven years earlier, at the height of the clamor to reserve seats
on People Express, one of the frustrated people at the other end of
the busy signal was Richard Branson, calling from his houseboat in
London. Branson was a recording industry executive who made fre-
quent trips to the United States. After Pan Am had put his fellow
Briton Freddie Laker out of business, Branson was eager to see how
People Express was performing on the same route, from Newark to
Gatwick.

At just 34 years old Branson in 1984 was one of Britain's most
successful entrepreneurs ever, undoubtedly the most successful of his
time. In the midst of the ferocious student insurgencies that swept
the public schools of England in the 1960s, Branson published a
magazine called *Student,* which he built with articles from leading
leftists and promoted to advertisers with an irresistible sales pitch:
"I'm Richard Branson, I'm eighteen, and I run a magazine that's

doing something really useful for young people." In an early display of a lifelong tendency, he sued Beatle John Lennon, claiming that Lennon's agent had reneged on a promise to provide an exclusive recording that Branson had intended to publish as a "flexidisc" in the magazine.

Student was financially overextended, and when it fell on hard times, Branson generated cash by launching a mail-order record business he called Virgin Music, a name meant to convey his utter unfamiliarity with the field. Among other mischief, he was fined and spent a night in jail for smuggling records into the country to evade import duties.

The profits were scant in the mail-order business, but Branson quickly realized that producing his own records might improve the equation. He bought a 16-track recording machine and a few microphones and installed them in a 17th-century castle near Oxford that he purchased cheap. He was 20 years old. A musician named Mike Oldfield moved in and labored for nine months on an album titled *Tubular Bells,* a runaway hit that became the soundtrack for *The Exorcist.* Branson was an instant millionaire.

Branson then signed the Sex Pistols, a group of spike-haired, vaguely sadomasochistic adolescents who played nihilistic, screeching ballads, one day to be dubbed punk music. Though the Sex Pistols were founded as a novelty act, the joblessness and economic stagnation gripping Britain in the 1970s made the times ripe for such a band to be taken seriously. Their breakout song was a "commemorative" number for the approaching silver anniversary of the coronation of Queen Elizabeth II.

> *God save the queen*
> *She ain't no human being*
> *There ain't no future in*
> *England's dreaming.*

The BBC banned the song and permitted it to appear in the pop charts only as a blank entry. Outlawed from every concert hall in England, the band began to tour the United States, where it soon fell apart. Band member Sid Vicious was arrested for the murder of his girlfriend and then died of a drug overdose.

Richard Branson, however, became a factor to be reckoned with in music publishing. He took the unusual step of signing a rock-and-roll drummer named Phil Collins, from the rock group Genesis, to a solo vocal album; he made Collins one of the biggest-selling artists of the 1980s. He signed up a songwriter named Gordon Sumner, who had adopted the stage name Sting and whose band, the Police, had become yet another of the decade's great rock acts. He signed a cross-dressing singer named Boy George, who was briefly the biggest pop star in the world.

And then he started an airline.

Freddie Laker had been out of business nearly two years when an American lawyer living in London came to Branson in 1984 with a plan to resurrect Laker's operating authority between Gatwick and Newark. Branson quickly bought into the idea, sticking the Virgin label on it, too. The two days he had spent trying to get through by telephone to People Express was the entire extent of Branson's market research. The failure of anyone to answer the phone at People Express told him that either there remained unrequited demand for cheap flights over the Atlantic or the service being provided was incompetent. Either way there was an opening.

Branson scheduled a lunch with Sir Freddie. The failed entrepreneur reeled off a litany of rules he said Branson must follow if he hoped to survive against the major carriers, especially British Airways: Compete on good service as well as low prices, because the major airlines can outlast you on price. Do not launch any more than two or three routes in a given year. Do whatever is necessary to break through the barriers around Heathrow. Use yourself to promote the airline. When they come after you, shout hard and shout long.

And finally, of particular importance, Laker said, when British Airways moves to crush Virgin, make sure you sue the bastards while you're still alive.

Branson acquired a single 747 for $28 million, a plane that had barely been used by its original owner, Aerolineas Argentinas. He intended to christen it *The Spirit of Sir Freddie,* but Laker talked him out of it, as if urging him to avoid a hex. Branson won his operating rights from the Civil Aviation Authority in London after a hearing at which he was scolded for showing up without a necktie.

In June 1984, seven years after he had cashed in on the Queen's jubilee, Virgin Atlantic was aloft. British Airways struck back with fares so low that the authorities in the United Kingdom deemed them injurious to Virgin. British Airways was pressured to restore its fares, giving Virgin a fighting chance to build a passenger base. Branson made a point of hiring flight attendants with arresting looks and figures and outfitted them as candy canes. Virgin had begun life as the Southwest Airlines of the North Atlantic.

Following Laker's advice, Branson applied for the authority to serve Heathrow but was told there was no room, not a single slot, available. He was stuck at Gatwick, just as Freddie Laker had been. Then in November 1990, Margaret Thatcher's government fell. The new Conservative Party government of Prime Minister John Major was immediately confronted with Branson's demand to get into Heathrow, and Major did not share the long-standing ties to British Airways that Thatcher had. At the same time United and American, in separate applications, were seeking the government's approval of their plans to begin operating the slots held by Pan Am and TWA. Although this latter issue seemed perfunctory, the new government resolved that nothing would change until it had completed a review of the entire slots scheme.

Branson, having waited seven years, would have to continue waiting, and the Americans with him.

Tom Plaskett urgently needed to close his deal with Stephen Wolf. Pan Am had to have its $400 million from United. But there was a hitch in London snagging the Pan Am–United deal, Plaskett learned. Not only was the British government evaluating its entire landing and takeoff scheme at Heathrow, but Sir Colin Marshall and his lawyers had been looking carefully at the Bermuda II amendments. Only Pan Am and TWA, the treaty said, could serve Heathrow—only they, that is, or their "corporate successors."

Was United the corporate successor to Pan Am? Was American the corporate successor to TWA? Absolutely not, said Sir Colin. Those companies were simply swapping assets. It was like trading ballplayers, selling a line of clothing, unloading a brand name in food, selling a factory; none of those exchanges altered the identity of any of the corporations involved. Sir Colin expressed his view to government officials as strongly as possible. To have United and

American counted as corporate successors, Marshall argued, the United States should give up something in return.

Marshall had been on easy street for years competing against Pan Am and TWA. British Airways, after its makeover in the mid-1980s, had one of the industry's most modern fleets and most skillful and dedicated workforces; the planes at Pan Am and TWA were wretched old money losers and the employees were as dispirited as any in commercial aviation. British Airways had developed the most sophisticated international marketing strategy in the world, designed to draw more passengers at premium prices; the marketing strategies at Pan Am and TWA involved selling at any price, meaning that their planes were jammed with low-fare passengers. In only five years, from 1985 to 1990, the U.S. carriers' share of the traffic between the United States and Heathrow had plunged to 47 percent from 57 percent—a free fall in an industry where battles were often won and lost on the east side of the decimal point.

The game would change drastically, Marshall knew, if United and American succeeded in replacing Pan Am and TWA. Wolf and Crandall were battle-hardened survivors of deregulation, the most cutthroat war in the history of commercial flying. They had the world's greatest arsenals of data-processing capability. Crandall, in particular, was a mean person—"Wretched Robert," as the irascible Lord King was known to call him. As for United, Marshall's valued code-sharing contract—assuring British Airways of many millions of dollars in additional passenger feed a year—was now clearly destined for the shredder with United planning to become a direct competitor in London.

In making his case to extract a price from the Americans, Marshall told his government that commercial aviation was a delicate, carefully balanced industry; that British Airways was one of the leading success stories in Britain's climb from economic oblivion; that severe, sudden change could risk British Air's leading role on the stage of international commerce and send it along the well-trodden path toward British industrial mediocrity. Happily for Marshall the government was obliged to listen: British airlines were customarily invited to participate directly in bilateral aviation negotiations. In contrast the United States didn't allow corporations in any industry such a voice in the diplomatic affairs of the nation. "When the

British government sits down to negotiate with the U.S. government, British Airways sits at the table," Crandall would later complain. "I'm not allowed in the room."

The diplomats negotiated on and off for weeks. On the Friday before Christmas in 1990, they reached an impasse. The negotiators went home. The Heathrow deals could not come to closing—not in 1990, in any case.

The wolf was soon baying at Pan Am's door. War in the Persian Gulf was imminent. There was too little money coming in, too much going out in fuel bills—payable in cash on delivery, in Pan Am's case. The company was now losing something like $2 million a day. Pan Am's personnel analysts observed a sudden, sharp increase in medical claims, apparently as employees hurried up elective medical attention on the expectation that their benefits might soon vanish.

"Who would ever have thought," Plaskett told a group of Harvard Business School alumni some time later, "that those two little words, 'corporate successor,' could generate so much debate, haggling, horse trading, intrigue, stalling, posturing, and negotiating between two governments?"

It was time to think about the unthinkable. Plaskett flew back to Dallas, where his family was still living, for the first weekend of the new year. He spent the weekend contemplating the weight of a momentous decision to put Pan Am into bankruptcy. He had to come to terms with the reality of it. Who would ever have thought? But there was $30 million in the till. The company was within days of having to shut down.

Plaskett was back in New York on Monday. "Let's go," he said.

Pan Am had been in bankruptcy two weeks when Britain agreed to reallocate the slots at Heathrow Airport, officially permitting new entrants. Within the United Kingdom the most conspicuous victor was Virgin Atlantic. John Major's government awarded Virgin 28 slots a week—only a third of what it had requested, but 28 more than British Airways wanted it to get. The authorities quickly increased Virgin's award to 40, enough to allow the upstart carrier to plan new routes to Tokyo, New York, and Los Angeles.

Richard Branson decided to celebrate the Heathrow conquest

with a "raiding party." He outfitted himself as a pirate, with a patch on one eye and a parrot on his shoulder. He approached the front entrance to Heathrow, where the huge scale-model replica of the British Airways Concorde was perched. With a crane, Branson lowered a carefully sewn sheet over the airplane, covering the British Airways markings with the logo and colors of Virgin Atlantic. In front of the entire display he planted a huge sign. It read simply: "This Is Virgin Territory."

British Airways was not exactly sporting. Lord King, who sometimes referred to Branson as "the boy," publicly called the award of slots to Branson a "tragedy." Sir Colin approved a payment of £50,000 for an outside PR firm to work up a dossier on Branson. The consultant's report cited speculation of "drug dealing, homosexuals, and male prostitutes" at a Branson-owned nightclub named Heaven. The report would have been a meaningless piece of competitive intelligence if it had remained in-house, but a British Air PR operative circulated the scurrilous information among Britain's news media. Stories questioning the financial security of the Virgin group of businesses began to fly. Branson meanwhile learned that British Airways had been poaching passengers by offering them inducements to break their plans to fly on Virgin.

A battle royal ensued in the British press and television media. Branson wrote a letter to the British Airways board complaining of "dirty tricks" and "a smear campaign in the press." Sir Colin answered with a marvelously patronizing letter that concluded, "Would it not be better if you were to devote your undoubted energies to more constructive purposes?" Lord King, for his part, publicly accused Branson of manufacturing the allegations.

Branson, the kid who had once sued John Lennon, then decided to take Freddie Laker's "sue the bastards" admonition to heart. He dragged British Airways to court, where the controversy would only continue to fester, proving, if nothing else, that the Yankees of the aviation world no longer had an exclusive license on bitterness in their business dealings.

The lifting of the barriers against new entrants at Heathrow touched off rejoicing in the United States amid hopes that Pan Am and TWA would soon get the cash for their London operations. But the celebration was short-lived. Officials from the U.S. State Department arrived in London a short time later expecting to conclude the diplomacy and were told that even if the slots matter had been decided, the issues of corporate successorship had not. To resolve this diplomatic standoff, the United States was still required to make a trade. Even as U.S. and British soldiers began fighting side by side in the Persian Gulf, diplomats from the two countries stared crossly at one another across the bargaining table.

The British price was soon clear.

British Airways had profited handsomely in its brief experience with code sharing. With unlimited code-sharing rights, Marshall could essentially turn the entire route system of a U.S. carrier into a feeder system for British Airways. Extending this blanket authority to British Airways would assure Marshall of the opportunity to replace the United code-sharing relationship that had been so fruitful with an even grander arrangement. And Marshall was in a position to make demands. Pan Am, already bankrupt, was inches from complete shutdown. Unless the British agreed to designate United as Pan Am's corporate successor, Pan Am would be inalterably dead.

When Bob Crandall found out that Sam Skinner of the Transportation Department was entertaining the British demand, he went wild. Crandall wanted to settle the succession issue as much as anyone on the U.S. side; his purchase of the TWA routes required the same British approval. Crandall in fact had people already stationed in London, going to work every day without knowing whether any planes would ever show up. But to Crandall no deal was worth capitulating to Sir Colin on code sharing.

No one had a more sophisticated appreciation for the power of a computer network than Crandall. In his view unlimited code sharing would give British Airways the right to serve any U.S. city through the proxy of another airline. In fact it was better than that: British Airways could go anywhere in the United States without having purchased a single airplane, without having hired or trained a single employee, without having wangled the necessary slots. Crandall thought he had been played for a fool: the hundreds of airplanes he had bought in the last 10 years, the tens of thousands of people he had trained—what were they worth when British Airways could scoop up passengers all over the United States without spending a dime in capital?

"Do not do that deal!" Crandall told the transportation secretary.

"Do not do it! It's a dumb deal!" The issue of corporate succession was a red herring, Crandall said. Corporate successors? "Tell them that means us!" Crandall snapped. Crandall suggested an alternate bargaining strategy to Skinner. "If United and American don't get certified to operate at Heathrow, then British Air isn't allowed to land in the U.S.!"

Skinner held out. The British held out. Soon it was February 1991, and the bombs at last were raining on Iraq. At various points President George Bush, Vice President Dan Quayle, and Secretary of State James Baker weighed in separately in the Heathrow battle, to no avail. Plaskett announced that Pan Am, though still flying, would cut its workforce 15 percent. Soon it was March 1991, five months after Wolf and Plaskett had first come to terms on the Heathrow deal. Pan Am missed a $100 million debt payment to Bankers Trust, exposing it to further possible foreclosures. Still the British and U.S. negotiators talked, and finally, on March 11, 1991, there was a deal.

The United States had caved. United and American would be allowed to serve Heathrow, although with a ceiling on their capacity levels. In exchange the airlines of the United Kingdom would have unlimited code-sharing rights in the United States, enabling them essentially to list any of their flights under the name and flight number of a U.S. partner.

How great a concession was that, really, despite Bob Crandall's protests? The cost of continuing to hold out had become too great. "Pan Am," said Transportation Secretary Skinner, "literally would have gone out of business tomorrow."

Within days of United's first landing in Heathrow, Stephen Wolf told Plaskett to forget it. United would make no deals for the whole of Pan Am.

The search for someone to buy Pan Am whole quickly became like the old Jimmy Durante punchline: everybody's trying to get in on the act. The unions, the creditors, various investment bankers acting officially and otherwise, and Plaskett himself were all bumping into one another in search of a way out. Through it all one company, hemming and hawing a bit—kind of shuffling, in fact—said that it might be interested in having a closer look. That company was Delta Air Lines.

That Delta was only now getting drawn into the great international takeover sweepstakes was perfectly in character. Delta was a follower—in fare moves, route applications, technology, takeovers, what have you. From the outside it appeared to have an unstinting company policy to let others innovate. Not that Delta was poorly managed—far from it. It controlled expenditures to the point of compulsiveness. ("We have zero paper-clip attrition," an official once boasted.) There were no budgets because the chief executive reviewed every expenditure over $1,000. Borrowing money was against Delta's corporate religion.

Its greatest strength was its people, in whom Delta bred a loyalty so powerful that it seemed almost creepy from the outside. Delta flight attendants were interviewed twice, then sent to the company psychologist, Dr. Sydney Janus, who explained that at Delta, "you don't just join a company, you join an objective." Like Southwest, Delta steeped its employees in corporate lore, dating to its origins as a crop-dusting service. Outside the headquarters building in Atlanta, a sky-high rendering of the triangular Delta logo looked down on the parking lot so that employees could not avoid the image as they marched toward the entrance. When employees reached the building, they entered by grasping a door handle in the shape of the corporate logo.

But Delta delivered for its employees. Delta people got jobs for life; the company had not laid off a soul in 34 years. There had been no BOHICA, no concessions, no b-scales. Delta paid its people exceptionally well, not only by the standards of the low-wage southern United States but by airline industry standards as well. On the initiative of the flight attendants, Delta's employees had once organized the purchase of a Boeing 767—a $30 million airplane—from their own paychecks.

It was only such a corporate environment that could produce an airline chief executive officer from the ranks of the personnel department. Ron Allen—like all his predecessors in the chairman's suite, a born-and-bred Delta product—fit Delta's trademark "Southern Gentleman" image to a *T.* Allen had an instinct for the superior customer service on which Delta so justly prided itself. On one of the company's new 757s Allen once rescued a passenger locked in the lavatory by using a knife from the galley. Considering flight at-

tendants an especially critical link, he sat through endless presentations on such vital subjects as meal cart optimization. Until a recent
diet, Allen enjoyed taking breakfast on the edge of the airport at a
blue-collar hangout called the Dwarf House.

Despite its reputation for following, Delta to its credit had been
among the earliest domestic U.S. airlines (though far from the first)
to begin spreading its wings overseas. But Delta had not exactly
taken the globe by storm. A Delta marketing executive in the late
1980s wrote an internal report saying Delta remained a nonentity in
its destinations in Europe. The company suffered from consumers'
"total lack of knowledge of who and what Delta is."

By April 1991 Allen was no longer content merely to do things the
ponderous "Delta way." Only so many international routes existed in
the world, and they were changing hands fast. Allen was late getting
into the game, but he had to get in, so when the pilots of Pan Am
were taking it upon themselves to find a buyer for their company,
Ron Allen was all ears.

By this time anybody who had ever thought of flying over water
was sizing up the remaining pieces of Pan Am. Plaskett found himself shuttling all over Manhattan meeting with bidders, investment
bankers, creditors, union leaders. The depressing part was that everyone wanted to pull off a chunk, but no one wanted to take on Pan
Am's people. They wanted nothing from Pan Am but little slips of
paper: certificates, many written in foreign languages, some half as
old as the industry's most experienced executives, entitling the bearer
to land airplanes and drop off or pick up passengers in a particular
city, and to collect a fare for doing so.

The frenzy reached its peak on a Tuesday in New York—July 23,
1991. Plaskett excused himself from a meeting with Carl Icahn of
TWA in order to join Ron Allen of Delta, who was waiting for him
on the 46th floor of the Pan Am Building. Stephen Wolf of United
had also made the scene. An extraordinary development had occurred: Delta and United were discussing a joint bid—for all of Pan
Am. It was Tom Plaskett's dream come true, for him and all of Pan
Am's employees. A joint takeover by United and Delta would pluck
Pan Am intact out of bankruptcy court, and Delta and United could
make a clean division of the assets and the liabilities *and the people.*

As twilight reached Manhattan, Plaskett went to work playing matchmaker.

Steve Wolf was suddenly stricken with déjà vu. He was, he realized, sitting in his old office on the 46th floor of the Pan Am Building, the same office he had occupied as a senior vice president for Pan Am a decade earlier, under Ed Acker.

But the place had lost its magic. The carpet had grown threadbare, the furniture upholstery was shiny and worn. And now here was Wolf, tearing apart the carcass of the once proud bird with the man from Delta.

What Wolf wanted very badly in this feeding frenzy was Latin America. Even in the downward slide of the past two years, even through Lockerbie and the Gulf War and the tarnishing of the Pan Am name, the Latin American operation had remained profitable, the only profitable division in fact in all of Pan Am. Wolf knew those routes could never be duplicated from scratch, and buying them was the only way to match Bob Crandall's move into South America on the old Eastern routes.

The irony was excruciating. Ron Allen and the rest of the Delta team were now down the hall, caucusing in Juan Trippe's old conference room—the very room in which Trippe, 25 years earlier almost to the day, had sold Pan Am's routes along the western side of South America to Braniff, which had subsequently sold them to Eastern, which had sold them to American—which was why Wolf had to get the other half, the eastern half, of the system that Juan Trippe and Charles Lindbergh had pioneered through South America.

Dividing the major pieces of Pan Am between them had been easy for Wolf and Allen: while United took Latin America, Delta would get a number of miscellaneous remaining Pan Am routes over the Atlantic, plus the East Coast flights. You get this, I get that. But there was one route on which the two men simply could not agree: London–Miami. Wolf would need it to feed Europeans into his new Latin American operation in Miami. He would need it to develop Miami fully into an intercontinental gateway for United. He would need it because Bob Crandall had picked up Continental's Miami–London route when he got Eastern's Latin division from Frank Lorenzo.

"Ron," Wolf said to the Delta chairman, "*you* wouldn't buy Latin America without the Europe feed. That's *got* to be in my package."

Remembering that these were markets they were trading for, and further realizing that the government frowned on corporations for subdividing markets, Wolf, at another point, turned to a United lawyer who was present.

"Is this legal?" he asked. (In fact, it was.)

Allen and Wolf were still hung up on Miami–London at 2:20 A.M., when Plaskett gave up on them.

"Screw it," he said.

There would be no joint deal for Pan Am. Wolf and Allen, United and Delta, went their separate ways.

Psychological stress overwhelmed the Pan Am organization at every level. Absenteeism rose. A psychologist from Cornell found elevated levels of headaches, sleeplessness, and digestive disturbances, symptoms she attributed to "grief." A flight instructor shot himself. "He loved that airline," his daughter said. A memo from the head of flight operations urged pilots and others to remain on guard against the effects of career anxiety on safety.

Plaskett, for his part, was rapidly becoming persona non grata among the creditors of Pan Am. They began saying that he was hard to reach, that he was spending too much time at his home in Dallas, too much time playing racquetball or golf. Plaskett could not understand the criticism. "I have never refused to take a phone call," he told *The Wall Street Journal*. "I wear a pager. I carry a portable phone. As to my reputation for golf, I have played golf maybe *twice* this year."

Leon Marcus, a lawyer representing some of Pan Am's creditors, turned to Plaskett during one meeting and called him "evasive and incompetent."

"Listen," Plaskett snapped, "we think we're doing the right thing. Anytime you want the keys, you can have them," to which Marcus said he would gladly take them right then and there. Plaskett, furious, began to stalk from the room; another participant coaxed him back.

As unpopular as Plaskett had become, there was no disputing his talent for keeping Delta's Ron Allen focused on what Pan Am had to offer. After failing to come to terms on a joint purchase with United, Allen was now more committed than ever to getting what he wanted from Pan Am and then some. Bidding principally against himself, Allen over the span of several days in late July and early August of 1991 raised his offer repeatedly, ultimately agreeing to buy nearly one half of the stock in a reorganized Pan Am. He agreed to take on many of Pan Am's liabilities. Best of all, he said he would absorb a legion of Pan Am employees.

Finally it had happened. The Blue Meatball strategy had worked. Delta was bailing out Pan Am, what was left of it. Pan Am would continue to fly—as an independent company! Delta would control it, throw money into it, reorganize it, and nurture it. The bidding process had begun at only a few hundred million; by the time it was over, Delta had agreed to cough up well over a billion— $1,289,000,000, to be exact—for Pan Am's remaining European routes, its East Coast service, and a controlling interest in the storied Latin American operation.

The ink was barely dry when Plaskett was pushed out the door by the creditors. Just like that, he was gone, left without a job in aviation for the first time since he had walked into American Airlines two decades earlier.

There was now one less player to take a chair the next time the music stopped.

Delta's purchase of Pan Am's East Coast routes closed on September 1, 1991. Delta took possession of Pan Am's remaining routes over the Atlantic on November 1, 1991. Although none of those routes went to Heathrow, they were sufficient in number to make Delta, in conjunction with the transatlantic routes it already had, the biggest airline to Europe. It now flew to Brussels, Bucharest, Geneva, Helsinki, Moscow, Rome, Tel Aviv, and several other new destinations. But the routes were losing money, and the Pan Am employees acquired with them were cranky and dispirited.

And a month after that, on the same day that the remnants of Pan Am were scheduled to emerge from bankruptcy as an affiliate of Delta, Ron Allen said never mind.

The rest of the deal, he announced, was off. Delta would have nothing further to do with Pan Am. There would be no more money for Pan Am, no purchase of equity, no saving of the 7,500 jobs remaining in the company. Pan Am's passenger traffic in November, Delta said, was breathtakingly below forecast. There was no way Delta could be expected to go through with the deal after that kind of performance.

The following day, December 4, 1991, a Wednesday, the *Clipper Juan Trippe* taxied through a gauntlet of water cannons and departed JFK for the last Pan Am flight from New York. Later the last Pan Am arrival reached Miami, where it made a low pass over the runway—a farewell to the world—before circling back to land. Pan Am employees waited at the gate, standing at attention.

Pan Am at last was dead.

The following evening back in Dallas, Tom Plaskett appeared before the Harvard Business School Club of Dallas. His remarks were full of blame casting and contrition.

> While some may preach "survival of the fittest" and "that's just business," in my view what happened to Pan Am is a tragedy, to be shared by many who brought it about—its board of directors, its management, its unions, our government, and fate. Our experiences in recent months did not swoop down on us suddenly, nor were they something unique to Pan Am. Indeed, the result was the culmination of a long process and series of events that began in 1978. That's when the drama really began. That's when the old script was thrown out the window and all of us in the airline industry were pushed out on stage together and told by our government to improvise.
>
> Now, more than a decade later . . . believe me, the show is far from over. . . .
>
> Whether you blame it on deregulation and excessive competition, recession, poor management, recalcitrant unions, or just plain bad luck, the reality is that the U.S. airline industry is in terrible trouble.
>
> In my view the state of our airline industry is a national embarrassment.

The judge in the bankruptcy case scheduled an emergency auction of Pan Am's assets a few days after Pan Am's final flight. Feverishly lawyers for all the principal airlines in the country milled around the courtroom in hopes of grabbing an asset here, an asset there, something to help fill in the route maps of their clients. Jeffrey Kriendler, a 45-year-old Pan Am executive who had experienced a stroke amid all the stress of the preceding months, turned out to observe the melancholy spectacle. "It was like a piece of flesh up there," he later said.

Because the scene was such a zoo, Stephen Wolf could not let himself attend. He was too conspicuous; he was sure people would recognize him. He remained instead at the Union League Club; his aides had to race to the courthouse pay phones to fill him in on what was occurring and obtain his instructions.

Before the night was out, the Latin American division of what was once Pan American World Airways wound up in the very large, very elegant hands of Stephen Wolf. The price was only $135 million, much less than United had offered Plaskett weeks earlier for the identical assets. Like Bob Crandall, Wolf was, at last, everywhere.

Each of them committed to victory, Wolf and Crandall had played to a tie. There was one round left.

CHAPTER 19

HARD LANDING

The ranks of the dearly departed were swollen by the early 1990s. Tom Plaskett was an entrepreneur in Dallas, devoting much of his attention to commercializing a breakthrough in car battery technology. In a sense he had returned to the automotive industry, which he had left to join American Airlines in 1974.

Frank Borman, also a car lover, was living in Las Cruces, New Mexico, helping to run the family automobile dealership. Charlie Bryan, laid off by the International Association of Machinists in the wake of Eastern's failure, grew a beard and worked occasionally as a golf course groundskeeper in Miami.

Marty Shugrue, still the court-appointed trustee in Miami, was studying a plan to put Eastern back in the air. Gerald Gitner, once his fellow vice chairman at Pan Am, was an investment banker raising capital for small and medium-sized businesses, including a helicopter manufacturer in Russia. Their boss at Pan Am, Ed Acker, went back into the business directly, purchasing a small commuter operation on the East Coast and turning it into a major feeder operation for United Airlines at Dulles Airport. Acker strolled into his office in the late morning in a cardigan sweater, led by a pair of pug dogs on a leash.

Dick Ferris was also a successful entrepreneur. He went into business with golfer Arnold Palmer and sports agent Mark McCormack, purchasing a Learjet and taking over a private airport in suburban Chicago. Ferris regularly commuted to the golf course from his home in suburban Chicago in a Porsche 928S-4, taking his corners fast.

Howard Putnam of Braniff, who had tape-recorded his conversation with Bob Crandall, was a consultant and motivational speaker. Putnam often yearned for an opportunity to explain to Crandall why he had tape-recorded that call in the first place, the only call he had ever recorded. In any case Putnam noticed that chief executives did not telephone him as frequently as they once did.

John Robson, who had taken the first meaningful steps to deregulate the airlines, became deputy treasury secretary in the Bush administration and later a fellow specializing in "regulatory reform" at the Heritage Foundation. Stephen Breyer, who had convinced Sen. Ted Kennedy to lead the deregulation charge in Congress, was appointed by President Clinton to the United States Supreme Court.

Breyer's protégé, Phil Bakes, remained in Miami. Though his association with Lorenzo effectively blocked him from running any airlines, he became the chief executive of a company that placed telephones and interactive videos on aircraft. Once at a Democratic Party function in Washington, Bakes was accosted by Senator Kennedy, who angrily accused Bakes of misleading him about the effects of deregulation.

Bob Carney, Frank Lorenzo's original partner, had cashed out of Jet Capital before the downfall of Texas Air and put his winnings into a company that sold discount tours and published travel and retirement magazines. Don Burr was divorced and living with Melrose Dawsey on Martha's Vineyard, where they collaborated on a book about the virtues of the six Precepts established at People Express.

Lorenzo made plans to launch a new low-fare airline at Baltimore-Washington International Airport. Friendship Airlines, he called it. Fifty-seven members of Congress wrote letters to Transportation Secretary Federico Peña demanding denial of an operating permit. Lorenzo appealed the order, but at last count Lorenzo's newly formed company had been deemed at every level of the process to be unfit to operate even a small airline.

Shortly after midnight on July 29, 1992, Lorenzo was driving the family's Ford Explorer along the bustling nightspots of Westheimer Road in Houston when a policeman noticed him driving erratically. Pulling him over, the officer got a whiff of alcohol through the window of Lorenzo's car. When the patrolman instructed him to step out, Lorenzo "stumbled out of vehicle," the arrest report said, "holding on to car door to keep from falling." Lorenzo pleaded no contest to drunk driving and was sentenced to two years' probation. Eventually he and his family left Houston.

But four of the leading, longtime principals—Crandall, Kelleher, Wolf, and Sir Colin—remained on the scene, each with his own battles to conclude and his own demons to exorcise. From 1992 to 1995 a final consolidation phase played out among the airlines, toppling a giant, elevating an upstart, and otherwise thrusting the world's aviation industry, after 25 years of trauma, into the state of delicate equilibrium in which it would approach the 21st century.

Even in the aftermath of the Gulf War, with airlines around the world losing billions of dollars annually, Colin Marshall could unabashedly proclaim British Airways the "world's most profitable airline." It distinguished itself as the last privately owned airline in the world to preserve an A rating from the credit agencies.

As part of a rearguard action against the invading American carriers, Marshall stepped up his strategy of promoting multiple "brands" within a single airplane. The company established a free valet service for passengers in premium classes, complete with luxury showers, changing rooms, and clothes pressing right inside Heathrow. Bob Crandall was angry that American did not know about the new facility until after the construction had been completed. "When those hammers started hammering, we should have been down there looking under the curtains!" he snapped during a meeting with employees in London.

Service was only part of the battle. With United and American attacking from the west and the surging carriers of Asia attacking from the east and Virgin Atlantic in his backyard, Marshall resolved to make British Airways the first global megacarrier not only by spanning the globe but also by collecting and transporting passengers within individual continents and countries. He bought control of a German airline that fed passengers into a British Airways hub at Berlin. He bought nearly half of TAT European Airlines in France, linking its operations at Charles de Gaulle Airport with long-haul British Airways departures. He picked up a major interest in Qantas, the Australian national carrier with the elegant, leaping kangaroo on the tail of its planes.

Even so, a gaping hole remained in Marshall's global expansion plans. It was the United States. He had briefly succeeded at breaking in through United, only to watch his code-sharing partner turn into his competitor. Every other airline in America was either bankrupt, in business against British Airways, or already hitched up with a European counterpart—except for USAir.

It was, if nothing else, a survivor. USAir by 1992 was the last of the original local-service operators. Few airlines had been more brilliantly managed or more consistently profitable in the years immediately preceding and following deregulation. Much of its success was due to its near-monopoly of Pittsburgh, which flourished as a medical and high technology center in the postindustrial economy of the 1980s. Pittsburgh was also one of the country's most valuable hubs, perfectly situated among the Great Lakes, New England, and mid-Atlantic regions. USAir was a short-haul airline, Chairman Ed Colodny liked to say, "because that's the way the country's built east of the Mississippi River."

Colodny assiduously resisted major acquisitions until, in the late 1980s, it was clear that USAir either had to begin swallowing other airlines or be devoured itself. It laid out a total of $2 billion to acquire PSA in California and Piedmont in the East, but it managed the mergers poorly. Because USAir had been so profitable for so long, workers refused to give meaningful concessions. The fuel-price surge following the invasion of Kuwait punished USAir severely because of its concentration of short-haul routes. Then to the rescue came riding Sir Colin.

Marshall proposed to invest in USAir the same $750 million he had tried to put into the ill-fated employee buyout at United. In exchange British Airways would have 21 percent voting control—safely within the legal limit. Together British Airways and USAir represented the largest airline in the world, with $16 billion a year in business. They served 339 cities in 71 countries. Marshall was convinced that within five years British Airways and USAir, on an operating basis, would become a single airline with one route system, one management, and possibly one name—British-American Airways, perhaps.

Marshall had spent enough years working in the United States to recognize the virtue of completing his USAir investment before the 1992 presidential campaign reached its peak, for the deal was politically vulnerable in one respect: although British Airways would have only 21 percent voting control, its massive contribution of cash would represent 44 percent of the equity in troubled USAir. That gave the U.S. Department of Transportation the power to wreck or wave through the deal.

The agency expressed no misgivings, until Bob Crandall threw a hissy. Crandall had seen such a deal coming; in the high-stakes trading over access to Heathrow a year earlier, the United States had approved unlimited code sharing by British carriers. Crandall's people did some quick arithmetic and came up with 20,000 pairs of cities for which British Airways theoretically could list its own flight numbers, even if USAir was flying all the segments within the United States. British Airways could, in theory at least, fill the travel agency screens of the world with artificially seamless flights—Milwaukee to London, say, or even Richmond to Riyadh. Crandall was convinced that Marshall had taken one of the most dramatic steps in the history of commercial aviation.

Fulfilling Marshall's worst fears, Crandall moved to engage the presidential candidates. Independent Ross Perot had catapulted himself ahead in the voter polls by demagoguing on the "giant sucking sound" of jobs going overseas. Crandall, who had recently built a massive maintenance facility on property owned by the Perot family, got a call through to the candidate just before the last of the presidential debates. When the rapt and massive audience was tuned in, Perot cackled, "We're getting ready to dismantle the airline industry in our country, and none of you know it!" The British Airways deal, Perot said, would be "terribly destructive to the U.S. airline industry." Stephen Wolf meanwhile worked the Clinton campaign, and before long, candidate Clinton declared that he had "real problems" with the deal.

Sir Colin knew he could preserve his deal for a price: giving up some of his landing slots at Heathrow to the American carriers. But that price was too great. Marshall considered the barrier around Heathrow to be the "ultimate bargaining chip," worth trading away only if British Airways won the right to fly anywhere or own anything within the United States.

Marshall announced the deal was off—but only to prepare a second maneuver, this one designed from the bottom up to be attack-proof in Washington. In January 1993 Marshall's people won the agreement of USAir's leaders to spread out British Air's big investment over several years. The first step would involve $300 million, representing only 19.9 percent of USAir's equity—safely within the law by any method of reckoning. In future years, as USAir's equity base swelled, Marshall could inject additional funds. The new terms left the U.S. government with no grounds on which to intercede.

Marshall announced that the deal had been completed on January 21, 1993, only hours after Bill Clinton had been sworn in as president. Crandall's PR people were instructed to plant suggestions in the press that Sir Colin was trying to slip a fast one past the new administration, though the timing appeared to be coincidental.

One step remained in Marshall's grand ambitions—mostly a formality, perhaps, but one that meant something to him. Although Marshall by 1993 had been running the show for nearly 10 years, the title that he had once confessed to coveting more than any in the world—chairman of British Airways—still belonged to the curmudgeonly Lord King of Wartnaby.

Shortly before completing the USAir deal, Lord King convened a meeting of the British Airways board in London at which the company's outside law firm reported on the suit that music impresario Richard Branson of Virgin Atlantic had filed nearly two years earlier, the suit charging British Airways with dirty tricks and Lord King with libel. To the astonishment of the board British Air's lawyers reported that Branson had a point. British Airways *had* poached Virgin's passengers. British Airways operatives *had* spread malicious stories about Branson. It was evident that British Airways would have to settle with Branson. If nothing else, the delicacy of British Air's efforts to crack into USAir demanded disposal of the Branson affair.

British Airways agreed to pay nearly $1 million in damages, one of the largest judgments ever paid in a British libel case. Of greater relevance to Branson was the assent to a public apology. "Both British Airways and Lord King apologize unreservedly for the injury caused to the reputation and feelings of Richard Branson and Virgin Atlantic," a lawyer for Lord King stated in court. In the orgy of congratulation that surrounded Branson, the Princess of Wales sent him a note from Kensington Palace scrawled with a single word: "Hurray!"

Within weeks, his retirement date accelerated, Lord King was gone. Marshall, having signed a statement disavowing any knowledge of the dirty tricks campaign, assumed at last the title of chairman—an almost eerie replay of the circumstances by which he had become the head of Avis two decades earlier.

After the machinery of Marshall's USAir agreement was bolted into place, British Airways flights were teeming with connecting passengers scooped up in the cities served by USAir—each a passenger that might otherwise have conducted his or her entire journey on United or American. For itself, however, USAir was operating poorly, though by 1995 it had finally finagled wage concessions from most of its labor groups. The airline was afflicted with a spate of tragic accidents, including one that killed 132 at its principal hub of Pittsburgh. But USAir's problems did not diminish the financial benefits of code sharing to Sir Colin, which he estimated to total £70 million in 1994 alone.

Branson, for his part, catapulted Virgin into a new phase of worldwide growth, adding Tokyo, Hong Kong, Los Angeles, Boston, Miami, and Orlando to his schedules. In 1992 his sale of Virgin Music to Thorn EMI for nearly $1 billion gave him all the money he could ever want to pour into Virgin Atlantic, although in the airline business it was possible to burn up money faster than even Branson could earn it. Though becoming the ninth wealthiest person in Britain following the sale of his label, Branson had acquired few pretensions. He still seldom wore a tie and ran from office to office in his Holland Park mansion with instructions to himself scrawled across the back of his hand.

The company's litigious history and its emphasis on festive flights strongly recalled Southwest Airlines. The two chairmen were even physically similar, with blue eyes, light hair, rumpled attire, and the look of men who had done some partying in their day.

"People keep saying I should meet Herb Kelleher," Branson once told a visitor from America.

When the 1990s hit, Herb Kelleher hit California.

Although Southwest Airlines was already flying into California on slots he had tricked out of the FAA, Kelleher had avoided the north-south corridor between Los Angeles and San Francisco. The busiest air corridor in the world, it had long been famous for bruising fare battles. When USAir began to cut back the service it had acquired from PSA—PSA, the very airline whose low-fare flights of the 1960s had inspired the creation of Southwest—Kelleher jumped into the void.

Southwest established itself first at the secondary airports of Oakland on the northern end and Ontario and Burbank on the southern. Cutting fares by two thirds and more, Southwest caused the number of Oakland-Ontario passengers to surge by 123 percent in only the first quarter of service. The route from Oakland to Burbank instantly became the 28th busiest aviation route in the United States (up from 272). As USAir cut back further, Southwest quickly rushed in, soon becoming the second largest carrier in California. United, the market leader, promptly began losing its shirt to keep what it had.

To Kelleher picking city pairs and launching massive operations had become a matter of formula, and although the formula succeeded to varying degrees, it never seemed to fail. Through 1992 and 1993, while the rest of the industry added up its losses, Kelleher continued reporting massive profits. In came more planes—737s all. Southwest's arrival in a new city not only sparked a surge in new travel but often an economic development boom. Spiegel, for instance, established a massive mail-order center in Columbus, adding 1,500 jobs to the local economy, in part because Southwest added service to the city. So many people made the 135-mile drive from Memphis to catch Southwest flights in Little Rock that a truck stop halfway in between, in Wheatley, Arkansas, began pumping 20 percent of its gasoline for Southwest passengers.

Kelleher's employees continued to worship him. A group of pilots passed the hat and bought Kelleher a chrome-plated Harley Davidson trimmed in Southwest's colors, presenting it to him at a company chili cook-off with 5,000 in attendance. Kelleher practically wept. He was perpetually looking for excuses to party, to loosen things up, to poke fun at himself. In 1992 Kelleher proposed to settle a minor trademark dispute with a sporting adversary by arranging an arm wrestling match, which he called "Malice in Dallas." Flight attendants in scoop-neck tops turned out as cheerleaders; Kelleher donned a white headband and twisted a cigarette between his lips. When Kelleher's wrist had been pinned, he keeled to the floor and was carried away on a stretcher, an intravenous line running from his arm to a bottle of Wild Turkey.

Wolf was as meticulous and precise in his early 50s as he had been when he positioned his food on the tray of his high chair. His friends nowadays preferred taking him to restaurants with limited menus so that he did not spend half the evening interrogating the waiter about the selections.

When he traveled overseas—something he did with tremendous frequency now, often crossing time zones by the dozens in a couple of days—Wolf carried a thick black binder that blocked out his schedule to the minute and contained seating charts and menus for his dinners, license plate and telephone numbers for the various cars meeting him, temperature ranges, locally preferred greetings and salutations, and the résumés of anyone he was likely to encounter. His briefing books, prepared by a Yale lawyer with an M.B.A. degree from Stanford, left little to chance. In Japan, for instance, Wolf's talking points reached all the way to the idiomatic: "It is a pleasure to meet you. . . . We must take care not to overreact to transitory circumstances. To use an American expression, we must be careful not to 'throw out the baby with the bathwater.' "

United's longtime middle managers, the people who actually kept the planes running, had grown accustomed in earlier years to seeing Dick Ferris wander into their offices and put his feet up on the nearest desk. Everyone called him Dick. These days United's veterans addressed the chairman as Mr. Wolf, expecting that he would correct them—please, call me Stephen—but he seldom seemed to. Mr. Wolf he remained.

Despite his sometimes off-putting manner, Wolf's most avowed enemies in organized labor admitted his brilliance in restructuring the airline. "The route structure that he put together for this airline is just unbelievable," Roger Hall, the leader of the pilots' repeatedly unsuccessful takeover effort, would one day remark. In addition to the overseas expansion, Wolf had reclaimed Bob Crandall's trophy as the number one U.S. carrier, although the companies were so nearly identical in size that the monthly rankings had become academic. Wolf also overhauled United's markings and colors, replacing the blue and orange *U* on bright white planes with a designer gray trimmed in blue and black—elegance itself, except that on an overcast day, United people complained, the airplanes seemed to vanish against the sky.

Despite these advances, by the spring of 1993 Wolf was very, very unhappy. His success in the international markets was being engulfed by failure at home. Despite its expansion, United was losing money hand over fist. One of the main reasons was the Southwest effect.

California was a killer. Wolf sent spies to the airports to count the people getting on Kelleher's planes while analysts estimated Southwest's costs of operating its flights. Southwest, they calculated, was at worst breaking even on a $59 flight. At that price United bled to death.

Southwest was only the most visible symptom of the problem. It was clear to Wolf that a cultural change had taken hold in America, one for which sociologists had not even begun to account. People were obsessed with living on the cheap. And to the extent that Herb Kelleher was positioned to cash in on that change—with his low costs and relentless efficiency and workforce dedicated to delivering a product for next to nothing—United Airlines would lose.

In searching for a strategy, Wolf called together the leaders of the principal unions at United. He told them that the more United flew in the United States, the more money it seemed to lose. There was no choice: unless it cut its labor costs, United had to get small. Getting small, of course, meant fewer planes and fewer promotion opportunities.

The pilots thought they were hearing the ghost of Dick Ferris. "Downsizing," Roger Hall of ALPA told Wolf, "means war." It would be one of the most cataclysmic labor wars ever, Hall vowed. It would make the pilots' strike of '85 look like a warm-up act. Hall warned Wolf that he had no idea how bad it could get: "You've never been involved in one of those, and I have."

War, Wolf knew, would get personal; it would call attention once again to his option position in United stock, worth something like $50 million. To avert war, Wolf decided once again to summon his powers of persuasion, as he had with such success at Republic Airlines and Tiger International.

On a brilliant late-winter morning in February 1993 a few hundred off-duty pilots and flight attendants gathered at a Marriott Hotel on the edge of Dulles International Airport to hear their distant and rather mysterious chairman speak. The parking lot was overflowing with Miatas and Mercedes Benzes. Inside the hotel waited a standing-room-only crowd of flight attendants in stretch pants and baggy sweaters and pilots in tweed and Ultrasuede.

For Wolf the presentation was an incursion behind enemy lines. The flight attendants were gravely upset by another of Wolf's moves: establishing crew bases overseas in order to recruit flight attendants who were in some cases less expensive but who in all cases were bilingual. Wolf was obsessed with the perfection of spoken language, to the point of rejecting a request by the flight attendants' union to open a crew base in Miami for United's new South American service instead of in Buenos Aires; even if there were plenty of qualified bilinguals in Miami, he pointed out, a different dialect was spoken in Argentina.

All heads in the audience turned when Wolf finally appeared at the back of the ballroom clad in a mile-long winter coat and scarf, holding a steaming cup of coffee to his lips. Wolf strode to the front, jerked his scarf from his neck with a snap, rested his cup on the lectern, and slowly peeled off his overcoat.

"The industry continues to be in nothing short of domestic chaos," Wolf told the group solemnly. The consumer now demanded ultralow fares. Three carriers, Continental, TWA, and American West, were in bankruptcy proceedings, each seeking to find a way to survive on low fares. And then there was the enigma of Southwest. "They are a competitor," he said, "that we don't know how to compete with."

Wolf reminded his people that in 1991 United had reported the biggest loss in its history; in 1992 the loss was three times greater. Now in 1993 the loss looked like it could be "staggeringly large."

Wolf paused. There was not a sound in the chamber. He sipped audibly from his Styrofoam coffee cup.

"In the history of America there's never been anything like what's happened in the aviation industry in the last three years."

Wolf concluded the presentation without making any firm requests and without offering solutions. He wished only to soften the ground, stirring enough empathy and anxiety that these rank-and-file employees might prevail on their leaders to consider some concessions. But this crowd would not give Wolf such truck. As soon as he asked for questions from the audience, the flight attendants, dozens of them, stood up in unison and stalked from the room in an organized protest. Wolf's appeal had failed.

United was slipping fast, and Wolf himself was perilously close to looking bad. It was the pilots who showed him a way out of his dilemma.

In June 1993 pilot officials at United resurrected their idea of an employee takeover, noting that the concessions Wolf wanted would be tolerable if employees were compensated for them in stock. The pilots, further, had a candidate whom they intended to elect as their new chief executive if they attained control: Gerald Greenwald, who had played an instrumental role with Lee Iacocca in the rescue and rehabilitation of Chrysler.

Wolf set to work designing a new, employee-owned United Airlines to compete with Southwest, knowing that if he were successful in selling the idea to the unions, he would be out of a job. At least he would be out cleanly, with $50 million or better in his pocket, leaving behind a company with a better chance.

Part of Wolf's solution involved a sleight of hand. United had suffered mightily from its lack of meaningful b-scales. So Wolf convinced the unions to establish a separate corporation—U2, it was called in the planning stages—which would look and act like Southwest, with quick turnarounds, reduced cabin service, and, most important, employees brought in at cut-rate wages. Regardless of the packaging, Wolf and his aides had talked the unions of United into b-scales. Ultimately, U2 operated in California under the name Shuttle by United.

Wolf seemed intent on bringing his own job to an end, as he ultimately had both at Republic and Tiger International. He even helped the pilots negotiate the employment contract for Greenwald, the man intended to take his job. "It's sort of a canned act," Kevin Lum, the president of the flight attendants' union at United, eventually decided regarding Wolf. "He paints the planes and then he sells them."

Some people thought the employees had no idea what the union leaders and Wolf were getting them into. Even two members of the United board—Andrew Brimmer, the former Federal Reserve official, and Frank Olson, who remained on the board even after returning to Hertz—ultimately voted against the buyout. Nevertheless, by the summer of 1994, the deal appeared at hand. The terms had been established. There would be severe pay cuts for existing employees (except the flight attendants, who declined to come in as owners) and b-scales for new hires. On his final day at United, Wolf put his pen in his pocket, went to the shareholders' meeting, awaited the official announcement of their approval, and went home, never to return to United Airlines. And when the deal closed, Wolf, age 53, walked away with his $50 million.

A short time later, when asked how he expected to spend his free time, he said perfectly seriously that he intended to bone up on personal finance. Would he also be reading more? Yes, he said, he had read six newspapers already that day. Wolf also accepted a major consulting engagement to assist in a turnaround attempt at troubled Air France. Wolf and his wife leased an apartment in Paris for a year.

"I'm not happy about leaving United," he commented. "But I accept it. I left it the best positioned airline in the world. If managed properly, it will work for everybody."

In April 1993 Kelleher announced that Southwest would expand in California by invading San Jose, the hub of the old AirCal operation that American Airlines had snatched seven years earlier. Informed of Southwest's plans, Crandall on the spot ordered a huge cutback in American's service at the hub, without waiting for even the first day of Southwest's operation.

Though seemingly powerless in a head-to-head matchup with Southwest, American was without doubt a beautiful machine. With close to 700 airplanes and 100,000 employees, it conducted nearly 2,500 takeoffs and landings daily in 338 cities, 72 of them outside the U.S. mainland. On an average day Crandall moved 230,000 passengers, the equivalent of transporting the entire population of Des

Moines, say, or Akron or Rochester for hundreds of miles; his people served 180,000 meals and handled 300,000 pieces of luggage. In a cavern in Oklahoma, behind a retina-scanning security device, the mainframes of Sabre were now connected to 200,000 reservations terminals around the world, handling as many as 3,600 transactions per second—the largest privately owned real-time network ever built, with every screen ringing up a fee on every reservation processed for another airline.

Crandall had also parlayed his yield management operation into a major business in its own right, with customers throughout the travel industry. The cutting-edge mathematical research American used to schedule flight crews and airplanes for maximum efficiency was being sold to dozens of clients. Keypunch operators at an American ticket processing center in Barbados were also processing insurance claims for Blue Cross and others.

The entire enterprise collected close to $15 billion in revenue a year, nearly five times the amount collected in 1980, when Crandall had become president. And yet on the bottom line, the only number that really counted, American, like every other airline except Southwest and British Air, was losing money. Why? A hard recession was raging, yes, but those two exceptions proved it was possible to profit through a recession. Southwest did it with low costs; British Airways did it with premium fares. Which course should Crandall attempt?

He had in fact already made his choice. The two-tier wage system by which Crandall had financed his Growth Plan had been slowly collapsing since the late 1980s, locking American into a higher labor-cost trend. Crandall had vowed never to let that happen. Time and again he swore publicly that American would take all the strikes it had to in order to defend b-scales. "We cannot yield on that and we will not yield on that," he had declared. But the Growth Plan, it turned out, had boxed Crandall in. Because of b-scales he had conducted the largest expansion in airline history, yet because of that expansion, there was no way that b-scales could last.

The Growth Plan had created a new union majority at American consisting of b-scale employees. Continuing b-scales benefited a-scale employees, but the a-scalers no longer carried the day in union affairs. At the same time American no longer had the financial power to push the issue all the way to a strike. While buying all those airplanes, American had doubled its long-term debt in 1990, more than doubled it in 1991, and increased it by half again in 1992—to $5.6 billion. Because the debt payments would not stop if Crandall allowed the pilots to walk out, a strike could bankrupt American in a matter of days. Crandall had no choice but to capitulate to the union wage demands. As the two-tier system withered, Crandall officially brought his Growth Plan to an end. As he would one day put it in his own delicate way, "The unions insisted on reversing all the good stuff and pissed it out the window."

The impasse on the cost side left Crandall only the revenue side: he could try to jump-start American's markets, try to extract more revenue from each airplane. Yet even the power of yield management seemed to be failing in the recession.

Crandall dispatched teams of researchers to find out why the growth in air travel had stopped so suddenly. He demanded "radical thinking," with all preconceived notions cast aside. The answers that came back were far from radical. Crandall's people reported that travelers were fed up with the ever-worsening complexity of the fare structure, a condition that no airline more than American was responsible for creating. American had carried complexity past the point of diminishing returns. A new generation of consumers brought up on Wal-Mart and double grocery coupons on Tuesdays—and peanuts fares and People Express fares and all the rest—were conditioned to expect prices that were plainly and visibly related to value. That quality had evaporated from airline pricing. Crandall and the other executives of aviation had managed to stifle the impulse to travel. Even worse, the most vital and most loyal segment of the marketplace—business travelers—were being forced to subsidize the cheap fares as never before. American was driving its best customers away.

After months of study, Crandall staged as big a press conference as American Airlines had ever held, unveiling what he called "value pricing." It was, at bottom, a price cut, particularly for the nation's disaffected business travelers, a welcome development to be sure. The plethora of complex rules and special deals was mostly eliminated, also arousing cheers. Discount fares for vacation travelers were reduced in variety—and in no event, Crandall decreed, would a discount fare ever again fall below 50 percent of the full coach price.

That way, American could stamp out the increasing practice of buying two round-trip tickets and flying on half of each.

"Simplicity itself," Crandall declared at his press conference, broadcast by satellite worldwide.

American had simply adopted the retailing strategy dignified as "EDLP"—everyday low prices, the same strategy that had made Wal-Mart magnate Sam Walton in his time the wealthiest man in America. It was also, purely and simply, little more than a duplication of the pricing at Southwest. An advertising budget of $20 million was set for the first two weeks, believed to be an industry record.

Crandall not only hoped but insisted that the rest of the industry follow his lead. Should anyone undercut American's fares, he declared, American would match, and its entire new fare structure would be proportionally reduced. There would be no more selective matching of special fare promotions. Airlines seeking to undermine American's new system, Crandall warned, would be stomped on by the world's biggest airline with the full weight of its fare structure.

There was absolutely no disputing that value pricing, however imbued with hype, held out tremendous appeals for the airline industry. And for a few days, it stuck. United rushed out new television spots so quickly that it had to recruit a substitute announcer until the company's usual narrator, Gene Hackman, could be scheduled into the studio. In the next few days reservations volume at American and elsewhere surged, although it was unclear whether this was a one-time gain triggered by publicity or the beginning of a permanent change in travel patterns.

Then while Crandall was running on his treadmill at home watching the early morning news, he saw the announcement of a 50 percent price cut by Northwest, couched as an "adults fly free" promotion. "Son of a bitch!" he cried. Northwest was spitting in the face of value pricing. It was precisely the kind of gimmicky, confusing, half-baked promotion that Crandall was trying to wipe out.

Crandall was now like Truman, contemplating whether to allow the long, bloody war to drag on or to drop the atomic bomb. He could simply copy the Northwest promotion by allowing American passengers to travel with a child for free, but that would require American to institute a new fare category, which he had vowed never to do. Or Crandall could lower the boom on Northwest. He could announce a 50 percent price cut on every leisure seat on every plane flying every route.

Crandall's people recognized that the company was on the cusp of a monumental decision. Someone might have spoken up to counsel against Armageddon. That speech might have come from Barbara Amster, Crandall's longtime pricing chief and one of his most trusted aides, but Amster was in Europe. No one apparently gave Bob Crandall that speech. No one appealed for peace, or if someone did, the performance was not convincing.

The bombs-away order went out, and suddenly it was possible to fly coast to coast for $100 on a full-service airline. The old "ninety-niner" was back, even after a decade of galloping inflation.

In the summer of '92 there was an electronic passenger riot in America—the telecommunications equivalent of shoppers tearing through soft goods in a sales bin. There had never been anything close to it. The long-distance telephone system of the United States literally locked up on calls to the airlines. On the peak day of the frenzy AT&T alone handled a record 177.4 million calls—1.6 billion over an 11-day period. American's Sabre system in one day created 1.2 million new reservations. People who couldn't get through by phone simply drove to the airport to buy tickets, often two, three, and four tickets. Within several days the airlines' inventory for the summer was sold out—virtually every seat filled. And a few weeks later, when those flights began taking off, there was another riot, an orgy of travel. Hotels were brimming. Rental car lots were cleaned out.

By autumn, when the kids at last were laying out their back-to-school clothes and the last of the sale seats had been flown, someone calculated that 11 percent of the households in the United States had at least one member who flew in those few weeks. And the airlines—most of them, anyway—went deeper into the red.

In the summer of 1993 Herb Kelleher finally announced that he would take Southwest, for the first time, to the East Coast. It was a juicy place to be because the low-fare revolution had long ago been put down in the East. His target was Baltimore-Washington International Airport, a center of high fares. Some of the established airlines at Baltimore-Washington were charging more than $300 for a one-way ticket; Southwest announced service to some of the same markets for as little as one tenth the full fare.

Kelleher had another reason to choose Baltimore-Washington. Southwest was now by any reckoning a huge airline, if still a niche player. But outside the cities it served, practically no one had heard of it. Moreover, the name Southwest carried little clout in Washington. Adding a destination 30 miles north of the nation's capital, Kelleher reckoned, would help Washington understand what Southwest was all about.

Kelleher was right. When the Clinton administration established a commission to investigate the problems of the airline industry, Kelleher was the only high-ranking airline executive appointed. Southwest's arrival on the East Coast caused many of the national media to discover Southwest, as if it had only recently come into being. Kelleher starred in a commercial for the American Express card. Before long Kelleher was on the cover of *Fortune* under a head-line asking, "America's Best CEO?"

By the end of 1993 Southwest was the eighth largest airline in the United States (behind United, American, Delta, Northwest, Continental, USAir, and what was left of TWA). But among the 100 largest airline markets in the country—the 100 city pairs traveled most frequently by the most passengers—Southwest was number one.

Southwest's success had by 1994 spawned a generation of imitators, companies established from the remains of Eastern, Pan Am, and other failures. Many went into business serving the New York–Florida market, where a low price was all that mattered, companies with names like Carnival Air Lines and UltraAir. A group of unemployed Eastern and Pan Am people, their companies killed in part by high labor costs, formed an airline they called Kiwi International, in honor of the bird that could not fly. Kiwi's pilots gladly went to work for lower wage levels than Ed Acker or even Frank Lorenzo had ever had the nerve to impose. The transformation of the passenger markets was especially evident in the name chosen by the most successful of the new entrants, based in Atlanta: ValuJet Airlines.

While some forgot (or were too young to know) that the upstarts constituted a second generation of Southwest imitators, there was no doubt that the new upstarts were benefiting from the errors of the earlier generation. Texas International, People Express, the post-bankruptcy Continental, and others had copied elements of the Southwest formula but had then strayed, lusting for the trappings of the established airlines: widebody airplanes, hubs, computers. The first generation of upstarts had tried to acquire for themselves the kind of presence that the major airlines had been awarded in the spoils conference of 1934. The second generation knew better than to overextend. The notion of critical mass had been discredited.

The second upstart revolution caused many to question whether Bob Crandall really knew what he was doing after all. The pilots' union at American hired a consulting firm that accused Crandall of overmanaging American Airlines. "The normal profit motive," the consultants' report said, "gave way to the notions that if two hubs are good then six must be better, and if 'bigger is better' then 'biggest must be best.' " Hubs, the consultants said, forced flight crews to sit and wait for airplanes. Hubs required the company to maintain a massive infrastructure. Southwest by contrast had no hubs and no reservation network. Southwest simply flew from one city to another and back again, over and over. American's problem wasn't high wages or restrictive work rules, the report concluded, but "structural problems within management's control."

Crandall bitterly resented his pilots' joining the "tulip craze" around Southwest. "You never see me on the line trying to fly *your* leg," he scowled at a meeting of captains. "You never hear me telling you how to fly airplanes! . . . We trust you with very expensive machines. We trust you every day with our lives."

Even his admirers began to doubt Crandall. Had he lost his touch? He and his team had always come up with the silver bullet for whatever problem plagued the company, whether charter operators or Braniff or People Express, whether the need to establish a computer reservation network or to institute b-scales or to break into the international markets. Had Crandall lost his creative spark? Had his organization atrophied? Or after 15 years of deregulation had all the original ideas at last been used up?

As if to comfort his doubters, Crandall in the fall of 1993 finally joined the battle he had been avoiding for so long: he attacked his profitability problems on the cost side, with labor as his target and Southwest as his new bogeyman. While waiting for the pilots' contract to expire, he resolved to make an example of the flight attendants. If he had to take a strike—his first strike ever—then so be it. Despite his unforgiving debt levels, he would take a chance that he could fly through a strike. Flight attendants, after all, were easy to replace. Nobody respected their picket lines. Flight attendants couldn't begin to shut down an airline.

Crandall, however, had not counted on two things. After years at the bottom of the industry's heap, the flight attendant profession was ready to extract revenge. In addition, Crandall was unprepared for Denise Hedges. In her 23 years as an American flight attendant, Hedges, age 46, had had three children, each born under a different company maternity policy. The shifting rules stirred her interest in union affairs. As American grew in the 1980s, flight attendants became numbers in complex scheduling formulas built on higher mathematics, making their work schedules dizzyingly unpredictable.

Crandall wanted even more control over scheduling—to eliminate hard-fought union staffing rules that promoted flight attendant hiring but compromised the perfect deployment of personnel. Crandall also wanted to block the union's attempt to erode further what remained of the b-scale provisions in the contract. And in keeping with the need to manage such great numbers efficiently, American insisted on their maintaining uniform weight standards, which failed to take account of the changing demographics of a flight attendant corps that included more mothers and older women all the time.

Hedges vowed to resist. She brought in labor consultants who had perfected telephone trees and other mass communication techniques. Rank-and-file flight attendants were indoctrinated in the evils—and dangers—of crossing any picket lines once a strike began, just as the United pilots had been in the great strike of '85. "You will be marked as a scab for life," the flight attendants' strike handbook said. "Strikers will know who you are. . . . You will not be forgiven."

The lapsing of the 30-day clock freed American to impose its own terms on the flight attendants in November 1993. But Hedges did not call a strike immediately, waiting instead until just before the long Thanksgiving weekend, the busiest travel period of the year. The strike, Hedges furthermore determined, would last only 11 days, her estimate of the time it would take American to train replacement workers. As Thanksgiving approached, the flight attendants also moved to curry public support—not easily done, since a holiday strike would terribly inconvenience passengers. Flight attendants distributed pamphlets pointing out that they earned a median salary of $23,007, "less than a mail carrier, or a roofer, or a security guard." They called attention to in-flight sexual harassment. And through a mixture of hyperbole and honesty, they called the public's attention to themselves as victims in other ways:

> We lift, push, pull, bend, and stoop in confined work areas. We are often required to work 14 hours on domestic flights, more on foreign trips. We are subject to constant changes in cabin temperature and humidity, vibration, turbulence, and time-zone changes that disrupt our work-sleep patterns. . . . And we pay for it all with back problems, foot, knee, and leg aches, eye, ear, nose, and throat maladies, headaches, high rates of colds and infections, hearing problems, skin irritations, menstrual and reproductive problems, varicose veins, fatigue, and depression.

This outpouring of grievances had an effect as well on the attitude of the flight attendants themselves. At one point someone distributed an essay comparing the company's behavior to that of an abusive husband.

If any managers sensed a groundswell of bitterness against the company, they were not reporting it to the people at headquarters, or if they were, no one there had the nerve to tell Bob Crandall. "They were regularly polled," Crandall would later say of the supervisors, "and they regularly expressed the opinion that flight attendants would come to work." As Thanksgiving approached, American blitzed its markets with messages that any strike would present only a slight, temporary disruption; there was no reason for anyone to change his or her travel plans.

On the night of the negotiating deadline, November 17, 1993, Crandall flew into Dallas from a meeting in New York and went to the office. His bargainers, meeting with the union's negotiators at a site in New Orleans, were still pressing his demands. About midnight, a time when American's operations had largely rolled to a stop for the day, the strike officially began.

About 4 A.M. Bob Baker, the airline's operating chief, traipsed to American's operating center, a gymnasium-size room filled with dispatchers, schedulers, mainframes, and video workstations. A computer was programmed to flash warnings when crews had not signed in for their flights on the electronic punch-in clocks scattered throughout the airline's realm. With daylight approaching, the system all but started smoking. Almost none of the flight attendants were coming to work. And the company had not trained replacements.

There was, moreover, a kind of double whammy hitting Crandall. The American fleet operated on such brilliantly efficient schedules that in order to operate any significant number of flights, American had to keep the entire system in operation; a selective shutdown, Crandall's people determined, would only "supercharge" the complexity of maintaining everything else. Thus American was enduring the punitive and improbable need to keep planes taking off and landing the world over with too few flight attendants, and therefore not a single paying passenger aboard. American was shut down by a strike but still had to pay to keep its operation going—and on top of that still had to service its debt.

To make matters worse, because American was able to board some flights with line crossers or management flight attendants, it continued urging passengers to maintain their travel plans; passengers were drawn to the airport only to watch planes take off without passengers. Even American's own labor negotiators had to fly back from their last bargaining session in New Orleans on Southwest. As angry passengers left the airport, they heard picketing flight attendants chant that management, not the strikers, were responsible for the inconvenience:

> *They lied to us*
> *They lied to you*
> *Now you know*
> *What we go through.*

At one point Federico Peña, the transportation secretary, blasted American for issuing a press release claiming it had "operated a normal schedule"; Crandall had scratched out a more moderate characterization in a draft of the press release and had substituted those words himself.

Crandall's strategists rationalized American as a victim of "a very angry group of people," as one later described it, a group prone to activism in part because of "the gay and lesbian component." "You set up a scenario," this executive said, "where you can get a lot of energy very quickly, and it can get out of control."

Crandall again had become his own victim. His ferocious temper had blocked the flow of vital information. The size and unforgiving perfection of his schedules had cost him dearly.

Four days into the strike, with Thanksgiving at hand and with Crandall expressing fears to his aides of falling into an "abyss," President Clinton personally intervened, asking whether both sides would submit the entire contract to arbitration. Crandall readily agreed. The full 11-day strike might well have killed American Airlines.

About the time of the flight attendants' strike, the cover of *The New York Times Magazine* showed an American plane flying off the page, leaving behind a quote from Crandall: "Unless the world changes, we will never buy another plane. We won't replace the airplanes that wear out. . . . The company simply won't be here anymore."

Some of Crandall's aides cringed at his rhetoric, but they knew it was bluster, calculated to worry the unions into relenting to his proposals. Bluster was all Crandall had left if he wished to cut his labor costs. If the flight attendants could beat him, any employee group could. Ultimately the pilot contract too would go to arbitration, so fearful of another strike had Crandall become. "That strike was a tragedy," Crandall told employees. "We must never have another."

The bluff in Crandall's threat to liquidate the airline was evident only a few blocks from American headquarters, where at the height of the tension with his employee groups Crandall presided over the dedication of an architectural masterpiece called the American Airlines C. R. Smith Museum. If Crandall had any expectation that American would shrink into oblivion, it was not evident in this museum— a memorial not only to C. R. Smith, but to R. L. Crandall.

At the front entrance the company had lashed down an American Airlines DC-3, the plane by which C. R. Smith had revolutionized the economics of air travel—a gleaming, silvery bird, with its endless wings and rounded deco features, meticulously restored by a group of retired American employees. "The most significant commercial airplane ever built," a plaque read. Inside the building was a steeply pitched theater, outfitted with leather airline seats and a towering Imax movie screen. The same film was shown hourly, every day of the week, with the employees of American Airlines presumed to be the people most often watching it at any time. As the music swelled, the film showed American baggage handlers trading high fives alongside their belt loader, while a newly graduated flight attendant shuddered with a thrill as her wings were pinned to her lapel.

In the museum's main hall was the exhibit on C. R. Smith's life (no mention of the Watergate checks, of course). One of the famous Wurlitzer organs, retrieved from a jumbo jet lounge, was placed under glass. Nearby a series of video screens told the story of how Al Casey had been brought into American 20 years earlier at a low point in the company's history—and how Casey had quickly come to anoint a new president:

> His eye fell on Robert Crandall. . . . Crandall proved to be the ideal choice to lead American in the unpredictable, rough-and-tumble airline industry of the 1980s. . . . Most observers credit him for American's successful passage through the post-deregulation years . . . Among his accomplishments [were] negotiation of innovative collective bargaining agreements . . . automation of travel agencies . . . creation of new hubs . . . expansion into key international markets . . .

The curators' script did not comment on Crandall's skill at exploiting the leverage of the airline business. But in late 1994, with the recession finally well past, with American's labor costs moderated if not reduced, with the battle against the upstarts largely played out for the time being, something extraordinary occurred. American Airlines reported the highest quarterly profit figure in its history—the highest, indeed, of any airline in the history of the airline business. And the surge continued into 1995. American, it appeared, was not so badly broken after all.

For Crandall the only disappointment was in thinking how much bigger the score would have been, if only his employees had done it his way.

One morning in June 1994 passengers began gathering in a gate area bathed in the first sunlight of the day, waiting to board the early

American Airlines flight from Dallas to LaGuardia. Twenty minutes before departure a nondescript white-haired man in a sports shirt ambled into the gate area with a Styrofoam coffee cup, a hanging bag, and a briefcase. He began chatting with the strangers seated and standing nearby. He could have been anybody, but he was Herb.

Buckling into a first-class seat, Kelleher noted that Crandall had packed another airplane. Kelleher himself was flying on American because his own airline did not serve New York. A 20-minute turn-around, much less one half as long, was an impossible dream in New York.

On this particular morning Southwest happened to be in the news, and as a consequence once again people were questioning whether the company could forever survive. For years Southwest had refused to pay fees for any bookings through the major computer reservations systems, other than certain slight fees to American's Sabre. The two other leading systems, Apollo and System One, finally announced that they were kicking Southwest out. Kelleher said fine. Any lost sales, he estimated, would be trifling in comparison to the tens of millions of dollars that the networks wanted to charge to preserve his visibility in the travel agency computers. The fact was, passengers didn't particularly need travel agents (and travel agents didn't particularly want clients) for $19 flights. The computers were part of the full-service airline industry—the equivalent of cable television. Kelleher only needed rabbit ears.

One unwelcome effect of the computer fracas was a plunge in the price of Southwest stock, which hurt the company's employees and none among them more than Kelleher, whose holdings had ballooned to well over a million shares. Over the course of several months the price would tumble from $40 to $20, causing Kelleher's net worth to deflate by better than $40 million, and the price would soon plunge even further, as the bloody California price battle raged with Shuttle by United. Not to worry, Kelleher sighed. "Being a millionaire ain't what it was in the 1890s."

Kelleher asked a flight attendant for a glass of milk to go with his macadamia nut cookie. "I'm coating my stomach for this evening," he explained.

Kelleher was flying to New York for an industry conference, but he had arranged another piece of business while he was there. People had been telling him for years that he should meet Richard Branson of Virgin Atlantic Airways. Kelleher spent a few minutes of the flight memorizing the lyrics of the Sex Pistols' "God Save the Queen" so he could impress Branson.

A pilot emerged from the cockpit with a message transmitted from American's operations center in Dallas and printed out by the onboard computer. It read, "Smooth ride whole way. Tell Herb we said hi."

Kelleher opened his briefcase and spent a few minutes reviewing traffic figures from the company's flights at Baltimore-Washington, opened a year earlier. "There was some expressed dubiety as to whether our coming to the East Coast would be successful," he said. The figures showed that in the fourth quarter of 1993 traffic to Chicago totaled 150,480, an increase of 1,052 percent. "Just a preliminary indication," he noted. As he stowed away the paperwork, his latest reading material slipped out, betraying Kelleher's plans for new service in Salt Lake City. It was a history of the Mormons.

As the plane turned into its final approach, one of the flight attendants leaned over to Kelleher with an extra macadamia nut cookie wrapped in a napkin. He lunged for the cookie but stopped short. "I'm not taking this from *you,* am I?" he asked her. When she said no, Kelleher practically inhaled the dessert.

He left the plane and entered the gate area at LaGuardia fantasizing about his first cigarette in four hours. At the end of a long, up-hill concourse, Kelleher approached a small throng of limousine drivers holding signs with the names of arriving passengers. Huffing and puffing like any four-pack-a-day man bearing a suitcase and briefcase, Kelleher angled past the limo drivers and walked outdoors to light up and stand in line for a cab into the city.

POSTSCRIPT: MAGIC ACT

The history of marketing and technology is the history of ourselves. While marketing reveals what we want as a society, technology determines what we are capable of fulfilling.

What do we want from our airlines? We want them to take us wherever we choose anytime we like, and we want them to do so at a low price. With their superb use of information technology, the airlines go a long way toward fulfilling these wants, but with an important limitation: they cannot satisfy both demands simultaneously. The passenger must sacrifice cost for flexibility, flexibility for cost.

It is for this reason that flying has remained—and doubtless will remain for years—an industry of two components, one serving those motivated by convenience and comfort, another serving those motivated by price. By the mid-1990s, when the settling-in process was well along, aviation was bifurcated as cleanly as the restaurant industry, in which the customer could choose an establishment with a full menu, a bar, and meals prepared to order, or a fast-food restaurant at a high-volume traffic intersection. Or like the television industry, which gave consumers the choice of uniformly consistent reception on dozens of channels for a fee or uneven access to a few channels through a set of inexpensive rabbit ears.

Certainly, there remained occasions when the two separate components of commercial aviation crashed together. Among the major "network" airlines, many of the most strategic hub cities had at last come under the dominion of a single airline: American in Miami, Delta in Atlanta, USAir in Pittsburgh, Northwest in Minneapolis, and United in Denver, among others. As points of connection, these hubs competed vigorously with one another; whenever passengers had the choice of hubs through which to reach their destination, fares remained moderate. The story was different for people who started or ended their journeys in a hub city. These hapless passengers were forced to pay monopoly prices—until a low-cost airline such as Southwest was finally drawn into the market. Then a battle ensued, and fares were quickly brought under control.

Fares had become purely market-driven, as sensitive to supply and demand as a Middle Eastern bazaar. Airline prices no longer bore the slightest relation to the cost of providing the service, which was why a 300-mile trip beginning and ending at a hub airport might cost three times that of a 1,000-mile trip *through* a hub airport. Instead, airline pricing depended almost entirely on what the market in any place and at any moment would bear. The major "network" airlines could only hope that when they had added together their $59 fares, their $1,200 fares, and everything in between, the sum exceeded the cost of having provided the service. For Southwest and other point-to-point carriers the exercise was no different, except that the fares—and their costs—were so much lower to begin with.

As the network airlines and the point-to-point carriers were settling into their respective roles, a new worry emerged for them all. In the first half of the 20th century the airlines had put trains and ocean liners out of business. In the second half they had made intercity auto and bus travel all but anachronistic. As the century drew to a close, it was the airlines who faced a terrifying new competitor: fiber-optic cable.

Notwithstanding that one transmits voices, images, and data and the other whole human beings, telecommunication bears an uncanny resemblance to flight. The telephone system, like the air transport system, was developed as a regulated public utility. Both began by offering products that were remote and prohibitively priced. (Charles Lindbergh devoted two pages of *The Spirit of St. Louis* to the cost and marvel of long-distance telephony.) Both industries were deregulated at a time when new entrants—Southwest and MCI—were demonstrating the marketing virtue of low prices. In both industries the upstarts emerged only after succeeding in protracted legal battles against entrenched competitors. Both industries were swept up in deregulation drives. To create brand loyalty in a newly competitive world, the airlines introduced frequent-flier programs, and when the long-distance phone companies created their own repeat-usage programs, they too began awarding frequent-flier miles.

The aviation chieftains have long looked warily on phones, as well as the kindred technologies of telex, fax, and modem. But for most of the airlines' history the phone proved a friend rather than a foe. Just as moviegoing stimulates book buying and television viewing stimulates newspaper buying, so had telecommunications always seemed to promote air travel. More and better and faster information only made business people want to have more meetings, not fewer.

By the mid-1990s that had begun to change. After studying the matter for decades, American Airlines detected that for the first time in history businesses were sometimes choosing video and audio conferencing over flying. Electronic communications, American's studies showed, was poised to reduce business travel by as much as 11 percent by 1998, representing $1.3 billion in business vanishing from American alone—a sum vastly exceeding its entire profit in an excellent year.

American was wise to remain on guard, for telecommunication technology had finally begun to accomplish what the airlines could not: uniting low cost and flexibility of use in the same product. Fiber-optic cable (and even some conventional wiring) became capable of transmitting so much digital information that a dozen people could meet face-to-face, in real time, while writing on the same document and studying the same engineering drawing or X-ray. Moreover, by 1995 they could do all this by loading $1,995 in off-the-shelf software into each of their desktop PCs.

How could the airlines ever begin to cut their costs to meet such a challenge?

Aircraft technology had largely run its course, at least so far as anyone could see. New airplane models could transform the cost structure of the airline industry only by flying at much greater speeds or with vastly increased seating capacities. And although there was much talk of "monster jets" and "super jumbos" flying at supersonic speeds, the airlines, it appeared, faced financial pressures too challenging in the short term to gamble on such long-term solutions.

Labor-saving technology was also largely played out; by the 1990s it was possible to fly almost any distance with only one engine on each wing, saving maintenance costs, and only two pilots in the cockpit. Herb Kelleher remarked that if the Wright brothers were alive, "Wilbur would have to fire Orville to reduce costs." But it was hard to imagine any passenger content to board a flight with a solo pilot.

With flying technology static, the industry turned its attention to seating technology. At the airlines' request, Boeing rolled out the 777 in 1995 with galleys and lavatories that could be removed to make way for more seats, should any airline wish to step up service in a densely traveled short-haul market. Refining cabin flexibility even further, British Airways developed individual seats that could be made two inches narrower, instantly adding an additional seat to every row when the time came to switch an aircraft to a vacation route (to Barcelona, say) from a business route (perhaps to Paris). In the cost-saving drive ValuJet introduced "ticketless travel," recalling Phil Bakes's "airport of the future" project nearly a decade earlier at Continental. Passengers received a confirmation number by phone, which they presented at a boarding gate as if checking into a hotel. Other airlines copied the practice.

Finally, the airlines turned their attention to the one major category of expense that had long escaped the ax. For years they had been paying travel agents a 10 percent commission on every ticket, plus special sweeteners. But by 1995 the nation's 33,000 travel agents could hide no longer. The airlines imposed a $50 commission cap, a policy that had the effect of cutting the airlines' costs by billions of dollars annually—a major breakthrough, it would appear. Unfortunately, the effect on the passenger, in whose interest this move was purportedly conducted, was quickly blunted if not negated: the major agencies announced that they would simply begin making passengers pay fees on top of the ticket prices.

Southwest even tread into the sacrosanct area of safety in the search for further efficiencies. It began lobbying for permission to push away from boarding gates while passengers were still taking their seats, arguing that the four minutes that this requirement added to the average flight cost the company $182 million a year in lost flying revenue—the equivalent of roughly $4 a ticket. Buses roar through city streets with passengers standing, Southwest argued, which was true, of course, except that buses are equipped with gripping devices for precisely this purpose, and bus passengers do not hoist heavy bags overhead while the vehicle is moving, and buses rarely hit the brakes with the suddenness that an airplane taxiing backward might.

There came a point when all such cost-cutting endeavors took on the air of disingenuousness. Even if consumers were demanding lower and lower fares, was it really worth consciously making a safety trade-off? Was it worth alienating the travel agent distribution channel? Was it worth a new round of ugly battles with organized labor, all to cause a few more people to fly a little more often?

No. It was time for the airlines to moderate their obsession with costs. They had whacked enough already. They had nearly cut to the core. It was enough for the airlines to dedicate themselves to preventing an increase in costs. Further cutting endangered the most basic and fundamental product provided by the airlines. That product is magic.

The magic is most abundant in the airlines' safety record. In America alone the airlines hurtle their more than 1 million a day over tremendous distances with injuries no worse than a few broken nails. To relentlessly attack costs year upon year, with no letup, only invites compromise, and even a single compromise is one too many. Merely establishing a dialogue about loosening on-board safety procedures—to invite so explicit a trade-off between safety and costs—is a first step down a slippery slope that the airlines, if they stop and reflect, would wisely choose not to take.

How we feel when we fly is another part of the magic. Complaints come loud and long from some of those who became spoiled in the regulated era, when seats were wide, meals were elegant, and flight attendants had college degrees. But for most people, the mystical quality remains. Flying, the novelist Joyce Carol Oates wrote in 1995, fosters "fantasies of childhood, of omnipotence, rapid shifts of being, 'miraculous' moments; it stirs our capacity for dreaming." Those who claim otherwise are either liars or cynics. The journey itself remains part of the richness of travel—except to the extent that we are distracted by the annoyances and miseries of obnoxious service, late arrivals, lost bags, crowded seats, long waits for the bathroom, and endless dashes through hub airports, all of which can only become more common as the airlines continue to cut costs.

If the airlines feel compelled to cut costs further in order to make flying as accessible as a phone call, they risk debasing their product to the same level. The airlines have legitimate reasons to worry about the advent of video telephones and other new communications technologies. But they will lose a certain amount of business to new rivals no matter what. So long as the airlines preserve their magic quality—including, above all, their safety and reliability—they will be guaranteed a significant role in the workings of the world. Science will never digitize an embrace. Electronics will never convey the wavering in the eye of a negotiating adversary. Fiber-optic cable can do many things, but it cannot transport hot sand, fast snow, or great ruins.

Consumers will always pay to fly at a half-reasonable price, unless the people providing the service drive them away.

Are the leaders of commercial aviation up to the task? Can they control their costs without debasing their service? Can they motivate their workers without alienating them? The answers are neither simple nor clear.

The past 25 years in aviation history was an extraordinary period, demanding an extreme sort of executive. From the moment the jumbo jets appeared the gloves came off, first in the competition to provide the most absurdly solicitous service, then to provide the lowest price. The brutal fare wars that gave so many their first taste of flying would never have been so significant without the likes of Frank Lorenzo, Phil Bakes, and Don Burr. It took a Bob Crandall to develop the sophisticated pricing necessary to fill up the airplane cabin. Sir Colin Marshall set a vital example for quality and consistency. Only the macho aggressiveness of a Dick Ferris could keep organized labor from taking all. A compulsive organizer such as Stephen Wolf was exactly the kind of leader required to extend an airline around the globe. Ed Acker displayed the keenest sense of growth.

But that was then. The airline markets are different now. Though it took nearly two decades, the shocking effects of deregulation have largely run their course. There will always be battles, of course; in a business won and lost in the margins, the fight over a single point of market share will always assume life or death proportions. But these titanic struggles have become, and will remain, far fewer. Today, the airlines need leaders willing to commit themselves to the customer as an end in himself rather than as a prize in a contest of adversaries.

The relentless efficiency of history and economics has gone a long way toward making the necessary adjustments at the top. The great airline leaders of the past 25 years—men for their time—are nearly all gone now. Within this special group of leaders, only three remain: Herb Kelleher, Sir Colin Marshall, and Bob Crandall. And in Crandall's case, the impossible had occurred in 1995. The title of president of American Airlines, which Crandall had long vowed never to yield so long as he remained the chairman, went to Donald Carty, one of the architects of American's fabulous expansion in the 1980s. Carty was a man of obvious intellect, perhaps even Bob Crandall's equal. And although Carty was capable of flashing anger and aggression, in those respects he did not come close to matching Crandall.

As for Kelleher and Marshall, they were men of ego every bit as much as the others. They too pursued their goals with fervor: the chairmanship of a global airline in Marshall's case, and the creation and survival of a niche airline in Kelleher's. Neither Marshall nor Kelleher had an unblemished career; both displayed a knack for pushing to the edge of the rulebook of business. But they also distinguished themselves with dignity. They were satisfied to win without killing off their adversaries. They were content to profit without profiteering. They saw themselves as part of something larger: an intricate economic system that depends on the worthy intentions of its participants.

Business, after all, is business. It is the space in which technology and marketing unite, in which man conducts the serious work of fulfilling the physical needs of society. Business is not sport, is not amusement, is not a toy—least of all the delicate business of flying.

POSTSCRIPT TO THE PAPERBACK EDITION

The danger in writing about a dynamic industry is that the story never ends. The tableau shifts constantly. The best a writer can accomplish is capturing an accurate snapshot of the moment when the final lines are committed to paper.

The airline industry has continued to evolve, although the pace of change has slowed from the halcyon days following deregulation. Stephen Wolf, who led, turned around, and reaped tremendous profits at more airlines than perhaps any executive in aviation history, agreed to try his hand one more time, at the long-suffering USAir. The assignment encompassed both of the main obstacles that Wolf had overcome in his previous campaigns: a high cost structure and a mishmash of a route map. The employees of USAir were urgently hoping that Wolf would not order a new paint job for the fleet, the first signal, it had always seemed, in his past efforts that he was getting ready to sell an airline.

Wolf's move to USAir was fraught with a certain irony, as it threw him into partnership with one of the airlines that had maneuvered so vigorously against him during his tenure at United: British Airways. The marketing alliance between British Airways and USAir remained a favorable arrangement for both companies, but its future was thrown into question as yet a different marketing agglomeration occurred, this one between the unlikely partners of British Airways and American Airlines.

These were the same two airlines that had fought so bitterly when American moved to plant its flag at Heathrow and British Airways maneuvered so desperately to keep it out; the fight had been just as nasty when British Airways was buying into USAir, and American cried foul. And although protégés were coming up rapidly behind both of them, Sir Colin Marshall and Robert Crandall remained the chairmen of BA and American, respectively. There had been no love lost between them over the years. Crandall, of course, had been known to some British Airways loyalists as "Wretched Robert." But by June 1996, when the two airlines announced they would coordinate their schedules and feed passengers into one another's systems, the commercial imperatives at last had begun to outweigh the personality issues and the legacy of feuding. As partners, American and BA became an airline powerhouse unlike any the world had ever seen. The two airlines dominated the vital North Atlantic. They forged a vibrant link between Europe and the rapidly developing economies of South America. British Airways helped begin to fill the biggest hole in the American route map, in the Far East.

Whether USAir would be ultimately cast aside or fully absorbed into the BA-American alliance—indeed whether it might even be acquired outright—remained unclear. But to the people who followed the industry's personnel lineup, the involvement of three personalities with so much history—Wolf, Crandall, and Marshall—could only make things more interesting.

Partnerships were taking hold throughout the global industry, recreating in a sense the kind of unified air-transport system that existed before the winds of deregulation had blown. Northwest and KLM had a powerful marketing partnership, although towering egos on both sides had sparked a bitter control dispute. United had cast its lot with Lufthansa, and Delta with Swissair, and various European and American lines were making deals in Asia. There remained a certain cheat in these arrangements—passengers would make a reservation with one airline, only to find themselves flying under the colors of another. Indeed the two leading practitioners of this marketing artifice, British Airways and American, had once been its staunchest foes. But disclosure cures all: so long as travelers were informed of the precise nature of their flying arrangements—and too often they weren't—they benefited from the linkup of international airlines, if for no other reason than because the odds were better that they could change airlines without having to claim and recheck their baggage.

There were other hopeful signs in 1996. The airlines at last seemed to be coming to terms with the off-putting effects of their poor service. Inspired by the benign internal culture of Southwest and the thrilling (if tentative) outbreak of harmony at employee-owned United, many airlines began trying to patch things up with their disaffected employee groups. The best proof was American's preliminary agreement in September 1996 on a conciliatory contract with its pilots—an agreement that had remained pending since about the time of the 1993 flight attendants' strike. The late 1990s was a period of heightened management sensibility throughout the industry, and although the major airlines were late getting with the program, they were at last getting in. No one remembered that nearly two decades earlier, a brilliant if emotional founder named Donald Burr had built what was briefly a fine airline on the principles of trust and empowerment.

The second generation of startups—the heirs to People Express—remained a vibrant force. Here too the major airlines appeared to be changing their spots, controlling, to some degree, the blood lust they had once exhibited when an upstart dared encroach on their turf. But the competition remained vigorous. Perhaps the most pitched battle was between Delta and the upstart ValuJet, which after a surprisingly strong beginning lost a plane in the Florida Everglades in the spring of 1996, with the deaths numbering 110. While investigators continued to probe, many people could not avoid drawing a comparison to the Air Florida crash in Washington, D.C., at the dawn of deregulation—another case of an airline brought down to earth following a furious growth campaign.

And what of the original upstart, Southwest Airlines? Herb Kelleher had taken it into Florida and the Northwest (although, conspicuously, not into New York). In the summer of 1996 he hosted a huge soiree to celebrate the company's twenty-fifth anniversary, asking guests to come dressed in tuxedo jackets and jeans. Southwest had grown into the seventh largest airline in America, and it showed little indication of slowing down.

There were other signs that the industry's leadership had learned some lessons. Despite the booming economy of 1996, the airlines kept their capacity under rigorous control instead of ordering every new airplane in sight, at last overcoming the "sex appeal" factor that Alfred Kahn had once identified. This fact, combined with ever more powerful yield management systems, helped the airlines sell a larger proportion of their seats than at any time since Juan Trippe put wicker chairs in the back of the mail planes to Cuba. The majority of flights, in fact, were flying virtually 100 percent full. The fare wars were few and far between. And although the business traveler was still getting gouged, there remained bargains for families and other leisure passengers who could plan their travels ahead.

Of course, all these positive developments were occurring in a time of strong economic expansion and relentless globalization. It was easy to forget that the airline industry—that management tightrope, that balancing act—had as much leverage in good times as in bad. Only when the economy again moved into the minus column would anyone know for sure whether the leaders of the industry had changed their war-mongering ways, or whether, at last, they, and their industry, had matured.

NOTES

This book is based on hundreds of hours of interviews with the principal characters, as well as tens of thousands of pages of published materials—court records, private correspondence, articles, studies, and other books. To keep this section from overtaking the entire book I have tried to limit the number of citations within the goal of satisfying a skeptical reader, one who might ask, "I wonder how he knows that?" I have particularly emphasized citing sources for the thoughts and words I attribute to my characters. Every one of these comes from somewhere—from one or more parties to a conversation, a published quotation, an assertion in a legal affidavit, a speech. Where no citation is given for someone's words or feelings it is usually because I have judged the source to be obvious from the context or from nearby citations.

In the case of articles I have generally provided a full reference, including the headline and byline, on the first appearance of a citation within a chapter and an abbreviated note for any subsequent appearance within the same chapter. The following abbreviations appear throughout the notes: *BW* for *Business Week, NYT* for *New York Times,* and *WSJ* for *Wall Street Journal.*

I have not followed a uniform style for captioning speeches and correspondence. Instead I have generally described these in the form in which they appeared on the documents themselves.

Prologue
page xvii "a single gesture": Saint-Exupéry, *Flight to Arras,* in *Airman's Odyssey,* page 383.

page xviii more adult Americans: Extrapolated from vehicle registration figures and Gallup surveys.

page xix world's biggest industry: "Travel and Tourism Is Top Employer," *Travel Weekly,* Apr. 6, 1992.

page xix "godlike power": Lindbergh, *The Spirit of St. Louis,* page 94.

page xx "savagely competitive": Quoted in "The Airline Mess," by Wendy Zellner and Andrea Rothman, *BW,* July 6, 1992.

page xx "don't have the stomach": Baker 4/23/93 interview.

page xx offers from the White House: Borman, *Countdown,* page 260.

page xx 43 vice presidents: Eastern Air Lines, Inc., 1968 annual report to shareholders.

page xxi 9 mm handgun: Borman 1/29/94 interview.

Chapter 1: Takeoff

page 3 unsteady his hand: Ross, *The Last Hero,* page 69.

page 4 "airlines radiating": Lindbergh, *We,* page 61.

page 4 "passengers for half-price:" *Ibid.,* page 79.

page 4 "What would you think": Quoted in Lindbergh, *The Spirit of St. Louis,* page 74.

page 4 "I've got a reputation": *Ibid.,* page 61.

page 4 "I made it": Quoted in Solberg, *Conquest of the Skies,* page 70.

page 4 baseball games: *Ibid.,* page 71.

page 4 the Lindy hop: Sann, *The Lawless Decade,* page 162.

page 4 "most cherished citizen": *Time,* Jan. 2, 1928.

page 5 four million New Yorkers: "A Little of What the World Thought of Lindbergh," by Fitzhugh Green, appendix to Lindbergh, *We,* page 300.

page 5 window in the Union Club: Daley, *An American Saga,* page 62. For Trippe's background, including the formation of Pan Am, see also Solberg, *Conquest of the Skies;* Bender and Altschul, *The Chosen Instrument;* Davies, *Airlines of the United States Since 1914;* and Gandt, *Skygods.*

page 5 fraternity brothers: "The Only Way to Fly," by T. A. Heppenheimer, *Audacity,* Spring 1995.

page 5 bidding low: Johnson, *Airway One,* page 13; "United Air Lines," by F. Robert van der Linden, in *Encyclopedia of American Business History and Biography.*

page 6 4,000 guests: Green, "A Little of What the World Thought."

page 6 Trippe . . . distinguished himself: Daley, *An American Saga,* page 62.

page 6 retainer of $10,000: Herrmann, *Anne Morrow Lindbergh,* page 58. Lindbergh entered into a similar arrangement as technical advisor to TWA, which for a time called itself "the Lindbergh Line."

page 6 traffic jam: Daley, *An American Saga,* page 67.

page 7 "bathe in Bacardi": Quoted in Solberg, *Conquest of the Skies,* page 80.

page 7 Al Capone: *Ibid.,* page 80.

page 7 elegant civilian clothes: Bender and Altschul, *The Chosen Instrument,* page 136.

page 7 aunt named Juanita: *Ibid.* page 26.

page 7 public relations operative: Daley, *An American Saga,* page 73.

page 8 wet blotters: Rickenbacker, *Rickenbacker,* page 176.

page 8 Christmas cards: Davies, *Airlines of the United States Since 1914,* page 43.

page 8 busiest airport: Remarks by Robert L. Crandall before the Rotary Club of Tulsa, July 12, 1978.

page 8 "stars weren't right": Quoted in *Aircraft Year Book for 1933,* page 56.

page 9 followed railroad tracks: Solberg, *Conquest of the Skies,* page 106.

page 9 whirling propellers: *Ibid.,* page 115.

page 9 hosed down: Solberg, *ibid.,* page 115.

page 9 a presidential commission: "Walter Folger Brown," by David D. Lee, *The Encyclopedia of American Business History and Biography.*

page 9 Brown changed the rules: Brown's maneuvers are described, among other places, in "U.S. Aviation and the Air Mail," *Fortune,* May 1934; Davies, *Airlines of the United States Since 1914;* Serling, *Eagle;* and H. Smith, *Airways.*

page 10 "If we were holding this meeting": Quoted in H. Smith, *Airways,* page 242.

page 11 12 army fliers perished: *Ibid.,* page 256.

page 11 last their lifetimes: The bitterness between Lindbergh and Roosevelt intensified their conflict over U.S. intervention in World War II. The feud is detailed in Lindbergh's *Wartime Journals.*

page 11 a dozen skeletons: The cartoon is reprinted in Allen, *The Airline Builders,* page 90.

page 12 hard-drinking Texan: Smith's background is told, among other places, in "Interview with C. R. Smith," Dec. 4, 1975, on file in American Airlines historical records; "There's More Than One Way to Run an Airline," by Perrin Stryker, *Fortune,* February 1961; Serling, *Eagle;* and Allen, *The Airline Builders.*

page 12 ragtag fleet: "Interview with C. R. Smith," Dec. 4, 1975.

page 12 increased the cost: The economics of the DC-3 are detailed in Miller and Sawers, *The Technical Development of Modern Aviation,* pages 100–103.

page 12 "Brooklyn Bridge": Quoted in Serling, *Eagle,* page 103.

page 13 Shirley Temple: Solberg, *Conquest of the Skies,* page 171.

page 13 "He still loves me!": Quoted in Serling, *Eagle,* page 103.

page 13 best route: The North Pacific flight of Charles and Anne Lindbergh is chronicled in Ross, *The Last Hero;* Herrmann, *Anne Morrow Lindbergh;* and Daley, *An American Saga.*

page 14 no mail contract: Daley, *An American Saga,* page 144.

page 14 Trippe chartered: The account of Pan Am's South Seas adventure is based on a 42-page internal Pan Am account called "History of the Transpacific Air Service to and through Hawaii," dated Aug. 12, 1944, on file in the Pan Am Collection at the University of Miami Library.

page 14 "imagination of a Jules Verne": Quoted in *ibid.*

page 15 "That's illegal!": Rickenbacker, *Rickenbacker,* pages 218–21. Serling, *From the Captain to the Colonel,* page 149.

page 15 commodity markets: Serling, *Eagle,* page 81.

page 16 "prevent the . . . system from crashing": Quoted in Richard H. K. Vietor, "Contrived Competition: Airline Regulation and Deregulation, 1925–1988," in *Business History Review,* Spring 1990.

page 16 Interstate Commerce Act: Breyer, *Regulation and Its Reform,* page 199.

page 17 Louis J. Hector: This CAB case is described in Johnson, *The Abominable Airlines,* pages 224–26.

page 18 installment loan contract: Solberg, *Conquest of the Skies,* page 349.

page 18 "Present rates": "A Statement of Certain Policies of the Executive Branch of the Government in the General Field of Aviation," Air Coordinating Committee, Report to the President, Aug. 1, 1947.

page 18 "the best impression": "The Cautious Pioneer," *Forbes,* June 1, 1956.

page 19 "most important . . . since Lindbergh's": Quoted in Bender and Altschul, *The Chosen Instrument.*

page 19 Puerto Ricans: Solberg, *Conquest of the Skies,* page 346.

page 19 Second only to Coca-Cola: "Pan Am Corp. Will Sell World Services in Attempt to Give Plaskett More Time," by James T. McKenna, *Aviation Week,* Jan. 23, 1989.

page 19 spaceship: "An Airline of Firsts Folds Wings Which Once Sought Moon," by Asra Q. Nomani, *WSJ,* July 12, 1991.

page 19 largest commercial office building: Daley, *An American Saga,* page 440.

page 20 "future of mankind": *Text of Remarks of Participants at Christening Ceremony for Clipper Young America,* Dulles International Airport, Chantilly, Va., Jan. 15, 1970, on file in the Pan Am archives at the University of Miami.

page 20 days later in New York: The ill-starred maiden voyage of the 747 is described, among other places, in a variety of articles in *WSJ, NYT,* and *Aviation Week.*

page 20 "A dozen bathrooms": Quoted in "Jumbo and the Gremlins," *Time,* Feb. 2, 1970.

page 20 the orchids . . . were dead: "The Tardy 747 Debut Makes the Going Grate," by John Mullane and Doug Ireland, *New York Post,* Jan. 22, 1970.

page 21 largest . . . commercial purchase: Daley, *An American Saga,* page 433.

page 21 "smell normal": "Nation's Airlines Split Over Youth Fares," by Ronald G. Shafer, *WSJ,* Dec. 5, 1969.

page 22 "the all-steak airline": Field 1/16/93 interview.

page 22 Bloody Mary mix: Serling, *Eagle,* page 377.

page 23 ramming them into the wall: Hedges 6/13/94 interview.

page 23 Robert D. Timm: "Under New Chief, CAB Bids to Lift Profits of Airlines, Annoying Consumer Advocates," by Albert R. Karr, *WSJ,* Aug. 7, 1973.

page 23 golf junket: The scandal is detailed in "CAB Chief Takes Self Out of Investigation of Nation's Airlines," *WSJ,* Aug. 21, 1974; Brown, *The Politics of Airline Deregulation;* and a series of letters between Timm and the Ford White House, published in *Aviation Daily.*

page 23 In a burst of reform: Robson's background and his tenure at the CAB were described in the Robson 1/7/93 interview; in the Cohen 2/16/93 interview; and in numerous articles in *Aviation Daily.*

page 23 *The Last Hurrah:* "The Move to Airline Deregulation," by John Robson, *The Bureaucrat,* Summer 1982.

page 24 During the evening: These discussions were described in the Cohen 2/16/93 interview.

page 24 absolutely no idea: Robson 1/7/93 interview.

page 24 fact-finding trip: "CAB Chairman Tours Braniff, TXI Facilities," *Aviation Daily,* Feb. 2, 1976.

Chapter 2: Cheap Thrills, Low Fares

page 25 over cocktails: Southwest Airlines has created an entire mythology about Kelleher's meeting over cocktails with Rollin King. Kelleher likes to tell people that the meeting occurred in a bar, although he's not positive that it did. It is a fair bet, however, that alcohol was involved. It's most likely that Kelleher and King were having cocktails in Kelleher's office. See "Is Herb Kelleher America's Best CEO?" by Kenneth Labich, *Fortune,* May 2, 1994.

page 26 this particular day: The account of the meeting is based on the Kelleher 10/13/93 interview; the Barron, Barrett, and Parker interviews of 4/26/93; a variety of memorabilia hanging on the wall of Southwest

Airlines headquarters; and "A Boy and His Airline," by Jan Jarobe, *Texas Monthly,* Apr. 1989.

page 26 turboprop airplanes: Southwest's original business plan contemplated the use of Electras. "A Study of Air Southwest Co.," by Matthews, Nowlin, MacFarlane & Barrett, Sept. 30, 1967.

page 26 Kelleher was born: The details of Kelleher's upbringing, education, and early career were described in the Kelleher 10/13/93 interview.

page 27 refused to take the shot: This fact, confirmed by Kelleher in the 10/13/93 interview, was reported in Jarobe, *Texas Monthly,* Apr. 1989.

page 28 "ancient truth": "The Great Airline War," by James Fallows, *Texas Monthly,* Dec. 1975.

page 29 split four molars: Kelleher 10/13/93 interview.

page 29 "undue prolongation": Quoted in Fallows, *Texas Monthly,* Dec. 1975.

page 29 show those bastards: Kelleher interviews of 10/13/93 and 10/14/94.

page 29 cocktail party: Kelleher 10/13/93 interview.

page 30 "if the sheriff": Parker 4/26/93 interview.

page 30 congregation in San Antonio: Kelleher 6/14/94 interview.

page 30 fill a fogger: Kelleher 10/13/94 interview.

page 30 airplane hangar: The anecdotes of Southwest's slapdash beginnings come from *Twenty Years of Luv,* a video program produced by Southwest.

page 32 "Our love service means": *Ibid.*

page 32 "Raquel Welch look-alikes": Barrett 4/26/93 interview.

page 32 shot from behind: *Twenty Years of Luv.*

page 32 denied a job: Nielsen, *From Sky Girl to Flight Attendant,* page 8.

page 32 "It strikes me": Quoted in Musbach and Davis, *Flight Attendant,* pages 259–60.

page 33 four-page guidebook: *Ibid.,* page 262.

page 33 comforting properties: This purported attribute was identified in a court case involving Pan Am. "Court Lets Stand Order That Airlines End Anti-Male Bias in Hiring Cabin Attendants," *WSJ,* Nov. 10, 1971.

page 33 "give-and-take of marriage": "The Jet Age Stewardess," unsigned internal article, circa 1960, on file in the archives of American's corporate communications department.

page 34 "want your daughter": Quoted in "Jets Across the U.S.," *Time,* Nov. 17, 1958.

page 34 alarm system: Serling, *Eagle,* page 284.

page 34 demanded comeliness: "Ex-Pilot Bob Six Uses Iron Hand, Tough Talk at Continental Airlines," by W. Stewart Pinkerton, *WSJ,* June 11, 1970.

page 34 Meadows . . . was responsible: Davies, *Continental Airlines: The First Fifty Years,* page 51.

page 34 "really move our tails": Sexist airline advertising is described in a *WSJ* roundup of July 11, 1974.

page 34 "we've got you": Kelleher 10/13/93 interview.

page 35 extraordinary proposal: The birth of Southwest's "10-minute turn-arounds" was described in the Barron and Parker interviews of 4/23/93. The particulars of the ground-handling procedures are described in "Southwest Cites Productivity as Key Factor in Profitability," *Aviation Week,* Feb. 9, 1976.

page 35 "brush their hair": *Aviation Week,* Feb. 9, 1976.

page 36 Lamar Muse: Muse's background is based on, among other sources, Larry D. Sall, "Marion Lamar Muse," in *Encyclopedia of American Business History and Biography.*

page 36 bothered him: Barron 4/26/93 interview; Kelleher 10/14/93 interview.

page 36 "chicken coop": Testimony of Charles Murphy, executive director, Texas Aeronautics Commission, U.S. Senate, Subcommittee on Administrative Practice and Procedure, *Oversight of Civil Aeronautics Board Practices and Procedures,* Feb. 14, 1975.

page 37 In addition to matching: Parker and Barrett 4/26/93 interviews; Kelleher 10/14/93 interview; Fallows, *Texas Monthly,* Dec. 1975.

page 37 Chivas Regal distributor: Sall, "Marion Lamar Muse."

page 37 first employee-owned airline: Kelleher 10/14/93 interview.

page 38 beauty parlor: The business background of Lorenzo's family was described by Bakes, Burr, O'Donnell, and other people who worked closely with Lorenzo over the years.

page 38 walls of his bedroom: "Top Gun," by William P. Barrett, *Texas Monthly,* Mar. 1987. Other published accounts of Lorenzo's early years include "TWA's Rescuer Is a Street Fighter," by James R. Norman, *BW,* July 1, 1985; and "Take-Off for Texas?" *Dun's,* Oct. 1972. A number of details of Lorenzo's life were also obtained from people who were close to him.

page 38 buying airline shares: Norman, *BW,* July 1, 1985.

page 38 Frankie Smooth Talk: Barrett, *Texas Monthly,* Mar. 1987.

page 38 gentile fraternities: "Sophomore Elections Conspiracy: Decline and Fall of a Machine," by Arnold Abrams, *Columbia Daily Spectator,* May 1, 1959.

page 38 "discussed . . . voting twice": *Ibid.*

page 39 biographies of . . . Carnegie: Barrett, *Texas Monthly,* Mar. 1987.

page 39 Lorenzo, Carney: Lorenzo's early ventures were described by a number of former associates and detailed in a Jet Capital amendment to

Form S-2, filed with the SEC on Nov. 19, 1969, and in a Jet Capital prospectus dated Jan. 22, 1970.

page 39 flew to New Orleans: Burr 9/16/93 interview.

page 40 approached by Bob Carney: *Ibid.*

page 41 fly over Mount Whitney: *Ibid.*

page 41 gin-and-cigar junket: *Ibid.*

page 42 Shares of Jet Capital: Lorenzo and Carney's machinations with Jet Capital are described in Jet Capital's Jan. 22, 1970, prospectus, as well as in a number of earlier and later filings that survive on microfiche at the SEC.

page 42 flash money: Jet Capital Jan. 22, 1970, prospectus.

page 42 Then one day: Lorenzo described his thought process in "Take-Off for Texas?" *Dun's,* Oct. 1972.

page 42 Mohawk . . . was the first: "Mohawk Airlines," by William M. Leary, in *Encyclopedia of American Business History and Biography.*

page 42 Lorenzo met with . . . Peach: The account of Lorenzo's dealings with Mohawk and the sale to Allegheny is based on the Murray 9/4/93 interview and on interviews with other participants and eyewitnesses.

page 43 killed himself: Leary, "Robert E. Peach," *Encyclopedia of American Business History and Biography.* The fact of Lorenzo's lunch date was confirmed by two close friends of Lorenzo.

page 43 Vietnam troop buildup: Higgins 6/8/94 interview. Higgins piloted Trans-Texas DC-3s in the troop movements.

page 44 Burr had an idea: Burr 9/16/93 interview.

page 44 prescription . . . urged: The account of Texas International's restructuring, including Jet Capital's ownership arrangements and the contest with Hughes, were described by a number of participants and observers and detailed in a collection of decisions and exhibits filed as a CAB proceeding, *Control of Texas International Airlines,* 60 C.A.B. 20, decided Aug. 9, 1972. Additional details were obtained from Jet Capital's 10-K report for 1971.

page 44 The board . . . looked warily: CAB, *Control of Texas International.*

page 44 Kelleher showed up: Kelleher 6/14/94 interview.

page 45 hog-tied . . . with conflicts of interest: CAB, *Control of Texas International.*

page 45 a proud moment: Lorenzo's pride in his defeat of Howard Hughes was described by an eyewitness.

page 45 youngest president: *Dun's,* Oct. 1972.

page 45 Burr had passion: Burr's background and character are based principally on interviews with him and with many people who worked with him, including Bakes, Murray, Gitner, Dawsey, O'Donnell, Plaskett, Sullivan, and Lavender. Burr made a number of revealing comments about himself in speeches and interviews with others, including on a privately produced videotape, *The People Remembered,* by JR Productions; "Bitter Victories," an interview with Burr by George Gendron, *Inc.,* Aug. 1985; and "A Conversation with Don Burr," *Scorecard: The Revenue Management Quarterly,* Fourth Quarter 1992. Burr has additionally been the subject of many in-depth profiles, the best of which include "Rapid Ascent: People Express Flies into Airlines' Big Time in Just Three Years Aloft," by William M. Carley, *WSJ,* Mar. 30, 1984; "That Daring Young Man and His Flying Machines," by Lucien Rhodes, *Inc.,* Jan. 1984; and "A Yankee Preacher in the Pilot's Seat," by Stephen Koepp and Frederick Ungeheuer, *Time,* Jan. 13, 1986.

page 45 ferocious statewide election: Burr 9/16/93 interview.

page 46 became a father: *Ibid.*

page 46 *dirty and bad:* Burr 9/17/93 interview.

page 46 his arms flailed: Burr 9/16/93 interview.

page 47 One weekend: *Ibid.*

page 47 windowless building: Life in the Blue Barn was described by many of the people who worked there.

page 47 full partnership: Burr 9/16/94 interview.

page 47 visit to Alvin Feldman: *Ibid.*

page 47 yesterday's news: Based on an interview with someone familiar with the relationship.

page 47 Frank was the godfather: Burr 9/16/93 interview.

page 48 "feel despicable": *Ibid.*

page 48 "Frank, great news": *Ibid.*

page 49 $10 million in mutual aid: Footnote 7, *Texas International Airlines 1975 Annual Report.*

page 49 "needed the strike": Burr 9/16/93 interview.

page 49 South Padre Island: Sall, "Marion Lamar Muse."

page 49 sparing nothing in the effort: Coats 6/9/94 interview; O'Donnell 6/9/94 interview; Fallows, *Texas Monthly,* Dec. 1975.

page 49 didn't . . . carry U.S. mail: Kelleher 10/14/93 interview.

page 50 dozens of Harlingen residents: Barron 4/26/93 interview.

page 50 funeral director: Coats 6/9/94 interview.

page 50 passengers from Mexico: "Business Soars Where Airline Flies," by Del Jones, *USA Today,* Sept. 17, 1993.

page 50 Southwest University: Coats 6/9/94 interview.

page 50 Gatling Gun Gitner: J. Arpey 9/8/93 interview.

page 51 started his career: O'Donnell 6/9/94 interview.

page 52 eager for the acceptance: Many accounts have suggested that Lorenzo had an impulse to slash fares from the time he came into the airline industry. By contrast most informed sources say that Lorenzo, desirous of the approval of his peers, was a reluctant price cutter, particularly in his early years of controlling Texas International and, later, Continental. In several years Lorenzo's annual letter to the stockholders of Texas International emphasized the virtues of fare increases.

page 52 special on permanents: O'Donnell 6/9/94 interview.

page 52 Flying back to Houston: *Ibid.*

page 52 as much as 600 percent: "Texas International Air Plans Discount Fares on Seven Routes in March," *WSJ*, Feb. 11, 1977.

page 53 Surveys showed: "Super Saver Swells Discounts," by David M. North, *Aviation Week*, Feb. 20, 1978.

page 53 "chickenshit fares": Apr. 26, 1978, internal report by Donald Burr and Edwin Cathell, Texas International Airlines.

page 53 *not . . .* an argument: "Texas International Asks 50% Fare Cut on Selected Flights," *WSJ*, Dec. 16, 1976.

Chapter 3: Network Warriors

page 55 "Be ruthless": R. L. Crandall, address to marketing meeting, Aug. 2, 1988.

page 55 "crunch our competitors": Remarks by R. L. Crandall to Sabre Travel Information Network, Apr. 23, 1988.

page 55 he inspired fear: Crandall 4/23/93 interview.

page 55 black wings: Crandall speech to marketing meeting, Inn of Six Flags, Dallas, Feb. 25, 1981.

page 55 Crandall loved bridge: Plaskett 8/31/93 interview.

page 55 misuse, and grammatical lapses: Becker 9/3/93 interview.

page 55 tools hung precisely: Crandall 4/23/93 interview.

page 55 "drives her batshit": *Ibid.*

page 55 "When I was born": Crandall 9/1/93 interview.

page 56 Robert Lloyd Crandall: Crandall provided most of the details of his life and career in interviews. Additional facts were compiled from a number of other significant in-depth treatments, including D. Reed, *American Eagle;* "Frequent Flier," by Paulette Thomas, *Avenue,* Summer 1988; "Battle of Titans," by Bridget O'Brian and Judith Valente, *WSJ*, Oct. 10, 1989; "Bob Crandall Soars by Flying Solo," by Kenneth Labich, *Fortune,* Sept. 29, 1986; and "American Rediscovers Itself," *BW,* Aug. 23, 1982.

page 56 His father was rescued: Crandall 4/23/93 interview.

page 56 a fat boy: Crandall 6/13/94 interview.

page 56 A decent fistfight: Crandall 4/23/93 interview; Thomas, *Avenue,* Summer 1988.

page 56 how fast he could ring: These and other details of Crandall's early working life were described in the Crandall 9/1/93 and 6/13/94 interviews.

page 56 "noted for arguments": Barrington High School *Arrow* for 1953.

page 57 "They sold the shit": Crandall 9/1/93 interview.

page 57 C. R. Smith had agonized: The story of Sabre's birth was detailed in the Hopper 4/22/93 and 10/13/93 interviews and, among other published sources, in Serling, *Eagle;* Bashe, *IBM's Early Computers;* "Airline Automation: A Major Step," by C. E. Ammann, *Computers and Automation,* Aug. 1957; "American Airlines Automates Reservations for the Jet Age," by Arnold E. Keller, *Management and Business Automation,* Jan. 1959; and "The Sabre System," by R. W. Parker, *Datamation,* Sept. 1965. A number of unpublished monographs, bulletins, and other internal records of American Airlines and IBM were also used, including "American Airlines' 'Sabre' Electronic Reservations System," by W. R. Plugge and M. N. Perry, circa 1962, and "American Airlines, Inc., and The Teleregister Corp. Present the Magnetronic Reservisor," circa 1952.

page 58 "reservations theory": Wolfe, *Air Transportation Traffic and Management,* page 495.

page 58 20 separate communications: *Ibid.,* page 503.

page 59 a grand contraption: D. G. Copeland, R. O. Mason, and J. L. McKenney, "SABRE: The Development of Information-Based Competence and Execution of Information-Based Competition," *IEEE Annals of the History of Computing,* 1995; Ammann, *Computers and Automation, August 1957.*

page 59 nicknamed Girlie: *Ibid.*

page 60 "unfavorable proportions": Plugge and Perry, "American Airlines' 'Sabre' Electronic Reservations System."

page 60 Blair Smith: Copeland, *IEEE Annals of the History of Computing,* 1995; Bashe, *IBM's Early Computers,* page 517.

page 60 14,000 . . . computers of any kind: "On Line in Real Time," by Gilbert Burck, *Fortune,* Apr. 1964.

page 60 "space age brain": "SABRE: A Plane Seat—Presto!" by Ted Ward, *New York Post,* Sept. 15, 1964.

page 61 "new mechanical monsters": Copeland, *IEEE Annals of the History of Computing,* 1995.

page 62 Passed over: D. Reed, *American Eagle,* page 16.

page 62 lost its way: Crandall 9/1/93 interview.

page 62 succeed . . . Marvin Traub: D. Reed, *American Eagle,* page 43.

page 62 exquisitely boring: Crandall 9/1/93 interview.

page 62 "fast-paced, high-risk": quoted in "Competitive Anger," by Suzanne Loeffelholz, *Financial World,* Jan. 10, 1989.

page 63 succeeded by . . . Spater: Spater is profiled in Serling; *Eagle;* and in "Goodbye to Robin Hood?" *Forbes,* Feb. 15, 1968.

page 63 the most erudite: Wheatcroft 2/24/94 interview.

page 64 dinner invitation: The account of American's Watergate finance involvement is based largely on "Memorandum of American Airlines Regarding Campaign Contributions During 1971–72," Aug. 20, 1973, and "Prosecutive Memorandum Re American Airlines," to Archibald Cox from Thomas F. McBride and John G. Koeltl, Watergate Special Prosecution Force, Oct. 9, 1973. These documents and others were obtained from the National Archives under the Freedom of Information Act.

page 64 terra incognita: Quoted in Lucas, *Nightmare*, page 174.

page 64 nudge from C. R. Smith: Smith's involvement is detailed in "Memorandum of American Airlines," Aug. 20, 1974. The report of the Senate Select Committee on Presidential Campaign Activities, page 448, says that Spater obtained the $5,000 checks "from a friend."

page 64 "five in cash": Quoted in "Memorandum of American Airlines," Aug. 20, 1973.

page 65 spared from criminal charges: "Three Firms Plead Guilty on Campaign Gifts," by Paul E. Steiger, *Los Angeles Times*, Oct. 18, 1973.

page 65 "brightest young financial men": Quoted in Serling, *Eagle*, page 439.

page 66 Casey's . . . apartment: Crandall 9/1/93 interview; D. Reed, *American Eagle*, page 106.

page 66 Casey was looking: Lloyd-Jones 3/10/94 interview; Serling, *Eagle*, page 443.

page 66 a planning exercise: "Industry Appraises American's Marketing," by William H. Gregory, *Aviation Week*, Sept. 2, 1974.

page 66 purposefully contentious: Crandall 9/1/93 interview.

page 66 terminated within days: Baker 6/10/94 interview.

page 67 tightest possible connections: Crandall, text of presentation to the American Airlines board of directors, June 18, 1975; Presentation to 1976 Management Meeting, undated text.

page 67 1,000 cathode ray tubes: Hopper 10/13/93 interview.

page 68 top data processing executive: *Ibid.*

page 68 William A. Patterson: "There's More Than One Way to Run an Airline," by Perrin Stryker, *Fortune*, Feb. 1961.

page 68 remote and confrontational: Luce 8/26/93 interview.

page 68 Keck's standing sank: Luce's downfall and Carlson's hiring are described in Johnson, *Airway One;* Carlson, *Recollections of a Lucky Fellow;* "Sic Transit Gloria: George E. Keck Found United Air Lines' Skies Could Turn Unfriendly," by Todd E. Fandell, *WSJ*, Sept. 11, 1972; "How a Hotelman Got the Red Out of United Air Lines," by Rush Loving, Jr., *Fortune*, Mar. 1972; and "Losses Spark Shakeup at United," by Laurence Doty, *Aviation Week*, Jan. 4, 1971.

page 69 going down the drain: Luce 8/26/93 interview.

page 69 hidden agenda: *Ibid.*

page 69 one of Gleed's close friends: Carlson, *Recollections,* page 249.

page 69 Carlson was fresh blood: Carlson's background and turnaround moves were detailed in interviews with Ferris and others who knew him; Johnson, *Airway One;* "A Life of Hard Work and a Stroke of Luck Aided Edward Carlson," by Todd E. Fandell, *WSJ,* Oct. 18, 1971; and Loving, *Fortune,* Mar. 1972.

page 70 self-described hero-worshiper: Carlson, *Recollections,* page 215.

page 70 "Ready Eddies": McAnulty 2/25/94 interview.

page 70 186,366 miles: Loving, *Fortune,* March 1972.

page 71 born with verve: The account of Ferris's background is based primarily on interviews with him and people who knew him well. Additional details were obtained from "Winning His Wings: United Airlines' Ferris Sets Expansion Plans, Alarms Carrier's Rivals," *WSJ,* Mar. 2, 1979; "Foodservice Career Profiles: Richard J. Ferris," by James R. Myers, *Cooking for Profit,* Aug. 1967; "Friendlier Skies? United Airlines Hopes Pilots' Vote This Week Will Be Turning Point," by John Curley, *WSJ,* Aug. 10, 1981; and "Friendly Skies over Pacific: How United Did It," by Carol Jouzaitis, *Chicago Tribune,* Apr. 7, 1986.

page 71 his father had scraped: Letter, Jesse W. Ferris to Dick Ferris, Aug. 28, 1957.

page 71 Ferris . . . landed: Ferris 6/7/94 interview.

page 72 Rocker Four Club: Ferris 5/27/93 interview.

page 72 legendary Dan London: Ferris 5/28/93 interview; Carlson, *Recollections,* pages 226, 234.

page 72 "work at the Olympic": Ferris 5/28/93 interview.

page 72 brash letter: Richard J. Ferris to Edward E. Carlson, Feb. 26, 1962.

page 73 "show business": Ferris 5/28/93 interview.

page 73 "full of myself": Ferris 5/27/93 interview.

page 73 a fabled enterprise: Nielsen, *From Sky Girl to Flight Attendant,* page 17; Solberg, *Conquest of the Skies,* pages 219–20.

page 74 membership in the Fortune 500: The food operation would have ranked roughly 400 on the list, comparable to such household name companies as Mattel, Green Giant, and Max Factor.

page 74 jabbing his finger: Putnam 10/13/93 interview.

page 74 reducing . . . steak: *WSJ,* March 2, 1979.

page 74 shared his thinking: Carlson, *Recollections,* pages 236–38.

page 74 spent weeks agonizing: *Ibid.,* page 237.

page 75 "reservations about Ferris": *Ibid.,* page 238.

page 75 " 'boy wonder' success": "New UAL Chief Must Earn Wings," by Leonard Wiener, *Chicago Tribune,* May 2, 1979.

page 75 Crandall was jarred: Hopper 10/13/93 interview; Copeland, *IEEE Annals in the History of Computing,* 1995.

page 78 Ferris . . . looked warily: Ferris 5/27/93 and 5/28/93 interviews.

page 78 months studying the issues: Ferris 5/27/93 interview; Zeeman 7/23/93 interview.

page 78 ordered his field managers: Crandall, speech to management meeting, DFW, 1976.

page 78 United was warning agents: Hopper 4/22/93 interview.

page 79 "Where do we go": Crandall, speech to management meeting, DFW, 1976.

page 79 "short white socks": Gunn 9/1/93 interview.

page 79 $800,000 worth: "Automation: The First 25 Years," *ASTA Agency Management*, Nov. 1989.

page 79 Crandall blew his stack: The harried takeover was described in the Murray 9/4/93 interview, the Hopper 10/13/93 interview, and in a speech by Crandall to First Boston Clients, Mar. 11, 1986.

page 79 enticing agents: The birth of "override" commissions in the CRS wars was described in interviews with Lazarus, Zeeman, and Gunn, and in a variety of industry and government publications about the growth of the CRS industry.

page 80 "highly confidential": Gunn, speech to 1984 American Airlines marketing meeting.

page 80 United had no idea: This point is conceded by Ferris and Zeeman.

page 80 a questionable business practice: Zeeman 7/23/93 interview.

page 81 generation of charter operators: "Charter Growth Sparks Concern," by Rosalind K. Ellingsworth, *Aviation Week*, Feb. 28, 1977.

page 82 no panacea either: "American Fare Bid Draws Fire," by Laurence Doty, *Aviation Week*, Feb. 21, 1977.

page 82 Crandall finally decided: Baker 4/23/93 interview; Plaskett 4/21/93 interview.

page 82 "pretend the empty part": The account of the origins of super savers is based on the Crandall 4/23/93 interview and the Kaldahl 4/27/93 interview. Varying accounts also appear in Serling, *Eagle;* Reed, *American Eagle;* and Peterson and Glab, *Rapid Descent.*

page 84 glared through a window: The venetian blind incident was partially described in "Frequent Crier: American Airlines Boss Blossoms as Champion of the Poor Passenger," by Francis C. Brown III, *WSJ,* Mar. 4, 1988. The circumstances of Crandall's outburst and the order for a special computer instruction against TWA were described in the Murray 9/4/93 interview.

Chapter 4: "In the Public Interest"

page 87 a brilliant day: Bakes 5/11/93 and 6/16/94 interviews.

page 89 Breyer wondered: Breyer's line of inquiry is detailed in "Memorandum to Thomas McBride from Stephen Breyer," Aug. 2, 1973, made available by the National Archives under the Freedom of Information Act.

page 89 lost its way: Breyer's views are detailed in Breyer, *Regulation and Its Reform,* and in "Airline Deregulation in America," by Stephen Breyer, *ITA Magazine,* May 1986.

page 89 resurrect . . . Watergate: Bradley Behrman, "Civil Aeronautics Board," in Wilson, *The Politics of Regulation,* page 100.

page 90 most vexing problem: *Ibid.,* page 102.

page 90 "nonglamorous . . . job": Breyer, *Regulation and Its Reform,* page 323.

page 90 "let's get rid": Bakes 5/11/93 interview.

page 91 bow and scrape: *Ibid.*

page 91 "the inherent tendency": Keyes, *Federal Control of Entry into Air Transportation,* page 326.

page 92 "unnecessarily high fares": "Is Air Regulation Necessary?" by Michael E. Levine, *Yale Law Journal,* July 1965.

page 92 "raise cost to the level": Kahn, *The Economics of Regulation,* page 209.

page 92 "rat is a bird": Lazarus 6/10/93 interview.

page 92 Ferris had an open mind: Ferris described his thought process in the 5/27/93 interview and in "Proposed Policy on Regulatory Reform," presented to United board of directors, Aug. 26, 1976.

page 92 Ferris presented . . . a long report: "Proposed Policy," Aug. 26, 1976.

page 93 growing enamored: Zeeman 7/23/93 interview.

page 93 Bakes felt the same . . . compulsion: Bakes 5/12/93 interview.

page 94 hotel fire alarm: Lazarus 6/10/93 interview; Bakes 6/11/93 interview.

page 94 For eight days: The hearing record is contained in U.S. Senate, Subcommittee on Administrative Practice and Procedure, *Oversight of Civil Aeronautics Board Practice and Procedure,* Feb. 6, 14, 18, 19, 25, and 26, Mar. 4 and 21, 1975.

page 94 officials were carefully chosen: Brown, *The Politics of Airline Deregulation,* page 107; Breyer, *Regulation and Its Reform,* pages 327–28.

page 95 "find a scandal": Bakes 5/11/93 interview.

page 95 "The only word . . . flashing": Transcript, U.S. Senate, Subcommittee on Administrative Practice and Procedure, *Inquiry into the Failure of the CAB to Investigate Fully Certain Violations of the Federal Campaign Laws,* Mar. 21, 1975.

page 95 "dishonor of the fool": Letter from William Gingery to subcommittee staff, Feb. 15, 1975, appearing in *ibid.*

page 95 "Total deregulation": "Borman to the Rescue," by James Conaway, *New York Times Magazine,* May 9, 1976.

page 96 the same rhetoric: Bakes 5/11/93 interview.

page 96 47 flight attendants: *Ibid.*

page 96 Bakes . . . relentlessly flirted: *Ibid.*

page 96 rendezvous with Al Casey: *Ibid.*

page 97 one of Bakes's colleagues: Bakes 6/16/94 interview.

page 97 "naturally competitive": "Options on Airline Regulation Reform," memo to the President-elect from Simon Lazarus, Mary Schuman, and Harrison Wellford, Dec. 22, 1976.

page 98 strengthened the call: Cohen 2/16/93 interview; "American Fare Bid Draws Fire," by Laurence Doty, *Aviation Week,* Feb. 21, 1977.

page 98 United held back: Lazarus 6/10/93 interview; "Airlines Unable to Agree on Regulatory Reform Stance," *Aviation Daily,* Mar. 3, 1977.

page 98 quit frolicking: Boies 11/11/93 interview.

page 98 three to four years: Ferris 5/27/93 interview.

page 98 "Properly written": Remarks by Monte Lazarus to United board meeting, Jan. 27, 1977.

page 99 began to applaud: Lazarus 6/10/93 interview.

page 99 "first question": Quoted in "Washington Roundup," *Aviation Week,* Feb. 28, 1977.

page 99 "As a first step: "Airline Industry Regulation," *Public Papers of the Presidents: Jimmy Carter.*

page 99 speech at the Commonwealth Club: "Chief of UAL's United Favors 'Philosophy' of Regulatory Reform," *WSJ,* Mar. 14, 1977.

page 99 "the greatest thing": Quoted in "Winning His Wings: United Airlines' Ferris Sets Expansion Plans, Alarms Carrier's Rivals," *WSJ,* Mar. 2, 1979.

page 99 scheduling their bosses together: Bakes 5/11/93 interview; Lazarus 6/10/93 interview.

page 100 inserted whole: Lazarus 6/10/93 interview.

page 100 turned to Al Feldman: *Ibid.*

page 100 buy off the unions: Bakes 5/11/93 interview.

page 100 "hardest to destroy": From "Essay on Bureaucracy," by Max Weber, in Rourke, *Bureaucratic Power in National Politics,* page 58.

page 100 only sensible course: Robson 1/7/93 interview.

page 101 furiously lobbied: Cohen 2/16/93 interview.

page 101 writing a dissent: *Ibid.*

page 101 visibly startled: Brown, *The Politics of Airline Deregulation,* page 113.

page 101 "mesmerized by computer models": U.S. Senate, *Hearings Before the Subcommittee on Aviation,* Apr. 1, 1977.

page 102 "fucking academic eggheads": Bakes 5/11/93 interview. Crandall does not recall the comment but does not deny making it.

page 102 In contemplating candidates: *Ibid.*

page 103 "free-fire zone": "CAB Proposes 50% Fare Cut Zone," *Aviation Week,* Apr. 10, 1978.

page 103 "get big quick": Ferris 5/28/93 interview.

page 103 death of the senior senator: "Washington Update," *National Journal,* Dec. 3, 1977.

page 104 "help raising some money": Bakes 5/12/93 interview. Mineta's staff, though confirming Kennedy's appearance at a fundraiser, said it was unrelated to his stance on deregulation.

page 104 a $433,000 tax reimbursement: Bakes 5/11/93 interview. Bakes recalls Frontier seeking a $10 million subsidy but contemporaneous accounts cite $433,000.

page 104 a thumbs-up: Lazarus 6/10/93 interview.

page 104 Bakes and . . . Kennedy pressed themselves: Bakes 5/12/93 interview.

page 105 "For the first time": Quoted in *Congressional Quarterly Almanac,* 95th Congress, 2nd Session, 1978.

page 105 spectacle ensued: "Airline Emissaries Rush to CAB Offices for Dormant Routes," *WSJ,* Oct. 20, 1978; "The Line Forms Here for Air Routes," *BW,* Nov. 6, 1978; and "Dormant Authority Rush Begins," *Aviation Week,* Oct. 30, 1978. The CAB remained in existence in shrunken form for several years as its powers were taken away or, in a few cases, shifted to other federal agencies.

page 105 carrying a gun: Bakes 5/12/93 interview.

page 105 no one holding a place: Gitner 3/16/93 interview.

Chapter 5: Start-ups and Upstarts

page 106 baby elephant defecated: Hicks 6/14/93 interview.

page 106 Deregulation, in his view: Lorenzo 5/5/88 interview.

page 106 "somebody else's sandwich": *Ibid.*

page 107 Burr . . . worshiped him: Burr 9/16/93 and 9/17/93 interviews.

page 107 true soul mate: Bakes 5/12/93 interview.

page 107 impressed by Burr's ability: Quoted in "Growing Pains at People Express," by Reggi Ann Dubin, *BW,* Jan. 28, 1985.

page 107 Idi Amin: Burr compared Lorenzo to any number of dictators in the interviews of 9/16/93 and 9/17/93.

page 107 veins in his temples: Burr 9/16/93 interview.

page 107 Who's going to get it: Dawsey 9/16/93 interview.

page 108 "run a lawn mower": Burr 9/16/93 interview.

page 108 had been wrapped up: Burr 9/17/93 interview.

page 108 plan to reform: Burr's scheme was detailed in the 9/16/93 interview. A copy of the plan was made available to the author by another party.

page 110 "Don, come here": Burr 9/16/93 interview.

page 110 "Carney rolls the spitballs": Coats 6/9/94 interview.

page 110 The next four: Based on 1978 rankings according to revenue passenger miles.

page 110 fact that appalled Lorenzo: "Texas International's Lorenzo Believes He Has a National Grasp," by Nicholas C. Chriss, *Los Angeles Times,* Oct. 29, 1978.

page 111 never been a hostile: Davies, *Continental Airlines,* page 85.

page 111 Slowly and imperceptibly: Russell, *Miami Herald,* Aug. 6, 1978.

page 111 hands were trembling: J. Arpey 9/8/93 interview.

page 111 breathtaking route map: Shugrue 9/8/93 interview; Plaskett 8/31/93 interview.

page 112 "to our side": Quoted in Halaby, *Crosswind,* page 275.

page 112 making things worse: Pan Am's travails in the Carter years and other periods are detailed in many publications and were described in a number of interviews. The best accounts include "Deep-Rooted Causes of the Current Crisis," *Lloyd's Aviation Economist,* June 1986, and "Bumpy Flying: Plagued by Problems, Pan Am Fights Rivals as Well as Internal Ills," by William M. Carley, *WSJ,* Jan. 10, 1979.

page 112 "airline . . . without a country": Daley, *An American Saga,* page 444.

page 112 tussled for weeks: The takeover battle is detailed, among other places, in "Merger Politics: It's a High-Stakes Game of Power, Pressure, Persuasion," by James Russell, *Miami Herald,* Nov. 19, 1978.

page 113 underdog strategy: Coats 6/9/94 interview.

page 113 Don Burr realized: Burr 9/16/93 interview.

page 113 "gobble up United": Quoted in "Lorenzo the Presumptuous," by James Cook, *Forbes,* Oct. 30, 1978.

page 113 at the house of . . . Bob Six: Lorenzo's encounter with Six was described in the Bakes 5/12/93 interview and in Murphy, *The Airline That Pride Almost Bought,* page 21.

page 114 greatest living figure: Six is profiled in "Last of a Breed: Ex-Pilot Bob Six Uses Iron Hand, Tough Talk at Continental Airlines," by W. Stewart Pinkerton, Jr., *WSJ,* June 11, 1970, and in Davies, *Continental Airlines, passim.*

page 114 reaching for the ashtray: "How Bob Six Keeps Continental Humming," by Joseph S. Murphy, *Air Transport World,* Apr. 1965.

page 114 covert operations: Sampson, *Empires of the Sky,* page 108.

page 114 breakfast at the Hotel Carlyle: Lorenzo's encounter with Smart is described in "Texas International, Thwarted in Bid for National, Eyes Bigger Target—TWA," by William M. Carley, *WSJ,* Sept. 14, 1979, and in "Top Gun," by William P. Barrett, *Texas Monthly,* Mar. 1987.

page 115 "Thirty-nine!": O'Donnell 6/9/94 interview.

page 116 "piece of shit": Burr 9/16/93 interview.

page 116 put his people plan: *Ibid.*

page 116 "I resign": *Ibid.*

page 117 "Frank would . . . kill us": *Ibid.*

page 117 needed to raise money: Detailed in "That Daring Young Man and His Flying Machines," by Lucien Rhodes, *Inc.,* Jan. 1984.

page 118 strewn with garbage: Burr 9/16/93 interview; Rhodes, *Inc.,* Jan. 1984.

page 118 "No one has ever made it": Burr 9/16/93 interview.

page 118 wide-open markets: "People Express Discounts Fares Heavily," by James Ott, *Aviation Week,* Apr. 13, 1981.

page 118 Burr . . . traveled to Boston: Burr and Dawsey 9/16/93 interview.

page 119 "The plain truth": Quoted in "True or False: Air Safety Is Worse Than Ever," by Robert E. Machol, *WSJ,* Sept. 10, 1987.

page 119 with Christmas approaching: Stich, *The Unfriendly Skies,* pages 1–4.

page 120 far west as Denver: "Airlines Fear Broad Flight Cancellations as Delays Eat Up Pilots' Hour Quotas," *WSJ,* July 23, 1968.

page 120 vacuums . . . on the East Coast: The strategic origins of New York Air were described in interviews with O'Donnell, Bakes, and Gitner, as well as in the company's Feb. 20, 1981, prospectus and in a number of contemporaneous articles, including "New York Air: Troubled Airline Fights Back," by David Corbin, *Airline Executive,* Sept. 1982.

page 121 turn cold: Quoted in Corbin, *Airline Executive,* Sept. 1982.

page 121 path of Southwest: Lorenzo 5/5/88 interview.

page 121 matter of the unions: The antiunion intentions of New York Air were affirmed by nearly every executive remotely affiliated or familiar with it.

page 121 airplanes . . . Burr had ordered: Bakes 6/11/93 interview.

page 122 "upstreamed" from Texas International: Bakes 5/12/93 interview.

page 122 patterned after Southwest: "Special Situation" report on New York Air by Robert A. LaFleur, Rotan Mosle Inc., New York, June 30, 1981.

page 122 breakfast at the Jockey Club: Bakes 5/12/93 interview.

page 123 looking for . . . a brother: *Ibid.*

page 124 got . . . Kennedy to insert: *Ibid.*

page 124 fashion models: *Ibid.*

page 124 kept the sum small: Burr 9/16/93 interview.

page 124 "sex appeal": Quoted in "CAB's Ex-Chairman, Alfred Kahn, Looks at Airline Industry He Helped Deregulate," by Bill Richards, *WSJ,* Oct. 4, 1983.

page 125 William Hambrecht: Burr 9/16/83 interview; Rhodes, *Inc.,* Jan. 1984.

page 125 "This fucking guy": Burr 9/16/93 interview.

page 125 human forms making love: *Ibid.*

page 125 loaners against: Baker 10/14/93 interview.

page 125 "whores and bastards": Burr 9/16/93 interview.

page 126 appointment with Murdoch: *Ibid.*

page 126 710,000 founder's shares: Prospectus for People Express stock offering, Nov. 6, 1980.

page 126 privacy of his bedroom: Burr 9/16/93 interview.

page 127 brash New Yorker: Bakes 6/16/94 interview.

page 127 "Runaway shop!": Raymond Rogers, letter to the editor, *NYT,* June 14, 1981.

page 127 rented a billboard: A photo of the billboard was provided by Higgins.

page 127 widow of . . . La Guardia: Bakes interviews of 5/12/93 and 6/11/93.

page 127 champion of the pilots' union: Hopkins, *Flying the Line,* page 50.

page 127 pilots' union railed: Bakes 6/11/93 interview.

page 128 Eastern fought back: "Pan Am to Cut Fares Between Washington, Newark, N.J., to $29," *WSJ,* Jan. 8, 1981.

page 128 captured one quarter: "Upstarts in the Sky," *BW,* June 15, 1981.

page 128 An ad . . . in Buffalo: Rhodes, *Inc.,* Jan. 1984.

page 128 they would all go down: Burr 9/16/93 interview.

page 129 "no potholes": From early People Express ad, included in JR Productions's *The People Remembered.*

page 129 ultimate frill: "A Champ of Cheap Airlines," by Peter Nulty, *Fortune,* Mar. 22, 1982.

page 129 chief financial officer: "Manager's Journal," by Donald Burr, *WSJ,* Jan. 7, 1985.

page 129 "quality of attractiveness": Burr 9/16/93 interview.

page 129 "a character flaw": Burr 9/17/93 interview.

page 130 "very disruptive": "Bitter Victories," an interview with Burr by George Gendron, *Inc.,* Aug. 1985.

page 130 "thinks he's John Madden": Sullivan 6/8/94 interview.

page 130 "Be Luke Skywalker": Burr 9/17/93 interview.

page 130 "fall in love at work": Burr 9/16/93 interview.

page 130 alcohol flowed freely: The party, including the sex, was described in the Burr 9/17/93 interview.

page 130 wept with joy: "Up, Up and Away?" by John A. Byrne, *BW,* Nov. 25, 1985.

page 131 utterly transform: The secondary effects of the firing are described, among other places, in *Eight Years of U.S. Airline Deregulation,* by Frank

A. Spencer and Frank H. Cassell, Transportation Center, Northwestern University, Jan. 1987, and in "Suicide Pact at Eastern Air Lines," by Thomas Moore, *U.S. News,* Mar. 20, 1989.

page 131 Germany with their wives: The account of People Express's response to the PATCO strike is based on the Gitner 3/31/93 interview; Burr 9/17/93 interview; "Rapid Ascent: People Express Flies into Airlines' Big Time in Just Three Years Aloft," by William M. Carley, *WSJ,* Mar. 30, 1984; and Nulty, *Fortune,* Mar. 22, 1982.

page 131 Gitner and his wife boarded: Gitner 3/31/93 interview.

page 131 "Come up with a new plan": Burr 9/17/93 interview.

page 131 dining room table: Gitner 3/31/93 interview; Nulty, *Fortune,* Mar. 22, 1982.

page 132 out of the question: Carley, *WSJ,* Mar. 30, 1984.

page 133 Kennedy . . . flew People: Nulty, *Fortune,* Mar. 22, 1982.

page 133 Montreal residents . . . began driving: "U.S. Fares Pull Canadians Across Border," by Alan Freeman, *WSJ,* Mar. 18, 1983.

page 133 eschewed such technology: Burr 9/17/93 interview.

page 133 "for hours, days, and weeks": Quoted in Carley, *WSJ,* Mar. 30, 1984.

page 133 the gospel of People Express: Burr 9/17/93 interview and Rhodes, *Inc.,* Jan. 1984.

page 134 "Gerry loves planning": Nulty, *Fortune,* Mar. 22, 1982.

page 135 first progeny: Midway Airlines is sometimes cited as the earliest of the post-deregulation carriers, although the company was actually founded well before the law took effect. Midway failed after several very successful years.

Chapter 6: The Empire Strikes Back

page 136 affinity for solving puzzles: Olsen 9/2/93 interview.

page 137 apocalyptic flare-ups: Plaskett 1/14/93 interview.

page 137 in a horse race: Crandall 9/1/93 interview; Lloyd-Jones 3/10/94 interview; and D. Reed, *American Eagle,* pages 112–17.

page 137 Lloyd-Jones intervened: Lloyd-Jones 3/10/94 interview.

page 137 problem was resolved: Crandall, in the 4/23/93 interview, confirmed receiving and considering the offer from Lorenzo. The timing, however, is unclear; Crandall recalled that Lorenzo already controlled Continental and wanted Crandall to run it; other events strongly suggest that Lorenzo made the offer before gaining control of Continental.

page 138 "Each of us wanted": Crandall 9/1/93 interview.

page 138 "Christians and lions": Crandall speech to marketing meeting, Inn of Six Flags, Dallas, Feb. 25, 1981.

page 138 "bleed American red": *Ibid.*

page 138 "person of ideas": Crandall 9/1/93 interview.

page 138 Crandall began every week: The description of Crandall's staff meetings is based on interviews with many who participated over the years.

page 139 "turn the pages": Baker 6/10/94 interview.

page 139 in his pajamas: Serling, *Eagle,* page 456.

page 139 cup after cup: "Bob Crandall Soars by Flying Solo," by Kenneth Labich, *Fortune,* Sept. 29, 1986.

page 139 "mankind's biggest bladder": Quoted in "America's Toughest Bosses," by Peter Nulty, *Fortune,* Feb. 27, 1989.

page 139 knots in their stomachs: G. Arpey 9/2/93 interview.

page 140 "screen science": Murray 9/4/93 interview.

page 140 agents now selected: "November Line of Sale Analysis," memo to R. E. Murray from S. D. Nason, American Airlines, Dec. 3, 1981.

page 140 programmed to score: Robert L. Crandall, text of remarks before Aviation Subcommittee, June 23, 1983.

page 141 "Trust the machine": Murray 9/9/93 interview.

page 141 One study found: "Proposal: Travel Agency Commercial Account Automation," American Airlines, Oct. 3, 1978.

page 141 "need-to-know basis": Memo to T. G. Plaskett from R. W. Baker, American Airlines, Oct. 1, 1981.

page 141 "We must achieve": *Ibid.*

page 141 Braniff flight first: Details of the moves against the Braniff flight are taken from Deposition of Richard E. Murray, U.S. Justice Department, CID No. 5087, June 22, 1983.

page 141 "adjust our Sabre display": Memo to Dick Murray from Mike Gunn, American Airlines, Aug. 22, 1980.

page 142 "bulk of the displacement": Memo to R. E. Murray from B. R. Amster, American Airlines, Jan. 15, 1982.

page 142 getting greedy: Murray June 22, 1983, deposition.

page 142 use some confidential . . . data: American's purported theft of confidential data from Texas International was described in the Murray 9/4/93 interview and June 22, 1983, deposition.

page 142 "too late now": Hopper, in the 10/13/93 interview, did recall using travel agency sales data pertaining to Texas International's operations but says he does not recall American using any proprietary data.

page 143 3,500 travel agencies: 1981 Sabre appropriations request.

page 143 "flow of passengers": *Ibid.*

page 143 "Factory of Ideas": Serling, *Eagle,* page 460.

page 143 The galling thing: Crandall, speech before the Airport Operators Council International, Mexico City, Sept. 30, 1980. Crandall expressed such views against upstarts in several other forums.

page 143 "breed apart": *Ibid.*

page 143 angrily ordered: Murray 9/4/93 interview.

page 144 bottom of the screen: "Motion of the Justice Department for an Extension of Time," *In Re Advance Notice of Proposed Rulemaking— Airline Computer Reservations Systems,*" Docket 41686, Civil Aeronautics Board, Oct. 5, 1983.

page 144 mortal threat: Crandall 4/23/93 interview.

page 144 Among the options: The origins of American's b-scales concept were detailed in the Crandall 4/23/93 and 9/1/93 interviews; the Carty 4/29/93 interview; the Plaskett 1/14/93 interview; the LaVoy 10/12/93 interview; the Hedges 6/13/94 interview; Crandall's speech to the 1985 American Airlines Fall Planning Meeting, draft dated Sept. 26, 1985; "The Volatile Airline Industry," speech by Crandall to the Economic Club of Detroit, Feb. 23, 1987; "American Air's New Contract with Union Seen Aiding Other Carriers in Labor Talks," by Dean Rotbart, *WSJ,* Mar. 7, 1983; and D. Reed, *American Eagle.*

page 145 "If we can't create": Crandall 9/1/93 interview.

page 146 winners and losers: Carty 4/29/93 interview.

page 146 scabs ... standing by: "What Labor Gave American Airlines," *BW,* Mar. 21, 1983.

page 146 booing and hissing crowd: "Competitive Anger," by Suzanne Loeffelholz, *Financial World,* Jan. 10, 1989.

page 146 huge proportion of the pilots: LaVoy 10/12/93 interview.

page 147 intimidate the rabble-rousers: Plaskett 1/14/93 and 4/21/93 interviews.

page 147 "emotional, visible level": Plaskett 1/14/93 interview.

page 147 every secretary in ... headquarters: D. Reed, *American Eagle,* page 203.

page 147 Finland in the shadow: "Sky King," by Sally Giddens, *D,* November 1989.

page 148 "I don't want to hear": Crandall 9/1/93 interview.

page 148 under the bright lights: Crandall, script for videotaped address to new employees, June 26, 1986.

page 148 the year 217 A.D.: Griffin and Ebert, *Business,* page 229.

page 149 the regulated past: Quoted in "How American Mastered Deregulation," by Colin Leinster, *Fortune,* June 11, 1984.

page 149 Acker stood out: The account of the careers and turnaround moves of Acker, Wells, and Lawrence is based on the Acker 1/7/93 and 6/3/93 interviews; Nance, *Splash of Colors;* Brown, *Ling;* Bender, *At the Top;* "On Loveable Madison Avenue With Mary, Dick, and Stew," by Philip Siekman, *Fortune,* April 1966; and "As the World Turns on Madison Avenue," by Carol J. Loomis, *Fortune,* Dec. 1968.

page 151 $40,000 in hundred-dollar bills: The political finance activities of Acker and Lawrence are detailed in several records of the Watergate Special Prosecution Force released by the National Archives under the Freedom of Information Act, including "Prosecutive Memorandum Re Braniff Airways," from Thomas F. McBride and Roger M. Whitten to Henry S. Ruth, Jr., Oct. 26, 1973, and "Braniff Airways, Inc.," Federal Bureau of Investigation File N. 56-4756, Nov. 27, 1973.

page 151 called before a grand jury: Acker 6/3/93 interview.

page 151 yearned to escape: *Ibid.*

page 151 protect Lawrence: "The Great Airline War," by James Fallows, *Texas Monthly,* Dec. 1975.

page 151 without its ballast: This assertion, though evident from the record, is persuasively argued in Nance, *Splash,* pages 84–85.

page 151 olive trees: *Ibid.,* page 140.

page 152 flight attendants . . . lost track: *Ibid.,* page 122.

page 152 rubbing his hands: Crandall 4/23/93 interview.

page 152 issue was delicate: Olsen 9/2/93 interview.

page 152 as a baggage handler: *Ibid.*

page 153 "de-peak DFW?": The description of the DFW hubbing project is based mainly on the Plaskett 4/21/93 interview, on the Olsen 9/2/93 and 6/10/94 interviews, and on "Should We De-Peak DFW?" presentation by Schedules Department, American Airlines, Oct. 20, 1980. An extensive discussion of the project also appears in Reed, *American Eagle.*

page 153 total of $13,140: "Should We De-Peak DFW?" Oct. 20, 1980.

page 154 "show this to Mr. Crandall": Olsen 9/2/93 interview.

page 154 a third party . . . Delta: Crandall 4/23/93 interview; "Delta Air's Aggressive Growth Contrasts with Large Losses for Ailing Competitors," by Janet Guyon, *WSJ,* Sept. 8, 1980.

page 154 It can't be done: Kaldahl 4/27/93 interview. Kaldahl himself was a vital player in the hub buildup.

page 155 40 percent of its business: These are standard industry figures, cited in *Winds of Change,* Transportation Research Board, 1991.

page 155 honorary Texas Ranger: Serling, *Eagle,* page 99.

page 155 "Do we even know": Plaskett 4/21/93 interview. The birth of American's frequent-flier program was also told in the Gunn 4/28/93 interview; the Crandall 4/23/93 interview; Serling, *Eagle;* D. Reed, *American Eagle;* "Targeting for AAdvantage," speech by Plaskett to Business and Professional Advertising Association, Anatole Hotel, Dallas, Sept. 26, 1983; and "American Rediscovers Itself," *BW,* Aug. 23, 1982.

page 155 about 150,000: Gunn 4/28/93 interview.

page 156 "What is that?": Plaskett 4/21/94 interview.

page 156 passing out scrip: "For Free Plane Trip to Mexico, Just Fly to St. Louis Three Times," *WSJ,* Sept. 26, 1979.

page 157 punch cards: "Western Air Hopes Carwash Rebate Plan Can Help It Clean Up," *WSJ,* June 13, 1980.

page 157 filled . . . with dread: Gunn 4/28/93 interview.

page 157 "on individual greed": Plaskett 4/21/93 interview.

page 157 like the Secret Play: Gunn 4/28/93 interview.

page 158 Runway 13L: The same ribbon of concrete was known as 31R when used in the other direction.

page 158 "what have I done?": Plaskett 4/21/93 interview.

page 158 Crandall thrust himself: The account of Crandall's thoughts and actions in the Runway 13L fracas, including his comments against Southwest, are based partly on a "Letter from R. L. Crandall to all American Airlines Employees in the Dallas–Fort Worth Area," June 24, 1981, and on "A Conversation with President Robert L. Crandall," KNBN-TV, Dallas, June 26, 1981.

page 159 Kelleher . . . hosted a meeting: "A Boy and His Airline," by Jan Jarobe, *Texas Monthly,* Apr. 1989.

page 159 among the 10 largest: *Ibid.*

page 160 demanded hearings: Kelleher 10/14/93 interview.

page 161 old pal . . . Bob Packwood: Kelleher 10/13/93 interview; Barrett 4/26/93 interview.

page 161 "pain in the ass": Quoted in "Is Herb Kelleher America's Best CEO?" by Kenneth Labich, *Fortune,* May 2, 1994.

page 161 did not . . . bother Kelleher: Kelleher 10/14/93 interview.

page 161 dinner and drinks: Kelleher 6/14/94 interview.

page 162 a little too uppity: The firing of Lamar Muse was described in the Kelleher 10/14/93 interview; the Barrett 4/26/93 interview; "Muse Air's M. Lamar Muse Returns, Ready for Fight to Strengthen Troubled Carrier," by Laurie P. Cohen, *WSJ,* Dec. 20, 1984; "Muse Air Founder Competes Against His Own Creation with an Aura of Class," by Danna K. Henderson, *Air Transport World,* Oct. 1981; and Jarobe, *Texas Monthly,* Apr. 1989.

page 162 double . . . the company overnight: Barrett 4/26/93 interview.

page 162 "king of Siam": *Southwest Airlines, Twenty Years of Luv* video.

page 163 Putnam learned to fly: Putnam 10/13/93 interview.

page 163 wanted to run something: *Ibid.*

page 163 his mission: Putnam described his moves at Southwest in the 10/13/93 interview and in his memoirs, *Winds of Turbulence, passim.*

page 163 three-page report: Putnam, *Winds of Turbulence,* page 66.

page 164 "unique, feminized image": Quoted in "Southwest Air Told to Make Its Hiring—Like Love—Blind," *WSJ,* June 15, 1981.

page 164 became an issue: "Why Herb Kelleher Gets So Much Respect from Labor," *BW,* Sept. 24, 1984.

page 164 Olympic scorecards: Southwest Airlines, *Twenty Years of Luv.*

page 164 "felt good": Putnam, *Winds of Turbulence,* page 119.

page 164 "No one expects Braniff": "Rough Weather: Braniff's Cash Shortage Is Becoming Desperate, Leaving Lasting Scars," by William M. Carley and Roger Thurow, *WSJ,* July 30, 1980.

page 164 Putnam . . . walked through the doors: Putnam 10/13/93 interview.

page 165 10 days' worth of cash: The desperation of Braniff's finances, and Putnam's turnaround moves, were described in the Putnam 10/13/93 interview; Nance, *Splash;* D. Reed, *American Eagle;* and an interview with Putnam broadcast on the *MacNeill/Lehrer Newshour.*

page 165 flew into a rage: Crandall's rage was evident in his public comments and in comments made by his subordinates.

page 165 $7 million: Notice from Albert V. Casey and Robert L. Crandall to All Employees, American Airlines, Nov. 16, 1981.

page 166 away from Braniff: Murray June 22, 1983, deposition.

page 166 "make them go away": Plaskett 4/21/93 interview.

page 166 "not good-spirited": *Ibid.*

page 166 strange things: The allegations that American committed dirty tricks in the fight against Braniff received widespread attention and investigation. Many of these allegations were undoubtedly enlarged in the retelling; a number seem patently impossible. Those enumerated here were repeated by credible accusers and make sense within the context of the competitive battle. Many of the principals were interviewed about these events; worthwhile accounts also appear in Nance, *Splash;* D. Reed, *American Eagle;* and "American Airlines Gets a 'Bad Guy' Image in Dallas from its Harsh Attacks on Braniff," by Brenton R. Schlender, *WSJ,* Mar. 12, 1982.

page 166 whole new route system: Putnam expressed his views in the Feb. 1, 1982, conversation with Crandall.

page 166 "American only gives you": The spot appears in the Public Broadcasting System production *Tailspin,* Jan. 1982.

page 166 Crandall . . . saw the ad: D. Reed, *American Eagle,* page 189.

page 167 "raise your drink prices": Putnam 10/13/93 interview. According to former government lawyers, Putnam also disclosed the conversation to the U.S. Justice Department. In a May 22, 1995, letter to the author, Crandall called Putnam's recollections "flawed and slanted," but otherwise declined comment. Anne McNamara, the general counsel of American, said she was unaware of an earlier conversation ever occurring with Howard Putnam.

page 167 Ferris too was dismayed: Ferris, in the 6/7/94 interview, recalled Putnam's informing him of the conversation with Crandall but did not recall his response.

page 167 "dumb as hell": This account of the conversation is based on a transcript included in *United States* v. *American Airlines Inc. and Robert L. Crandall,* U.S. District Court, Northern District of Texas, CA383-0325D, Feb. 23, 1983. Stammers appearing in the transcript have been removed by the author. Crandall has long declined to discuss this conversation with any reporter.

page 168 "need your support": PBS production *Tailspin.*

page 168 sneered at by salesclerks: The hazing of American employees was described in the Becker 9/3/93 interview, the Plaskett 8/31/93 interview, the Gunn 9/1/93 interview, the Crandall 9/1/93 interview, and the Kaldahl 4/27/93 interview.

page 168 children were harassed: Kaldahl 4/27/93 interview.

page 168 local media war: Becker 9/3/93 interview.

page 168 casually remarked: Schlender, *WSJ,* Mar. 12, 1982.

page 169 Sunday night at Billy Bob's: Appears as a scene in the PBS production *Tailspin.*

page 169 "parking ticket": Quoted in *BW,* Aug. 23, 1982.

page 169 "We're getting off": Crandall 9/1/93 interview.

page 170 dabbing his eyes: PBS production *Tailspin.*

page 170 American was soon carrying: *BW,* Aug. 23, 1982.

page 170 a system restart: Murray 9/4/93 interview.

page 170 remembered the incident: *Ibid.*

Chapter 7: Workingman's Blues

page 173 "command approach": Magurno 3/11/94 interview.

page 174 "mission control": "Borman to the Rescue," by James Conaway, *New York Times Magazine,* May 9, 1976.

page 174 came into the world: Eastern's history is told in "History of Eastern Air Lines," an internally produced article dated January 1986; Davies, *Airlines of the U.S. Since 1914;* Rickenbacker, *Rickenbacker;* and Serling, *From the Captain to the Colonel.*

page 174 stopped at nothing: Rickenbacker, *Rickenbacker,* pages 190–95.

page 175 Laurance became Rickenbacker's principal: Collier and Horowitz, *The Rockefellers,* pages 217–18.

page 175 "bums on seats": Quoted in Sampson, *Empires of the Sky,* page 19.

page 175 a *no-reservation* Merry-Go-Round: The birth of the Eastern shuttle is detailed in Johnson, *The Abominable Airlines,* pages 84–86.

page 176 "social calls": *Ibid.,* page 85.

page 176 "the greatest advance": Quoted in *ibid.,* page 86.

page 176 celebrity-spotting venue: "The Northeast Corridor After Eastern" by Barbara Sturken Peterson, *Frequent Flier,* May 1993.

page 176 hopelessly late: "Another Tailspin at Eastern," by Neil A. Martin, *Dun's,* Nov. 1973; Borman, *Countdown,* page 270.

page 176 W.H.E.A.L.: Serling, *From the Captain,* page 277.

page 176 "The Great Stingy Fleet": "Floyd Hall's Problems at Eastern," *BW,* Aug. 18, 1973.

page 177 drowning himself in martinis: Serling, *From the Captain,* page 331.

page 177 nipping quite a bit: *Ibid.,* pages 383–84.

page 177 "scientific management": *BW,* Aug. 18, 1973.

page 177 Rosenthal china: Serling, *From the Captain,* page 406.

page 178 born in Gary: The facts of Borman's early life and military career are based principally on his memoir, *Countdown.* Borman is also profiled in "Lost in Space," by Rowland Stiteler, *Florida,* Nov. 1, 1987, and "Frank Borman: Is He Really Captain America?' " by Nancy Webb Hatton, *Miami Herald,* July 31, 1977.

page 178 happiest moments: Conaway, *New York Times Magazine,* May 9, 1976.

page 178 sponsorship of a judge: "Frank Borman," by W. David Lewis, from *Encyclopedia of American Business History and Biography.*

page 178 threatened to kill him: Borman, *Countdown,* page 29.

page 178 an alcoholic: Bryan 5/13/93 interview. Most of the details of Bryan's early life and career are based on this interview.

page 180 sleeping on an army cot: "Charlie Bryan Has Ideas—And Lorenzo Is Listening," by Pete Engardio and Aaron Bernstein, *BW,* Nov. 21, 1988.

page 180 "deserted island": Bryan 5/13/93 interview.

page 180 engraved invitation: Rickenbacker, *Rickenbacker,* page 207.

page 181 seminal event: Bryan 5/13/93 interview.

page 182 Charles Leader: Bryan in the 5/13/93 interview said he listed his surname as "Leader" because at the moment the phone company asked him to designate a name, he was holding a record album cover identifying the recording company as a "leader" in high fidelity.

page 182 *extemporaneous: Ibid.*

page 182 overtime records: *Ibid.*

page 182 "awesome experience": Quoted in "Paradise Tossed," by Alex Gibney, *Washington Monthly,* June 1986.

page 182 1 billion people: Lewis, *Encyclopedia of American Business History and Biography.*

page 183 dousing her fears: Borman, *Countdown,* page 295.

page 183 "didn't blow it": Quoted in Serling, *From the Captain,* page 468.

page 183 "below average" rating: Borman, *Countdown,* page 276.

page 184 two warring camps: The management strife at Eastern was described in the Borman 1/29/94 interview, the Kaldahl 4/27/93 interview, and the following publications, among others: Borman, *Countdown;* Serling, *From the Captain;* and "Can Frank Borman Make Eastern Take Off?" *BW,* Dec. 22, 1975.

page 184 Borman was shocked: Borman 1/29/94 interview.

page 184 "impossible to manage": Quoted in Borman, *Countdown,* page 280.

page 184 "like the Captain": Quoted in Serling, *From the Captain,* page 480.

page 185 nothing less than a spy: Borman, *Countdown,* page 318; Serling, *From the Captain,* page 467.

page 185 pull the plug: Deposition of Frank Borman, *In the Matter of: Preliminary Investigation of Texas Air and Its Subsidiaries,* U.S. Department of Transportation, Docket No. 45581, Apr. 26, 1988.

page 185 "the only man": Quoted in Stiteler, *Florida,* Nov. 1, 1987.

page 185 "I'll do my best": Quoted in Serling, *From the Captain,* page 472.

page 186 "a certain romanticism": Memo to senior staff from Frank Borman, Eastern Air Lines, Nov. 5, 1976.

page 186 a paperweight: "Eastern Sticks to Its Gamble," *BW,* Jan. 11, 1982.

page 186 dismissed as "dipshits": Conaway, *New York Times Magazine,* May 9, 1976.

page 186 "Have you fixed it": Quoted in Serling, *From the Captain,* page 487.

page 186 a cup of coffee: Borman, *Countdown,* pages 336–37.

page 186 not a trace of ostentation: A number of these examples appear in Borman, *Countdown,* and Conaway, *New York Times Magazine,* May 9, 1976.

page 186 "Everyone whose mission": " 'Moon Man' Turns Around Eastern," *Time,* Feb. 7, 1977.

page 187 memorable ˙ . . . television advertisements: Kunstler 9/7/93 interview; Serling, *From the Captain,* page 505.

page 187 struck him as weird: Borman 1/29/94 interview.

page 187 "never go anywhere": *Ibid.*

page 187 Borman quit anyway: A decade later Borman would get the last laugh as Thayer became one of the first people sent to jail in Wall Street's insider trading scandal.

page 187 fired or demoted: Borman, *Countdown,* page 323.

page 187 curtly fired . . . Nicklaus: Borman 1/29/94 interview.

page 187 most lucrative airplane deal: The terms are described in "Eastern to Pay No Lease Fee for Airbus A-300s," by Jeffrey M. Lenorovitz, *Aviation Week,* May 30, 1977; and "Airbus Cracks the U.S. Market," by Rosalind K. Ellingsworth, *Airline Executive,* May 1978.

page 188 "kiss the French flag": Quoted in *BW,* Jan. 11, 1982.

page 188 "One of the great joys": Borman, letter to employees, Eastern Air Lines, Jan. 25, 1977.

page 188 "meet our payroll": Memo from Frank Borman to employees of Eastern Air Lines, June 10, 1975.

page 188 "very serious threat": Frank Borman, letter to employees of Eastern Air Lines, July 1, 1976.

page 188 "It's quite clear": Frank Borman, letter to employees of Eastern Air Lines, Nov. 2, 1978.

page 189 "he alone resuscitated": Hatton, *Miami Herald,* July 31, 1977.

page 189 "remarkable turnaround": *Time,* Feb. 7, 1977.

page 189 "Magellan of our time": Bryan 5/13/93 interview.

page 189 "Earth to Frank": "IAM District 100 vs. Eastern and the Banks," by Andrew R. Banks, in *Labor Research Review,* Winter 1984.

page 190 When Lyndon Johnson: Reggi Ann Dubin Associates, *The IAM: Another Look,* for Texas Air Corporation, Feb. 1988.

page 190 "utmost respect": Quoted in *Charlie Says . . . ,* published privately by Eastern Air Lines.

page 190 "Gestapo tactics": *Ibid.*

page 190 briefcase . . . of proxies: "Labor-Management Cooperation at Eastern Air Lines," by Beverly Smaby *et al.,* Harvard University, U.S. Department of Labor contract, May 1987.

page 190 "just to get attention": Bryan 5/13/93 interview.

page 190 "You made history": Quoted in Banks, in *Labor Research Review,* Winter 1984.

page 191 "Quit fucking with people": Bryan 5/13/93 interview.

page 191 Borman had been smarting: Borman, *Countdown,* page 351.

page 191 reverse thrust: Borman 1/29/94 interview; Borman, *Countdown,* pages 351–52.

page 192 slot machine: Bryan 5/13/93 interview.

page 193 in the Florida Keys: Borman 1/29/94 interview.

page 193 "take me . . . feet first": Quoted in "Grinning and Bearing It," by Jess Blyskal, *Forbes,* July 21, 1980.

page 193 spent several days: Acker 6/3/93 interview.

page 194 best moneymaker: "Braniff Leads Medium Trunk Assault on International Airline Economics," by Joseph S. Murphy, *Airline Executive,* May 1978.

page 194 fire the guilty party: "Eastern's Smooth Latin Landing," *BW,* Dec. 13, 1982.

page 194 pronunciation guide: *Falcon,* Eastern Air Lines, May 12, 1982.

page 194 noisily demonstrating: "Eastern Air Had 1st Period Loss of $51.4 Million," by John D. Williams, *WSJ,* Apr. 28, 1982.

page 194 "here it comes again": Barber 6/21/94 interview.

page 194 "a few six-packs": Smaby *et al.,* May 1987.

page 195 NO DEPOSIT, NO RETURN: Banks, in *Labor Research Review,* Winter 1984.

page 195 aides were jubilant: Magurno 3/11/94 interview.

page 195 Both groups indicated: Borman, *Countdown,* page 390.

page 195 "kill these guys": Magurno 3/11/94 interview.

page 195 *In good faith I took*: The poem appears in Banks, in *Labor Research Review,* Winter 1984, and is used with permission.

page 196 "the end of Eastern": Borman, *Countdown,* page 389.

page 196 "If the union doesn't accept": Quoted in Smaby *et al.,* May 1987.

page 196 "personal guru": Borman, *Countdown,* page 385.

page 196 Born in Wyoming: Barber 6/21/94 interview.

page 197 "In business schools": Quoted in Borman, *Countdown,* page 385.

page 197 brought in some pals: Barber 6/21/94 interview.

page 198 12 days' worth of cash: Smaby *et al.,* May 1987.

page 198 contract to kill: Borman 1/29/94 interview.

page 198 9 mm . . . pistol: *Ibid.*

page 198 fact-finding mission: Borman 1/29/94 interview.

page 199 Willard C. Butcher: *Ibid.* Borman also discussed the meeting in Deposition of Frank Borman, Apr. 26, 1988.

page 199 not a strikebreaker: Borman 1/29/94 interview. Butcher denies making any inflammatory remarks but does not dispute the gist of Borman's account.

page 200 ballots recounted: Smaby *et al.,* May 1987.

page 200 lording their victory: Banks, in *Labor Research Review,* Winter 1984.

page 200 "We were raped!": Borman, *Countdown,* page 391.

Chapter 8: Stormy Weather

page 201 "Safety . . . lay in speed": Lindbergh, *The Spirit of St. Louis,* page 290.

page 202 cigarette smoke: Grey, *The Facts of Flight,* page 24.

page 202 Each square foot: Serling, *Loud and Clear,* page 40.

page 202 Air Florida Flight 90: The account of the crash is based mostly on the *Aircraft Accident Report* of the National Transportation Safety Board, NTSB-AAR-82-8, Aug. 10, 1982. Additional insights were obtained from an excellent reconstruction in Nance, *Blind Trust.*

page 202 after leaving Braniff: Though not affirming legal travails as the reason for his departure from Braniff, Acker provided the details of his post-Braniff career in the 6/3/93 interview.

page 203 reminded Acker of . . . Southwest: *Ibid.*

page 203 "worse than dope": Quoted in "At the Controls of Pan Am," by Thomas L. Friedman, *NYT,* Aug. 28, 1981.

page 203 controlling interest: Acker's turnaround moves at Air Florida were detailed in the Acker interviews of 1/7/93 and 6/3/93 and, among other places, in "Air Florida, Soaring Out of Obscurity, Becomes Profitable,

Feisty Contender," by Roger Thurow, *WSJ,* Aug. 17, 1978; and Friedman, *NYT,* Aug. 28, 1981; "Air Florida's Fortunes Soar in Six Market Areas," by Joseph S. Murphy, *Airline Executive,* May 1980.

page 203 "a warm climate": Thurow, *WSJ,* Aug. 17, 1978.

page 203 "flights for a kiss": "Highly Publicized Cuts in Airline Fares Mask Rapid Escalation of Ticket Prices," by William M. Carley, *WSJ,* Oct. 8, 1980.

page 203 dog-eared copy: Friedman, *NYT,* Aug. 28, 1981.

page 204 "darling of deregulation": *Ibid.*

page 204 "ablest of the entrepreneurs": "Putting Pan Am Back Together Again," by Louis Kraar, *Fortune,* Dec. 28, 1981.

page 204 "corporate success stories": "Air Florida's Future Open to Question Following Acker's Surprise Departure," by Chester Goolrick, *WSJ,* Aug. 27, 1981.

page 204 profits were subsidized: Lloyd-Jones 3/10/94 interview.

page 204 "talked to Cunard Lines": Quoted in "Pan Am's Brash New Pilot," *Newsweek,* Sept. 7, 1981.

page 205 dentist in Key West: Air Florida System, Inc., proxy statement, Dec. 29, 1978.

page 205 access in the Keys: Acker 6/3/93 interview.

page 205 "kids are just crapping": The NTSB transcript says "are just # . "

page 208 reservations evaporated: "How Two Airlines Lost Their Way," *BW,* Apr. 19, 1982.

page 208 revenue vanished: *Ibid.*

page 209 saw no merit: The account of Acker's turnaround moves is based on the Acker 6/3/93 interview; "Risky Flying: In Bid to Save Pan Am, New Chief Trims Fares Instead of Operations," by William M. Carley, *WSJ,* Dec. 11, 1981; and "Putting Pan Am Back Together Again," by Louis Kraar, *Fortune,* Dec. 28, 1981.

page 209 flight to . . . Bermuda: Shugrue 9/8/93 interview.

page 209 "just *tell* them": Acker 6/3/93 interview.

page 209 cigarette butts: Shugrue 9/8/93 interview.

page 209 counted his chauffeur: Acker 6/3/93 interview.

page 209 hundreds of ticket stubs: Shugrue 9/8/93 interview.

page 210 away from the gate: C. Edward Acker, speech to Pan Am Management Club, Miami, Oct. 13, 1981.

page 210 "powerful force": Quoted in "Clipped Wings: Is Pan Am's Strategy the Airline's Salvation or Its Death Sentence?" by William M. Carley, *WSJ,* Feb. 12, 1986.

page 210 "does he work for us?": Wolf 6/4/93 interview.

page 210 turned around to see: Gitner 3/31/93 interview.

page 210 "What's that doing here?": *Ibid.*

page 211 search plane: Shugrue 5/14/93 interview.

page 211 Wolf's . . . sanctimony: Wolf 6/4/93 interview.

page 211 "no choice": Kraar, *Fortune,* Dec. 28, 1981.

page 211 "terrific travel bargain": Acker speech, Oct. 13, 1981.

page 212 flipped the pages: Acker 6/3/93 interview; Kraar, *Fortune,* Dec. 28, 1981.

page 212 Laker's operation was dead: Laker's failure, which was due to a number of causes, generated a thicket of antitrust litigation as well as a U.S. grand jury investigation that caused diplomatic stress between the United States and Britain. Ultimately President Reagan quashed the probe at the urging of Prime Minister Thatcher. These intrigues are worthy of a book in their own right, but not a glossed-over account in this one.

page 212 "I didn't mind": Acker 6/3/93 interview.

page 212 ACKER BACKER: Kriendler 5/12/93 interview.

page 213 "dedicate ourselves": Letter from C. Edward Acker to Pan Am employees, May 10, 1982.

page 213 heavily unionized airline: "The Golden Years," *Avmark Aviation Economist,* June 1986.

page 213 operate forklifts: Shugrue 5/14/93 interview.

page 214 close family friend: Shugrue 9/8/93 interview.

page 214 serious bind: The description of the lie is based on the Shugrue 9/8/93 interview; "Pan Am Strike by TWU Is Viewed as Stemming from Personality Conflicts and Economic Woes," by William M. Carley, *WSJ,* March 6, 1985; Carley, *WSJ,* Feb. 12, 1986; and *Pan American World Airways, Inc., Financial Analysis,* Lazard Frères & Co. Jan. 31, 1985.

Chapter 9: Continental Divide

page 215 imagined himself a builder: Lorenzo 5/5/88 interview.

page 216 51 percent: Bakes 5/12/93 interview. In 1982 Texas Air completed the takeover by exchanging some of its own shares for the remaining shares of Continental. The financial mechanics of the Continental perchange are detailed in *Continental Airlines Preliminary Prospectus,* Mar. 18, 1983.

page 216 called Bob Six: Murphy, *The Airline That Pride Almost Bought,* page 25.

page 216 Feldman was an engineer: The description of Feldman's career and his turnaround moves at Frontier are based on several interviews with his friend Travis Reed and on a number of published accounts, including "Frontier's Planning Serves It Well in Good Times and Bad," by

James P. Woolsey, *Air Transport World,* August 1980; and Murphy, *The Airline That Pride Almost Bought,* pages 9–11.

page 216 purple vulture: Reed 5/31/94 interview.

page 216 threw himself into his work: "Continental Air Chairman Found Dead in His Office, Apparently a Suicide," by Roy J. Harris, Jr., *WSJ,* Aug. 11, 1981.

page 217 "first time . . . I've ever lost": Quoted in Murphy, *The Airline That Pride,* page 47.

page 217 hottest free agent: Reed 6/2/94 interview.

page 217 "necessary to renegotiate": Quoted in Murphy, *The Airline That Pride,* page 38.

page 218 "must tell you": Letter from A. L. Feldman, Continental Airlines, to Francisco A. Lorenzo, Apr. 3, 1981.

page 218 Lorenzo was bothered: "Texas Air's Lorenzo Hopes to Pilot Continental Airlines into His Hangar," by Roger Thurow, *WSJ,* Apr. 23, 1981.

page 218 prove himself worthy: Bakes 5/12/93 interview.

page 218 angry Continental employees: Murphy, *The Airline That Pride,* page 110.

page 218 filled with dread: Bakes 5/12/93 interview.

page 218 "authorized representative": Bakes's remarks, and those of Dennis Higgins that follow, are based on videotape shot by a television crew and later presented to Higgins.

page 219 thronged by microphones: Lavender 6/16/93 interview.

page 219 chilling glare: Bakes 5/12/93 interview.

page 220 "made you feel dirty": Bakes 5/12/93 interview.

page 220 "Get the fuck:" Bakes 5/12/93 interview. Bakes is also the source of the Maxine Waters anecdote.

page 220 around the Senate chambers: "How Texas Air Won Its Fight," *BW,* Oct. 26, 1981, and Murphy, *The Airline That Pride,* pages 187–88.

page 221 brother-in-law: *BW,* Oct. 26, 1981.

page 221 see Rostenkowski: Bakes 5/12/93 interview.

page 221 with Sen. Lloyd Bentsen: Lavender 6/16/93 interview.

page 221 Bakes and Lorenzo collapsed: Bakes 5/12/93 interview.

page 221 adventurous . . . vacations: Reed 6/1/94 interview.

page 222 "100 percent immersed": Reed 6/2/94 interview.

page 222 "big drinks": *Ibid.*

page 222 nine banks . . . were withdrawing: Harris, *WSJ,* Aug. 11, 1981.

page 222 before 6 P.M.: The facts of Feldman's death are detailed in the report written by the Los Angeles County Medical Examiner's Office, Case No. 81-10225, Aug. 9, 1981.

page 222 Lorenzo . . . had resisted: Bakes 5/12/93 interview.

page 223 first for breakfast: *Ibid.*

page 223 "I've just gotten word": *Ibid.*

page 223 "You killed him!": *Ibid.* Lavender, in the 6/16/93 interview, recalled a member of his group turning to Bakes and shouting, "Are you happy now?"

page 223 color vanish: Bakes 5/12/93 interview.

page 223 "next plane out": *Ibid.*

page 223 "despondent since the death": L.A. County Medical Examiner, Case No. 81-10225.

page 224 "Why did you": Reed interviews of 6/1/94 and 6/2/94. Ferris declined to discuss Feldman's death.

page 224 their first meeting: Bakes 5/12/93 interview; "Unfriendly Skies: Frank Lorenzo Tries to Navigate 3 Airlines Through Stormy Times," by Roger Thurow, *WSJ,* Feb. 18, 1982.

page 224 "Judging from these projections": Bakes 5/12/93 interview.

page 224 Fifteen percent: "Continental Air Lays Off 1,500, 15% of Employees," *WSJ,* Jan. 26, 1982.

page 225 give up $90 million: *Continental Airlines Preliminary Prospectus,* Mar. 18, 1983.

page 225 "The fact is": Letter from Frank Lorenzo to the Hon. Don Sebastiani, July 28, 1981.

page 225 Lorenzo was eager: Bakes 5/12/93 interview.

page 226 "going to be announcing": *Ibid.*

page 226 mother would later tell: The anecdote attributed to Wolf's mother was told by her to a close acquaintance who prefers to remain anonymous.

page 226 father walked out: Wolf detailed his early years in the 6/4/93 and 8/25/94 interviews.

page 227 caught the attention: Casey 3/6/92 interview.

page 227 walking down a . . . street: Gunn 4/28/93 interview.

page 227 Wolf would take delight: Wolf 6/4/93 interview.

page 227 Some of his peers: Baker 4/23/93 interview.

page 227 wanted a promotion: Wolf 6/4/93 interview; Plaskett 1/14/93 interview.

page 227 wanted to run something: Wolf 6/4/93 interview.

page 227 "profound financial strengths": Quoted in "Frank Lorenzo Lures a Copilot to Continental," *BW,* Dec. 6, 1982.

page 228 dry cleaner: Murray 9/4/93 interview.

page 228 mastery of intricacy: J. Arpey 6/16/94 interview.

page 228 sprawled on the floor: This story, heard by many Continental executives, was also reported in "Up in the Air," by Mike Steere, *Chicago,* May 1991.

page 228 One Sunday night: Bakes 6/16/94 interview.

page 228 end runs around Wolf: Bakes 6/11/93 interview.

page 228 calling him Steve: Murray 9/4/93 interview.

page 228 "no plans to move": Letter from Frank Lorenzo to the Hon. Don Sebastiani, July 28, 1981.

page 229 month-to-month lease: Wolf 6/4/93 interview.

page 229 Burr read aloud: Burr 9/16/93 interview.

page 229 eagerly seeking: Bakes 6/11/93 interview; Burr 9/16/93 interview.

page 229 "one more of Frank's deals": Burr 9/17/93 interview.

page 229 "way to jab Frank": *Ibid.*

page 229 swamp Lorenzo: *Ibid.*

page 230 had a child: Dawsey 9/17/93 interview.

page 230 "a screwup": Murray 9/4/93 interview, and Deposition of Richard E. Murray, U.S. Justice Department, CID No. 5087, June 22, 1983.

page 230 "suppression of all Continental fares": Memo from J. L. Ott to L. A. Iovinelli *et al.,* "Subject: Continental Fares," American Airlines, Dec. 1, 1981.

page 230 sheepishly approached Murray: Murray 9/4/93 interview.

page 230 "sworn to secrecy": *Ibid.*

page 230 meeting with Bob Crandall: Murray 6/11/93 and 9/4/93 interviews.

page 231 "put them out of business": *Ibid.* Anne McNamara, the general counsel of American, said she was unaware of this conversation ever occurring. In his May 22, 1995, letter to the author, Crandall called Murray's recollection "flawed and slanted."

page 231 wanted to join: Murray 9/4/93 interview.

page 231 tales of tweaking: *Ibid.*

page 231 smoking gun: *Ibid.*

page 231 touch on Wall Street: Continental's extensive financing moves are described in *Continental Airlines Preliminary Prospectus,* Mar. 18, 1983.

page 232 "laid on all the charm": Bakes 6/11/93 interview.

page 232 fitting metaphor: *Ibid.*

page 232 average Continental pilot: Wage rates and work rules are taken from Affidavit of Philip J. Bakes, Jr., *In re Continental Airlines Corp.,* U.S. Bankruptcy Court, Southern District of Texas, Sept. 24, 1993.

page 232 use of a private airplane: Bakes 6/11/93 interview.

page 232 changed overnight: *Ibid.*

page 233 "prepare for a strike": *Ibid.*

page 233 Lorenzo and Bakes were rejoicing: Bakes 6/16/94 interview.

page 234 appellate court decision: Bakes 6/11/93 interview.

page 234 "awfully big stick": Quoted in "Continental Air Official Saw Chapter 11 as 'Stick' Against Unions, Hearing Told," by Bryan Burrough, *WSJ,* Dec. 14, 1983.

page 234 Lorenzo was nervous: Bakes 6/16/94 interview.

page 235 "alarming rate": The text of Lorenzo's speech is attached as an exhibit to the Bakes affidavit of Sept. 24, 1993.

page 235 veins were popping: Bakes 6/16/94 interview.

page 236 "press the test": Higgins 6/8/94 interview.

page 236 all the head banging: Wolf 6/4/93 interview.

page 236 perfectly modulated voice: Wolf's manner on such occasions, described by many who have seen him speak over the years, was also observed by the author.

page 237 stomach for . . . confrontation: J. Arpey 6/16/94 interview.

page 237 "Frank is bashing them": Wolf 6/4/93 interview.

page 237 downright naive: Bakes 6/11/93 interview.

page 237 no amount of concessions: Murray 9/4/93 interview.

page 237 Lorenzo sat Wolf down: Wolf refused to discuss this meeting with Lorenzo. The dialogue is reconstructed from interviews with Bakes, Murray, and others who later spoke to Lorenzo and Wolf about the conversation.

page 237 a severance check: Lorenzo told Murray that he gave Wolf a check for one year's salary. Murray 9/4/93 interview.

page 237 "take him very seriously": Wolf 6/4/93 interview.

page 237 Wolf then telephoned: Murray 9/4/93 interview.

page 237 BMW sedan: Wolf 6/4/93 interview.

page 238 somebody's grave: Bakes 6/11/93 interview.

page 238 "welfare agency": Quoted in Thurow, *WSJ*, Feb. 18, 1982.

page 239 Braniff II rates: Bakes 6/11/93 interview. The salary levels cited here are taken from "Bitter, Deadly Dogfights," by John S. DeMott, *Time*, Oct. 10, 1983.

page 239 "blow-your-mind number": Bakes 6/11/93 interview.

page 240 inserted "The New": *Ibid.*

page 240 deeply depressed: *Ibid.*

page 240 admission of failure: Bankruptcy case testimony of Frank Lorenzo, cited in Burrough, *WSJ*, Dec. 14, 1983.

page 240 "It's your baby": Bakes 6/11/93 interview.

page 241 Just cut: *Ibid.*

page 241 protesting the arbitrariness: Murray 9/4/93 interview.

page 241 instantly joyous: Burr 9/16/93 interview.

page 242 forces of good: Sullivan 6/8/94 interview.

page 242 "don't have enough": Bakes 6/11/93 interview.

page 242 "vilest enemy": Quoted in Hopkins, *Flying the Line*, page 52.

page 242 cheer went up: Bakes 6/11/93 interview.

page 242 50 deep in Houston: DeMott, *Time*, Oct. 10, 1983.

page 242 "threat of a strike": "Continental Air Union Leaders for Pilots and Flight Aides Vote to Strike Tomorrow," by George Getschow and Charles F. McCoy, *WSJ*, Sept. 30, 1983.

page 242 instructed . . . Bruce Hicks: Bakes 6/11/93 interview.

page 243 requisite training: Detailed in *60 Minutes*, CBS Television Network, Apr. 15, 1984.

page 243 peculiar individual: Baxter's behavior was described by his fellow ALPA leader in Houston, Dennis Higgins, in the 6/8/94 interview. Several elements of Higgins's account were corroborated by Jim Sullivan, who was also an ALPA leader at Continental, in the 6/8/94 interview. In 1994 ALPA informed the author that it had no idea of Baxter's whereabouts.

page 243 "like wind shear": Sullivan 6/8/94 interview.

page 244 "Frank's past lies": Passage taken from an untitled memo to striking Continental pilots dated Nov. 18, 1983.

page 244 head of an elk: This and other episodes of violence against Continental scabs are detailed in *Continental Airlines* v. *Air Line Pilots Association,* in Re: Continental Airlines Corp., U.S. Bankruptcy Court, Southern District of Texas, Houston Division, No. 83-2386-H3, Jan. 30, 1984.

page 244 a U-turn . . . in San Antonio: Aspects of this incident were described in the Higgins 6/8/94 interview; First Amended Complaint, *Continental Airlines* v. *Air Line Pilots Association;* and "Militant Fliers: Pilots' Bitter Strike Against Continental Changed Their Union," by Leonard M. Apcar, *WSJ,* March 17, 1986.

page 245 "with the gear up": Babbitt 8/26/94 interview.

Chapter 10: Breaking Ranks

page 246 "Superman of Now": Herrmann, *Anne Morrow Lindbergh,* page 201.

page 246 official history: Hopkins, *Flying the Line,* page 23.

page 246 "a man's job": Saint-Exupéry, *Wind, Sand and Stars,* page 166.

page 246 had to be accompanied: Boase, *The Sky's the Limit,* page 68.

page 247 airlines' farm club: U.S. Department of Transportation, *Labor Relations and Labor Costs in the Airline Industry: Contemporary Issues,* May 1992.

page 247 a barnstormer: The facts of Behncke's life were taken principally from Hopkins, *Flying the Line.*

page 247 "Public safety calls": Quoted in *ibid.,* page 21.

page 247 went to Behncke's head: *Ibid., passim.*

page 248 "the pilot's life": Quoted in Solberg, *Conquest of the Skies,* page 174.

page 249 "getting to be a pilot": Quoted in "United Boss Dreams of Piloting a 747," by Dick Griffin, *Chicago Daily News,* Apr. 28, 1976.

page 249 how to fly: Ferris 5/27/93 interview.

page 249 starting flag: *Ibid.*

page 249 "He listens": Quoted in "United President Takes to Skies for Fun, Profit," by Todd Fandell, *Chicago Tribune,* Sept. 22, 1976.

page 249 "fearless Dick Ferris": "Businessmen in the News," *Fortune,* May 1977.

page 249 Boeing 767 jet: Ferris 5/28/93 interview.

page 249 failed to gain: Carlson, *Recollections,* pages 209–10.

page 249 losing an engine: Ferris 6/7/94 interview.

page 250 Ferris gave money: "United's Pilots Borrow Ferris's Idea to Whip Up Unity," by Bill Barnhart and Sally Saville Hodge, *Chicago Tribune,* May 8, 1985.

page 250 "your golf games": Quoted in "Friendlier Skies? United Airlines Hopes Pilots' Vote This Week Will Be Turning Point," by John Curley, *WSJ,* Aug. 10, 1981.

page 250 "blue skies" contract: "Management, Labor Debate Work Issues," by James Ott, *Aviation Week,* Sept. 7, 1981; "United Takes on the Up-starts," Oct. 19, 1981.

page 250 "a new era": "United Air Pilots Clear Pact Granting Carrier Job-Rule Concessions," by John Curley, *WSJ,* Aug. 14, 1981.

page 250 "Eighty to 90 percent": Richard J. Ferris, *Distinguished Executive Lecture,* Krannert Graduate School of Management, Purdue University, 1979.

page 251 squirmed and fidgeted: Griffin, *Chicago Daily News,* Apr. 28, 1976.

page 251 a podium: Ferris 5/28/93 interview.

page 251 "What the hell": Luce 8/26/93 interview.

page 251 "worked too hard": *Ibid.* Luce was the principal source of the dialogue reconstructed here. Ferris, though not confirming all of the words exchanged, does confirm secretly proposing an LBO at United at this time; he says employee groups would have been partners in the transaction.

page 252 Ferris could see: Ferris 6/7/94 interview.

page 252 "Well, Dick": Luce 8/26/93 interview.

page 252 "This is a takeover": *Ibid.*

page 253 "don't make many mistakes": *Ibid.*

page 253 "shook the board": *Ibid.*

page 253 backlash on his hands: Babbitt 8/26/94 interview.

page 253 still seething: Rick Dubinsky, speech to the Harvard Trade Union Program, Feb. 28, 1991.

page 254 dead anyway: Ferris 5/27/93 interview.

page 254 Chicago Action Plan: Testimony of Robert L. Crandall, *AMR Corp.* v. *UAL Corp.,* U.S. District Court, Southern District of New York, 91 Civ. 7773, Mar. 4, 1992.

page 254 well over $100 million: Based on spending of $75 million after 1988, as disclosed in *ibid.*, plus $32 million paid to United for 12 slots in 1992.

page 254 mattered immensely: Ferris 5/27/93 interview; Testimony of Donald J. Carty, *AMR Corp.* v. *UAL Corp.*, Mar. 4, 1992.

page 254 giant soiree: "United and American Vie to Expand Share of Market at O'Hare Airport," by Harlan S. Byrne, *WSJ,* Aug. 27, 1984.

page 254 civic activities: Zeeman 7/23/93 interview.

page 255 "Get along peaceably": Letter from Jesse W. Ferris to Dick Ferris, Aug. 28, 1957.

page 255 deeply hurt: Ferris 5/27/93 interview.

page 255 pounding on tables: "Revolt at Allegis: How Labor and Wall Street Stopped Ferris," by Mark Hornung, *Crain's Chicago Business,* Nov. 30, 1987.

page 255 "You match the American": Ferris 5/27/93 interview.

page 255 actually canceling: "The Dogfight Between United and Its Pilots," by Carol Jouzaitis, *Chicago Tribune,* May 12, 1985.

page 255 "lost his balance": Luce 8/26/93 interview.

page 255 Dick's toughness: Carlson, *Recollections of a Lucky Fellow,* page 270.

page 256 "love affair gone bad": Zeeman 7/23/93 interview.

page 256 role that wives played: "United Pilot Unity Starts at Home Front," by Gary Washburn, *Chicago Tribune,* June 13, 1985.

page 256 fully 1,000 pilots: First Officer David Cook, speech before United Pilots Teleconference, May 5, 1985.

page 256 household finance: "Video Technology Rallies Striking United Pilots," by Beth Ann Krier, *Los Angeles Times,* May 24, 1985.

page 257 piggy bank: *Pan American World Airways, Inc., Financial Analysis,* Lazard Frères, Jan. 31, 1985.

page 257 "Employees will not trust": *Ibid.*

page 257 "I want to talk": Ferris 5/27/93 interview.

page 258 commissioned a study: *Ibid.* Ferris's thinking is also detailed in "The Pan Am-United Deal: Truly a 'Win-Win' Situation," by Reggi Ann Dubin, *BW,* May 6, 1985.

page 258 intervention of . . . Reagan: Carlson, *Recollections,* page 224.

page 259 that was okay: Shugrue 9/8/93 interview.

page 259 "The Continental situation": Quoted in "Pan Am Reaches Back-to-Work Accord with Pilots; Mechanics Remain on Strike," by William M. Carley, *WSJ,* Mar. 7, 1985.

page 259 required a cushion; Acker 6/3/93 interview.

page 260 "fucking believe it": Zeeman 7/23/93 interview; Ferris 6/7/94 interview.

page 260 Ferris . . . readily agreed: Gitner 3/31/93 interview. Ferris, in the 6/7/94 interview, confirmed quickly accepting Acker's price, although not before he had conducted a quick and discreet due-diligence review.

page 260 emotionally wrenching: Acker 6/3/93 interview.

page 261 "could always argue": Coleman 2/16/94 interview.

page 261 could not imagine: Crandall 9/1/93 interview.

page 262 Ferris knew the timing: "Pan Am Agrees to Sell United Its Pacific Unit," by William M. Carley and Harlan S. Byrne, *WSJ*, Apr. 23, 1985.

page 262 high gear: "United Tries to Keep 'Em Flying During Strike's War of Nerves," by Carol Jouzaitis and Gary Washburn, *Chicago Tribune*, May 23, 1985.

page 262 casual slacks: "United Chief Takes Two-Tiered Pay Show 'on the Road,' " by Bill Barnhart and Sally Saville Hodge, *Chicago Tribune*, Mar. 13, 1985.

page 262 intimidating my pilots: Ferris 5/27/93 interview.

page 262 satellite production: ALPA, United Pilots Teleconference, May 5, 1985. The author viewed a videotape of the production.

page 264 agreed to b-scales: "There's No Turning Back at United," by Aaron Bernstein and Ellyn E. Spragins, *BW*, June 3, 1985.

page 264 50 percent of capacity: "United Airlines, Pilots' Union Agree to Hold Talks with Mediators in Strike," by Harlan S. Byrne, *WSJ*, May 20, 1985; "Pilots Go on Strike at United," by James Warren and Carol Jouzaitis, *Chicago Tribune*, May 17, 1985.

page 265 lodging the strikebreakers: ALPA's countertraining operation in Denver was described in the Babbitt 8/26/94 interview and the Higgins 6/8/94 interview.

page 265 "nuclear reactor": Babbitt 8/26/94 interview.

page 265 double agents: Higgins 6/8/94 interview.

page 265 Haas . . . expressed reservations: Zeeman 7/23/93 interview; Ferris 6/7/94 interview.

page 266 Six showed up: Byrne, *WSJ*, May 20, 1985.

page 266 30 management pilots: *Ibid.*

page 266 Twenty-four-hour security: Ferris 5/27/93 interview. Ferris also described the acts of intimidation against strikebreakers.

page 267 "I am the chairman": Quoted in " 'Friendly Skies' Now Cloudy," by Carol Jouzaitis and Gary Washburn, *Chicago Tribune*, June 23, 1985.

page 267 "back to the Dumpster": Babbitt 8/26/94 interview; "Settlement Pleases United's Chief Exec," by Gary Washburn, *Chicago Tribune*, June 21, 1985.

page 267 Ferris would . . . deny: Ferris 5/27/93 interview.

page 267 "ALPA can't win": Warren and Jouzaitis, *Chicago Tribune*, May 17, 1985.

page 267 called his senior managers: Zeeman 6/23/93 interview.

page 268 "tank of gasoline": Luce 8/26/93 interview.

page 268 "not a strike": Zeeman 7/23/93 interview.

page 269 "pile of cash": Olson 6/28/94 interview.

page 270 landed in London: Ferris 6/7/94 interview; Zeeman 7/23/93 interview.

page 270 Ferris's own managers: Marianne Lazarus 6/10/93 interview.

page 270 "own the world": Ferris 5/27/93 interview.

Chapter 11: Gloom over Miami

page 271 direct electronic tie-in: "The Other Reason Frank Lorenzo Wants TWA," by Chuck Hawkins, *BW,* Dec. 30, 1985.

page 271 30,000 travel agencies: U.S. Department of Justice, *1985 Report to Congress on the Airline Computer Reservation System Industry,* Dec. 20, 1985.

page 272 "competitive raison d'être": Robert L. Crandall, written statement, U.S. Congress, House Aviation Subcommittee, June 23, 1983.

page 272 ways to play games: "Aerial Combat: Major Airlines, Tired of New Lines' Inroads, Cut Fares, Woo Public," by Francis C. Brown III, *WSJ,* Feb. 28, 1986.

page 272 concentration of terminals: Hopper 10/13/93 interview.

page 272 "Whether bias exists": Michael Gunn, American Airlines, presentation to 1984 marketing meeting.

page 273 greater motive: Hawkins, *BW,* Dec. 30, 1985.

page 273 gypsies play cards: *Ibid.*

page 273 walked away: Bakes 6/11/93 interview.

page 274 "no intent or motive": Quoted in "Continental Air Wins Defense of Chapter 11," by Bryan Burrough, *WSJ,* Jan. 18, 1984.

page 274 judge would soon accept: "Judge in Texas Air Unit's Case Says Talk of Job Came Weeks After His Rulings," by Jonathan Kwitny, *WSJ,* Oct. 6, 1986.

page 274 imploring Bakes: Bakes 6/11/93 interview.

page 274 inferiority complex: A number of Lorenzo's former associates used these terms to describe his ambivalence about cutting Continental's levels of cabin service.

page 275 jumped all over Bakes: Bakes 6/16/94 interview.

page 275 marketing innovations: *Ibid.*

page 275 "airport of the future": *Ibid.*

page 275 "wasting money on this shit": *Ibid.*

page 275 pictured in *Business Week:* "Continental Is Soaring Out of Chapter 11," by James R. Norman, *BW,* July 7, 1986.

page 275 "a real high": "Continental Air's Lorenzo Has New Image with Aides a Year After Chapter 11 Filing," by Bryan Burrough, *WSJ,* Sept. 24, 1984.

page 275 30 percent of his time: Bakes 6/16/94 interview.

page 276 same budget hotel: "Continental Air Reorganization Plan Is Accepted by Most of Firm's Creditors," by Mark Zieman, *WSJ,* Sept. 6, 1985.

page 276 "running the zoo": Quoted in Gibney, *Washington Monthly,* June 1986; "Lost in Space," by Rowland Stiteler, *Florida,* Nov. 1, 1987.

page 276 moved to restrict: Smaby *et al.,* May 1987.

page 276 Within hours: By Barber's recollection, Borman privately first issued his Chapter 11 threat about two days before the Continental Chapter 11, although there is little doubt that Continental's icebreaking maneuver emboldened Borman to take his threat public.

page 277 "à la Continental": Quoted in "Future of Eastern Air Lines Hinging on Chief's Credibility with Unions," by Margaret Loeb and Thomas E. Ricks, *WSJ,* Sept. 29, 1983.

page 277 fanned out: Magurno 3/11/94 interview.

page 277 intimidate . . . its customers: Gibney, *Washington Monthly,* June 1986.

page 277 "Borman, Resign Now": "The Fall Crisis at Eastern," by Paul J. Baicich, *Labor Research Review,* Winter 1984.

page 278 teach some reason: Magurno 3/11/94 interview.

page 278 Crisp . . . made a point: Bryan 5/13/93 interview.

page 278 Bryan would later admit: *Ibid.*

page 278 "largest experiment": Gibney, *Washington Monthly,* June 1986.

page 278 "extensive employee participation": "Frank Borman's Most Difficult Days," by Leslie Wayne, *NYT,* Feb. 17, 1985.

page 278 "off by 10 years": Kelleher 6/14/94 interview.

page 279 "war is over": Quoted in "Eastern's Kansas City Hub Is Proving to Be a Bright Spot," by Gary Conn, *WSJ,* Apr. 20, 1984.

page 279 dying inside: Borman admitted to his secretly negative feelings in Deposition of Frank Borman, *In the Matter of Preliminary Investigation of Texas Air Corp.,* U.S. Department of Transportation, Docket No. 45581, Apr. 26, 1988.

page 279 so much "crap": Borman 1/29/94 interview.

page 279 had shaken him: Barber 6/21/94 interview.

page 280 "the only pilot": Frank Borman, transcribed remarks to Eastern ALPA Master Executive Council, Miami, Aug. 19, 1985.

page 280 cancel . . . 500 flights: Smaby *et al.,* May 1987.

page 280 Colonel's long-range vision: Kunstler 9/7/93 interview.

page 280 Crandall's coterie: Kaldahl 4/27/93 interview.

page 281 "Caribbean marketing": Gunn, presentation to 1984 marketing meeting.

page 281 "beyond Band-Aids": Quoted in Smaby *et al.*, May 1987.

page 281 just $3,000: "Eastern Air Union Leaders Are Taking Steps Toward Possible Bid for Control," by Gary Cohn, *WSJ*, Jan. 9, 1986.

page 282 "Fix it": Magurno 3/11/94 interview; Borman, *Countdown, passim.*

page 282 "talk to you": Borman, *Countdown*, page 420.

page 282 Lorenzo wanted System One: Borman 1/29/94 interview. Borman and Lorenzo discussed the possibility of using System One as the foundation of a multiairline reservations network to compete with Sabre and Apollo. Lorenzo had assumed an active role among the non-CRS airlines in proposing this system, known as the Neutral Industry Booking System, or NIBS. According to Richard Murray, who represented Lorenzo in these discussions, "We were using NIBS as a way of getting to System One. We knew NIBS would never happen: there were too many different philosophies and cultures. . . . NIBS was a way of keeping a finger on System One."

page 282 Borman took . . . to Lorenzo: Borman, *Countdown*, page 421.

page 282 as if . . . making a joke: Borman reconstructed his conversation with Lorenzo in Deposition of Frank Borman, Apr. 26, 1988. Additional details are based on Borman, *Countdown*, page 421, and in the Borman 1/19/94 interview.

page 282 "ace in the hole": Borman, *Countdown*, page 421.

page 282 Borman excitedly described: Magurno 3/11/94 interview.

page 283 "just using me": Borman, *Countdown*, page 423.

page 283 potential buyers: Borman 1/19/94 interview.

page 283 "loony tunes": *Ibid.*

page 283 "What do you think?": Bakes's conversations with Lorenzo, and Lorenzo's state of mind, were described in the Bakes 6/11/93 interview; Deposition of Phillip [sic] Bakes, *Air Line Pilots Association* v. *Eastern Air Lines*, U.S. District Court for the District of Columbia, Civil Action No. 87-2002, Aug. 10, 1988, as well as numerous public comments by Lorenzo.

page 284 remotely plausible: "Sabre Rattling," *Economist*, Nov. 7, 1987.

page 284 Borman had known . . . Winpisinger: Borman, *Countdown, passim.*

page 285 "Charlie hears voices": Quoted in Borman, *Countdown*, page 377. Winpisinger confirms making the remark.

page 286 bulletproof vest: Borman 1/19/94 interview.

page 286 Bryan . . . was vomiting: Bryan 5/13/93 interview.

page 286 pondered the variables: *Ibid.;* Barber 6/21/94 interview.

page 287 On Sunday: The account of the fateful Eastern board meeting is based, among other sources, on copious contemporaneous notes by Randy Barber, who was an eyewitness to many of the events, as well as on a 23-page monograph written by Barber on Mar. 7, 1986; on the Borman 1/19/94 interview; the Bryan 5/13/93 interview; the Magurno 3/11/94 interview; Borman, *Countdown;* Bernstein, *Grounded;* and the first in-depth published account of the meeting, "Classic Mistake: Eastern Air's Borman Badly Underestimated Obduracy of Old Foe," by Gary Cohn, *WSJ,* Feb. 25, 1986.

page 288 track down someone: Magurno 3/11/94 interview.

page 288 "change his mind": Barber notes.

page 288 Borman pulled Bryan: *Ibid.*

page 289 offered a proposal: Bryan 5/13/93 interview.

page 289 "What's going on?": The account of the phone conversation is based on the Bryan 5/13/93 interview; the Borman 1/19/94 interview; and Borman, *Countdown,* pages 430–31. Winpisinger confirms the gist of the conversation and provided some details.

page 290 "you destroyed this airline": The exchange is based on the Barber notes. A similar account appeared in Cohn, *WSJ,* Feb. 25, 1986.

page 291 clients some comfort: Magurno 3/11/94 interview.

page 291 "Hold it!": Bryan 5/13/93 interview.

page 292 "Bryan's offer": Borman, *Countdown,* page 435.

page 292 in the open: *Ibid.*

page 292 "Any allegation": *Ibid.*

page 292 "Don't you agree": Magurno 3/11/94 interview.

page 292 "submit my resignation": Borman, *Countdown,* page 436.

page 292 "volunteering to leave": Barber notes.

page 292 "promises are no good": Barber monograph, Mar. 7, 1986.

page 292 "They did it!": Barber notes.

page 293 "sorry to tell you": Quoted in Bernstein, *Grounded,* page 50.

page 293 tears streaming: Babbitt 8/26/94 interview.

page 293 "I'm sorry": *Ibid.*

page 293 "might be surprising": Quoted in "Editorial: The Eastern Strike," by James Woolsey, *Air Transport World,* May 1989.

page 294 never receive an answer: Bernstein, *Grounded,* page 53.

page 294 "union buster": A transcript of the press conference appears in the *Falcon,* Eastern Air Lines, Mar. 5, 1986.

page 295 Colonel wanted . . . to remain: Borman 1/19/94 interview.

page 295 No, Lorenzo said: *Ibid.*

page 295 sick to his stomach: Bakes 6/16/94 interview.

page 295 a cesspool: *Ibid.*

page 295 reputation had suffered: Bakes 6/11/93 interview.

page 296 "got to have a meeting": Bakes 9/7/93 interview.

page 296 "Get to the point!:" An account of the exchange appears in the IAM District 100 newsletter of Jan. 12, 1987.

page 297 sat down with Lorenzo: Memo to file from David Kunstler, Eastern Air Lines, July 22, 1986.

Chapter 12: Nosedive

page 298 "I'll shoot you!": Burr 9/16/93 interview.

page 299 In the New York area: "Rapid Ascent: People Express Flies into Big Time in Just Three Years Aloft," by William M. Carley, *WSJ,* Mar. 30, 1984.

page 299 Hundreds of passengers: The scene is described in "That Daring Young Man and his Flying Machines," by Lucien Rhodes, *Inc.,* Jan. 1984.

page 300 "High growth is important": Quoted in "Arrant Burr," by James K. Glassman, *New Republic,* Oct. 6, 1986.

page 300 "two bull elephants": Quoted in "People Express's Newark-Chicago Entry Underscores Shift in Strategy of Carrier," by William M. Carley, *WSJ,* Aug. 9, 1984.

page 301 6,000 potential passengers: Carley, *WSJ,* Mar. 30, 1984.

page 302 Burr . . . finally got religion: Burr 9/17/93 interview.

page 302 "mini–Manhattan Project": *Ibid.*

page 302 "a dry hole": *Ibid.*

page 302 "give a shit": *Ibid.*

page 302 little rhyme and reason: *People Express Airlines: Rise and Decline,* Harvard Business School Case No. N9-490-012, Mar. 1, 1990.

page 302 evaluated against the Precepts: Burr 9/17/93 interview.

page 302 from *The Greatest:* Harvard Business School Case, Mar. 1, 1990.

page 302 shoes and socks removed: *Ibid.*

page 302 "personally and painfully": Quoted in *Ibid.*

page 303 "brought together": Quoted in *Ibid.*

page 303 Crandall had not forgotten: Crandall 4/23/93 interview.

page 304 nearly 1,500 departures: "Revenue Control: Mining Gold at the Margin," by Samuel M. Fuchs, *Airline Executive,* Jan. 1987.

page 304 assigned to Barbara R. Amster: Amster 4/29/93 interview.

page 305 had to be eradicated: Crandall 4/23/93 interview; "American on the Offensive," *Financial World,* Feb. 20, 1985; "American Tries to Muscle In on the Low-Cost Carriers," by Reggi Ann Dubin, *BW,* Feb. 4, 1985.

page 306 Crandall was concerned: Crandall remarks to 1985 Fall Planning Conference, American Airlines, draft dated Sept. 26, 1985.

page 306 "brains of Southwest": Amster 4/29/93 interview.

page 306 "devised the fare": Carty 4/29/93 interview.

page 306 new pricing strategy: "American Airlines Slashes Fares on Many Routes; Industry Stock Prices Slip as Rival Carriers Follow," by Laurie P. Cohen, *WSJ,* Jan. 18, 1985.

page 306 Within minutes: "Airlines' Bookings Soar on Discounts, But Increases in Profits Aren't Certain," by Laurie P. Cohen, *WSJ,* Jan. 28, 1985.

page 307 "the price card": Remarks by T. G. Plaskett to Lenders' Meeting, May 7, 1986.

page 307 "across our bow": Burr 9/17/93 interview. Some of Burr's comments also appear in "A Conversation with Don Burr," *Scorecard: The Revenue Management Quarterly*, Fourth Quarter 1992.

page 307 posing as American customers: Burr 9/17/93 interview; Speech by Burr to the Wings Club, transcribed and printed in *Airport Press*, Feb. 1989.

page 308 Burr was shocked: Burr 9/17/93 interview.

page 308 dying at the thought: "Bitter Victories," an interview with Burr by George Gendron, *Inc.*, Aug. 1985.

page 308 "had your Kool-Aid": Burr interview, *Inc.*, Aug. 1985.

page 308 Burr's mother called: Burr, Wings Club.

page 309 tennis club: Burr 9/17/93 interview.

page 310 "air bridge": Quoted in "Will Frontier's Fall Ground People Express, Too?" by Mark Ivey, James E. Ellis, and Chuck Hawkins, *BW*, Sept. 8, 1986.

page 310 "Over time": Quoted in Byrne, *BW*, Nov. 25, 1985.

page 310 his horror: Burr, Wings Club.

page 311 "remarkable offer": "People Express Merger Might Cause Problems," by William M. Carley and Teri Agins, *WSJ*, Oct. 14, 1985.

page 311 standing ovation: *Ibid.*

page 311 day's notice: "People Express, Signaling New Strategy of Acquisitions, Will Purchase Britt Air," by William M. Carley, *WSJ*, Dec. 30, 1985.

page 311 buying time: Burr 9/17/93 interview.

page 311 "raider-type stuff": *Ibid.;* Byrne, *BW*, Nov. 25, 1985.

page 311 "new wave capitalist": Byrne, *BW*, Nov. 25, 1985.

page 312 10-foot screen: *Ibid.*

page 312 "most comprehensive": Quoted in *ibid.*

page 312 Burr had vowed: Burr 9/17/93 interview.

page 312 like Herb Kelleher: *Ibid.*

page 312 Some pilots swore: Lavender 6/16/93 interview.

page 312 century-old home: Burr 9/16/93 interview.

page 312 "my moat": Burr 9/17/93 interview.

page 313 "Kibbles'N Bits": Dempsey, *Airline Deregulation and Laissez-Faire Mythology*, page 97.

page 313 boxed lunches: "Continental Air Will Offer Rivals' Fliers Free Lunch," *WSJ*, Mar. 14, 1986.

page 313 "boom" the market: Burr 9/17/93 interview.

page 313 anywhere from Denver: "Skirmishing That Only Looks Like a Fare War," by Todd Mason, *BW*, Dec. 2, 1985.

page 313 "beat the shit": O'Donnell 6/9/94 interview.

page 313 "change this board": *Ibid;* "How I Spent My Spring Under a Bill-board," by Francis C. Brown III, *WSJ,* Apr. 8, 1986.

page 313 stink lines: O'Donnell 6/9/94 interview.

page 314 elderly woman had clunked: "Bumpy Flights: Many Travelers Gripe About People Express, Citing Overbooking," by William M. Carley, *WSJ,* May 19, 1986.

page 314 grew tardy: Dempsey, *Airline Deregulation,* page 83.

page 314 Death Star: Burr 9/17/93 interview.

page 314 "my children": *Ibid.*

page 314 "fucking minds": *Ibid.*

page 314 "I kept this": Burr 9/16/93 interview.

page 315 a go-between: "People Is Still Carrying Some Heavy Baggage," by Chuck Hawkins, *BW,* July 28, 1986.

page 315 titanic egos: *ibid.*

page 315 "a final salute": Reed 9/16/94 interview.

page 316 "bittersweet moment": "Texas Air Corp. Agrees to Buy People Express," by William M. Carley, Teri Agins, and Daniel Hertzberg, *WSJ,* Sept. 16, 1986.

page 316 flipped on: Burr 9/17/93 interview.

page 316 they argued: Burr 9/16/93 and 9/17/93 interviews.

Chapter 13: The Southwest Shuffle

page 319 Consultants and academics: Barron 4/26/93 interview.

page 319 "Kelleher's bullshit": Bakes 4/23/93 interview.

page 320 resolved to strike west: Southwest's strategy is detailed, among other places, in "Flying on the Cheap: Southwest Airlines Is a Rare Air Carrier—It Still Makes Money," by Bridget O'Brian, *WSJ,* Oct. 26, 1992; "A Boy and His Airline," by Jan Jarobe, *Texas Monthly,* Apr. 1989; and "Changing Fortunes of a Dallas Star," by Harold Shenton, *Avmark Aviation Economist,* Aug. 1987.

page 320 He boned up: Kelleher 10/14/93 interview.

page 320 "Those were the rules": *Ibid.*

page 321 visiting his daughter: *Ibid.*

page 322 austerity program: "Southwest Airlines to Drop Flights, Limit Hiring to Cut Costs," *WSJ,* July 23, 1984.

page 323 dilute the purity: Barrett 4/26/93 interview.

page 323 "involved in a crusade": Kelleher 10/14/93 interview.

page 323 screening procedure: The description of Southwest's hiring procedures is based in part on the Barrett and Barron 4/26/93 interviews as well as on information from lower-level Southwest employees.

page 324 every employee's paycheck: Kelleher, "Life as an Airline Commissioner," Address to National Press Club, Washington, D.C., June 8, 1994.

page 324 *William Tell Overture:* "Air Chortle Is Now Boarding," by Adam Bryant, *NYT,* Oct. 2, 1994.

page 324 leprechaun costumes: Jarobe, *Texas Monthly,* Apr. 1989.

page 325 McGregor . . . encountered Kelleher: McGregor 6/10/94 interview.

page 326 Kelleher's own office: Kelleher 10/14/93 interview.

page 326 different wall: Ed Stewart, Southwest public relations official.

page 327 48,860 pairs: Brenner, *Analysis of Airline Concentration Issue,* July 1990.

page 328 "whale shit": Barrett 4/26/93 interview; Jarobe, *Texas Monthly,* Apr. 1989.

page 329 "growing disadvantage": "Southwest Air Is Facing Challenge of Its Making," by Ralph Blumenthal, *NYT,* Mar. 17, 1986.

page 329 "American now has fares": Kelleher interviews of 10/14/93 and 6/14/94.

page 330 office on Fridays: "These Two Airlines Are Doing It Their Way," by Joseph Weber, *BW,* Sept. 21, 1987.

page 330 "I'm immortal": Quoted in O'Brian, *WSJ,* Oct. 26, 1992.

page 330 "lost my color": Kelleher made the comment during a cocktail party in front of a *60 Minutes* camera.

page 331 "battle . . . is essentially over": Airline Economics, Inc., "Airline Consolidation: Where It Stands, What's to Come," 1987.

page 331 "kill him": Kelleher 10/14/93 interview.

page 332 "You're too young": *Ibid.*

page 332 say "up yours": Kelleher 6/14/94 interview.

page 333 "Dr. Ruth spoof": Quoted in Jarobe, *Texas Monthly,* Apr. 1989.

Chapter 14: Operation Stealthco

page 334 day of fishing: Reed 9/16/94 interview.

page 334 "Being second": *Ibid.*

page 335 some of Crandall's people: Gunn 4/28/93 interview.

page 335 "to my grave": Ferris 5/27/93 interview.

page 335 glass of gin: Reed 5/31/94 and 6/1/94 interviews.

page 335 no reason to doubt: Ferris 5/27/93 interview.

page 336 "pass the dividend": Luce 8/26/93 interview.

page 336 "when does *management*": *Ibid.*

page 336 withholding the name: *Ibid.*

page 336 favorite color: Ferris 5/28/93 interview.

page 336 Linked by satellite: "United Air's Parent Flies off Handle at Its PR Concern," by Michael J. McCarthy, *WSJ,* Feb. 19, 1987.

page 336 "It's a name": Quoted in *Ibid.*

page 337 Egregious Corporation: "How Dick Ferris Blew It," by Kenneth Labich, *Fortune,* July 7, 1987.

page 338 glasses of wine: ALPA's takeover effort is intricately detailed in "Revolt at Allegis: How Labor and Wall Street Stopped Ferris," by Mark Hornung, *Crain's Chicago Business,* Nov. 30, 1987.

page 338 "new toy": Roger Hall, "History of the ESOP," in May 1994 newsletter of ALPA's United affiliate.

page 338 hired help: Rick Dubinsky, speech before the Harvard Trade Union Program, Feb. 28, 1991.

page 338 an also-ran: Interview with Rick Dubinsky by Richard Rolfe, *Airline Business,* Dec. 1989.

page 338 Eastern unions . . . provided: Hall, May 1994 newsletter.

page 338 "buy our jobs": Rolfe, *Airline Business,* Dec. 1989.

page 338 Operation Stealthco: "United Airlines Pilot F. C. Dubinsky Flies Unfriendly Skies in Buyout Effort," by Judith Valente, *WSJ,* Apr. 8, 1987; "How Labor, Wall Street, Changed Allegis's Course," by Robert Kearns, *Chicago Tribune,* Sept. 21, 1987.

page 339 flying to Des Moines: Ferris 5/27/93 interview.

page 339 three-page letter: Kearns, *Chicago Tribune,* Sept. 21, 1987.

page 339 "chain reaction": "Cloudy Skies: Rising UAL Turmoil Threatens Ferris's Job as the Chief Executive," by Judith Valente, John Koten, and Scott Kilman, *WSJ,* Apr. 17, 1987.

page 339 "in jeopardy": *Ibid.*

page 339 Luce was horrified: Luce 8/26/93 interview.

page 339 community of interests: "Coniston to Seek Control of Allegis Board, Says It Would Sell All or Part of Concern," by Laurie P. Cohen and Judith Valente, *WSJ,* May 27, 1987.

page 340 must not divide: Luce 8/26/93 interview.

page 340 drafted a response: *Ibid.*

page 340 "anti-management bias": Charles F. Luce, "UAL Board Backs Chairman," letter to the editor, *WSJ,* Apr. 20, 1987.

page 340 Boeing now had two thirds: "Boeing's Roll to Continue, Analysts Agree," by Mark Lyon, *Airline Executive,* Dec. 1986.

page 341 clinch its standing: "Boeing's Accord with Allegis Reflects Stiff Competition Among Aircraft Firms," by Eileen White, *WSJ,* May 14, 1987.

page 341 "Coniston Schmoniston": Ferris 5/27/93 interview.

page 341 Allegis Visa card: Kearns, *Chicago Tribune,* Sept. 21, 1987.

page 342 under advisement: "Canceled Flight: Allegis Shakeup Came as Shareholder Ire Put Board Tenure in Doubt," by Judith Valente, Laurie P. Cohen, and Scott Kilman, *WSJ,* June 11, 1987.

page 342 win a proxy fight: *Ibid.*

page 342 "sell something": Olson 6/28/94 interview.

page 343 "own the company": Hornung, *Crain's Chicago Business,* Nov. 30, 1987.

page 343 "Don't worry": Luce 8/26/93 interview.

page 343 "lost our confidence": Quoted in "Allegis Considers Raising Payout Offer in Wake of Pilots' Proposal," by Judith Valente and Laurie P. Cohen, *WSJ,* June 8, 1987.

page 344 Cooley . . . agreed: Luce 8/26/93 interview.

page 344 "alternative to Dick": Olson 6/28/94 interview; Luce 8/26/93 interview.

page 345 "If you don't": Olson 6/28/94 interview.

page 346 "principal motivation": Luce 8/26/93 interview.

page 346 "getting weird": *Ibid.*

page 346 "my friend": Olson 6/28/94 interview.

page 346 "best interests": Luce 8/26/93 interview.

page 346 McGillicuddy . . . suggested: *Ibid.*

page 347 "there's no point": *Ibid.*

page 347 "You got it": Ferris 5/27/93 interview.

page 347 "big bad wolf": Lum 6/7/94 interview.

page 347 fabulously lucrative: Olson 6/28/94 interview.

page 348 Teton Valley: Reed 6/1/94 interview.

page 348 "human being": *Ibid.*

page 348 more than $4 million: The company paid Ferris a settlement equal to his salary of $650,000 over five years, plus $792,640 in stock-option profits. Allegis Corp. proxy statement, Apr. 27, 1988.

Chapter 15: Fly Now, Pay Later

page 349 feeder airlines: "The New 20,000-Pound Gorilla," by Alison Chambers, *Commuter World,* Dec. 1987.

page 349 17,000 . . . terminals: Lee Howard, "The Changing U.S. Airline Picture," presentation to *The Future of Aviation,* Fifth International Workshop, National Academy of Sciences, Oct. 6–8, 1987.

page 350 assembled with debt: Statistics on the magnitude of Texas Air's debt are taken from "House of Mirrors: Lorenzo's Texas Air Keeps Collecting Fees from Its Ailing Units," by Thomas Petzinger, Jr., and Paulette Thomas, *WSJ,* Apr. 7, 1988.

page 351 "merger escapades": Robert Crandall, American Airlines, address to Fall Planning Conference, 1986.

page 352 "legalized warfare": Plaskett, American Airlines, address to Fall Planning Conference, 1986.

page 352 into a mausoleum: Bakes 6/16/94 interview.

page 353 revitalization plan: Bakes 9/7/93 interview.

page 353 "one-trick pony": *Ibid.*

page 354 "a cancer": "Texas Air Demands Deep Cost Cuts at Eastern," by Paulette Thomas, *WSJ,* Jan. 22, 1989.

page 354 "a nonissue": *Ibid.*

page 354 "Weapons formed": A transcript of Bryan's comments at the rally was published in the IAM District 100 newsletter of Jan. 12, 1987. The exact King James scripture is, "No weapon that is formed against thee shall prosper." Isaiah 54:17.

page 354 company ID badge: Letter from John Adams to Charles E. Bryan, Eastern Air Lines, Jan. 13, 1987; memo from A. M. Shade-Griffith to security officers, Jan. 13, 1987.

page 354 "public soap operas": Adams to Bryan, Jan. 13, 1987.

page 354 "white paper": Reggi Ann Dubin Associates, *The IAM: Another Look,* Mar. 1, 1988.

page 354 "false pretenses": Memo to Clark Onstad, Texas Air Corp., from Reggi Ann Dubin, Mar. 1, 1988.

page 355 "never tells one person": Murray 9/4/93 interview.

page 356 "If we can't cut": Quoted in Bernstein, *Grounded,* page 59.

page 356 simply stopped coming: Magurno 3/11/94 interview; Bakes 7/16/94 interview.

page 357 Lorenzo blew up: Magurno 3/11/94 interview.

page 357 arguably more in the interests of Texas Air: The examples of cash and assets taken from Eastern are detailed in "Examiner's Analysis of Pre-Petition Transactions and Relationships," *In the Matter of Ionosphere Clubs, Inc.,* U.S. Bankruptcy Court, Southern District of New York, Mar. 1, 1990, and in Petzinger and Thomas, *WSJ,* Apr. 7, 1988.

page 357 million . . . gallons: Based on invoices totaling $19.4 million from April 1987 to December 1988. Report of the Examiner.

page 357 commodity markets: "Debtors' Submission to the Examiner," *In the Matter of Ionosphere Clubs, Inc.,* Feb. 16, 1990.

page 357 People Express notes: The Eastern directors were assured by Texas Air that independent Wall Street investment bankers had found the terms of the sale fair to Eastern; all of the firms in question, however, had a previous relationship with Texas Air. "Examiner's Analysis," Mar. 1, 1990.

page 357 repaying Texas Air: Magurno 3/11/94 interview. In defending the transaction in Eastern's bankruptcy proceedings, Texas Air noted that the People Express takeover had "removed the competitive threat People Express . . . presented to Eastern." "Debtors' Submission to the Examiner," Feb. 16, 1990.

page 357 "flipped it": Plaskett 4/21/93 interview.

page 358 only $100 million: A consulting firm provided an after-the-fact opinion to the Eastern board and to a group of Eastern's creditors affirming the $100 million price as fair, but the opinion was based on a plethora of erroneous assumptions. These are documented at length in "Examiner's Analysis," Feb. 16, 1990.

page 358 rail strikes: Nielsen, *From Sky Girl to Flight Attendant,* page 26.

page 359 cover of *Business Week:* Bakes 9/7/93 interview.

page 359 "We don't acknowledge": "Texas Air Corp.'s Eastern Unit Seeks Steep Pay Cuts from Machinists' Union," by Paulette Thomas, *WSJ,* Oct. 6, 1987.

page 360 written record: "American Air, Chief End Antitrust Suit, Agree Not to Discuss Fares With Rivals," *WSJ,* July 15, 1985.

page 360 "very carefully": D. Reed, *American Eagle,* page 208.

page 360 Crandall . . . was mortified: Though Crandall has never publicly discussed the case, he has made his views known to others, including Plaskett and Becker.

page 360 "in my obituary": Becker 9/3/93 interview; D. Reed, *American Eagle,* page 210.

page 360 cosmetic dentistry: Kaldahl 4/27/93 interview; "Battle of Titans: Crandall's American Is Unlikely Recipient of $8 Billion Trump Bid," by Bridget O'Brian and Judith Valente, *WSJ,* Oct. 6, 1989.

page 360 "rage less": "American Rediscovers Itself," *BW,* Aug. 23, 1982.

page 360 "I've never felt": Crandall 6/13/94 interview.

page 361 burning inside: Plaskett 4/21/93 interview.

page 361 discreetly negotiating: *Ibid.*

page 361 10 hottest executives: "New Airline Empire Will Test Lorenzo as a Manager," by Paulette Thomas, *WSJ,* Dec. 26, 1986.

page 361 "like a Stradivarius": "Rescue Party," by Howard Banks, *Forbes,* Dec. 1, 1986.

page 361 slide show: "Continental Air Dismisses Plaskett; Lorenzo to Step In," by Paulette Thomas, *WSJ,* July 22, 1987.

page 361 by the book: "Plaskett Replaced as Continental Chief; Lorenzo Takes Over," *Aviation Week,* July 27, 1987.

page 361 round of golf: Bakes 9/7/93 interview.

page 362 "biggest . . . giveaway ever": Quoted in "New York Officials Ground Continental Air Giveaway," *WSJ,* Jan. 29, 1987.

page 362 "wanted a scene": Quoted in *ibid.*

page 362 "Frank was adamant": Plaskett 4/22/93 interview.

page 362 the "big bang": Peterson and Glab, *Rapid Descent,* page 206.

page 362 32 different galley: The service breakdown at Continental is detailed in "Texas Air's Rapid Growth Spurs Surge in Complaints About Service," by Paulette Thomas, *WSJ,* Feb. 26, 1987, and "Lorenzo Again

Faces Problems at Helm of Continental Airlines," by Carole A. Shifrin, *Aviation Week,* Aug. 3, 1987.

page 363 "never *intentionally* overcommit": "Flight Ops Pipeline," Continental Airlines, July 1987. Emphasis added.

page 363 Johnson & Johnson: "Lorenzo: In the Cockpit," interview with Frank Lorenzo, *Time,* Nov. 23, 1987.

page 363 "lived through a lot": Letter to Continental Pilots from Frank Lorenzo, Sept. 11, 1987.

page 363 tried to overcome: Plaskett 4/22/93 interview.

page 363 dumped Tom Plaskett: Thomas, *WSJ,* July 22, 1987.

page 364 they knew would hurt: Baker 4/23/93 interview.

page 364 "window of opportunity": Remarks by Crandall, 1987 Fall Planning Conference, Harvey Hotel, Dallas, Oct. 14, 1987.

page 364 15,000 reprints: "Shop Talk: Bookish Airline Is Magazine Fan, Too," by Francis C. Brown III, *WSJ,* Mar. 3, 1987.

page 364 "abusing employees": Quoted in "Crandall Hits Budget Lines for Cost Cuts at Employees' Expense," by Barbara Sturken, *Travel Weekly,* Aug. 12, 1987.

page 364 "treat . . . people dreadfully": Quoted in "Continental: Full Planes May Not Mean Full Coffers," by Jo Ellen Davis, James E. Ellis, and Chuck Hawkins, *BW,* Mar. 16, 1987.

page 364 "have no chance": "Chairman of American Airlines Seeks Regulations on Employee Benefits," by Scott Hamilton, *Airline Executive,* June 1987.

page 364 "it wasn't success": Quoted in Sturken, *Travel Weekly,* Aug. 12, 1987.

page 364 "can't fix prices": Quoted in *ibid.*

page 365 had a problem: G. Arpey 9/2/93 interview; Kaldahl 4/27/93 interview.

page 365 Crandall feared, the door: Crandall 9/1/93 interview.

page 365 overpaid for AirCal: Presentation by Frank Lorenzo, Quarterly Pilots' Meeting, Continental Airlines, Houston Intercontinental Airport, Dec. 2, 1986.

page 365 "Lorenzo's raiders": Remarks by R. L. Crandall to Sabre Travel Information Network, Apr. 23, 1988.

page 365 sum of $250 million: Murray 9/4/93 interview.

page 366 "hate to lose": R. L. Crandall, Address to Sales and Marketing Meeting, Aug. 2, 1988.

page 366 replacement altimeters: "Labor-Management Relations in the 1990s: Yesterday's Tactics With Today's Psychology and Tomorrow's Technology," Texas Air Corp., unpublished monograph, July 13, 1990.

page 366 $2 million subsidy: "The Eastern Pilot Group TAC Attack," presented by Jack Bavis to ALPA Executive Committee, Washington, D.C., Jan. 20, 1987.

page 366 inundated with postcards: " 'Max Safety' Shows Little Headroom for Pilot Tolerance," by Paulette Thomas, *WSJ,* Oct. 28, 1987.

page 367 "make Frank . . . the issue": Memorandum to Mary Jane Barry and Charlie Bryan from Joe Uehlein and Randy Barber, Feb. 8, 1988.

page 367 Jesse Jackson got: Barber 6/21/94 interview; Kenneth M. Jennings, "Union-Management Tumult at Eastern Air Lines: From Borman to Lorenzo," *Transportation Journal,* Summer 1989.

page 367 "full investigation": House Concurrent Resolution 262, 100th Congress, Mar. 10, 1988.

page 368 extremely favorable terms: A new unit of Texas Air proposed to buy the shuttle for $125 million in cash and a note of $100 million. By contrast, when Eastern ultimately did sell the shuttle to Donald Trump, the price was $365 million.

page 368 into a stupor: "Airline Backfire: Texas Air Triggered Investigation of Itself with Shuttle Gambit," by Paulette Thomas, Bob Davis, and John E. Yang, *WSJ,* Apr. 15, 1988.

page 368 "noise level": Frank Lorenzo, Remarks to International Aviation Club, Washington, D.C., May 4, 1988.

page 369 "discord and complexity": Memorandum to the Transportation Secretary from the FAA Administrator, June 1, 1988.

page 369 "Nobody'd believe it": Bryan 5/13/93 interview.

page 370 referring to as "D-Day": Guy Uddenberg, Memo to All Employees, Eastern Air Lines, Toronto, Feb. 1, 1988.

page 370 "Eastern goes under": Olsen 9/2/93 interview.

page 370 American's internal studies: G. Arpey 9/2/93 interview.

page 370 Crandall seemed intent: Olsen 9/2/93 interview.

page 370 schedules were removed: *Ibid.*

page 370 "positioning ourselves": Olsen 6/10/94 interview.

page 371 as mendacious a denial: An American spokesman told the *WSJ,* "This is not part of a strategy aimed at moving in on Eastern or anyone else." "American Air Will Use Miami as a Crew Base," by Paulette Thomas, *WSJ,* Aug. 11, 1988.

page 371 sense of disconnect: Bakes 9/7/93 interview.

page 371 "two scorpions": Quoted in "Feud Between Bryan, Lorenzo Explains Much, but Not All," by Bridget O'Brian, *WSJ,* Mar. 6, 1989.

page 371 Continental was cratering: Bakes 6/16/94 interview.

page 372 about $10 million: The estimate is based on a list of Lorenzo's stock sales from Sept. 17, 1986, to Sept. 16, 1987, at prices ranging from

$25.88 to $49.25. *Official Summary of Security Transactions and Holdings,* U.S. Securities and Exchange Commission.

page 372 had cost $70 million: Estimate based on pre-strike budget data, contained in undated Eastern Air Lines records.

page 373 "There's no way": J. Arpey 6/16/94 interview.

page 373 "When push comes": *Ibid.*

page 373 "The best answer": Quoted in "Judge Won't Order Eastern Pilots to End Strike Backing Machinists," *WSJ,* Mar. 8, 1989.

page 373 business textbook: Griffin, *Business,* page 222.

page 373 pen in his hand: "Eastern Woos Pilots to Break Planned Strike," by Bridget O'Brian, *WSJ,* March 2, 1989.

page 374 Manhole covers: Peterson and Glab, *Rapid Descent,* page 247.

page 374 onto a rooftop: Bakes 6/16/94 interview.

page 374 Cable News Network: *Ibid.*

page 374 couldn't "imagine": Quoted in "A Boss They Love to Hate," by John Schwartz, Erik Calonius, David I. Gonzalez, and Frank Gibney, Jr., *Newsweek,* Mar. 20, 1989.

page 375 "build the company": Quoted in "Peripheral Collective Bargaining at Eastern Airlines," by Kenneth Jennings, *Transportation Journal,* Spring 1990.

page 375 meeting in New York: Bakes 9/7/93 interview.

page 375 100 cents: Robinson, *Freefall,* page 59.

page 376 infuriating Crandall: Reed, *American Eagle,* page 250.

page 376 70 boxes: Baker 4/23/93 interview.

page 376 "complete shambles": Crandall 4/23/93 interview.

page 377 most profitable piece: Olsen 9/2/93 interview.

page 377 "Frank factor": Plaskett 8/31/93 interview.

page 377 "last nickel": Bakes 6/11/93 interview.

page 377 "Any means": Burr 9/16/93 interview.

page 378 "If I were you": O'Donnell 6/9/94 interview.

page 378 five . . . repayment schemes: "Creditor Group Seeks Trustee for Eastern Air," by Bridget O'Brian, *WSJ,* Apr. 11, 1990.

page 378 "no longer tolerate": Quoted in *Ibid.*

page 378 plundered Eastern: "Report of the Examiner," *In the Matter of Ionosphere Clubs, Inc.,* U.S. Bankruptcy Court, Southern District of New York, Mar. 1, 1990.

page 378 "smacking of fraud": Quoted in "Answer of the Air Line Pilots Association," *Application of Friendship Airlines, Inc.,* U.S. Department of Transportation, Docket 48723, Apr. 26, 1993.

page 378 "outstanding job": Quoted in "Ruling Lorenzo Team 'Incompetent,' Judge Orders Trustee to Run Eastern," by James T. McKenna, *Aviation Week,* Apr. 23, 1990.

page 378 "issue in reality": "Examiner's Analysis," Mar. 1, 1990.

page 379 burned up $1.2 billion: Cited in "Answer of the Air Line Pilots Association," Apr. 26, 1993.

page 379 pay phone: Bakes 6/16/94 interview.

page 379 establishing a foothold: SAS had previously purchased an interest in Texas Air and established a joint marketing arrangement with Continental.

page 380 once reckoned: Murray 9/4/93 interview.

page 380 Texas Air joined Continental: By the time it had filed for bankruptcy, Texas Air has been renamed Continental Airlines Holdings, Inc.

page 380 "We can say to them": Crandall videotaped presentation to new captains, *Facing Crucial Issues,* Mar. 15, 1994. When passenger demand is strong and flights are selling out, American has the power to restrict the assignment of seats. Favored travel agencies can be rewarded with special treatment at such times.

Chapter 16: "To Fly, to Serve"

page 382 remained decidedly imperial: "Nostalgia Is Not What It Was!" by Capt. Laurie Taylor, *Air Line Pilot,* Nov. 1992.

page 382 separate computer . . . system: A. Reed, *Airline,* page 134.

page 382 gentleman's airline: A. Reed, *Airline;* Campbell-Smith, *The British Airways Story.*

page 383 "management by consent": Wheatcroft 2/24/94 interview.

page 385 a drab, depressing place: Marshall 3/1/94 interview.

page 385 sailed 21 voyages: Campbell-Smith, *The British Airways Story,* page 82.

page 385 as he would later suggest: Interview with Marshall in *BA News,* Jan. 21, 1983.

page 385 then in Toronto: Marshall's titles and assignments through the years are drawn in part from the British *Who's Who,* published by A&C Black, London.

page 385 a pan-European market: Marshall's view of Hertz's evolving European market was described by Frank Olson, who ultimately became the chairman of Hertz, as well as by Marshall himself. Olson 6/28/94 interview; Marshall 3/1/94 interview.

page 386 "fiefdoms": Marshall 3/1/94 interview. Marshall also discussed his Hertz years in "Managing Across Borders," by Joan M. Feldman, *Air Transport World,* June 1, 1992.

page 386 get lost: Marshall 3/1/94 interview.

page 386 barely a dozen: Marshall 3/1/94 interview.

page 387 dirty knuckles: James 6/20/94 interview.

page 387 free cars: This and other questionable practices are detailed in an amendment to a Form S-8 registration statement filed by Avis, Inc., with the SEC in Nov. 1976.

page 387 "a paste jewel": James 6/20/94 interview.

page 387 secret file: James 7/1/94 interview.

page 388 "ambition was tickled": Morrow 3/7/94 interview.

page 388 "improper" . . . payments: Details of the audit committee report to the SEC are included in the amendment to Avis's SEC Form S-8.

page 388 attention of the SEC: The existence of an investigation by the SEC was confirmed by the SEC in a response dated Sept. 6, 1994, to a Freedom of Information Act request submitted for this book. In addition, the fact of the investigation was reported in "Avis Inc. Discloses $470,958 Payment Studied by the SEC," *WSJ*, May 3, 1977. Marshall, in the 3/1/94 interview, said, "I don't recall an SEC investigation." He subsequently declined to discuss the matter whatsoever. Morrow discussed the payment in the 3/7/94 interview. Additional details are reported in the amendment to Avis's SEC Form S-8. The Italian tax payment was first publicly revealed in "Audit Aftermath: Avis's Payoff Inquiry Has a Lingering Effect as Questions Remain," by Priscilla S. Meyer, *WSJ*, Mar. 15, 1977.

page 389 reached any government officials: Amendment to Avis's SEC Form S-8.

page 389 "confidence in Mr. Marshall": "Avis's Trustee Endorsed President, Chief Officer," *WSJ*, Mar. 28, 1977.

page 389 "deep odor": Morrow 3/7/94 interview.

page 389 prosaic brands: Marshall 3/22/94 interview.

page 389 complaining to others: Olson 7/11/94 interview.

page 389 Gravely unhappy: *Ibid.*

page 389 "like to be the chairman": Marshall 3/1/94 interview.

page 390 time traveling: *BA News*, Jan. 21, 1983.

page 390 When his old boss at Avis . . . heard: Morrow 3/7/94 interview.

page 390 vaguely noble: Campbell-Smith, *The British Airways Story*, page 25.

page 390 hunted in Leicestershire: "Co-Pilots on a Private Flight," by Arthur Reed, *Industry Week*, Jan. 23, 1984.

page 390 attacked . . . with abandon: A. Reed, *Airline*, pages 40–41.

page 390 like an archaeologist: The description of Marshall's state of mind as he joined British Air is based on interviews with Marshall; on the text of the Royal Aeronautical Society R. J. Mitchell Lecture given by Marshall on Mar. 4, 1992; on an account written by Marshall and published in *NYT* on Sept. 19, 1988; and on extensive comments by Marshall in Corke, *British Airways: The Path to Profitability.*

page 391 internal politics: Marshall, *Times*, Sept. 19, 1988.

page 391 "morale outweighs matériel": *Ibid.*

page 391 "Putting People First": The courses were described in interviews with Marshall and other British Air employees; various editions of *BA News;* and Corke, *British Airways*, pages 113–16.

page 391 groaning and shrugging: Marshall 3/1/94 interview.

page 391 "there will be a businessman": Comments of Dr. Nick Georgiades, British Air's director of human resources, in Corke, *British Airways,* page 114.

page 392 "Caledonian girls": Coltman 3/17/94 interview.

page 392 emphasis . . . on youth: Campbell-Smith, *The British Airways Story,* page 148.

page 392 requirements . . . were reduced: A. Reed, *Airline,* page 80.

page 392 "grooming room": *BA News,* June 22, 1984.

page 392 "look right": *Ibid.*

page 392 "warmth of the welcome": Quoted in Sampson, *Empires of the Sky,* page 281.

page 392 same design firm: James 6/20/94 interview.

page 392 horrible and garish: "British Pride Hurt in BA's Color Change," *Airline Executive,* Jan. 1985.

page 393 Marshall instructed: Marshall 3/22/94 interview.

page 393 would be three classes: Detailed in Batt 3/2/94 interview.

page 394 British Airways suffered: The account of terrorism's cost to British Air and the company's marketing response is based on Harvard Business School Case No. 9-589-089, as well as on interviews with company officials and contemporaneous press coverage.

page 394 American behavior: Marshall 8/31/94 interview.

page 395 15 percent more revenue: Batt 3/2/94 interview.

page 395 American picked up: American had also briefly served Europe in the C. R. Smith era. The evolution of American's international strategy was detailed in interviews with Crandall, Carty, Olsen, and G. Arpey, and is described in "Competitive Anger" by Suzanne Loeffelholz, *Financial World,* Jan. 10, 1989.

page 396 power of the hub: Olsen 9/2/93 interview.

page 396 "fragment the market": *Ibid.*

page 396 Crandall instantly grasped: Crandall 6/13/94 interview.

page 396 they would allow: Carty 4/29/93 interview.

page 396 "betting on the come": G. Arpey 9/2/93 interview.

page 397 nearly half: "Wolf at the Gateway," by Robert McGough, *Financial World,* May 14, 1991.

page 397 20 percent ownership: Ferris 5/27/93 interview; Marshall 3/1/94 interview.

page 398 fastest friends: Olson 7/11/94 interview.

page 398 "intrinsically deceptive": Comments of British Airways on PDSR-85, Notice of Proposed Rulemaking, Docket 42199, cited in David A. Schwarte, *Global Alliances: Compatibility with U.S. Antitrust Law,* presented to International Aviation Symposium, Apr. 13, 1994.

page 399 employed Acker's son: Acker 1/7/93 interview.

page 399 little enthusiasm: "Pan Am, Passed Over as a Merger Candidate, May Be Running Out of Time to Show Profit," by Randall Smith, *WSJ,* Mar. 26, 1987.

page 399 "clock is ticking": Shugrue 9/8/93 interview.

page 400 at war: "Pan Am Board Battling Over Proposed Braniff Merger," by William M. Carley, *WSJ,* Dec. 7, 1987.

page 400 sky-high wages: Coleman 2/16/94 interview.

page 400 Acker's head: *Ibid.*

page 400 clean sweep: *Ibid.*

page 400 committee of the board: "Pan Am Is Said to Be Seeking New Chairman," by William M. Carley, *WSJ,* Jan. 5, 1987.

page 401 broke Plaskett's heart: Plaskett 8/31/93 interview; "An Airline of Firsts Folds Wings Which Once Sought Moon," by Asra Q. Nomani, *WSJ,* July 12, 1991.

page 401 "When I arrived": Plaskett, text of remarks, 1988 Employee Meetings.

page 401 no marketing plan: *Ibid.*

page 401 by the bucket: *Ibid.*

page 401 looked with foreboding: "Will Plaskett Save Pan Am?" *ASTA Agency Management,* June 1988.

page 401 with Malev: "DOT Confirms Approval of Pan Am–Malev Code-Sharing Agreement," *Aviation Daily,* June 23, 1988.

page 402 partners said no: "Pan Am, Covia Group Trade Charges in CRS Dispute," *Aviation Daily,* June 23, 1988.

page 402 "inconvenienced them": Plaskett, 1988 Employee Meetings.

page 402 every 45 days: *Ibid.*

page 402 "a believer": *Ibid.*

page 402 "professional manager": Plaskett described himself thus in explaining his decision to leave American. Becker 9/3/93 interview.

page 402 "counting on you": Plaskett, 1988 Employee Meetings.

page 403 led the pilots: Gandt, *Skygods,* page 271.

page 403 Flight 103 that day: The account of the disaster is based principally on Johnston, *Lockerbie, passim.*

page 404 cries of sorrow: Cross 1/16/94 interview. Cross was working as a consultant in the Pan Am building at the time.

page 405 "used to be enough": Remarks of Thomas G. Plaskett, Harvard Business School Club of Dallas, Dec. 5, 1991.

Chapter 17: The Gilded Cockpit

page 407 "Could I interest you": Olson 6/28/94 interview. Marshall declined to discuss the overture from United.

page 407 Olson's motivation: Olson 6/28/94 interview.

page 407 wrestled with the question: *Ibid.*

page 407 its blessing: Luce 8/26/93 interview

page 407 cared deeply: An executive who deals regularly with Crandall says he was rankled by the wealth that Wolf had accumulated in the industry.

page 407 exceeding $12 million: This is the author's estimate, based on Crandall's saying the figure was greater than the counteroffer he received from American, which was then valued at nearly $12 million.

page 407 Segall . . . proposed: Crandall 9/1/93 interview.

page 407 golden handcuffs: The details of Crandall's stock award are taken from the Apr. 6, 1988, proxy statement of AMR Corp.

page 408 less money: Crandall 9/1/93 interview.

page 408 "thought very seriously": *Ibid.*

page 408 executive-search consultant: Olson 6/28/94 interview.

page 408 "very unusual": "Up in the Air," by Mike Steere, *Chicago,* May 1991.

page 408 Wolf was lionized: "Union Busting vs. Unionism," by F/O Jerry Baldwin, *Air Line Pilot,* Oct. 1985.

page 408 "*unusual* route structure": Quoted in "Republic's Stephen Wolf, the Right Man at the Right Time," by David L. Brown, *Airline Executive,* Jan. 1985.

page 408 five box tops: "Republic Air Offers Rides to Youngsters for Cereal Boxtops," by John Curley, *WSJ,* Feb. 3, 1982.

page 409 not look proper: Wolf 8/25/94 interview.

page 409 95,000 shares: Wolf's 1984 options award is detailed in various amendments to his employment contract, on file at the SEC, as well as in the March 28, 1986, Republic Airlines proxy statement.

page 409 "tasteful": Wolf 8/25/94 interview.

page 409 "hit it off": Quoted in "Republic Air's Wolf Tackles Labor Costs, Undirected Growth to Cure Ailing Carrier," by Harlan S. Byrne, *WSJ,* May 24, 1984.

page 409 "into their fold": Brown, *Airline Executive,* Jan. 1985.

page 409 perfect moment: Wolf 6/4/93 interview.

page 410 family steak house: The account is based on *ibid* and on a telephone interview with Rothmeier on May 3, 1995.

page 410 $2 million in option profits: Republic Airlines proxy statement, Mar. 28, 1986.

page 410 not so fortunate: Northwest's operating problems are detailed, among other places, in "Flying Solo: The Autocratic Style of Northwest's CEO Complicates Defense," by Richard Gibson, *WSJ,* Mar. 30, 1989.

page 411 Sperry computer system: "Northwest's Merger Has Passengers Fuming," by Patrick Houston, *BW,* Nov. 24, 1986.

page 411 "dangerously close": Quoted in Gibson, *WSJ,* Mar. 30, 1989.

page 411 organically grown tomatoes: Wolf 7/20/93 interview.

page 411 all-cargo airline: The history of the Flying Tiger Line is told in *Flying Tigers: 1945–1989,* published by a group of Tiger employees.

page 412 "It's over!": Nagin 6/6/94 interview.

page 413 studying French: Wolf 8/25/94 interview.

page 413 visited regularly: Coltman 3/17/94 interview.

page 413 especially Burgundies: Wolf 6/4/93 interview.

page 413 compelling business reasons: Wolf gave these reasons to Coltman, whom he hired to run United's European operation. Coltman 3/17/94 interview.

page 414 "keep our arrangement": Wolf 7/21/93 interview; Marshall 3/1/94 interview.

page 414 one or two routes: Interview with Colin Marshall by Nadine Godwin, *Travel Weekly,* July 10, 1989.

page 414 "bizarre thing": Quoted in Steere, *Chicago,* May 1991.

page 414 "if not strange": Wolf 7/20/93 interview.

page 414 "Iacocca of the Airways": "Taking Off: Under Its New Chief, United Airlines Begins to Pick Up Altitude," by Robert L. Rose, *WSJ,* July 28, 1988.

page 414 Wolf as the bad guy: Babbitt 8/26/94 interview.

page 415 microphone cord: Wolf 8/25/94 interview.

page 415 Anti-Wolf stickers: "Strange Bedfellows: Can UAL Pilots Bury Their Old Animosities as Firm's Co-Owners?" by Randall Smith and Judith Valente, *WSJ,* Sept. 18, 1989.

page 415 "Sweet Sixteen": Quoted in "United Air's Performance Has Taken Big Dive, Hurt by Pilots' Union Action," by Asra Q. Nomani, *WSJ,* Sept. 18, 1989.

page 415 pilots . . . invited him: Wolf 7/20/93 interview.

page 416 wanted no part: *Ibid.*

page 416 25 percent of Northwest's flights: Houston, *BW,* Nov. 24, 1986.

page 416 "play with toys": Quoted in Smith and Valente, *WSJ,* Sept. 18, 1989.

page 416 "board has concluded": Wolf 7/20/93 interview.

page 417 "greedy son of a bitch": *Ibid.*

page 417 "not an inch": Wolf 7/21/93 interview.

page 417 "very serious decision": Wolf 7/20/93 interview.

page 417 "must now demonstrate": Quoted in Smith and Valente, *WSJ,* Sept. 18, 1989.

page 417 "just a Wolf": Quoted in "Inside Group Favored to Win Fight for UAL," by Judith Valente, *WSJ,* Sept. 5, 1989.

page 418 75 percent of the equity: "UAL Buyout Group Begins Campaign to Maintain Stake for British Airways," by Randall Smith and Laurie McGinley, *WSJ,* Sept. 29, 1989.

page 418 "underestimated by 4,000 percent": Wolf 7/20/93 interview.

page 419 second test: "A Slice of Skinner," by Mead Jennings, interview with Sam Skinner, *Airline Business,* July 1991.

page 419 Mitsubishi Bank: "Flawed Portent: Banks Rejecting UAL Saw Unique Defects in This Buyout Deal," by Jeff Bailey, Asra Q. Nomani, and Judith Valente, *WSJ,* Oct. 16, 1989.

page 419 ministry of finance: Wolf 7/21/93 interview.

page 419 bankers . . . began studying: Bailey, Nomani, and Valente, *WSJ,* Oct. 16, 1989.

page 420 not been warned: Olson 6/28/94 interview.

page 421 "I remind you": R. L. Crandall, Address to Sales and Marketing Meeting, Aug. 2, 1988.

page 421 buy Air Wisconsin: McNamara 6/10/94 interview; Nagin 6/6/94 interview.

page 421 singling out United: Wolf 7/21/93 interview.

page 422 "Bashing of this type": Letter to Hon. Sam Skinner from Stephen M. Wolf, March 27, 1989. Obtained from the U.S. Department of Transportation under the Freedom of Information Act.

page 422 friendly thank-you: Letter to Stephen M. Wolf from Samuel K. Skinner, May 8, 1989. Obtained from the U.S. Department of Transportation under the Freedom of Information Act.

page 422 only a single U.S. carrier: Wolf 7/21/93 interview.

page 422 some $6 million: "American Means Business in War for UAL's O'Hare Turf," by Mark Hornung, *Crain's Chicago Business,* June 25, 1990.

page 422 Crandall . . . personally fired: D. Reed, *American Eagle,* page 260.

page 422 "worst screwing": Crandall 4/23/93 interview.

page 423 "There was a sense": Baker 4/23/93 interview.

Chapter 18: London Calling

page 424 crazy quilt: McAnulty 2/25/94 interview.

page 424 55 control centers: "Europe's Sky Wars," by Kenneth Labich, *Fortune,* Nov. 2, 1992.

page 425 diluting the noise: House of Commons, Transport Committee, "The Future of the Air Services Between the United Kingdom and the United States of America," Mar. 17, 1984.

page 425 a bank of video cameras: "Heathrow's Terminal 4: A Simple Showplace," by Jerome Greer Chandler, *Airline Executive,* Apr. 1987.

page 426 demanded some amendments: "Air Wars," by John Newhouse, *New Yorker,* Aug. 5, 1991.

page 426 bizarre organization: The description of the attire, menu, and activities at the Conquistadores is based on interviews with Borman, Burr,

Bakes, Plaskett, and Shugrue; on photos and other details appearing in the organization's yearbooks; and on "Aviation Bosses Belong to Secret Club Where Dressing in Pink Frocks Is Okay," by Roy J. Harris, *WSJ,* Sept. 17, 1985.

page 427 special . . . work rules: LaVoy 10/12/93 interview.

page 427 Plaskett considered: Plaskett 4/22/93 interview.

page 427 Plaskett approached . . . Wolf: Plaskett 8/31/93 interview; Wolf 7/21/93 interview.

page 427 not yet ready: Plaskett 1/14/93 interview.

page 428 cryptic proposal: Plaskett 8/31/93 interview.

page 428 evident to Plaskett: Plaskett 4/22/93 interview.

page 429 "That's interesting": Plaskett 8/31/93 interview.

page 429 absolutely no interest: Wolf 7/21/93 interview.

page 430 busy signal: Branson 3/1/94 interview.

page 430 most successful entrepreneurs: The account of Branson's background is based on the Branson 3/1/94 interview; the Whitehorn 2/28/94 interview; Brown, *Richard Branson;* Sampson, *Empires of the Sky;* "How Richard Branson of Virgin Group Ltd. Is Taking Off in Britain," by L. Erik Calonius, *WSJ,* Aug. 29, 1984; and "High Flier: Adventure Capitalist Is Nipping at the Tail of Big British Airways," by Ken Wells, *WSJ,* May 22, 1992.

page 430 "I'm Richard Branson": Quoted in Brown, *Richard Branson,* page 66.

page 431 sued . . . Lennon: *Ibid.,* page 73.

page 431 night in jail: *Ibid.,* page 107.

page 432 unrequited demand: Branson 3/1/94 interview.

page 432 lunch with Sir Freddie: Laker's advice to Branson was described in the Whitehorn 2/28/94 interview and the Branson 3/1/94 interview.

page 432 Laker talked him out: Whitehorn 2/28/94 interview.

page 432 without a necktie: *Ibid.*

page 433 deemed them injurious: Brown, *Richard Branson,* page 299.

page 433 Marshall and his lawyers: Marshall 8/31/94 interview.

page 433 Absolutely not: *Ibid.*

page 433 expressed his view: *Ibid.*

page 434 plunged to 47 percent: "Action on the North Atlantic," by Perry Flint, *Air Transport World,* June 1991.

page 434 "Wretched Robert": This epithet has been publicly attributed to Marshall, but people inside British Air insist that it was the invention of Lord King.

page 434 leading success stories: "Wolf at the Gateway," by Robert McGough, *Financial World,* May 14, 1991.

page 435 "I'm not allowed": Crandall 4/23/93 interview.

page 435 medical claims: "Lost Horizons: A Grand Tradition Can Make a Fall That Much Harder," by Brett Pulley, *WSJ*, Sept. 16, 1991.

page 435 "Who would ever": Remarks by Plaskett, Harvard Business School Club of Dallas, Dec. 5, 1991.

page 435 weekend contemplating: Plaskett 4/22/93 interview.

page 436 "raiding party": A photograph of the draped Concorde is on display in Branson's home. The "attack" is also described in "King's Last Days," by Nick Rufford, David Leppard, and John Harlow, *Times*, Feb. 28, 1993.

page 436 "the boy": Quoted in Rufford, Leppard, and Harlow, *Times*, Feb. 28, 1993.

page 436 approved a payment: "BA Paid 50,000 Pounds for Virgin Slurs," by Frank Kane, *Guardian*, Jan. 15, 1993. Marshall refused to discuss any aspect of the Virgin dispute because it remained in litigation.

page 436 "drug dealing": The report was obtained by Virgin, which provided the author with a copy.

page 436 PR operative circulated: "Agreed Statement in Open Court," In the High Court of Justice, Queen's Bench Division, *Between Virgin Atlantic Airways Ltd. and British Airways plc*, 1992 V no. 434, Jan. 11, 1993.

page 436 poaching passengers: *Ibid.*

page 436 "dirty tricks": "An Open Letter to the Non-Executive Directors of British Airways plc," from Richard Branson, Dec. 11, 1991.

page 436 patronizing letter: Letter to Richard Branson from Colin Marshall, Dec. 12, 1991.

page 436 touched off rejoicing: "Pan Am Misses $100 Million Payment as Talks Continue on Pact with United," by Asra Q. Nomani and Laurie McGinley, *WSJ*, Mar. 11, 1991.

page 437 stationed in London: Feeser 3/3/94 interview.

page 437 played for a fool: Crandall 6/13/94 interview.

page 438 "dumb deal": *Ibid.*

page 438 "that means us": Crandall 4/23/93 interview.

page 438 George Bush: "U.K. Lifts Airline Curb at Heathrow, Aiding Pan Am, TWA Route-Sale Plans," by Laurie McGinley, *WSJ*, Mar. 6, 1991.

page 438 missed a $100 million: Nomani and McGinley, *WSJ*, March 11, 1991.

page 438 forget it: Letter to the Hon. Samuel K. Skinner from Thomas G. Plaskett, Aug. 2, 1991.

page 439 "zero paper-clip": Quoted in "Pinching Pennies Keeps Profit Flying at Delta Air Lines," by John Koten, *WSJ*, Mar. 7, 1980.

page 439 "join an objective": Quoted in " 'Family Feeling' at Delta Creates Loyal Workers, Enmity of Unions," by Janet Guyon, *WSJ*, July 7, 1980.

page 440 "lack of knowledge": "Recommendations: International Advertising and Promotional Support," Delta Air Lines, Oct. 31, 1988.

page 442 *"you* wouldn't buy": Wolf 7/20/93 interview.

page 442 "Is this legal?": Wolf 7/21/93 interview.

page 442 "Screw it": Plaskett 4/22/93 interview.

page 442 no joint deal: Some of the participants believed United and Delta did come to an understanding later that night, although within a day or two the deal was off.

page 442 Psychological stress: Pulley, *WSJ,* Sept. 16, 1991.

page 442 persona non grata: "Plaskett Is Attracting Flak for His Piloting of Pan Am," by Asra Q. Nomani, *WSJ,* Aug. 12, 1991.

page 442 "evasive and incompetent": Quoted in *ibid.*

page 443 raised his offer: "Higher Flier: Delta, Despite Victory in Pan Am Bid, Faces Some Big Challenges," by Bridget O'Brian, *WSJ,* Aug. 13, 1991.

page 444 water cannons: Pan Am's final flights were described in Gandt, *Skygods,* page 316, and in a number of memos to the author from former Pan Am employees via America Online.

page 444 "some may preach": Remarks by Thomas G. Plaskett, Harvard Business School Club of Dallas, Dec. 5, 1991.

page 445 "piece of flesh": Kriendler 5/12/93 interview.

page 445 too conspicuous: Wolf 7/21/93 interview.

Chapter 19: Hard Landing

page 447 Putnam noticed: Putnam 10/13/93 interview.

page 447 accosted by Senator Kennedy: Peterson and Glab, *Rapid Descent,* pages 244–45.

page 447 Lorenzo made plans: "Still Grounded: For Lorenzo, Getting a New Airline Aloft Is Proving Treacherous," by Bridget O'Brian, *WSJ,* Jan. 25, 1994.

page 447 Shortly after midnight: The DWI incident is detailed in "Current Information Report, Non-Public," Houston Police Department, Incident No. 081184992, July 28, 1992.

page 448 pleaded no contest: O'Brian: *WSJ,* Jan. 25, 1994.

page 448 "most profitable airline": "British Airways Has Time to Mull Moves," by Brian Coleman, *WSJ,* Apr. 27, 1992.

page 448 an A rating: "Airline of the Year: British Airways," *Air Transport World,* Feb. 1, 1993.

page 448 "started hammering": Crandall, "President's Conference," Earl's Court Park Inn, London, Mar. 2, 1994.

page 448 first global megacarrier: "G-GLOBAL: Britain's Role in World Air Transport," address by Colin Marshall, Royal Aeronautical Society R. J. Mitchell Lecture, Mar. 4, 1992.

page 449 "east of the Mississippi": Quoted in "USAir's Business Strategy Succeeds in Deregulation," by Carole A. Shifrin, *Aviation Week,* May 14, 1984.

page 449 represented the largest airline: "USAir Will Get $750 Million from British Air," by Brett Pulley, *WSJ,* July 22, 1992; "Air Raid," by Paula Dwyer *et al., BW,* Aug. 24, 1992.

page 450 a single airline: Dwyer *et al., BW,* Aug. 24, 1992.

page 450 20,000 pairs: Robert L. Crandall, "International Aviation at the Crossroads," Remarks to Economic Club of Detroit, Nov. 11, 1992.

page 450 Crandall was convinced: Letter from R. L. Crandall to Hon. Jim Lightfoot, Aug. 28, 1992.

page 450 maintenance facility: D. Reed, *American Eagle,* pages 235–36.

page 450 Clinton campaign: Address by Stephen Wolf to United pilots and flight attendants, Marriott Hotel, Dulles International Airport, Mar. 12, 1993.

page 451 "bargaining chip": Marshall 8/31/94 interview.

page 451 Lord King convened: Lord King's downfall is detailed in "King's Last Days," by Nick Rufford, David Leppard, and John Harlow, *Times,* Feb. 28, 1993, and Gregory, *Dirty Tricks, passim.*

page 452 Princess of Wales: A photograph of the note appears in *ibid.*

page 452 signed a statement: *Ibid.,* page 350.

page 452 ninth wealthiest person: "High Flier: Adventure Capitalist Is Nipping at the Tail of Big British Airways," by Ken Wells, *WSJ,* May 22, 1992.

page 453 "People keep saying": Branson 3/1/94 interview.

page 453 28th busiest: "The State Bird of Texas," by Thomas G. Donlan, *Barron's,* Oct. 19, 1992.

page 453 Spiegel . . . established: "Business Soars Where Airline Flies," by Del Jones, *USA Today,* Sept. 17, 1993.

page 454 friends nowadays preferred: Coltman 3/17/94 interview.

page 455 "just unbelievable": Roger Hall, "History of the ESOP," *The Leading Edge,* UAL-MEC, May 1994.

page 455 Wolf sent spies: Wolf speech, Dulles International Airport, Mar. 12, 1993.

page 455 cultural change: Wolf 7/21/93 interview.

page 455 called together the . . . unions: Preliminary Prospectus, UAL Corp., June 1994.

page 455 "Downsizing . . . means war": Hall, *Leading Edge,* May 1994.

page 456 "You've never been": *Ibid.*

page 456 crew base in Miami: Lum 7/7/94 interview.

page 458 "canned act": *Ibid.*

page 458 ultimately voted against: Olson 7/11/94 interview; Preliminary Prospectus, June 1994.

page 458 bone up: Wolf 8/25/94 interview.

page 458 "I accept it": *Ibid.*

page 459 in Barbados: "Course Correction: Tired of Airline Losses, AMR Pushes Its Bid to Diversify Business," by Bridget O'Brian, *WSJ,* Feb. 18, 1993.

page 459 "will not yield": transcript of question-and-answer period, Crandall speech to American Airlines Management Club, Jan. 28, 1986. Crandall made the point in equally strong terms in "The Volatile Airline Industry," speech to Economic Club of Detroit, Feb. 23, 1987.

page 460 "out the window": Crandall 4/23/93 interview.

page 460 "radical thinking": Amster 4/29/93 interview.

page 460 answers that came back: The results of the marketing studies conducted at American in the summer and fall of 1991 were described in interviews with American executives, as well as in speeches by Crandall, published interview comments, and a series of papers, entitled "Critical Issues," prepared for American employees in 1992.

page 461 pricing at Southwest: American itself acknowledged this point in "Joint Statement of Issues," *Continental* v. *American,* U.S. District Court for the Southern District of Texas, Case No. G-92-259, Feb. 8, 1993.

page 461 $20 million: "American Airlines Flies with Value Strategy," by Jennifer Lawrence, *Ad Age,* Apr. 27, 1992.

page 461 scheduled into the studio: "Airlines' Ad Spending Takes Off, But It May Be Just a Short Flight," by Joanne Lipman, *WSJ,* April 21, 1992.

page 461 on his treadmill: Crandall 4/23/93 interview.

page 462 Amster was in Europe: Amster 4/29/92 interview.

page 462 handled a record: AT&T 1992 Annual Report.

page 462 drove to the airport: "Flying Low: Simplifying Their Fares Proves More Difficult Than Airlines Expected," by Bridget O'Brian and James S. Hirsch, *WSJ,* June 4, 1992.

page 463 help Washington understand: Kelleher 6/14/94 interview.

page 463 100 city pairs: Michael Gunn, presentation to managers, American Airlines, Oct. 5, 1993.

page 464 "normal profit motive": Simat, Helliesen & Eichner, Inc., *Review of AMR Transition Plan,* July 27, 1993.

page 464 "never see me": Crandall, videotaped presentation to new captains, *Facing Crucial Issues,* Feb. 22, 1994.

page 466 "less than a mail carrier": Pamphlet by Association of Professional Flight Attendants, Euless, Texas, Aug. 1993.

page 466 abusive husband: "Coffee, Tea, and Solidarity," by Judy Mann, *Washington Post,* Nov. 26, 1993.

page 466 "regularly polled": Crandall 6/13/94 interview.

page 467 "supercharge": Baker 6/10/94 interview.

page 467 own labor negotiators: *Ibid.*

page 467 "lied to us": Edwards 6/13/94 interview.

page 468 "strike was a tragedy": Crandall, "President's Conference," Mar. 2, 1994.

page 469 most often watching: Gunn 9/1/93 interview.

page 470 Kelleher's net worth: Southwest's May 18, 1995, proxy statement lists Kelleher's stock and option holdings at 2,758,268 shares.

Postscript: Magic Act

page 473 uncanny resemblance: I am grateful to Jim O'Donnell for this analogy.

page 474 moviegoing stimulates: "The Twain Shall Meet," by Paul Klebnikov, *Forbes,* Feb. 27, 1995.

page 474 promote air travel: Carty 4/22/93 interview.

page 474 11 percent: Michael Gunn, videotaped presentation to management conference, American Airlines, Irving, Texas, Oct. 5, 1993.

page 475 "monster jets": "Monster Jets Are Coming!" *Weekly Reader,* Sept. 11, 1992.

page 475 "fire Orville": Quoted in "Kelleher Mixes Wit, Wisdom," by Del Jones, *USA Today,* June 8, 1994.

page 475 with galleys and lavatories: "You Can Look but You Can't Touch," by Fred Reed, *Air & Space,* Apr./May 1994.

page 475 two inches narrower: Demonstration for the author at the British Airways Cabin Service Development Center, Mar. 2, 1994.

page 476 $182 million: "Tracking Travel," by Daniel Pearl, *WSJ,* May 3, 1994.

page 476 "fantasies of childhood": "Coming Home," by Joyce Carol Oates, *USAir Magazine,* May 1995.

BIBLIOGRAPHY

Books

Allen, Oliver E. *The Airline Builders.* Alexandria, Va.: Time-Life Books, 1981.

Bashe, Charles J., Lyle R. Johnson, John H. Palmer, and Emerson W. Pugh. *IBM's Early Computers.* Cambridge, Mass.: MIT Press, 1986.

Banks, Howard. *The Rise and Fall of Freddie Laker.* London: Faber and Faber, 1982.

Bender, Marilyn. *At the Top.* Garden City, N.Y.: Doubleday, 1975.

Bender, Marilyn, and Selig Altschul. *The Chosen Instrument.* New York: Simon & Schuster, 1982.

Bernardo, James V. *Aviation in the Modern World.* New York: E. P. Dutton, 1960.

Bernstein, Aaron. *Grounded: Frank Lorenzo and the Destruction of Eastern Airlines.* New York: Simon & Schuster, 1990.

Boase, Wendy. *The Sky's the Limit: Women Pioneers in Aviation.* New York: Macmillan, 1979.

Borman, Frank, with Robert J. Serling. *Countdown: An Autobiography.* New York: William Morrow, 1988.

Braybrook, Roy. *Pocket Book of Aircraft.* London: Kingfisher Books, 1985.

Breyer, Stephen. *Regulation and Its Reform.* Cambridge, Mass.: Harvard University Press, 1982.

Brown, Anthony E. *The Politics of Airline Deregulation.* Knoxville: University of Tennessee Press, 1987.

Brown, Mick. *Richard Branson: The Inside Story.* London: Headline, 1989.

Brown, Stanley H. *Ling: The Rise, Fall, and Return of a Texas Titan.* New York: Atheneum, 1972.

Bruck, Connie. *The Predators Ball.* New York: The American Lawyer/Simon & Schuster, 1988.

Campbell-Smith, Duncan. *The British Airways Story.* London: Hodder and Stoughton, 1986.

Carter, Jimmy. *Public Papers of the Presidents of the United States.* Washington, D.C.: U.S. Government Printing Office, 1977.

Caves, Richard E. *Air Transport and Its Regulators, An Industry Study.* Cambridge, Mass.: Harvard University Press, 1982.

Collier, Peter, and David Horowitz. *The Rockefellers, An American Dynasty.* New York: Holt, Rinehart and Winston, 1976.

Corke, Alison. *British Airways: The Path to Profitability.* New York: St. Martin's Press, 1986.

Daley, Robert. *An American Saga: Juan Trippe and His Pan Am Empire.* New York: Random House, 1980.

Davies, R.E.G. *Airlines of the United States Since 1914.* London: Putnam, 1972.

———. *Continental Airlines: The First Fifty Years.* The Woodlands, Tex.: Pioneer Publications, 1984.

———. *Rebels and Reformers of the Airways.* Shrewsbury, England: Airlife Publishing, 1987.

Davis, Sidney E. *Delta Air Lines: Debunking the Myth.* Atlanta: Peachtree Publishers, 1988.

Dempsey, Paul Stephen, and Andrew R. Goetz. *Airline Deregulation and Laissez-Faire Mythology.* Westport, Conn.: Greenwood Publishing Group, 1992.

Derthick, Martha, and Paul J. Quirk. *The Politics of Deregulation.* Washington, D.C.: Brookings Institution, 1985.

Earhart, Amelia. *The Fun of It: Random Records of My Own Flying and of Women in Aviation.* Chicago: Academy Chicago, 1932.

Eglin, Roger, and Berry Ritchie. *Fly Me, I'm Freddie!* London: George Weidenfeld and Nicolson, 1980.

Epstein, Joseph. *Ambition: The Secret Passion.* New York: E. P. Dutton, 1980.

Feldman, Jesse. *A New Air Transport Policy for the North Atlantic: Saving an Endangered System.* New York: Atheneum, 1976.

Gandt, Robert. *Skygods: The Fall of Pan Am.* New York: William Morrow, 1994.

Green, William, Gordon Swanborough, and John Mowinski. *Modern Commercial Aircraft.* New York: Portland House, 1987.

Gregory, Martyn. *Dirty Tricks: British Airways' Secret War Against Virgin Atlantic.* London: Little, Brown, 1994.

Grey, Jerry. *The Facts of Flight.* Philadelphia: Westminster Press, 1973.

Griffin, Ricky E., and Ronald J. Ebert. *Business.* Englewood Cliffs, N.J.: Prentice-Hall, 1989.

Halaby, Najeeb E. *Crosswinds: An Airman's Memoir.* Garden City, N.Y.: Doubleday, 1978.

Herrmann, Dorothy. *Anne Morrow Lindbergh, A Gift for Life.* New York: Ticknor & Fields, 1992.

Hopkins, George E. *Flying the Line: The First Half-Century of the Air Line Pilots Association.* Washington, D.C.: Air Line Pilots Association, 1982.

Johnson, George. *The Abominable Airlines.* New York: Macmillan, 1964.

Johnson, Robert E. *Airway One: A Narrative of United Airlines and Its Leaders.* Chicago: United Airlines, 1974.

Johnston, David. *Lockerbie: The Tragedy of Flight 103.* New York: St. Martin's Press, 1989.

Kahn, Alfred E. *The Economics of Regulation: Principles and Institutions.* New York: John Wiley & Sons, 1971.

Keyes, Lucile Sheppard. *Federal Control of Entry into Air Transportation.* Cambridge, Mass.: Harvard University Press, 1951.

Leary, William M., ed. *The Encyclopedia of American Business History and Biography: The Airline Industry.* New York: Facts on File, 1992.

Lewis, W. David, and Wesley Phillips Newton. *Delta: The History of an Airline.* Athens: University of Georgia Press, 1979.

Lindbergh, Charles A. *The Spirit of St. Louis.* New York: Charles Scribner's Sons, 1953.

——. *The Wartime Journals of Charles A. Lindbergh.* New York: Harcourt Brace Jovanovich, 1970.

——. *We.* New York: Grosset & Dunlap, 1927.

Lukas, J. Anthony. *Nightmare: The Underside of the Nixon Years.* New York: Viking, 1976.

Miller, Ronald, and David Sawers. *The Technical Development of Modern Aviation.* New York: Praeger, 1968.

Murphy, Michael E. *The Airline That Pride Almost Bought: The Struggle to Take Over Continental Airlines.* New York: Franklin Watts, 1986.

Musbach, Alice, and Barbara Davis. *Flight Attendant: From Career Planning to Professional Service.* New York: Crown, 1980.

Nance, John J. *Blind Trust.* New York: William Morrow, 1986.

——. *Splash of Colors: The Self-Destruction of Braniff International.* New York: William Morrow, 1984.

Newhouse, John. *The Sporty Game.* New York: Alfred A. Knopf, 1982.

Peterson, Barbara Sturken, and James Glab. *Rapid Descent: Deregulation and the Shakeout in the Airlines.* New York: Simon & Schuster, 1994.

Pritchard, Capt. J. Laurance. *The Book of the Aeroplane.* London: Longmans, Green, 1926.

Reed, Arthur. *Airline: The Inside Story of British Airways.* London: BBC Books, 1990.

Reed, Dan. *The American Eagle: The Ascent of Bob Crandall and American Airlines.* New York: St. Martin's Press, 1993.

Rickenbacker, Edward V. *Rickenbacker.* Englewood Cliffs, N.J.: Prentice-Hall, 1967.

Robinson, Jack E. *Freefall: The Needless Destruction of Eastern Air Lines and the Valiant Struggle to Save It.* New York: HarperCollins, 1992.

Ross, Walter S. *The Last Hero: Charles A. Lindbergh.* New York: Harper & Row, 1964.

Rourke, Francis E., ed. *Bureaucratic Power and National Politics.* Boston: Little, Brown, 1965.

Rowan, Hobart. *Self-Inflicted Wounds.* New York: Times Books, 1994.

Saint-Exupéry, Antoine de. *Flight to Arras.* In *Airman's Odyssey.* New York: Harcourt Brace Jovanovich, 1942.

———. *Wind, Sand and Stars.* New York: Harcourt Brace Jovanovich, 1940.

Sampson, Anthony. *Empires of the Sky: The Politics, Contests and Cartels of World Airlines.* London: Hodder & Stoughton, 1984.

Sann, Paul. *The Lawless Decade.* New York: Crown, 1957.

Serling, Robert J. *Eagle: The Story of American Airlines.* New York: St. Martin's Press, 1985.

———. *From the Captain to the Colonel: An Informal History of Eastern Airlines.* New York: Dial Press, 1980.

———. *Loud and Clear.* New York: Dell, 1969.

Smith, Henry Ladd. *Airways: The History of Commercial Aviation in the United States.* New York: Alfred A. Knopf, 1944.

Solberg, Carl. *Conquest of the Skies: A History of Commercial Aviation in America.* Boston: Little, Brown, 1979.

Stich, Rodney. *The Unfriendly Skies: An Aviation Watergate.* Alamo, Calif.: Diablo Western Press, 1980.

Thomson, Adam. *High Risk: The Politics of the Air.* London: Sidgwick & Jackson, 1990.

Wescott, Lynanne, and Paula Degen. *Wind and Sand: The Story of the Wright Brothers at Kitty Hawk.* New York: Henry N. Abrams, 1983.

Wilson, James Q. *The Politics of Regulation.* New York: Basic Books, 1980.

Wolfe, Thomas. *Air Transportation Traffic and Management.* New York: McGraw-Hill, 1950.

Studies and Papers

Airline Economics, Inc. *Airline Consolidation: Where It Stands, What's to Come.* Washington, D.C., 1987.

America West Airlines, Inc. *Airline Market Power: Its Impact on Competition and the Consumer.* Phoenix, Ariz., May 2, 1991.

Aviation Systems Research Corp. *The U.S. Airline Industry: Reassessing and Rebuilding.* Golden, Colo., March 1993.

Brenner, Melvin A., Associates Inc. *Analysis of Airline Concentration Issue.* Presented to American Airlines, Inc., Rowayton, Conn., July 1990.

Brenner, Melvin A., James O. Leet, and Elihu Schott. *Airline Deregulation.* Eno Foundation for Transportation, Inc., Westport, Conn., 1985.

Civil Aeronautics Board. *Report of the CAB Special Staff on Regulatory Reform.* Executive summary published in *Journal of Air Law and Commerce,* Dallas, 1975.

Copeland, D. G., R. O. Mason, and J. L. McKenney. "SABRE: The Development of Information-Based Competence and Execution of Information-Based Competition." *IEEE Annals of the History of Computing.* 1995.

Dubin, Reggi Ann, Associates. *The IAM: Another Look.* Prepared for Texas Air Corp., February 1988.

Harvard Business School. *People Express Airlines: Rise and Decline.* Case N9-490-012. Cambridge, Mass., March 1, 1990.

———. *British Airways.* Case 9-585-014. Cambridge, Mass., March 6, 1991.

———. *British Airways: "Go for It, America!" Promotion.* Case 9-589-089. Cambridge, Mass., December 5, 1991.

House of Commons, Transport Committee, *The Future of the Air Services Between the United Kingdom and the United States of America.* London, March 17, 1984.

Kaspar, Daniel M. *BA-USAir: Network Effects and Other Public Policy Considerations.* Harbridge House, Inc., Boston, September 1992.

Lazard Frères & Co. *Pan American World Airways Inc., Financial Analysis.* New York, January 31, 1985.

Levine, Michael E. "Is Air Regulation Necessary?" *Yale Law Journal.* New Haven, July 1965.

———. "Alternatives to Regulation: Competition in Air Transportation and the Aviation Act of 1975." *Journal of Air Law and Commerce.* Dallas, 1975.

McShane, Rosa. *Computer Reservations Systems: A Study of Their Impact on Competition in the United States Airline Industry.* Department of Business Administration, University College, Dublin, Ireland, December 1987.

Morrison, Steven, and Clifford Winston. *The Economic Effects of Airline Deregulation.* Brookings Institution, Washington, D.C., 1986.

National Academy of Sciences, Transportation Research Board, *The Future of Aviation.* Fifth International Workshop. Washington, D.C., October 6–8, 1987.

Schwarte, David A. *Global Alliances: Compatibility with U.S. Antitrust Law.* Presented to the International Aviation Symposium, April 14, 1994.

Science Applications International Corp. *Labor Relations and Labor Costs in the Airline Industry: Contemporary Issues.* Prepared for Volpe National Transportation Systems Center, U.S. Department of Transportation. Washington, D.C., 1992.

Simat, Helliesen & Eichner. *Review of AMR Transition Plan.* Prepared for Allied Pilots Association, Grand Prairie, Tex., July 1993.

Simon, Julian L. *Airline Service Improves Under Deregulation.* Center for the Study of American Business, Washington University, St. Louis, October 1992.

Smaby, Beverly, Christopher Meek, Catherine Barnes, Joseph Blasi, and Preeta Bansal. *Labor-Management Cooperation at Eastern Air Lines.* U.S. Department of Labor Contract. Harvard University, Cambridge, Mass., May 1987.

Spencer, Frank A., and Frank H. Cassell. *Eight Years of U.S. Airline Deregulation: Management and Labor Adaptations; Re-Emergence of Oligopoly.* Transportation Center, Northwestern University, Evanston, Ill., January 1987.

Transportation Research Board, National Research Council. *Winds of Change: Domestic Air Transport Since Deregulation.* Washington, D.C., 1991.

TravelTechnics, Ltd. *A Failed Partnership: Factors Contributing to Failures in the U.S. Airline Industry.* Prepared for the International Institute of Tourism Studies, George Washington University, Washington, D.C., October 1992.

U.S. Air Coordinating Committee. *A Statement of Certain Policies of the Executive Branch of the Government in the General Field of Aviation.* Washington, D.C., August 1, 1947.

U.S. Department of Justice, *1985 Report to Congress on the Airline Computer Reservation System Industry,* Washington, D.C., December 20, 1985.

U.S. Department of Transportation, Office of Economics. *Study of Airline Computer Reservation Systems.* Washington, D.C., May 1988.

U.S. General Accounting Office. *Airline Scheduling: Airlines' On-Time Performance.* Washington, D.C., June 1990.

Vietor, Richard H. K. "Contrived Competition: Airline Regulation and Deregulation, 1925–1988." *Business History Review,* Spring 1990.

Interviews

This list identifies the principal sources of this book, giving the locations and dates of each in-person interview. The list does not include follow-up and fact-checking conversations conducted by telephone or hundreds of interviews conducted as part of my work for *The Wall Street Journal.* A few substantive telephone interviews are also noted.

I have identified the corporate and institutional affiliations of these sources, although for simplicity I have listed only those companies of relevance to this book. In cases where my sources worked for and were interviewed about multiple companies, I have listed the companies roughly in their order of significance to the book.

Finally, this list does not include a number of people who spoke with me on the condition that they not be identified as sources. Though valuable for gaining insights and for developing other information, material from confidential sources has been used sparingly.

Acker, C. Edward. Pan Am, Braniff, Air Florida, United Express. Sterling, Va., Jan. 7, 1993; June 3, 1993.

Amster, Barbara R. American. Irving, Tex., Apr. 29, 1993.

Arpey, Gerard J. American. Irving, Tex., Sept. 2, 1993; June 10, 1994.

Arpey, James. Continental, Texas International, TWA, Eastern. Miami, Sept. 8, 1993; June 16, 1994.

Babbitt, Randolph. Air Line Pilots Association. Herndon, Va., Aug. 26, 1994.

Baker, Robert W. American. Irving, Tex., Jan. 14, 1993; Apr. 23, 1993; Apr. 26, 1993; Oct. 14, 1993; June 10, 1993.

Bakes, J. Philip, Jr. U.S. Senate, Civil Aeronautics Board, Texas Air, New York Air, Continental, Eastern. Coconut Grove, Fla., May 11, 1993; May 12, 1993; June 11, 1993. Coral Gables, Fla., Sept. 7, 1993; June 16, 1994.

Barber, Randy. Eastern. Washington, D.C., Oct. 20, 1992; June 21, 1994.

Barrett, Colleen C. Southwest. Dallas, Apr. 26, 1993.

Barron, Gary A. Southwest. Dallas, Apr. 26, 1993.

Batt, Michael. British Airways. Hounslow, Middlesex, England, Mar. 2, 1994.

Becker, Al. American. Irving, Tex., Sept. 3, 1994.

Boies, Mary Schuman. U.S. Senate, Civil Aeronautics Board. By phone, Nov. 11, 1993.

Borman, Frank. Eastern. Washington, D.C., Jan. 29, 1994.

Bowler, Peter M. American. Hounslow, Middlesex, England, Mar. 3, 1994.

Branson, Richard. Virgin Atlantic. London, Mar. 1, 1994.

Bryan, Charles. Eastern. Miami, May 13, 1993.

Burr, Donald C. Texas International, People Express. Edgartown, Mass., Sept. 16, 1993; Sept. 17, 1993.

Carty, Donald J. American. Irving, Tex., Jan. 13, 1993; Apr. 22, 1993; Apr. 29, 1993.

Casey, Albert V. American. Washington, D.C., Mar. 6, 1992.

Coats, Sam. Texas International, Braniff, Southwest, Muse. Houston, June 9, 1994.

Cohen, Howard A. Civil Aeronautics Board. New York, Feb. 16, 1993.

Coleman, William T., Jr. Pan Am, United, U.S. Department of Transportation. Washington, D.C., Feb. 16, 1994.

Coltman, David. United, British Overseas Air Corp., British European Air, British Airways, British Caledonian. Herndon, Va., Mar. 17, 1994.

Crandall, Robert L. American, TWA. Irving, Tex., Jan. 13, 1993; Apr. 23, 1993; Sept. 1, 1993; June 13, 1994.

Cross, Robert G. Texas Aeronautics Commission, Delta. Atlanta, Jan. 16, 1994.

Dawsey, Melrose. People Express, Texas International. Edgartown, Mass., Sept. 16, 1993; Sept. 17, 1993.

Doke, Timothy J. American. Irving, Tex., June 10, 1994.

Edwards, Randy. American, Association of Professional Flight Attendants. Euless, Tex., June 13, 1994.

Feeser, Barbara F. American. Hounslow, Middlesex, England, Mar. 3, 1994.

Ferris, Richard J. United. Northbrook, Ill., May 27, 1993; May 28, 1993. By phone, June 7, 1994.

Field, Katherine M. Delta. Atlanta, Jan. 16, 1994.

Gardner, Sandy. British Airways. Washington, D.C., Mar. 16, 1994.

Gitner, Gerald L. Texas International, People Express, Pan Am, TWA. New York, Mar. 16, 1993; Mar. 31, 1993.

Gunn, Michael W. American. Irving, Tex., Apr. 28, 1993; Sept. 1, 1993.

Hedges, Denise. American, Association of Professional Flight Attendants. Euless, Tex., June 13, 1994.

Hicks, Bruce. Texas International, Continental. Houston, June 16, 1993.

Higgins, Dennis. Texas International, Continental, Air Line Pilots Association. Memphis, June 8, 1994.

Hopper, Max D. American, United. Irving, Tex., Apr. 22, 1993; Oct. 13, 1993.

Jackman, William E. Air Transport Association. Washington, D.C., Aug. 17, 1992.

Jamail, Joseph D., Jr. Northwest. Houston, June 15, 1993.

James, Russell. Avis. By phone, May 24, 1994; June 20, 1994.

Kaldahl, Wesley. American, Pan Am, Eastern, Capital. Dallas, Apr. 27, 1993.

Kelleher, Herbert D. Southwest. Dallas, Oct. 13, 1993; Oct. 14, 1993. Aboard American Flight 126 from Dallas to New York, June 14, 1994.

Kriendler, Jeff. Pan Am. Miami, May 12, 1993.

Kunstler, David. Eastern. Coconut Grove, Fla., Sept. 7, 1993.

Landry, James E. Air Transport Association. Washington, D.C., Aug. 18, 1992.

Lavender, Robert J. Continental, People Express. Kingwood, Tex., June 16, 1993.

LaVoy, Richard T. American, Allied Pilots Association. Grand Prairie, Tex., Oct. 12, 1993.

Lazarus, Marianne. United. Ft. Lauderdale, June 10, 1993.

Lazarus, Monte. United, Civil Aeronautics Board. Ft. Lauderdale, June 10, 1993.

Lloyd-Jones, Donald. American, Air Florida, Western. New York, Mar. 10, 1994.

Lorenzo, Francisco A. Texas International, Continental, Eastern. Houston, May 5, 1988; Nov. 7, 1988. These interviews were conducted as part of the author's reporting for *The Wall Street Journal*. Lorenzo declined repeated requests to be interviewed for this book.

Luce, Charles. United. New York, Aug. 26, 1993.

Lum, Kevin D. Association of Flight Attendants, United. Rosemont, Ill., June 7, 1994.

Magurno, Richard. Eastern. New York, Mar. 11, 1994.

Marshall, Sir Colin. British Airways, Avis. London, Mar. 1, 1994. By phone, Mar. 22, 1994; Aug. 31, 1994.

McAnulty, Frank. United. Hounslow, Middlesex, England, Feb. 25, 1994.

McGregor, Steve. American. Irving, Tex., June 10, 1994.

McNamara, Anne H. American. Irving, Tex., June 10, 1994.

Melancon, David. Association of Flight Attendants. Washington, D.C., Feb. 24, 1993.

Miller, Ron. American, United, Continental. Irving, Tex., Apr. 29, 1993.

Morrow, Winston V. Avis. By phone, Mar. 7, 1994.

Murray, Richard. American, Continental, Mohawk. Arlington, Tex., Sept. 4, 1994. By phone June 11, 1993.

Nagin, Lawrence. United, Tiger International. Elk Grove Village, Ill., June 6, 1994.

O'Donnell, James V. Continental, Texas International, Mohawk. Galveston, Tex., June 9, 1994.

Olsen, Melvin E. American, Western. Irving, Tex., Sept. 2, 1993; June 10, 1994.

Olson, Frank A. United, Hertz. Park Ridge, N.J., June 28, 1994. By phone, July 11, 1994.

Onstad, Clark. Texas Air, Continental. Washington, D.C., Feb. 17, 1993.

Parker, James F. Southwest. Dallas, Apr. 26, 1993.

Plaskett, Thomas. American, Continental, Pan Am. Irving, Tex., Jan. 14, 1993; Apr. 21, 1993; Apr. 22, 1993; Aug. 31, 1993.

Putnam, Howard D. Braniff, Southwest, United, Capital. Dallas, Oct. 13, 1993.

Robson, John. Civil Aeronautics Board. Washington, D.C., Jan. 7, 1993.

Samuel, John. American. Irving, Tex., Apr. 29, 1993.

Shugrue, Martin R. Pan Am, Continental, Eastern. Miami, May 14, 1993; Sept. 8, 1993.

Sullivan, Jim. Continental, People Express, Air Line Pilots Association. Memphis, June 8, 1994.

Wheatcroft, Stephen. British European Air, BOAC. London, Feb. 24, 1994.

Whitehorn, Will. Virgin Atlantic. London, Feb. 28, 1994.

Wolf, Stephen. United, American, Continental, Republic, Pan Am, Tiger International. Washington, D.C., June 4, 1993. Elk Grove Village, Ill., July 20, 1993; July 21, 1993. Chicago, Aug. 25, 1994.

Zeeman, John. United. Tequesta, Fla., July 23, 1993.

INDEX

ABOUT THE AUTHOR

THOMAS PETZINGER, JR., grew up in Youngstown, Ohio, and received his journalism degree from Northwestern University. For the last seventeen years he has been a reporter and editor for *The Wall Street Journal*. His wife, Paulette Thomas, is also a *Journal* reporter. They have three children.